DANTE'S
SWIFT AND STRONG

DANTE'S
SWIFT AND STRONG

ESSAYS ON INFERNO XV

by
Richard Kay, 1931-

THE REGENTS PRESS OF KANSAS
Lawrence

Library of Congress Cataloging in Publication Data

Kay, Richard, 1931–
Dante's swift and strong.

Bibliography: p.
Includes index.
1. Dante Alighieri, 1265–1321. Divina commedia.
Inferno: XV. I. Title.
PQ4445.15th.K39   851'.1   77–6795
ISBN 0–7006–0158–9

Publication of this book was assisted
by the American Council of Learned Societies
under a grant from the Andrew W. Mellon Foundation

TO THE MEMORY OF MY FATHER

LORIN L. KAY

Preface

I take it to be a measure of Dante's greatness that he cannot be understood objectively. One cannot stand outside his work and thought with any hope of comprehending what has been said. The poet's very originality creates the ground from which it must be viewed in true perspective. To be sure, the historian can locate this in a larger cultural context, but it is nonetheless an enclave, a spot that one mind, through *poesis*, has made peculiarly its own.

The scholar who seeks to explain the *Divina Commedia* in terms of something else can at best only approximate the poet's meaning, for the work is more than the sum of its sources: through the force of creative intellect, old and familiar concepts, both ancient and medieval, are placed in a new configuration, which constitutes at once the originality and the problem of the work. The reader is challenged to try to comprehend the work's *Gestalt*; if he succeeds, he participates in the mind of the author. It is as if two persons are viewing a distant object from literally different points of view. One discerns something that is not visible from the standpoint of the other and invites him to see things in the same perspective by assuming the same viewpoint. To refuse such an invitation is to miss the point altogether.

Desperately, Dante wanted to communicate his point of view to the reader. His invitation to art was emphatically an invitation to life, to fulfillment in this world and the next. But it has not been an easy invitation to accept, for Dante was not content to have his reader learn by rote. Rather, the reader must make the poet's thoughts his own by reasoning to the same conclusions. Once the reader sees the world as the poet did, the art of the poem will at last make sense. Because Dante's art follows nature and her God, to appreciate the poem's art one must first comprehend the twofold truth of Dante's philosophy and theology which molds the poem.

Dante did not imagine that his message was self-explanatory. The scholastic *divisiones* of the *Vita nuova*, the commentary of the *Convivio*, and the epistle to Can Grande all go to prove that Dante felt his works did require commentary. Yet he did not provide the *Commedia* with an apparatus, but instead he deliberately left the reader to discover the meaning for himself. Still, the poet took care to provide assistance through devices by which the reader is incited to think, or rather to understand, for himself. The great allegorical puzzles are the most obvious instances. For centuries the Veltro and the DXV have intrigued readers, excited their curiosity, and provoked their ingenuity. Yet no one, I think, would be so rash as to claim that either of these enigmas has been completely opened to our understanding. And that circumstance was Dante's way of warning us that we have not yet comprehended the underlying truth of his philosophy and theology. Indeed, we are told so explicitly by Beatrice, who explained to the pilgrim that she spoke in obscure riddles "so that you may know that school which you have followed, and see if its teaching can follow my words, and see your way to be as far from God's way as the heaven that spins highest is parted from the earth" (*Purg.* xxxiii, 89–90). The poet, therefore, contrived puzzles in the poem that would tease the reader out of his complacent incomprehension.

This book is an attempt to solve one of these puzzles, albeit a minor one, for the supposed sodomy of the runners in *Inferno* xv–xvi does pose a similar problem. One is led to expect sodomites and finds only intellectual and political leaders who had no reputation as sexual perverts. Had the device been successful, the ideal reader would have worried the matter until some other solution presented itself. But men, it would seem, are ever inclined to believe the worst of their fellows, and although there is some evidence that Dante's apparent judgments did elicit the resentment of contemporaries, particularly in the case of Francesco d'Accorso, still the discrepancy between poetry and history has never been generally admitted to be a problem that required explanation with anything like the urgency of the major allegories.

Dante anticipated his readers' blindness, and indeed appears in the poem as one of us. Willy-nilly, we are identified with the pilgrim, for we must see with his eyes and understand with his limited but expanding comprehension. Therefore, as we approach *Inferno* xv, we must be conscious that the pilgrim of A.D. 1300 was still a citizen committed to a corrupt society that obscured his vision and consequently ours. As Brunetto warns, with Virgil's approval, the pilgrim must purge himself before he can see with whole vision (*Inf.* xv, 69, 97–99). In the following essays, I have tried to see the runners in a new light, though it still remains the half-light of Hell. Nonetheless, I hope that through the gloom one can discern that the middle cantos of the *Inferno* form an essential unity with the rest of the *Comedy* and with Dantesque thought.

If I am correct, it is not a flattering light for either Dante's age or our own. Our scholars still squint and sprint, while our statesmen still maneuver for advantage instead of considering the common welfare of mankind. As I write these lines, the world in which I live—both the small world of academe and the great world of politics—are racked with doubt, despair, and a rising sense of frustration, betrayal, and alienation.

In these troubled times, scholarship has been for me a preoccupation, and literature a comfort. As a historian, I fear that the past is too often my refuge from the present: but not so with Dante. In his work I see reflected the world on which I have turned my back, and I see it moreover with the clarity that one experiences in a highly polished, slightly concave glass: sharper though smaller than life. I cannot help feeling that this is what the poet would have wished: to turn his readers, through comprehension, from literary to social criticism. This is not to deny that his poem has many facets, but to affirm that the ultimate purpose of the work has ever been to induce men to live rightly, both collectively in a just society and individually in the pursuit of intellectual and spiritual perfection. Thus, I have been sustained in this study by the hope that others may feel the force of these cantos as I have and that they will also recognize in them the evils of our own troubled humanity.

This is not to say that I have tried to read my own view of society into the *Comedy*. Quite the reverse, for I mean, rather, that my reading of the poem has shaped my perception of the contemporary world. Since I believe that every act of historical understanding—and literary criticism is for me but one species of inquiry into the past—is successful only insofar as it comprehends the past as it actually was, I doggedly have tried to arrive at an interpretation that, on the one hand, would account for all the facts within the poem and, on the other, would correspond to Dante's own thought and to other relevant data external to the work. In both respects I am only too conscious of my own limitations, and for this reason I have chosen the modest form of the tentative essay to advance my interpretation.

The principal merit of my view, I believe, is that it does explain in Dante's own terms why the scholars and statesmen are divided into two mutually exclusive bands. Although I am attached to the answer, I would insist more upon the question. And I hope that those who find my explanation unacceptable for one reason or another will nevertheless recognize the necessity for providing an alternative answer. Those who maintain that Dante has here introduced a superfluous and meaningless distinction, as a most distinguished Dantologist once assured me, are warned that this is not a book for them. I can only remind them that Dante in his art sought to follow nature, which does nothing in vain.

In short, I think I have had the good fortune to hit upon the right question. The means of answering it are hardly original: they are provided by the cumulative efforts of generations of Dante's devoted editors and careful commentators, not to mention other areas of medieval studies. While I have by no means exhausted the store of Dantology, still I have sampled enough of the work of the giants of the past to suspect that my path leads to a point on which their several approaches converge, and thus it may provide a *via media* in which apparently disparate views may eventually be harmonized. Or more simply, I feel that the time is not far off when the poem shall at length yield its meaning.

It may seem strange for an author to begin with an estimate of his own work. I do so because I do not wish to be misplaced, as was André Pézard, my most distinguished predecessor, among those authors of *travaux dantesques* whose excessive claims were caricatured by a reviewer in *Les lettres romanes*: "Voici six siècles que l'on commente tel ou tel passage de la *Divine Comédie*; on n'y a jamais rien compris; on a méconnu la véritable pensée de Dante; cette pensée, je l'ai découverte, moi et moi seul, et je vous la livre dans toute sa splendeur nouvelle" (5 [1951]: 104). Rather, I would say that I have asked a single question more persistently than any have before me, and I gratefully acknowledge that my answers have been drawn for the most part from the common treasury of Dante scholarship, to which in turn my question will, I trust, prove a worthy contribution. For those who seek to maintain the traditional view of the runners, this should become a decisive question: How can sodomy account for the division of the runners into two mutually exclusive bands?

Books, like people, have a personality, but not always that of their author. Indeed, some scholars favor an impersonal style of presentation suggesting that their work is impartial, objective, and thoroughly scientific. This featureless mask may be appropriate to works of reference and other purely factual utterances, but I feel that it would be a deceptive pose to assume when discussing a work of literature the meaning of which is by no means beyond doubt. What I can hope to do is share my point of view with others, and this, I conceive, can best be done by inviting the benevolent reader to place himself at my side and view the poem from my perspective. At best he will be persuaded that he himself sees more from that point of view than from another and will make it his own. Since no two readers are quite the same and many differ widely, I hardly expect that any reader will see the poem quite as I do. Instead, I hope that having led others to view Dante's work as I do, they will see much that I have overlooked. In sum, I have termed my studies "essays" because I regard them as personal attempts.

These essays, then, are the record of one effort to reread a canto of the *Comedy*. By stressing that the viewpoint is a personal one, I do not mean to imply that it is an original, unheard-of approach to the poem. Just as the approaches to an unconquered mountain peak are limited, so also are those to this mighty poem. Surely I have often trod along familiar paths, and used tools, techniques, and concepts that have been tried before, perhaps more often than I realize, for I cannot pretend to know all the efforts of my predecessors. I have, I believe, scrupulously acknowledged every debt that I am conscious of; but given the vast extent of previous scholarship, it is more than likely that observations which I believe to be original have in fact been made before.

Probably a more extensive study of my predecessors would have spared me some errors, and certainly my arguments could profitably be extended along lines that others have pursued, but for the most part I have simply not had the resources for retrospective research at my disposal. With the exception of a year at the Johns Hopkins University, I have worked in libraries that did not have so much as a complete file of *Studi danteschi*, much less the early commentators, standard bibliographies, and recent monographs. Such conditions have imposed limits of a practical order upon my approach: perhaps it is better for being necessarily focused on the text of the poem. Happily chapters 3 and 4, which required the greatest amount of historical research, were written under all but ideal conditions, from which the other chapters have profited in lesser measure. For these deficiencies, I have consoled myself with the words of Benvenuto da Imola, perhaps the wisest single sentence ever written in explanation of the *Commedia*: "It is rather great wit than great learning that is needed for the understanding of this book."

For better or for worse, then, the crux of this study lies in my understanding. Hence I must acknowledge that my heaviest obligation is to those who formed that understanding: my parents, my teachers, my family and friends, my students and colleagues—all deserve my thanks no less than those whose specific assistance can be recognized in the notes. Only an autobiography would suffice to acknowledge them all, but some few deserve special thanks in this foreword.

First, my teachers: and at the beginning, the late Edwin White Webster, the historian who introduced me to Dante. Next, William F. Bottiglia, from whom I learned to read Dante, and all literature, critically; his help was also invaluable at the initial stages of this book. Further, the encouragement of Basil Busacca provided me with the impetus to undertake these essays. My debt to these, my teachers at Ripon College, is exceeded only by that owed to my masters in medieval history at the University of Wisconsin. There the lively example of the late Robert Leonard Reynolds taught me how literature can profit from history. But of all my benefactors, the greatest is surely Gaines Post, who led me into the intricacies of medieval political and legal thought. My debt to Reynolds and Post can be measured by chapters 1 and 2, which were, respectively, dedicated to them when published separately.

Many scholars have read portions of this book and offered comments from which I have profited. Foremost is André Pézard, whose long and generous critique of chapter 1 shaped the final course of my argument. Hardly less stimulating has been the sustained interest of John F. McGovern and Charles T. Davis. Both Helene Wieruszowski and Charles S. Singleton honored me with extensive criticism, and at particular points I learned from John Baldwin, Richard Fauber, David Heimann, Stephan Kuttner, Edward Peters, Sesto Prete, Donald Queller, Jan Rogozinski, Jerry Stannard, and many others.

The first two chapters were written while I was teaching at the universities of Kentucky and Colorado, and both were first read as papers to the Conference on Medieval Studies at Western Michigan University in Kalamazoo (1966 and 1968). The rest of the book profited immeasurably from a fellowship at the Humanities Center of the Johns Hopkins University during the year 1968/69. The greater part of the work, comprising chapters 5–10, was composed at the University of Kansas, to which the author is grateful for research grants and unremitting interlibrary-loan services.

Credit is also due to those publishers through whose courtesy material under copyright has been used. Chapter 1 was first published in *Mediaeval Studies* 31 (1969): 262–86; chapter 2 in *Studies in Medieval Culture*, vol. 4, pt. 2 (1974), pp. 338–52; and chapter 3 in *Studia Gratiana* 15 (1972): 147–200. All, especially the first, appear here in somewhat revised form. I must also acknowledge the kindness of those publishers who have granted me permission to quote from the following copyrighted works: The Bodley Head, for John D. Sinclair's translation of *The Divine Comedy*; J. M. Dent & Sons Ltd., for the Temple Classics translations of the *Inferno*, the *Convivio*, and *A Translation of the Latin Works of Dante Alighieri*; the

McGraw-Hill Book Company, for Thomas Aquinas, *Summa Theologicae*, vol. 40, published by Blackfriars in conjunction with the McGraw-Hill Book Company, New York, and Eyre & Spottiswoode, London, 1968; the Oxford University Press, for *Dante's Convivio*, translated by William W. Jackson, and for *Dantis Alagherii Epistolae: The Letters of Dante*, translated by Paget Toynbee; the Soncino Press, of London, for *The Babylonian Talmud* and the *Midrash Rabbah*; Weidenfeld & Nicolson Ltd., of London, and the Dial Press, of New York City, for Donald Nicholl's translation of *Monarchy and Three Political Letters*.

Finally, I am grateful for the support, forbearance, assistance, and interest of my daily companions. Many a burden has been made lighter by the cheerful labors of my research assistants Mary Catherine Elliott and Walter Willmert. My parents, my children, and my wife, Sherry, have all sustained me with their love. Over the years every aspect of the work benefited from stimulating hours of discussion with Miryam Neulander Kay. The tedium of proofreading and indexing this work was shared, with diligence and patience, by Sherry Needham Kay.

To all of my benefactors I express heartfelt gratitude, together with the hope that they, and the benevolent reader, who will also participate in the following adventure, will draw from it due satisfaction.

RICHARD KAY

Lawrence, Kansas
29 June 1971

Contents

List of Abbreviations

The reader who is unfamiliar with the bibliographic complexities of the major medieval historical series (marked [*] below) is advised to consult the *Repertorium fontium historiae mediae aevi*, vol. 1: *Series collectionum*, ed. Istituto storico italiano per il medio evo (Rome, 1962).

ad v(v).	*ad verbum (-a)*, "at the word(s)": in references to legal and Biblical commentaries, this indicates a lemma, that is, a word of the text at which a comment is given.
at n. 1	Cross references in this form refer to the *text* at the point where the note number occurs.
AV	*The* [Authorized Version of the] *Holy Bible containing the Old and New Testaments and the Apocrypha, translated by His Majesty's special command* [King James I, A.D. 1611].
BEFAR[2]	Bibliothèque des Ecoles françaises d'Athènes et de Rome; Deuxième série in-4°: Registres et lettres des papes du XIIIe siècle (Paris, 1883 ff.). [*]
Berger	A. Berger, *Encyclopedic Dictionary of Roman Law*, in *Transactions of the American Philosophical Society*, n.s., vol. 48, pt. 2 (Philadelphia, 1953).
Busnelli-Vandelli	*Il Convivio*, ed. G. Busnelli and G. Vandelli, in *Opere di Dante . . .* , ed. V. Branca et al., vols. 4 and 5, 2d ed., rev. A. E. Quaglio (Florence, 1964).
C.1 q.1 c.1	Causa 1, questio 1, canon 1, in *Decretum Gratiani*, ed. Friedberg, vol. 1.
CCL	*Corpus Christianorum, series Latina* (Turnhout, 1953 ff.). [* and Dekkers]
Cod.	*Codex Justinianus*, ed. P. Krueger, in *Corpus iuris civilis*, vol. 2 (Berlin, 1880).

Par.	*Paradiso*, ed. Petrocchi, Ed. naz., pt. 7, vol. 4 (Milan, 1967). English translations: (1) *The Divine Comedy of Dante Alighieri with Translation and Comment* by John D. Sinclair, vol. 3: *Paradiso* (London, 1948; reprint ed., New York, 1961); (2) *The Paradiso of Dante Alighieri*, trans. P. H. Wicksteed, Temple Classics (London, 1899).
Parma ed.	*Sancti Thomae Aquinatis Doctoris Angelici Ordinis Praedicatorum Opera Omnia secundum impressionem Petri Fiaccadori Parmae 1852–1873 photolithographice reimpressa* (New York: Musurgia, 1948).
Petrocchi	*La Commedia secondo l'antica vulgata*, ed. G. Petrocchi, Ed. naz., pt. 7, vols. 1–4 (Milan, 1966–67).
Pézard	André Pézard, *Dante sous la pluie de feu (Enfer, chant xv)*, Etudes de philosophie médiévale, no. 40 (Paris, 1950).
Purg.	*Purgatorio*, ed. Petrocchi, Ed. naz., pt. 7, vol. 3 (Milan, 1967). English translations: (1) *The Divine Comedy of Dante Alighieri with Translation and Comment* by John D. Sinclair, vol. 2: *Purgatorio* (London, 1939; rev. 1948; reprint ed., New York, 1961); (2) *The Purgatorio of Dante Alighieri*, trans. T. Okey, Temple Classics (London, 1901).
RIS[2]	*Rerum Italicarum Scriptores*, 2d ed. [*s.v. "Muratori"]
RSV	*The Holy Bible: Revised Standard Version . . . being the version set forth A.D. 1611, revised A.D. 1881–1885 and A.D. 1901 . . .* , as incorporated in *The Oxford Annotated Bible*, ed. H. G. May and B. M. Metzger (New York, 1962).
Sapegno	*La Divina Commedia*, ed. N. Sapegno, in *Letteratura italiana: Storia e testi*, vol. 4 (Milan-Naples, 1957).
Scartazzini-Vandelli[19]	*La Divina Commedia . . . col commento Scartazziniano rifatto da G. Vandelli*, 19th ed. (Milan, 1965).
Sinclair	*The Divine Comedy of Dante Alighieri with Translation and Comment* by John D. Sinclair, 3 vols. (London: The Bodley Head, 1939–48; paperback reprint as Galaxy Books by Oxford University Press, New York, 1961).
S.T.	*Summa theologica* of Thomas Aquinas: cited by part, question, and article. The two subdivisions of the second part are conventionally cited as I-II (prima

	secundae partis) and II-II (secunda secundae partis). See also "Parma ed." above.
Temple Classics	See above under *Inf., Purg., Par., Conv.* and *De vulg. eloq.*
Toynbee-Singleton	*A Dictionary of Proper Names and Notable Matters in the Works of Dante,* by P. Toynbee, rev. C. S. Singleton (Oxford, 1968).
X 1. 1. 1	*Decretales Gregorii IX* [traditionally called "Extravagantes" = X], Liber 1, titulus 1, canon 1, ed. Friedberg, vol. 2.
1300 × 1310	between the years 1300 and 1310.
< > and [ ]	In quoted passages, pointed brackets enclose an emendation of the text, whereas square brackets contain matter that has been interpolated, either by an editor or by the present author.
: and /	Figural relations, e.g., the analogy of Adam to Christ, are represented by joining the two terms with a colon—Adam:Christ. A solidus is used instead to express antithetical relations—Satan/Christ.

Occasionally I have revised the translations that are used; any changes that are substantial have been signaled in the notes.

The works of Dante are cited according to the divisions made by the editors of the Latin or Italian texts that are listed above. These divisions sometimes vary from those appearing in the English translations of the *Monarchia,* the *Convivio,* and the *Vita nuova,* all of which were made from earlier editions. When such differences occur, a page reference to the translation is also given. In the case of the *Epistolae,* however, I cite first by Pistelli's numbers and then add Toynbee's in parentheses.

The Bible is quoted from the Vulgate Latin text, ed. C. Vercellone, *Biblia sacra vulgatae editionis* . . . (Rome, 1861; reprinted, Paris, 1891), and from its literal English translation made at Douay (OT, 1609) and Rheims (NT, 1582), rev. R. Challoner (1749–50): *The Holy Bible translated from the Latin Vulgate.* Citations are made in English (e.g., Kings, not Reg.) according to the Douay-Rheims system, which differs from that of the AV in these noteworthy respects:

Douay-Rheims		*AV*
1 and 2 Kings	=	1 and 2 Samuel
3 and 4 Kings	=	1 and 2 Kings
Paralipomena	=	Chronicles
Canticle of Canticles	=	Song [of Songs] of Solomon
Abdias	=	Obadiah
Sophonias	=	Zephaniah
Apocalypse	=	Revelation

The numbers of chapter or verse also occasionally differ (e.g., almost all Psalms disagree by one number). The English transcription of Biblical names is not uniform, since the Douay-Rheims forms are retained in quotations and citations, e.g., Isaias, Jeremias, Ezechiel, Osee, Esdras; whereas I have preferred elsewhere to use the more familiar AV forms: Isaiah, Jeremiah, Ezekiel, Hosea, Ezra. The only abbreviations susceptible to confusion are Eccl(esiast)es and Eccl(esiastic)us.

DANTE'S
SWIFT AND STRONG

The Sin of Brunetto Latini

Half of Dante's day in Hell had already passed when he came to a plain of sterile sand upon which fire perpetually fell in flakes like snow. When he arrived, he knew in a general way what sins were punished on this desert. Somewhat earlier, Virgil had explained that the circle through which they were now passing contained those who had injured someone by force rather than by fraud. The crimes of violence punished in this seventh circle were of three kinds, corresponding to the three parties to whom injury could conceiveably be done: injuries to one's fellow man, injuries to one's self, and injuries to God. The seventh circle was accordingly subdivided into three rings (*gironi*). The first was the river Phlegethon, a ring of boiling blood, in which were plunged tyrants, murderers, bandits, and merciless soldiers, all of whom had done violence to their neighbors (*Inf.* xii). In the second ring lay the dolorous wood of bleeding trees that embodied the souls of those who had destroyed their bodies (*Inf.* xiii). In accordance with the Roman legal concept that a man's property is an extension of his body, profligates who had wantonly wasted their substance were also punished in the wood, through which they were forever pursued by a pack of hellhounds.

As Dante passed from the wood of the suicides and approached the third and final ring of the circle of the violent, he may have recalled Virgil's description of the sins punished there. And so may the reader, for it is the only explicit definition that he will be given in the poem:

> One can do violence to the deity with heart negating and blaspheming it, and disdaining nature and its goodness; and hence the smaller round seals with its sign both Sodom and Cahors and him who, disdaining God, with heart, speaks.

> Puossi far forza ne la deïtade,
>   col cor negando e bestemmiando quella,
>   e spregiando natura e sua bontade;
> e però lo minor giron suggella
>   del segno suo e Soddoma e Caorsa
>   e chi, spregiando Dio col cor, favella.

(*Inf.* xi, 46–51)

Just as in the two preceding rings an injury to property was treated as an injury to its owner, so here an offense against nature is an injury to nature's Creator. A life that is contrary to nature is an indirect denial of God Himself. Virgil explained that his broad definition of injury to God included not only the sin of blasphemy but also the sins of sodomy and usury, or to repeat his precise words, the round "seals with its sign both Sodom and Cahors."

Arriving at the plain itself, Dante found a scene that was reminiscent of the destruction of Sodom and Gomorrah (Genesis 19:23–25). Suffering there beneath an eternal rain of fire were three groups of sinners, each with a characteristic action:

> Supin giacea in terra alcuna gente,
>   alcuna si sedea tutta raccolta,
>   e altra andava continüamente.

(Inf. xiv, 22–24)

The blasphemers, who once had exalted themselves by daring to judge God, now were literally abased in their particular mode of punishment, for here they were laid low, supine upon the burning sands. The usurers sat huddled up in a place apart, on the very edge of the precipice, motionless even as they had lived without laboring. Both the supine blasphemers and the squatting usurers remain forever fixed in one spot, but the third class of sinners must run forever. They do not all run together, however, for Dante met two bands of runners, and there may well have been more.

What was the sin of these runners? That, I think, is a good question. Most critics find the answer self-evident and the subject embarrassing.[1] After all, did not Virgil specify three sins that are punished in this ring—blasphemy, usury, and sodomy? Since the blasphemers are lying in one place and the usurers are sitting in another, must not all the runners be sodomites? This conclusion, however, soon places the commentator in an awkward position. The inference is logically valid only if Virgil's enumeration of the crimes punished on the plain was an exhaustive catalogue. It is possible, however, that he selected a *characteristic* sin from each of the three categories in order to illustrate his definition. If this were the case, the runners would include not only sodomites but also those who disdained nature and her bounty in other ways as well. From Virgil's reference to Sodom, we may infer that *some* are sodomites, but not that they *all* are. His ambiguous words provide nothing more than a preliminary orientation. Like the pilgrim Dante, we must see for ourselves what was meant.

THE RUNNERS AS A SURPRISE

Dante the narrator describes his encounter with the runners in cantos xv and xvi. For the reader who has anticipated a scathing exposé of unnatural vice, they are a disappointment. The sin of the runners is never explained. Indeed, neither canto mentions it at all, either directly or indirectly. The Virgilian ambiguity remains unresolved. In the absence of an explicit amplification of Virgil's explanation, most commentators have taken it literally to mean sodomy and nothing more.[2]

Now this interpretation is based on a single ambiguous line in canto xi. Cantos xv and xvi, in which the sin should be treated, contributed nothing but silence. Yet if the interpretation is correct, it should be the key to those cantos. Armed with the hint that the sin is sodomy, the reader should be able to see the sin mirrored in the place and manner of punishment, in the character of the inmates, and in Dante's reaction to them. But as a matter of fact, it is hard to see that sodomy is the vice that is appropriate to the passage in any of these respects. At best, one can say that the setting is reminiscent of the Biblical plain of Sodom. Nothing in the punishment itself is peculiar to sodomy. The endless running is appropriate to all those who are the slaves of their appetites. If sodomy alone were to be punished by a characteristic action, little imagination would have been required to provide a more striking image. Some commentators have observed the generality of the imagery, from which they have concluded that "the Sodomites are chosen as the image of all perverse vices which damage and corrupt the natural powers of the body."[3] Nonetheless, they continue to suppose that those runners whom Dante encountered were in fact sodomites.

If that was what Dante had intended, then some distinction between *kinds* of sodomy should have been the basis for his classification of the runners. As he and Virgil crossed the plain, they encountered two distinct groups of runners. They were told explicitly that the members of the first band

> were all clerks, both great literati and of great fame, defiled on earth by one same sin.[4]

> In somma sappi che tutti fur cherci
>   e litterati grandi e di gran fama,
>   d'un peccato medesmo al mondo lerci.

(Inf. xv, 106–8)

Dante's informant was the Florentine scholar Brunetto Latini, who recognized Dante and lingered behind the first band in order to trot alongside his former protégé. Among his fellow sufferers, he identified only two by name: Priscian, the greatest Latin grammarian, and Francesco d'Accorso, a professor of Roman law at Bologna. Contemptuously, Brunetto added that the bishop whom Pope Boniface VIII had transferred from Florence to Vicenza was also in the group, although he was not worthy to be named, much less seen. All four conform to Brunetto's definition: the first three were laymen famous for their learning; the bishop was a clergyman infamous for his lack of it.

The composition of the second band of runners is not explicitly defined in the poem, but its nature can easily be inferred by comparison with the other. We may be sure that the two groups are mutually exclusive, for when Brunetto saw the second troop approaching across the sands, he hastily excused himself with the words:

> I would say more, but our walk and talk cannot be longer: because there I see new smoke arising from the sand. People are coming with whom I ought not to be.[5]

> Di più direi; ma 'l venire e 'l sermone

più lungo esser non può, però ch'i' veggio
là surger nuovo fummo del sabbione.
Gente vien con la quale esser non deggio.

(*Inf.* xv, 115–18)

As he hastened to catch up with the first runners, the other group came into view. Three Florentines detached themselves from the main body and ran to Dante to learn how their city fared, for by his dress they knew him to be their fellow citizen. All three were prominent statesmen in Florence about the time that Dante was born. Unlike the scholars in the preceding group, they were all men of action, the political leaders of the last generation. Moreover, they were all of the Guelf faction, as was Dante's father, who shared their exile in 1260. Two were of noble birth, but the third, Jacopo Rusticucci, was not. Only Guido Guerra was a military leader. What all three have in common is their prominence in Florentine politics, and particularly in the Guelf party. The three mention only one person who shares their fate: Guiglielmo Borsiere (*Inf.* xvi, 70), a Florentine gentleman of Dante's own generation, also a Guelf, with a reputation as a peacemaker and matchmaker in high society. Like the others, he had political talents, although he was more a courtier than a statesman.[6]

The runners, then, are divided into two mutually exclusive groups: one for clerks, and the other for political laymen. Since we are explicitly told that the clerks are all being punished for one sin (*Inf.* xv, 108), the politicians, too, must have their characteristic sin. What could these vocationally determined vices be? If one maintains that all the runners are sodomites, then it should follow that each group has its characteristic variety of sodomy. Few recent commentators have ventured thus far, however.[7] They agree that the two groups are differentiated by profession, but they have had little success in finding a characteristic sexual perversion for each. No doubt the cleric and the academic have always been suspected of pederasty because their work with young people offers special opportunities, but so far as I know, no one has yet been able to suggest a sexual perversion that is peculiar to politicians. Happily for the dignity of all involved, the attempts to find one have been few.

We have reached a point where it might seem better to change the subject, as has been the convenient practice of most commentators. But let us not do so before observing that we have been led into this absurdity by a literal interpretation of Virgil's reference to the sin of Sodom. Perhaps sodomy should be understood figuratively after all. To do so would at least remove the hedge of inhibitions that presently surrounds the so-called cantos of the sodomites.

What is more, by not insisting on sodomy, we can resolve an embarrassing conflict between poetry and history. For not a single one of the eight persons who are placed among the runners has any record of homosexuality outside of the *Divine Comedy*. The grammarian Priscian is the clearest case in point. He lived some eight hundred years before Dante, so the poet's sources must have been much the same as ours; but the accusation of sodomy is peculiar to Dante alone. Surely it was not his own invention, the critics argue. "It is an insult to Dante," says one, "to assume that he condemns Priscian merely because, as a grammarian and teacher of youth, he was specially liable to fall into the vice here condemned. There must have been some medieval tradition to account for Priscian's position in this circle."[8] Yet even so indefatigable a literary historian as Ernst Curtius could not find that legend, although he did not doubt that it existed.[9] Since Dante was a contemporary of the other seven suspected sodomites, all but one of whom were fellow Florentines, presumably he knew more about them than we do, and hence must be believed. Yet commentators and biographers, duly noting that Dante *is* the only source for the accusations, have thought this "a curious fact, considering the prominence of Guido" and the others.[10]

Because of their reverence for Dante, his commentators have not considered the possibility that the charge of sodomy was in fact so outrageously false that the poet insinuated it with deliberate intent to shock his contemporary readers.[11] Let us suppose that the poet made Virgil's reference to Sodom artfully ambiguous in order to create in the reader a false expectation. As the runners approach, the curious reader wonders who of the many classical homosexuals shall be among them—Hylas, Alcibiades, Caesar, Alexander? And who of his own generation? What will his reaction be if the first shade whom he meets was instead a man of irreproachable virtue? In surprise and disbelief, would not the startled contemporary exclaim as does Dante the character in the poem, "Siete voi qui, ser Brunetto?" ("Are you *here*, Ser Brunetto?"; *Inf.* xv, 30). The latter-day reader must take his cue from Dante and *be* surprised at the discovery that the runners are not the notorious homosexuals he had expected to meet.[12] And in his bewilderment, the surprised reader should begin to wonder *why* he was mistaken. Dante's commonsense audience would not be apt to think that Florentine public opinion had been mistaken about the morals of six prominent citizens. Rather, on finding that the runners included Brunetto and the rest, Dante's ideal reader would be brought to realize that the poet's conception of unnatural vice was something more subtle than sodomy. Consequently, as he reads the rest of the passage, this question should be uppermost in his mind: In what sense could such honorable men be said to have sinned against nature?

Needless to add, as far as we know, Dante's original audience contained no such ideal readers. Our hypothetical device was apparently too sophisticated for minds habituated to respect the authority of the written word, but there is good reason to believe that the poet wrote in the expectation of being largely misunderstood. We know, for example, that he purposely posed a riddle to his readers in order that they might gauge their understanding, and since the poem's *enigma forte* has in fact gone unsolved for six hundred and fifty years, it would appear that few if any of his readers have measured up to the poet's mark.[13] Whether Dante realized that his poem would seldom if ever have its ideal reader must be a moot question. But there can be no doubt that he did regard most men as blind to the truth that was his theme.[14]

[7]

UNNATURAL VIOLENCE AGAINST PHILOSOPHY OR THE EMPIRE

Before we proceed in our search for the sin of Brunetto Latini, let us have well in mind what we are looking for. The range of possible sins is clearly set by Virgil's definition: the runners did violence to nature, which is to say they violated some natural law. The only such offense that we can exclude categorically is usury, since the usurers are already seated at the edge of the burning sands. We have examined at considerable length the traditional view that the offense is sodomy. Although there might possibly have been a band of sodomites running about somewhere on the plain, Dante does not seem to have met them, because the runners whom he encountered have no reputation for that sin in either history or legend. Instead, the two groups of runners he met were composed of scholars and statesmen. Each group had its own characteristic sin, and neither group dared to mix with the other. The sin of sodomy does not explain these distinctions, so we must seek some other explanation.

One way that we might proceed would be to look for another sin, or more precisely, two other sins, one for each group of runners. From scholastic sources we could collect a list of likely suspects and hope to hit upon an appropriate pair. Such a method would be based on two assumptions: (1) that Dante did indeed have two specific sins in mind, not a nameless class of sins; and (2) that the sins in question were not original with Dante but were derived from other sources. Should either prove to be false, we would have learned much about scholasticism and little about Dante. Happily, greater certainty can be obtained with less risk. Undoubtedly the best approach is to confront the text of the poem directly. Now that we have defined the question, cantos xv and xvi may appear in a new light when subjected to an *explication de texte*. Such a textual analysis was, in fact, my first approach to the problem, and it provided an approximate solution. However, in this case the original method of discovery is neither the clearest nor the shortest means of exposition.

The very terms of our problem suggest a shortcut. Essentially, we want to know how scholarship and statesmanship are related to Dante's concept of nature. That should explain why he divided the violators of natural law into two mutually exclusive groups of statesmen and scholars. The answer will be related to Dante's attitude towards two subjects dear to his heart—philosophy and politics. Doubtless his views on both find their highest artistic expression in the *Comedy* itself, but he also expounded these subjects explicitly and systematically in two treatises: philosophy in the *Convivio* and politics in the *Monarchia*. Both abound in problems of their own that could easily turn our shortcut into a permanent detour. Fortunately, we have a guide, almost as wise as Virgil himself, to lead us through these uninviting tracts of scholastic learning. Thirty years ago, scholasticism's most distinguished historian, Professor Etienne Gilson, was faced with a problem not unlike our own. In a book entitled *Dante et la philosophie*, Gilson sought to explain why the Latin Averroist philosopher Siger of Brabant was placed by Dante in Paradise. The argument was based on an expert analysis of Dante's fundamental views on the relation of philosophy to theology and politics. These tools, forged as they were by the hand of a master, will serve our purpose, and I shall proceed to unpack them without further apology.[15]

Gilson's basic contention is that Dante had a view of philosophy peculiar to himself. To be sure, Dante borrowed concepts from Aristotle, Averroës, and Aquinas, among others, but he recast these elements into a new system that was uniquely his own. The *Banquet* and the *Monarchy* expound portions of this original synthesis in formal scholastic terms. The *Comedy* is based on it, and consequently the poem must be interpreted in terms of Dante's philosophy, not in those of some rival system, as has too often been done. The cantos that we are discussing are a case in point. They are based on Dante's singular conception of the goals that mankind should strive to attain, and of the function of the scholar and the states-man in mankind's common pursuit of happiness. This conception is fundamental to Dante's philosophical thought, and accordingly it pervades his writings, but its essential outlines can be found in the concluding chapter of his treatise *On Monarchy*.[16]

The argument is based on the familiar concept that every man is a compound composed of two parts *(partes)*—body and soul. Each part has its own nature *(natura)*: the body is corruptible, and the soul is incorruptible. Man partakes of both natures, being neither one nor the other exclusively. This double nature of man gives him a double goal, because every nature is directed to its own ultimate end. Unique among God's creatures, man has two final goals *(hominis duplex finis; duo ultima)*: one appropriate to his corruptible compound of body-and-soul, and the other to his incorruptible soul. Dante breaks with the scholastic tradition, and particularly with Aquinas, by refusing to reduce the two ends of man to only one by subordinating the good of the body-and-soul compound to the good of the soul. Instead, he maintains that the two are coordinate, each with its own inde-pendent fulfillment or beatitude *(beatitudo)*. One end finds fulfillment in this life, the other in eternal life. The happiness of this life consists in the life of reason, the exercise of man's highest and characteristic power *(operatio propriae virtutis)*. The happiness of eternal life, on the other hand, consists in the enjoyment of the beatific vision, which human reason cannot attain unless aided by grace. Sym-bolically, the two states of felicity correspond to the Earthly Paradise and the Heavenly Paradise.

Having established a double goal for man, Dante next explains how each goal can be achieved. Just as the ends are distinct, so also are the means by which man reaches them. Both are attained by the practice of virtue, but each has its appropriate virtues. Man gains his earthly happiness by living in accordance with the moral and intellectual virtues. Collectively these may be termed *natural* virtues because they have been discovered by human reason, unaided by grace.[17] Human reason alone has been sufficient to make these ethical teachings *(philosophica documenta)* known in their entirety *(tota)*. They were discovered by the great philosophers of antiquity, especially by Aristotle, whose *Nicomachean Ethics* was, for Dante, the highest authority in this domain.[18] A second set of truths guides man to his other goal of heavenly happiness. These are spiritual teachings *(documenta spiritualia)*, from which man learns how to live in accordance with the three theological virtues—faith, hope, and charity. Spiritual truths cannot be discovered by human reason but have been revealed to mankind by the Holy Spirit through prophets, sacred writers, Christ himself, and his disciples. Unlike the natural truths of the philosophers, these supernatural truths are *not* known to us in their entirety; instead, we know only as much of them as is necessary for our eternal salvation.[19]

Throughout this argument, Dante has been carefully separating human activity into two distinct orders—one natural and the other supernatural—based on the twofold nature of man. Mankind, then, has two goals, which are reached by two paths. The natural truths, which have been discovered by the philosophers, who used only human reason, teach man the virtues by which he can attain happiness in this life. The supernatural truths, which have been revealed by God through His spokesmen, teach man the virtues by which he can attain eternal life through grace.

Reason and revelation have provided mankind with all the knowledge that is necessary for attaining temporal and eternal felicity. But, for Dante, knowledge is not virtue. Man knows his true goals and how to pursue them, but he does not act on this knowledge because he is led in the other direction by his greed *(humana cupiditas)*. He will never attain his goals unless human passions are restrained. Like horses who wander at the mercy of their bestial appetites, men must be kept on their true course by bit and bridle. Providence has accordingly given mankind two drivers to direct it to its double destination. The pope leads mankind to eternal life in accordance with revealed truth; the emperor directs mankind to temporal felicity in accordance with the teachings of philosophy. In the *Monarchia*, the stress is on the need for an emperor who will provide a supreme political authority over the human community. Mankind as a whole must be regulated if individual men are to attain happiness in this life, for without the necessary preconditions of universal peace and freedom, individual self-realization will be difficult, if not impossible. The principal function of the emperor is to maintain peace and freedom by restraining human greed. The final step in Dante's argument is the demonstration that the emperor's authority must be derived directly from God, not indirectly through the pope. At each stage of his argument, Dante has distinguished the natural order from the supernatural. The two hierarchies culminate only in God. We need not follow Dante to the ultimate conclusions of his treatise, for here we are concerned, not with the relationship between the two orders, but only with the order of nature.[20]

We have been looking for a principle, explicitly stated by Dante in his philosophic works, that will explain the classification of sins against nature in cantos xv and xvi. Why are scholars and statesmen and usurers the only professions to violate nature? And what do the runners have in common that distinguishes them from the usurers? And why do they run in mutually exclusive bands? Dante's concept of the natural order provides the answers. In the Dantesque dichotomy of orders, philosophy and temporal government both pertain properly to the natural, rather than to the supernatural, order. They are the two coordinate authorities that guide man to mortal happiness. Each has its proper function. The philosopher shows men the road to mortal virtue, and the emperor makes sure that they travel along it. The human intellect should be subject to philosophy, but man's will is to be subject to the emperor. One authority governs theory; the other, practice. Neither has competence in the other's domain. "Now taken together, Philosophy and the Empire govern the entirety of human life in the realm of nature, and against them there is no appeal. Within this sphere nothing evades their suzerainty, since Aristotle shows men what is their natural aim, while the Emperor subjects their wills to it."[21]

Those who recognize philosophy and the emperor as man's supreme guides respectively in the theory and practice of the natural virtues will live in accordance with nature. Those who deny the supremacy in the natural order of the monarch or the philosopher will in effect reject God's provisions for the temporal well-being of mankind. They do violence to God, to use Virgil's words, by "disdaining nature and its goodness" (*Inf.* xi, 48). In place of the natural authority, which they do not acknowledge, they will set up for themselves an *un*natural authority. Since there are but two natural authorities, one governing the human intellect and the other the will, perversions of natural authority will also be of two distinct types. Any unnatural authority must necessarily constitute a denial either of the true authority of philosophy over the intellect or of the true authority of the empire over the will.

This twofold division of the means of doing violence to nature is implicit in Dante's concept of nature. Now we must inquire whether it corresponds to the classification of sins against nature in cantos xv and xvi. We may begin by recalling that only the runners are violent against nature alone. The usurers, who sit at the edge of the burning desert, are in a class by themselves, as Virgil expressly declared (*Inf.* xi, 94–111), because usury does violence not only to nature but also to art, which should follow nature:

> And because the usurer takes another way, he despises nature in itself and in its follower [art], since he puts his hope in another.

> e perché l'usuriere altra via tene,
>   per sé natura e per la sua seguace
>   dispregia, poi ch'in altro pon la spene.

(Inf. xi, 109–11)

Violence against nature, then, can be either simple or compound. Simple violence against nature alone is the sin of the runners, while compound violence against nature *and* against art is the sin of the usurers.

As we saw earlier, the runners are divided into at least two exclusive groups, one containing intellectuals and the other, politicians. Previous interpretations of the poem have failed to provide a coherent explanation of why the sins against nature should be committed only by these two professions. The twofold Dantesque division of natural authority seems to provide the principle on which the distinction is based. The politicians have refused to recognize the natural authority of the empire, and the intellectuals have done the same to philosophy.

On the face of it, this appears to be a plausible explanation, since the professional character of each group in the poem corresponds to the two forms of natural authority in Dante's authentic thought. But can we be sure that this is the correct explanation and not merely an ingenious hypothesis? The architectonic character of Dante's art should provide the means of verification, for we expect that a structural principle employed by Dante will govern his treatment of the parts subsumed under it. Since we have discovered just such a principle that appears to explain the classification of sins in a pair of cantos, it should also explain those cantos in detail. The parts will elaborate the principle and will be appropriate to it; the principle will pervade the parts and give them coherence and articulation. In short, the principle, if we have hit upon the correct one, should explain the parts as well as the whole. In the present case, if the sins of the individual runners can be seen to conform to the pattern that we have detected, our hypothesis will be confirmed. Let us begin with the relatively simpler problem of the three Florentine statesmen, and then return to the more difficult case of Brunetto Latini himself.

THREE INSUBORDINATE NOBLEMEN

In our discussion of sodomy, we have already remarked the high regard in which the three Florentine statesmen were evidently held by everyone save Dante and his commentators. Certainly they had no reputation for sodomy outside of the poem, and canto XVI contains no clear reference to that sin. Indeed, when we read that canto without preconceptions, it is difficult to see why they are in Hell at all, for Dante emphasizes the nobility of their character.[22] Virgil sets the tone even before the trio has arrived, saying that courtesy is their due; by rights Dante should hasten to them rather than they to him (*Inf.* XVI, 15–18). When Dante learns who they are, his first impulse is to leap down and embrace them (*Inf.* XVI, 46–48), but since that is impossible, he does the next best thing and plainly affirms that he has always held them in the highest respect. His exact words are significant, for they expressly exclude the possibility of a scandalous reputation:

> I am from your land, and ever with affection have I always repeated and heard your deeds and honored names.

> Di vostra terra sono, e sempre mai
>   l'ovra di voi e li onorati nomi
>   con affezion ritrassi e ascoltai.

> (*Inf.* XVI, 58–60)

Even in their torment, the three remain perfect gentlemen. Although bitterly disappointed by Dante's denunciation of Florentine morals and appalled at his bluntness, they still speak with dignity and courtesy.

The contemporary reader might well have wondered why such admirable men were among the damned, but a careful reading of their speeches could have suggested to him the true nature of their besetting sin. Like all damned souls, their personalities have been deformed by the characteristic vice which was the cause of their damnation. In Hell this fatal defect continues to pervade their words and actions, and because this is so, the nature of the sin can be known through its effects on the sinner. In the case of the three Florentines, we do not have to look long for such a motif: they are obsessed with fame. This theme emerges quite early in the episode as their spokesman, Rusticucci, introduces himself and his companions. He identifies the three because he is sure that their fame (*la fama nostra*; *Inf.* xvi, 31) will impress a fellow Florentine and induce him to answer their questions. This appeal to fame suggests the importance that Rusticucci attaches to reputation, but the full extent of his obsession becomes evident only in his second speech. Dante the character has explained the purpose of his journey with a metaphor:

> I leave the gall and go for sweet apples promised to me by my veracious guide; but it is necessary first that I fall all the way to the center.

> Lascio lo fele e vo per dolci pomi
>   promessi a me per lo verace duca;
>   ma 'nfino al centro pria convien ch'i' tomi.

(Inf. xvi, 61–63)

The pilgrimage from evil to good cannot be comprehended in Hell, however. Literally, the explanation tells Rusticucci nothing more than that Dante must pass through Hell to attain some desideratum. The object of the search is unstated, but in his response, Rusticucci assumes that Dante's *dolci pomi* are long life and fame thereafter:

> Se lungamente l'anima conduca
>   le membra tue, rispuose quelli ancora,
>   e se la fama tua dopo te luca, . . .

(Inf. xvi, 64–66)

Thus the pilgrim's conception of human happiness is replaced by Rusticucci's own. By this misunderstanding, he inadvertently discloses his own false values: *fama*, for Rusticucci, is the crown of life. Only at the end of the episode do we learn that his companions also share this obsession. Then, as the trio departs, all three in chorus admonish the traveler to "see that you speak of us to men" ("fa che di noi a la gente favelle"; *Inf.* xvi, 85). Personal reputation is their last as well as first thought in the encounter.

The theme of fame, however, is only one aspect of their character. Throughout the scene their primary concern is Florence itself. Rumors of its moral decline (*Inf.* xvi, 70–73) caused them to approach Dante simply because he was a fellow citizen. After introductions are exchanged, they get to the point:

> Tell us whether courtesy and valor abide within our city as once they truly did, or whether they have departed altogether out of it.

> cortesia e valor dì se dimora
>   ne la nostra città sì come suole,
>   o se del tutto se n'è gita fora;

(Inf. xvi, 67–69)

[13]

Dante replies that pride and excess—*orgoglio e dismisura*—the vices opposed to *cortesia e valor*—now flourish in their stead (*Inf.* xvi, 73–75).[23] Having heard their worst fears confirmed, the Florentines have no further interest in the conversation and quickly take their leave (*Inf.* xvi, 77–87). They had come to verify a rumor, nothing more.

We have gleaned the raw materials of an interpretation from the text. Let us summarize what can be said with certainty of the three Florentines as they appear in the poem: (1) they are men who are famous in Florence for their deeds and honored names; (2) they regard fame as the goal of life; and (3) they are concerned that courtesy and valor no longer flourish in Florence. Do these data all point to some fundamental sin against nature? Guided by a knowledge of Florentine history, the reader might reason out the answer from these establishted facts, but we shall take a shorter route, for the time has come to test our hypothesis. If it is correct, it will enable us to coordinate these data. Let us assume, then, that the sin against nature is a failure to recognize the political supremacy of the empire. To be sure, nothing in the poem suggests that the three statesmen were distinguished for their opposition to the Roman emperor, but every Florentine knew it to be true. The modern reader may need *un peu d'histoire*.

These three Florentines were all leaders of the Guelf party during the years that saw the climax of its struggle with the Ghibellines in Florence. They were the men who fought for Florence and the Guelfs at Montaperti in 1260,[24] and in the wake of that great Ghibelline victory, they fled into exile as the first Florentine republic, the Primo Populo, collapsed. Florence became a Ghibelline city and supported Manfred in his attempt to dominate Italy. It was to be the last chance for a union of Italy under the Hohenstaufen and the Ghibellines, for with the defeat and death of Manfred in 1266, the Ghibelline cause became an anachronism. The next year, the Guelf exiles returned to Florence, and from that day on the city remained Guelf.[25] Never again was a Ghibelline Florence to look to the Roman emperor for leadership. This was the political legacy of our three Florentine statesmen, who led the Guelfs through their darkest hour to ultimate triumph. For Dante's generation, which remembered them as the leaders who had freed Florence forever from the shadow of imperial control, their political careers constituted a singularly appropriate symbol of insubordination to the emperor's authority.[26]

From the poem's ideal perspective of 1300, these statesmen of the preceding generation also represented a type of leader that had all but vanished from the political scene. All three belonged to the aristocratic wing of the Guelf party, which was purged therefrom, or at least deprived of political influence, by the Ordinances of Justice in 1293. The old Florentine nobility had been a feudal aristocracy whose wealth was based on land and whose profession was chivalry. By 1300, economic and social changes were making them obsolescent. As a cavalry force they were already obsolete, for the battle of Campaldino in 1289 "was the last in which the Florentine nobles were the deciding factor."[27] Economically, they were being replaced by the middle classes, whose wealth was based on commerce and banking. Socially, their prestige was also on the wane. The first *nouveaux riches* had sought to assimilate themselves to the old nobility by adopting their ideals and way of life. Rusticucci was one of these who became noble in all but birth.[28] But as the new plutocrats grew in numbers and power, they were less inclined to ape the aristocrats, for the military obsolescence of the noble knight stripped chivalry of its raison d'être, leaving it nothing but the social graces. Some new men still did seek to acquire noble manners, but in Dante's generation they distinguished themselves as courtiers like Guiglielmo Borsiere (*Inf.* xvi, 70), rather than as soldiers and statesmen like Rusticucci. In short, by 1300 the old aristocratic values of *cortesia e valor* no longer paved the road to political leadership in Florence. In their stead, hubris prevailed because the elite had failed to resist the temptations occasioned by an influx of population and wealth:

> La gente nuova e i sùbiti guadagni
>   orgoglio e dismisura han generata,
>   Fiorenza, in te, sì che tu già ten piagni.
>
> (Inf. xvi, 73–75)

The nobles themselves were to blame. Had they remained loyal to their traditional moral and political values, the greed of the ignoble would have been restrained by the emperor and his natural allies, the local nobility. Instead, the Guelf nobles had allied with the people and brought about the destruction both of the emperor's authority and their own class. What led them to upset the natural hierarchy of authority wherein the emperor rules the nobles and the nobles rule the people? Precisely that hunger for fame which obsessed the three Florentine statesmen. Leadership of the Guelf party offered them scope for their political and military talents; partisanship endowed them with an importance that they would not have enjoyed had the Florentine nobility remained united. Florence, too, gained fame as an independent political entity, which it would not have enjoyed as a constituent part of the empire. To gain distinction for themselves and their city, the Guelf nobles had perverted the natural political structure, which for Dante was the foundation of human peace, justice, virtue, and happiness. The result was the disordered Florence of Dante's generation,[29] which the three Guelfs themselves deplored in their first words to the traveler from "our perverse country" ("nostra terra prava"; *Inf.* xvi, 9). In Hell they are still enslaved by their false values; they appear not to realize that they themselves had precipitated the ruin of their class and its way of life. At this point in the poem, the character Dante also fails to comprehend their crime, for the true principles of natural polity are not to be learned in Hell.

THE GOAL OF BRUNETTO LATINI

When we turn back to canto xv, its stress on individual and personal values is at once apparent in contrast to the societal values of the nobles. Dante speaks to only one scholar, Brunetto Latini, who is portrayed in individual detail. The intensely personal character of their interview contrasts significantly with the impersonal politeness of the three Florentines, who after the manner of politicians had regarded

Dante as a fellow citizen, a presumed admirer, a source of information; in a word, as a type but not as an individual. Brunetto, however, recognizes the pilgrim, not as a Florentine, but as Dante himself (*Inf.* xv, 23–24). What he seeks is news of Dante, not of their city, for the greater part of the conversation concerns Dante's future (*Inf.* xv, 46–99).

Like Rusticucci, Brunetto begins by asking, "What fortune or destiny" ("Qual fortuna o destino"; *Inf.* xv, 46) brings Dante to Hell while still he lives. By putting the question in terms of Dante's personal fortune or destiny, he focuses our attention on the part that this journey will play in the pilgrim's later life. Dante replies that he had gone astray in a valley and that when he failed to find his way out, Virgil had appeared and is now leading him back (*riducemi*; *Inf.* xv, 49–54). Brunetto pointedly ignores Virgil and instead assures Dante that he will gain his goal if he but uses his own natural talents. All that another can do is to supply comfort (*conforto*), which he himself would have done had he not died (*Inf.* xv, 55–60). Like Rusticucci, he has interpreted Dante's figurative description of the journey in accordance with his own preconceptions. The goal that Brunetto has in mind can be reached by developing one's special talents. In his own words, "If you follow your star, you cannot fail to attain a glorious port" ("Se tu segui tua stella, / non puoi fallire a glorïoso porto"; *Inf.* xv, 55–56). Now we know that Dante was born under the sign of the Gemini, which astrologers believed predisposed man to a life of study and letters.[30] In Paradise, Dante himself invoked the twin stars as the origin of his genius:

> O glorious stars, O light impregnated with mighty power, from which I derive all my genius, such as it is.

> O glorïose stelle, o lume pregno
>   di gran virtù, dal quale io riconosco
>   tutto, qual che si sia, il mio ingegno.
>
> <div align="right">(<i>Par.</i> xxɪɪ, 112–14)</div>

By telling Dante to follow his star, then, Brunetto was urging him to apply his intellectual gifts, to live the life of letters as Brunetto himself had done. This life of work (*opera*; *Inf.* xv, 60) is not all that Dante's fortune has in store for him, however. Prophetically, Brunetto adds that fortune has reserved for Dante such honor that he will become the envy of his fellow Florentines:

> La tua fortuna tanto onor ti serba,
>   che l'una parte e l'altra avranno fame
>   di te;
>
> <div align="right">(<i>Inf.</i> xv, 70–72)</div>

He has been so richly endowed by nature that he can expect to achieve great things, for which fame shall be his reward. Once again the theme of fame is sounded, faintly but distinctly suggesting that Brunetto, no less than the noble trio, works for applause.

Brunetto imagines that Dante's goal in life is to win fame through intellectual achievement, and by the close of the episode he has made it clear that the ideals he imputes to Dante are in fact his own. When forced to break off the interview in great haste, Latini condenses his advice to Dante into a single self-revealing sentence: "Let my *Tesoro*, in which I still live, be commended to you, and more I ask not" ("Sieti raccomandato il mio Tesoro, / nel qual io vivo ancora, e più non cheggio"; *Inf.* xv, 119–20). His last and only wish is that his book shall continue to be an influence on future generations of scholars. The intellectual lives on in the works he leaves to posterity: they are his contribution to the community, but they are also his claim to fame. Brunetto's recommendation reveals that for him the stress lay on reputation rather than on contribution. He is content neither with the knowledge that he had done his best nor with the satisfaction of a job well done: above all, he must have recognition. Precisely because he placed his hope of immortality in his writings, he now fears that they will be forgotten, and consequently that his fame among men will fade into oblivion. Like the three Florentines, Brunetto had totally dedicated his native talents to the pursuit of *fama*: he had worked for the greater glory, not of God, but of Brunetto.

The author of the *Tresor* sought to gain immortality in the natural rather than the spiritual order, and divine justice does not deny him his due, for in his book he does live on as an influence on its readers. This passionate desire to exert an intellectual influence on future generations is given essential expression in his parting reference to his book, but it pervades his whole character. In canto xv, it finds its fullest development in the scholar's concern for Dante's career, which he regards as an offspring of his own.[31] At the beginning of their conversation, Brunetto twice calls Dante his son (*figliuol*; *Inf.* xv, 31, 37), emphasizing by this repetition the paternalistic spirit in which he counsels the younger man in the long passage that follows (*Inf.* xv, 55–78). Moreover, his advice is not altogether objective. As is often the case with advisers who seek to live through their advisees, Brunetto tends to maximize his own influence on Dante and to exclude that of all others. Brunetto would himself have been the best guide in Dante's work, he seems to say, but since he is no longer available, Dante should follow his star to the goal that Brunetto had foreseen, and in default of the master himself, the *Tresor* will guide him. There is the implicit suggestion that Virgil's intervention was not altogether necessary, as indeed it was not, in order for Dante to achieve the goal that Brunetto had in mind. The more Dante's greatness is the product of Brunetto's, the better the maestro will like it.

Dante is quick to acknowledge his indebtedness to Brunetto in the most touching terms:

> Were my desire all fulfilled . . . you had not yet been banished from human nature: for in my memory is fixed, and now goes to my heart, the dear and kind, paternal image of you, when in the world, hour by hour, you taught me how man makes himself eternal; and while I live, it is proper that my tongue should show what gratitude I have for it.

> Se fosse tutto pieno il mio dimando,

> rispuos' io lui, voi non sareste ancora
> de l'umana natura posto in bando;
> ché 'n la mente m'è fitta, e or m'accora,
> la cara e buona imagine paterna
> di voi quando nel mondo ad ora ad ora
> m'insegnavate come l'uom s'etterna:
> e quant' io l'abbia in grado, mentr' io vivo
> convien che ne la mia lingua si scerna.

(*Inf.* xv, 79–87)

With this speech, Dante confirms the interpretation we have put upon Brunetto's career, for the poet testifies that Brunetto had been the pilgrim's very model of the dedicated intellectual. The crucial phrase is the statement that hourly Brunetto taught him "come l'uom s'etterna," literally "how man eternizes himself" (*Inf.* xv, 85). Obviously, this does not refer to the eternal life of the soul after death, since man does not attain happiness in the spiritual order through his natural powers alone but only with the assistance of grace. Man can be the cause of his own immortality only in the natural order, where his own powers suffice to attain his ends. On earth, then, man can make himself immortal through works that live after him.[32] This was the lesson that Dante acknowledged, and as we shall see, it was written in Brunetto's life as well as in his doctrine.

PERVERSE WORKS OF BRUNETTO LATINI

But was this dedication to a lifework of scholarship the sin for which Brunetto was damned? A comparison with the case of the three statesmen suggests that the ideal is not in itself bad. Rather, it was the desire for fame that led them to turn their talents to unnatural ends. The sin itself was evident only after we turned from the text to examine their role in history, and then judged it in the light of Dante's concept of natural political order. Let us follow a similar procedure to determine the sin of Brunetto. If our hypothesis is correct, his writings should pervert the true place of philosophy (or some part of it) in the natural order. Dante himself has pointed the way, for he has the departing scholar recommend one of his writings above all others as his enduring claim to fame, and we may suspect that ironically it constitutes his claim to infamy as well.

The work entitled *Li livres dou tresor* is an encyclopedia written between 1260 and 1266, when Brunetto was in France as a Guelf exile. It is a relatively compact work, filling only 422 octavo pages in its modern critical edition.[33] The general character of the *Tresor* may be illustrated by comparing it with two famous encyclopedias compiled about the same time. One, the *Speculum naturale*, prepared by a team of Dominicans under the direction of Vincent of Beauvais, was meant to be a comprehensive work of reference; the other, the *Opus maius* of Roger Bacon, was one individual's original reinterpretation of the scientific knowledge of his day. Brunetto's work occupies a position between these two, for it is the work of one man, as was Bacon's, but the *Tresor* reproduces its sources almost verbatim without any pretense at originality. In contrast to the *Speculum*, it is a summary of knowledge that was meant to be read from cover to cover, not merely consulted. Unlike either of its companions, the *Tresor* was intended for laymen rather than clerics and consequently was written in the vernacular rather than in Latin. In the introductory chapter, Brunetto explains that he used French instead of his native Italian for two reasons: because he was in France when he wrote the work and because French "is the most charming and most commonly known of all languages" ("est plus delitable et plus commune a tous langages"; *Tresor* 1. 1. 7).

Carmody has shown that the book is not original either in content or in plan, for both are derived from recognized sources.[34] If Brunetto committed an intellectual sin in preparing such a derivative work, it could only be an error of judgment in his selection of materials.[35] A brief description of its contents will suffice to reveal such a fault. The *Tresor* is divided into three books. The first is devoted to the theoretical sciences, and the last two to the practical sciences. The stress is accordingly on practical knowledge, to which half the pages of the book are devoted. Only two forms of practical knowledge are in fact treated: ethics in book 2 and politics in book 3. Brunetto repeatedly explains that the highest of all the sciences is the art of government, which is the end to which all other knowledge is directed. It is the goal and conclusion of his *Tresor* as well. For the layman who wished to learn the art of government from the ground up, Brunetto's treasury would provide all the knowledge necessary for the practice of his political art. The first book lays the theoretical foundations, the second teaches the ruler how to govern himself and his household, and the final book expounds the art of governing others. Book 3 is subdivided into two parts: rhetoric and political science. The inclusion of rhetoric among the arts of the ruler was, of course, suggested by its importance in the political life of the ancient city-state, and it is duly justified with a citation from Cicero (*Tresor* 3. 1. 2) and buttressed by a false etymology and spelling—*rectorique*—the art of the *rector*, or ruler.[36] In a manual for the instruction of a medieval monarch, this stress on rhetoric for the ruler might seem to be a strange anachronism, but when we turn to the culminating treatise on political science proper, we discover that rhetoric is in fact essential to the ruler for whom Brunetto wrote. The head of state that he had in mind was not a feudal monarch but the elected ruler of a thirteenth-century Italian city-state, the official known as the podesta.

Brunetto introduces his discussion of politics by distinguishing between various forms of government. He will treat just one of them, for only that one concerns him and the friend for whom the book was composed. This type of government, he explains, is that found "in Italy, where the citizens and the burgesses and the community of the city elect as their podesta and their lord [*signour*] whosoever they think will be most profitable to the common welfare [*preu*] of the city and of all their subjects."[37] The treatise that follows is a manual on how to be a podesta; it was probably derived from one composed early in the thirteenth century.[38] Rhetoric, it develops, is a necessary administrative art for the preparation of documents, forms for which are given in the manual.

This was the notarial art in which Brunetto himself excelled and which he put to the service of the Florentine Guelfs as chief secretary of the republic in the years after his return from France. For he, like the three Florentines, was a leading Guelf who was exiled after Montaperti and who returned to share in the ultimate triumph of his party over the Ghibellines. Not an aristocratic statesman, he was an intellectual who not only made his career in the civil service but also taught others how to do so. Contemporaries acknowledged the value of his professional services, but they remembered him primarily as the political philosopher of the autonomous Florentine city-state. His obituary by the chronicler Giovanni Villani leaves no doubt that book 3 of the *Tresor*, with its double emphasis on rhetoric and politics Italian style, quite literally epitomized his contribution to Florentine culture:

> In the said year 1294 a talented citizen died in Florence, who was named Ser Brunetto Latini. He was a great philosopher and in rhetoric was an accomplished master of the art of good speech as well as that of good composition. This man expounded Tully's *Rhetoric* and made the good and useful book called *Tesoro*, and the *Tesoretto*, and the *Chiave del Tesoro*, and still other books on philosophy and about the vices and virtues; and he was our commune's secretary [*dittatore*]. He was a man of this world but we have made mention of him because he began the refinement of the Florentines and was their teacher in making them distinguished for good speech and in knowing how to guide and govern our republic according to the principles of politics.[39]

Villani's estimate has been substantiated recently by Charles T. Davis, who shows Brunetto to have been the fountainhead of Florentine civic humanism.[40] Although as an author Brunetto seldom went beyond the sources that he compiled and translated, nonetheless on occasion he did imprint his own character on these materials, if only in passing. By comparing Brunetto's work with his sources and with Florentine education before and after him, Davis has been able to single out those original elements that Villani had in mind.

"For Brunetto, education in general and rhetorical education in particular was a preparation for politics," Davis says.[41] This attitude constituted nothing less than a revival of the Hellenic concept of liberal education, which was appropriate to the free citizen who participated in the government of his city-state. After the rise of the Hellenistic monarchies had rendered this ideal education obsolete in the Greek world, the aristocracy of the late Roman republic adopted it as their own. Among the Latins, Cicero in his life and works exemplified this application of deliberative rhetoric to public affairs. Indeed, the Roman republic hardly outlived its greatest rhetorician, for with the establishment of the monarchistic principate, meaningful opportunities for the orator to deliberate in political assemblies with his fellow citizens dwindled rapidly into insignificance, as Tacitus bitterly complained a century later in his *Dialogus de oratoribus*. To be sure, rhetoric remained the basis of ancient education, but not for its value in civic assemblies. The medieval image of Cicero, as Davis points out, is indicative of the altered role of rhetoric in a monarchical society. From the age of Augustine and Orosius almost down to the end of the thirteenth century, Cicero was honored as a master of rhetoric and of ethics, but never of politics.[42]

Brunetto Latini was the first rhetorician in centuries to return to Cicero's view of rhetoric as the basis of political action. The revival was eminently practical, inasmuch as the conditions of political life in Cicero's Rome bore a strong resemblance to those in Brunetto's Florence. Accordingly, treatises of Cicero on rhetoric spoke directly to the needs of Brunetto Latini, and he studied them well, translated some, and above all took Cicero as his own model of the rhetorician as statesman.[43]

Dante surely did not disapprove of this revival. On the contrary, it would appear that he was deeply influenced by it. Certainly he often honored Cicero much as Brunetto had done,[44] though it was Virgil whom he took as his supreme classical model. Nonetheless, Dante may well have conceived himself to be, as Davis suggests, a virtuous rhetorician who, like Cicero, devoted his talents to public service.[45] But I cannot agree with Davis that the poet of the *Comedy* considered the political career of Brunetto Latini no less worthy of emulation.[46] Dante could readily accept Brunetto's ideal of public service through rhetoric and yet maintain without contradiction that Brunetto's efforts to put these principles into practice were misdirected, not to say perverted.

For Brunetto differed from Cicero in one essential respect: he was not loyal to Rome. The crux of the matter for Dante was political, since the Rome that the poet felt commanded the political loyalty of all men was the Roman empire. Although Brunetto in his private writings did acknowledge that Rome was "the head of the world and the commune of everyone," his loyalty to her would seem to have been cultural rather than political.[47] Without question the commune that he served had flatly refused to recognize that the Roman emperor had any right to the political loyalty of Florence. In no uncertain terms, the Florentines had written in 1281 to the vicar of Rudolf of Habsburg: "Nunquam Comune Florentie fidelitatem fecit alicui imperatori ... quia semper vixit et fuit liberum" ("The Commune of Florence has never given allegiance to any emperor: it has always been free").[48] To be more precise, I should have said that this treasonable assertion was written *in the name of* the Florentines by their government and, still more precisely, that the letter was composed by that official whom the commune retained to draw up its documents— the *dittatore*, chief notary and scribe of the council of the commune, who in effect was head of the secretariat of the Florentine republic and in all but title was its chancellor. And who was the man who held this position in 1281? Beyond doubt— Brunetto Latini.[49] In all probability, a composition of such major importance would have been executed by the best Latinist available; certainly the final responsibility for the work would have rested on Brunetto as chief of the notarial staff. Either way, one cannot escape the implication that Brunetto was professionally responsible for the letter.[50] One could not wish for a clearer example of the sin of Brunetto Latini: he had perverted his profession of rhetoric by turning it against the natural lord of the world, the Roman emperor.

Dante himself provided a contemporary model of the truly virtuous rhetorician, for his political epistles supplied the antidote to Brunetto's. To the Italians, Dante

Alighieri in his own name wrote: "Be ye not like the ignorant, deceiving your own selves, after the manner of them that dream, and say in their hearts, 'We have no Lord.' "[51] And he does not leave us in doubt as to the identity of these self-deceived, ignorant dreamers. They are, above all, the Florentines whose folly Dante exposed to them in another letter. The commune had recently defied an emperor again, this time Henry VII, "refusing the duty of submission due to him" ("debitae subiectionis officium denegando"). The alleged reason simply was the plea of "prescriptive right" ("iure praescriptionis"), which is to say that Florence had rested its case on a precedent of long standing. No doubt Brunetto's letter, written thirty years earlier, was itself a mainstay of the argument. But in refutation, Dante replied that the emperor had an imprescriptable right to the loyalty of his subjects:

> Have you to learn, senseless and perverse as you are [*ignorantis, amentes et discoli*], that public right can be subject to no reckoning by prescription, but must endure so long as time itself endures? Verily the sacred precepts of the law declare, and human reason after inquiry has decided, that public control of affairs, however long neglected, can never become of no effect, nor be superseded, however much it be weakened. For nothing which tends to the advantage of all can be destroyed, or even impaired, without injury to all—a thing contrary to the intention of God and nature, and which would be utterly abhorrent to the opinion of all mankind. Wherefore, then, being disabused of such an idle conceit, do you abandon the Holy Empire, and, like the men of Babel once more, seek to found new kingdoms, so that there shall be one polity of Florence, and another of Rome?[52]

For Dante, time was not a factor in this case: what was wrong in 1311 had been wrong in 1281 and always had been and always would be contrary to the intent of God and nature: "Et hoc Deus et natura non vult." This, then, is how Brunetto Latini can be said to have done violence to nature: by ignoring the superior claims of the Roman emperor on his loyal professional services. I do not mean that Brunetto runs in Hell because of one isolated letter. Like the *Tresor,* which he compiled for the rulers whom he recognized, it is a typical, concrete expression of the political ideals that had molded his entire life and character. For what *was* Brunetto Latini if not a rhetorician dedicated to the cause of the Florentine Guelfs? He is in Hell because the poet profoundly believed that such a life constituted a tragic waste of natural talent, which it misdirected against the imperial order sanctioned by God and established by Him in nature itself.

Brunetto emerges as the intellectual counterpart of the three Florentines. Between them, they have led Florence into political and moral disorder, impelled by their desire for fame. Their presence in Hell must have been calculated to shock the contemporary reader and urge him to reflect deeply on the cause of their damnation, since he presumably knew that their sexual reputations were spotless. The Florentine regarded these men as the highest fulfillment of the political and intellectual ideals of his society. He was right, and that was precisely the point. They were truly the product of the society in which they lived, for they valued the good opinion of their fellow citizens above all else. To achieve the fame that they longed for, they listened to public opinion rather than to nature. Thus they became the slaves of the society that by nature they were destined to lead. In the context of that corrupt society, their vices were honored as virtues, since only in the true perspective of a society obedient to natural law would their sins be evident. Their presence in Hell was an invitation to every Florentine to reconsider the values of the society in which he lived and to rediscover the true principles of the natural order.

To turn the reader's thought in this direction, the poet placed a warning against the Florentines at the center of canto xv, as the conclusion to Brunetto's prophecy of Dante's future (*Inf.* xv, 61–78). The words, although addressed to Dante, stand as a general warning against the dangers of society for the man of intellectual genius. The naturally base part of society will hate him for his good deeds, and with good reason, for the sweet fig cannot bear fruit among the bitter sorb trees:

> An old saying [*fama*] on earth calls them blind; they are a people that is avaricious, envious, and proud: be sure to cleanse yourself of their customs.

> Vecchia fama nel mondo li chiama orbi;
>   gent' è avara, invidiosa e superba:
>   dai lor costumi fa che tu ti forbi.

> *(Inf.* xv, 67–69)

Dante, having grown up in corrupt Florence, has himself been tainted and must be purged. Brunetto prophesies that Dante will achieve such honor that both parties will seek to destroy him, but he will be beyond their reach—a veiled allusion to his proud exile. Brunetto concludes with a striking metaphor based on the legend that the Florentine people were a mixture of noble Romans and ignoble folk from Fiesole: Let the beasts of Fiesole forage for themselves and not touch the plant which springs from the holy seed of the Romans, if indeed such a plant can still grow up in their manure:

> Faccian le bestie fiesolane strame
>   di lor medesme, e non tocchin la pianta,
>   s'alcuna surge ancora in lor letame,
> in cui riviva la sementa santa
>   di que' Roman che vi rimaser quando
>   fu fatto il nido di malizia tanta.

> *(Inf.* xv, 73–78)

Brunetto, as becomes a seer (*vates*), does not recognize how truly he speaks, for his sharp words can cut with the double edge of irony. Their import will emerge more fully as the poem and our study of it progress,[53] but we can already catch the drift. Could Brunetto dissociate himself from the Florence which he condemns? Only if, true to his name, Latino had proved loyal to his proud heritage as the oldest, most honorable and trustworthy ally of the Roman imperium. Manifestly, such was far from his historic role, so we must conclude that the character stands condemned unwittingly by his own mouth.

[2]

Natural Grammar and Priscian's Perversity

With the discovery of the sin of Brunetto Latini, the first essay attained our prime objective. Dante's conception of the twofold role of philosophy and the emperor in leading man to his natural beatitude on earth has provided a key to cantos xv and xvi. With it we have been able to explain the damnation of the principal characters of the twin cantos. Brunetto and the three statesmen now appear, respectively, as intellectual and political leaders who had established an autarchic civic society that was contrary to nature.

The interpretation improves upon earlier ones in several important respects. (1) The characters now appear in the poem as historical figures who are being punished, not for unattested vices, but for the veritable part they played in the history of Florence. The strain formerly placed on the reader's credulity is now removed. One no longer needs to agonize over the poet's motives in condemning these honorable men. They are damned for those acts that in life constituted their claim to fame. (2) One no longer has difficulty in seeing why Dante condemned these rebels against the principles of natural polity, since we have his solemn word that such crimes as theirs merit nothing but damnation.[1] (3) The closing chapter of the *Monarchia* permits us to understand the principle that divides the runners into two distinct bands. This in itself marks an advance beyond earlier interpretations, which have not been able to correlate this division with the sin of the runners. In short, our answer offers an account that integrates the characters' history, the poet's political philosophy, and Hell's moral structure into a single, coherent interpretation.

Nonetheless, few if any will be persuaded by these advantages alone. And rightly so, for partial coherence is hardly enough: at the least, the new interpretation must prove applicable to the lesser characters as well as to the major ones. Therefore, our next concern will be to examine each of Brunetto's companions in turn. Their cases must be tried separately, for if my line of argument has been correct, then the three defendants should each represent a distinct form of professional activity. If Priscian the grammarian, d'Accorso the lawyer, and Mozzi the bishop each proves to have perverted his profession in a way that Dante believed to be unnatural, then the proposed reinterpretation will have provided an account that is consistent on the literal-historical level.

The three cases are by no means of equal complexity. Indeed, if we adhere to the poet's arrangement and treat the three characters in the order in which they were named in the poem, each case will appear to be more difficult than the preceding one. Moreover, the ascent will have the appearance of being so graded that each contributes to the understanding of the next. Whether by accident or design, this progression will at length lead us from the problem of Mozzi's damnation (chap. 4) to the surprising discovery that his transfer has in the poem a significance all of its own (chap. 5).

Since the poet's subject was "the state of souls after death,"[2] I have thought it best to see first of all whether my hypothesis applies to the several members of Brunetto's band. Though laborious, this method will permit us to enlarge our understanding gradually through an accumulation of concrete biographical details. There is, however, another approach available, through poetic images rather than through historical biographies. The evidence of imagery will serve to confirm and refine the results obtained from the consideration of individual cases (chaps. 6–9). This arrangement somewhat arbitrarily postpones to the end of the book a question to which some readers may require an answer before they can seriously entertain any thought of a nonsexual interpretation of the runners' sin. Those who cannot conceive that the image of Sodom might imply anything but unnatural sexuality should at this point be assured that the apparent obstacle will be surmounted eventually in chapters 8 and 9. The final argument will, I hope, be all the more persuasive when read with the characters and images of the runners already in mind.

With this orientation, let us turn to consider the minor characters of *Inferno* xv. To avoid misunderstanding, at the outset it should be recognized that, because the immediate context of the poem offers no clue as to the particular vices of these lesser figures, any attempt to identify their sins must necessarily proceed by means of conjecture to conclusions that are at best only probable. The reader, for example, was given only the name "Priscian" to ponder, as if the implicit meaning might be deduced by reflection on the familiar facts of this sinner's history, his place of punishment, and Dante's views on the vice in question. Strictly speaking, an inference drawn from such evidence can establish nothing more positive than the *possibility* that such was the author's intention. For the interpretation of these secondary characters, however, no greater certainty should be required, inasmuch as the burden of proof must be borne by those major characters whose cases can be argued directly from the text. Thus, while a reinterpretation cannot begin with the lesser figures, it can be corroborated by them if the new explanation, which for the major personae is already probable, proves to have possible application to the minor ones as well. In other words, although we cannot hope to discover conclusive proof of Dante's view of Priscian, d'Accorso, and Mozzi, still we may be able to discern in their life and works something that *l' autentico pensiero dantesco* might condemn as an intellectual perversion of nature. Our first task must be, then, to see whether the principle that explained the sin of Brunetto Latini can also be applied to the case of Priscian.[3]

[26]

TWO BYWORDS: DONATUS AND PRISCIAN

"Priscian goes with that wretched crowd," declared Brunetto, as he identified the most noteworthy clerks who shared his punishment.[4] "Priscian sen va con quella turba grama": from this bare statement we can only be certain that someone named Priscian ran with the clerks who were all famous literati.[5] Now, although many lesser Latinists have been named Priscian, only one was so famous in Dante's day that his name alone would identify his profession.[6] This was Priscian of Caesarea, who taught Latin grammar in Constantinople during the first quarter of the sixth century. To the European Middle Ages he was the author of the authoritative advanced Latin grammar, the *Institutiones grammaticae*, and accordingly his name was a byword for grammar itself, just as Euclid's was for geometry.[7] Earlier writers had used Priscian to personify grammar, but only Dante saw him as the type of the perverse grammarian.[8]

The cause of his damnation can be found within the *Comedy* itself, but not in the obscurity of Hell, for his sin, like so many others, is revealed only by contrast to virtues that appear later in the poem. As has often been observed, Priscian is not the only grammarian in the *poema sacro*, for Dante has provided his perverse grammarian with an ideal counterpart among the souls in Paradise. For that role he selected Donatus, who throughout the Middle Ages was familiar to every schoolboy as the author of the standard beginning and intermediate textbooks on Latin grammar. In the mid 300s this Aelius Donatus taught at Rome, where Saint Jerome was his most famous pupil. The rules of grammar were not his sole interest, for among his extant works are a commentary on Terence and fragments of another on Virgil,[9] but in the Dantesque Heaven he is only remembered as an elementary grammarian: "that Donatus who deigned to set his hand to the first art" ("quel Donato / ch'a la prim' arte degnò porre mano").[10]

In the *Paradiso* he is placed in the heaven of the Sun, that symbol of intellectual illumination, and with him are other saints who in one way or another were distinguished for their wisdom. They include not only such conventional scholars as Aquinas, Gratian, Boethius, and Peter Lombard, but also less obvious types of human wisdom, ranging from Bonaventure and Solomon down to the enigmatic figures of Siger of Brabant and Joachim of Flora. Collectively they have been characterized as doctors, as scholars, as wise men—*sapientes*.[11] Each represents the proper approach to his subject, with an implied contrast to its malpractice. This theme is exemplified in the mission of the mendicant orders, which is expounded to Dante in the solar heaven: friars who are true to their ideal of poverty are praised, but false friars who pursue worldly things are condemned.[12] Like the praiseworthy friar, the *sapiens* has the wisdom to practice what he professes. Because he understands the proper function of his chosen profession, the wise man directs his efforts towards the fulfillment of that goal. The *sapientes* of the solar heaven, then, typify different forms of intellectual activity in accordance with nature. In this company of ideal professional types, Donatus is expressly presented as a grammarian, for he "deigned to set his hand to the first art." From this we can safely infer that, for Dante, he represented the ideal grammarian.

What that ideal was may be seen from the subdivision of the doctors into two circles of lights, one led by Aquinas, the other by Bonaventure, and animated respectively by the spirits of Dominic and Francis: "The one was all seraphic in his ardor, the other by his wisdom was on earth a splendor of cherubic light." The wisdom of the cherubic band was based on learning (sapientia) alone, while the seraphic wisdom was expressed as love (ardor charitatis) derived from knowledge, although not necessarily imparted by formal learning.[13] Now the reader may be perplexed to find Donatus among the ardent rather than the merely learned; but Dante left no doubt as to the explanation: this grammarian thought it worthy (degnò) to write the most elementary of textbooks. From these circumstances of Donatus' salvation, we may conclude that Dante's ideal grammarian devoted himself to the elements of language, and that he did so not for the sake of learning but in order to teach others.

Priscian and Donatus: their names were frequently coupled as typical grammarians by medieval writers.[14] In the Comedy, too, they represent their profession, but with a distinction peculiar to Dante. The one is condemned for some unnatural malpractice, the other praised for his dedication to the teaching of elementary grammar. This contrast, though not a commonplace, was intelligible to Dante's contemporaries. To grasp the poet's meaning, the puzzled medieval reader had only to reconsider his old school books; but Priscian and Donatus are empty names for the modern reader, who has been tutored by other authorities, and he must make their acquaintance if he would comprehend the implicit contrast.

Priscian's majestic Institutiones grammaticae is a magisterial treatise of imposing length. The standard modern edition extends over some 974 pages. As in systematic Latin grammars today, a twofold division is employed: words and their forms are treated in the first sixteen books (702 pages) and syntax is the subject of the two remaining books (272 pages).[15] Compared to this, Donatus' work is puny. In the same format, his Ars maior runs to 36 pages, his Ars minor to but 12.[16] Morphology forms the whole matter of his lesser work and the bulk of the greater, which concludes, not with a systematic syntax, but with an anatomy of common faults (bk. 3). In scope and intention, the methodical treatment of the eight parts of speech in the Ars maior is about on a level with Bennett's New Latin Grammar less the paradigms. "The object of this book is to present the essential facts of Latin grammar in a direct and simple manner, and within the smallest compass consistent with scholarly standards."[17] With these words, Bennett might have introduced Donatus' systematic school grammar instead of his own, had he excepted syntax and prosody. Both books were intended as practical reference grammars that stick to the certainties and avoid philological discussion. Donatus, in his devotion to teaching, produced a solid, simple textbook, but he stooped even lower, to epitomize the rudiments of his subject in a form suitable for catechizing beginners. This is his Ars minor, in which the core of his longer work (bk. 2) is condensed by one-third, from 19 pages to 12, and presented in question-and-answer form.

Priscian, on the other hand, did not write for students but for fellow grammarians. He undertook to reform the rules of Latin grammar in accordance with the latest developments of Greek philology. Most notably he initiated the systematic study of Latin syntax;[18] but he also revised and refined morphology—the traditional concern of Latin grammar—often reducing to rule a usage that his predecessors had explained as idiomatic. His was no mere textbook but a monument of erudition that was comparable in scale and spirit to the Teubner *Historische Grammatik der lateinischen Sprache*.[19]

In short, Priscian wrote a theoretical work for fellow grammarians; Donatus, a practical grammar for students and everyday Latinists. In its general outlines the contrast is clear enough to permit anyone who is familiar with the two works to grasp Dante's meaning simply by reflecting on the character of each. Hence I think that the poet, in opposing Donatus to Priscian, relied on the general impression that each would have made on those who had studied them. Donatus was a vade mecum for any Latinist, whereas Priscian could profit only the professional grammarian. Thus, Dante would glorify in Donatus the self-effacing teacher who enables his students to acquire Latin as a second language by presenting them with a manageable set of rules; while on the other hand, he would condemn in Priscian all clever and industrious scholars who endeavor to convert the grammarian's craft into a science as perfect in every respect as human reason can make it. In grammar, Dante seems to say, theory exists for the sake of practice: the perfect language, *grammatica*, is the most functional, not the most rational.

THE GRAMMARIAN'S ROLE

Such a reading can be justified and refined at length by a consideration of the theory of language that Dante set forth in the *De vulgari eloquentia* and, to a lesser extent, in the *Convivio*,[20] but a single passage will serve to confirm the main point, namely that Dante assigned to Latin grammar a definite role, which Donatus fulfilled but Priscian did not. At the opening of the treatise *De vulgari eloquentia*, Dante established a contrast between the primary, vernacular speech, learned by all as the mother tongue, and Latin, learned by literati as a second language:

> We say that the vernacular speech is that which we acquire without any rule, by imitating our nurses. There further springs from this another secondary speech, which the Romans called grammar. . . . Few, however, acquire the use of this speech, because we can only be guided and instructed in it by the expenditure of much time, and by assiduous study.[21]

After explaining in detail the origin and nature of human speech in general, he takes the Romance vernaculars as a particular case of progressive linguistic differentiation, which he sees as a necessary consequence of having unlearned speakers separated in space and/or time. The secondary language, which is learned as Latin grammar, he regards as a conventional artifact, instituted to bridge the ever-widening gaps between divergent vernaculars. This at least is my understanding of the four sentences into which Dante compressed his whole account of the origin and function of Latin grammar:

> If, therefore, the speech of the same people varies (as has been said) successively in the course of time, and cannot in any wise stand still, the speech of people living apart and removed from one another must needs vary in different ways; just as manners and dress vary in different ways, since they are not rendered stable either by nature or by intercourse, but arise according to men's inclinations and local fitness. Hence were set in motion the inventors of the art of grammar, which is nothing else but a kind of unchangeable identity of speech in different times and places. This having been settled by the common consent of many peoples, seems exposed to the arbitrary will of none in particular, and consequently cannot be variable. They therefore invented grammar in order that we might not, on account of the variation of speech fluctuating at the will of individuals, either fail altogether in attaining, or at least attain but a partial knowledge of the opinions and exploits of the ancients, or of those whom difference of place causes to differ from us.[22]

This is the sole coherent expression we have of Dante's theory of language, which other scattered references only serve to elucidate. Our immediate problem is solved by the last sentence, which plainly states the function of Latin grammar as Dante conceived it. Grammar was instituted to provide a uniform common language that, because it transcends time and place, will render intelligible the *auctoritates atque gesta* of times and places not our own.[23] The stress is on communication: grammar puts the Latinist in contact with a wide range of significant facts and ideas.

Armed with this Dantesque concept of grammar as a rational construct designed to maximize communication between diverse times and places, we may return to Priscian and ask whether his *Institutiones grammaticae* does indeed serve this purpose. The answer is emphatically No, since the treatise was written for those who have already attained the goal that Dante set for Latinity. A knowledge of Donatus, followed by a diligent reading of the *auctoritates,* should suffice to form a Latin style adequate to Dante's requirements.[24] In this view, a diligent study of Priscian would do more harm than good, since his advanced grammar overshoots the Dantesque mark. The rules formulated by Priscian either introduce stylistic refinements that are unnecessary for effective communication, or else they are philological descriptions rather than grammatical prescriptions. In either case, they unnecessarily complicate the practical exercise of Latin, making it the private preserve of the professional grammarian rather than a lingua franca. If, as Dante asserted, Latin grammar existed to unite diverse times and places by a common, artificial tongue, then it ought to be simple, straightforward, uniform. Dante perceived that this ideal would be lost in stylistic snobbery and overregulated preciosity, and he was not wrong: Latin subsequently suffocated in the corset, or rather strait jacket, of Renaissance neoclassicism.[25] Thus, Dante's theory of language explains how he could regard the great Priscian as a professional grammarian who was guilty of malpractice. Instead of making Latin a living second language for all who learned its elements, Priscian and his breed excluded all but a few from such benefits by creating a pluperfect language for grammarians rather than for all men.

According to Dante, corrupt grammarians, like other professionals, are motivated by selfish greed, whether for glory or for wealth. Such is the express charge that he alleged in the *Convivio* as a reason why a Latin commentary to his canzoni would serve no purpose. Were he to expound his didactic poems in Latin, only one in a thousand Latin literati would partake of his feast of philosophy,

> so prone are they to love of gain, and thus devoid of all nobleness of mind, which is most of all required for this food. And I say to their reproach that they ought not to be called men of letters, since they do not acquire a knowledge of letters for their proper use, but only so far as they may employ it to gain money or rank; just as no one should be called a lute-player who keeps a lute at home in order to lend it on hire, and not to use it for playing on it.[26]

As the type of a grammarian who writes to gain glory, Priscian was particularly apt, because he had revealed such damnable motives in the dedicatory epistle prefixed to his *Institutes*. The opening paragraphs disclose the fatal attitude:

> I have come to realize that the Latins have extolled, in their own language, the teachings of every form of eloquence and every manner of study that reflects the light of wisdom only after it had been derived from Greek sources, and that the Latins have followed their footsteps in every branch of these liberal pursuits, imitating them not only where they have produced error-free publications, but even some of their mistakes, taken in by their open admiration for such learned men. In this respect it is primarily the very ancient art of grammar that stands accused of such shortcomings, a discipline whose authorities, though more recent [*iuniores*], are for all that more gifted with insight and, in the judgment of the best educated, are admittedly the greatest in natural endowment and the most painstaking in their application, for what could be more well founded than the arts of Herodian or what could possibly be more thorough than the scrupulous disquisitions of Apollonius? Accordingly, since I find that they have expurgated almost all the mistakes that chanced to have been handed down in the Greek commentaries on grammar and have corrected them in terms of a rigorous and disciplined methodology, but that on our own side of the ocean no one has come forward to imitate their work because the study of letters has greatly suffered for lack of writers, I have made every conceivable effort (however much boldly, but not I should think presumptuously) in behalf of a most exacting undertaking—but an enterprise quite in keeping with the objectives of my profession—namely to examine the teaching of the above mentioned authorities and translate the pertinent sections of their work into Latin, and also, by assembling all the related materials that ought certainly to be represented in our own specialized treatment of grammar. I felt it would be a welcome commingling of two points of departure if the more elegant achievements of the masters of both tongues could be combined into one body as a result of my scholarship; for I do not believe there is

any cause for criticism in imitating those who are in the very first ranks of the Greek authorities on grammar, especially after our own scholars of a former generation, as I have pointed out above, have deserved the highest praise even where they reproduced the Greeks' mistakes.

I also purposed to provide an example here lest others, in their efforts to further the common progress of our literary profession, be discouraged from enlisting all due effort to add to whatever I have perchance neglected to mention in my ignorance or to correct whatever I may have put down only poorly—for I firmly believe that nothing in our human endeavor can ever be perfect on every count. Actually I have been forced to publish these writings rather sooner than I had hoped and planned, by reason of the threatening danger of some people who prey upon the efforts of other men, appropriating their written work by stealth and open brigandage, treacherously changing but a single name on the title page in order to steal the glory of the entire publication. Finally, since it is impossible in a work of such magnitude to make a really concise presentation of the material, I beg the indulgence of some small space, although compared to the veritable ocean of Herodian's output and the spacious volumes of his father Apollonius, the contents of my books must indeed seem more in the nature of a brief compendium.[27]

Priscian here presents his work with the conscious pride of an innovator who desires his just share of credit. In the preface he carefully enumerates those features that set this work above all its Latin predecessors, but he also scrupulously acknowledges scholarly debts. Priscian explains that he has borrowed the latest Greek linguistic theories and has applied them for the first time to Latin grammar. Moreover, he has incorporated all the pertinent observations of earlier Latin grammarians, together with new discoveries of his own. These authorities will be regularly cited in the body of the work,[28] but from the outset the reader must understand that, although the content is largely derivative, Priscian alone deserves credit for the conception and execution of this ambitious project. So jealous is he of his due that the work has been published prematurely to forestall the appearance of a pirated edition under the name of some plagiarist. Clearly Priscian believed that glory was the reward for outstanding scholarship. This impression grows as the *gloria* motive recurs in the dedicatory act itself, for our proud author assures his patron, the consul Julian, that the work has been offered to him so that he may share "whatever glory God shall grant me for performing this labor."[29]

Let there be no doubt: the *Institutiones grammaticae* is a great work of scholarship. But what is more important for Priscian's damnation, he meant his work to be great so that it might reflect glory on its author. This thirst for recognition was Priscian's flaw, for in his desire to impress his colleagues, the just and proper function of grammar was forgotten. The author pursued his subject, not as a good in itself or to others, but as an occasion to exhibit his *virtù*.

UNNATURAL GRAMMAR

Now we have half of our answer. It is clear that, to Dante's mind, Priscian was a misguided grammarian; but this does not explain why Priscian qua grammarian was placed among those who violated nature. To discover how Dante might have conceived that a grammarian could violate nature, we must inquire more deeply into Dante's convictions about the nature of language in general and of grammar in particular. It will be a hazardous enterprise, for in these matters his utterances are unfortunately incomplete and all too often are enigmatic. When Dante wrote about language, Italian was his primary concern, and he developed his views on language and Latin only insofar as they were necessary for his argument. From these fragmentary indications, we must seek to reconstruct the theories that he undoubtedly held but never fully expressed. This is a risky business at best, and it is all the more difficult because these theories appear to differ from one work to another. Now, although it must be admitted that Dante's thought may have developed or even reached new conclusions, I think that one must assume consistency unless faced with irreconcilable statements, and I shall accordingly endeavor to harmonize statements that he made at different times and in various contexts.[30]

My contention will be that Priscian was included among nature's violators because Dante believed that Latin grammar was by its nature subject to change, and hence that any attempt to stabilize it completely would be contrary to nature. To begin with, we may note that this position seems implicit in the account of the origin of grammar in *De vulgari eloquentia* 1. 9. 11 (quoted above at n. 22). In support of this, we may note that Dante categorically asserted in the section (§ 10) just preceding that passage, that "language changes . . . nor can it by any means stand still" ("sermo variatur . . . nec stare ullo modo potest"). From this it would seem that grammar, which was invented to overcome certain disadvantages accruing from this inevitable linguistic flux, could impart to language only relative stability. And indeed, Dante claimed no monolithic unity for grammar, but instead carefully qualified his definition: "Grammar is nothing else but a kind of unchangeable identity of speech in different times and places" ("gramatica nichil aliud est quam quedam inalterabilis locutionis idemptitas diversis temporibus atque locis"). To be sure, in *some* respects grammar is inalterable, but not in all, as the qualifying *quedam* warns. This is but a hint: the explanation is to be found elsewhere.

To discover in what respects Dante thought grammar was subject to change, we must turn to *Convivio* 2. 13, where it is shown that a comparison exists between each of the several sciences and the ten heavens. Grammar, the first of the seven liberal arts, is likened to the lowest heaven, that of the moon, with this explanation:

> I say that the heaven of the Moon resembles Grammar because it may be compared with it. For if the Moon is carefully observed, there may be seen in it two things peculiar to it, which are not seen in the other stars; the one is the shadow in it, which is nothing else but rarity of its substance, upon which the rays of the sun cannot be brought to a stand and reflected back as in the other parts; the other is the variation in its brilliancy, which shines now on one side, now on the other, according as the sun looks upon it. And Grammar has these two properties, because on account of its infinitude the rays of the reason are not brought to a stand in any direction,

[33]

especially in the case of words; and it shines now from this side, now from that, in so far as certain words, certain declensions, certain constructions are in use which formerly were not, and many formerly were in use which shall hereafter be in use again, as Horace says in the beginning of the *Poetry*,[31] when he affirms that "many words shall revive which formerly have lapsed, &c."[32]

Perhaps it was inevitable that the first art should be equated to the first heaven, but it is nonetheless significant that scholastic cosmology accounted the moon to be the only imperfect planet precisely because of its shadows and phases, the two properties from which Dante draws his comparisons.[33] The comparable characteristics of grammar likewise make that study an imperfect science. First, its possibilities are unlimited, especially with regard to vocabulary; therefore, finite human reason cannot pretend to comprehend this infinite subject. The grammarian will never have the last word. In contrast to the first property of grammar, which considers the potential scope of the subject, the second describes its actual condition. This is a state of constant flux, in which grammar apparently resembles the primary languages. What is more, grammar appears to be subject to change in all of its parts—words, their formation, and syntax. Finally, there is the suggestion not only of flux but of reflux: grammatical fashions come into being, pass away, and then return. When any one of the infinite number of possible words comes into actual use, its grammatical status is still not assured, for although the grammarian may attest its use or disuse in the past and the present, his art cannot determine whether it will remain in usage in the future.

From *Convivio* 2. 13 we now know that some of the vocabulary, declensions, and constructions of grammar are not in constant use. The assertion of *De vulgari eloquentia* 1. 9. 10 that "language changes . . . nor can it by any means stand still" had already suggested that this might be so, but the case can be most firmly established from Dante's final pronouncement on the nature of language, which he made in the *Paradiso*. There the relation between nature and language is unequivocally expounded to the pilgrim by Adam, who explains that the *lingua* that he first spoke in the Terrestrial Paradise had changed even before the Confusion of Tongues:

> The tongue I spoke was all extinct before Nimrod's race gave their mind to the unaccomplishable task; for no product whatever of reason—since human choice is renewed with the course of heaven—can last forever. It is a work of nature that man should speak, but whether in this way or that nature then leaves you to follow your own pleasure.[34]

> La lingua ch'io parlai fu tutta spenta
>   innanzi che a l'ovra inconsummabile
>   fosse la gente di Nembròt attenta:
> ché nullo effetto mai razïonabile,
>   per lo piacere uman che rinovella
>   seguendo il cielo, sempre fu durabile.
> Opera naturale è ch'uom favella;

ma così o così, natura lascia
poi fare a voi secondo che v'abbella.

(Par. xxvi, 124–32)

Here the natural law of language is clearly, if broadly, defined. Nature governs human speech in two respects at least: first, it is by nature that man is a speaking animal; and second, it is a work of nature that whatever speech man uses is bound to change. Both ideas had been developed in Dante's earlier works, but the role of nature is most clearly expressed in this passage. The faculty of human speech is natural to man, and specifically it is an effect of his rational nature.[35] Self-expression in words is for Dante a fundamental human need, so basic, indeed, that he opined it to have been Adam's first act, spontaneous and unhesitant.[36] Note here especially that nature does not prescribe any specific form of human speech. Man's nature impels him to express ideas in sounds, but the means of expression is purely arbitrary and conventional.

In the *Paradiso*, linguistic change appears as an inevitable law of nature. Because nature leaves men free to make up any language that suits them, languages are a product of the human mind; and since men can change their minds, they can also change their fashions of speaking.[37] In the *De vulgari eloquentia*, we were simply told that since "homo sit instabilissimum atque variabilissimum animal" (1. 9. 6), this changeable animal alters his language as he does his customs and fashions. But now we have learned from Adam in Paradise that men's tastes do not change haphazardly but are governed by the movements of the heavens.[38] By the introduction of a cosmic cause, linguistic change becomes an inevitable law of nature. This natural law not only permits men to construct whatever language they choose, but also makes it impossible for them to preserve the language of their choice free from change. Thus the variability that the *Convivio* represented as a property of grammar now proves to be a property inherent by nature in *all* human language, of which grammar is but one manifestation. The process is exemplified as Adam goes on to explain that although the first word he uttered was *J*, the name of God, yet soon after his death the form *El* replaced it:

> . . . and that is fitting, for the usage of mortals is like a leaf on a branch, which goes and another comes.[39]

> . . . e ciò convene,
> ché l'uso d'i mortali è come fronda
> in ramo, che sen va e altra vene.

(Par. xxvi, 136–38)

Perhaps there are other natural linguistic laws that Adam omitted to mention, but from him we have learned two respects in which nature can be violated by interfering with "freedom of speech"—either by denying man the power of speech or by ignoring the reality of linguistic change. Either attitude would be perverse enough, but clearly neither could hope to be successful in practice, for both the faculty of speech and the tendency to change its means of expression are inevitable.

[35]

That indeed is the meaning of natural law: it is the way things are and how they operate.

One can, however, violate nature by doctrines as well as by deeds, and in a teacher and authority like Priscian, such an intellectual vice would have particularly pernicious effects. As has already been remarked, Priscian conceived his *Institutes* as a definitive treatise on the Latin language, and for the most part, his definitions are presented as descriptions of the inherent nature of that language, systematized moreover in accordance with certain universal linguistic laws discovered by his Greek predecessors. Priscian treats language as a natural phenomenon, governed by the unchanging laws of its nature, which human reason can discover both for the genus *lingua* and for the species *latina*. Once known, these are natural laws that state the constitution of things linguistic, not merely bylaws that are descriptive of arbitrary human conventions.

To Dante, however, Priscian's attempt to discover a "natural grammar" would appear as an illegitimate, unnatural, and presumptuous enterprise, because in Dantesque thought, language has no fixed nature of its own but is the by-product of human nature. From his anthropology, the good grammarian should derive but two laws of "natural language": that language must consist of significant signs because the rational animal can only communicate his thought by means that are perceptible to the senses; and that these signs are nothing more than human conventions that vary because human tastes are swayed by the changing heavens. Moreover, observant of Dante's second law, the true grammarian will not claim for his craft the authority of a natural science: to do so would constitute an intellectual perversion of nature. Hence Priscian violated nature by treating linguistic phenomena, which by nature are relative, dynamic, and manmade, as if they were absolute, static, and autonomous.

THE RULES OF GRAMMAR

Having discovered how Dante could regard Priscian as a violator of nature because of his professional activity as a Latin grammarian, our inquiry has reached its goal. The damnation of Priscian, like that of Brunetto Latini, can be explained as an intellectual rather than a sexual perversion.

To attain this goal, we have examined Dante's views on language, Latin, and grammar only so far as was necessary to establish a new basis for Priscian's sin. The proposed explanation, if acceptable, should itself cast new light on the obscurities of Dante's linguistic thought; but to pursue these implications is beyond the scope of this essay. It is only proper, however, since our argument has stressed the element of change in Latin grammar, to redress the balance by adding some concluding remarks on the *stability* of grammar, which after all was for Dante the distinguishing characteristic of a grammatical language.[40]

How can an artificial language possibly be stable if astral influences are continually altering human taste? Apparently Dante foresaw this objection to his definition of grammar, since directly after the proposed definition he provided this response, as it were, to an unstated difficulty. Grammar, "having been settled by the common consent of many peoples, seems exposed to the arbitrary will of none in particular, and consequently cannot be variable" (quoted above at n. 22). By a common act of will, the many peoples who use Latin as a secondary language have agreed that it be governed by a set body of rules *(regulata)*. Because the group as a whole has consented, no individual or subgroup may now dissent. By what may be called a "linguistic contract," the users of Latin have, in the interests of intercommunication, surrendered their natural right to speak as they please. The resultant uniformity is a human law of the same order as other laws governing human conduct that are neither repugnant to nature nor positively required by natural law. That the regulation of Latin grammar was a species of legislation is suggested in *De vulgari eloquentia* by Dante's use of the term *positores* as a synonym for the *inventores gramatice facultatis*.[41] The legislative function of the *positores* is not evident in *De vulgari eloquentia*, but the equivalent Italian term *ponitori* is used in the *Convivio* for those who frame laws for the common good:

> And, moreover, to give to many is impossible without giving to a single individual, inasmuch as the many include the one, but it is quite possible to give to a single individual without giving to many. Therefore whoever helps many confers both benefits, whoever helps an individual confers only one benefit; and hence we see that the framers [*ponitori*] of laws, in drawing them up, keep their eyes chiefly fixed on the most universal benefits.[42]

The stability of grammar, then, is achieved through rules established by common consent for the general welfare.

Thus far Dante is clear, but he is mysteriously noncommittal about how the rules were formulated and by whom. The originators are simply called by terms that are descriptive of their function—*inventores* or *positores*, the inventors or builders of grammar. Attempts have been made to identify them as the Greeks who discovered the general linguistic theories on which grammar is based and/or as the Latins who, like Priscian, applied these specifically to their own language.[43] If our interpretation of Priscian's sin is correct, those who treated grammar as a branch of natural science may at least be ruled out. It may be that for Dante the true *inventores* were poets and other literary artists who "regulated" their language by being the first to realize its potentialities and to provide models for the future.[44] Probably, however, Dante shrewdly evaded this historical question for which he could provide no definite and demonstrable answer. Whatever his reasons, he chose to leave the matter vague, and in view of this we cannot be sure that he did in fact have a more precise notion of the historical origins of Latin grammar than the one that he expressed. We must be content with the nebulous assertion that the rules of grammar were imposed on an otherwise changing language at some period in the past by certain unspecified individuals.

Finally, we may ask, What were the rules of Latin grammar that Dante recognized as binding? The answer might seem self-evident were it not for his condemnation of Priscian, which could imply disapproval of the rules no less than of their author. Now, it is altogether possible that Dante regarded many of Priscian's dicta as superfluous refinements, alien to the true function of grammar, since the scrupulous observance of the vast body of prescripts imposed by the *Institutiones* would make communication difficult if not impossible. On the other hand, it seems more probable that although Dante objected to the pseudoscientific spirit which animated that work, still he accepted its regulations, however perversely conceived, because their acceptance by the Latin-speaking world had made them authoritative. The question might be resolved if one had but the patience to determine by comparison how closely Dante's Latinity was in practice regulated by the finer points laid down by Priscian,[45] but such a desperate expedient is fortunately not necessary for the present study, since the conception of a linguistic contract permitted Dante to accept the rules while condemning their inventor. From his definitions of grammar in *De vulgari eloquentia* 1. 1 and 1. 9, one would expect that Dante himself would identify the rules of Latin grammar simply as those we learn in school, certainly from Donatus, perhaps later from Priscian or some other advanced grammar, or preferably from the study and imitation of classical models.

[3]

Francesco d'Accorso the Unnatural Lawyer

The notary and the grammarian did not practice their respective professions as God and nature intended, and thereby rose to fame in this world and fell into damnation in the next. With them ran another famous professional, the lawyer Francesco d'Accorso. This we know because Brunetto told Dante the traveler that "Priscian goes on with that wretched crowd, and Francesco d'Accorso also" ("Priscian sen va con quella turba grama, / e Francesco d'Accorso anche;" *Inf.* xv, 109–10).[1] From Brunetto's description of his group, it follows that this man was, like the rest, a clerk, a great man of Latin letters, and a personage of great fame.[2] Moreover, Brunetto linked his name with that of Priscian. The order is perhaps significant, for Francesco's name is loosely subjoined to the main clause, as if it were an afterthought: "and Francesco d'Accorso also."

This subtle subordination reflects the train of thought of the speaker, Brunetto Latini. As such, it is but one of several indications which remind the reader that his informant at this point is not the pilgrim turned poet but rather one of the squinty-eyed scholars, whose subjective point of view may color this account of his comrades. The first words of his response do in fact warn us that Brunetto consciously intends to select only certain of his companions according to his own criteria:

> ... Saper d'alcuno è buono;
>   de li altri fia laudabile tacerci,
>   ché 'l tempo saria corto a tanto suono.

To know of some is good; of the others it will be laudable to be still, as the time would be too short for so much sound.

(Inf. xv, 103–5)

That his choice is indeed colored by his own subjective opinions becomes evident a few lines later, when he pointedly omits to name a bishop of Florence because Latini assumes that the pilgrim would agree with him that the man merits the abusive term *(tigna)* with which Brunetto chooses to dismiss him.[3] Brunetto Latini, then, had his own reasons for bringing certain scholars to the attention of his former protégé.

What were Brunetto's criteria? Two factors determined each choice, both of which he plainly distinguished. He would name only persons about whom, in his opinion, it would be (a) good that Dante know and (b) not unpraiseworthy that Brunetto speak. Thus the choice depended on Brunetto's estimate of what he ought to say and the pilgrim to hear. Clearly the choice is relative both to the speaker and to his audience. Less clear are the operative terms *buono* and *laudabile*, which tell us nothing in themselves, for both involve subjective value judgments on Brunetto's part. One can only discover what "good" and "laudable" meant to Latini by examining the choices he actually made.

Therefore he considers it good that Dante should know, and not unpraiseworthy that Brunetto should mention, first of all that Priscian shares his fate, "and Francesco d'Accorso also." No doubt he is proud to be found in such distinguished company, for were not Latinity and law his stock in trade as a notary? Further, it accords well with Brunetto's classical humanism that he should regard Priscian as the most notable of his infernal colleagues. A difficulty appears, however, when we ask why he thought it good that Dante should know what fate had befallen Francesco d'Accorso. The poet and the notary can readily be presumed to have had a common interest in Priscian, but not in Francesco. The case of d'Accorso, then, poses a special problem, which we can hope to answer after we have learned in what way, other than sodomy, this man might be said by Dante to have done violence to nature.

WHO WAS FRANCESCO D'ACCORSO?

Our work divides into two parts: first, we must search the life, works, and reputation of the historical Francis Accursii for suspiciously unnatural thoughts and deeds; secondly, by examining Dante's opinions on these questionable acts, we may hope to account for his damnation of Francesco d'Accorso. But before beginning, we must identify our suspect, for until recently there appeared to be several persons who bore that name in the thirteenth century. The most prominent was the author of the *Glossa ordinaria* to the *Corpus iuris civilis*, who has repeatedly been confused with his son, the genuine Francesco d'Accorso. The father's Christian name, however, was simply Accorso—Accursus being the original Latin form, which was later altered to Accursius.[4] From his birthplace near Florence, the glossator was surnamed either Fiorentino or da Bagnolo. In a painstaking notice, Piero Fiorelli drily notes that earlier biographers have called him Francesco without any justification.[5] The distinction between father and son is clearly present in the inscription on their joint tomb, which dates from the latter's death in 1293: "SEPVLCRVM ACVRSI GLOSATORIS LEGVM FRANCISCI EIVS FILII."[6] Fiorelli has also determined the long disputed question of the dates of the Glossator's birth and death (born 1181 × 1185, died 1259 × 1263). These *minima* vitiate the argument of André Pézard, who sought to identify Dante's Francesco with the Glossator by supposing that Accorso da Bagnolo was his father, as would have been possible if, as was once believed, the first Accursius had been born in 1151.[7] This still does not leave the Glossator's son in full possession of his name, for Accorso da Reggio (fl. 1263–1279) has long been supposed to have had, like his homonym and contemporary the

Glossator, a son named Francesco, who now has been proven to be a fiction compounded of errors.[8]

With the elimination of these ghosts, we are left with only one Francesco d'Accorso who lived before 1300, the ideal date of the *Comedy*, namely the Glossator's eldest son. Some have sought to disqualify even him on the grounds that his death has occasionally been dated after 1300, but there is now general agreement that he died in June 1293.[9] This identification is supported by those of Dante's early commentators who do not confuse Francesco with his father. Jacopo della Lana, a Bolognese who wrote between 1323 and 1328, presents the earliest account that is free from internal contradictions:

> This man was a great Bolognese legist; he was the son of Master Accursius, who was a Florentine and made the apparatus to the *Corpus iuris civilis*.

> Questo fu un gran legista bolognese, lo quale fu figliuolo di messer Accorso, che fu fiorentino, e fe' li Apparati al Corpo di ragione civile.[10]

Half a century later, Benvenuto da Imola, whose work was largely done in Bologna, unhesitatingly and unmistakably identified Dante's Francesco d'Accorso as the Glossator's son.[11] Thus we can at least be sure that an allusion to one Francesco d'Accorso, dead by 1300, could refer Dante's contemporaries to only one man.

Before we proceed to examine the historical Francis Accursii, we would do well to pause briefly and reflect upon his name. Since Dante left his readers no clue other than this, it would seem reasonable to suppose that contemporaries were expected to divine his meaning in at least a general way by pondering "Francesco d'Accorso" and its common associations. To be sure, a detailed knowledge of the man and his works should substantiate the popular image if the condemnation was a just one, but first impressions must be indicative if the name alone was to suggest the sin. It may be objected that this approach is extremely subjective, as indeed it is; nonetheless it can be successful if the poet relied upon stereotyped associations that he could expect the mention of a name would evoke from his intended reader. We have already seen that Priscian was invoked to conjure up visions of a grammatical treatise that had no practical utility. Should this approach be valid, those of my readers who know Francis Accursii as more than a name should be able to anticipate my conclusions by attempting a simple mental experiment: consider for a moment what in your mind distinguishes this man from all others. Meanwhile, for those who are unfamiliar with him, I shall hasten to add biographical details.[12]

IN HIS FATHER'S FOOTSTEPS

The career of Francis Accursii is inseparable from that of his father, the great glossator, whose achievements so overshadow those of his son that the next generation could hardly distinguish between them.[13] From his father, Francis inherited both the fame and the fortune that were the controlling factors in his life, and to appreciate this patrimony, we must first consider the career of Accursius *antiquus*.

Born in modest circumstances near Florence, Accorso through his *virtù* became the most famous, if not the most learned, Roman lawyer of the Middle Ages. His reputation was assured because his glosses to the whole of Justinian's *Corpus* were so useful that for four centuries the *Glossa ordinaria*, as the Accursian apparatus came to be called, was the standard companion to the text of the civil law. For the medieval law student, Accursius' gloss was the standard interpretation, which he read before class, where both text and gloss were explained to him by the professor. Until 1627, this Accursian apparatus was printed in the margins of every edition of the *Corpus iuris civilis*.[14] Thus, successive generations of students knew the author as the basic interpreter of the civil law. Like Donatus, Accursius provided his discipline with the essential tool for instruction and thereby earned the gratitude that awaits the author of a successful school book.

Other textbooks have brought their authors equal fame, but the material benefits realized by Accursius have never been equaled, for his career yielded profits beyond the dreams of even the most affluent American professor. By the end of his life, the Glossator had established himself and his sons as the economic and social peers of the greatest Bolognese aristocrats. Of this success, his town house and his country villa were the outward signs. The *palazzo* that he built was so commodious that it was later acquired from his heirs by the commune and became the core of the city hall. Significantly, the neighborhood was Ghibelline, with the Lambertazzi, leaders of the local party, across the piazza, and the Guezzi adjoining Accursius' own property. In the country he acquired a villa, the Riccardina, which was on the Idice near Budrio and was surrounded by 271 hectares of land. This country house, to which he retired after forty years of teaching, was also a considerable mansion, for eventually it came to house a Franciscan convent.[15] Yet another index of his prosperity is his library, the greatest owned by any medieval lawyer.[16] His rise to fame and fortune can be measured in social prestige as well, for he married his eldest son to Aichina Guezzi, the girl next door, whose house was both aristocratic and Ghibelline.[17] In a word, Accursius established his family as one of the greatest in Bologna. Moreover, from a letter which he addressed to Pier della Vigna, we know that his attachment to the Ghibelline cause was neither nominal nor merely local.[18]

As the eldest son of the Glossator, Francis inherited his father's academic and social prominence. The patrimony was shared with three stepbrothers, but of all the Accursii, Francis identified himself most closely with his father. The magnificent father-and-son mausoleum that he built in the Franciscan cemetery, to which his father's remains were transferred from their original Dominican resting place, manifests the son's determination both to perpetuate his father's fame and to associate himself therewith.[19] That contemporaries accepted this father-son equation is most clearly evident in the tribute that was paid to them by the Guelf commune in 1309, when their joint contribution to the community was recognized as sufficient reason to exempt their descendants from the penalties to which other former Ghibelline families were subject:

... descendentes venerande memorie domini Accursii et domini Francisci de Accursiis, patrum et dominorum omnium scolarium et studentium in iure civili per universum mundum, qui tantum onorem fecerunt civitati Bononie, glosando in civitate Bononie et illuminando ius civile et scolares de toto mundo ex hoc ad civitatem Bononie convocando, ita quod ipsa civitas honoratur, et divulgatur eius fama per mundum universum.[20]

This close identification, which was apparently encouraged by Francis and the later Accursii, does much to account for the tendency of all but the best informed of Dante's commentators to confuse son and father. Selmi's Anonymous (1321 × 1337), for example, thought that Francis had "glossed all the books of the laws," when in fact he had not.[21] Indeed, only rarely does one find Francis praised apart from his father. One of the few to do so was the notarist Pietro de' Boattieri (1260–1334), who eulogized him in the proem to his commentary on the notarial art.[22] In legal literature, Francis is rarely cited as an authority, which strongly suggests that his opinions were hardly original. In the anecdote by which he was best remembered in Bologna's classrooms, he appears as a pious mediocrity, vainly defending his father's gloss against the best legal mind of the day. The incident occurred at a French university (probably Orléans in 1274), where he was slyly drawn into a disputation on an extremely obscure title of the *Codex* (7. 47) with Jacques de Révigny, who, though a great jurist, had for the occasion disguised himself as a student. Cino da Pistoia, Dante's friend, reports the encounter thus:

> Glossa per praedictam ratione non potest sustineri, nec potuit eam defendere Franciscus Accursii dum legeret hanc legem ultra montes, dum fuit cum Rege Angliae, et Jacobus praedictus in forma discipuli poneret sibi, nimirum non erat in mundo adversarius durior nec subtilior.

A generation later, Bartolus retold the tale in a way that brings out even more clearly the son's dependence on his father:

> Quidem, ut dominus Franciscus Accursii, cum semel fuerit advocatus pro rege Angliae, in studio Tolosano[23] repetiit istam legem et recitavit, et tenuit opinionem patris sui prout iacet. Dominus Jacobus de Ravenis qui erat ibi magnus doctor, in forma discipuli surrexit contra eum, et opposuit sic.[24]

The impression left by this glimpse of Francis in the classroom is reinforced when we turn to examine his works. Despite his great reputation, he produced no legal writing of any great importance. Quite probably he did write the abstracts *(casus)* for the *Digestum novum*, though his claim to similar summaries for other parts of the two laws ranges from dubious to outrageously anachronistic.[25] Useful though these summaries are, they hardly constitute a great work of jurisprudence. A pair of surviving *consilia* testify to his employment as a jurisconsult.[26] Putting these indications together, it would seem that his work, compared with that of the other great jurists of his day, did not rise above mediocrity either in quantity or quality. Evidently his reputation was far greater than his accomplishments, and we can only conclude that by attaining a modicum of competence, Francis was able to participate in the reflected glory of his illustrious father.

Nothing that we have found thus far would in itself cause Dante to condemn a man. Our poet certainly did not subscribe to the principle of publish or perish; far from it, he quite probably would have accorded Francis an honorable place in Purgatory if he had been content to live off the accumulated prestige and capital that was his heritage, for it was a worthy occupation to expound the Roman law as his father had done. What we have discovered suggests, nonetheless, that we are on the right track, for Francis was evidently eager for a fame that he could not attain through his own powers, and the *Inferno* is filled with those who sinned to attain fame or fortune that was not their due. Whether Francis succumbed to the temptation of his false position remains to be seen.

Accursian Avarice

Since the *Divine Comedy* was not written for the Bolognese alone, much less for lawyers, Dante could not assume that evidence such as we have examined thus far would be available to his ideal reader, whom I take to be a literate Italian, not necessarily a Latinist. If, as I think likely, Dante considered the name of Francesco d'Accorso enough to suggest his meaning to such a reader, then the clue must lie in the popular image of the man. Here we are fortunate, considering how elusive such evidence can be, in that Francis was the subject of one of the anecdotes collected shortly before his death in the *Cento novelle antiche*.[27] We are told that when Master Francis returned from England, where he had been for a long time, he proposed to the commune of Bologna that, since by law an absent father was entitled to any profits realized by his sons during his absence, the commune ought to recognize that he had an analogous claim to the possessions of his former students, who in his absence and with great profit had themselves become masters.

Whether true or not, the story certainly suggests that in his lifetime Francis had a reputation for putting his legal knowledge to serve his avarice. The tale does not tell what response the commune gave, so we may be sure that the humor of the story lies in the request alone. Taken by itself, the anecdote is susceptible of various interpretations, but a contemporary document places the point beyond dispute. In 1291, Pope Nicholas IV responded to Francis' petition for papal absolution from the sin of usury. He had confessed to the pope that both he and his father were guilty of sin, inasmuch as they had lent money to students at interest and had, as examiners, received bribes in the form of gifts. Both father and son are absolved on the condition that they make restitution *(iniqui foenoris)*: directly to laymen, but to clerics indirectly, through pious donations.[28] Evidently Francis complied at least with the second condition, because in his will he provided benefactions for churches and charities in England, France, and Spain as well as in Bologna and other Italian cities.[29] The details of his shady business operations need not concern us,[30] for two documents suffice to establish the point. From the bull it is clear that Francis did in fact exploit students for his financial advantage, and the *Novellino* leaves no doubt that, however widespread such practices may have been among his colleagues, Francis was to the popular mind the very type of the avaricious professor.

Have we discovered the cause of Francis' damnation? It is possible that Dante was either unaware of Francis' repentance or perhaps did not think him sincere. But in either case, the crimes for which he received papal absolution were punished elsewhere in the *Inferno*. Usury, though related to the unnatural sin of Francesco d'Accorso, is patently distinct from it, being an offense against not only nature but also art, as Virgil explains in *Inferno* xi, 97–111. The usurers, moreover, have all been identified beyond question as those who sit at the inner rim of the circle of the violent, laden with purses bearing the arms of great banking houses (*Inf.* xvii, 43–75). Likewise, it is not possible that d'Accorso was condemned as a corrupt examiner, for that would qualify him for a lower place in Hell, among the fraudulent. Hence we may be reasonably certain that Francis was not condemned for the crimes he confessed to Nicholas IV.

The *Novellino* suggests, however, that Francis' avarice knew no bounds, and it may well have led him to obtain money from students by other means for which he was neither repentant nor forgiven. When one considers that the great wealth of the Accursii was derived in no small part from student fees, one of the medieval maxims on which Professor Gaines Post has lavished his learning cannot but come to mind: "Scientia donum dei est, unde vendi non potest."[31] Could it be that d'Accorso's crime consists in receiving more than the just price for his services as a teacher? To investigate this possibility, we shall first ascertain what doctrine Accursius and his son professed, and no doubt practiced, concerning the remuneration of masters, and this position we shall then compare with that of Dante and the scholastic interpreters of Aristotle.

The *Glossa ordinaria* admits that the civil law cannot by its nature be sold. Like other forms of wisdom, *civilis sapientia* is a gift of God (*donum dei*); and legists, the gloss maintains, are true philosophers who scorn money.[32] Francis himself summarized the legal fiction by which these ideals were in practice circumvented: "Item nec doctoribus legum ius reddent, qui petunt a discipulis suis salarium constitui et solvi et redditur ratio in litera. Si tamen discipuli velint aliquid sponte dare doctori suo, doctor potest recipere."[33] Thus, in Post's words, "neither philosophers nor doctors of law can legally ask students to pay their salaries, but they can accept whatever the students wish to give of their own free will (*sponte*)." Accursius' apparatus leaves no doubt that at Bologna this spontaneous giving was highly institutionalized. When the student began his course of study, he promised certain gifts (*dona*) to his professor, and this promise was legally binding, for the teacher could bring suit if the promise was not fulfilled. Moreover, there was a formula that determined the size of the fee: "The salary ought to be given according to the means and dignity of the giver and of him to whom it is given."[34] The ideal apparently imposed a certain propriety upon the professor, but not much. Although professional ethics forbade him to request a promise from the new student, still the *Glossa ordinaria* gave him a legitimate opportunity to discuss the question on the first day of class. Accursius himself recalls that legists are true philosophers, and he refers to Papinian's statement that "vere philosophantes pecuniam contemnunt" (*Dig.* 50. 5. 8. 4); but he hastens to remind his class that "we do not reject money" ("licet pecuniam non abiiciamus"; *Dig.* 1. 1. 1. 1, ad vv. "nisi fallor").

If Dante had wished to condemn the legists' customary gratuities as a system, it is hard to see why the elder Accursius would not have been placed among Brunetto's band, since the son merely echoed his father's apparatus, which authorized the practice. But surely the Glossator was not with Brunetto, for Francesco would not have been named in preference to his more illustrious father, whose Florentine birth would have ensured the pilgrim's interest. From this circumstance, it follows that Francis' sin must have been one that did not taint his father.[35]

Since the two are hardly distinguishable in doctrine or professional ethics, one may wonder whether Francesco's fault was perhaps that he somehow followed too closely in his father's footsteps. We have seen that the son not only owed his position and reputation to his father's efforts far more than to his own, but also that he was disposed to assume his father's *dignitas* as his own. Since custom required Bolognese law students to proportion their gifts to the dignity of their professor, it would seem that Francis would be offered gifts more suitable to his father, and we may imagine him saying, if he had any twinge of conscience, "licet pecuniam non abiiciamus." No doubt he accepted as his due whatever was offered.

According to the teaching of the thirteenth-century scholastics, however, he should have received no more than the worth of his labor. Although the schoolmen agreed with Aristotle that truth and knowledge cannot be measured in terms of money, they were not content with his recommendation that the question of recompense be left entirely to the student. Instead, following Aquinas, the scholastics insisted that the work involved in teaching provided a measure of the just price in philosophy as in other fields of human endeavor.[36] Dante, we may be sure, made this labor theory of value his own, for in the *Inferno* it provided the justification for his condemnation of usury (xi, 97–111). The usurer "despises nature both in itself and in its follower," namely art, because instead of toiling by the sweat of his brow, he lets his money work for him, which is contrary to nature, since money is sterile. Dante expressly cites Genesis as his authority that man is obliged to gain his living from nature and his own labor, apparently referring to 3:17b, 19a: "In laboribus comedes ex ea [terra] cunctis diebus vitae tuae. . . . In sudore vultus tui vesceris pane." Unlike the usurers, Francis did no violence to nature through art, for insofar as he labored, he did so honestly. On the other hand, he did do violence to nature by accepting the just price for his father's labor as if it were his own.[37]

FRANCIS' EXILE AND REPATRIATION

Is this, then, our conclusion? To me it seems possible but nonetheless improbable. Though the last step of the argument is certainly debatable, perhaps endlessly, still it is not impossible. Yet even if the argument were in itself flawless, I would not be satisfied with the conclusion, because the case seems to me to be special rather than typical. How many legists, not to mention other intellectuals, find themselves in the position of Accursius' son? So few, I think, that his special case seems hardly worth a place in the *Comedy*. Since all of Brunetto's companions are professional intellectuals, one would suppose that the sins of individual members of the group typify the failings of the intelligentsia in general and each profession in particular to fulfill its function in the natural order. The case that we have constructed against Francis, however, is based on a sin that is neither limited to intellectuals nor particularly typical of his profession. Thus the reputation of a famous craftsman might enable his son to sell mediocre work for more than it was worth, though the culprit would not find a place among the *cherci* and *litterati* of Brunetto's company.

In short, we must continue our search for the sin of the unnatural lawyer. The false lead we have pursued can serve to suggest a more profitable line of inquiry, because the reasons that suggested the hypothesis and then rendered it inacceptable do in fact permit us to define more clearly the sin that we are looking for. On the one hand, as Francis was a legist, we must expect that the sin was common in that profession; on the other hand, since his father does not share the son's fate, we may be sure that the sin consists in something that distinguishes son from father. With these qualifications in mind, let us look again at the *Novellino*'s tale about Francis to see whether his contemporaries were struck by anything that distinguished him from his father. The opening words of the anecdote provide the clue: "Maestro Francesco, figliuolo del maestro Accorso de la città di Bologna, *quando ritornò d'Inghilterra, dove era stato longamente*, fece una così fatta proposta dinanzi al Comune di Bologna, e disse. . . ."[38] There may have been many avaricious professors of Roman law who might have sought to share in their students' success, but the story would fit only one who was known to have absented himself from Bologna for a long time, and the travels of Francis were so familiar that the storyteller could sketch the situation without further explanation. the tale takes place at the moment "when he had returned from England, where he had been for a long time." We can be sure that Francis' absence in England was the one episode in his career that was common knowledge during Dante's lifetime, for his friend Cino thought that Francis' presence in France was sufficiently explained by remarking that the disputation with Révigny had taken place "dum fuit cum Rege Angliae," as though every student in Bologna knew about that.[39] Even today Francis is remembered as a councillor of the first Edward no less than as a son of the Glossator, and indeed if the mental experiment I proposed earlier has been successful, many of my readers have impatiently had this in mind through the foregoing preliminaries. Since it was the one event of his career that would distinguish Francis from his father for Dante's contemporaries, we may suspect that it contains the clue to the damnation of Francesco d'Accorso, and we shall accordingly consider this aspect of his life in greater detail.

The episode as related by his modern biographers readily suggests a plausible solution.[40] According to most authorities, Edward met Francis when the king was passing through Bologna in May 1273 on his way home from the Holy Land to assume the crown that he had just inherited. Francis, in this version, remained behind to settle his affairs and then joined Edward in France.[41] In May 1274 he witnessed a notarial process in the king's presence at Limoges; and during the next seven years he lived in England, serving Edward as *consiliarius* and *secretarius*, and receiving, among other benefits, an annual salary of £200.[42] He sold his services dearly, for the constable of the Tower of London received only half as much, and Edward's papal notary commanded barely a quarter of Francis' fee.[43] His service in England ended in 1281, when he returned to Bologna to resume his teaching, but he agreed at that time to serve Edward's interests in Italy for a lifetime annuity of 40 marks.[44]

No contemporary record tells us either why he left Bologna or why he returned. The evidence for this is all circumstantial, consisting for the most part of legal and official documents from London and Bologna that tell us where he was, what he was doing, and how much he was paid, but they leave us to guess what his motives might have been. Since we already know his reputation for avarice, it is all too easy to explain his decision to leave Bologna with reference to that alone. Recent accounts give the impression that Edward was able to persuade Francis in the space of a very few days, presumably by offering an irresistibly high salary. That might explain why he left Bologna, but not why he returned. The facts, however, are susceptible to quite another interpretation, which although it does not exclude the profit motive, will permit us to see Francis as something worse than a legal mercenary.

From Bologna to England

The English interlude in Francis' teaching career was for him more than a lucrative venture: it provided him with an alibi during the fiercest civil war in Bolognese history. Accursius, it will be recalled, belonged to the aristocratic Lambertazzi faction, the local Ghibelline party. In Accursius' day, the Lambertazzi had already begun their rivalry with the Geremei, leaders of the Guelfs of Bologna, who in domestic politics represented the commercial interests of the new plutocracy of guild masters against those of the old aristocracy of birth and landed wealth. Both sides struggled for control of the communal government that ruled the city, and in 1270 the Geremei won a constitutional victory by excluding the nobles from membership in the companies of arms, which were the communal militia that, together with the guilds, elected the communal officials. For the next four years, the commune was split by a great debate over whether it should make war on Guelf Modena or Ghibelline Forlì. Each party urged war on the allies of its rival, and as the tension between the opposing factions grew progressively worse, brawls and street fights between their adherents became increasingly common. The conflict assumed legendary proportions, for a later century would tell the tale of Imelda Lambertazzi and Bonifazio Geremei, two lovers who, if they were not the prototypes of Romeo and Juliet, at least shared with them the same folk motive.[45] In the spring of 1273 the will of the Geremei prevailed, and the commune laid siege to Ghibelline Forlì in May.

At this juncture, Edward I appeared on the scene. As he was returning from his crusade in the Holy Land, news of his father's death had met him halfway, in Sicily (December 1272). The following February he arrived at the papal court in Orvieto, and early in the spring he crossed the Apennines and proceeded northward on the Via Aemilia during May, somewhat retarded by sickness.[46] His first recorded stop after leaving Orvieto was at besieged Forlì, where he showed himself favorable to the Ghibellines, first by attempting to persuade the Bolognese to make peace, and then, when the Geremei refused, by honoring their enemies, for he knighted Ottavio de' Lambertazzi and nine other Bolognese nobles.[47] Progressing northward, he passed next through Faenza and Bologna, where he knighted still others.[48] By 20 May he had reached Reggio,[49] and after a brief detour to Milan, he crossed the Mount Cenis pass into France on 1 June 1273.[50] There he remained for over a year, principally settling affairs in Gascony before finally crossing on 2 August 1274 to Dover and his coronation.[51] During his Italian progress, the imperial throne was vacant, for his uncle, Richard of Cornwall, who for twenty years had been the titular *rex Romanorum*, had died in April 1272. In October 1273 Rudolf of Habsburg was of course elected, but at the time of Edward's passage, many great princes were prospective candidates, including the king of France.[52] No one seems to have remarked that some Italians apparently sought to encourage Edward himself to succeed his hapless uncle, for an English chronicler recalled that some communes of Tuscany and Lombardy had greeted him with trumpets and *laudes:* "Vivat imperator Edwardus."[53]

At what point did Francis enter the king's service? In May 1274, while Edward was still in France, at the king's court in Limoges the legist witnessed a notarial process between the royal seneschal of Gascony and Gaston VII de Béarn, the greatest of the king's French vassals.[54] Presumably, Francis was already in Edward's employ, but we cannot be certain of his status before his next appearance in the royal records, on 2 September 1274, when the king issued letters of credit on the Paris Temple "ad salarium advocatorum" to Francis and a colleague, who were his proctors at the Parlement of Paris.[55] In connection with the same business, on 18 January 1275 Francis and the seneschal of Gascony were accredited to the king of France as Edward's proctors in all cases at the court of France against Gaston.[56] Later that year, in June, Francis was one of the "discretos viros et familiares nostros" whom Edward further empowered to represent his interests before the Parlement of Paris by both a general mandate and a special one for the suit with Gaston.[57] Since the case against the viscount of Béarn that was heard on appeal at Paris was the same one that Francis had witnessed earlier at Limoges, in all likelihood his connection both with the case and with Edward began no later than May 1274.[58]

The mounting hostilities between the Lambertazzi and the Geremei in Bologna seem to have decided Francis to leave the city. Edward had passed through just at the moment when the Geremei had demonstrated their predominance in external as well as internal affairs, and Francis would have been receptive to an offer from one who not only had favored his party a few days before at Forlì, but also was being hailed as the next emperor. We cannot be sure that Edward made him any

[49]

offer in Bologna, however, nor is it necessary to assume that one was made; for there is good reason to believe that he would have left Bologna within the year in any case, because as the civil storm gathered, both his brothers also sought refuge elsewhere. Francis was probably the first to depart: in July 1273 he made his will, liquidated his capital, and empowered proctors to look after his interests.[59] About two months later, in September, Cervottus, his eldest stepbrother, contracted to teach law for the coming academic year at Padua.[60] It is not known when another stepbrother, William, fled, but in later years he claimed that he had been *ultra montes*, more than twenty days' journey from the city, when the civil war finally broke out in April 1274.[61] Francis was safely with Edward before the fighting ended, and probably well before it began.

Chroniclers tagged the war "the beginning of the destruction of Bologna,"[62] as indeed it was. It began in mid April when the Lambertazzi refused to renew the campaign against Forlì and the Geremei thereupon attacked them as traitors to the commune. For more than forty days Bologna was the battlefield of the two factions, and only the intervention of Ferrara gave the Geremei the upper hand. Early in June 1274 the Lambertazzi fled the city and were declared exiles.[63] The sons of Accursius, being absent Ghibellines, were naturally accounted exiles, though not public enemies, for they had not fought against the commune. By their timely withdrawal, the Accursii had been able to avoid an open break with either the commune or their party.

The emigration of the Accursii brothers was probably conceived as a temporary expedient, since Francis had left his wife and children behind in Bologna.[64] Aichina apparently did not share the exile of her father's family after the civil war in June 1274, for the communal records attest her receipt of 108 marks sterling from Francis in November 1274 and another 50 marks in April 1275, both sums having been delivered by bankers from Pistoia who did business in France and England.[65] Taken together, these payments total a little more than half the annual salary of £200 that we know Francis was receiving at a slightly later date. At first it would seem that he attempted to maintain his family in Bologna while he represented Edward's interests in Paris, but by the end of the year another arrangement had been worked out; for on 7 December 1275 Edward granted him the use of Beaumont Manor in Oxford "to inhabit with his wife and household."[66] Edward himself sent Aichina an elegant invitation to bring her family at his expense to England, where honor awaited her for the sake of her husband, who now was titled *consiliarius* to the king.[67] The fact that the king provided this housing expressly with her in mind seems to be sufficient proof that the offer was accepted. Francis certainly was residing in Oxford the next spring, when the king provided him with firewood and made sure that the professor properly restocked the gamepark;[68] a month later Francis was commissioned to hear the grievances of the Jews of Oxford against an extortionate sheriff and do them justice.[69] His presence in Oxford, of which nothing more is known, led Anthony Wood to conjecture that Francis had taught Roman law at the university, but most recent writers have doubted this. More than likely he chose to live in an academic community because there he could converse comfortably in Latin.[70]

Services to Edward I

How he served Edward during the six years that he spent in England is something of a mystery. In writing to Aichina, Edward had styled him *dilecti consiliarii sui*, and in this capacity Francis appeared as king's councillor at the Michaelmas parliament of 1276. He was present when the earl of Gloucester's claims to Bristol were judged there *in pleno consilio regis*,[71] and he was also among the councillors who examined the statute *De bigamis* before it was presented to the king.[72] During his last five years in England, however, we know of only one piece of royal business that he was engaged in, a diplomatic mission to the Roman curia in 1278–79. Occasionally he does appear on the royal rolls, to be sure, but the entries merely concern private affairs. One of them styles him *secretarius* to the king,[73] and the nature of his confidential work is somewhat clarified by the oath that he swore to Edward upon leaving England for the last time in 1281, wherein he promised: "I shall faithfully conceal all his counsels and secrets that have been or shall be revealed to me."[74] From the fact that he was rarely entrusted with specific commissions, and those only in affairs of the greatest importance such as the process against Gaston de Béarn and the Roman mission, it would seem that the services for which Edward paid so much were almost wholly those of a jurisconsult. In view of the cost, it is hardly surprising that the king did not assign him to routine work that less highly feed royal clerks could do as well.[75] Thus, when we find that Edward sent him to the court of Pope Nicholas III on a mission that kept him from England for six months (September 1278 to February 1279), we may be sure that the king placed a high value on this assignment.

The primary objective of this Roman mission was to obtain the pope's consent to the election of Robert Burnell, the royal chancellor, as archbishop of Canterbury. Francis presented this request in a formal harangue *(arenga)*, the rhetorical genre that was particularly cultivated by Italians in the thirteenth century, and especially at Bologna.[76] His mastery of the outward forms of Italian diplomacy was no doubt an asset, though not a unique one at Edward's court;[77] but no other English clerk could rival his personal connections within the curia, which of course was largely staffed by graduates of Bologna who would receive him honorably for his father's sake no less than for his own. Although it was not uncommon for nuncios to be persons of high rank, yet Francis' students at Bologna had never imagined that a turn of fortune's wheel would convert their professor into an English ambassador. Such unexpected alterations were the laughingstock of the age, and the pope himself brought out the humor of the situation. Once, when Francis was delivering the king's latest letter, Nicholas announced before reading it that he would not change his mind, whatever the king might have written, "et ridendo dixit: 'Et hoc vobis *nuncio*, domine Francisce.' "[78] The English agent who reported this to the king did not neglect to testify in his dispatch that Francis had done all that anyone could do.[79] Nonetheless the mission failed; for despite Francis' energy and influence, the pope provided Canterbury with an archbishop, John Pecham, who was decidedly not the king's man.

Return to Bologna

During the months that Francis was at the curia, Nicholas was mediating between the Geremei and the Lambertazzi. The émigrés had taken refuge in the Ghibelline cities of the Romagna and, with the assistance of their hosts, had been trying for four years to conquer Bologna. What had begun as a civil war within one city had been spread throughout the province by the expulsion of the Lambertazzi, and the pope now hoped to end the conflict, or at least to contain it, by repatriating the exiles. Their prospects were already favorable when Francis left the curia in January 1279, although the actual negotiations took place that summer, and in September the exiles returned. This reconciliation hardly lasted three months: after a day of battle in the piazza, the Lambertazzi again fled the city, taking refuge in Faenza.[80] Although driven once more from the city, the Lambertazzi had good reason to believe they could still return as conquerors; for during their first exile the Ghibellines of the Romagna had been winning before the pope had intervened. Now, less than a year later, their hopes were dashed by an abrupt shift in the balance of power. Faenza, the Ghibelline mainstay and base of operations, was betrayed to the Geremei and became a Guelf city through the treachery of Tebaldello Zambrasi, who opened the gates to the besieging army in November 1289, for which crime Dante finds him frozen among the traitors in Antenora.[81] For the Lambertazzi, the loss of Faenza was an epoch-making event. It stands as the climax of the contemporary *Serventese dei Lambertazzi e dei Geremei*, a partisan ballad that ends with the survivors of the massacre making their way to Forlì, "lamenting as does the lamb behind its mother."[82] Although Ghibelline power in the Romagna was by no means destroyed by the event, it was weakened enough to give the Guelfs a permanent advantage, which they would hold for almost twenty years. For the Lambertazzi, the fall of Faenza shattered all hope of an early victory over their rivals. They were condemned to exile until Ghibelline power revived.

Not a year had passed since this upheaval when we find Francis preparing to return to Bologna, and the circumstances of his repatriation plainly show that this was no mere coincidence but rather was a direct result of the now hopeless position of his party. We must follow the progress of Francis' rehabilitation with particular attention, for these events clearly reflect the cause of his damnation.

On 1 October 1281, he entered into a new relationship with Edward. That day he acknowledged that he had received from the king for services rendered, both past and future, the sum of 400 marks plus the promise of a lifetime annuity of 40 marks. In return for this he swore that for the rest of his life he would be faithful to the king, that he would not reveal the counsels and secrets of the king, and that he would undertake to represent the king's interests overseas without any further fee (*feodum*), it being understood nonetheless that he would have an expense account.[83] A few weeks later the annuity "of 40 marks yearly at the Exchequer" was entered on the patent rolls.[84] In the meantime, Francis had been putting his affairs in order: on 10 September and 24 October, loans that he had made to a rector and a chaplain were acknowledged by them and entered on the close roll.[85]

By 19 April 1282 he was back in Bologna buying himself a house and apparently both teaching and participating in public affairs, for the *Album doctorum* lists Francis among the doctors attached to the city council for 1282.[86] At some time during the same year the commune drew up a list of the adherents of the Lambertazzi in which Francis was named as one of those who were in exile,[87] but two years later the following note was appended to the blacklist:

> MCCLXXXIV indict. XII decimo intr. Jun. Non molestetur non gravetur predictus dn. Franciscus dn. Accursii in aliquo ob hoc quod sit scriptus in isto presenti libro vel aliquo alio cum appareat ipsum iurasse partem Ecclesiae homagium et fidelitatem in romana curia in manu dn. pp. Martini IV.[88]

By swearing homage and fealty to Pope Martin IV, who was the mainstay of the Guelf cause in the Romagna, Francis at least dissociated himself from Ghibelline politics if he did not at that time actually become a Guelf. Thereafter his old ties with the Lambertazzi rapidly dissolved. Less than a month after Francis' submission to the pope, the Bolognese passed a new law that excluded the reconciled members of the Lambertazzi faction from public office, but the statute expressly exempted Francis and no one else.[89] This extraordinary provision set him apart not only from the Lambertazzi in exile but also from those who had made their peace with the commune. Two years later, in 1286, he renewed his oath, this time in the presence of the municipal magistrates and council.[90]

Meanwhile he was actively allying himself by marriage with the leading families of the Geremei party. Francis' Ghibelline wife, Aichina Guezzi, was already dead when their son Castellano was betrothed to a Lambertini girl in 1284; and a few months later, Francis himself married the widow of Rigucio Gallucci (Galuzzi), a noble adherent of the Geremei. These family alliances were strengthened by his daughters, one of whom married a Lambertini while another was given successively to a Gallucci and a Malavolti.[91] All of these houses had stood with the Geremei at the time of the second expulsion of the Lambertazzi; and although the third and eldest of Francis' daughters, Dotta, married into a noble house in which loyalties were divided, the match almost certainly would have been with the Guelf branch that remained in Bologna.[92]

THE LOYALTIES OF A ROMAN LAWYER

How much of all this did Dante and his contemporaries know? In Bologna we may be sure that it was not soon forgotten that the Accursii had once belonged to the Lambertazzi faction, and indeed they were still subject to the civil disabilities imposed on reconciled Ghibellines. Only Francis himself had been exempted in

1284; for more than twenty years thereafter the city treated the other members of his family as former Lambertazzi partisans. Finally, in 1306, the university petitioned the city to remove the names of the surviving male Accursii from the Lambertazzi list and to accept them as Geremei without qualification. Evidently feelings still ran high, for the bill met substantial opposition, passing in the council by a vote of 197 to 104.[93] The question of the loyalty of the Accursiani must have enjoyed a certain notoriety, for the petition was presented to the council with a veiled threat that if it were not granted, the students might move their university elsewhere.[94] Since the Ghibelline skeleton in the Accursian closet had thus been something of a cause célèbre in Dante's day, we may be reasonably certain that for contemporaries the name Francesco d'Accorso would, more than that of any other Bolognese legist, evoke the image of a Roman lawyer who through expediency had become a Guelf.

The means by which Francis effected this transfer of loyalty was also fixed in the common memory, for as we know, his withdrawal to England was the one event of his life that gave rise to anecdotes that outlived him. In view of the facts presented above, I think there can be no doubt that for the historical Francis, England was nothing more than a convenient, though lucrative and even honorable, refuge from the hazards of civil war. He left Bologna when strife appeared inevitable; he remained absent and uncommitted until the issue was no longer in doubt; he returned to cast his lot with the victors.

We may fairly assume, moreover, that Dante knew that Francis had served the king of England and that he had become a Guelf, since it is hardly credible that the poet would have ventured to condemn a contemporary without at least being familiar with those events in his life that were notorious. This is not to say that Dante perceived the historical connection between the two events, for such an inference, however probable, is unnecessary for our argument. It is of course quite possible that Dante knew a great deal more about Francis than we shall ever know, but I can only reiterate that it seems unlikely that the poet would condemn a character without explanation unless the grounds were common knowledge. This seems all the more probable in Francis' case because he was not only Dante's contemporary but also was one so well known that Brunetto singled him out as particularly noteworthy among many "di gran fama." If one doubts the traditional inference that his sin was sodomy (and there is no evidence independent of the poem to support this), one can only assume that to convey his meaning the poet relied upon the connotations of the name Francesco d'Accorso that were most familiar to his readers. Accordingly, I have sought to retrieve the associations that the name had for Dante's generation. Let us recapitulate the results.

Before all else, the patronymic d'Accorso establishes the profession of this *litteratus* as that of Roman law. As a scholar, this Francesco was closely identified with his father, sharing his fame and often being credited by the uninformed with his father's work. His reputation for avarice earned him a place in the *Novellino*, which represents him as one who twisted the law to make the utmost profit from his teaching. Finally, two events in his life were commonly remembered, and they were in fact the outstanding features in his one great crisis. That he had been retained for some years by the king of England made a lasting but apparently not unfavorable impression. More controversial was his prompt shift of allegiance to the Guelf-Geremei faction as soon as it was securely in control of Bologna.

These, then, are the associations that clung to the name Francesco d'Accorso. Do they explain why Dante placed this man among the intellectuals who violated nature? We have already discovered that neither the avarice nor the fame Francis inherited from his father suffices to explain his presence in Brunetto's band. What remain are his service to Edward and his adhesion to the Guelfs, and we must now inquire whether either or both of these would constitute for Dante a violation of the natural order. The basic structure of authority in the poet's political thought suggests that, for him, both are in fact contrary to nature.

Dante on Imperial Jurisdiction

In the *Monarchia*, it will be recalled, Dante argued that mankind has two goals, one natural and the other supernatural, and that the emperor and the pope have been established by God to lead mankind to these respective ends. The political order, headed by the emperor, is entirely natural, and hence those who subvert imperial authority also pervert natural law. The *Monarchia* explains that the principles governing this natural polity are discovered by philosophers and are applied by the emperor, "qui secundum phylosophica documenta genus humanum ad temporalem felicitatem dirigeret."[95] To ascertain more precisely the place that Dante assigned to the *Corpus iuris civilis*, we must turn to the fourth book of the *Convivio*, where Dante develops his doctrine of *ratio scripta*. This was discovered (*trovata*), he tells us, to inform men of what is equitable and to command them to observe equity in those actions wherein their will is subject to reason.[96] He further explains that an official is placed on earth to formulate this written reason, to promulgate it, and to impose it: this of course is the emperor.[97] Earlier in the treatise, the nature of the imperial office had been defined in more general terms:

> And this office is called by pre-eminence empire, without any qualification, because it is the command of all the other commands. And hence he who is appointed to this office is called emperor because he is the commander who issues all the commands. And what he says is law [*legge*] to all, and he ought to be obeyed by all, and every other command draws its strength and authority from his.[98]

The emperor, then, is the ultimate authority for the whole of *ragione scritta*. But what is this mysterious written reason? According to Dante it was nothing less than *ius* itself; for Celsus' celebrated maxim, "Ius est ars boni et aequi," he turns thus into Italian: "la *ragione scritta* è arte di bene e d'equitade."[99] For Dante, therefore, "written reason" was a generic term, and presently he explains that it comprises two species—*ius civilis* and *ius canonica*.

> And what else is the one and the other Reason, I mean the canonical and the civil, intended to contemplate so much as to make defence against the greed which grows as riches are amassed? Verily the one and the other

Reason manifests it sufficiently if we read their beginnings—I mean the beginnings of their scripture.[100]

Hence it would follow that the emperor is equally responsible for both branches of the *ratio scripta*. Presumably they are distinct because their sources are different, the one being discovered by the natural light of unaided human reason and the other being revealed to it. Although man knows each from a different source, ultimately of course both forms of positive law originate in the divine law of God, and therefore they should not contradict one another. In Dante's ideal cosmos, however, they were given a single source on earth as well as in heaven—"quello imperador che là sù regna"[101]—thus assuring harmony in practice as well as in theory.

In contrast to the emperor, who directs mankind to temporal happiness, the pope functions as the spiritual guide of the human race, who in accordance with revelation leads men to eternal life.[102] In the concluding chapter of the *Monarchia*, the sources of this revealed truth are carefully itemized: both our supernatural end and the means to it have been made known by the Holy Spirit through the prophets and holy writers, through Christ, and through his disciples.[103] These are "documenta spiritualia que humanam rationem transcendunt"; they teach men the theological virtues of faith, hope, and charity.[104] It should be particularly noted that the pope teaches men solely those things that transcend human reason. Clearly the inference is that *la ragione canonica* lies outside his sphere of competence; and should any doubt remain, the *Monarchia* goes on to conclude that mankind will attain neither its temporal nor its eternal goal unless cupidity is repressed, "and this is the task to which that protector of the world must devote his energies who is called the Roman Prince."[105] As we already know from *Convivio* 4. 12. 9, the purpose of the two laws is the same as that of the emperor who imposes them: "a riparare a la cupiditate."

Although Dante does not say so, the roles thus assigned to pope and emperor correspond respectively to the *forum internum* and the *forum externum*. In Dante's day, canonists distinguished by these terms what we might call the private and public aspects of a case. Canon law was concerned exclusively with "the exercise of the judicial power of the Church in the interests of society," with the external consequences of a moral act; so far as it affected only the salvation of the agent, it was a case of conscience, to be heard privately in the *forum internum* by a priest. The latter is the jurisdiction exercised, *inter alia*, in the sacrament of penance. It is characterized by other names: the *forum conscientiae* and, because it concerns salvation, the ultimate goal of the individual, also the *forum poli*.[106] Enough has been said to show that the canonistic distinction corresponds exactly to the functions assigned to pope and emperor in *Monarchia* 3. 15. As I have said, Dante does not invoke the distinction between the two forums in this connection, but in the *Paradiso* we are told that Gratian, the founder of canon law, "helped the one forum and the other so that it is pleasing in Paradise" ("Grazïan, che l'uno e l'altro foro / aiutò sì che piace in paradiso"; *Par.* x, 104–5). Gratian's two forums once were taken to be lay and ecclesiastical, but they have been convincingly, if not conclusively, identified by Brandileone as external and internal.[107] Certainly Gratian's textbook, the *Concordantia discordantium canonum*, though largely concerned with external matters, did render service as well to the *forum conscientiae* through its extensive treatment of penitence,[108] whereas it is difficult to see how it could be said to have aided the *forum civile* at all. It would carry us far from our theme to pursue further this source of Dante's political thought, but the traces would surely lead into the dense thicket of publicist literature produced by Dante's contemporaries.[109] For our purpose, it is enough to know that Dante accorded the emperor full and unequivocal jurisdiction over the external forum of canon law and thereby resolved with a single stroke the conflict of interest between *imperium* and *sacerdotium*.

Now let us return to Francis of Bologna and ask whether his service to Edward and his adhesion to the Guelf party can be construed as contrary to this political order that for Dante was established by nature and its Creator. As a teacher of civil law, Francis' first duty evidently would be to interpret the will of the emperor as expressed in the *Corpus iuris civilis*. If he held that secular princes, such as the king of England, are not subject to the emperor and his *ratio scripta*, he would clearly be advocating insubordination in the natural order. Likewise, if he denied to the emperor his rightful jurisdiction in the external forum, he would subvert the natural function of the *curator orbis*. Such false doctrine in a Roman lawyer would surely qualify him for a place among the intellectuals who perverted the teachings of nature.

Dante himself rebuked jurists who presume to read their own opinions into the law, particularly to minimize the authority of the emperor, and he bade them render their counsels and judgments according to the sense of the law: "Videant nunc iuriste presumptuosi quantum infra sint ab illa specula rationis unde humana mens hec principia speculatur, et sileant secundum sensum legis consilium et iudicium exhibere contenti."[110] These presumptuous jurists were, for Dante, unnatural lawyers: they expounded the law according to their own perverse ideas, which were contrary both to the natural political order and to the sense of the laws that were its positive expression. Since as a political philosopher he condemned them, we may suppose that the poet wished to include at least one such in that band of intellectuals who violated nature, but the specialized character of their crime created a problem. How could he suggest the quality of the crime to readers who were familiar with the offending lawyers as personalities yet were ignorant of their technical writings? Symbolism, of course, provided the answer. Francis was accordingly selected because his popular image was an appropriate symbol of his perverse teaching. Seen thus, his subjection to king and pope is not in itself a sinful act but suggests both the occasion and the nature of his intellectual sins. To Dante's contemporary reader, the name Francesco d'Accorso recalled a Roman lawyer who had left Bologna to serve a foreign king and had later returned to shift his allegiance to the papal party. Once the reader further grasps Dante's political vision—which he shall not learn in Hell—the lawyer's new loyalties seem unnaturally placed. At this point the common reader may jump to conclusions, but the scholar must either substantiate the charge implicit in this symbolic innuendo or else dismiss it altogether.

FRANCIS' ARENGA TO NICHOLAS III

Francis Accursii was not a prolific writer. Savigny hesitated to attribute to him any work that goes under his name save only the *casus* to the *Digestum novum*, and the other surviving writings that bear his name hardly constitute an impressive list: additions to the *Glossa ordinaria*, a *repetitio*, several *consilia* and *quaestiones*, a report to Edward I, and the *arenga* that he delivered to Nicholas III.[111] Of these, Dante is unlikely to have known any save the work last named. Obviously he had no access to English state papers, and there is no reason to believe that he had read any Romanist legal texts other than the *Corpus iuris civilis* and just possibly the *Glossa ordinaria*.[112] The *arenga*, on the other hand, was a work that Dante was apt to have encountered, if, as seems probable, he had studied Latin rhetoric at Bologna.[113]

Francis, we know, had a reputation for eloquence among the teachers of the *ars notarilis* at Bologna. One of them, Pietro de' Boattieri, told his students that "the eloquence of Francis flows like the dew, as if a shower on the green or droplets on the grass."[114] Only one work could justify that good opinion, and indeed it survives because of it. This is the *arenga*, or harangue, that he addressed to the pope as Edward's nuncio in October 1278. The brief oration, scarcely six printed pages in length, is preserved in three manuscripts, all of the fifteenth century. In each case, the copy forms part of a collection of *arengae* in which those of Pier della Vigna are the most prominent. All the manuscripts are Italian in origin, and since the rest of their contents are legal in nature, we may infer that the collections were made at some Italian center of legal and rhetorical studies, of which Bologna was by far the greatest.[115] No matter where in Italy these late copies of Francis' oration originated, it seems likely that this particular *arenga* would have been known at Bologna if anywhere, since the author spent his last years there, where his eloquence was admired. Certainly it must have represented his best efforts as an *arengator*, for it was the keystone of the mission that consumed some six months of Francis' highly paid services. As such, we may easily suppose that Francis preserved the text and circulated it with pride among those connoisseurs of *Kunstprosa* whom he knew at Bologna. Moreover, during the period when he was trying to live down his Ghibelline past, it would be distinctly advantageous to make it known that his sympathies had already been decidedly Guelf at the time when the fortunes of the exiled Lambertazzi had been at their height. Every circumstance suggests that the *arenga* was familiar in just those circles at Bologna in which Dante presumably moved. This argument of course does not prove that he knew Francis' *arenga*; it does establish the possibility and a certain degree of probability, which can best be enhanced by confronting the document itself.

The *arenga* introduces a petition in which the pope is requested by the king to approve the election of a new archbishop of Canterbury.[116] The harangue proper (§ 1–29) consists of generalities which were intended to dispose the pope to listen favorably to the argument of the case that followed in the original but that has been omitted in the surviving texts; a brief conclusion submits the petition formally

(§ 30–31). The *ars arengendi* required that the orator touch upon four matters in his introduction: the person of the petitioner, the person of the grantor, the nature of the request, and its justification. His art consisted in hitting upon a theme that related all four with appropriate flattery and grace. Francis chose the means recommended by one of his contemporaries at Bologna, Jacob of Dinant, who would have the *arenga* be a blend of preaching and advocacy, the union of the arts of Cicero the forensic orator and of Solomon the preacher of Ecclesiastes. Accordingly, Francis expounded for the pope a passage of Scripture, first literally and then figuratively, applying it to the case at hand.[117]

As his text he took 1 Kings 8:4–7: the elders of Israel beg the prophet Samuel to give them a king, "ut iudicet nos." Samuel turns to God and is told, "Audi vocem populi in omnibus que loquuntur tibi" (§ 1). After a perfunctory exposition of the literal sense, the arengist shows first how the passage typifies all petitions, and then he applies it to the present instance. The king and peers of England, like the spokesmen of Israel, approach their Samuel and beg for a ruler in their new archbishop. The argument proceeds to justify at length each of these three similarities, but having established the resemblance between the two cases, the orator stops short of his conclusion and tactfully leaves the pope to infer that his decision should be governed by the maxim *Vox populi, vox dei.*[118]

If the argument was to be taken seriously, it would determine a *figura* or essential relationship established in the nature of things by God's ordinance.[119] Not every *figura* had this intention, however. Often one was employed as nothing more than a rhetorical device to be appreciated simply for the ingenuity and virtuosity with which it was developed. It would be hard to say how Francis meant his analogy to be taken, but we may be sure that Dante would have taken it seriously, for in his own art the *figura* is always essentially true, never an ornamental fiction. If, as seems likely, Francis adopted the figural method as a rhetorical device that was appropriate for the occasion and the audience—that is, if his text was only a pretext for flattery and virtuosity—he might then find a sympathetic audience in Nicholas III but decidedly not in Dante. For the poet, art must be true to nature, and the orator who made the false appear true, whether to display his talent or persuade his audience, would merit a place among the perverse intellectuals.

Francis' fault, however, appears to have lain less in his thesis than in the arguments by which he sought to justify it. Here he employed his knowledge of Roman law to support his own opinions, and this display permits us to identify him as one of those presumptuous jurists of whom Dante complained in *Monarchia* 2. 9. 20. Three of these opinions, when compared with Dante's convictions, will suffice for him to damn their defender.

(1) To establish the resemblance between Israel and England, Francis recalls that Moses urged his people to offer God more than was strictly necessary.[120] The English imitate them in this, for they are incomparably more generous than any other Christian people. Among other proofs of this, he declares that the English "do not observe the rules of civil law on donations to churches and to their ministers, . . . but by imperial authority they use <that rule> in which immensity is approved

by imperial authority as the best measure."[121] This argument was based on a law of Justinian's (*Cod.* 1. 2. 19) and the accompanying ordinary gloss. The purport of the *lex* is to ensure that all considerable donations to pious causes be conveyed in writing. No written act is required for pious donations of less than five hundred solidi; above that amount, the transaction must be formally recorded. An express exception is made from the latter provision, however, in the case of an imperial donation: "excepta scilicet imperiali donatione."[122]

In explanation, the *Glossa ordinaria* adds: "for the emperor is able without acts to give pious places more than five hundred solidi," alleging *Novella* 7.[123] The cross reference leads us to the other rule that Francis said the English followed: his paraphrase echoes it so closely there can be no doubt. This novel permits the confiscation of ecclesiastical property for the common welfare, but the emperor will compensate for the loss by an amount equal or even greater in value ("aequa aut etiam maiore"). To justify this departure from the strict equity of distributive justice, the legislator added: "Quid enim causetur imperator, ne meliora det? cui plurima deus dedit habere et multorum dominum esse et facile dare, et maxime in sanctissimis ecclesiis, in quibus *optima mensura* est donatarum eis rerum *immensitas*."[124] The words stressed by italics in the final clause are those used by Francis in his *arenga*, and it is significant that without this identity, Francis' references to the civil law in section 10 would be obscure.[125]

Indeed, the whole section adds so little to the ostensible argument that it might seem that it has no other purpose than to embellish the oration with an apt allegation from the civil law. The preceding sections had already established that the English did in fact resemble the Israelites inasmuch as they fulfilled the Mosaic injunction to give God more than was necessary. After listing examples of English generosity to the Church (§§ 8–9), Francis by way of conclusion introduced the words of Justinian to affirm that the liberality of the pious English knew no bounds. In the structure of his main argument, this is hardly more than an apt and erudite quotation, but had it been meant to be that and nothing more, he might simply have said that the English, like Justinian, used "pro mensura optima immensitas."

Francis, however, was not content with a mere simile. The *Anglicani* actually exercise (*utuntur*) a privilege reserved to the emperor alone. Neither the Romans nor other peoples enjoy this prerogative, for the one is bound to observe the *iuris civilis regulas*, whereas the others have their own customs.[126] Apart from these peoples the privileged emperor stands, "to whom it was given by God to have many things and to be lord of many and to give easily," and with him stand the English. In Francis' argument, however, *populus Anglicanus* is an ambiguous term that signifies not only the whole nation but also the king and his barons, as is evident from the terms in which he formulated his thesis: "Et certe sub nomine maiorum seu populi Israel significari possunt rex et proceres Anglie necnon universus populus anglicanus" (§ 5). Nowhere does he justify the equation of *populus* with *rex et proceres*, but he did not need to; for "generally it was assumed that the greater men were the effective *populus*,"[127] and in Roman law the prince was taken to represent his people by virtue of the *lex regia*.[128] Thus, since the king in this context stands for or represents his people, the assertions made in *Arenga* 10 about the *populus Anglicanus* must be understood to apply to the king as well.

This substitution yields two correlative propositions that relate the king of England respectively to the *ius civilis* and the *imperator*: he does not observe the rules of Roman law; instead he enjoys the exempt status that, according to the gloss, is an imperial prerogative. Taken together, these statements declare the independence of England from the empire, for they affirm that England's king is not subject to the emperor but is himself the emperor in his own realm. Of this there can be no doubt, for they correspond quite precisely to the pair of maxims that constituted for jurists of Francis' generation the twin attributes of national sovereignty: "rex superiorem non recognoscens" and "rex imperator in regno suo." As Gaines Post has shown in an essay that is now famous, the first to justify the independence of the national monarchies from the empire were canonists and theologians. "But a few legists of France, from the mid-thirteenth century on, . . . asserted that the king of France was not subject to the emperor and was emperor in his own realm."[129] Chief among them was that same Jacques de Révigny who confounded Francis at Orléans.[130] The doctrines of his school are supposed by Meijers to have been brought back to Italy by Francis and his fellow émigrés,[131] though no one as far as I know has yet seen Francis as the disseminator of this particular doctrine. It was certainly contrary to the teachings of the Bolognese glossators whom his father epitomized, for they were champions of imperial authority, especially as embodied in Roman law. The indications of the *arenga* are too slender to bear a reconstruction of his doctrine in any detail, but it may well be that he, like Révigny and Cino, held that the national monarchs' independence was de facto rather than de jure,[132] as indeed is suggested by his choice of verbs in our passage: the English do not *observe* civil law, they *use* the imperial prerogative ("non observant . . . utuntur").

The relevance of the *rex-imperator* theme to Francis' mission is not hard to guess. While ostensibly praising the pious works of Edward and the English, Francis contrived through this obiter dictum to remind the curia that the petitioner was no mere kinglet within the empire but an emperor in his own realm. The allusion, though strange on the lips of an Italian legist, would be eminently acceptable to an audience of canonists and theologians, for they had originated the doctrine.

One cannot be so sure, however, that the allusion would unhesitatingly be grasped by Dante. The text, at least in the form that has come down to us, does not expressly state that only the emperor is entitled to take immensity as the best measure in pious acts. If, as seems likely, Dante read the *arenga* at Bologna, there would be many at hand who could have explained the implications of the passage to him, however; and it is also possible that the point was explicitly made in the text that he would have seen almost a century before our earliest extant manuscript, which at this point is patently corrupt.[133] Even without these suppositions, Dante could have seen for himself that Francis had asserted that the English *rex-populus* did not observe the rule of Roman law, and this would have been enough to convince him that this Roman lawyer was serving the interests of his client against the intent of both civil and natural law. If such was the poet's line of reasoning, his conclusions were based solely on the text of the *arenga* and his own concept of the natural order. Since he is not known to have been deeply learned in the two laws, this explanation contains more likelihood than one involving reference back to the *Corpus iuris civilis* and the *Glossa ordinaria*, and further analysis of the *arenga* will reinforce this impression.

Although the emperor was denied his due by Francis, the pope received from him far more than Dante thought to be either just or natural. The contrast is the orator's own, for after having suggested that England is independent of the empire, he immediately goes on to praise her obedience to the Church. Henry III had manifested his devotion in many ways, one of which was "in venerating the Roman church and its envoys"; his son Edward has inherited these virtues and is distinguished, among other things, by his "obedience towards the Roman church and its envoys."[134] Indeed, the whole English people has been obedient to God and his vicar, both by paying tithes and by obeying papal mandates to provide nonresident foreigners with ecclesiastical benefices.[135] Their devout subjection to the vicar of God provides Francis with his final proof that the English can be likened unto the people of Israel who petitioned Samuel in the text that the *arenga* expounds.

To carry out his theme he must next demonstrate that the pope, to whom the petition was addressed, resembles the prophet Samuel.[136] A good third of the speech (§§ 14–25) is devoted to establishing this congruence by seven extended analogies, the first five of which concern the pope's person rather than his office. Nonetheless it is clear from the start that Samuel is to be taken as the type of all popes, although Nicholas III resembles him more perfectly than any of his predecessors.[137] Only the two last analogies need concern us, for these alone concern the papal office, and two examples will suffice to show how repugnant to the mind of Dante this figure would appear.

(2) The sixth similitude is based on the fact that Samuel "was high priest and renewed the empire and anointed princes among his race," and the first text alleged to support this is 1 Kings 10:1, wherein Samuel anointed Saul king, just as Pope Nicholas anointed princes in his time.[138] We do not need to guess what Dante's reaction to this would have been: the whole of *Monarchia* 3. 6 is devoted to refuting those who cite this very passage to prove that the pope, like Samuel, is God's vicar with power to create and depose kings. Dante emphatically denies that Samuel was God's vicar with full authority to bestow temporal power and take it away again. Instead, the *Monarchia* maintains that Samuel acted, "not as vicar, but as a special *ad hoc* legate, or nuncio bearing the express mandate of the Lord."[139] A vicar, Dante explains, is entrusted with a definite jurisdiction by his master, and within it he can, at his own discretion and without referring back to his master, exercise the powers delegated to him. A nuncio, on the other hand, is empowered to do only the will of his master and has no discretionary power whatsoever. Since in making Saul king, Samuel did and said only what God told him to, he evidently was a nuncio. This distinction enables Dante to deny the validity of the analogy between

Samuel and the pope, for "it does not follow, therefore, that if God did this through the nuncio Samuel, that the vicar of God is able to do so as well." He reasons that God is known to have used nuncios to accomplish things that lie outside the jurisdiction of his vicar, because often he has acted through the agency of angels, whose very name indicates that they are divine messengers or nuncios. Obviously no one can claim that the pope can do whatever has been effected by an angelic agent, and consequently, since *some* acts of divine nuncios fall outside the pope's jurisdiction as *vicarius Dei*, one cannot determine by logic alone whether or not any particular mission entrusted to one of God's nuncios, such as Samuel, also falls within the pope's competence.[140] For Dante, then, Samuel's coronation of Saul cannot be taken as the prototype of papal kingmaking: it was, rather, the direct intervention of God in human affairs through an agent sent to do his will.

This argument of course clears the way for the radical separation of papal and imperial power that concludes the treatise *On Single Government*. Moreover, it was offered as an express refutation of those "who assert that the authority of the Empire is derived from the authority of the Church, as the inferior artisan is dependent on the architect."[141] On the strength of Francis' sixth similitude, he would accordingly be numbered among those who seek to subordinate emperor to pope. Yet of all people he should have known better, for the argument is invalidated by a distinction drawn from Roman law. Dante based his refutation on the legal concept of the nuncio, whom Roman law distinguishes from the procurator by just the criteria that Dante invoked: the proctor acts in his own name, but the nuncio acts in the name of his principal.[142] Since this distinction was made explicit by the elder Accursius, Francis unquestionably knew it, and had he expounded his text according to the letter, he should have seen, as Dante did, that Samuel was a nuncio and therefore could not be compared to the vicar of God. At least so it would seem to Dante. Yet the lawyer had preferred to draw a specious analogy that, for the poet, implied the subjection of emperor to pope. It does not matter that these political implications are not expressly recognized in the *arenga*: as a lawyer, Francis should have known that the text would not bear the interpretation he placed upon it.

(3) In Dante's court, Francis cannot plead that his errors appear only by implication, for his seventh similitude between Samuel and the pope attributes to the latter a jurisdiction that is contrary to the Dantesque natural order. Scripture tells us that Samuel "judged the congregation in the law of the lord and in the [Christian] faith of the lord."[143] The application to Nicholas, though obscure in its details, clearly represents both the man and the office in a role that Dante reserved to the emperor alone, for Francis attributes to the pope jurisdiction over all mankind: "Iudicatis etiam congregationem, id est gentem humanam." These words, which declare Francis' thesis, are the theocratic antithesis to Dante's *Monarchia*. But lest there be any doubt, let us view them in their context:

> You also judge the congregation, i.e., the human race, in the law of the
> Lord and in divine faith, both by making decrees against the unfaithful and
> by standing beside others who make decrees as their helper. In such cases,

you supplant the judge even though others appointed him, on the ground that he was not able to have produced the desired effect.[144]

Francis might have interpreted *congregatio* narrowly to mean the *congregatio fidelium*, the Church, but this restricted sense would not have displayed the full scope of the papal *plenitudo potestatis*. According to the canonists of the thirteenth century, of whom Hostiensis is in this respect typical, the pope had the power to intervene in cases that came under the ordinary jurisdiction of the temporal courts if justice could not be done otherwise ("propter defectum iustitie"). For example, he might take cognizance of the case "wherever a lord treats his man unjustly or judges unjustly, and wherever a civil judge is lacking; and if the ordinary judge be rejected as suspect."[145] The last case would seem to be the one contemplated by Francis in his encomium. But in view of Dante's conviction that the emperor was the supreme judge in canon as well as civil law, violence would be done to the natural judicial order even by the more modest statement that in canon law the pope exercised a jurisdiction that was independent of imperial authority. Either way, Dante could take this statement as prima facie evidence of Francis' complicity in diminishing the emperor's jurisdiction. Whether Dante knew it or not, under Roman law the pope's jurisdiction *propter defectum iustitiae* was not what Francis represented it to be, for a novel of Justinian's had accorded it, not to the pope alone, but to all bishops.[146] Thus it could be argued that this jurisdiction was exercised by the courts Christian as an imperial concession under the emperor's authority. This Francis undoubtedly knew, but in his *arenga* he adduces such interventions as an example of the universal jurisdiction of the pope, without a hint that it was exercised as the emperor's immediate vicar, not as God's.

Francis' harangue contains other passages that might have offended Dante's convictions, but we have seen enough to know that before the judgment seat of Dante's just God, the orator would stand patently guilty of subverting Roman law and perverting natural polity. The principal subjects of the emperor's authority appear in Francis' discourse as independent powers. The king of England is emperor in his own realm and knows no secular superior; the pope is the emperor's superior and exercises over mankind a jurisdiction that by natural right belongs to the *curator orbis*. Moreover, it has been shown that Francis could only maintain these opinions by ignoring the letter, or by misrepresenting the sense, of the laws on which he was a professed authority. Whether Dante knew Francis' opinions from this document or from some other source makes little difference to our argument, for we can be sure that the historical Francis deserved the place occupied by Francesco d'Accorso in the Dantesque afterworld.

FRANCIS AND GRATIAN

In Dante's eyes, Francis was an unnatural legist, and as the title of this chapter indicates, something more as well—an unnatural lawyer. By this I mean that he represents the errors of those who profess "the one and the other reason," the canon as well as the Roman lawyers. Since Dante uses *ragione scritta* to translate *ius*, these professionals as a class would more accurately be called jurists than lawyers, though "unnatural jurists" hardly conveys in English the essence of their offense. It would be instructive to compare Francis with other jurists whom Dante mentions, but to do so would entail a treatise on Dante and law, which in turn would be incomplete unless it were related to these progressively larger themes: Rome and her empire; man and his political, intellectual, and spiritual goals; and finally the laws of nature and her God, by whom all is ordained. The foundation for the least of these inquiries has been firmly laid by André Pézard, who under the title "Légistes d'enfer et saints légistes" has collected the jurists mentioned in the *corpus Dantescum*. Only one of these can directly illuminate the case of Francesco d'Accorso. The others— Justinian, Benincasa, and Hostiensis, to name only the principals—reflect more general aspects of Dante's views on the rule of law.[147] The canonist Gratian, however, stands in the heaven of the Sun among the *spiriti sapienti* as the counterpart of our unnatural lawyer, much as Donatus does to Priscian.[148] The father of canon law, as we have already seen, pleased paradise by serving both forums, the internal and the external, in one of which the priesthood, headed by the pope, hears cases of conscience; while in the other, the jurists, under the emperor, maintain the rule of justice on earth through law.[149] Although Gratian treated penitential matters separately, he of course neither distinguished between the two forums *expressis verbis*— the Decretalists were to do that two generations later[150]—nor consequently could he have perceived, as Dante did, that it could serve to define the competence proper to *sacerdotium* and *imperium*. To me it seems that he owes his place in the Dantesque Heaven to quite another virtue—his lack of *presumption*. No legislator like Justinian, Gratian collected the sources of canon law into a textbook, the objectivity of which was neither impaired nor significantly colored by the intrusion of his own dicta. Gratian's saving virtue, then, was the honesty that Dante demanded of the jurists who presumed to interpret the law contrary to its sense. As such, he appears as the blessed antithesis of Francesco d'Accorso, that type of the *iuristae praesumptuosi*.

Ap Appropriate Choice

In conclusion, we must observe that the sin of Francesco d'Accorso was hardly an uncommon error, and in consequence we may wonder why this particular man was singled out among many who held the same commonplace opinions; for by 1300, Dante's assertion of imperial supremacy was distinctly an anachronism, whereas the prevailing view was that condemned in Francesco. The independence of the national monarchies from the empire was accepted de facto and justified de jure; the jurisdiction of the pope *in spiritualibus* was likewise hardly open to question. The great issue lay between them: whether the papacy could in some sense exercise a superior jurisdiction over the secular powers *in temporalibus*. Dante, I believe, advocated a radical solution that eliminated the foundations of this conflict by returning to Caesar what was rightfully his by nature, while leaving God's vicar to exercise his proper function as the spiritual adviser of humankind. To exemplify the intellectual errors that generated the false assumptions of his contemporaries,

Dante selected a Roman lawyer, partly because in the poet's ideal natural polity legists were the appointed guardians of that order, which found its positive expression in the imperial law; partly because in Dante's day those who taught the civil law still expounded their texts literally and thus preserved, in class at least, the Byzantine ideal of Caesaropapism. The poet's problem, then, was to hit upon a Roman lawyer whose name would stand for the whole profession and whose life would suggest the presumption of those who assumed that neither kings nor popes were subject to the empire. Francis, son of Accursius, most certainly fulfilled all these requirements and probably did so better than any other candidate.

Yet one further consideration would seem to have governed this choice: of all notable legists who had died before 1300, Francesco was the one to whom Dante was most attached by personal ties. Francis, it will be recalled, took a second wife in 1284, marrying at that time the widow of Rigucio Gallucci, a prominent Bolognese Guelf. This woman, of a famous Guelf family from Ferrara, was born Remgarda di Papazzone Aldighieri.[151] These same Aldighieri of Ferrara are the line from which the Alighieri of Florence took their name, or at least so Dante thought; and consequently Francesco was related to the poet, very distantly to be sure, by marriage.[152] The precise relationship would appear to have a special significance for the *Divine Comedy*, for Dante's link with the Aldighieri was formed by the marriage of Alighiera degli Alighieri to Dante's crusading ancestor, Cacciaguida, who in the heaven of Mars represents true nobility in contrast to the three Florentines of *Inferno* xvi.[153] Thus in Francesco, who like these three nobles runs with the violent against nature, albeit in another band, Dante found an infernal counterpart to the kinsman he had placed in heaven. The selection of one to whom the poet was bound by kinship precluded all question of spite. Since similar considerations are even more strongly in evidence in the case of Brunetto Latini, for whom the pilgrim-poet displays both reverence and affection, one may further conjecture that Dante had a place in his heart for Priscian as well. But to catch the last nuance, one would better say that within the context of the poem the choice of Francesco and Priscian reflects Brunetto's judgment as to which of his many famous and scholarly companions would (or should) possess the greatest personal interest for his friend and former pupil. We may turn to the last case on our docket, wondering why Brunetto went on to recall a clerk whom both he and Dante despised.

[4]

The Pastoral Misrule
of Bishop Mozzi

At last we have come to the text that is, as Giovanni da Serravalle remarked, "valde fortis et difficilis." The other minor characters in *Inferno* xv were both mentioned by name. Priscian and Francesco d'Accorso, like Brunetto, proved to be famous intellectuals who violated Dante's concept of natural order in their writings. In contrast to them, Brunetto does not name the third of his companions; instead he alludes to him in a scornful riddle, as if the man were infamous. Still further differences appear when that personage turns out to be a bishop whose only opus was a career in ecclesiastical administration and whose *fama* was local at best and indeed amounted to infamy, since neither his contemporaries nor posterity respected him. Still worse, his career ended in disgrace, for in the last year of his life, that bishop was transferred under obscure circumstances by Boniface VIII from Florence to the far less important diocese of Vicenza. Because Brunetto used this incident to identify the man, it would seem that the poet intended a contrast between the bishop's unfortunate end and the successful careers of his companions. Not a famous author but a cleric somehow worthy of Brunetto's scorn, he is unlike the rest of Brunetto's known associates. In only one respect does this bishop resemble the others: nothing in his vita suggests that he was a homosexual.

These marked contrasts suggest that the last case is in truth a special one, distinct in kind from the others, and they lead us to expect that his figure represents quite a different aspect of the violence done to nature by "cherci / e litterati grandi e di gran fama," so we may suspect that the poet reserved this exceptional case for the end because of its difficulty. Be that as it may, the case of Andrea de' Mozzi constitutes the supreme test of our hypothesis, for we must not only show how this bishop did egregious violence to Dante's natural order, but we also have to account for those special difficulties connected with the case that have puzzled earlier critics. To make the full extent of our task apparent from the start, let us ascertain the problems that are peculiar to this case. Some, raised by the text itself, must be our primary concern; but others, which may be termed secondary problems, arise from the external evidence that forms the historical context of the poem. Let us then first acquaint ourselves with the primary questions posed by the passage itself and then attempt their solution.

BRUNETTO'S RIDDLE

Priscian sen va con quella turba grama,
    e Francesco d'Accorso anche; e vedervi,
    s'avessi avuto di tal tigna brama,
colui potei che dal servo de' servi
    fu trasmutato d'Arno in Bacchiglione,
    dove lasciò li mal protesi nervi.

                                         (Inf. xv, 109–14)

Priscian goes with this wretched throng, and Francesco d'Accorso also;
and if you had had any hankering for such a *tigna*, you would have been
able to see him who was transferred by the servant of servants from the
Arno to the Bacchiglione, where he left his badly strained nerves.

The speaker is Brunetto Latini. Obvious though this may seem, I must insist
upon the point at the outset, for it colors all subsequent interpretation of the passage.
At the close of the preceding chapter, we observed that it was in keeping with
Brunetto's courteous character that he singled out Priscian and Francesco as persons
in whom the pilgrim would have a special interest. On the other hand, this, his
final example, manifests a strong personal distaste, also presumably shared with the
pilgrim. Perhaps Brunetto was correct in this assumption, but we must not overlook
the possibility that Dante's reasons for condemning the bishop might have been
quite different from the causes of Brunetto's scorn. Since we have already seen that
Brunetto is blind both to his own vice and to the pilgrim's mission,[1] we can hardly
suppose that he will abhor transgressions against a natural order that he does not
recognize. On the contrary, one might suspect that Brunetto's scorn arose from his
own misplaced values. Thus, I doubt that we can depend upon this speech to reveal
the poet's reasons for condemning the bishop. At best, the evidence will be ambiguous, for if Dante contrived to superimpose his own meaning upon that of
Brunetto, the passage will at best yield a double entendre rather than a univocal
certainty. Hence the question of Brunetto's scorn is better postponed until we have
determined by other means the cause of the bishop's damnation.

    Two phrases in particular require explanation. One, *li mal protesi nervi*, has
long been seen as a reference to the bishop's unnatural, and presumably sodomitical,
practices. At this point we need only grasp the most general sense, which is that the
bishop, by the end of his life, had somehow exerted his mortal powers badly. As
there are innumerable ways in which man can abuse his natural powers, we shall
have to rely on the life and reputation of the individual in question to give specific
content to this generality.

    In the second case, however, the possibilities are more limited, and it would be
well to have them in mind before we proceed. I hesitated above to translate the term
tigna, because I suspect it conceals two or perhaps three meanings. Scartazzini-
Vandelli had no doubt that it is "a loathsome malady, with which name such a
filthy sinner is designated."[2] The word comes from the Latin *tinea*, a gnawing
worm of any sort, including moths, bookworms, silkworms, and lice. In medieval

medical Latin, the same word signified the fungus disease known as ringworm or, by extension, any other fungus skin disease. The Italian *tigna* retains only this medical sense, which extends to cover still more general skin conditions such as mange, scurf, scabs, and the itch. Moreover, Italians variously apply it as a term of abuse. To judge from Tommaseo-Bellini, Dante is singular in having Brunetto use the name of the disease to signify a thing or person to which one has an aversion. Far more common is the popular use of the term in Tuscany to signify a miser *(avaro)*; and other dialects, notably Roman, apply it to a "pig-headed, obstinate individual."[3] The meaning that we choose as the translation of Brunetto's *tigna*, I think, cannot be determined from the passage itself; once again we can only bear the possibilities in mind until we have seen which one best suits the historical figure to whom the epithet was applied.

Although the specific meaning of the passage is thus ambiguous, it can still yield the general certainties upon which a firm interpretation can be based. From the start there is a marked contrast between the first two minor characters and the last one. Not only is the final name suppressed with a sneer, as would be evident even in the most corrupt of texts, but a notable refinement of *Inferno* xv, 110, in the latest edition also links Francesco more firmly to Priscian in contrast to their anonymous fellow:

| e Francesco d'Accorso; anche vedervi, | (1921) |
| e Francesco d'Accorso anche; e vedervi, | (1965) |

The nuance is slight but perceptible, and its significance is amplified by the perception of Petrocchi, the new editor, who remarks that the contrast is also evidenced in a structural parallel between cantos xv and xvi. The three noble Florentines in the latter canto have Guiglielmo Borsiere (*Inf.* xvi, 67–72) as their pendant personality; their counterparts in the adjacent canto are the three *litterati grandi*—Brunetto, Priscian, and Francesco—and again the fourth party is distinctly inferior.[4] Because the contrast is thus inherent in the structure of the poem, we can be certain that it reflects the intention of the author and not merely the prejudices of the speaker, Brunetto.

It is one thing to establish that a contrast was intended and quite another to discover its intent. Again the text can be our guide. Let us trust only those elements in Brunetto's speech that are matters of fact and not of opinion. Whatever he meant by *tigna* and *li mal protesi nervi*, the terms clearly express value judgments, and the two lines containing them are in consequence nothing more than affective utterances. Between these subjective husks, however, lies a pair of lines that contains the kernel of objective information we require:

> s'avessi avuto di tal tigna brama,
> colui potei che dal servo de' servi
>   fu trasmutato d'Arno in Bacchiglione,
>   dove lasciò li mal protesi nervi.

> (*Inf.* xv, 111–14)

It is, to be sure, a riddle, but the very terms in which it is cast provide the contrast we are seeking. All that we are told of this person is that the servant of servants transferred him from the Arno to the Bacchiglione. Even if we cannot identify the man, still from this description we know him as a member of a class. The key expression, seized on by the early commentators, is the epithet *servo de' servi* (servant of servants), which can refer only to a pope, for the bishop of Rome in his letters distinguishes himself from all other bishops by the formula, invariable since the sixth century, *N. episcopus servus servorum Dei. . . .*[5] It was a pope, then, by whom our unknown *fu trasmutato*, and in a papal context this technical term applies almost exclusively to the transfer, or "translation," of a bishop from one diocese to another, which by Dante's day was an administrative act that could be authorized only by the sovereign pontiff.[6] As both *servus servorum* and *translatio episcoporum* were familiar terms to Dante's contemporaries, it would be evident from the text alone that Brunetto was referring to a bishop who had been transferred by the pope from one diocese to another. The reference to the rivers narrows the possibilities still further, to the point where the early commentators correctly guessed that Florence on the Arno and Vicenza on the Bacchiglione were intended. Significantly, two of them—Bambaglioli and Lana—both writing less than five years after the poet's death, reached these general conclusions but still could not identify the bishop by name.[7] Consequently it would appear that neither of them brought to this text anything but the general knowledge we have posited for our hypothetical reader, which nonetheless proved sufficient for them to grasp the general import of Brunetto's allusions.

It is no coincidence, I think, that the text enabled them to know the character by his office—bishop of Florence—though not to know him as an individual. We have seen that Priscian and d'Accorso had famous names that were synonymous with their professions, but the same was not true of Andrea de' Mozzi, whose fame was no more than regional, though in the course of his life he occupied several prominent offices. By introducing him by an allusion to his episcopate, the poet overcame both these difficulties. The reader would at least know that Brunetto's execrable companion was a bishop, and in this he stands in contrast to the three laymen who share his fate. This, I submit, is the fundamental contrast that distinguishes him from the others.

Why should a bishop be sharply differentiated from the rest of Brunetto's band? The obvious distinction between cleric and laic would not seem to apply here, since we have been told that they "all were clerks and great scholars and of great fame."[8] Rather, the stress would seem to be hierarchical and, more specifically, episcopal, for in the passage both the bishops of Rome and Florence/Vicenza figure in their official capacities, stripped of all individuality. What then distinguishes a bishop qua bishop from those other *cherci* whose cases we have already studied? Each had a natural function that not only was professionally determined but also corresponds to distinctions that Dante recognized in the natural order. All three contribute to the *beatitudo huius vitae* of *Monarchia* 3. 15: ideally Brunetto should have taught the *philosophica documenta* to mankind and its monarch, the emperor; Priscian should have taught men how to communicate in accordance with nature; and d'Accorso should have taught them the emperor's will as embodied in law. Of the three, Francesco's sin alone relates to the ecclesiastical hierarchy, for he attributed to the pope a jurisdiction that by nature belonged to the emperor. In Dante's just society, however, the pope has but one function: to guide humanity to its other goal, the *beatitudo vitae aeternae* (*Mon.* 3. 15. 7), in accordance with the *documenta spiritualia*. The essence of Francesco's offense was that he recognized the pope as mankind's spiritual *and* temporal guide. This perverted the natural, but not necessarily the supernatural, order; for conceivably the pope might fulfill his legitimate spiritual functions at the same time that he exercised the emperor's natural powers illegitimately. It remains to be seen how the supernatural order itself can be corrupted, and this form of professional corruption would of course take place solely within the ecclesiastical hierarchy. Thus the principle of natural order, which already has accounted for the sins of the other characters, could also explain the contrast that we have remarked between the bishop and his companions. This does not explicate Brunetto's scorn, which we may suspect proceeds from other causes, but it does suggest why the characters of the twin cantos are grouped in the pattern 3:1 :: 3:1. In short, the text itself indicates that the last of these unnatural intelligentsia did violence to nature qua bishop.

THE CAREER OF ANDREA DE' MOZZI

Brunetto's riddle has structured our approach to the problem. To answer it, one proceeds logically from the general to the specific, from the office to the man. Since the first stage defined the scope of our inquiry, we may hope that at the second the offense itself will become apparent. Let us therefore turn forthwith to the career of this character in the expectation that he will prove to have been the antithesis of Dante's ideal bishop.

The riddle itself was soon solved by the early commentators. By 1324 both Jacopo di Dante and Guido da Pisa had the answer, which was repeated by all subsequent commentators, with but one exception,[9] and its correctness can hardly be doubted, for as of 1300 only one bishop of Florence had been translated to Vicenza. This was Andrea de' Mozzi, who filled the see for over eight years (1287–95) and then was translated by Boniface VIII to Vicenza, where he died about the first of September 1296, less than a year later. Thus, our prelate was contemporary not only to Dante but also to all the runners save only Priscian.[10]

The Mozzi Family

The main line of Mozzi's career was delineated some forty-five years ago by Eletto Palandri in the *Giornale dantesco*,[11] and indeed a generation earlier the prodigious Davidsohn had already vividly represented the man's essential characteristics.[12] Both his career and character were the product of birth, for Andrea was born into one of the great Florentine banking families of the thirteenth century—the Mozzi clan. Although its origins had been modest, early in the century the family had acquired great wealth, and with it nobility.[13] At one time the Mozzi must have been Ghibellines, inasmuch as the family arms on our bishop's tomb were an imperial double-headed eagle,[14] but by 1260 the sons of Mozzo were staunch Guelfs who went into exile after Montaperti.[15] The reason for this realignment of loyalties is not far to seek; for, like the other bankers of Florence, they had financed the papacy in its struggle against Frederick II and his descendants.[16]

The earliest traces of Mozzi commercial operations survive in England, where they were active as merchants and bankers throughout the second half of the thirteenth century. The foundations of these English interests appear to have been laid in the decade 1253–63 by Andrea's uncle, Rucco di Cambio de' Mozzi, who during that period appears almost annually in English royal documents, usually paired with a member of the Spini family, with which the Mozzi had a partnership.[17] Among their other English transactions, Rucco and his partners were already acting as bankers to the papacy,[18] and while they were exiled with the other Florentine Guelfs, this bond was reaffirmed by a formal oath of allegiance to Urban IV in 1263.[19] With the Guelfs' return to Florence in 1267, the house of Mozzi, headed by Tommaso Spigliati di Cambio de' Mozzi, Andrea's brother, began a generation of unparalleled power and prestige, which was to last until its financial empire collapsed in bankruptcy shortly after the turn of the century.[20]

The importance of the family both in Florentine and papal affairs was dramatized in 1273, when Pope Gregory X, then passing through the city on his way to the Council of Lyons, made the Mozzi Palace his residence in Florence and obligingly laid the cornerstone for the new church of San Gregorio, of which Tommaso was the principal benefactor. At the Mozzi Palace he negotiated a brief reconciliation between the Guelfs and Ghibellines, which, though abortive, provided a model for future papal interventions.[21] The same residence was chosen by the two papal legates who in the next generation were sent to pacify the city—Cardinal Latino in 1279–80[22] and Matthew of Aquasparta in the spring of 1300.[23] These visits were a public expression of the importance of Mozzi money to the papacy during this period. Under Martin IV, theirs was one of four Italian banks that collected the papal census in England, Scotland, Germany, and Portugal;[24] and in 1295 Boniface VIII named the Mozzi and Spini, together with the Chiarenti of Pistoia, as exclusive bankers to the papacy.[25]

Tommaso himself supported a succession of popes in their Italian policies. In 1282 he put a company of three hundred soldiers at the disposal of Martin IV for service in the Romagna;[26] in 1285 he used the opportunity of a business conference with Honorius IV to seek the new pope's support of Florentine aggression against Pisa;[27] and in the reign of Nicholas IV, Tommaso was one of the great bankers who financed the War of the Vespers for the papacy.[28]

No less great was Tommaso's influence in domestic politics. In 1273 he was numbered among the ten Guelf leaders who, as heads of the greatest families, dominated Florentine politics.[29] This small oligarchy governed Florence for the next twenty years, until the Ordinances of Justice were framed in 1293 to limit the power of these families.[30] It would seem that Tommaso accommodated himself to the new political situation of the 1290s, for he did not share the fate of his partner, Vanni de' Mozzi, who was the only Mozzi to be exiled along with Dante and the other White Guelfs in 1302.[31] Vanni, it would seem, was singled out because he had been one of the three captains who had led an armed demonstration of the *magnati* against the Ordinances in July 1295, which had a limited success, in that the restraints upon the magnates were somewhat moderated.[32] Tommaso no doubt had supported Vanni in 1295, but by remaining in the background, he avoided the appearance of open resistance,[33] and hence also the vengeful ban of 1302.

Nonetheless, for all his prudence, Tommaso was unable to avert the financial disaster that engulfed the family in bankruptcy at about the time that Vanni was exiled. Indeed, as Masi suggests, the two events may be related,[34] although the connection can by no means be certain, because for a decade Florentine banking firms had been falling like dominoes, and more than likely the Mozzi interests had already been severely shaken.[35] The cause of their collapse remains unknown, although the close association of the Mozzi bank with the papacy suggests to me that Philip the Fair's efforts to reduce papal revenues during his second struggle with Boniface, which began in 1302, may well have been the decisive factor. Economic historians may in time ferret out the cause of the collapse from the Mozzi account books, but for our inquiry the answer is not essential. The evidence at hand traces the career line of the Mozzi fortunes clearly enough to put that of our bishop in perspective. At mid century, the Mozzi were but one of many families of Italian merchant-bankers who were acting for the papacy in England. During the last third of the century, however, they were preeminent. Although one can see that their fall was being prepared by events in the 1290s, still at the curia they maintained their influence past the turn of the century.[36]

Papal Protégé and Curialist

Borne on the rising tide of the family fortune, Tommaso's brother, Andrea Spigliati di Cambio de' Mozzi, came to be bishop of Florence. Some time before 1248 he became a canon of the Florentine cathedral chapter, most likely through family influence. The Mozzi bank was more than a local power, however, and nothing molded his career more than business contacts with the Roman curia. Also before 1248, these had secured for young Andrea the highest of all ecclesiastical patrons—the pope himself. Innocent IV had ordered that a benefice worth thirty marks a year be provided in the Scottish diocese of Saint Andrews for "Andrew, canon of Florence, son of Spigliati, citizen of that city." When the appropriate vacancy occurred, however, the bishop had conferred it on another papal protégé whose claim was stronger, but in compensation Innocent decided that the bishop must pay young Andrea twenty marks annually until a suitable living could be found.[37] This pension was paid intermittently over the next six years, until in 1254 Innocent directed his English agent to see that the original mandate be fulfilled.[38] Eventually, though we do not know when, Andrea was provided with two English benefices; for by 1276 he was rector of Saint Botolph's church in Boston and of

Rayleigh parish in the diocese of London. Moreover, between 1276 and 1283 the papal taxes on his income from these livings were paid directly to the Mozzi bank rather than to the pope's local collectors, which was an acceptable though not a routine procedure.[39]

Family connections probably exerted their usual influence in obtaining one of these benefices, for a papal nominee frequently had some connection, however tenuous, with the church to which he was recommended.[40] In the case of Saint Andrews, Andrea's claim had been quite literally nominal, but Saint Botolph's was a church that was much patronized by the foreign merchants who came to Boston for England's greatest fair, and in consequence the appointment of Andrea probably served the interests of the church's benefactors at least as well as the appointment of any Englishman would have done.[41] As we shall see, during the years that the taxes on his English benefices were being paid, Andrea was busy in Italy, and I can find no indication that he ever was in England, while on the contrary, there are strong reasons to suppose that he never was. Mid century saw the high tide of papal provisions for Italians to English benefices, which provided livings for members of the curia, and since other sources attest Andrea's presence in Italy as a curial official during the years in which he sought and held English benefices, he undoubtedly was one of those nonresident Italians against whom the English complained with bitter indignation.[42] Indeed, this aspect of his life should not have detained us so long had not Davidsohn fallaciously inferred from Innocent's letters of 1248 and 1254 that Andrea was in England during that period.[43] In fact, the letters in Mozzi's favor closely resemble those papal provisions that were issued explicitly to sustain scholars at the university,[44] and although he is not expressly described as a scholar, the evidence of his Italian career, to which we must now turn, leaves no doubt that such was his occupation at the time.

Andrea was educated as a canon lawyer at Bologna. One might have guessed as much from his subsequent employment, but the Bolognese connection is placed beyond doubt by a curious document printed by Palandri. It is a letter addressed to the chapter of Florence by two of its absent members, Alberto degli Scolari and Andrea Spigliati, who second the pope's recommendation that a canonry be provided at Florence for Guiglielmo d'Accorso, son of the Glossator.[45] Though neither place nor date is stated, both may be inferred from the context. The latter must be 1251, for only in that year was there a thirteenth-century bishop-elect of Florence named Johannes.[46] Thus the date of the letter falls between Innocent's two letters in Andrea's behalf, which were issued in 1248 and 1254. The indications of place, while less evident, all converge on Bologna. That one of the writers was beneficed there is a faint clue, which is strongly reinforced by the reference to Guiglielmo d'Accorso, who at this time was certainly a minor living at home, though perhaps not as young as Sarti supposed, for by his reckoning, in 1251 the boy would have been only five years old.[47] Since the writers had *seen* the letters written for him by the pope and the bishop-elect, which would have been in the recipient's possession, it would follow that they too were in Bologna, where, from their desire to oblige a distinguished professor, we may guess that they were students.

When next we hear of Andrea, five years later, in 1256, he is styled for the first time *magister*, which would indicate that he had attained an academic degree.[48] In the same year he received the title *capellanus papae*, which was an honorary title conferred, though not exclusively, on papal clerks of some importance.[49] Bearing it, Andrea appears as assessor to the papal governor of the Marches of Ancona, which leaves no doubt that he was making a career in papal service.[50] The last doubt as to his qualifications is removed when we find him, in 1264, sitting in judgment at the curia as a judge-subdelegate,[51] which clearly identifies him as a professional canonist.

Taken together, the indications yield a consistent picture of his early career. A younger son, he was destined for the Church, but the wealth and influence of his family assured him a good education and papal patronage. During his student days at Bologna, the papacy provided him to benefices, and when his studies in canon law were completed, an honorable place in the papal bureaucracy awaited him. All this had occurred before the family fortunes rose spectacularly during the last third of the century, at a time when the Mozzi were hardly distinguishable from the several dozen Italian banking families that also did business with the curia. The preferment that Andrea secured was no sinecure but rather an administrative post in the central government of the Church, where ability counted for more than birth. No doubt the family thought it a good investment to have one of their number within the organization with which the bulk of their business lay; the papacy would also appreciate his value as a liaison with the banking world on which its policy depended, and indeed quite possibly it patronized his education because he was intended for this role.[52]

Of his thirty years of service to the papacy, we know next to nothing, but judging from his later preoccupation with fiscal matters as bishop of Florence, one may guess that earlier he had specialized in financial matters. Beyond that, there is little to say of his years at the curia,[53] and his connections with Florence are still more obscure. During the long episcopate of Giovanni de' Mangiadori (1251-75), Andrea only once subscribed to an episcopal document, and that was in 1273, probably as he passed through the city in the entourage of Gregory X, who was a guest of Andrea's brother.[54]

Only one episode of Andrea's papal service brought him into prominence before he became bishop. This occurred in the pontificate of Nicholas III (1277-80), when Andrea was attached to the staff of Cardinal Latino during his famous legation[55] and was stationed in Florence to represent the legate there. In this capacity, Mozzi played a supporting role in the great events of the day. Nicholas III, the Orsini pope to whom Francesco d'Accorso addressed his *arenga*,[56] attempted during his brief reign to reorient the Italian policy of the papacy.[57] Unlike his immediate predecessors and successors, he disengaged the pope from dependence on Charles of Anjou and instead endeavored to establish Rome as an independent and leading power in Italian affairs. To this end, Nicholas enlarged the papal states by acquiring the Romagna from Emperor Rudolf in June 1278, and the following September he forced the Angevin to resign his office as imperial vicar in Tuscany. The next step was to restore peace to these areas by exercising the spiritual and temporal authority of the papacy to mediate between the warring Guelf and Ghibelline factions. Such was the mission that Nicholas entrusted to his nephew, Latino Malabranca, whom he had made bishop of Ostia, and hence dean of the college of cardinals, in March 1278.[58] In September, Cardinal Latino was accredited as Nicholas' legate in Tuscany, Romagna, and Venetia,[59] and a few weeks later he was further entrusted with temporal power in the Romagna as its rector.[60] His first concern was with the Romagna, where he spent a year bringing the Bolognese Lambertazzi and Geremei and their allies to an uneasy peace, but in the meantime Tuscany was not forgotten. Latino subdelegated his powers there to Andrea de' Mozzi, who was acting as Latino's agent as early as March 1279.[61] On 31 May the Tuscan commune of San Gimignano notified Andrea that it was at the legate's disposal,[62] and on 22 June he was mentioned in a Pisan charter.[63] In October 1279, Latino himself came to Florence, and for the next eight months he made the Palazzo Mozzi his headquarters while he negotiated the Peace that bears his name.[64] Andrea and his colleague, the canonist William Durandus the elder, spent the month of February receiving pledges of adherence from both parties.[65] Latino's work of mediation having been accomplished, the legate hastened back to Bologna (26 April 1280),[66] leaving Andrea behind to represent the legation in Tuscany, as before.

The death of Nicholas III on 22 August brought an abrupt change of policy. Latino was recalled to Rome, his legatine commission withdrawn, and the Orsini program in North Italy was abandoned. Latino's last known act as legate was issued on 10 September,[67] and Andrea no doubt ceased to act as his agent in Tuscany at about the same time. The new pope employed Mozzi's administrative talents elsewhere, for on 27 January 1282 Martin IV announced that he had appointed Mozzi as rector of Campagna and Marittima, the southernmost provinces of the Papal States.[68] Manifestly, the curia considered his administration of Tuscany a success and in consequence now entrusted Latino's late lieutenant with an independent command. Increased responsibility was not the only recognition of his recent services; he also received material reward, for about this time a canonry at Cambrai was added to his collection of benefices.[69]

Five years later, Andrea de' Mozzi was elected bishop of Florence. The circumstances surrounding his promotion are complex. Davidsohn, who was not overly perceptive of internal ecclesiastical polity, laid too great stress on the political factors that favored Andrea.[70] Undoubtedly in 1286 the influence of Tommaso de' Mozzi stood at its height, both in Florence and at the curia,[71] but his brother had more than favoritism to recommend him as the right man for the present situation of the see. For eleven years, from 1275 to 1286, Florence had been without a bishop— a situation that, while not uncommon, was rightly considered hazardous to the spiritual well-being of a diocese, for which its pastor, the bishop, was responsible; and as a practical matter, the temporalities of the see were no less threatened. On 28 May 1286 a new bishop had been appointed, one Giacomo Castelbuono of Perugia, but within four months he was dead (16 August), and the church of Florence was faced with the prospect of yet another extended vacancy.[72] Under these conditions, the *maior et sanior pars* of the chapter elected Andrea de' Mozzi, with two canons dissenting. In contrast to the last bishop, they now had chosen one of their own members, who was moreover a Florentine by birth and seemingly assured of the respect of the community, no less for his recent role in Latino's legation than for his close connection with the Guelf *grandi* who were then in control of the city government. The chapter could be certain that the pope would support their choice, and not just as a favor to the Mozzi interests, for Andrea had been the devoted servant of the papacy for the past thirty years, and such a career often deserved a bishopric back home.[73] All these considerations converged to favor Andrea, so before the see had been vacant five months, the election was confirmed by Honorius IV on 29 December 1286.[74]

Early in 1287 Andrea de' Mozzi, then nearly sixty years of age, was consecrated bishop of Florence. The new office gave Mozzi his first opportunity to exercise authority in his own name, for during the previous three decades he had always been responsible to some superior official in the papal administration. His conduct during the next eight years, then, reflects for the first time his own character and independent judgment, and both require our particular attention because, as has already been remarked,[75] it is in his capacity as bishop that Mozzi is presented to the reader of the *Inferno*.

The Canonist as Bishop

At Andrea's accession, Florence had been without a bishop for the better part of twelve years,[76] and in consequence the new pastor was faced with an extraordinary backlog of official duties. He was placed in a situation that reveals his true character, for his efforts were allocated by his judgment alone. As might be expected of one who had been trained as a canonist and who had, moreover, served thirty years as a papal administrator, he devoted his talents to the reorganization of the fiscal and legal affairs of his diocese.

Before the end of his first year in office, the new bishop had collected all the documentary evidence of his predecessors' temporal rights into a chartulary entitled *Memoriale reddituum et iuramentorum fidelium episcopatus florentini*. This brought up to date a similar compilation made about fifty years earlier by Bishop Ardingo (1231–49).[77] Not content to garner the occasional acknowledgments made in the past, the lawyer-bishop initiated an ambitious program to secure fresh legal recognition of all the bishop's rights *in temporalibus*. Every obligation to the bishopric was attested by a notarial act, and by 1292 some 180 of these *recognitiones* were collected into a separate register, which was for several centuries to constitute the authentic record of the see's temporalities.[78] What is more, Mozzi was determined to exercise these and all other rights of his office, and this course inevitably brought him into conflict with his clergy, particularly with the cathedral chapter.

These legal conflicts began with his enthronement in 1287 and were still raging when Andrea was transferred to Vicenza in 1295. Our knowledge of the disputes is at best fragmentary, and many of the documents have not been published, but the general outlines can be sketched from the studies made by Sanesi and Davidsohn.[79] These struggles between the pastor of Florence and his flock deserve our special attention because they constitute the historical record of Mozzi's failure as a professional.

Although the bishop contended with many antagonists over a variety of issues, his struggles with the canons of the cathedral chapter are outstanding because their length and complexity left many records and a bitter residue of malevolence. The feud apparently originated in a dispute over who should bear the cost of the bishop's enthronement. In 1287 Andrea had borrowed two thousand gold florins from the Mozzi bank to cover the costs entailed by his promotion, and once he was in office he levied a tax on his clergy to defray the expenses not only of his own consecration but also that of his short-lived predecessor. The cathedral clergy, however, disputed the bishop's assessment and refused to pay the tax. Andrea replied with sentences of excommunication, suspension, and interdict against them, which they in turn appealed to Rome. Their proctor in Rome, Cambio delle Panche, soon reported that canonists at the curia privately considered the bishop's action to be illegal and the chapter's case against him to be strong.[80]

Despite this optimistic report, Rome had still reached no decision when the case was settled out of court in 1292. In the meantime, the friction between bishop and chapter generated further quarrels and at least two more appeals to Rome. Because the rights and duties of bishop and chapter frequently overlapped, each had abundant opportunities to challenge the authority of the other, and as hostility deepened to rancor, each side multiplied pretexts to harass the other. The dispute over the tithe was probably already raging when the bishop exercised his right to fill a vacancy in the cathedral chapter by appointing his own nephew, Aldobrandino Manetti de' Cavalcanti. The canons refused to receive the bishop's nephew because they had not been consulted. Again Bishop Mozzi invoked the canonical sanctions against his chapter, and this sentence also was appealed to Rome.[81] Yet another appeal arose from the bishop's claim that he had the right to confirm the chapter's choice of a rector for the church of Sant' Andrea.[82]

Mozzi's leading opponent in the chapter was the archpriest Tebaldo. In March 1290 this man was in Rome representing the chapter against its bishop, and the two reports that he wrote to his colleagues in Florence serve to characterize both Mozzi and his principal antagonist.[83] Tebaldo pictured himself as the dedicated defender of the diocesan clergy: "Ego procuro salutem cleri in quantum possum." The archpriest had no doubt as to the bishop's intentions: he was seeking to increase his jurisdiction as much as possible. Moreover, whatever the episcopal rights might be, Tebaldo observed, the bishop had weakened his case by the deplorable methods to which he had had recourse and "especially because of the injuries and afflictions which he has inflicted on the clergy."[84]

Tebaldo's reports, tendentious though they are, also afford us a few precious glimpses of our bishop at the curia, whence he had gone to defend himself against his accusers. "The bishop went to the cardinals," the archpriest wrote on 15 March

1290, "and to other high curial officials. And the cardinals' chaplains say that the cardinals did not appear pleased to see him. And all the Florentines who were at the curia and saw the bishop say that he seemed completely dumbfounded."[85] Evidently he was no longer an insider, and his personal influence with his old associates was not as great as he had imagined. But whatever his disappointment, it did not deter him from his program, for the contest with his chapter passed through many rounds after this one.

Even by the end of March, Andrea had taken a new tack. He presented a rich gift to the pope and another to Cardinal Benedetto Gaetani, the future Boniface VIII, who accepted the gift but would not receive the donor.[86] Mozzi also paid court to Giacomo Colonna, then the most influential cardinal—Tebaldo calls him "the other pope"—only to find his eminence attended by three other cardinals, whose presence made intrigue impossible, and by Mozzi's rival the archpriest as well, whom Andrea pretended to ignore, though by many sidelong glances the bishop betrayed that he was all too conscious of the situation.[87] The two cardinals, each in his own way—Benedetto in characteristically blunt fashion, and Giacomo with a certain humor by receiving both importunate favor-seekers simultaneously—demonstrated that although gifts were always acceptable to them, still they would not let bribes sway their judgment. The only promise of assistance that Tebaldo could secure was hardly more helpful, for Cardinal Napoleone Orsini agreed to urge Giacomo Colonna to recommend an investigation of the bishop's conduct.[88] The promise was in fact illusory, for the Colonna and Orsini bitterly opposed one another in the curia at this period: within the decade their rivalry led to the compromise election of Celestine V and to the harrying of the Colonna by Boniface VIII, with his excommunication of their cardinals. Hence it is not surprising that the case was still pending when Nicholas IV died in April 1292.

Meanwhile, both sides tried new expedients to gain some decisive advantage over the other. Andrea refused to repay the loan his brother had made to him, quite possibly hoping that Tommaso would exert his influence with the curia to make the chapter pay the tithe with which the bishop had meant to repay the loan. If so, the scheme backfired, for the banker simply used his influence at court to force the bishop to pay. On 20 January 1291, Nicholas IV ordered that Andrea was to be excommunicated if he did not satisfy his creditor. Presumably the threat alone sufficed, for nothing more is heard of the debt.[89]

Not content with insisting on their rights, the chapter sought to limit the discretionary powers of their bishop. To a commission of papal judges-delegate in Florence, the cathedral chapter claimed that it ought to be consulted by the bishop in all matters concerning ecclesiastical appointments, excommunications, and interdicts; that the chapter had the right to present clerics to the bishop for ordination; and that the chapter ought to receive from the bishop an annual subsidy to provide for the paschal candle. Further, the troublesome Tebaldo, whom Mozzi had suspended from his office of archpriest, brought suit against him in the municipal courts.

After five years of bickering, both parties agreed, in a compromise dated 11

September 1292, to drop their claims and return to the status quo ante. Mozzi withdrew his several sentences of excommunication, interdict, and suspension, while the chapter renounced the claims made to the papal commissioners, and Tebaldo dropped his civil suit. The bishop conceded that the chapter could confirm the rector of Sant' Andrea, and he also let the canons keep as a gift £100 and 23 measures (*modii*) of grain for which he had sued them. His claim to a *decima* was tacitly dropped, and in return the chapter at last received the bishop's nephew.[90]

The compromise permitted the bishop to disengage himself from a struggle in which he had little chance of success. He did not abandon his objectives, however, and a year later he launched a new attack. The goods of the chapter had been administered theretofore by one of the chaplains of the church, who was chosen by the chapter and was not himself a member thereof.[91] Under normal circumstances the chapter could have ignored the wishes of the bishop, but whenever the office of provost was vacant, as it was from late 1291 until early 1295, certain of his functions as head of the chapter were, as required by statute, performed by the bishop.[92] On 31 August 1293 Andrea accordingly presided over a chapter meeting that commissioned the bishop and two canons to establish and fill a new office of chapter treasurer. As the first incumbent, the commissioners chose none other than the bishop's nephew, Aldobrandino, who was invested the following day.[93] The new fiscal officer promptly took possession of the chapter's official papers, and it appeared that for the moment the bishop was in remote control of capitular affairs.

Throughout 1294 the dissenting canons continued to resist ineffectually, but early in 1295 their efforts were rewarded by the election of Tebaldo, the bishop's *bête noire*, as provost of the Florentine church. Andrea soon contrived a means to remove this new obstacle. He claimed that "whenever he wished to come and visit the provost and canons, the provost ought to serve lunch to the bishop and his family," which Tebaldo maintained neither law nor custom bound him to do. Thrice Tebaldo was commanded to comply, and finally the bishop suspended and excommunicated the contumacious provost and instituted proceedings both to depose him from his office and to deprive him and another canon of their benefices.[94] The provost could hardly have been surprised by this course of events; for, as archdeacon, he had already sustained a similar attack, and now he responded much as he had done before. Again he appealed to the civil authorities, this time to the Signoria itself, alleging instances in which the statutes of the chapter had been violated and petitioning that they be enforced by the city. On those matters which concerned only the internal affairs of the chapter, the Signoria obligingly intervened and restored order in a manner reminiscent of an American court pacifying a disorderly university by injunction. The office of treasurer was not abolished but merely deprived of all fiscal functions, which were entrusted to *distributores*. Thus, the bishop's attempt to reform the financial structure of his chapter was effectively blocked, and a generation later the abortive office of treasurer was eliminated altogether by papal command in 1337.[95]

Of the quarrel between the provost and the bishop, the provisions of the Signoria made no mention whatsoever.[96] The reason for this silence would seem to be quite simply that the dispute had been settled unexpectedly before the Signoria issued its decree in May 1296.[97] The feud between bishop and chapter ended abruptly when Andrea was removed from the scene by Boniface VIII. On 13 September 1295 a bull was dispatched from the curia, notifying the bishop that he had been transferred from the see of Florence to that of Vicenza,[98] which recently had been vacated by the death of the incumbent.[99] No reason was given for the move, but evidently it was part of a coordinated plan, for on the same day Pope Boniface translated the bishop of Orvieto, Francesco Monaldeschi, to Florence.[100] Thus, the Florentine chapter had no voice in the new appointment, which was effected exclusively at the pope's discretion.

Andrea's surviving *acta* as bishop of Vicenza are few but nonetheless characteristic of the man. (1) In March 1296 the new bishop confirmed his predecessor's nephew in the possession of some property at Bassano, which the nepotist had held from the Vicenza chapter. Further, since the Bassanesi persisted in pressing their claims to this same property, they were excommunicated by Andrea. (2) He disposed the temporalities of the bishopric with less difficulty, leasing out his rights to tolls collected at the gates of Vicenza and to a fishery. (3) At Vicenza as in Florence, he attempted to rationalize the fiscal operation of the cathedral chapter. Since the capitular endowment had proved insufficient, Mozzi by statute reduced the number of canons to fit their fixed income—a reform that was eventually confirmed by the papacy. Thus his administration on the Bacchiglione, no less than on the Arno, was devoted to the business affairs of his diocese. As before, he appears to have avoided local politics, for he does not figure in the conflicts that were current between Guelf and Ghibelline in Vicenza during his episcopate.[101]

Less than a year after Andrea's transfer, the new bishop of Vicenza was dead. Already in February 1296, Boniface VIII had anticipated his death by reserving the appointment of the next bishop of Vicenza for the Holy See. About the first of September 1296, Andrea died,[102] and on 13 October 1296 Boniface conferred the Vicentine see on a papal chaplain, Rainaldo Concoreggi of Milan.[103] Andrea's brother Tommaso had the old bishop's remains returned to Florence and interred there in the family church of San Gregorio with the simple epitaph: "Sepulcrum venerabilis patris domini Andree de Mozzis, Dei gratia, episcopi florentini et vicentini."[104] Some years later, Tommaso fulfilled his brother's will by making a large donation in his name to the Ospedale di Ricorboli.[105]

MOZZI AS DANTE'S PASTORE-LUPO

Contemporary documents adequately attest the career line of Bishop Mozzi. In them he appears as a type that was increasingly familiar during the second half of the thirteenth century—the ecclesiastical administrator. Davidsohn estimated him to be "ein tüchtiger Mann der Geschäfte und der Politik."[106] Palandri concurred in this judgment, and I would too, for certainly these facets of his character are uppermost in the documents. The younger son of a well-to-do merchant-banker, a canonist by education and a curialist by experience, he rose in papal service through undoubted merit to become bishop of Florence. As an expert administrator, he made financial reform the keynote of his episcopate. Like a true bureaucrat, Andrea valued efficiency and order in business operations, and accordingly he sought to rationalize the fiscal structure of his bishopric. His inventory of the episcopal fisc was a conspicuous and lasting success, but when he sought to force his reforms on an unwilling cathedral chapter, he evinced yet another aspect of his character: unbending determination. There can be no doubt that he preferred to fight for his administrative reforms rather than to pontificate in a spirit of peace and concord. "But it is historically certain," Palandri observed, "that, impetuous and imperious by nature, he more than once debased and compromised his pastoral authority" by insisting on having his way.[107]

The sources tell us clearly enough how this bishop behaved, but they do not characterize his behavior with a name. Those who share his values will see him as a practical man who gets things done by determined and realistic effort. Others will account him a worldly man, more concerned with temporal matters than with things spiritual; to them his concern with the fiscal welfare of his church will appear as avarice, his methods will seem litigious and uncharitable, and the decisive and resolute qualities that are the virtues of a hard-headed businessman will be deemed vices, more or less serious depending on the moral judgment of the critic, who could qualify Andrea as dogged, obstinate, stubborn, willful, or even pig-headed. For the present purpose we need not form our own estimate of this man's character: it is more important that we be aware of the range of interpretations that the moralist can place upon the bishop's conduct. With this in mind, we can now ask the principal question of this inquiry: Do contemporary sources reveal anything in the life of Andrea de' Mozzi that would justify Dante to condemn him *as bishop*?

The key, I think, lies in the epithet by which he is characterized in the poem— *tigna*. This, as we have seen, denotes not only diseases of the skin, and especially of the scalp, such as scurf and mange, but also moral conditions that are analogous to a persistent itch. Italian dialects offer two such figurative meanings, both of which admirably fit the case of our bishop: the Tuscans apply *tigna* to one who is consumed by avarice, *un avaro*, while the Romans use it to signify a person who is obstinate or pig-headed.[108] Sensitive as our poet was to dialectical nuance, both senses may have served his purpose, perhaps even to reflect Andrea's image respectively at home and at Rome; therefore, until we can find reason to prefer one before the other, we must retain both. The text, then, recalls with this word the traits that characterized Andrea as bishop—his pertinacious efforts to provide for the financial welfare of his institution, whose members he did not hesitate to excommunicate for the sake of his administrative reforms. Evidently he valued the temporal well-being of his church more highly than the eternal salvation of its individual members.

To Dante such an attitude was anathema. The poet's work is pervaded with the conviction that the Church by its nature should be exclusively a spiritual body. In the preceding chapter we found Francesco d'Accorso condemned for attributing to the Church the temporal authority and jurisdiction that by natural right belong to the emperor alone. Throughout the *Comedy*, Dante complains with many voices that the pursuit of temporal wealth and power has corrupted the Church, which he recalls to apostolic poverty;[109] but the greatest of these complaints will suffice to justify his condemnation of Bishop Andrea de' Mozzi.

In the heaven of the Fixed Stars, after the pilgrim had witnessed a vision of the Church Triumphant and had been examined on the theological virtues (*Par.* xxii–xxvi), Saint Peter exposed to him the besetting weakness of the Church Militant, which was, in a word, avarice.

> Non fu la sposa di Cristo allevata
>> del sangue mio, di Lin, di quel di Cleto,
>> per essere ad acquisto d'oro usata;
> ma per acquisto d'esto viver lieto
>> e Sisto e Pïo e Calisto e Urbano
>> sparser lo sangue dopo molto fleto.
> Non fu nostra intenzion ch'a destra mano
>> d'i nostri successor parte sedesse,
>> parte da l'altra del popol cristiano;
>
> .   .   .   .
>
> In vesta di pastor lupi rapaci
>> si veggion di qua sù per tutti i paschi:

The Bride of Christ was not nurtured with my blood and that of Linus and Cletus to be used for gain of gold; but for gain of this happy life Sixtus and Pius and Calixtus and Urban shed their blood after many tears. It was not our intention that one part of Christ's people should sit on the right hand of our successors and the other on the left. . . . Ravening wolves in shepherds' clothing are seen from here above through all the pastures.[110]

(Par. xxvii, 40–48, 55–56)

Principally these words were directed at the papacy, and specifically at the pope then reigning, Boniface VIII, whom Peter denounced as a usurper, declaring that in the sight of God the apostolic see was vacant (*Par.* xxvii, 22–24). Flushed with anger, the first pope began his indictment by contrasting the true purpose of the Church with the misuse to which it was being perverted: the Church was meant to bring salvation to its members, not gold to its head. In second place on the Petrine bill of particulars stands the abuse of excommunication: the early popes did not pretend to divide their flock into sheep and goats, into the blessed and the damned. Peter further condemned the paradox of a papal army and the sale of papal privileges, but these do not concern our bishop, whereas the first points apply to the lower members of the hierarchy no less than to its head. Indeed, verses 55 and 56 expressly extend the condemnation from the pope to the bishops. From the heights of heaven one can discern wolves in shepherds' clothing (*vesta di pastor*) ravening through all the pastures.

Of such bishops I take Andrea to be Dante's type. Certainly Mozzi's episcopate was dedicated to the financial affairs of his see, which for Dante was to use the Church for gain of gold rather than of salvation. Moreover, to attain this improper end, he coerced the recalcitrant by excommunicating them, contrary to the intention of the founding fathers of the Church, as expounded by Dante's St. Peter. Both aspects of Mozzi's ministry are, as we have observed, compacted in the epithet *tigna*.

The correspondence of these concepts cannot be attributed to random coincidence, for they were repeatedly associated by the poet. A pair of further examples will illustrate and extend this conceptual complex. In Epistle xi, addressed in 1314 "To the Italian Cardinals" assembled near Avignon to elect a new pope,[111] Dante exhorted them to purify the papacy and return it to Rome:

> It seems then . . . that I have kindled the blush of confusion in you and in others, chief-priests in name only (if so be that shame has not been wholly rooted out throughout the world), since among so many who usurp the office of shepherd, among so many sheep who, if not driven away, at least are neglected and left untended in the pastures, one voice alone, one alone of filial piety, and that of a private individual [i.e. Dante's own], is heard at the obsequies as it were of Mother Church.
>
> And what wonder? Each one has taken avarice to wife, even as you yourselves have done; avarice, the mother never of piety and righteousness, but ever of impiety and unrighteousness. Ah! most loving Mother, Spouse of Christ, that by water and the spirit bearest sons unto thy shame! Not charity, not Astraea, but the daughters of the horseleech have become thy daughters-in-law. And what offspring they bear thee all save the Bishop of Luni bear witness. Your Gregory lies among the cobwebs; Ambrose lies forgotten in the cupboards of the clergy, and Augustine along with him; and Dionysius, Damascenus, and Bede; and they cry up instead I know not what *Speculum*, and Innocent, and him of Ostia. And why not? Those sought after God as their end and highest good; these get for themselves riches and benefices.[112]

The elements of Peter's expostulation are already here in combination: the blush of shame, the bride of Christ, the wolfish pastor, and avarice, the root of evil. To these, another theme is added: the motives of the clergy can be judged by the authorities they study. The Church Fathers, whose goal was God and the *summum bonum*, are neglected in favor of the Decretalists, the commentators on the papal decretals of the last century and a half, the mastery of which assured material rewards. Dante singles out three among the latter authors, easily the greatest canonists of the thirteenth century: Pope Innocent IV and Hostiensis, whom we encountered in the previous chapter, and the Speculator William Durandus, colleague to Andrea de' Mozzi in Latino's legation.[113]

This theme reappears in a new and significant context in the heaven of Venus, where the pilgrim's informant remarks that the pope seldom remembers the Holy Land, and the observation is amplified thus:

> La tua città, che di colui è pianta
> che pria volse le spalle al suo fattore
> e di cui è la 'nvidia tanto pianta,
> produce e spande il maladetto fiore

c'ha disvïate le pecore e li agni,
    però che fatto ha lupo del pastore.
Per questo l'Evangelio e i dottor magni
    son derelitti, e solo ai Decretali
    si studia, sì che pare a' lor vivagni.
A questo intende il papa e ' cardinali;
    non vanno i lor pensieri a Nazarette,
    là dove Gabrïello aperse l'ali.

Thy city, which is a plant of his who first turned his back on his Maker and from whose envy come such lamentation, brings forth and spreads the accursed flower that has led astray the sheep and the lambs, for it has made a wolf of the shepherd. For this the Gospel and the great Doctors are neglected and only the Decretals are studied, as may be seen by their margins. To this Popes and Cardinals devote themselves. Their thoughts do not go to Nazareth, whither Gabriel spread his wings.[114]

(*Par.* ix, 127–38)

Here the bibliography has been reduced to a simple contrast between the Gospel and the great doctors on the one hand and the decretals on the other. Again the theme is associated with the *topos* of the *pastore-lupo*, but both are joined to a new, third theme that in turn leads back to Mozzi. The clerical avarice that inflames the shepherd to prey upon his flock is here linked to Florence, the center of papal finance. The city's coin—the florin, which bore a fleur-de-lis—is represented as the ultimate corrosive force in Christendom; for its sake the pastor has become the enemy of his flock, which untended goes astray. And as we know, in the generation before 1300, chief among the Florentine houses that made this possible was the family of Andrea de' Mozzi, who, with appropriate irony, became in his turn just such a pastor of Florence.

In sum, the historical Andrea embodied the complex of qualities that Dante associated with the misgovernment of the Church. As such he could provide the poet with a perfect type of the perverse pastor. Yet, though one can admit the possibility that Mozzi could typify for Dante the failings of the episcopate, one still can doubt that this was actually the poet's intention. As the coincidences accumulate, however, this doubt should diminish; but it can be resolved more completely by internal indications of the author's intention, which can most readily be discerned in the patterns he imposed on his work. If Mozzi was meant to be taken as the type of Dante's bad bishop, then we may expect to find his antitype, the good bishop, exemplified in Paradise. But who in Heaven stand to Andreas as Donatus stands to Priscian?

One might expect those two great patristic bishops, Ambrose and Augustine, but neither are characters in the poem. The answer is—significantly—not far to seek, for the passage last quoted was spoken by one who was the antithesis of Andrea de' Mozzi. Named Folco in the poem, in life he was Folquet de Marseille, a contemporary of Saint Francis, a troubadour, Cistercian, and bishop of Toulouse during the Albigensian Crusades. Of his life we need recall only those features that will bear comparison with the career of Mozzi.[115] Like Andrea and Francis, Folquet was the son of a prosperous merchant. His early life was devoted to love and poetry in Provence, where he became one of the great troubadours of the age. That Dante appreciated this aspect of his career there can be no doubt, for he adduced one of Folquet's canzoni as an example of the highest degree of *constructio*, the appropriate ordering of words, "which has flavor and grace and also elevation, which belongs to illustrious writers."[116] It is not for this alone that he was placed among the *spiriti amanti* in the heaven of Venus, however. After a conventional series of courtly loves, apparently unconsummated, upon the death of his *domna* he entered a religious order and persuaded his wife and sons to do the same. For himself he chose the Cistercian order, distinguished for the unworldly love of its austere rule, the *Carta caritatis*, exemplified in the life and works of its most famous member, Bernard of Clairvaux. Within a few years, Folquet rose to be abbot of Torronet, but his true vocation proved ultimately to be secular rather than monastic. In 1205 he was translated by Innocent III from his abbacy to the see of Toulouse, whose bishop the pope had just deposed on the eve of the first Albigensian Crusade. Folquet's diocese was the heartland of the heresy, and his long episcopate (1205–31) was dedicated to the spiritual renewal of his flock.[117]

Dante's Folco reflects this crusading zeal in the passage analyzed above, though it appears as a general concern for the Holy Land rather than for crusades in Christian lands. To contemporary Christians, such as William of Tudela, a Provençal poet who chronicled the first Albigensian Crusade in verse, Folquet appeared to be the ideal bishop, "who had no rival for his degree of goodness."[118] In his concern for heresy, this Cistercian resembles, not Saint Francis, but the founder of the other great mendicant order, Saint Dominic, who received his vocation in the same milieu. Unlike Dominic, however, Folquet was a bishop who provided moral leadership within the recognized structure of ecclesiastical authority. As such, he was an exception in Languedoc, where the heresy had grown because the bishops not only failed to provide the spiritual food for which their congregations hungered but also were prepared to tolerate the Cathari, who offered the poison of heresy instead. In contrast to this episcopal laxity, Folquet was, by medieval lights, a model of episcopal action *in spiritualibus*.

This is enough to assure us that, given his denunciation of the lupine canonist-bishops of Mozzi's day, who cared more for florins than for their flocks, Folco was meant to stand as their proper counterpart. The contrasts to Andrea's episcopal career are already apparent, but they do not exhaust the full range of correspondences between the two men. Presently we shall see that Mozzi, too, had a reputation as a rhetorician and pastor to which Folco's stands as the obverse of the coin.[119] But these additional parallels, though they will confirm the resemblance we have noted and will extend our interpretation in other directions, are not essential to the principal hypothesis, with which we are now concerned. For the present, our argument requires only that we recognize that Dante linked Andrea and Folco through the latter's denunciation of the sins that were typical of the former; for from this we can infer that he intended one to stand as the type of improper, and the other of proper, episcopacy.

My thesis, then, is that Andrea de' Mozzi is to be taken as the type of all bishops who pervert their office by preying on their flocks. Taken out of context, the gloss of the early commentator known as the False Boccaccio might seem agreeable to this interpretation, for he wrote that Andrea "could signify all prelates, because this vice is widespread among them."[120] The context makes clear, however, that this commentator considered sodomy to be the vice in question. The originality of the comment lies in the perception, applied to Priscian as well, that the character represents his profession.[121] In effect, I am proposing that "this vice" was not sodomy but something improper to the profession of the sinner in the sense that it perverted the essential nature of that profession. As has already been noted in our preliminary analysis of the problem,[122] for Dante the true sphere of episcopal action lay, not in the natural, but in the supernatural order. How then, we may ask, could Mozzi's conduct be condemned as unnatural? Because, it would seem, the bishop did not observe the distinction, profound for Dante, between the realms of nature and grace. Instead, Andrea and his ilk overstepped the limits of nature by governing the Church Militant as if it were just another human institution to which the natural principles of economics and politics might licitly be applied. But for Dante, thus to "naturalize" the Church was a confusion of divinely separated orders: and he would let no man join together what God has put asunder. Hence, Andrea de' Mozzi can be seen as one who did violence to nature by putting it to uses for which it was not intended.

THE RIDICULOUS PREACHER

Because of the complexity of Mozzi's case, I have proceeded directly from the contemporary evidence to its interpretation in the previous section. The conclusions we have just arrived at, however, must be regarded as hardly more than a working hypothesis that further analysis shall either refine or refute. To become acceptable, our thesis must be examined in three respects: it must be consistent with Dante's text, with itself, and with other evidence external to the poem.

(1) We have yet to account for several of the questions raised in our preliminary analysis of the problem, notably with Brunetto's scorn and Mozzi's *mal protesi nervi*. One would hardly expect that the worldly sins we have attributed to the bishop would excite in a *mondano uomo* such as Brunetto the degree of contempt that he expresses in the poem.[123] While a humanist would not be apt to praise either avarice or obstinacy, neither would someone flawed by them be despised as vehemently as is Andrea by Brunetto. Therefore we must inquire whether this animus proceeds from another source; we may suspect that on Brunetto's lips, the term *tigna* might have quite another meaning. Similarly, we have yet to explain Brunetto's other epithet, for it is not apparent from the proposed reinterpretation why the remains of Mozzi could appropriately be described as his "badly stretched nerves."

(2) Yet another point can be raised from the text. The poet identified the bishop by reference to his translation, but although it thus figures prominently in the poem, this event as yet plays no part in our interpretation. Presumably Andrea would have been damned as the perverse pastor of Florence had he remained its bishop to his dying day. The reference would be apposite, however, if the sins for which Dante condemns him were the cause of his translation; but this would create a curious internal contradiction in our argument, for it would be inconsistent if Boniface VIII had punished in a bishop the very sins that Dante explicitly attributes to that pope.[124] To resolve this paradox, we must investigate the cause of Mozzi's translation, which for commentators both medieval and modern has constituted a problem in itself.

(3) Finally, we must confront in Dante's trecento commentators a battery of witnesses whose hearsay reminiscences give Mozzi a character that differs markedly from the impression we have gained from contemporary sources. The earliest of them offered vague and sketchy explanations of both Andrea's transfer and his damnation, but the second generation of commentators added circumstantial details that yet a third generation embroidered. In general, they tend to represent Mozzi as a degenerate simpleton who hardly resembles the man of affairs we have met in contemporary sources. On the basis of an extensive analysis of the successive variations in these commentaries, Palandri concluded that this tradition grew by supposition and misunderstanding into a legend "that the historian is continually constrained to doubt."[125] These sources are not, I think, to be altogether avoided for that reason, for more than likely the legendary husk conceals a grain of historical fact, but this I have felt can be distinguished only by comparison with the undoubted facts, and at best the legendary evidence should be regarded as probable rather than certain. Hence, before confronting the tradition of the commentators, I have sought to form a judgment of Mozzi's character from the authentic materials provided by his contemporaries; but now the time has come to hear the testimony of the secondary sources, for they preserve the clues that can explain both Brunetto's scorn and Mozzi's translation.

Trecento Commentaries

There is no need to repeat Palandri's systematic presentation of the early commentators on this passage. Suffice it to say that all who identify the bishop's sin are agreed that it is sodomy, though in no case is there any reason to believe this opinion has any basis except in their reading of the poem itself. Of far greater importance is the external evidence that they incorporate in explanation of Mozzi's translation, and it is with these possibly historical facts that we shall be concerned. Only one is found among the first generation of commentators, from the gloss known as Selmi's Anonymous (1321 × 1337): "And this [transfer] Mozzi's relatives procured to remove from their presence the disgrace of his sodomy by not having to see him every day."[126] Written within living memory of the translation of 1296, this may well reflect the interpretation that contemporary observers in Florence put upon the event, though Vaticanology, then as now, is by no means an exact science. At worst we can be sure that the explanation, even though an uninformed guess, must have seemed plausible to contemporaries. Subsequent commentators found it no less attractive, and as we shall see, it was duly repeated by the next two generations.

Boccaccio, whose commentary dates from 1373 × 1375, accepted family influence as the efficient cause of the translation, but he was less certain that the reason was scandalous sodomy. Apparently he had heard folk tales about some "foolish deeds" ("sciocchezze") by which the bishop had scandalized the Florentines, and these Boccaccio suggested were more likely to have been the cause of the translation:

> This is said to have been one messer Andrea de' Mozzi, bishop of Florence, who both for this defect [sodomy], which sin—perhaps—made him a public scandal, and also for his many other foolish deeds, which are commonly told about him, was changed from bishop of Florence into bishop of Vicenza by the pope at the instance of messer Tommaso de' Mozzi, his brother, who was an honorable knight and highly regarded by the pope, in order to remove such an abomination from his sight and that of his fellow citizens.[127]

What sort of foolishness the bishop had been up to, Boccaccio did not say, apparently assuming that his Florentine audience knew well enough the oral tradition. These particulars, however, were soon collected by another commentator writing in the 1370s. Benvenuto da Imola came to Florence in 1373 to hear Boccaccio lecture and then returned to Bologna, where he himself expounded the *Divine Comedy* to private classes. Much of his material comes from Boccaccio and often is supplemented by inquiries made during his year in Florence.[128] These early Bolognese lectures have not survived. Instead we have two later redactions made by the author, probably at Ferrara between 1379 and 1383. Only fragments have been published from the earlier and shorter of the two versions (A), but happily one of these is the passage concerning Mozzi.[129] When compared with the longer and better-known second recension (B),[130] it is apparent that A is the more reliable of the two, for not only did B discard precious details (§ 2) but it also diffused and softened the clarity of the earlier redaction through rhetorical embellishments.[131]

A	B
1. The person in question was a citizen of Florence and bishop of Florence. This bishop was Andrea de' Mozzi, of good family.	1. To understand this passage I want you to know with more than a modicum of laughter that this spirit was a Florentine citizen, born de Modiis, who was called Andrea.
2. This man was a good simpleton. He said that he did not want to be punished by God for neglecting his people; therefore he wished to preach, and all Florence ran to hear him. And when he preached, he went into profound matters of theology.	2. This simple and foolish man often preached publicly, saying many ridiculous things to the people.

3. Afterwards he said, "Do you know what the providence of God is? I say to you, it is like a mouse that stands on a roof-beam and sees but is not seen.

4. The grace of God is like the dung of a wild she-goat that stands on a height and defecates: part falls, part remains, etc.; some have a little and some much."

5. Further, to illustrate the power [of God] he had a turnip seed and then held up one huge turnip.

6. In short this bishop was continually doing such things, but among others [he offended] one of his relations, the wife of Lord Nicholas de' Mozzi, a great doctor. She wished to go to Rome and when he preached he said: "Please pray for the Lady Tessa, for she was somewhat inconstant and complaisant but now is repentant."

7. So that brother arranged with Pope Nicholas Orsini for his transfer.

3. Among other things, he said that the providence of God was like a mouse who, while standing on a roof-beam, sees whatsoever happens below him in the house and no one sees him.

4. He said also that the grace of God was like the dung of wild she-goats, which falling from on high breaks dispersedly into divers parts.

5. Likewise he said that divine power was immense, and wishing to illustrate this by an obvious example, he held up a turnip seed and said, "You can see how very small and tiny this seedlet is." Then from beneath his cope he produced an enormous turnip, saying, "Behold how wonderful is the power of God, who from so small a seed made such a fruit."

. . . .

6. And note here [at *Inf.* xv, 112–13] that the author not without reason describes him thus by this transfer, for you must know that once when Bishop Andrea preached publicly to his people, he said at the end: "Ladies and gentlemen, please remember in your prayers my relative, the Lady Tessa, who is going to Rome, for in truth if she was momentarily somewhat inconstant and complaisant, now she has mended her ways and therefore is going to gain an indulgence."

7. This I know: When his brother, the great jurist Lord Thomas de Modiis, could no longer bear Andrea's blunders and because the scandal of the [bishop's] vice was increasing, he prudently set to work to have him transferred to Vicenza by Pope Nicholas Orsini.

A

1. Iste de quo loquitur fuit civis Florentie et episcopus Florentie. Fuit iste episcopus Andreas de Moçis bona domo.

2. Iste fuit bonus, simplex: dicebat quod nolebat ferre penam apud Deum propter suos; ideo volebat predicare, et tota Florentia currebat. Et quando predicabat intrabat profundam materiam theologie.

3. Postea dicebat: "Scitis quomodo facta est providentia Dei? Dicam vobis: est facta sicut mus qui stat in trabe, et [MS. nec] videt nec videtur.

4. Gratia Dei est sicut stercus capre: capra stat in alto et stercoriçat; pars cadit, pars remanet etc.; aliqui habent parum, aliqui multum."

5. Postea de potentia: habebat semen rape, et ostendebat unam rapam magnam.

6. Breviter ita faciebat iste episcopus. Sed inter alia cum una sua cognata, uxore domini Nicholai de Moçis doctoris magni. Ista voluit ire Romam: quando fecit predicationem, dicit: "sit vobis recomendata domina Tessa, nam bene fuit aliquantulum vaga et placens, sed vere emendata est."

B

1. Ad cuius cognitionem volo te scire cum non modico risu, quod iste spiritus fuit civis florentinus, natus de Modiis, episcopus Florentiae, qui vocatus est Andreas.

2. Iste quidem vir simplex et fatuus, saepe publice praedicabat populo dicens multa ridiculosa;

3. inter alia dicebat, quod providentia Dei erat similis muri, qui stans super trabe vident quaecumque geruntur sub se in domo, et nemo videt eum.

4. Dicebat etiam, quod gratia Dei erat sicut stercus caprarum, quod cadens ab alto ruit in diversas partes dispersum.

5. Similiter dicebat, quod potentia divina erat immensa; quod volens demonstrare exemplo manifesto, tenebat granum rapae in manu et dicebat: bene videtis, quam parvulum sit istud granulum et minutum; deinde extrahebat de sub cappa maximam rapam, dicens: ecce quam mirabilis potentia Dei, qui ex tantillo semine facit tantum fructum.

. . . .

6. Et hic nota, quod autor non sine quare describit ipsum taliter ab ista transmutatione; nam debes scire, quod semel episcopus Andreas, cum praedicasset egregie populo suo, dixit in fine: O Domini et Dominae, sit vobis recommendata monna Thessa, cognata mea, quae vadit Romam; nam in veritate si

fuit per tempusculum satis vaga et placibilis, nunc est bene emendata; ideo vadit ad indulgentiam.

7. Iste frater ita scivit facere cum papa Nicola de Orsinis quod permutavit eum.

7. Hoc scito [?scite], dominus Thomas de Modiis frater eius, magnus iurista, non valens [?volens] ulterius ferre ineptias eius, et quia crescebat infamia vitii, dedit operam prudenter quod transmutaretur in episcopum vicentinum per papam Nicolaum de Ursinis. . . .

It would seem that Benvenuto, having heard Boccaccio's allusion to "molte altre sue sciocchezze che di lui si raccontano nel vulgo," made inquiry at Florence and was told two distinct anecdotes, which he dutifully repeats. Both concern Andrea's public appearances in the pulpit. The first consists of three parables by which the bishop attempted to illustrate theological concepts, evidently not to the edification of his audience (§§ 2–5); the second represents him as an indiscreet confessor who inadvertently reveals to the congregation the secret sins of Tessa, one of his relatives (§ 6). After relating both tales, Benvenuto repeats Boccaccio's explanation of the translation, attributing it to the influence of the bishop's brother.

The first and last sections are paraphrased from Boccaccio, while the intervening pair of anecdotes is in effect a gloss on his *sciocchezze*. Benvenuto is no surer than was Boccaccio about why the bishop was transferred. The A text represents the Tessa incident as the brother's motive (A, 2: *ita*), but B returns to Boccaccio's noncommittal explanation, in which Tommaso is motivated not only by Andrea's ineptitudes in general (*ineptias*) but also by the supposed scandal of his vice. In short, Benvenuto had nothing new to say on this score.[132]

The earlier commentators, then, ascribed the transfer to the influence of the Mozzi clan, which Boccaccio, probably by shrewd conjecture, individuated as its then head, Tommaso. Since the motives of the family are vaguely and variously described, we may suspect that they were not public knowledge. At the most, it would seem that it was whispered about Florence that the family was behind the mysterious transfer, and this rumor the commentators most probably seized upon and enlarged without further information. As Palandri has pointed out, the bishop can hardly have been the embarrassment to the family that the commentators pretend, for Tommaso had his remains returned to Florence and buried in the family church;[133] moreover, we have seen that the banker executed his brother's will and associated himself with Andrea in philanthropic and pious donations.[134] On the cause of Andrea's translation, then, the commentators say nothing that can be considered an established fact. Their immediate contribution is rather that they reflect the popular image of the bishop's character.

At first glance, it would seem that the man whom Benvenuto describes can hardly be the historical Andrea de' Mozzi whom we met in the contemporary sources. That obstinate canonist might be called many things but scarcely *bonus* or *simplex* (A, 2)—at least if we are to take these terms literally. More probably, how- ever, their sense is better conveyed by the expression *vir simplex et fatuus*, which was substituted in B, 2. Then Benvenuto would represent the bishop as one who was clumsy though well intentioned, which assuredly is more charitable, not to say discreet, than to bluntly call him a fool *(stultus)*. The same tendency is still more plainly evinced in his treatment of Boccaccio's *sciocchezze*, which in Benvenuto's Latin becomes, not *stultiae*, as we might expect, but only *ineptiae* (B, 7).

Benvenuto's meaning, then, is clear enough; and indeed he was only putting into words what was implicit in the anecdotes themselves, for in both the bishop means well but, through a lack of common sense, bungles miserably. If this is the meaning, we must accordingly ask whether such behavior is consistent with what we know of the historical Mozzi. To me it seems highly probable that an ecclesi- astical administrator who had exercised no cure of souls for thirty years would, upon becoming a bishop, prove deficient in the practical judgment that is proper to a preacher and confessor, not to say a pastor. Such would seem to be the interpretation laid upon his conduct by a commentator of the third generation, Fanfani's Anonimo Fiorentino, who about 1400 summarized Benvenuto's B version:

> This was messer Andrea de' Mozzi, bishop of Florence, who was on account of this sin [sodomy] most disgraceful [*disonestissimo*] and as a result of it he was moreover a man of little sense [*di poco senno*]. And he was not con- tent to conceal his defect and his lack of common sense; on the contrary, he wished to preach daily to the people, saying foolish and colorless words [*parole sciocche et dilavate*]. Whence the pope, having learned of his miser- able life, took away the bishopric of Florence . . . and made him bishop of Vicenza. . . . And it seemed that the pope did this at the request of his brother, who was a worthy knight and wealthy.[135]

By exaggeration, this comment brings a most important point into relief: we are told here that Andrea wished to preach *every* day *(ogni di)*. Surely this is an overstatement of the frequency, for B, 1, has him "preaching publicly often [*saepe*]," while A, 1, merely signifies by the imperfect tense that the action was a repeated one. Nonetheless, both Benvenuto and the Anonimo agree that the decision to preach frequently was the bishop's own *(volebat A, 1; volea)*. This might seem self-evident were it not that the bishop of Florence was at this period obliged by the statutes of the cathedral church to preach only on three great spring feasts, namely Easter, May Day (the kalends of May), and the feast of San Zanobi (25 May).[136] The rest of the year was apparently ad libitum, and our self-willed bishop apparently made himself conspicuous where a more prudent man would have satisfied the minimum requirement and left his pulpit to more capable preachers for the rest of the year. Why he chose to make a fool of himself is a question that has not occurred to modern commentators for the simple reason that Benvenuto, in the familiar B version of his work, stripped the preaching anecdote of its context, which has been preserved, however, in the little-known, earlier version (A, 2): "Dicebat quod nolebat ferre penam apud Deum propter suos; ideo volebat predicare, et tota Florentia currebat. Et quando predicabat intrabat profundam materiam theologie." There can be no doubt about Andrea's motives: he often stated them, probably from the pulpit in explanation of his extraordinary decision: "He said that he did not want to be punished by God for neglecting his people; therefore he wished to preach." The statement has an authentic ring. These are not the words of a foolish man, much less of a storyteller, but rather the sober statement of a conscientious medieval bishop. They echo a long tradition in Christian thought about the responsibility of a bishop. To investigate the genealogy of this remark might seem a superfluous excursus were we not prompted to do so by Dante himself. Previously in our inquiry we have found it profitable to follow up the poet's literary references, notably Brunetto's allusion to his book. In the preceding section we encountered another such reference that was associated with his complex of ideas on episcopal office, for Dante rebuked the pastors of his day because they preferred to read the Decretalists rather than the Fathers of the Church.[137] Let us not neglect to do so then, in the hope that we may not only elucidate Mozzi's motives but also discover how Dante's ideal bishop might have been guided in his office by Christian tradition.

Preach or Perish

Mozzi preached because Holy Scripture itself had instilled in him the fear of God. For Christian bishops, the *locus classicus* that enjoined them to preach or be damned was found in the prophet Ezekiel:

> So thou, O son of man, I have made thee a watchman to the house of Israel: therefore thou shalt hear the word from my mouth, and shalt tell it them from me. When I say to the wicked: O wicked man, thou shalt surely die: if thou dost not speak to warn the wicked man from his way: that wicked man shall die in his iniquity, but I will require his blood at thy hand. But if thou tell the wicked man, that he may be converted from his ways, and he be not converted from his way: he shall die in his iniquity: but thou hast delivered thy soul.

> Et tu, fili hominis, speculatorem dedi te domui Israel: audiens ergo ex ore meo sermonem, annuntiabis eis ex me. Si me dicente ad impium: Impie, morte morieris; non fueris locutus ut se custodiat impius a via sua: ipse impius in iniquitate sua morietur, sanguinem autem eius de manu tua requiram. Si autem, annuntiante te ad impium, ut a viis suis convertatur, non fuerit conversus a via sua: ipse in iniquitate sua morietur: porro tu animam tuam liberasti.[138]

Jerome, after expounding the passage literally, explains that it can be applied to any person having authority over the Lord's people, whether a king or prophet of Israel, or a bishop or priest of the Church.[139] For churchmen he points out the moral: they are unworthy appointees who have no right to be either negligent or idle; still less ought they to receive and enjoy the honor of their office without performing the functions proper to it. Augustine made the same passage from Ezekiel the text of a sermon preached on the anniversary of his consecration, in which he stressed the burdens that a bishop must bear: "Praedicare, arguere, corripere, aedificare, pro unoquoque satagere magnum onus, magnum pondus, magnus labor."[140]

The early Latin Doctors, then, had taken Ezekiel the Watchman as the type of ecclesiastical prelates, who were accordingly enjoined to preach as he had prophesied. These implications were most fully developed two centuries later by Gregory the Great in his *Homilies on Ezechiel*, where the passage (or rather its doublet) occasioned this classic statement of the obligation of the prelate to preach:

> We should note and carefully reflect on the meaning of these words [Ezech. 3:18], and what else can it be than this? Neither does the subject die because his director is at fault, nor is his director without fault when the subject dies by his own fault without having heard how he might live. For the wicked man deserves death, but the [Lord's] watchman should proclaim to him the way of life and denounce his iniquity. If the watchman is silent, the wicked shall die in his iniquity, for because of his iniquity he did not deserve what the speech of the watchman might have accomplished. But the Lord requires his blood from the hand of the watchman, because he killed this man, for by being silent he betrayed him to death.[141] Consider in both these cases how greatly the sins of subject and rulers are interconnected, because whenever the subject dies by his own fault, his supervisor who was silent is held to be his murderer. Consider, dear brethren, consider therefore that it is your fault also if we, your prelates, are not worthy shepherds; and if you fall into iniquity, this also is our offense, who have not stood in your way and called you back. Therefore you spare both yourselves and us if you desist from evildoing; we spare both you and ourselves when we do not leave unsaid what displeases.[142]

Patristic exegesis, then, developed the words of Ezekiel into the precept that prelates must preach or perish. In subsequent centuries, bishops especially were reminded that their own salvation, no less than that of their flocks, depended on incessant preaching. Thus, Alcuin exhorted an unknown bishop to be diligent in his office: "Your tongue is the key of heaven: hence about good things let it never be still; may it never cease from uttering admonitions."[143] As Christ preached in all manner of places, so his bishop should seize every opportunity to exercise his office. Moreover, he should be always mindful of those terrible penalties for negligence in the *officia praedicationis* with which the Lord had threatened Ezekiel—whereupon Alcuin quotes Ezekiel 3:17-18.

Now it is evident that when Mozzi "said that he did not want to be punished by God for neglecting his people" (A, 2), he was but repeating a patristic commonplace. Where did he get it? Not, one suspects, directly from the Church Fathers, with whom, as we shall presently see, he had little familiarity. Curiously enough, it does not appear in the canonistic corpus that formed his professional training. Indeed, in Gratian's *Decretum* I can find only one passage that enjoins preaching specifically on bishops or prelates, and there it is listed along with reading and prayer simply as an occupation that is more appropriate to the office than are worldly pursuits.[144] There is but one other work that he surely knew wherein it is clearly stated that bishops must preach or perish, namely the *Pontificale Romanum*.

To perform his ritual functions, every medieval bishop had a collection of liturgical texts known as the bishop's book, or *pontificale*. Although there are many compilations of this type, Mozzi almost certainly would have used one that followed the Roman use to which his years at the curia would have accustomed him and which, moreover, was the use of his metropolitan, since Florence was then an immediate subject of the Holy See. Several versions of the *Pontificale Romanum* were current in Andrea's time, but all contained, as an appendix to the service for the consecration of bishops, a form letter that the newly consecrated bishop was to receive in writing from his metropolitan.[145] Since the *Pontificale Romanum* attests that this was the custom of the bishop of Rome, no doubt Andrea himself received a copy at the time of his consecration, and most likely this letter is what impressed upon him the idea that his own salvation as a bishop depended upon frequent preaching.

This form letter, usually entitled *Edictum quod dat pontifex episcopo cui bene-dicit*, was probably written in the ninth or early tenth century, certainly before 964.[146] The writer, presumably an archbishop, has been asked to consecrate a newly elected bishop, and he writes him some general words of advice on how to fulfill the office:

> Know that you have undertaken the heaviest load of work, which is the burden of the direction of souls, and to be subject to the needs of many, and to become the least and servant of all, and to render account on the day of reckoning and judgment for the talent entrusted to you.[147]

After stressing the general responsibilities of a pastor, the writer touches on several specific cases. The bishop must preserve the faith; he must ordain only worthy priests and never charge for his services; his private life must be free from scandal; he must devote himself to preaching, study, and prayer; and moreover he should practice as he preaches. Discipline must be maintained firmly but with mercy, and the goods of his church must be devoted to charity but not wasted. If he does all this with zeal and impartiality, the exhortation concludes, at the last judgment he will enjoy the reward of a good and faithful servant. Preaching, then, is only one of many pastoral duties upon which the bishop's salvation depends: it is treated in this single sentence: "Devote yourself to preaching; to the people committed to you do not cease to preach the word of God fluently, sweetly, and distinctly, insofar as you shall have been steeped in the celestial dew [of eloquence]."[148]

To be sure, this is a pale reflection of the patristic precept, but that, I think, may be precisely the point. Take the sentence in the *Edictum* on preaching and consider it for a moment out of context, as Mozzi might have taken it. Is it not the justification for his pastoral program? He did indeed devote himself to preaching, and with his characteristic obstinacy he persisted despite ridicule. All that the *Edictum* required of him was persistence—not talent or success, for he was only urged to do the best he could.

Whether this particular sentence suggested such a course to him is of no great importance, for he could easily have encountered the Gregorian interpretation of Ezechiel 3:18 elsewhere—perhaps from some theologian or preacher at the curia.

The point is rather that his conduct was obviously an oversimplification that fulfilled the letter rather than the spirit of the precept. Andrea's concern was for his own salvation rather than for his flock, and hence his sermons did not speak to the spiritual needs of his congregation; instead they were scandalous, yet he did not mind. Such an attitude, of course, is legalism of the worst kind: to seize upon a text and interpret it in one's own favor. It is what one might expect of the *pastore-lupo* who devoted himself to the Decretalists rather than to patristics.[149]

The preaching of Andrea de' Mozzi, then, would seem to have been completely in character. The popular image of Mozzi as an inept preacher, which the trecento commentators have handed down to us, accords so well with what we have already learned about the man from strictly contemporary sources that this legend, at least, must contain a kernel of historical fact.

Gregory on the Ideal Bishop

We have already found in the case of Francesco d'Accorso that the poet relied in part upon the popular image of a character to convey his meaning, and we may with some justification expect that the same will be true in Mozzi's case as well. For d'Accorso, such evidence enabled us to secure a first glimpse of his fault, but since in the present inquiry our hypothesis has already been framed, the folk image of our man will serve to clarify and confirm what we already suspect to be his fault.

I take it for granted that Dante was well aware of the bishop's gauche sermons, for a contemporary Florentine could scarcely have remained ignorant of a scandal of such magnitude that it had not been forgotten in the city two generations later. According to our hypothesis, the bishop's place in Hell was primarily determined by his perverse exercise of his office, which, contrary to its exclusively supernatural and spiritual nature, he reduced to temporal and natural terms. It is not clear, however, that this ridiculous preaching was an instance of such malversation. Quite to the contrary, it might seem that, more than many an ecclesiastical administrator, he was concerned, at least *pro forma*, with the spiritual side of his office; and if he failed through ineptitude, still his good intentions should not have merited damnation. Now if we are convinced that Dante knew of Mozzi's preaching, we must suspect that, as in the case of d'Accorso, the poetic image was conceived as an extension and refinement of a preexistent public image. Such, indeed, was the poet's expressed intention, for we are told by Cacciaguida that the poem contains "only souls that are known to fame; because the mind of one who hears will not pause or fix its faith for an example that has its roots unknown or hidden or for other proof that is not manifest."[150] Therefore we must ask why Mozzi's preaching is a patent case of pastoral perversion.

Let us begin with an obvious question. What would Dante's ideal bishop have done? Surely he, too, would have preached to his flock frequently, but how could he have avoided Mozzi's scandalous performance? Folquet, the ideal bishop of the *Comedy*, is ready with a cue: avoid the Decretalists dear to the *pastore-lupo* and instead read the Church Fathers.[151] To whom, then, among *i dottor magni*, should the inexperienced bishop turn for guidance in the performance of his pastoral office?

In all Latin patrology, one treatise has for centuries stood as the classic manual for bishops: the *Regula pastoralis* of Gregory the Great. For example, more than once Alcuin recommended it to his episcopal correspondents as the single guide to their duties:

> Let your tongue never be still from preaching holy words; let your hand never be idle from doing good works: and wherever you go, let the pastoral book of Saint Gregory go with you. Read it often and re-read it, since through it you may become so familiar with yourself and your work that you will never forget how you ought to live or teach. For it is a mirror of the bishop's life and medicine for every wound of diabolic deception.[152]

That Alcuin closely associated the *Regula pastoralis* with preaching suggests that we are on the right track, and a cursory glance at its contents places this beyond doubt: Gregory devotes more than half of his treatise to the art of preaching.[153]

The general character of the treatise is evinced by the opening sentence. Gregory proposes to expound the burdens of pastoral care "in order both that he who is free from them may not unwarily seek them, and that he who has so sought them may tremble for having got them."[154] Since Andrea, we know, was conscious that the responsibilities of his office endangered his salvation, he would have known from the outset that this was the book he needed; and before he had finished the first page he would have been prevented from becoming the laughing stock of Florence:

> But inasmuch as there are many, like me in unskilfulness, who, while they know not how to measure themselves, are covetous of teaching what they have not learned; who estimate lightly the burden of authority in proportion as they are ignorant of the pressure of its greatness; let them be reproved from the very beginning of this book; so that, while, unlearned and precipitate, they desire to hold the citadel of teaching, they may be repelled at the very door of our discourse from the ventures of their precipitancy.[155]

The book is not long—less than sixty pages in Migne's format—and its instruction is pointed and practical. One who is unsympathetic with Gregory's figural method will find the argument tedious, but this would hardly deter either Dante or a proper bishop. The instruction is graded into four phases. (1) The conscientious bishop first learns his responsibilities: he must lead his flock by life and doctrine. Once these goals have been defined, Gregory proceeds to advise the bishop of how to attain them. (2) In the next part the bishop learns how he should live, and then (3) he is instructed in "the proper performance of his teaching office [*magisterium*]." Finally, (4) an epilogue warns the successful bishop against pride in his accomplishments.

What counsel might Andrea have found here? Assured that he needed instruction, he should at least have discovered from Part 1 whether he was fit to hold such an office. Less than six pages would have told him that he lacked the essential qualifications. Gregory left no doubt as to that, for he plainly states what manner of man ought not come to rule (*Reg. past.* 1. 11). This catalogue of character faults that are unacceptable in a bishop takes the form of an exposition of Leviticus 21:17–20, which lists those physical defects that disqualify one of priestly birth from handling holy bread or otherwise ministering to the Lord. Gregory allegorizes each physical blemish into a moral fault that is intolerable in a bishop; in the penultimate one, Mozzi would have recognized his own fundamental sin—avarice.[156] Indeed, in this instance he could not plead ignorance, for Gratian transcribed the whole of this chapter into his *Decretum,* where Mozzi the canonist unquestionably had studied it.[157] This alone should have deterred him from accepting the fatal office, or at least have sent him to profit from the whole of Gregory's book. *De vita pastoris,* the second part of the *Pastoral Care,* would have taught Mozzi how to moderate his behavior, hold his tongue, and conduct himself with Christian charity. But as preaching is our present concern, let us hasten on to the third and longest part, without dwelling on our bishop's every fault.

Already we have seen what importance Gregory attached to preaching in his *Homilies on Ezechiel,*[158] and the same theme dominates the *Regula pastoralis,* more than half of which is devoted to a detailed discussion of "how the bishop of upright life ought to teach and admonish his subjects." His treatment of the subject proceeds on the principle that specific remedies are more effective than general ones. "Therefore according to the quality of the hearers ought the discourse of teachers to be fashioned, so as to suit all and each for their several needs, and yet never deviate from the art of common edification." To illustrate his point, he concludes the prologue with a metaphor that shall prove to be not without significance in our inquiry:

> For what are the intent minds of hearers but, so to speak, a kind of tight tensions of strings in a harp, which the skilful player, that he may produce a tune not at variance with itself, strikes variously? And for this reason the strings render back a consonant modulation, that they are struck indeed with one quill, but not with one kind of stroke. Whence every teacher also, that he may edify all in the one virtue of charity, ought to touch the hearts of his hearers out of one doctrine, but not with one and the same exhortation.[159]

In accordance with this principle, Gregory next enumerates some thirty-six distinctions that the pastor should recognize in his flock, and then systematically explains the special approach that each type requires. The repertory is long and varied: he must discriminate between men and women, rich and poor, young and old, sick and healthy, quarrelsome and peaceful, obstinate and inconstant, and thirty more antinomies. As far as we know, Mozzi observed none of these distinctions in his pastoral work (though we can believe that he was a respecter of persons); in his sermons, as far as we know, he attempted instead to popularize theological abstractions such as grace, providence, and omnipotence. However, we may note that Gregory would afford Andrea some insight into his own obstinacy, and the discussion may be quoted in passing, as it explicates one sense of the word *tigna* that proves to fit the historical Mozzi even more closely than we had perceived:

> The former [the obstinate] are to be told that they think more of themselves than they are, and therefore do not acquiesce in the counsels of others. . . . Those are to be told that, unless they esteemed themselves better than the

rest of men, they would by no means set less value on the counsels of all than on their own deliberation. . . . To the former it is said through Paul, "Be not wise in your own conceits [Rom. 12:16]. . . . For obstinacy is engendered of pride. . . . The obstinate are therefore to be admonished, that they acknowledge the haughtiness of their thoughts, and study to vanquish themselves; lest, while they scorn to be overcome by the right advice of others outside themselves, they be held captive within themselves to pride.[160]

When Gregory has considered the last of these particular pastoral problems, his book is almost at an end; five brief chapters and the epilogue will complete the work. All that remains is to consider those situations that could not be treated as contrasting passions. Had Mozzi persevered to the end, he would have found two chapters that should have remedied the faults of his Florentine sermons. The first concerns the problem of a general audience (*Reg. past.* 3. 36). Mozzi's solution was to discourse on theological generalities, but Gregory will have none of that. For him, a pastoral sermon always aims at the improvement of morals, and when the audience contains a diversity of character faults, the preacher must say something that speaks to each need; but this task is far more difficult than when each is addressed separately, for the presence in the same audience of any pair of opposites requires that the preacher maintain a mean between two extremes:

> For in this case the speech is to be tempered with such art that, the vices of the hearers being diverse, it may be found suitable to them severally, and yet be not diverse from itself; that it pass indeed with one stroke through the midst of [opposed] passions, but, after the manner of a two-edged sword, cut the swellings of carnal thoughts on either side; so that humility be so preached to the proud that yet fear be not increased in the timid; that confidence be so infused into the timid that yet the unbridled licence of the proud grow not. . . .[161]

In sum, for Gregory a general sermon is the rhetorical equivalent of the Aristotelian ethic: the preacher must balance between opposing vices just as he ought to strive for moderation in all things. Here, then, was what Mozzi should have been doing. Despite the difficulties of addressing a mixed audience, the preacher should not deal in generalities that are devoid of moral application; instead he should circumspectly endeavor to reprove the several faults of his congregation.

But Gregory's advice does not end there. He singles out one topic that the preacher should avoid above all others, and of course it is Mozzi's favorite theme. This chapter more than any other reveals that Mozzi's preaching marked him as an irresponsible pastor:

> *Reg. past.* 3. 39. *That deep things ought not to be preached at all to weak minds.*
>
> [1] But the preacher should know how to avoid drawing the mind of his hearer beyond its strength, lest, so to speak, the string of the soul, when stretched more than it can bear, should be broken. For all deep things should be covered up before a multitude of hearers, and scarcely opened to a few.

[100]

[2] For hence the Truth in person says, "Who, thinkest thou, is the faithful and wise steward, whom his lord has appointed over his household, to give them their measure of wheat in due season?" Now by a measure of wheat is expressed a portion of the Word, lest, when anything is given to a narrow heart beyond its capacity, it be spilt.

. . . .

[4] Hence Moses, when he comes out from the sanctuary of God, veils his shining face before the people; because in truth He shows not to multitudes the secrets of inmost brightness.

[5] Hence it is enjoined on him by the Divine voice that, if any one should dig a cistern, and not cover it, and an ox or ass should fall into it, he should pay the price, because when one who has arrived at the deep streams of knowledge covers them not up before the brutish hearts of his hearers, he deserves to be punished if through his words any mind, whether clean or unclean, is scandalized.

[6] . . . he who preaches aright cries aloud plainly to hearts that are still in the dark, and shows them nothing of hidden mysteries, that they may then hear the more subtle teaching concerning heavenly things, when they draw nigh to the light of truth.[162]

Surely the Mozzi whom Florence remembered in Benvenuto's day had notoriously failed to profit from this advice. The bishop's sermons erred by commission no less than omission, for from his pulpit he expounded profound theological concepts that were incomprehensible and useless to his congregation. They needed pastoral, not dogmatic, theology. For lack of spiritual direction, the Florentines continued their perverse course and, if anything, were led into still other errors by the discourses of their perverse pastor. From Gregory he should have learned to conceal the sacred arcana from the mass of mankind, men whose narrow minds and brutish hearts lack the capacity to comprehend such occult mysteries. There is no mistaking the Latin Doctor's advice to the preacher: "intimae arcana non indicat; nil de occultis mysteriis indicat" (§§ 4, 6).

Moreover, Mozzi was warned to disregard this injunction at the peril of his immortal soul. If scandal results from an attempt to popularize theology, the preacher will be held responsible: "poenae reus addicitur" (§ 5). It matters not whether he scandalizes the pure or the impure, for a bishop deserves condemnation if he but cause doctrinal scandal to his flock.[163] Unquestionably the sermons of Andrea de' Mozzi were a scandal to his Florentine flock, and hence, if for no other reason, his damnation was deserved.

"Li mal protesi nervi"

Once again a literatus stands condemned by written authority. Brunetto's *Tresor*, Priscian's *Institutes*, and Francesco's *Arenga*, however, condemned their authors; Mozzi's *opera* were foolish sermons, which the *Regula pastoralis* reveals to be a just cause for his damnation. Admittedly we have come to Gregory by a devious route, and although the clues have been drawn from internal evidence and although the results correspond exactly to the case of Mozzi, one may wonder whether this is a happy coincidence or Dante's actual design. The poet, I think, foresaw this difficulty and provided the reader with a built-in assurance that he was on the right track, which served moreover to direct him onward in his search. I allude to the opening words of *Regula pastoralis* 3. 39, which we must now savor in the original: "Sciendum vero est praedicatori, ut auditoris sui animum ultra vires non trahat, ne, ut ita dicam, dum plus quam valet tenditur, mentis chorda rumpatur."[164] There at the end of Part 3, Gregory returned to the metaphor of the harpist, which he had first introduced into his prologue to the same part:[165]

> Quid enim sunt intentae mentes auditorum, msi ut ita dixerim, quaedam in cithara tensiones stratae chordarum? quas tangendi artifex, ut non sibimetipsi dissimile canticum faciat, dissimiliter pulsat. Et idcirco chordae consonam modulationem reddunt, quia uno quidem plectro, sed non uno impulsu feriuntur.

The harper *topos* has the same basic application in both passages. The preacher is likened to a performing artist *(artifex)*; his audience to the *cithara*, whose strings *(chordae)* represent the several minds upon which he works his art *(animi* or *mentes auditorum)*. The similitude arises, as the prologue suggests, from the double sense of the verb *intendere*, which can signify either the stretching of a harpstring, as in *Aeneid* 9. 776—"Crethea Musarum comitem, cui carmina semper / et citharae cordi numerosque *intendere nervis*"—or directing one's thought or attention to anything, for example, "digna est res ubi tu *nervos intendas* tuos."[166] In *Regula pastoralis* 3. 39, Gregory played on the underlying notion of physical and mental strain: just as harp strings will break if stretched beyond their strength, so the attention of the listener will be lost if the subject is beyond his understanding. We must note here the precise words, for they mark our trail. The preacher must not draw the auditor's intellect beyond its strength: "animum ultra vires non trahat" (§ 1). Otherwise, so to speak, while stretched more than it can bear—"dum plus quam valet tenditur"— the mind's attention may be broken *(mentis chorda rumpatur)*.

To one coming to the passage, as we have, in search of Mozzi's fault, and thus with the words of *Inferno* xv, 110–14, ever in mind, this tension imagery evokes Brunetto's cryptic reference to the *mal protesi nervi* that the bishop left in Vicenza, where he died *(Inf.* xv, 114). Whatever the phrase "the badly stretched-out nerves" may mean, surely the same general notion of tension that we find in Gregory's metaphor underlies this phrase as well. The equivalence is even more specific, for *protesi* derives from the Latin *protendere*, which in its basic meanings is hardly distinguishable from *intendere*. Moreover, Latin *nervus* is, as in the Virgilian example quoted earlier, a synonym for *chorda*. What is more, used figuratively in the plural, as by Brunetto in the poem, it can also signify *vires*, powers of body, mind, or expression.[167] At the verbal level, then, a remarkable correspondence exists between the two passages. Let us note yet another, which I think will be decisive.

Some twenty-five years ago, André Pézard subjected the phrase *li mal protesi nervi* to a searching analysis in terms of both historical semantics and topical imagery.[168] By a complex argument that is better read than reported, he arrived at the conclusion that *protesi nervi* refers to a drawn bowstring *(protensus nervus arcus)*, a common classical and patristic metaphor for mental intention, but in the sense of purpose rather than attention. The argument is gravely weakened, if not vitiated altogether, by a fundamental flaw: in Latin and Italian, as in French and English, a bow has but a single string. Yet, since the words *protesi nervi* are plural, they must correspond to a tension metaphor involving many strings rather than just one. Hence the image of the many-stringed cithara suits Brunetto's words better than the archery image.[169] Added to the resemblances we have already noted, this final congruence urges us to understand Brunetto's dark trope in the light of the Gregorian metaphor. Taken in this sense, *lasciò li mal protesi nervi* would mean that Mozzi had overtaxed his powers or, to paraphrase Gregory, had drawn his mind beyond its strength.

A difficulty immediately appears in this interpretation, for a transitive relation has become reflexive: the mind of the auditor has become the mind of the preacher. How can we justify this transfer? We may begin by noting that Gregory himself does as much when it suits his purpose. In *Regula pastoralis* 3. 2 he remarks that a gentle admonition may sometimes be appropriate for a proud and rich man, just as sores are soothed by gentle lotion and as a madman is calmed by the physician's soothing speech. The principle is confirmed by the figure of Saul, whom David tranquillized by playing on his harp, "since, when the senses of men in power are turned to frenzy by elation, it is meet they should be recalled to a healthy state of mind by the calmness of our speech, as by the sweetness of a harp."[170] Here the cithara is likened to the pastoral allocution itself. But no number of instances from other writers will prove that Dante himself had in mind the sense we desire. Let us turn then to his own works for help.[171]

Although the harpist appears not infrequently in the Dantesque corpus, the figure of the stretched harp cord is found only once, in *De vulgari eloquentia* 2. 4. 9, an exhortation to the poet who proposes to undertake the highest and most difficult form: "Having first drunk of Helicon, let him, after stretching the strings to the utmost [*tensis fidibus ad supremum*] take the plectrum and then begin to ply it."[172] The context makes the meaning of the figure plain: let the poet summon up his highest powers. But to be sure of this interpretation, let us view the passage in the context of the whole chapter.

De vulgari eloquentia 2. 4 introduces Dante's treatment of the canzone, which he has already established as the highest form of vernacular poetry. Since the form has not been explained by poets before, our instructor proposes to take us into his workshop (§ 1), where he shall teach us to regulate by art the language of poetry, which he significantly defines as "an invention expressed in verse according to the arts of rhetoric and music" (§§ 2–3):[173]

> 4. Before all things therefore we say that each one ought to adjust the weight of the subject to his own shoulders, so that their strength may not be too heavily taxed, and he be forced to tumble into the mud. This is the advice our master Horace gives us when he says in the beginning of his

Art of Poetry, "Take up a subject [equal to your powers, o you who write (verses 38–39)]."[174]

After this admonition, Dante considers which style is most appropriate to the form, and he settles on the tragic (§§ 5–8). Having defined the scope of his inquiry, Dante pauses to insist that no one undertake the most difficult poetic form without adequate preparation (§§ 9–11). It is in this second admonition that the figure of the harpist occurs:

> 9. Let every one therefore beware and discern what we say; and when he purposes to sing either of these three subjects [proper to the canzone, namely *salus, amor,* and *virtus*] exclusively, or of those things which directly and properly follow after them, let him first drink of Helicon, and then, after adjusting the strings, boldly take up his plectrum and begin to ply it.
> 10. But it is in the exercise of needful caution and discernment that the real difficulty lies; for this can never be attained without vigorous intellect [*strenuitas ingenii*] and constant practice in the art, and the habit of the sciences. And it is those [so equipped] whom the poet in the sixth book of the *Aeneid* [verses 126–31] describes as beloved of God, raised by glowing virtue to the sky, and sons of the gods, though he is speaking figuratively.
> 11. And therefore let those who, innocent of art and science, and trusting to genius alone, rush forward to sing of the highest subjects in the highest style, confess their folly and cease from such presumption; and if in their natural sluggishness they are but geese, let them abstain from imitating the eagle soaring to the stars.[175]

The earlier warning (§ 4) was directed to those who lack the natural endowments necessary for the highest poetic achievement. They are again reproved in the second admonition, for the poet should first have drunk the inspiring waters of Helicon; he cannot attain his goal without *strenuitas ingenii*: lacking this, he is a goose by nature. Other geese are not ungifted but only lazy. They have not studied the art of rhetoric assiduously and are not habituated to the sciences. Though gifted, they have not worked to capacity, or to revert to the metaphor, they have failed to stretch their strings to the utmost. The strings, then, are here equivalent to *vires*, which we already know to be another sense of *nervi*. The strings of the lazy are slack, whereas by implication (one recalls in this connection *Reg. past.* 3. 39) those of the ungifted are unequal to the strain required. Either type is immune to both art and science; each trusts solely in his own *ingenium*, which for one reason or the other is insufficient.

Several significant details support this reading and link it more closely to Gregory and Mozzi. The verb *intendere* introduces the figure of the harpist, whom the poet resembles "when he intends to sing" ("quando . . . cantare intendit"), so both types of poetic inadequacy—one by excess and the other by defect—are cases of misplaced intention, or in other words, both can be described in terms of *nervi-vires*, as we have done. Another notable echo may be discerned as Dante ascribes their ill-considered efforts to foolishness—*stultitia*—a term, as we know, that aptly describes Andrea's preaching.[176] Finally, we may observe that the passage alleged from the *Aeneid* (easily identified by the echo a few lines earlier) turns out to be the famous lines:

> ... facilis descensus Averno:
> noctes atque dies patet atri ianua Ditis;
> sed revocare gradum superasque evadere ad auras,
> hoc opus, hic labor est. pauci, quos aequus amavit
> Iuppiter aut ardens evexit ad aethera virtus,
> dis geniti, potuere.[177]

Dante tells us to take it figuratively: accordingly, the sense would be that, while it is easy to write bad poetry, only those who are gifted can attain the heaven of high poetry, and even then they must work at it.

The others are damned. Is it only coincidence that Mozzi shares their fate? They aspired to the highest form of profane rhetoric; he, to the highest form of sacred rhetoric. But why is the offense against secular letters only damned figuratively, while that against divine letters is, in Mozzi, literally damned? In Pézard's interpretation, the answer would be that the difference was blasphemy *in ore*: he is supposed to be essentially nothing more than a jesting Capaneus.[178] But if such were the case, we should have expected that Mozzi's offense would be touched on in Beatrice's denunciation of false preachers in *Paradiso* xxix, 88–93. She has just denounced philosophers who, because they would rather appear to be wise than actually be so, sustain theses in which they do not believe:

> E ancor questo qua sù si comporta
>   con men disdegno che quando è posposta
>   la divina Scrittura o quando è torta.
> Non vi si pensa quanto sangue costa
>   seminarla nel mondo e quanto piace
>   chi umilmente con essa s'accosta.

> and even this is borne with less anger up here than when the divine Scripture is neglected or perverted. There is no thought among you what blood it cost to sow the world with it or how acceptable he is who approaches it with humbleness.[179]

(*Par.* xxix, 88–93)

Evidently a perversion of the revealed truth of *la divina Scrittura* is less to be condoned than the distortion of philosophic truth. She then proceeds to denounce false preachers:

> Per apparer ciascun s'ingegna e face
>   sue invenzioni; e quelle son trascorse
>   da' predicanti e 'l Vangelio si tace.

> Each tries for display, making his own inventions, and these are discoursed on by the preachers and the Gospel is silent.[180]

(*Par.* xxix, 94–96)

Her first examples are of preachers who feed their flocks on wind, that is, who teach fables as doctrine (*Par.* xxix, 97–114); she further complains against those who "go to preach with jests and gibes, and if only there is a good laugh the cowl inflates and they ask no more" (*Par.* xxix, 115–17). Mozzi committed neither offense. The doctrine he presented was not unsound; nor, in view of his stated intention to preach for his own soul's sake, can he be assimilated to the second type. He did not set out to play the fool, so the laughter he provoked was neither anticipated nor desired. He did not, in short, preach *per apparer*, and therefore cannot be subsumed under Beatrice's complaint. What *was* reprehensible in Mozzi's sermons was not bad theology but bad rhetoric. Had he been able to convey divine truths to simple minds in a seemly manner that did not scandalize but in fact edified his audience, he would then have been a successful preacher.

The point may be underscored by a brief reference to the *Convivio*. There Dante, too, undertook to popularize difficult doctrine. Unlike Mozzi, however, he took care to restrict his audience to those who could digest his banquet (*Conv.* 1. 1. 12). But the teacher also must be qualified, and he concluded the first chapter by begging that "if the banquet be not so splendid as beseems its profession, they [who are invited to this supper] will impute every fault not to my will but to my want of power, because my will here aims at perfect and precious liberality."[181] That Dante did undertake to expound philosophy in the vernacular (and in the *Commedia* undertook to do the same for theology), represents his considered judgment that it lay within his powers to do so; for we can safely assume that in his own undertakings he observed the advice of *De vulgari eloquentia* 2. 4 by not attempting what seemed beyond him. By contrast, Mozzi undertook a task that surpassed his natural powers, and when it was evident that he had overreached himself, he still persisted obstinately. This I take to be the true meaning of *li mal protesi nervi*.

Brunetto's Scorn

The significance of the phrase can be made still more precise by considering *li mal protesi nervi* in context. The words are put in the mouth of Brunetto Latini, and accordingly we would expect them to be in character. Since Brunetto was a teacher of rhetoric, we may further suspect that he viewed Mozzi's ineptitude in the pulpit from his own professional perspective. This suspicion grows when we further observe that he takes it for granted that the pilgrim, whom Latini regards as a disciple, shares his scorn for the unmentionable bishop: "and if you had had any hankering for such a pig-headed fool, you would have been able to see him" ("e vedervi, / s'avessi avuto di tal tigna brama, / colui"; *Inf.* xv, 110–12). Since we have already seen that *li mal protesi nervi* are linked by the *fides-vires-nervi* complex to Dante's teaching that the rhetorician should perfect his natural powers but not exceed them, we may once again accept the recommendation Brunetto made in parting (*Inf.* xv, 119) and turn to his *Tresor* to confirm and complete our interpretation.[182]

First let us see how his introduction to rhetoric compares with the counsels of *De vulgari eloquentia* 2. 4. The third book of the *Tresor* is entirely devoted to rhetoric, and the first chapter explains the value and limitation of rhetorical instruction:

> 10. Now it is proven that the knowledge of rhetoric is not at all acquired by nature or by use, but by instruction and by art, wherefore I say that each ought to study his genius [engien] to know it.
>
> 11. [Cicero says that the power of speech is natural in man.]
>
> 12. Nonetheless the proverb says that "Nurture surpasses nature"; for according to what we have found in the first and second parts of this book, the soul of all men is naturally good, but its nature is changed by the badness of the body that encloses it, just as wine that is spoiled by the foulness of the vessel. And when the body is of good nature, its goodness lends aid and comfort to the soul, and then art and experience [us] are worth having. For art teaches the soul the rules appropriate to it, and experience makes it ready and keen for the work.
>
> 13. And for this reason the teacher wishes to recall to his friend the rules and teaching of the art of rhetoric, which shall greatly aid him to [exercise] the subtlety that is in him through his good nature.[183]

Like Dante, Brunetto insists that rhetoricians are made, not born. Natural endowments and experience in using them are both necessary prerequisites, but the science of rhetoric is an art that is acquired by instruction. It is not enough simply to have the natural power of speech, for not all persons are equally apt for instruction. Latini attributes differences in natural aptitude to the nature of the body rather than to the nature of the soul. By nature the soul is good; but its good nature can be corrupted if the body, whose nature is variable, is bad rather than good.[184] Only when both soul and body are good can the person profit from instruction in an art and from experience; presumably those who cannot are hopelessly corrupt.

Was Brunetto the character justified in assuming that the pilgrim would share his view of Mozzi the preacher? That they at least agreed on which factors determine success in rhetoric can be seen from Dante's list of the qualities that are essential for high achievement in one branch of rhetoric: "nunquam sine strenuitate ingenii et artis assiduitate scientiarumque habitu fieri potest" (De vulg. eloq. 2. 4. 10). If we accept Brunetto's word us as the equivalent of Dante's Thomistic habitus,[185] we find that they both conceive the problem in terms of genius, art, and experience. This is not to say that they agreed at every point, for obviously the poet's phrase habitus scientiarum bears only a family resemblance to the practical experience implied by the word usus. However much the two theories may differ in matters of detail, both do agree that nature must be perfected by art and by some form of experience. Furthermore, Dante and Brunetto would concur in asserting that some men are, by their peculiar natures, imperfectible. They might disagree on the natural origin of Mozzi's deficiencies, but still they would be in substantial agreement that as a rhetorician he was not qualified either by talent or by training.

We have already heard Dante caution the aspiring poet not to exceed his powers (De vulg. eloq. 2. 4. 4). In the Tresor, Brunetto explains in still greater detail how to use one's abilities with discretion. The following *sententiae*, which are culled from Cicero's *De officiis*, occur in his discussion of moderation:

> Tully says, Each ought to direct his efforts to things to which he is suited; and, even though some other thing may be better or more honorable, he always should govern his studies according to this rule.
>
> Example: If his body is weak and he has a good intellect [*engien*] and quick memory, he should not pursue chivalry but the study of letters and of science [*clergie*]. For we ought neither to go against nature nor pursue that which cannot be attained.
>
> But if we are forced by necessity to attempt things not proper to our genius [*engin*], we ought to take care to do them well and without fault, or at least without dishonor, [since] we ought to try not so much to achieve those goods which we are not given as to avoid faults.[186]

Now there can be little doubt about why Brunetto Latini in the *Comedy* despised Mozzi as a pig-headed fool for his performance in the pulpit: the bishop violated every counsel of discretion in his immoderate use of his limited natural powers. First, Andrea attempted what for him was, as the phrase *mal protesi nervi* implies, against nature. Instead of trying to avoid faults, Mozzi strove to achieve what for him could have been at best a qualified, wasteful, and unnecessary success. Still worse, he did not even attempt to make the best of what little talent he had, but blundered ahead without either experience or instruction in the art of rhetoric. Finally, he obstinately persisted in making a fool of himself even after it was apparent that his efforts were ridiculous.

We have accounted, then, for Brunetto's scorn. He condemned Andrea de' Mozzi qua rhetorician, and with good reason assumed that the pilgrim would agree with this judgment. But we must be careful not to impute this judgment to the poet without qualification, for in our first chapter we discovered that in Hell, Brunetto is still imbued with the perverted values by which he lived. He was, as Villani remarked, a worldly man, and Dante depicts him as such in the poem.[187] Thus it would be in character for him to see Mozzi exclusively in humanistic, this-worldly terms. The bishop's lack of *virtù* had made him infamous in Florence, and when we recall Brunetto's preoccupation with earthly *fama*, it is entirely characteristic that he refuses to utter the name of Andrea de' Mozzi. Instead, he describes the man by an elaborate periphrasis that draws appropriately upon the two arts in which Latini excelled. As he was a rhetorician, he employed metonymy in speaking of Mozzi's bishoprics; as he was a notary, he designated the pope by alluding to the superscription formula of the papal chancery—*servus servorum Dei*. Also it is suggestive of his worldly outlook that he does not complete the formula but omits the name of God, saying only *servo de' servi*, as if the hierarchy were nothing more than an administrative machine that exists for its own sake. Such a man would not appreciate the cause we have assigned to Mozzi's damnation, any more than he could perceive the reason for his own presence in Hell.

Are we then to trust his perception and suppose that Mozzi was placed among the violent against nature because he did not respect the limits that nature had placed upon his rhetorical powers? No. Just as Brunetto's worldly virtues received their due reward through fame in this life, so the worldly aspects of Mozzi's offense were similarly punished by infamy. For in the *Tresor*, Brunetto, in his own variation on the Ciceronian theme, represents the man of moderation as one who seeks to discharge his office with as little dishonor as possible *(a poi de deshonour)*, by which he means one should avoid vices (2. 73. 5). In the poem, Brunetto projects his own system of values on Mozzi as well as on Dante, with equal irrelevance, for we know that Mozzi, unlike the false preachers whom Beatrice condemned, did not take to the pulpit for applause but for his own eternal salvation.

The infamy Andrea earned as a rhetorician survives him on earth; it was his just punishment for that aspect of his offense. We must accordingly look to some other reason for his damnation in Hell. The answer we know already: he earned eternal punishment for his soul qua bishop. Gregory assured us that the preacher who scandalized his congregation deserved as much, but we know that this was but one facet of Mozzi's perverted pastorate. Thus, after a long excursion, we return to our original hypothesis. The evidence we have collected en route now lends it color. Above all, the trail that Dante laid to and from the *Regula pastoralis* (especially 3. 39) convinces me that Mozzi must be interpreted primarily as the perverted pastor of Florence. In him are condemned all bishops who perversely annexed their supernatural office to the natural sphere—an inversion of their proper function, which the poet expressed through the apposite image of the shepherd turned wolf.[188]

[5]

"Dal servo de' servi fu trasmutato"

The few words that the poet expended on Andrea de' Mozzi all concern his transfer from Florence to Vicenza, yet we have been able to determine his fatal vice completely without reference to that event in his life. And indeed the transfer appears to be quite incidental to his damnation, since he would have been damned as surely had he died before the transfer. Why, then, did the poet lay such emphasis on an event that was apparently irrelevant to his theme? To be sure, the transfer—as an event both unique and notorious—provided an unmistakable clue to the bishop's identity. But was it something more? We have repeatedly found that Dante relates even the slightest details to his larger message, and consequently we may reasonably expect that the transfer had for him a significance that was commensurate with its relative prominence in the poem.

WHY WAS MOZZI TRANSFERRED?

The obvious answer is that the act was the *result* of the bishop's besetting sin. The trecento commentators drew this inference, though not with equal assurance, since only the earliest commentators attributed the transfer to this unique cause. Boccaccio was less certain, for he attributed the transfer to two causes: "both for this defect [sodomy], which sin—perhaps—made him a public scandal, and also for his other foolish deeds."[1] Benvenuto went still further: originally he assigned but a single cause to the act, namely the intervention of Andrea's brother, but in his next recension, the brother was motivated by two distinct sources of scandal, one the bishop's ineptitude and the other his infamous vice.[2] Finally, Fanfani's Anonymous subordinated one to the other, alleging that sodomy was the primary fault, while Andrea's lack of good sense was a by-product of that vice.[3]

Since the charges of sodomy have proved to be ill founded for Mozzi as well as for his companions, it follows that the commentators simply imputed to him whatever violence against nature the name Sodom suggested to them. These assertions, accordingly, have no independent value and may be disregarded as historical evidence. We are left with the memories of Mozzi's foolish behavior, which Boccaccio,

Benvenuto, and Fanfani's Anonymous agree was the cause of his transfer. Since we have found good reason to accept Mozzi's preaching as a historical fact, must we also accord equal credibility to the tradition of family influence that is associated with the tales of Mozzi's *sciocchezze* from Boccaccio on?

I would think not, because in the first generation of commentators, Selmi's Anonymous reports that Mozzi's relatives procured his transfer "to remove from their presence the disgrace of his sodomy by not having to see him every day."[4] The tradition of family influence thus is seen to be earlier than, and independent of, the silly behavior to which Boccaccio makes the first allusion. Since no two commentators quite agree on what the family's motives were, I think it safe to conclude that these were not public knowledge, and accordingly the most we can affirm with assurance is that less than a decade after Dante's death there was a Florentine tradition to the effect that the Mozzi family had been embarrassed by Andrea's presence and consequently had influenced the pope to transfer him to Vicenza.

The tradition may be authentic and nonetheless be mistaken, for common rumor feeds on conjecture and malicious invention. As far as I know, there is not a scrap of evidence that can either confirm or deny this rumor. At best we can judge, much as the Florentines did, whether it accords with what is known of the circumstances. Enough has been said of the relations of the Mozzi bank with the curia to make the view entirely plausible. Two objections can be raised to the contrary and then laid to rest.

(1) Davidsohn asserts that in 1294 there was a discernible split between the Mozzi and their banking partners, the Spini, and moreover that the latter were favored by Boniface VIII, because they alone had handled his financial affairs when he was a cardinal. The evidence, however, consists solely of a petition to the commune of Perugia, dated 5 March 1294, made jointly by "Domini Medicus" and "Gerardus, mercatores Domini pape et Domini Benedicti cardinalis de sotietate Spine."[5] I am not so sure that the evidence will bear this interpretation, for certainly the representatives of the Mozzi-Spini partnership were known sometimes under one name and sometimes under another.[6] At all events, both Mozzi and Spini appear to have been held in the highest favor by Boniface after his accession, for on 14 July 1295 they and the Chiarenti of Pistoia were named exclusive bankers to the papacy.[7]

(2) This fact, I think, is also fatal to the other, more formidable, objection raised by Palandri's thesis. He argued that since we cannot be sure that the family's role in the transfer is anything more than a legend, the contrary might be true: that Mozzi's transfer was in fact a reprisal against the Mozzi clan for the part played by Vanni de' Mozzi in the magnates' demonstration on 5 July 1295 against the Ordinances of Justice.[8] The chronological difficulty is at once apparent: the pope's immediate reaction would seem to have been to bind the Mozzi house still closer to the curia by the privilege dated at Anagni on 14 July 1295. Moreover, he was deeply in their debt and literally could not afford to offend them; more likely the transfer of Andrea the following September is to be coupled with the privilege of

July as a mark of their influence at the curia. This does not exclude the possibility, of course, that Boniface gradually disengaged himself from his alliance with the Mozzi; but it asserts that no breach was visible in 1295.

These objections notwithstanding, then, the Mozzi interests appear to have been influential with Boniface during the first year of his pontificate. This being the case, one would expect that Boniface would at least have consulted the family before humiliating Andrea. Thus far we can agree with the Florentine tradition of the commentators, but it does not necessarily follow that the Mozzi family took the initiative. We can only guess how and why Boniface reached his decision to transfer Andrea from Florence to Vicenza. As an informed guess, Sanesi's estimate of the situation seems to come closest to the mark. He stressed the various complaints against Andrea that had been made to the curia during the pontificates of Nicholas IV and Celestine V. If one adds to this the fact that Boniface, when a cardinal, had not been favorably inclined to Andrea,[9] then it does indeed seem significant that the transfer was effected less than eight months after Boniface became pope. I would agree with Sanesi, then, that Boniface himself probably provided the initiative[10] and that the decision was based on the cumulative evidence of Andrea's incompetence.

Sanesi's reconstruction, however, took no account of the alleged influence of the Mozzi family. As I have said, it seems more than likely that they would have been consulted, and I would suggest that they exercised their influenced at the curia in favor of moderation. The dossier assembled by Sanesi proves that Andrea was an incompetent bishop, and as such he did not deserve another see, however inconsequential, but instead deserved deposition.[11] Why did he receive a penalty less severe than he deserved? Since Boniface himself had little regard for Andrea, we may suspect that he was not personally inclined to treat the bishop with mercy rather than justice. Moreover, as Sanesi's documentation also suggests that Andrea had little personal influence at the curia,[12] we are encouraged to look elsewhere for an effective influence on Boniface's decision. Who but another Mozzi would have been disgraced by the well-deserved deposition? And what other interested party would have had enough prestige with Boniface to avert the sword of justice?

TRANSLATION AS SIMONY

This reconstruction represents the traditional approach to the problem. We have adopted and extended Sanesi's conclusions by reconciling them to the tradition preserved in the commentators. The net result simply is that the rumor of family influence now appears plausible. For those who were already disposed to accept the testimony of the early commentators, this historical excursus will have been unnecessary, for we shall now return to the assertion of Selmi's Anonymous and proceed from there.

We have, then, a popular tradition that Mozzi's relatives procured his transfer because his presence was a disgrace to the family. Although I think it historically more probable that the initiative came from Boniface, still for the interpretation of the poem I take this to be a moot question. All that I shall insist on is that the charge of sodomy did not form part of the popular tradition, which, as we have seen from the Ashburnham recension of Benvenuto, did in fact explain the family's embarrassment quite otherwise.[13]

To begin from this point, let us observe that there is no reason to believe that the *Divine Comedy* was written for political insiders. Even if Dante knew something more than we have been able to discover about the translation of Mozzi, he could not assume that his contemporary reader knew as much. Therefore I think it safe to assume that the poet expected his readers to grasp the significance of Mozzi's translation from such facts of the case as were common knowledge. More than likely he knew the popular interpretation that attributed the transfer to the influence which the Mozzi family enjoyed with the *servo de' servi*. Since public opinion has led us to Dante's meaning in the past, perhaps it contains the significance of Mozzi's translation as well. Let us consider, then, the implications of the rumor when taken in conjunction with our earlier conclusions on the nature of Mozzi's sin.

Dante, we concluded, thought Mozzi was an unworthy bishop. How, then, would he regard the transfer? It was, in itself, an improper act, for Boniface conferred the bishopric of Vicenza upon a man whom he knew to be unworthy of episcopal office. That much should have been plain to anyone who was familiar with Mozzi's Florentine pastorate. Add to this the assertion of Selmi's Anonymous— "E questo proccacciaro i Mozzi suoi consorti. . ."—and it appears that Boniface's decision was prompted by his Florentine bankers. It was no secret that the bond between them was none other than the almighty florin. It is irrelevant whether the Mozzi actually bribed Boniface or whether he simply wished to oblige the bankers who were at once his principal fiscal agents and his largest creditors. Either way, money was the decisive consideration that secured for Andrea his new, if unwanted, bishopric.

In effect, then, Mozzi's transfer involved the sale of an ecclesiastical office. The name for such transactions is simony, and for just this offense Dante anticipated the damnation of Boniface VIII among the simoniacs of *Inferno* xix. Thus it would appear that the translation of Mozzi is a concrete example of the sin for which Boniface himself was to be condemned. This in itself is a noteworthy discovery, for although Boniface is accused of two other crimes in the poem, neither offers a clear instance of the simony that damned him. Guido da Montefeltro tells how Boniface abused the power of the keys by absolving a sin that was committed for his benefit;[14] and in Paradise, Peter reveals what the poet has long hinted, that Boniface had usurped the papacy.[15]

Popes as Translators

Having hit upon one instance of the sin for which Boniface was to be damned, we may well wonder whether it was an isolated lapse or, as seems more likely, whether it was typical of his administration. Was he unique in this, or did he conform to the practice of his predecessors and successors? To answer this question we need a detailed study of episcopal translations from Innocent III to the Great Schism, but if such exists, I have not been able to discover it. For our purposes, however, the deficiency can easily be suppiled by counting the translations listed in Eubel's *Hierarchia catholica*. To place the practice of Boniface VIII in a sufficiently broad context, I have tabulated the papal translations of bishops for the entire period from 1198 to 1378. Further, because Florence was a see immediately subject to the papacy—that is, with no intervening ecclesiastical superior, such as an archbishop—I have distinguished between translations from such sees and those from

PAPAL TRANSLATIONS OF BISHOPS, 1198–1378

PONTIFICATE		BISHOPS TRANSFERRED		
Years	Pope	Immediate Subjects	Mediate Subjects	Total
1198–1216	Innocent III	3	27	30
1216–27	Honorius III	2	15	17
1227–41	Gregory IX	3	23	26
1241	Celestine IV	0	0	0
1243–54	Innocent IV	6	30	36
1254–61	Alexander IV	2	13	15
1261–64	Urban IV	2	10	12
1265–68	Clement IV	3	14	17
1271–76	Gregory X	0	7	7
1276	Innocent V	0	0	0
1276	Hadrian V	0	0	0
1276–77	John XXI	1	1	2
1277–80	Nicholas III	4	8	12
1281–85	Martin IV	0	3	3
1285–87	Honorius IV	7	7	14
1288–92	Nicholas IV	5	10	15
1294	Celestine V	0	0	0
1294–1303	BONIFACE VIII	25	47	72
1303–4	Benedict XI	0	9	9
1305–14	Clement V	3	52	55
1316–34	John XXII	21	184	205
1334–42	Benedict XII	1	33	34
1342–52	Clement VI	8	180	188
1352 62	Innocent VI	10	133	143
1362–70	Urban V	8	111	119
1370–78	Gregory XI	11	122	133

NOTE: Based on translation (or retranslation) as the cause of a vacant see, as indicated in C. Eubel, *Hierarchia catholica medii aevi*, vol. 1. Promotions to the cardinalate are excluded. The simultaneous transfer of a pluralist from his several bishoprics has in principle been counted as a single transaction. The sees that were immediately subject to the papacy are usually so designated by Eubel at the head of each diocesan entry; in his Appendix 1 (pp. 540–45), they are either listed as "in Italia media" or marked by an asterisk.

mediate subjects. The results of this statistical survey, summarized in the accompanying table, show that Boniface did indeed play a pivotal role in the development of episcopal translation.

These figures throw into relief Boniface's use of episcopal translation.[16] In terms of total translations, Boniface made twice as many as any other pope that his contemporaries could remember. His predilection for transferring bishops would already have been apparent at the ideal date of the poem, and by the actual year of composition the poet could have further perceived that Boniface had established a precedent for Clement V.[17] Episcopal translation in itself, then, had a topical interest for a critic of church government, and as every departure from customary usage is by one definition an abuse,[18] we may suspect that Dante was not only aware of the trend but also viewed it with disapproval. In short, we must consider the possibility that Dante, critical as he was of both popes, was moved by their lavish use of the transfer power to consider whether they acted rightly in this. In other words, since Mozzi's translation was neither an isolated case nor a routine affair but rather marked the beginning of a new and unmistakable trend, the event in the poem is apt to typify all such acts.

In effect we have established by historical research an association that the mention of Mozzi's transfer might have evoked from a contemporary of the event less than twenty years later. If he had paid any attention to the pattern of higher appointments during 1295, the first year of Boniface VIII, the new trend toward frequent transfer would have become apparent to him at just the time when Mozzi's translation was announced.[19] Florentines, who both lost and gained a bishop by transfer that year, would have been especially conscious of the new tendency. Moreover, had such a reader lived to read the *Inferno*, he would still have associated Boniface with episcopal translation, for he, more than any other pope in the entire period surveyed, had translated bishops from those sees of central Italy that were immediately subject to the Holy See. His policy in this respect must have been conspicuous to those Italians who were affected, all the more so because his immediate successors did not imitate him in this.

In short, what we have laboriously attained would have suggested itself to a contemporary who, finding translation to be only accidently related to Mozzi's sin, considered whether it might instead relate to the general theme of the canto. Could a bishop's transfer be yet another instance of some violation of the divinely established order?

The reader, modern or medieval, who has inferred this question from the context, will find after further reflection that the text itself urges him to pursue this train of thought and that it even points the way. At first the thesis appears doubtful, because Boniface will be condemned among the simoniacal popes for his part in the affair, and perhaps Clement also committed simony in his translations.[20] But canto xv cloaks the translator in the anonymity of his official title: "dal servo de' servi fu trasmutato." Inevitably, one is reminded of the medieval distinction between the office and the man. Since elsewhere the poet left the reader an elaborate reminder that Boniface is not to be confused with his office but should be judged separately,[21] we have good reason to think that he drew the same distinction in his own judgment of Boniface as a simoniac. It would seem, therefore, that we are urged to consider the translation in canto xv in relation to popes in general, not to Boniface in particular. In other words, the context of canto xv implies that episcopal translation by any pope whatsoever is a usurpation of authority. Thus the stress on the papal office serves to confirm our earlier suspicion that Dante here is suggesting that translation *in se* is offensive.

DANTE'S CRITIQUE OF THE DECRETALISTS

If translation is the offense, who then is the offender? If we adhere to the letter, we must say it is the *servo de' servi*, which signifies an office rather than a man. But implicit in the distinction between man and office is the doctrine that the office is incapable of moral acts, as exemplified in the English legal maxim "The king can do no wrong" or in the Roman-law concept of the prince as *legibus solutus*. Although these civil applications of the doctrine are better known, there can be no doubt that it applies to ecclesiastical office as well, for in origin it was an ecclesiological concept that was first applied to bishops and reached its fullest development in the theories of papal sovereignty that were evolved by Dante's contemporaries.[22]

If the incumbent of an office exercises powers that do not pertain to that office and if he does so in good faith, he cannot be blamed as an individual. The blame rests rather on the theorists whose arguments permit the officer to act in good faith. We have already met such irresponsible intellectuals in Brunetto and his fellow literati, each of whom did violence to nature by exceeding the natural limits of the discipline he professed. Their ecclesiastical counterpart should be the culprit who is appropriate to this place in Hell.

If Boniface had been asked to justify his right to translate a bishop, to what profession would he have turned for help? His own, of course, the discipline of canon law. And so, for that matter, would his predecessors for the past four generations, but not more, since canonistics as a profession only came into existence in the second half of the twelfth century, when canon law became an academic discipline at Bologna. The canons themselves had been in existence for centuries, and individuals had collected and studied them; but the Christian *auctoritates* were neither studied nor taught as a system of jurisprudence until the appearance of Gratian's *Decretum* in the early 1140s. This was "a comprehensive canonical collection and a didactic text book in one,"[23] on which the professional education of canonists at Bologna was founded. In 1159 one of the first masters of the new science became Pope Alexander III, and from then on, the Church was administered chiefly by men who had made canon law their career. At least half the popes of the thirteenth century were themselves trained as canonists, including the three most famous—Innocent III, Innocent IV, and Boniface himself.[24] During the century and a half following Gratian's *Decretum*, the infant science of canon law was perfected by the new professionals, a process that was all but completed by 1300. The papacy itself played an active part in the process by clarifying obscure points and turning classroom theories into official doctrine. This was accomplished almost wholly through judicial decrees,[25] which immediately became part of the law of the Church and eventually were collected into official compilations of *decretales* that supplement Gratian and joined his work in the standard curriculum. Since these decretals represented the latest refinements in the common law of the Church, Gratian was relegated in the schools to the position of an introductory course and a basic repertory of older sources; whereas the new theories were more conveniently explained while expounding the various decretal collections. Under the influence of the existing model of Roman law, the new jurisprudence tended increasingly to equate the position of the pope in the Church to that of the emperor in the empire, thus exalting the pope to the position of an absolute monarch. For all practical purposes, in Dante's day the powers of the papacy were those that had been defined and justified by this now-perfected body of jurisprudence.

Dante was outspoken against the new science. We have already heard him reprove the clergy for studying Hostiensis, Innocent, and Durandus rather than the Church Fathers (see above, p. 84), and by the example of Mozzi we have discovered that such studies could produce perverted pastors. The reasons for Dante's hostility are a matter of record, and as one might expect, they derive from the fundamental principles of his religio-political thought which we found in *Monarchia* 3. 15. Had he accepted the authority of the canonists, these conclusions would have been untenable, as well he knew, for he took care to disarm them before undertaking his own definition of papal power. Although the *Monarchia* is concerned with papal power only in relation to the empire, his critique of the canonists has no such limitation, since it establishes general criteria for evaluating and interpreting the sources of canon law. From it we can accordingly learn the standards by which Dante would judge the pretended right of the papacy to transfer bishops. The chapter has still further claims on our attention, however, as almost every sentence casts new light on canto xv; therefore, I shall expound it in full.

Monarchia 3. 3 begins by explaining why men do not understand the just relationship between pope and emperor: their involvement in the issues has blinded them to reason, or as Dante puts it, "here it is the quarrels that cause the ignorance." He then pauses to anatomize intellectual prejudice in more general terms that may surprise us:

> It is always the case with men whose will runs ahead of their rational insight that their affections become perverted through their having put the light of reason behind them, and they are then drawn along by these affections like blind men who obstinately deny their blindness. Thus very often not only is the kingdom of their own souls invaded by error but they in turn transgress the bounds of their own territories and come rioting within other people's settlements. Here, since they understand nothing, nothing they say

is understood; consequently they provoke some people to anger, some to indignation and not a few to laughter.[26]

Surely the reader who has groped with me through four chapters in an effort to define the sin of Brunetto's band will here recognize Dante's own general description of the vice that we have so laboriously deduced from a consideration of particular cases! Obsessed with their drive for fame, the literati have all been blind to the limits that nature has imposed on their fields of endeavor, and each has, in his own way, blindly established himself and his subject as an authority in a sphere that lies outside the limits of his professional competence. Indeed, the first impression we receive of these runners is that their vision is defective: "Each looked at us as men look at one another under a new moon at dusk, and they puckered their brows on us like an old tailor on the eye of his needle" (*Inf.* xv, 17–21). In the case of Mozzi, we have heard that not a few were provoked to laughter by one who obstinately denied his blindness, and from Dante's perspective the irrational perversity of the other runners must have stirred both anger and indignation.

But to return to the *Monarchia*: having characterized intellectual perverts in general, Dante next distinguishes "the main three classes of men who resist the truth on this issue" of the relation of papacy and monarchy:

> The first class includes the Supreme Pontiff, Vicar of Our Lord Jesus Christ and successor to Peter (to whom we should render not what is due to Christ but what is due to Peter), and certain pastors of the Christian flock. Perhaps it is through his zeal for the keys that the former opposes the truth I am to demonstrate and I well believe that the latter are motivated solely by zeal for Mother Church. As I have said, this class may be inspired by zeal rather than pride.
>
> But there is a second class whose obstinate greed has extinguished the light of reason; though they profess themselves to be sons of the Church they have the Devil for their father. . . .
>
> Then there is a third class, known as the Decretalists, who are totally ignorant of both theology and philosophy; relying entirely upon the Decretals, to which they have devoted all their attention [*intentio*]—and which [Decretals] I myself hold to be venerable—they imagine—so I believe—that the force of the Decretals justifies their attacks upon the Empire.[27]

Now, although all three classes belong to the general family of those described in the preceding passage, whose perverted will has blinded them to the light of reason, yet not all forms of intellectual prejudice deserve damnation. Only members of the second class, who are motivated by *obstinata cupiditas*, are unqualified sons of the Devil and will, as a group, be damned. The motives of the first class are open to question; and though in reverence for ecclesiastical office, Dante gives popes and prelates the benefit of the doubt, presuming that they are respectively motivated by zeal for the papal office and for the Church universal, still he does not exclude the possibility that their motives are instead reprehensible and indeed damnable. This presumption of zeal I take to be his regular attitude towards the papal office.[28] The intention of the Decretalists, who compose the third class, is of quite another kind; it is based, not on official zeal or pride, not on obstinate cupidity, but entirely on their decretals: "suis decretalibus . . . tota intentione innixi." This intention is not moral but intellectual; it defines the scope of their study, which falls short of first principles in either the natural or the supernatural order, for "they are totally ignorant of both theology and philosophy" ("theologie ac phylosophie cuiuslibet inscii et expertes").

Having grouped his opponents into three classes, Dante goes on to define his attitude towards each, from last to first. The Decretalists present a formidable obstacle, because they base their arguments on the authority of papal decretals, which, they maintain, represent the tradition of the Church. One might easily assume that Dante employs the label *Decretalistae* in the specific sense of those who expound the decretal letters that were issued subsequent to Gratian's *Decretum*, but in fact he uses it as a generic term to denote all those who attribute to any papal decretal, regardless of date, an authority such that it can prevail over the other *auctoritates* from which Gratian collected his canons, namely Holy Scripture, the Councils, and the Fathers of the Church. By directing his attack against those who misapprehend the authority of the decretals, Dante avoids a direct critique of the decretals themselves. He can affirm his veneration for these papal decisions while denying the authority that their interpreters have falsely imputed to them.

Dante clearly recognized that many papal prerogatives rested on no other basis than the pronouncement of a papal letter that had become part of the accepted *traditio* embodied in the canon law of the Church. Moreover, he knew that unless the authority of certain of these decretals could be neutralized, the third thesis of the *Monarchia* would not be tenable. Characteristically, he questioned, not their historical authenticity, but rather their divine authority. Although Dante was quick to profess veneration for the decretals as a body, he ranked them below more authoritative writings. Foremost he placed the Old and New Testaments, which had existed from eternity as the Divine Word and thus were prior to the Church itself. Contemporaneous with the Church were those Christian writings made with divine assistance: the principal councils of the whole Church and the writings of such doctors as Augustine. The ecumenical councils derive their authority from Christ's promise that he should be with the Church even unto the end of time (Matt. 28:20); the teachings of the Fathers, by contrast, have no a priori guarantee of authority but rather are judged by their *effects* to have been prompted by the Holy Spirit. Lowest in the scale of authoritative scripture, Dante places papal decretals, for these come after the Church and hence are not inspired. He admits they are venerable authorities but still insists that such authority as they possess is derived from the Church. From this it follows that the pope can neither exceed the authority of the Church nor augment it, for that authority is determined by the sources that Dante designates as prior to or contemporary with the Church. Since the decretal tradition is derivative, Dante concludes that it is irrelevant to an argument concerning the authority of the Church: for this, better and higher sources are available.

Against the decretals, Dante lodges no accusation of falsification or even usurpation of authority; nonetheless it is implicit in his argument. If the decretals faithfully reproduced the original sources, neither adding nor subtracting, one could rely on their authority; but manifestly Dante refused to do so. The Decretalists, whose only perversion consists in being too intent upon this inferior source in preference to the higher truths of theology and philosophy, he has already branded as ignorant of the truth about the authority of the Church; so we may be sure that this truth could not be learned from their decretals:

> Once the former [i.e., the Decretalists] have been excluded we must also exclude those others who, though covered in crows' feathers, come prancing into the flock of the Lord like white sheep. These are the sons of impiety who to further their profligacy prostitute their Mother, drive out their brothers, and finally refuse to recognize any judge. Why, then, should our argument be directed towards them when they are so firmly in the grip of their own greed that they cannot even see first principles? Which means that our dispute is restricted to those who are motivated by a certain zeal for Mother Church yet miss the very truth at issue.[29]

Having excluded the Decretalists because their intention was not directed to trust-worthy authorities, he retraces his steps to the second class, apparently secular princes opposed to the empire,[30] whose cupidinous intentions are evidenced by their evil deeds in the same way that inspired doctors are known from the good effects of their written works. The ignorance of these manifest sons of iniquity and impiety he considers to be invincible, and consequently he foregoes any attempt to convince them of their error. That leaves Dante with the task of addressing the class first named, which comprises popes and prelates who pervert the truth, presumably from an excess of zeal. Like the other two kinds of opponents, the prelates are ignorant of the truth but not to the extent that they are blind to first principles, as are the obstinately greedy. The Decretalists, I gather, are not blind to first principles but only preoccupied with their decretals. If they can be persuaded by Dante's critique of their chosen source to shift their attention to better sources of authority, they cease—by his definition—to be Decretalists.

Through this chapter, Dante establishes both his attitude and approach toward unwarranted pretensions to ecclesiastical power. Out of reverence and respect for the authority of the Church, he will assume that all its officers act in good faith, and their excesses he will impute to zeal. Moreover, he takes care not to let his own good faith be called into question. As a dutiful Christian, Dante gives the ecclesiastical authority all the respect to which it is entitled. These professions manifest his own zeal and guard him against *argumenta ad hominem*. If, as we suppose, Dante denied that the papacy possessed the right to translate bishops, his respectful attitude would necessarily control the expression of that opinion in the poem. It would, in the composition of the *Inferno*, restrain him from exemplifying such a usurpation in the person of any pope. Instead, the burden of guilt would be laid on the *Decretalistae* who justified the right by citing decretals in preference to revelation. Thus one phase of our preliminary analysis already finds confirmation in the thought of Dante.

The chapter also defines the criteria which enable Dante to determine whether any ecclesiastical power is exercised by right or by usurpation. Because decretals derive their authority from the more general authority of the Church, they can authorize nothing that is contrary to revealed truth. In other words, *decretales* repeat the revealed truth that is man's sole authority in the supernatural order; they themselves are not original sources of revealed truth. At the end of the *Monarchia*, Dante returns to this theme and classifies these sources of revealed truth. They are the *documenta spiritualia* that mankind has received from the Holy Spirit, "who has revealed the supernatural truth necessary for our salvation by means of the prophets and sacred writers, and through the Son of God, who is co-eternal with the Spirit, Jesus Christ, and through Christ's disciples."[31] Further, the pope's relation to revealed authority is there made explicit: "[He] is to lead mankind to eternal life in accordance with revelation" ("secundum revelata humanum genus perduceret ad vitam ecternam").[32] The pope cannot alter the content of revelation any more than the emperor can change the laws of nature. Thus we can be sure that any decretal insofar as it contradicts revelation will be considered false by Dante.

EPISCOPAL TRANSLATION

If the conspicuous use of the translation power by Boniface and his successors had prompted Dante to inquire whether the pope in fact possessed the right to transfer bishops, he would inevitably have had to consult and confront the authorities that were alleged by canonists who sought to justify that right. Since decretals in themselves were insufficient evidence by his standards, he would surely avoid the decretal collections of the thirteenth century and instead go directly to Gratian's *Decretum*, where he could be sure to find collected those conciliar and patristic sources that, together with Scripture, he trusted as the revealed constitutive documents of the Christian Church.[33]

Gratian's Decretum

Although no one suspected as much in Dante's day, many of the decretal letters included by Gratian were in fact forgeries, notably those deriving from the collection falsely ascribed to Isidore of Seville. Not a few of the powers exercised by Dante's papacy were, in the last analysis, justified by nothing more than these counterfeit documents, the historical authenticity of which was first challenged by the Magdeburg Centuriators in 1558.[34]

No doubt, what little Dante knew of the early history of episcopal translation he deduced from the pages of Gratian, but the modern reader will better grasp the development of the institution if our exposition moves forwards rather than backwards in time. Let us therefore sketch the historical evolution of episcopal transfers from the early Church down to the canons concerning translation that appear in the *Decretum*, and then we shall apply Dante's criteria to them.[35]

In 325 the council of Nicaea absolutely forbade the translation of bishops from one see to another:

It is not proper for bishops or other clergymen to migrate from city to city. Let no bishop, no priest, no deacon make a change. If, however, after [this] the definition of the great and holy council, anyone shall have attempted to do such a thing, and by actually doing it shall have emancipated himself, let this deed be deemed utterly void, and let him be restored to the church of which he was the ordained bishop or priest or deacon.[36]

In justification of this extreme position the explanation was soon advanced that the bishop was wedded to his church in mystical marriage,[37] and the metaphor persisted long after the rule had been relaxed. The uncompromising Nicene position was maintained by at least two of the Latin Doctors, for Augustine invoked "the prescriptions of the Fathers" against the proposed translation of his neighbor, the bishop of Fussala,[38] and Jerome not only cited the Nicene canon expressly and to the same effect, but also echoed the doctrine of mystical marriage by comparing translation to adultery.[39] In the West, hardly two centuries after Nicaea, the *Statuta Ecclesiae antiqua* incorporates a more moderate position, which was to become that of the Latin Church. On the one hand, upward mobility for the sake of ambition was condemned; on the other, a translation was permissible if it served the *utilitas ecclesiae*. The question then was, Who determined whether a move was useful? The *Statuta* assigned that function to a council of bishops.[40] The doctrine of utility was subsequently expanded by the forgers of the *Pseudo-Isidorean Decretals* to cover the case of necessity as well.[41] Two of these false decretals found their place in Gratian's collection, one with a significant addition from some intermediate source, which amended the traditional assertion of the supposed author, Pope Anterus—that neighboring bishops could authorize the transfer of a bishop—by inserting the all-important qualification "not however without the authority and licence of the sacrosanct Roman see."[42] Thus, in Dante's time, when the historical authenticity of the texts collected by Gratian was as yet unquestioned, episcopal translation appeared to have been a prerogative of the papacy since the pontificate of Anterus (A.D. 235–236).

Since all the relevant sources are grouped together by Gratian and occupy hardly more than a folio of text,[43] an hour's study of this book, which was available in almost any ecclesiastical library, would have sufficed to convince Dante that by his standards the papal pretensions were unjustified. Moreover, Gratian carefully records the source of each canon, so that Dante at a glance could have distinguished the revealed canons from mere decretals. The Nicene canon stands first in the series. Of the remaining twenty, he would, by his own definition, have been forced to acknowledge the authority of only one more, which was from another of the *concilia principalia*, and this act of the council of Chalcedon (451) does nothing but confirm the decision made at Nicaea.[44] Gregory is the only important Church Father whom Gratian excerpted on translation; that saintly pope applies the Nicene rule to a particular case.[45] In short, Dante's Razor—the criteria of *Monarchia* 3. 3— reduces to shreds the argument of the *Decretalistae* regarding episcopal transfer. All that remains after the decretal letters and lesser councils have been cut away is the core of truth revealed through the council of Nicaea: Let no bishop change his church for another one. Of this much, then, we can be positively certain: with a minimum of effort and no special skill except Dante's own criteria, his reader could have determined from Gratian that the *documenta spiritualia* absolutely prohibited bishops from changing churches.

Innocent III's Decretals

To transfer a bishop was therefore, by Dante's lights, to violate the revealed law embodied in the canons of the principal councils. But can we construe this in any sense to be a violation of the natural order? It might seem that we cannot, because Dante maintained that "since the Church is not caused by nature, but is the work of God . . . it is obvious that nature did not impose its law upon the Church."[46] It is possible, however, that the relation of the bishop to his church belongs to the realm of nature, in which the Church has no authority. Strange though this proposition may seem, it is in fact the case.

To arrive at such an apparently paradoxical conclusion, the reader has but to progress in his consultation of the canonists to the authority that Dante and his contemporaries would inevitably have turned to next after Gratian's *Decretum*, namely the decretal collections that were made as a supplement to that work. Although several such supplements had been officially promulgated by Dante's day, all but one can be eliminated, for the title *De translatione episcopi* appears only in the *Decretals of Gregory IX* (1234),[47] where four decretal letters of Innocent III stand together as the only official development of the law of translation between the time of Gratian and that of Dante. Since a separate title was devoted to the subject, we can be sure that even an amateur canonist could have located the passage; moreover, he could have mastered it as easily as the corresponding section in Gratian, which is hardly longer. Further, because copies were everywhere available, Dante would also have had this standard work at his disposal and could similarly have expected that his readers would also. Assured that our next step is plausible, let us therefore examine these decretals of Innocent III, together with their exposition by the *Glossa ordinaria*.[48]

Taken together, the four decretals provide a general theory of episcopal translation by papal authority. In Gratian, the papal right to supervise translation of bishops was simply asserted but not justified. In commenting on Gratian, the Decretists of the later twelfth century had attempted to discern the general principles on which such claims were based, but at the time that Innocent became pope, in 1198, none of these competing explanations had received official recognition. Innocent, who had been trained in canon law at Bologna, made the theories that he had learned in the classroom the basis for his decisions as pope. By incorporating these doctrines into his official pronouncements, he in effect decretalized them. Consciously, Innocent used his power as supreme judge to systematize the common law of the Church.

This intention is perhaps best perceived in the unprecedented care that he took to have his decisions collected, systematically arranged, and transmitted to Bologna for use in the courts and schools. Thus the title *De translatione episcopi*

(X 1. 7) represents Innocent's authorized selection of his translation decretals, which were arranged under his direction to present his thought systematically.[49]

Each decretal treats a case of considerable complexity, the details of which could long detain us, but this will not be necessary. In general, Innocent extended the papal jurisdiction over episcopal transfers by including borderline cases.[50] His method was that of the Decretists: to discern the general principles upon which the specific regulations of existing canons were based, and then to apply these principles to new cases. Our concern will be with the principles that he formulated rather than with his application of these principles to the particular cases in question.

The first of these four canons was issued less than a month after Innocent's coronation. Directed to the patriarch of Antioch, the decretal *Cum ex illo* asserts that the papacy has jurisdiction over all translations of bishops:

> By that general privilege which our Lord granted to Saint Peter and through him to the Roman Church, canons presently arose stating that the more important business of the Church should be referred to the Apostolic see, and consequently translations of bishops and changes of sees pertain de jure to the pope, and no changes of this sort are to be made without his consent.[51]

Innocent's claim to hear all important cases *(causae maiores)* is justified, the *Glossa ordinaria* explains, "because a question of religion and faith is to be referred only to Peter";[52] and the glossator took the opportunity to list all the cases that were reserved for the pope's judgment alone.[53] This right to reserve major cases for the pope is derived by Innocent "ex illo generali privilegio, quod beato Petro et per eum ecclesiae Romanae Dominus noster indulsit," and the glossator explains that Christ's general privilege to Peter was the one "by which he preferred it [the Roman church] to all the churches collectively."[54] This preference was expressed, of course, in the verse beginning "Tu es Petrus" (Matt. 16:18), which forms the basis for Peter's claim to primacy among the Apostles.[55]

For our purpose, it is important to note that Innocent does not claim that his right to move a bishop from one see to another is derived from this general privilege of primacy. Instead, he only maintains that by virtue of the primacy of Peter, lesser ecclesiastical authorities must refer cases of such importance to Rome.

For Innocent, it would seem that Peter's primacy did not entitle him to transfer bishops. For this a special privilege was necessary, as Innocent explained in his second translation decretal, *Quanto personam* (X 1. 7. 3), written half a year later:

> That bishop . . . transferred himself by his own authority, without regard for the truth declared in the Gospel: "Whom God has joined together, let man not separate." The Lord and Master thus retained for himself the power of transferring bishops, which by a special privilege he assigned and conceded to his sole vicar Saint Peter and through him to his successors, just as is attested by antiquity, to which the decrees of the Fathers sanctioned that reverence be shown, as the sanctions of the holy canons plainly assert. For not man but God separates what the Roman pontiff (who acts on earth not as a mere man but as the agent of the true God), after weighing the

necessity or utility of the churches, dissolves not by human but rather by divine authority.[56]

The argument is based on the assumption that the bishop is wedded to his church. From this it would appear, as it did to the Latin Fathers, that a bishop could be separated from his own church only by God, since Christ had stated that "quod ergo Deus coniunxit, homo non separet" (Matt. 19:6). However, from the translation canons in Gratian it appeared that the papacy had in fact moved bishops from see to see as early as the pontificate of Anterus (A.D. 235–236).[57] Since this could not licitly have been done by a mere man, Innocent inferred that the early popes had done so because Christ had conferred on Peter a special privilege to act in His place as agent of the true God (veri Dei vicem). This unique power to act in God's stead, Innocent identified with the title vicarius Christi, asserting that the privilege was entrusted to Christ's sole vicar, Peter, and to his successors.

Two weeks after Innocent celebrated his first anniversary as pope, he restated this argument in a third decretal, Inter corporalia (X 1. 7. 2), in which particular stress is laid on the nature of the bond in spiritual matrimony:

> We recognize this difference between things spiritual and corporal: that physical things are easier to destroy than to construct, while spiritual things are easier to construct than to destroy. Whence a lone bishop is able to give an honor, but he alone is not able to take it away. Bishops also are consecrated by their metropolitans, but cannot be condemned except by the pope. Since a spiritual bond is therefore stronger [fortius] than a carnal one, it ought not to be doubted that God omnipotent reserved for only his judgment the dissolution of the spiritual union [coniugium] between bishop and church, since he even reserved for only his judgment the carnal union between man and woman, by the warning "Whom God has joined together, let man not separate." For a spiritual union is dissolved not by human but rather by divine power, since through translation, deposition, or resignation a bishop is removed from a church by the authority of the Roman pontiff, who is well known to be the vicar of Jesus Christ. And hence these three cases stated above are reserved to the Roman pontiff alone, not so much by canonical constitution as by divine institution.[58]

Here the bond between the bishop and his church is expressly termed coniugium spirituale and is compared to the coniugium carnale that obtains between man and woman. After explaining, though not very convincingly, that spiritual bonds are stronger than carnal ones,[59] Innocent argues that a fortiori the injunction "Quos Deus coniunxit homo non separet" applies even more to spiritual than to carnal matrimony. Thus—Innocent concludes, condensing his earlier argument of Quanto personam—when the pope dissolves the bond between bishop and church, he exercises divine power as vicar of Christ. This potestas vicaria now has been broadened to include not only the translation but also the deposition or resignation of bishops.

Much ink, medieval and modern, has been spilled over the obscurities of this argument,[60] but these are not our concern. We need only remark that the main features of Innocent's earlier argument recur in its subsequent development. A year

[126]

later he himself provided an admirable summary of his doctrine in the fourth and last of his decretals on translation, *Licet in tantum*:

> Just as man is unable to dissolve the bond of legitimate matrimony that exists between man and wife, since the Lord said in the Gospel, "Whom God has joined together, let man not separate"; so also the spiritual covenant of union [*spirituale foedus coniugii*] that exists between bishop and church—which is understood to be initiated in election, ratified in confirmation, and consummated in consecration—cannot be broken without the authority of him who is the successor of Peter and the vicar of Jesus Christ.[61]

Perhaps it is folly to think that texts can speak for themselves, but I have tried to restrict my commentary to a paraphrase of the salient points in the hope that the two main themes would be thrown into relief by a close juxtaposition of the texts themselves. I have resisted the temptation to overlay the text with a detailed exposition, because in our previous analyses we have found that when Dante refers us to a text, its relevance is not concealed in an isolated passage but rather is conveyed by the whole import of the work. In the present case, Innocent's argument consists of two principal propositions: (1) only God can dissolve the spiritual bond between a bishop and his church, and (2) God has delegated this power to the pope as the successor of Peter, who was sole vicar of the very God, Jesus Christ. We could now proceed to inquire directly how acceptable these theses were to Dante Alighieri; but lest the reader imagine that we here are dealing with nothing more than some small detail of ecclesiastical administration, it would be well to make clear first of all that the argument Innocent developed to justify translation did in fact represent a major turning point in Latin ecclesiology.

VICARIUS CHRISTI BEFORE INNOCENT III

Historians have long recognized that Innocent III was the first pope to make frequent use of the title *vicarius Christi* in his correspondence. In the half-century before his accession, the papal chancery seems not to have used the term at all, and equivalent expressions, such as *Christi vices in terris agimus*, appear but three times.[62] In 1198, however, the phrase suddenly became a favorite of Innocent's chancery, as did the closely related term *plenitudo potestatis*.[63] From that time on, both expressions were staples of papal rhetoric, and it is generally agreed that the new usage marks the moment when the absolutistic ecclesiology of the Decretists, in which "plenitude of power" was the key phrase, was adopted for official use by the curia. The definitive history of this doctrine of "hierocracy," as it has been called, has yet to be written. The materials have been accumulating ever more rapidly in the past two generations, but many links in the development of the hierocratic doctrine are still obscure. In particular, Innocent's role in the curial adoption of these Decretist theories remains highly debatable. Some would maintain that he himself contributed "little, if anything" to the development of the doctrine but merely effected its adoption by the curia.[64] This hardly accords with the high opinion in which he was held by the early Decretalists, who knew both his decretals and the work of his predecessors, the Decretists. Hostiensis, for example, liked to call Innocent "the father of canon law,"[65] suggesting that the pope's personal contribution to his profession was radically creative. In particular respects it is known that the great legislator-pope departed from or developed the teaching of his teacher at Bologna, Huguccio of Pisa (whom Dantists know better as a lexicographer), and especially it has been observed that Innocent "tightened the notion of *plenitudo potestatis*."[66]

Although the Innocentian translation decretals were frequently cited by later writers in support of the hierocratic position, apparently no one has attempted to assess their function in the complex of interrelated texts that, taken together, constituted the hierocratic ideology. Dante has prompted me to review recent scholarship from this perspective, and the result will, I believe, reveal an unsuspected link in the hierocratic argument, indeed a crucial one, for it appears that the argument advanced in these early Innocentian decretals constitutes the very keystone of his hierocratic system. I cannot at present say whether that argument was altogether original with Innocent, since the answer lies in unpublished manuscripts, but if, as I suspect, it was Innocent's own contribution to the development of the hierocratic doctrine, then it would follow that in effect he provided the first proof that the hierocratic hypothesis was in fact demonstrably derived from revelation. If the Decretist argument for hierocracy was in effect incomplete until Innocent brought it to a successful conclusion, that would explain why the curia hesitated for half a century to make use of the argument, and then suddenly adopted it in 1198. Thus the interpretation of the Innocentian translation decretals that I am about to propose has a potential significance far beyond the interpretation of Dante. No doubt the subject deserves a monograph in itself, but here I shall confine myself to those aspects that seem essential to an understanding of Dante's ecclesiology. Presently we shall view these texts from Dante's standpoint, but in order to acquaint ourselves with the concepts involved, it seems best to gain first the broader, more familiar perspective of the historian of ideas and then to sketch successively the development of each of the two senses of the term *vicarius Christi* that Dante would have found respectively in Gratian's *Decretum* and the Gregorian *Decretales*.[87]

Gratian's Decretum

The Pauline doctrine that all power is from God (Rom. 13:1) encouraged the earliest Christians to regard all earthly authority as delegated authority. Hence it is not surprising that the common classical terms for agents or representatives were applied to ecclesiastical authority. Ignatius of Antioch expressed the basic idea as early as A.D. 108, when he spoke of the bishop as one who holds "the place of God." By the middle of the third century, Cyprian conceived of a succession of delegated powers in which the Apostles acted *vice Christi*, while each successive bishop was the vicar (or replacement) for his predecessor, and these powers he delegated in part to the clergy of his diocese, so that priests and deacons were, according to Cyprian, their bishop's vicars.[68]

Thus Cyprian approximated, but did not coin, the phrase *vicarius Christi*, which for centuries to come would convey his concept of a vicarious hierarchy of Christian authority. The phrase itself appears in Tertullian and again fleetingly in the tract *Adversus aleatores*, by an anonymous contemporary of Cyprian, but its use in the Cyprianic sense was established over a century later, in the age of Ambrose, by works that were attributed to the Latin Doctor of Milan during the Middle Ages but now are ascribed to the fictitious author "Ambrosiaster."[69] This writer used the term *vicarius Christi* to characterize ecclesiastical officers, especially the Apostles and their successors, the bishops, but he also applied it to priests. To designate secular, and particularly imperial, authority, Ambrosiaster employed the term *vicarius Dei*, which though superficially similar, had deep roots in the pagan ruler-cults of antiquity.

Ambrosiaster's usage of both terms predominated until the Investiture Struggle. Because *vicarius Christi* could, by this definition, refer to any ecclesiastical authority, none claimed it as a distinctive title, particularly not the papacy. Instead, the preferred papal title was *vicarius Petri*, which though implicit in the Cyprianic concept, only became an indubitable title in the fifth century,[70] and continued to be the preferred usage of the papal chancery down to the time of Innocent III.

Ambrosiaster's distinction between the vicariates of Christ and of God lost its clarity with the sacralization of Carolingian kingship,[71] and occasionally before 1050 the papacy was addressed by the prestigious imperial title *vicarius Dei*.[72] The emperor's claim to the title was effectually denied in the course of the Investiture Struggle and afterwards was recognized by neither Gratian nor later canonists.[73]

From the pages of Gratian, one would learn instead that all bishops were vicars of Christ "quia episcopus personam habet Christi" and that husbands are quasi vicars of Christ, who possess the *imperium Dei* to rule their wives because only males are made in God's image.[74] Other passages were understood to qualify all priests as Christ's vicars.[75] As for the pope, in Gratian's *Decretum* he is twice referred to as Peter's vicar but never as Christ's. Apparently Gratian had no reason to believe that the title *vicarius Christi* had any special significance for the papacy. The idea, though an old one, as Maccarone has shown, had been advanced infrequently but had never been elaborated.

The Circle of Eugenius III

Shortly after the completion of Gratian's compilation circa 1140, a chorus of voices began to insist that the pope was the *sole* vicar of Christ. This enthusiasm found its center in the court of the Cistercian pope Eugenius III (1145–53) and was, to all appearances, generated by his former abbot, Bernard of Clairvaux, who first addressed him as *vicarius Christi* in 1147, though previously that saint had been content to use the traditional title *vicarius Petri*.[76] The title had come to have special significance for Bernard because he associated it with the concept of *plenitudo potestatis*, and if I am not mistaken, he was the first to do so. The terms were linked by Bernard in the famous *De consideratione* that he composed for Eugenius. In book 2, written between 1148 and 1152,[77] Bernard devoted a chapter to the thesis that the pope excells the other bishops because the apostolic see has been given the unique prerogative of plenitude of power over all churches of the world, by virtue of which the successor of Peter is the *pastor pastorum*.[78] Bernard's principal argument attempts to provide a Scriptural foundation for the assertion, first made by Pope Leo I, that the pope is called to plenitude of power while the other bishops are called to part of the solicitude, which Bernard interpreted to mean that the pope has jurisdiction over the bishops.[79]

The Bernardine proof is based on Peter's commission as shepherd of all the sheep of Christ (John 21:17), with a counterproof that the bishops are subject to the power of Peter's keys (Matt. 16:19), since the pope can depose and excommunicate bishops. Having established that all bishops are subject to the pope because he possesses the prerogative of *plenitudo potestatis*, Bernard offers another proof, "that confirms the prerogative to you no less." This proof is accomplished by an allegorical interpretation of two Gospel episodes which placed Peter in a special relation to the peoples of the world and to the Church, which Bernard symbolized respectively by the sea and a ship. In the first, Peter commands the ship bearing all the Apostles, from which he swims to shore to greet his risen Lord (John 21:3–7). This signified that Peter's government should not be limited to a single local church, as was the case with the other Apostles, but should be world-wide. The peculiarities of the second incident (Matt. 14:29) yield a significant variation:

> The other time by walking on the water like Christ, he [Peter] designated himself to be the unique vicar of Christ, who ought to be over not one people but all of them, since many waters signify many peoples. So, because each of the others has his own ship, the one greatest ship is committed to you, the universal Church itself, made out of all and scattered throughout the entire world.

Taken by itself, Bernard's second proof would hardly convince anyone that the pope was entrusted with the government of the whole Church, but it was not intended to bear the weight of the argument. Rather, it was meant to confirm and refine Bernard's exposition of *plenitudo potestatis*, and to this concept it made a significant and enduring contribution. By linking the two terms, he suggested that the bearer of this prerogative might appropriately be entitled sole vicar of Christ. Almost certainly it was an afterthought, for as early as 1135 Bernard had already arrived at his definition of the plenitudinary power,[80] while the idea of the pope's unique vicariate appears only this once, in his last major work.

In all likelihood, Bernard acquired the new concept of *vicarius Christi* at the court of Eugenius III, during the pope's travels in France.[81] The most likely source is Anselm of Havelberg, a German bishop who in 1150 wrote, at the request of Eugenius himself, an account of the discussions that Anselm had had at Easter 1136 with the Greek archbishop of Nicomedia. Whereas Bernard sought to impress upon the pope the vast extent of his power, Anselm, as an apologist, interpreted the Petrine texts in a spirit of tactful restraint. At the beginning of the argument he conceded that all the Apostles had received the Holy Spirit from Christ, together with the power to loose and bind; but citing the verses in which Peter alone was given the keys and the sheep, Anselm insisted that this applied to Peter *specialiter*.[82] One suspects that he could have inferred from these texts much the same consequences that Bernard did, but Anselm leaves these implicit and instead develops his argument for Peter's primacy through a literal interpretation of the Scriptural evidences of Peter's position of leadership, the conclusion of which was:

> Wherefore none of the faithful should have the least doubt or call into question, but rather ought to maintain firmly, that Peter was constituted prince of the Apostles by the Lord. However, just as the Roman pontiff alone acts for Christ in Peter's place, so to be sure the other bishops do act for the Apostles under Christ, and for Christ under Peter, and for Peter under the Roman pontiff his vicar. Nor in this is there anything in the least derogatory to any of the Apostles, if the proper function of each is humbly recognized.[83]

The vicarial concept, which for Bernard was but an adjunct to his theory of *plenitudo potestatis*, is evidently Anselm's essential point. To define Peter's position as *princeps Apostolorum*, Bernard relied above all on his distinction between plenitude of power and the part of solicitude; Anselm, however, defined the same term by distinguishing between two senses of *vicarius Christi*. In one sense, the rest of the bishops derive their vicariates directly from the Apostles; in another, they represent Saint Peter, the sole vicar of Christ, and they stand lowest in a vicarial hierarchy descending through Peter to the pope. This latter sense is not without its ambiguity, for although the bishops are said to represent Christ and Peter and the pope, yet they are subordinated successively to all three. Probably this element of ambiguity was intentional; if unclarified, it rendered the formula acceptable to the Greeks, since in Anselm's dialogue the archbishop of Nicomedia replied, "What you say can be," and then changed the subject.[84]

Working from the same premises as Bernard, the bishop of Havelberg found a more tactful, though less trenchant, way to distinguish the papacy from the episcopate. Whether he or Bernard or some one else was first to maintain that the pope was Christ's sole vicar, Anselm's contribution was a significant one, for he was the first to expressly reconcile the broad, traditional concept of Christ's vicars to the new, exclusive one. Bernard more than likely was prepared to draw some such distinction, for he repeatedly entitled all priests *vicarii Christi*;[85] but Anselm enunciated the distinction, and what is more, his concept corresponds, as we shall see, so closely to that adopted by the Decretists that he must be regarded as the first exponent of their doctrine. Perhaps he also perceived the correlation between *plenitudo potestatis* and *solus vicarius Christi*, but in this case, Bernard was the first to make the express statement.

Fusion with Plenitudo Potestatis

The significance of their respective contributions can only be appreciated in the light of later developments. It may seem to the reader, for example, that because the uniqueness of the papal vicariate was not the principal point of Bernard's second argument, he can hardly be credited with uniting the two concepts. Yet there is good reason to believe that Bernard's argument suggested to at least one contemporary that *because* the pope alone possessed the plenitude of power, he in consequence was *solus vicarius Christi*. This, the earliest fusion of the two concepts that Bernard juxtaposed, occurs in a tract on the schism that was created by the double papal election of 1159. To all appearances written by Barbarossa's chronicler Rahewin, the argument is presented with at least a pretense of impartiality as a dialogue between the two rival popes; but to introduce the debate, the author argues *in propria persona* that both cannot be right since, as he endeavors to prove, there can be only one true pope:

> Quod ambo sint, quod dicuntur, putare vel astruere canonica atque catholica religione prohibemur. Nempe sicut una est columba, una formosa, una immaculata virgo et mater ęcclesia, sic unus et unicus eius sponsus, agnus sine macula [Cant. 6:8], cuius gerunt vicem in terris Petrus et Petri successores. Romanus siquidem pontifex solus vicarius Christi, successor Petri estimatur. Ceteri pastores ceterarum ęcclesiarum formam tenent apostolorum seu discipulorum Domini, vocati in partem sollicitudinis, non in plenitudinem potestatis.[86]

At first glance the resemblance to Bernard's argument is not striking, but a significant detail betrays the source. Both Bernard and Rahewin paraphrase the Song of Songs, and both insert the phrase *formosa mea*.[87] We need not be surprised that Rahewin was familiar with the *De consideratione* a decade or so after its completion in 1152 or 1153, since it had already been cited by his Cistercian master, Bishop Otto of Freising, in the *Gesta Friderici I Imperatoris*, which Rahewin himself continued.[88] Like Otto, Rahewin was disposed to keep abreast of modern ideas. The *Dialogus* is noteworthy for the use it makes of the first fruits of scholasticism, invoking, for example, Boethius' commentary on Aristotle's *Categories* in order to prove that one cannot, without equivocation, say there can be two popes simultaneously. Similarly, Rahewin draws on canon law, apparently from Gratian's *Decretum*.[89]

From Rahewin, therefore, we can learn how sophisticated contemporaries received the Bernardine argument. Only three elements are abstracted from Bernard's much lengthier discussion. (1) The Church is one and has but one spouse, Christ. (2) On earth he is represented by one vicar, Peter and his successors, which Rahewin supports by stating that the pope is held *(estimatur)* to be *solus vicarius Christi* as well as successor of Peter. (3) In contrast, the other bishops resemble *(formam tenent)* Christ's Apostles or disciples, because they have only partial responsibility and not the plenitude of power.

Although these elements were all present in Bernard's chapter, they were not integrated there, as they are here, into a single argument designed to prove Rahewin's point, namely that there can be but one living and true pope. Like Bernard, Rahewin relies basically on the distinction between *plenitudo potestatis* and *pars sollicitudinis*; but unlike Bernard, he wishes to stress the uniqueness of the papacy, and hence gives prominence to the striking claim that the pope is *solus vicarius Christi*. First we are told that this title is claimed for the papacy, and then we are told why it is justified, namely because the pope alone has *plenitudo potestatis*. Thus, the two concepts, which Bernard laid side by side, Rahewin intimately related to one another.

The precise relationship is of particular importance. For Rahewin, it is more certain that the pope alone has plenitude of power than that he is sole vicar of Christ: the former serves to define the latter. The reason for this is not far to seek; for, as Bernard remarked, the papal monopoly on plenitude of power was asserted by the canons, whereas the unique vicariate of Christ was still a new concept. In Rahewin's dialogue the two concepts are correlated for the first time as the distinctive office and power of the papacy.

It would be rash to credit Rahewin with this conception. His treatise never seems to have left the diocese of Freising; therefore it is more than likely that the combination originated elsewhere. It is not impossible that Anselm and Bernard held this view but for one reason or another did not make it explicit; quite possibly their primatial doctrines coalesced into a single theory at the court of Eugenius III. At least we can be certain that a third member of Eugenius' circle maintained a variant of their view and continued to maintain it long after the others were dead— long enough, in fact, to be remembered about 1192 by a canonist who was contemporary with Innocent III. "The cardinal of Santi Giovanni e Paolo used to say that the pope is called the vicar of Christ because Jesus Christ, and thus the pope, is set over the whole world." Most probably this cardinal was John of Sutri (Johannes Sutrinus), whom Eugenius promoted to the title, which he held for the next thirty years (1151–81).[90]

The use of the vicarial title also persisted after Eugenius' death, particularly at the papal curia. *Vicarius Christi* is applied to the pope, and notably to the late Eugenius himself, by chroniclers and papal biographers working at this time in Rome. Barbarossa's cardinals used it as a papal title during the schism, as he himself is reported to have done. On Maccarrone's evidence,[91] the usage cannot be said to have been widely diffused outside of Rome during the second half of the century. Indeed, Joachim of Flora aside, the other testimonia amount to two clusters in northern France: single references occur in three authors from the region of Amiens and in letters of John of Salisbury and Thomas à Becket. Admittedly, the sources for the period have not been surveyed exhaustively,[92] but Maccarrone's sample suggests that few outside Eugenius' circle attached any special significance to *vicarius Christi* as a papal title before the time of Innocent III.

This impression is strongly borne out by the use made of the title, or rather its equivalent *Christi vices in terris agimus*, by the papal chancery itself. Eugenius was the first pope to use that form in a public document, and then only once and with no suggestion that he had any exclusive right to the title.[93] In the forty-five years between the death of Eugenius and the accession of Innocent, the chancery employed the formula only twice again. One occasion was a simple repetition of Eugenius' bull, while the other was a letter addressed to Clairvaux, in which the echo reminiscent of the Cistercian pope may have been intended as a compliment.[94] Evidently the chancery felt no compelling reason to replace the traditional formula *vicarius Petri*, to which the papacy had an exclusive right, with the ambiguous new use of *vicarius Christi* or its equivalent. This hesitancy vanishes in 1198, however, when Innocent's decretal *Quanto personam* was issued, with its claim that a special privilege of acting for God, at least in certain cases, had been conceded by Christ "soli beato Petro vicario suo."[95]

Objections Raised by Decretists

Why, we must ask, did the chancery ignore the title *solus vicarius Christi* for half a century, well known though it was at the curia, and then suddenly and permanently adopt it in Innocent's first year? Did the forceful personality of the young pope brush aside objections that had tempered the enthusiasm of Eugenius? It would seem far more plausible to suppose that Innocent could meet those objections with reasons unknown to Eugenius.

The most obvious objection, of course, was that for centuries all bishops, and indeed all priests, had been recognized to be Christ's vicars. The Eugenian advocates of the *solus vicarius Christi* never expressly dealt with this difficulty, but whatever obstacle it might have presented was brushed aside by Innocent's teacher, Huguccio of Pisa. In his *Summa* (ca. 1190), that great Decretist inferred from a text in Gratian that all priests are vicars of Christ: "This is true with respect to the plenitude of power; otherwise, however, any priest is vicar of Christ and of Peter."[96] His interpretation of the text was the one common to his generation and was adopted by the *Glossa ordinaria.*[97]

Only one other Decretist seems to have pointed out the application to the papal vicariate. The *Summa Reginensis*, written about 1192, perhaps by Innocent's future vice-chancellor Petrus Collivaccinus of Benevento, first pointed out that priests as well as bishops represent Christ; it went on to note that this was an "argument against those who say that only the pope is vicar of Christ. For every priest is vicar of Christ and Peter (C.1 q.1 c.86). The cardinal of SS. Giovanni e Paolo used to say that the reason the pope is called vicar of Christ is because Jesus Christ, and so the pope, is set over the whole world."[98]

These two comments deserve our particular attention because they come from the canonists whom Innocent knew best; their observations are all the more remarkable because neither author apparently had anything more to say about *vicarius Christi* as a papal title.[99] Since Huguccio generally considered the pros and cons of those questions that had occupied his predecessors, his terse treatment of the papal vicariate would seem to indicate that the Decretists had attached no great significance to the title. Both Huguccio and Reginensis are principally concerned about defending the older claim of the whole sacerdotal order to be *quoad ordinem* vicars both of Christ and of Peter. Reginensis, it will be observed, does not argue the question himself; he only points out that this locus would be a useful argument against an unqualified claim that the pope alone was Christ's vicar. Instead of taking sides himself, Reginensis summarizes the thesis of Cardinal John of Sutri, most probably as an example of a suitably qualified statement. Huguccio, however, does not hesitate to commit himself to this qualified form of the proposition: *solus papa est vicarius Christi quoad plenitudinem potestatis*. But it was precisely in this respect that Bernard, Anselm, Rahewin, and John of Sutri made their claim. The point is that they made it tacitly, and hence they appeared to deny the vicariate to all but the *summus sacerdos*. Guided by the legal maxim *Exceptio probat regulam de rebus non exceptis*, both Decretists tested the assertion that the pope is sole vicar of Christ and found it wanting. From this, Reginensis apparently concluded that it would be better to discard *solus* from the formula, as in his example. Huguccio, however, retained the objectionable quantifier but removed the objection by qualification.

Innocent III appreciated their critique and, on occasion, took account of it. Before he became pope, he acknowledged in his treatise *De sacro altaris mysterio* that in certain respects all members of the sacerdotal order act *vice Christi*, "since they pray for sins and reconcile sinners through penitence."[100] In *Quanto personam*, however, Peter is stated to have been Christ's sole vicar without qualification, although manifestly some qualification is to be understood.[101] In this regard, *Quanto personam* is no more precise than the statements made earlier by the Eugenian circle. Thus we must conclude that the objection raised by Huguccio and Reginensis was not the impediment that had to be removed before the formula could be acceptable for official use.

The difficulty arose from quite another consideration. Essentially, the problem of the Decretists was to define the governmental powers of the papacy. By arguments based on the Petrine passages in the New Testament, the lawyers could show that Christ had entrusted Peter with the government of the whole Church. By the time of Huguccio, the Decretists identified this governmental power as the *plenitudo potestatis* that several canons asserted belonged to the pope but not to the other bishops. This asserted only that the papacy was the one highest authority in the Church; it did not indicate what could or could not be done by virtue of that authority. In comparison to other bishops, the pope had full authority—but authority to do what?

The Decretists were sure that a pope could, as Peter's successor, do whatever Peter could do; they were not at all sure, however, that Peter could do whatever Christ could do. Peter and his successors were men, while Christ was both man and God. Did Christ commit to Peter any of his divine power? and if so, all of it or only certain specific powers? From Christ's commission there was no way of telling just how extensive it was. Therefore the Decretists had to be content with a denotative definition that described the plenitude of power as the sum of such powers as could be discovered from Scripture or the canons. What the *auctoritates* stated had been done by Peter or his successors certainly was to be counted among the powers of the papacy. Further, this list of powers could be extended by inference, though this was a delicate dialectical process. Some of these powers were shared with the episcopate; others were not. The latter, the prerogative powers of the papacy, were of particular value in defining *plenitudo potestatis*, and of these the Decretists compiled lists. For example, Huguccio listed a dozen of such *causae maiores* that were reserved for the papacy alone: heading his list were the deposition, resignation, and translation of bishops.[102]

Nowhere in the *auctoritates* was it said that the pope alone was vicar of Christ. When Huguccio declared that this was nonetheless true *quoad plenitudinem potestatis*, he inferred as much from the existing doctrine of papal plenitude of power. Since it was established that Christ had committed the plenitude of power only to Peter and his successors, Huguccio conceded that it could properly be said that in this respect the pope was sole vicar of Christ. This deduction was a purely analytic statement, however; it added nothing to what was already known. Huguccio evidently thought the title, though justifiable, was of little value as a legal concept, and consequently he avoided it elsewhere in his work. Instead, he and other Bolognese Decretists in the last two decades of the twelfth century favored the concept of *plenitudo potestatis*.

Chancery usage, it should be noted, followed the new fashion at Bologna with little or no hesitation: *plenitudo potestatis* appears occasionally in bulls during the formative years of the Decretist doctrine in the 1180s, and regularly in the 1190s.[103] The chancery, it would seem, agreed with the Bolognese canonists that *solus vicarius Christi* was a title better avoided, since whatever meaning it had was derived from and comprehended in the venerable canonical expression *plentitudo potestatis* as defined by the Decretists. Moreover, the title *vicarius Petri* was already established and would serve as well as the other, since the pope could only do what Peter could do as vicar of Christ.

HOW INNOCENT III REDEFINED PLENITUDE OF POWER

In the hands of the Decretists, *plenitudo potestatis* was in effect a collective name for the prerogatives of the papacy as established by the canons. From Scripture they could prove that the pope possessed full power in the Church, as opposed to the partial power of the other bishops, but this was understood to mean that he had the care of the whole Church, whereas the others cared for particular churches.[104] The Decretists could not offer a comprehensive statement of what the pope *could* do by virtue of this power, for the simple reason that they could not be sure whether Peter could do whatever Christ could do, or only what Christ qua man could do. Innocent III revolutionized Latin ecclesiology by closing this gap. He discovered a Scriptural proof that Peter's commission did indeed include the power to do what only God could do. Once this was established, the Decretalists could define *plenitudo potestatis* as the broadest discretionary power: provided that the pope did not contravene the faith, "in all things and through all means he is able to do and say whatever he pleases."[105]

Innocent found the means to define Peter's commission among the *causae maiores*, those exceptional cases that were reserved by the canons for papal judgment. One of his earliest acts as pope was to assert in *Cum ex illo* that his jurisdiction in such cases, and especially in the translation of bishops, was not limited to the Latin church but extended throughout the universal Church, specifically including the patriarchate of Antioch, which might have been an exception because it was Peter's original see.[106] Thus the *causae maiores* were identified beyond doubt with the universal plenitude of power.[107] Were any of them a divine prerogative? Innocent, as we have seen, argued that because the bishop was united to his church in spiritual matrimony, no mere man could alter that relationship, since Christ himself had declared, "What therefore God hath joined together, let no man put asunder." This was a conclusion that had not been drawn in the Latin church since the days of Jerome and Augustine.

The Bishop as Sponsus

The spiritual marriage of each bishop to his church had, as we remarked previously, constituted an objection to episcopal translation for the early Fathers,[108] and for this view there was Scriptural basis in Paul's admonition to Timothy: "It behoveth therefore a bishop to be blameless, the husband of one wife. . . ."[109] The authority for taking this to be a reference to spiritual rather than carnal marriage was supplied by Eph. 5:22–33, where man and wife are urged to imitate the example of Christ's marriage to his Church. Just as Christ was bridegroom of the Church universal, so by analogy the bishop was *sponsus* of his particular church: he was a figure of Christ.

This patristic conception of the bishop's spiritual marriage had become an integral part of Latin ecclesiology. Notably, the marriage metaphor was employed in the liturgical rites whereby the bishop was consecrated to his see. The union was symbolized by the ring, which he was given with these words: "Receive the ring, the sign of faith, so that, adorned with pure faith, you may preserve without harm your bride, namely the holy church of God."[110] The Western church, however, had not followed the Fathers in drawing legal consequences from this mystical marriage. Thus, in support of the argument that the bishop's relationship to his church was lifelong, to be broken only by death or deposition for a capital offense, Gratian quoted several authorities that invoked the matrimonial analogy.[111] For him and most canonists of the twelfth century, the argument was not convincing in view of the established custom of translation not only by popes but also by provincial councils, especially since that custom was supported by weighty and apparently ancient authorities. Only towards the end of the century did the matrimonial metaphor come to play a crucial role in canonistic thought, and then it was first used to explain how and when the bishop's bond to his church was formed. The sacramental view, of course, held that the mystical union was effected by ritual consecration, but as this occurred after, often long after, the bishop's election, an earlier occasion had decided practical advantages. The solution was devised by Huguccio, who accepted the usual view that the bond was matrimonial, but then explained its formation by drawing an analogy to the Roman law of marriage, in which consent rather than consecration was the operative factor.[112] Thus a mystical allegory was taken to be a legal reality, to be interpreted according to the Romano-canonical law of marriage.

Huguccio's theory won general acceptance because it was adopted by his most distinguished student, Innocent III, who as pope made it part of the law of the Church by incorporating it, not without adaptation, in his decretals, most notably *Inter corporalia*.[113] For Innocent, if not for Huguccio, the *episcopus-sponsus* concept was more than a convenient legal fiction; in the Innocentian ecclesiology it provided the central, integrating idea whereby he related the episcopate, and especially the papacy, to the Church.[114] In Innocent's scholastic works, *matrimonium spirituale* is a recurrent theme, on which he wrote a special treatise; moreover, it served as the keynote of his sermon on the first anniversary of his consecration.[115]

In view of the major role that Innocent assigned to the bishop as bridegroom, most likely he, rather than his master, was the first to return to the view of the Fathers that the *episcopus-sponsus* was bound by the divine laws of matrimony as well as by the civil laws. At any rate, the revival is hardly a decade older than *Quanto personam*, and Innocent was undoubtedly the first pope, if not the first Latin for centuries, to insist that the bishop's status as husband of his church constituted a divinely ordained impediment to translation, which only God could remove.

The Superhuman Vicariate

Having reerected the patristic barrier to translation, Innocent converted it into a proof that the pope acts for God when he severs the bishop's union with his church. Translation was the leading case, but *Inter corporalia* expressly included deposition and resignation as well. All three, we are told, are justified "not so much by canonical constitution as by divine institution." Innocent, then, does not rest the weight of his argument on the Pseudo-Isidorian translation canons but instead on appeals to Scripture. But where is it said that the pope "veri Dei vicem gerit in terris"? Innocent states only that Christ reserved to himself the "power of transferring bishops, which by a special privilege he assigned and conceded to his sole vicar Saint Peter and through him to his successors." But what was this *speciale privilegium*? From the context of the decretal, one might imagine that it concerned only translation, but clearly it is broader, since it covers both deposition and resignation as well. Elsewhere, Innocent explains that all the *maiores ecclesiae causae* were reserved to the papacy by the Church Fathers, especially episcopal resignations and translations, "that he who alone obtained the plenitude of power might dispose concerning these things."[116] Thus the pope's canonical powers are taken to be patristic recognition of his plenitude of power. All that Peter received from Christ as a *speciale privilegium* was plenitude of power; the content of that power is still defined with reference to the canons, but Innocent has been able to infer from the canons that the Church Fathers recognized that his plenitude of power entitled the pope to act on earth "not as a mere man but as the agent of the true God . . . not by human but rather by divine authority." In short, because the patristic canons sanction papal action in a matter reserved to God alone, it follows that they recognized that Christ had committed to Peter the power to act in His divine as well as His merely human capacity.

At the least, the argument first adduced in *Quanto personam* established the existence of a particular *potestas vicaria*, heretofore unsuspected, by which the bonds of matrimony might be dissolved.[117] Innocent was prepared, however, to take his discovery as proof that the pope had a still broader discretionary power to intervene on God's behalf in human affairs. In the famous decretal *Per venerabilem* (X 4. 17. 13), issued in 1202, Innocent claimed that at his discretion he could exercise jurisdiction in secular cases that were either "difficult or ambiguous."[118] This novel claim was introduced by these words:

> A superior priest or judge is established, to whom the Lord, speaking to Peter, said: "Whatsoever you bind on earth shall be bound in heaven." Vicar of Him who in eternity is priest after the order of Melchisedech, constituted by God judge of the quick and the dead, [the pope] indeed distinguishes three types of judgment. . . ."

The claim to temporal jurisdiction that directly follows is justified because the pope, as Christ's vicar, is like Melchisedech—not only priest, but also king. Lest there be any doubt, we are told immediately after the claim has been made: "Paul also, that he might expound the plenitude of power, wrote to the Corinthians saying, 'Do you not know that you shall judge angels? How much more the things of this world.'"[119] Christ's vicar could, and thus did, claim superhuman powers. Innocent made the claim even more trenchantly in a sermon on the anniversary of his consecration: the pope is

> truly the vicar of Jesus Christ, successor of Peter, the christ of the Lord, the God of pharaoh: established midmost between God and man, on this side of God but beyond man; less than God but greater than man. All things are judged by him and he is judged by no one; in the words of the Apostle he says, "he that judgeth me is the Lord."[120]

In the Fourth Lateran Council, Innocent could, with good reason, abolish the ordeal, for the judgment of God was now available on earth. In *Per venerabilem* he asserted his appellate jurisdiction in civil as well as ecclesiastical cases, in temporal as well as spiritual affairs; and in so doing, he revealed for the first time that the vicar of Christ was a veritable hierocrat. Later popes, notably Innocent IV, were to develop this aspect of the vicariate,[121] but there can be no doubt that his great predecessor not only was the first to enunciate the principle of the superhuman vicariate but also was the first to derive therefrom the corollary hierocratic doctrine.

The Decretalists Concur

The great Decretalists of the next generation attest the significance of Innocent's translation canons in the development of the doctrine of *plenitudo potestatis*. Whereas Huguccio had seen *solus vicarius Christi* as a possible descriptive title for the bearer of the plenitude of power, though of no significance in jurisprudence, Pope Innocent IV, writing half a century later in his private capacity as the canonist Sinibaldo Fieschi, explained that the pope can exercise temporal jurisdiction when a secular prince has died or has failed to do justice, even if the office is not conferred by the papacy, but in that case "he does not do this by common law but by the plenitude of power which he has because he is vicar of Jesus Christ."[122]

The relationship between the office and its attendant power was elaborated by Hostiensis: "Jesus Christ left as his vicar-general Saint Peter and his successors, to whom he left plenitude of power." When the pope separates what God has joined together, "this is done not by man but by God, i.e. the vicar of the very God to whom he gave this power."[123] In support of both statements, be it noted, Hostiensis cites the translation decretals of Innocent III. In his other great work, the *Summa aurea,* Hostiensis attempted a general definition of both the office and its powers, from which we can learn in what respect Innocent's translation canons enlarged the concept of papal plenitude of power:

> The pope is full vicar, for although every bishop can be called vicar of Jesus Christ, he, however, is a particular vicar; but the pope is vicar general, whence he conducts all business concerning all persons just as he pleases; he judges and disposes. *Plenus,* i.e. having plenitude of power, to which he is called, while the others are called to part of the responsibility. Therefore say in short that, provided he does not contravene the faith, he is able to do and say whatever he pleases in all matters and through all means, even declining to do justice to whom he will, because no one dare say to him, Why do you do this? And he can take away every right [*ius*] and he can lawfully dispense beyond the law [*supra ius*] because he acts on earth in place of the very God. Although he can do this, let him fear that he not sin.[124]

The two concepts, so tentatively joined by Saint Bernard a century earlier, are now fused into one: the *plenus vicarius Christi*. Yet Hostiensis appreciates the specific value of the texts that Innocent III provided in *Quanto personam* and *Inter corporalia,* both of which are his only authority for the statement "Quia veri Dei vicem gerit in terris": it is in virtue of this office that he can deprive persons of their rights and can grant extraordinary dispensations from the ordinary course of the law. In other words, the pope, like the emperor, is not bound by the letter of the law; he is *legibus solutus,* and the laws from which he is free are not ecclesiastical only but human law in general: hence Innocent's assertion that he was *supra ius*.[125] To be sure, before *Quanto personam* the pope had claimed the right to this extraordinary power or that, afterwards he had a large, generalized, and unspecified discretionary power to act above and beyond—but never contrary to—the law. This absolute prerogative power was indeed what *plenitudo potestatis* signified to the thirteenth century: "*plenitudo potestatis plenissima,*" in Hostiensis' apt phrase.[126] Before Innocent, one could say that the pope had full power without being able to specify how full it was. Innocent plumbed the depths of his power by proving that traditionally it included the capacity to do what only God could do.

Thereafter the vicar of Christ was omnicompetent in human government, though by no means omnipotent in every sense.[127]

Quanto personam, in sum, was the keystone in the Innocentian arch of *plenitudo potestatis*. Remove this proof of the pope's omnicompetent jurisdiction over human affairs, and the general definition of plenitude of power would disintegrate into its component parts. Discrete powers, authorized by the canons of the *Decretum*, would remain, as would the indefinite claim to govern the whole Church with whatever authority Peter had. The overarching, hierocratic claims of the thirteenth-century Decretalists would be reduced to the dualism of the twelfth-century Decretists.[128]

DANTE AND THE INNOCENTIAN ARGUMENT

It would seem, therefore, that Dante has led us to a crux in Latin ecclesiology. He did not, of course, see it in the historical perspective that we have taken in the foregoing excursus. For Dante the connections would be far simpler and more obvious. There can be no doubt that he saw the papal claim to be *vicarius Christi* as one of the most dangerous, for he twice attacks it in *De monarchia*, both times insisting that the Decretalists claimed too much power for the vicariate. In one case, which we have already discussed in connection with Francesco d'Accorso,[129] he argued that Samuel did not prefigure the papal vicariate in making and unmaking kings, because he acted with an ad hoc commission and not as God's vicar-general. The other argument is still more apposite. Dante, in *Monarchia* 3. 7, concedes that the pope is vicar of God but contends that his commission does not enable him to do whatever God can do. For God cannot make another equivalent to himself in all things, and "no vicariate, whether human or divine, can be equivalent to the authority from which it originates." This he proves by instances in which the pope clearly lacks divine power, one of which is especially relevant to the interpretation of *Inferno* xv: "To take one example, we know that Peter's successor does not enjoy divine authority in regard to the workings of nature; for he could not make the earth rise or fire descend by virtue of the office entrusted to him."[130]

Dante does not venture an opinion as to what spiritual or temporal powers are exercised by Peter's successor in virtue of his vicariate, yet he is positive that the pope cannot act contrary to the laws of nature. But it is just in that connection that he draws the leading case of the *potestas vicaria* to our attention. If the association is no mere coincidence, if indeed it could be shown that the pope did violence to nature by transferring a bishop, then it would follow that God did not delegate that specific power to him, much less the whole range of discretionary powers that the pope claimed to exercise *supra ius*. If the keystone proves to be unnatural, the whole superstructure of *plenitudo potestatis* will come tumbling down.

That much I think Dante could see clearly. We know he thought that the powers claimed for the vicar of Christ were excessive. If Dante sought the basis of those claims in the *Decretales*, he would inevitably be referred to the single fountainhead, *De translatione episcoporum* (X 1. 7). There he had but to read

Innocent's four decretals and judge for himself. We already know that by Dante's standards, the translation of bishops was contrary to the *documenta spiritualia*. We must now ask whether, as he read the Innocentian argument, Dante discovered that it was also contrary to nature. To reconstruct his reaction, we must rely on his own statements about the peculiar features of Innocent's argument, notably spiritual matrimony. Though scattered, their evidence is unambiguous. Since we have been long in coming to the point, let us collect them without further delay and recreate the Dantesque response.

Innocent's treatment of translation differed radically from that of Gratian and the Decretists in that he returned to the patristic conception of spiritual matrimony between the bishop and his church and insisted, as his immediate predecessors had not, that this constituted a bond indissoluble by man. Our first question accordingly must be whether Dante would agree that each bishop was the spouse of his church. The fact that the conception was based on Scripture and approved by the Fathers immediately suggests that it would find favor with Dante.[131] This suggestion could be greatly strengthened by a survey of the matrimonial images that occur in Dante's works, for they play an extensive and important part in his imagery. Such a study would doubtless be valuable in itself, but for our present purpose it would be an unnecessary excursus. All we need to know is what Dante thought about the bishop's marriage to his church, and to discover this we have only to examine several passages in the *Commedia*. The clearest of these indicate that Dante considered the bishop of Rome to be, while living, the husband of Holy Church. Since this can be firmly established, let us make it our point of departure, starting first with the strongest evidence and then passing on to less obvious indications that can confirm the basic position and can extend it to cover the case of the other bishops as well.

The Pope as Spouse

Purgatorio XIX contains the leading case. On entering the circle that purges avarice, Dante and Virgil encounter a shade lying prone on the pavement, bound hand and foot, who identifies himself as Pope Adrian V (1276). Particular stress is laid on his office, which he announces in a Latin verse: "*scias quod ego fui successor Petri*" ("know that I was a successor of Peter"; *Purg.* XIX, 99). While the late pope is explaining the circumstances of his repentance and the rationale of his punishment, the pilgrim decides that he should show proper respect to such a personage, with this result:

Io m'era inginocchiato e volea dire;
    ma com' io cominciai ed el s'accorse,
    solo ascoltando, del mio reverire,
"Qual cagion," disse, "in giù così ti torse?"
    E io a lui: "Per vostra dignitate
    mia coscïenza dritto mi rimorse."

[142]

"Drizza le gambe, lèvati sù, frate!"
    rispuose; "non errar: conservo sono
    teco e con li altri ad una podestate.
Se mai quel santo evangelico suono
    che dice '*Neque nubent*' intendesti,
    ben puoi veder perch' io così ragiono."

I had kneeled down, and was about to speak; but as I began, and he perceived my reverence merely by listening, "What reason," he said, "thus bent thee down?" And I to him: "Because of your dignity my conscience smote me for standing." "Make straight thy legs, uplift thee, brother," he answered: "err not, a fellow-servant [*conservo*] am I with thee and with the others unto one Power. If ever thou didst understand that hallowed gospel sound which saith, '*Neque nubent*,' well canst thou see why thus I speak."

(Purg. xix, 127–38)

These lines do not yield their full meaning at once. It is clear enough that Dante kneeled because he felt that it was not proper for him to stand in the presence of a pope; it is equally clear that he was mistaken. The reason for his error, however, is stated explicitly only in the most general way: no honor is due because Adrian and Dante are equals, both being fellow servants of the same Lord. For a more complete explanation, Adrian refers the pilgrim (and the reader) to the words "*Neque nubent*" ("they shall neither marry") in the Gospels. The phrase is found in three parallel passages of the Synoptic Gospels (Matt. 22:30, Mark 12:25, Luke 20:34). All three recount Jesus' response to the Sadducees' question concerning the resurrection: if a woman had seven husbands in this life, whose wife would she be in the next life? No one's, was the answer, "for in the resurrection they shall neither marry nor be married; but shall be as the angels of God in heaven" ("in resurrectione enim neque nubent, neque nubentur: sed erunt sicut angeli Dei in caelo").[132]

What Adrian wanted the pilgrim to understand, therefore, was that in the afterlife none of the blessed is party to a matrimonial relationship. Thus he drew a distinction between his status in life and in death. While living, he was pope and Dante would have been bound to reverence him as such; now that Adrian is dead, however, he is no longer pope but instead is Dante's equal, because as one of the elect he can no longer be married. Evidently the argument is founded on the assumption that a man is pope by virtue of a kind of spiritual matrimony. Although this assumption is implicit, it is none the less present, for if the papacy were not essentially matrimonial in nature, Adrian would still be a pope in Purgatory. Thus, indirectly Dante revealed his conviction that a man is made pope through spiritual matrimony.

If the pope is a *sponsus*, who is his *sponsa*? To many, perhaps most, of Dante's commentators, the answer seems simply to be "the Church." Dante himself says as much in *Purgatory* xxiv, 22, where Forese Donati points out the gluttonous Pope Martin IV and, to indicate what his office had been, states that he "had the Holy

Church in his arms" ("ebbe la Santa Chiesa in le sue braccia").[133] There can be no doubt that "Holy Church" without qualification can only mean the whole Christian community on earth—the Church Universal. The image intended is no less clear: Martin embraced her, that is, had her to wife. That would settle the matter, had not Dante also suggested in an earlier passage that the pope's spouse was the Roman church. The lines occur in the pilgrim's denunciation of papal simony, which he addressed to Nicholas III.

> Di voi pastor s'accorse il Vangelista,
>> quando colei che siede sopra l'acque
>> puttaneggiar coi regi a lui fu vista;
> quella che con le sette teste nacque,
>> e da le diece corna ebbe argomento,
>> fin che virtute al suo marito piacque.

You shepherds it was the Evangelist had in mind when she that sitteth upon the waters was seen by him committing fornication with the kings, she that was born with the seven heads and had her strength from the ten horns so long as her husband [*marito*] took pleasure in virtue.[134]

(Inf. xix, 106–11)

Not a few commentators have assumed that this whorish wife of unvirtuous popes must represent the Church that has been corrupted,[135] but there are strong indications that she must be understood more precisely as the Roman church. John says that the woman he saw "is the great city, which hath kingdom over the kings of the earth" (Apoc. 17:18). This city he calls "Babylon," but evidently he alludes to Rome. Moreover, he is told by an angel that the waters on which the woman is seated "are peoples, and nations, and tongues" (Apoc. 17:15). Since the Universal Church includes its members, obviously she cannot be said to make them her throne; this can better be said of that part of the Church that rules the rest.[136] Accordingly, Pietro di Dante identified the woman as "the government of the Church" (*"gubernatio Ecclesiae"*), and Guido da Pisa expressed the same idea in significantly different terms: for him she is *"romana Ecclesia, idest prelati Ecclesie."*[137] This more restricted view of the meretricious woman of *Inferno* xix has been developed by Charles Davis, who concludes that Dante, under the influence of Joachite-Franciscan exegesis, transformed John's symbol of pagan Rome into a representation of papal Rome.[138]

Dante, therefore, seems to say in one place that the pope is married to the Universal Church and in another that his spouse is the Christian city of Rome. This is not to say that he contradicts himself, however, for in medieval usage the two statements are compatible. The apparent contradiction can be resolved because both cases can be comprehended in a single, albeit ambiguous, term by saying that the pope is married to "the Roman church." In one sense *Romana ecclesia* refers to the local church of the city of Rome; in another, wider sense it also can signify the whole community of the faithful who are subject to, and in communion with, the local Roman church.[139] Dante's contemporaries usually spoke of the pope as the *sponsus* in the latter, universal sense,[140] although the theorists recognized that his marriage to the local Roman church was more fundamental, because "the papal-Petrine powers are embodied in the Roman church, and it is by becoming bishop of Rome, by his spiritual marriage to the church in which his office consists, that each succeeding pope acquires them."[141] Since Dante's contemporaries understood that the pope could be married to the Roman church both in its local and in its universal sense, we can reconcile the apparently divergent statements of *Inferno* xix, 106–11, and *Purgatorio* xxiv, 22: the former refers to the local Roman church and the latter to the universal Roman church. Who then would Dante say was the pope's *sponsa*? One phrase could cover both cases that he recognized—"the Roman church."[142]

The Bishop as Spouse

This inquiry into the pope's matrimonial relation to his church may seem to be beside the point, for we are chiefly interested in learning whether Dante accepted Innocent III's major premise in *Quanto personam*, namely, that a bishop is spiritually married to his church. It is, in fact, the most direct approach, because Dante does not apply the matrimonial metaphor to any bishop other than the pope. This is enough, however, since the case of one bishop can stand for all the rest. The crux of our inquiry, then, has been to determine that in Dante's view the pope as bishop of Rome was married to his local church. Once that is clear, it follows that all other bishops must similarly be the husbands of their local churches.

The correctness of this conclusion can be verified by Dante's one generalization about spiritual matrimony. In the narrator's apostrophe that introduces the canto of the simoniacs, the poet applied the sponsal figure to all "the things of God" without qualification:

> O Simon mago, o miseri seguaci
>   che le cose di Dio, che di bontate
>   deon essere spose, e voi rapaci
> per oro e per argento avolterate, . . .

(*Inf.* xix, 1–4)

> Ah, Simon Magus, and you his wretched followers, who, rapacious, prostitute for gold and silver the things of God which should be brides of righteousness.

It is important to remember that these words are not spoken in the obscurity of Hell but rather were written by the enlightened poet after his journey. They are placed in a position of prominence at the head of a canto, and are further commended to our attention by the fact that no other canto of the *Inferno* opens with an apostrophe. The passage is commonly understood to mean that ecclesiastical offices and spiritual goods ought to be bestowed freely on those who are good, not sold to whoever can pay for them.[143] The reference to Simon Magus suggests that the passage applies particularly to bishops, since Simon sinned by wishing to purchase the *potestas* of imparting the Holy Spirit by the imposition of hands, which the Apostles alone possessed[144] and which is traditionally identified as the bishop's power to administer the sacrament of confirmation. This suggestion is strengthened later in the canto when the pilgrim reminds the simoniac Nicholas III that neither Peter nor the other Apostles took money from Matthias when he was chosen "for the place" (*"al loco"*) among the Twelve that was vacated by the death of Judas.[145]

The passage, then, not only includes bishops within its wide scope but also appears to have special reference to them. The primary message of these lines is that God's stewards on earth ought to be men who are good, but by expressing this in sponsal terms, the poet also conveys a secondary message, which for our present purpose is more important, namely, that all of God's officers are joined to their office in spiritual matrimony. For Dante, such officials certainly include emperors and kings,[146] who have charge of the temporal things of God, as well as popes and bishops, to whom the care of things spiritual is committed. Hence our earlier conclusion stands confirmed: the episcopate, in Dante's view, was a form of spiritual matrimony.

Popes Violate Nature by Transferring Bishops

Now it is clear that Dante had no quarrel with the fundamental assumption of Innocent's last three translation decretals (X 1. 7. 2–4), namely, that bishops were married to their churches. If he objected to Innocent III's argument, it had to be on other grounds. Since Dante agreed with Innocent that the bishop is bound to his church by spiritual matrimony, we must next inquire whether the poet also would have assented to the pope's claim that he, as vicar of Christ, had the power to dissolve that bond.

Dante's answer was positively and emphatically—No! Indeed, divorce was his leading example of an act that the pope was by no means able to perform. To refute those who maintained that "Peter's successor can bind and loose *all* things" (*Mon.* 3. 8. 3), Dante argued that there are *some* things that even the pope cannot do. If Christ had conferred on Peter the power to loose and bind all things whatsoever,

> then my adversaries' statement would be correct; not only would he be able to do the things they claim, he would also be able to loose a woman from her marriage to one man and bind her in marriage to another whilst the first was still alive; and this is quite impossible for him.

> verum esset quod dicunt; et non solum hoc facere posset, quin etiam solvere uxorem a viro et ligare ipsam alteri vivente primo: quod nullo modo potest.
>
> (*Mon.* 3. 8. 7)

Since Dante flatly denied that the pope could dissolve the bond of carnal matrimony, obviously he would reject the argument of Innocent's decretal *Quanto personam*, which was based on that assumption.

Dante does not explain why the pope could not release a wife from one marriage and bind her in another while her first husband lived. The most obvious reason is that Dante maintained that the authority of Scripture is superior to that of a pope (*Mon.* 3. 3. 11–16), and hence the pope, like any other man, would be bound by Christ's prohibition of divorce (Matt. 19:6 and Mark 10:9). To this I would add another reason, namely that the marital connection lies in the realm of nature, outside the jurisdiction of the Church, and especially of the papacy.

This follows from Dante's conception of the relation of the Church to nature, which he expounded in *Monarchia* 3. 13–14. There, of course, his principal concern is to prove that temporal authority cannot be derived from the Church; and he argues, first, that the Church has never possessed temporal power and therefore could not confer what it did not possess (*Mon.* 3. 13. 6) and, second, that "the power of conferring temporal authority is contrary to the nature of the Church" (*Mon.* 3. 14. 9). From the first argument we learn that the Church is not an effect of nature but of grace, as it was produced directly by God: "Ecclesia non sit effectus nature, sed Dei" (*Mon.* 3. 13. 3). From the second we further discover that the rule (*regnum*) of our mortality is contrary to the nature of the Church: "therefore it is not to be numbered among its powers."[147] Essentially, this proposition is proved by Christ's dictum, "My kingdom is not of this world," which Dante explicates:

> Which must not be taken to mean that Christ, who is God, is not lord of this kingdom [*regnum*], because the Psalmist says, "For the sea is His, and He made it, and His hands established the dry land." Rather it means that, as the model of the Church, He took no care for this kingdom.[148]

For Dante, the form or nature of the Church is the life of Christ; hence he set an example for the Church by his conduct, which constitutes a divine categorical imperative. Above all, the point to retain from this is that the Church has no authority in the "*regnum nostre mortalitatis*." This is another way of saying that Peter's keys can open and close only the doors of the kingdom of heaven; they have no authority over us while we live.[149]

Since this is the case, we have only to determine whether episcopal translation falls under the authority of the kingdom of this world or of the next. Pope Adrian has already given us the answer when he taught the reader that the bishop's spiritual marriage with his church is terminated by death. The *Neque nubent* verses of the Gospel, which he cited, leave no room for doubt: humans are married in their earthly life but not in the life to come. Consequently the Church, to which the care for our immortal life has been entrusted, has jurisdiction over the matrimonial relationship only insofar as the matter affects our status in the afterlife. Because Christ said "my kingdom is not of this world," Dante could conclude that the pope, Christ's vicar on earth, was not empowered to sever a matrimonial relation that existed only in "the realm of our mortality." Normally, God entrusted jurisdiction in this "*regnum nostre mortalitatis*" to the secular authorities, and above all to the emperor, who was God's supreme vicar in this realm of nature. According to Dante, the imperial vicariate, as we already know, included the external forum of canon law. Insofar as the canons govern the welfare of man in this world, they lie under the jurisdiction of the emperor. Only cases of conscience, which pertain to the eternal salvation of one individual, fall within the papal sphere of competence.[150] Divorce, however, was an exception. According to Scripture, God had reserved that right to himself and forbade any man to exercise it (Matt. 19:6, Mark 10:9). Consequently, the emperor, to whose rule of this world divorce would ordinarily pertain, had this particular power excluded from his jurisdiction by revelation. Although the pope was the vicar of Christ, he was not authorized to exercise the right of divorce that was reserved to God, because papal jurisdiction was limited to the internal forum of conscience and was excluded from the realm of nature, that of our mortality, which is the only realm in which human marriage exists.[151]

To have two autonomous jurisdictions over the affairs of this world would—and historically did—create jurisdictional disputes. According to Dante's political philosophy, nature dictates that in the interests of man's earthly welfare, all temporal jurisdiction must be subject to a single authority, the monarchical imperium. The imperial claim to jurisdiction in the external forum was not Dante's invention, for Justinian's *Corpus* more than justified such an opinion. As early as A.D. 380, the imperial Edict of Thessalonica declared that violations of divine law were punishable as sacrilege by the secular courts,[152] and the *Glossa ordinaria* explained that one offended the divine law by erring in the articles of faith. When issued, this may have been largely limited to disobedience to the law of the Gospel,[153] but the definition of divine law was expressly extended by Justinian to include the first four ecumenical councils, whose statutes were all decreed to be equivalent to Holy Scripture and likewise to have the force of civil law.[154] Moreover, these enactments proceeded from the imperial conviction, best expressed in prefaces to Justinian's constitutions, that the emperor has been entrusted by God with the care (*sollicitudo*) of Christian dogma and clerical discipline.[155] Thus, once again we find that Dante's convictions on imperial jurisdiction are rooted in Roman law.

Hence, in Dante's view the natural order is violated when the papacy assumes for itself the supreme jurisdiction in the external forum, for that belongs to the emperor alone among men. To be sure, the translation of bishops also violates the divine law revealed in the Nicene canon, for even the emperor cannot licitly transgress the laws committed to his care.[156] Therefore the papal claim that bishops could be transferred "by license and authority of the Apostolic See" usurped the prerogatives of both God and the emperor, which were established respectively by divine and natural law. Since this compound of violence to God and nature is precisely the sin of the runners, we can at last be sure that Mozzi's translation was itself an offense proper to the place in which it is mentioned.

The emperor does not enjoy all the rights of his principal, however, and so Innocent's claim that he has the right to dissolve the bonds of matrimony is not a real threat to imperial jurisdiction. Nonetheless it is an actual invasion of the realm of nature, from which the pope is altogether excluded as an authority. The pretension is all the more egregious because it wounds the divine majesty of the *Imperadore del cielo*,[157] for it is God's prerogative that Innocent would usurp.

[148]

THE ROOT OF ALL EVIL

At long last we can see clearly that a pope who translates a bishop does indeed commit an act of violence against nature and her God. The offense is entirely proper to the theme of *Inferno* xv. This crime of violence, which at first appeared to be a relatively minor case of the arbitrary exercise of administrative authority, now stands revealed as the most perverse of all the acts for which the runners were condemned. Its gravity within the scheme of the *Comedy* can best be comprehended from the discourse of Marco Lombardo, which is the parallel in *Purgatory* to this section. The pilgrim asks Marco to explain to him what the *cause* is of the wickedness of the world in Dante's day,[158] and Lombardo replies in a long and famous speech (*Purg.* xvi, 64-129) that discovers the root of all the evils of the age to be the avarice of the papacy. In particular, the church of Rome has usurped the function of temporal government, and therefore it corrupts both itself and the world it misgoverns:

> Dì oggimai che la Chiesa di Roma,
> per confondere in sé due reggimenti,
> cade nel fango, e sé brutta e la soma.
>
> (*Purg.* xvi, 128-30)

Though Marco has much more to say, this is his essential point: the prime perversion that has disrupted the natural order of society is none other than the hierocratic policy of the papacy. And it is precisely to this first cause that the theme of episcopal translation has led us.

The connection would not be evident to one who was unfamiliar with the *Decretales,* but once they are read with the criteria posited in *Monarchia* 3. 3 (see above, pp. 118-22), the conclusions are unmistakable. Episcopal translation in itself was forbidden by every authoritative source: by Holy Scripture, by the principal councils—which the civil law expressly undertook to uphold—and by the Latin Fathers. Further, Dante's philosophy and theology combine to forbid any ecclesiastical authority from acting as translator, since the Church has no jurisdiction in this world. Thus Dante might justly have said that translating popes "transgress the bounds of their own territories and come rioting within other people's settlements."[159]

Taken in itself, then, episcopal translation exemplifies the illegitimate claims made for the papacy by the *decretalistae*. It is far more than an example, however: it is the keystone of the hierocratic doctrine. Once the illegality of translations is recognized, it can no longer be demonstrated that the pope has power to do what only God can do. The papal vicariate shrinks to human size: there is no reason to believe that the vicar of Christ received anything save the keys of the Kingdom, which confer on him no power over things in this world. The plenitude of power can no longer be defined as more than the sum of the pope's canonical powers, which can further be pared away in detail by Dante's Razor—the criteria of *Monarchia* 3. 3. Thus *plenitudo potestatis* loses its character of being a discretionary power to act in God's stead above and beyond the law. In short, with the loss of his *ius transferendi*, the pope has been deprived of his suppositious warrant to interfere in the government of Church and state in this world. Hence the temporal involvement of the papacy, to which Marco Lombardo traced the troubles of his time, has no justification; to the contrary, it is plainly unnatural and simply unjust.

To this conclusion the reader has been drawn by the hint that translation of bishops might violate nature. If the reader is able to establish the connection between translation and contranatural violence, he will come thereby to comprehend the most perverse doctrine of the age. The root of all evil will be in his grasp, and since knowledge is power, it can then be eradicated. To effect this discovery is surely the main function of the translation theme in *Inferno* xv. Hence, the stress fell not on the offender but on the offense. Nonetheless, the offense cannot exist without an offender, since soulless ideas obviously cannot in themselves be condemned to perdition, however false they may be. The culprit must be a person, and to judge from our earlier experience, in this canto that person will represent a learned profession. In the present case, the profession is more readily determined than the individual, since Dante leaves no doubt about what profession fabricated false doctrines from papal decretals—certainly the *decretalistae*. Some of them, we may be sure, have been condemned to Brunetto's band, though we must wonder why no great canonist is identified by name as one of the runners. Surely it was no oversight; rather, since the poet seems rarely if ever to have been obscure without good reason, we may suspect that this too has its significance. Clearly he urges the reader to seek the culprit among the known characters of the canto, and the search need not be long, for one of them we know to have been a Decretalist.

MOZZI AND THE SERMON ON THE MOUNT

Up to now we have taken Andrea de' Mozzi to be the type of the perverted pastor, his profession being the clergy; but now a neglected detail of his biography assumes new significance, for Andrea was a canonist by training, and his career was made practicing this profession in the service of the papacy.[160]

Evidently Mozzi had not one profession but two—one to which he was false, and another to which he was true. But as no man can serve two masters, his devotion to a canonistic career was the cause of his pastoral failure.

"Nemo potest duobus dominis servire!" The words of the Sermon on the Mount describe his conflict of loyalties so appositely that we may wonder whether Dante had them in mind. On a hunch, let us consult the Vulgate version of the familiar words of the Gospel according to Matthew, beginning with the first contrast between spiritual and temporal care:

> Nolite thesaurizare vobis thesauros in terra, ubi aerugo, et tinea demolitur,
> et ubi fures effodiunt, et furantur. Thesaurizate autem vobis thesauros in

caelo, ubi neque aerugo, neque tinea demolitur, et ubi fures non effodiunt nec furantur.[161]

(Matt. 6:19–20)

A familiar word springs from the context to greet the reader who in the preceding chapter weighed with me the several senses of the epithet *tigna*: here is its Latin parent word, *tinea*, used in its primitive sense to denote the destructive moth.[162] Once detected, the allusion to the Vulgate reveals the poet's own view of Andrea, as distinct from that he attributed to Brunetto. Mozzi the Moth is a living figure of the corrosive effects of temporal concerns upon the clergy, who profess an exclusive devotion to the spiritual welfare of mankind. As he comments on canonists and false clergymen, the poet bids us to read the Sermon on the Mount: "For where thy treasure is, there is thy heart also."[163]

The antinomy of the treasures applies to any Christian, but the next contrast has a special application to the bishop, the "overseer" or eye of the church:[164] "The light of thy body is thy eye. If thy eye be single, thy whole body shall be lightsome. But if thy eye be evil thy whole body shall be darksome. If then the light that is in thee, be darkness: the darkness itself how great shall it be!"[165] And what blinds the bishop but avarice? The text continues with the maxim that we have already applied to Mozzi's professional ambivalence: "No man can serve two masters. For either he will hate the one, and love the other: or he will sustain the one, and despise the other. You cannot serve God and mammon."[166] The last sentence applies to all who would follow the spiritual way of Christ, but more especially to their leaders—the bishops—and, above all, to the vicar of Christ, whose function in the Danteque cosmos is to lead mankind as a whole to salvation.[167]

There follow the injunctions to live in apostolic poverty, which no incumbent of the Apostolic see exemplified in Dante's day, save only Celestine V. God feeds the birds of the air and clothes the lilies of the field: how much more will he not provide for you, "O ye of little faith."[168] Among those *modicae fidei*, do we not recognize our bishop, whose name in Latin is Andreas *de Modiis*?[169] Certainly he had no faith that God would provide for the church of Florence, but rather Mozzi was as solicitous for the morrow as any of the heathen *(gentes)*, despite his Lord's express command:

> Be not solicitous therefore, saying, What shall we eat: or what shall we drink, or wherewith shall we be clothed? For after all these things do the heathens seek. For your Father knoweth that you have need of all these things. Seek ye therefore first the kingdom of God, and his justice, and all these things shall be added unto you. Be not therefore solicitous for to morrow; for the morrow will be solicitous for itself. Sufficient for the day is the evil thereof.

(Matt. 6:31–34)

It would be tedious to exhibit every application of the sermon to worldly prelates and popes, but a few further allusions will show the possibilities. Spiritual leaders should not judge, lest they be judged by their own standards; they should look

[151]

first to their own great failings (Matt. 7:1–5). To describe the false shepherds, we find Christ using the original of the *pastore-lupo* theme: "Beware of false prophets, who come to you in the clothing of sheep, but inwardly they are ravening wolves. By their fruits you shall know them."[170] "A fructibus eorum cognoscetis eos": this is the essence of Dante's message. Rather than denounce the false spiritual leaders, he leads us to this passage and, out of reverence for their office, leaves us to decide whether by Christ's standards the labors of Mozzi and his kind have yielded good fruit or evil.[171] Nor are we left in any doubt as to the fate of the false shepherd: "Every tree that bringeth not forth good fruit, shall be cut down, and shall be cast into the fire."[172] Jesus leaves nothing to the imagination; vividly he anticipates the Last Judgment:

> Not every one that saith to me, Lord, Lord, shall enter into the kingdom of heaven: but he that doth the will of my Father who is in heaven, he shall enter into the kingdom of heaven. Many will say to me in that day: Lord, Lord, have not we prophesied in thy name, and cast out devils in thy name, and done many miracles in thy name? And then will I profess unto them, I never knew you: depart from me, you that work iniquity.
>
> (Matt. 7:21–23)

Then the finale, vibrant with the ecclesiological overtones of the *petra-arena* dichotomy:

> Every one therefore that heareth these my words, and doth them, shall be likened to a wise man that built his house upon a rock [viro sapienti, qui aedificavit domum suam supra petram] and the rain fell, and the floods came, and the winds blew, and they beat upon that house, and it fell not, for it was founded on a rock [fundata enim erat super *petram*]. And every one that heareth these my words, and doth them not, shall be like a foolish man that built his house upon the sand, and the rain fell, and the floods came, and the winds blew, and they beat upon that house, and it fell, and great was the fall thereof. [Et omnis, qui audit verba mea haec, et non facit ea, similis erit viro *stulto*, qui aedificavit domum suam super *arenam*: et descendit pluvia, et venerunt flumina, et flaverunt venti, et irruerunt in domum illam, et cecidit, et fuit ruina illius magna.]
>
> (Matt. 7:24–27)

Dante did not accept the Petrine interpretation that many of his contemporaries placed upon this passage. Thus in the *Monarchy* he wrote: "For the Church's foundation is Christ; hence the Apostle's words to the Corinthians: 'Other foundation can no man lay than that is laid, which is Christ Jesus.' He is himself the rock on which the Church is built."[173] Since Dante took the rock to be a figure of Christ, the wise man of the Sermon on the Mount would be one who built on Christ, in this case by taking his words as literally as they were intended. Opposed to the wise man *(vir sapiens)* is the foolish man—*vir stultus*—who built on sand: his life is founded on false doctrine. Dante exemplified him in a man who was known by his fruits to be a fool; that man's folly he reflected in an appropriate punishment, for Mozzi and his companions run ceaselessly over burning *sand*.[174]

Since Andrea de' Mozzi typifies the villain of the Sermon on the Mount, we can collect its contrasts and construct composite portraits of Dante's true and false *cherci*. The true clergyman confines himself to the spiritual world. He is altogether otherworldly, literally taking no thought for the morrow but rather placing his trust wholly in divine providence. He conforms his will to that of God, and most especially lives in apostolic poverty according to the teaching of Christ. False *cherci* do just the opposite. Laying up treasures on earth, they serve Mammon and trust that he, not God, is their best provider for the morrow. Their orientation is temporal, not spiritual: in a word, they are worldly. The faithful need not fear these wolves in sheep's clothing, for they betray themselves by failing to live in Christlike poverty; instead they regulate their lives by contrary principles that are false to the teaching of Christ, and they shall be rewarded accordingly.

Dante's contemporaries would recognize this as a variation on the theme that had been made familiar by the controversy within the Franciscan order as to whether the friars were bound to live like Francis, who had avidly pursued poverty no less than the other precepts of the Sermon on the Mount. Dante, however, went much further, if only by implication, for he took the Sermon on the Mount to be the canon or rule of life for all "who profess and call themselves Christians." Still, not all Christians profess Christ in the same degree, for some bind themselves to follow Christ's example more closely than others. These are the clergy in general, for whom Christian leadership is a profession, and more particularly the bishops, but most especially the pope. This ideal is reflected in the prayer for bishops that was composed in Dante's lifetime by Mozzi's one-time colleague—one might almost say alter ego—the elder William Durandus:

> Deus omnium fidelium pastor et rector, hunc famulum tuum quem ecclesie tue preesse voluisti, propitius respice, da ei, quesumus, verbo et exemplo quibus preest proficere, ut ad vitam una cum grege sibi credito perveniat sempiternam. Per Christum . . . Amen.[175]

Christ's life and doctrine, then, was for Dante the clergy's professional ethic. Chiefly, they are bound to observe the precepts of the Sermon on the Mount. This will be seen to be a corollary of the Dantesque doctrine of the two beatitudes.[176] All temporal jurisdiction is vested in the emperor, who guides mankind to its earthly happiness. This jurisdiction we already know includes not only civil law but canon law as well,[177] while the pope's authority is limited to the internal *forum conscientiae*.[178]

We now are in a position to grasp Dante's conception of papal authority in more positive terms. As the spiritual guide of mankind, the pope leads man to eternal life by word and deed (*verbo et exemplo*), which for Dante means that he preaches Christ's Gospel and, moreover, that he leads the spiritual life to which he exhorts others. In two key words, the pope can be said to be dedicated to a life of *preaching* and *poverty*. In this world, the ideal pope is an authentic exemplar of Christ's life and doctrine, and in this alone his earthly authority consists. To be sure, he does have the power of the keys; this, however, does not pertain to this

world but to the kingdom of Heaven. Precisely, it is the power of the spiritual direc-
tor, acting typically in the confessional, to absolve sinners authoritatively. Thus it
appears that Dante pressed his distinction between the realms of nature and of
grace to its logical conclusion: a radical rejection of the Church's claims to temporal
authority. Dante in this respect now appears not so dissimilar to Marsiglio of Padua
as some have thought.[179]

What need has such a spiritual pope for canon lawyers? His judgments are
delivered in the confessional. The laws he gives to mankind are those of Christ,
which he makes only in the Kantian sense that, by acting as he would have all men
act, he legislates for all men. Thus, to Dante the whole system of papal law that
was founded on the *decretales* appeared to proceed from a misconception of the
pope's office, and indeed of the Church itself.

This is the point we can at last make clearly: The Decretalists, for Dante, constitute a pseudo profession. They are false prophets who have erected for the Church
a legal system that is contrary to her spiritual nature. The temporal authority that
they impute to ecclesiastical officers, whose powers can only be spiritual, must
perforce be power usurped. In the eyes of Dante's God, their true profession is the
clergy, but this they neglect for the false one that they have created for themselves.
Since no man can serve two masters, they profess to serve God but instead serve the
decretals. In the poem, Mozzi, as both Decretalist and bishop, exemplies the illegitimate as well as the perverted profession.

Who, then, are the clerics condemned to run with Brunetto's band? not mere
parish priests, but rather their mis-leaders, the worldly bishops, with their myopic
guides, the Decretalists, who together impersonate ecclesiastical *auctoritas*. It is
Brunetto's definition that excludes the lesser clergy from the company of the *cherci*,
all of whom we know to be not only clerks but also great literati and men of great
fame.[180] The one sin that unites this band, "d'un peccato medesmo al mondo lerci"
(*Inf.* xv, 108), simply is that they have all transgressed the natural limits of their
professions. All are members of professions entrusted with the care of one form of
divine law or another.[181] Of such callings, the Christian ministry is the highest, but
for Dante not essentially different from the others. Hence all are punished together.

Mozzi, then, is Dante's figure of the Decretalist-prelate. By the prevalent
standard of his age, Mozzi was not remarkable except perhaps in his penchant for
preaching, however ineptly. Both as canonist and as bishop, his career was otherwise
altogether ordinary. Just because he was typical rather than outstanding, Dante
could condemn in Mozzi all Decretalist-prelates as a class. Had a great canonist
been named, such as Huguccio, Hostiensis, or either of the Innocents, the criticism
would seem to be directed against some doctrine that was peculiar to the man.
Instead, Dante wished to condemn the *decretalistae* in general, just as he treated
them as a body in *Monarchia* 3. 3 without singling out any particular member. For
this purpose, Mozzi was a better figure than any distinguished member of his
profession. As a competent Decretalist and little else, his scandalous episcopate exemplified Dante's fundamental point: good Decretalists made bad bishops.

AN ALTERNATE ROUTE

This essay has, for the most part, proceeded along historical lines. In conclusion, let us return to the analytic approach with which it began[182] and reconsider a clue that passed unobserved. At the time it would doubtless have seemed idle speculation to pursue it, but now that our problem has been resolved by more conventional means, we can indulge our intuition, discover a shortcut to the solution, and gain thereby both deeper insight into the poet's meaning and keener appreciation of his methods.

Our first impression of *Inferno* xv, 109–14, was that it posed a riddle, which with the aid of the most general knowledge we determined to be: What bishop was transferred by a pope from Florence to Vicenza? This much we could assume that any contemporary reader could have reasoned out for himself, as indeed the earliest commentators did. Now it should be observed that by asking this question, the poet artfully structured our approach to the passage. Everyone who would understand it must first solve the riddle, the answer to which is nothing more than the bishop's name. In other passages, one may well wonder which of many clues to follow first, but here there can be no doubt whatsoever. One must begin by discovering the name of that bishop of Florence. The poet thus ensured that our first step would be in the right direction.

The next step Dante left to the reader. What should we do with the name *Andreas episcopus Florentinus* once we have hit upon it? Few if any have considered that question; instead, most if not all have taken the obvious path of biography, seeking, as we did, to ferret out a suitable sin in the life of Andrea de' Mozzi. But wait! Could it be that his name is significant *in itself*? Could the poet's intention be divined by a contemporary Florentine who simply reflected on this bishop's name and nothing more? It would not, of course, have for him all the biographical connotations that we have laboriously retrieved, but at least he would know the family background and the tales of ludicrous preaching. Beyond this, are there any associations that an early trecento Florentine could make with the scanty information to be derived from the riddle and its answer?

The discovery that this bishop of Florence was named Andrea would surely cause a native reader to recollect that yet another bishop of Florence had once borne the same name, and Florence's first Bishop Andrew was as saintly as Mozzi was sinful. That contrast is at once apparent: two bishops of Florence, both named Andrea, one in Hell and the other revered as a saint. Since both are bishops, the interpreter can infer that Mozzi's sin relates to his episcopacy. To discover the nature of the sin with this clue, one can omit all biographical considerations except folklore and pass directly to the *Regula pastoralis*. Thus far the line of reasoning parallels for the most part our course in chapter 4; the shortcut avoids the subsequent technical discussion of translation and leads one directly to the same conclusion.

This alternate route begins with the vita of Sant' Andrea, to which one would naturally turn, since the fault of the perverse pastor, once known, immediately invites comparison with the virtues of his sainted predecessor. The task is light, for the saint's legend consists of but a single brief episode. Successor to Saint

Zenobius,[183] Andreas was pastor of the Florentine flock during the unsettled years of the *Völkerwanderungen* early in the fifth century. In the year 405, when a barbarian army under Radagaisus threatened Florence,[184] Bishop Andreas feared that the remains of Saint Zenobius would not be safe, and having consulted with the clergy and people, he determined to move the saint from an outlying church into the cathedral. The relics proved recalcitrant, however, and the reliquary refused to enter the cathedral until the bishop dropped to his knees at the head of the waiting procession and prayed for divine assent.[185]

What, then, is the sole recorded act of the holy bishop Andreas? Nothing more than a relocation of relics, or to give the act its proper technical name, a *translatio*; and since the remains were those of a bishop, it was neither more nor less than a *translatio episcopi*! In this case, however, Bishop Andrew is the agent rather than the patient. We have already encountered a similar reversal of roles in the application of Gregory's metaphor of the cithara to Mozzi,[186] and it would now appear that both inversions were contrived by the poet for ironic effect.

Does the discovery of this antitype to Mozzi's translation put that event in a new perspective? In the translation of Saint Zenobius, the agent is not the pope but the bishop of the place: hence, it is an exclusively diocesan drama. Moreover, the bishop did not act arbitrarily on his own authority but rather consulted his clergy and people; even more, their human authority proved insufficient, so in the end the translation could only be accomplished after Andreas had secured the consent of God Himself. Significantly, the role of the agent, Saint Andreas, is reduced in the legend to that of an intercessor. The shepherd by himself or in agreement with his flock has no authority over the things of this world, for the body of Saint Zenobius belongs to the realm of our mortality, whereas the bishop is God's vicar only *in spiritualibus*. In short, Andreas, like all bishops, was restricted to moral leadership in the supernatural sphere. When his plans are blocked, it is a sign from heaven that he had attempted to exceed his authority. Humble rather than obstinate, the saint swiftly perceives his error and rectifies the situation by reverting to his proper function: interceding, he at last does what is within his competence, namely to pray God that His Will be done on earth.

The quality that differentiates the latter-day bishop from his sainted namesake is simply self-will. The earlier Andrew was capable of error, but he did not persist in the face of divine displeasure. If Mozzi had received the laughter of his congregation with humility and had pondered the cause, he should have discovered his own inadequacies and acted thereafter within his limitations. At the least, he would have preached according to Gregory's prescriptions, and a thorough consideration of the *Regula pastoralis* should have convinced him that basically he was altogether unsuited for episcopal office and that he ought to resign. Instead, he persisted and, as a result, was himself translated.

Mozzi's translation, then, was the consequence of his sin. In the *Comedy*, his life is compressed into this single symbolic event, as if to invite comparison with the only recorded act of Sant' Andrea. The glimpse of the primitive Florentine church afforded by the single known deed of Sant' Andrea stands in evident antithesis to the perverted pastorate of Andrea de' Mozzi. So dissimilar are the two events, that the contrasts far exceed the few points of contact. In both cases a bishop of Florence is translated, and a bishop Andrea is responsible. Beyond that, one can only contrast the two cases, and the points of opposition are numerous and various.

Of the bishops translated, one is a dead saint and the other a living sinner; the first enters Florence in honor, the other is ejected in disgrace. One comes to safety with honor; the other goes dishonored to his death. The former case is purely a diocesan affair, whereas the latter from first to last involves the Roman curia, where Mozzi made his career, in consequence of which he was an acceptable candidate for the Florentine see; later he returned to Rome while quarreling with his clergy and was at last transferred by the Roman *servo de' servi*.

Mozzi's translation was determined secretly in consultation with his influential relative, while the saint's removal was decided in public consultation with the clergy and people of Florence. On the one hand, Saint Zenobius was translated by another bishop, his successor and equal, who could act only after divine sanction had been expressly given; on the other, Mozzi was transferred by his superior, a pope and indeed a pseudo pope, who acted in this contrary to the canons.

Both translations were arbitrary human acts that were contrary to the will of God. In Mozzi's case, God's will in the matter had been manifest for centuries in Scripture and the conciliar canons; in Saint Zenobius' case, God's will was at first hidden but was respected as soon as it was revealed through the miraculous resistance of the relics. Boniface, the translator in Mozzi's case, acted without consulting either clergy or people, much less their interest, and he acted in the false confidence that God would acquiesce in the decisions of his vicar.

In a flight of fancy, one might imagine the two translations on the exterior panels of a diptych painted in the manner of Hieronymus Bosch. The first panel would be a conventional representation of the translation of Saint Zenobius. To the amazement of clergy and people, the procession is halted at the doors of the church, because the reliquary will move no farther; but Saint Andreas has already dropped to his knees and is interceding with a contrite heart. In contrast to this serene panel would stand the other, set on the same scene but painted now in lurid hues. As the gouty bishop leaves his church forever, the papal bull of translation in hand, he is mocked by spiteful clerics and jeered by a populace depraved for want of spiritual leadership; but Mozzi is obstinate and unrepentant to the end.

When such a diptych is opened, the outer Florentine scenes are found to have their parallels in the Roman church. One inner panel depicts Saint Peter bearing the keys at the gates of Heaven, where he admits the worthy and refuses the impenitent. The serenity of this scene contrasts with the lurid pandemonium of the other, in which another *claviger* attempts to rule the earth with Peter's keys. Boniface VIII himself dominates this disordered composition. Behind him flies the banner of the Keys, as his soldiers massacre Palestrina and he absolves Guido da Montefeltro with the golden key of *potestas*, while on the ground the silver key of *scientia* lies neglected. In its stead, Boniface holds a third, counterfeit key, with which he has already forced the lock of an imperial treasure chest. Looking closely at this false key, one perceives it to be a brazen devil whose tail is coiled into a grotesque simulacrum of the interlaced symbol of the Trinity. With this monster key the pseudo pope is even now unloosing the bonds of wedlock between a bishop and his church.

[6]

The Swift and the Strong

The weary though benevolent reader may be thankful that Brunetto named but three companions; as he observed, "de li altri fia laudabile tacerci, / ché 'l tempo saria corto a tanto suono" (*Inf.* xv, 104–5). To consider still more offenders would indeed be a proof by exhaustion, but the cases of the four *literati* have more than justified our efforts. Every one has been found to have violated the principles of his profession, perverting it and, with it, the leadership of society. By examining them in the order that the poet presented them in, we have let Dante program our investigation; and it was well we did so, since in retrospect it is evident that they were ordered according to their complexity, or rather their obscurity.

The sin of Brunetto Latini was relatively easy to hit upon, because the insubordination of Florence to the empire is one of Dante's clearest complaints. Repeatedly he expounded their proper relationship; moreover in the *Convivio* he wrote at length on the function of philosophy in the government of the empire. The case of Priscian was more difficult because our knowledge of Dante's linguistic theory is fragmentary, but still Dante's ideal reader could grasp the general sense from the contrast between Priscian and Donatus, both authors being familiar to all *literati*. The damnation of Francesco d'Accorso required a far greater knowledge of particulars, though it could be approached either through biography and local history or through his *arenga*. The fame of Francesco made his case less obscure than that of Mozzi, whose reputation was limited to Florence. Moreover, our understanding of Andrea's sin was further complicated because Dante chose to refer his readers to ecclesiastical *auctoritates* such as Gregory, Gratian, and the Vulgate rather than to expound an ecclesiology in his own name.

Once grasped, none of the solutions is difficult. The philosopher should teach the emperor how to rule; the grammarian should make Latin a functional medium of learned communication; the legist should interpret the civil law; and the bishop should lead his flock by word and deed, through preaching and poverty, to eternal salvation.

Yet it is no wonder that Dante's interpreters failed to comprehend the poet's message, for comprehension required nothing less than an intellectual revolution. The reader was asked to judge the intellectual establishment of his day by the criteria of reason and more fundamental authority. But the errors that Dante discerned were deeply embedded in Latin culture, some so deeply that they have persisted to the present, and the respect for authority among scholars, modern no less than medieval, does not dispose the literati to discover their own misconceptions. Dante would not be surprised, for he recognized that his age was blind to the simplest truths and made no exception for himself. Brunetto warned him against the blindness of the Florentines, and Marco Lombardo more clearly saw that Dante was as blind as the world from which he came: "lo mondo è cieco, e tu vien ben da lui."[1] Disillusionment is perhaps possible only if one is already alienated from this world. For Dante, I think, the moment of truth came when exile cut short his successful career; reflecting on the injustice of it all, he was led to trace the cause of his frustration to its ultimate roots.

If today we can at last grasp his meaning, it is because the Latin clerical culture of the thirteenth century is far more alien to our generation than to any before ours. Latinity can no longer be regarded as a measure of general culture, and the forces of *aggiornamento* have instilled Dante's doubts into the minds of many. Mine, then, is a contemporary thesis in the sense that it has been made possible by the present climate of opinion. This, more than anything else, may explain why the sin of the runners has eluded interpreters for six and a half centuries.

All the characters now have been accounted for; all the passages that favor the sodomitical interpretation have yielded a more profound meaning. To be sure, much more could be said, and I hope others will investigate aspects that I have left unexplored. For example, I have not attempted to expound the fourfold sense of the canto, though from time to time it has been evident that a figure could be understood at more than one level. Again, I have not pursued many tempting clues that would no doubt nuance our appreciation of the poem. One instance can stand for the rest: Does not the verb *trasmutato* echo a scholastic, and specifically a Thomistic, terminology? For Innocent's claim to do what God alone could do verges on a *transmutatio miraculosa*.[2] Lines that I would myself pursue are the riddle of the DXV[3] and Dante's use of canon and civil law, particularly his close agreement with Cino of Pistoia on certain fundamental points.[4]

One could, I suppose, begin anywhere in the *Commedia* and proceed to explicate the whole in terms of the part, so closely does Dante interweave his thematic thread, but the interpretation of the part must first be acceptable before one proceeds to exfoliate its consequences for the rest of the work. Therefore it has seemed best not to elaborate the implications of my theory, as Pézard did his, lest my main point come to be lost in a maze of attractive speculations.

We have accordingly arrived at the point where I would have my critics pause and declare their verdict, for the rest is either prologue or epilogue. Still, I think Dante would object that what follows is integral to an understanding of his work; for once, however, I consider it wiser not to meet him on his own terms, but rather on those of the audience for whom I write. For this chapter, like the closing section of the one just concluded, will proceed, not by historical research, but by imagination. The very thought is abhorrent to the academic mind, my own included, which is persuaded by objective demonstration and is always wary of subjective impressionism. Yet I propose to treat here the images of *Inferno* xv–xvi, and it is difficult, perhaps impossible, to develop this theme without a large measure of imagination. Just as the reader of the *Comedy* is often forced to reason his way to Dante's conclusions, to discover the reasons for himself, and thus make the author's arguments his own, just so he must also be something of a poet, so that through his imagination he can recreate or recapture the poet's intentions.

My distinction here can best be understood in reference to the close of the last chapter. The antinomy of the two Andrews may very well be the high road to an understanding of the passage, but few scholars today would be persuaded by this alone; nor would they be inclined to entertain seriously an argument that was premised on such a perception. We find it plausible only as an illustration of the strict demonstration, to which it can add a poetic dimension. Some Dantists, such as d'Entrèves,[5] refuse as a methodological principle to admit allegorical interpretation as a reliable indication of Dante's thought. Such caution assuredly has merit, and I have myself adopted it in my foregoing exposition, lest my argument be faulted for subjectivity. In this I feel somewhat like Galileo, who cast his discoveries in the conventional academic form of geometrical demonstration, though originally he had arrived at his conclusions by quite another method. But now that my case rests, these seminal perceptions need no longer be excluded, and indeed I think it may profit others if I confess that my thesis was suggested by the analysis of concrete images rather than of abstract concepts. This, I suspect, was the poet's design or, better, his veritable poetic art—to compact his meaning in poetic images that convey the general sense long before the inner reasons can be comprehended.

The poet wrote the *Comedy*, I believe, in conscious imitation of God the Creator.[6] His book purports to be a species of revelation; and like Holy Scripture, as medieval men understood it, the poem speaks to the reader at several levels. The mind of the omniscient demiurge never is wholly revealed to his reader, though his reason underlies and informs its verbal expression, which is the poet's creation. The message is proportioned to the mind of the reader: often it is expressed in plain, practical terms, without theoretical explanation. Thus Marco Lombardo clearly states the practical conclusion of Dante's critique of the papacy, but without reference to the underlying ecclesiology. Such plain statements, like God's commandments, contain what is essential for salvation. Less crucial matters are often expressed as figures, as images, or even as echoes from which the perceptive reader can glimpse the intention of the creator. In particular they indicate pattern, and thus serve to correlate apparently disparate, discrete terms. The two Andrews and their papal counterparts, for instance, are related by this technique; similarly we have heard the significant echoes of *nervi* in Gregory and *tigna* in the Vulgate.

We have not, however, considered the fundamental images of our cantos, nor have we scrutinized the names of the other characters against the possibility that these are no less significant than that of Andreas de Modiis. This will be the business of this essay. It might have stood as the prelude to the whole enterprise, which in fact had its origin in an analysis of the characteristic actions of each group of runners, but because these images also interrelate the middle cantos of the *Inferno* to other portions of the poem, it is no less fitting that we analyze those images in a postlude, which will perhaps enable others to better exfoliate the consequences of this interpretation for the poem as a whole. That work must be shared by many hands, for I think it likely that the larger significance of my thesis will prove to be even more controversial than its basic contention. But enough of apologies.

Each group of sinners in *lo minor giron* has a characteristic activity that is the outward expression of its dominant fault. Lying, sitting, and running are the three principal forms under the rain of fire, as every commentary duly notes. But few go on to observe that each band of runners also has its characteristic behavior. The politicians act as a group, but the scholars act as individuals. As the *cherci* run past Dante, they peer at the poet and squint to sharpen their weak vision, "as an aged tailor does at the eye of his needle" (*Inf.* xv, 17–21). Myopia is the mark of their profession, no less figuratively than literally. To be sure, it would be difficult to deduce that profession from this metaphor, but there is no need to do so because they are categorized explicitly in the poem (*Inf.* xv, 106–7). The politicians' actions, by contrast, help the reader to define the nature of their sin. The three Florentines leave their band together (*insieme*; *Inf.* xv, 4), speak twice in chorus (*Inf.* xv, 8–9, 79–81), and collaborate by organizing themselves into a ring, the better to run in place while talking with the poets (*Inf.* xv, 21). Even in Hell they retain the habit of concerted action, which is the basis of political life.

This propensity marks them as politicians but not as sinners, since cooperation directed to proper ends is necessary for the perfect society. Such a truly harmonious and productive community living in accordance with nature is evoked in the opening lines of the canto by the alter image of a humming hive of bees (*Inf.* xvi, 1–3).[7] Compared to this, the cooperation of the three Florentines is only superficial, as their actions prove. They form their ring facing inward, and then circle sideways, keeping their eyes on Dante, so if they were sidestepping leftwards, their heads turned slowly to the right:

> fenno una rota di sé tutti e trei.
> Qual sogliono i campion far nudi e unti,
>   avvisando lor presa e lor vantaggio,
>   prima che sien tra lor battuti e punti,
> così rotando, ciascuno il visaggio
>   drizzava a me, sì che 'n contraro il collo
>   faceva ai piè continüo vïaggio.
>
> (Inf. xvi, 21–27)

Described thus, their action appears to be a strange, inexplicable dance;[8] but the poet makes his meaning clear by the metaphor: their slow and deliberate circling reminds him of naked and anointed fighters who are feeling one another out in order to discover some advantage before coming to grips or blows. The politicians do in fact act together, but as suspicious antagonists rather than as harmonious co-workers, for they are infected with the divisive spirit of faction and strife which informs party politics.

The athletic analogy not only explains the image of the wheel, or *rota* ("così rotando"), but also comments on it. The nobles are likened, not to fighters in general, but specifically to champions (*i campion*; *Inf.* xvi, 22), because the knight's proper function is to champion the just cause of his community in combat. The appointed champions of Florence, however, perversely serve their own interests to the detriment of the community by turning their arms against one another rather than against their common enemy.

FIGHTERS AND RACERS IN *MONARCHIA* 2

The figure of the champions has a still wider significance than is evident from within the context of the poem, for it permits us to correlate the episode of the runners with Dante's political thought as formulated in the *Monarchia*. There, ordeal by champion forms the basis of one of the principal arguments of the thesis of book 2, that the Roman people acquired its empire by right. Dante seeks to prove that Rome's victories constitute a judgment of God, and he begins by expounding the various forms of divine judgment upon human affairs. The just man can discover the divine will as it is made unmistakably manifest in the general judgments of natural and scriptural law; but in any particular case, human reason requires special grace to be certain that God has intervened. Although it is not always apparent, God does judge particular cases, both *directly*, by revealing his will either expressly or through signs and answers to prayer, and also *indirectly*, by settling differences between men when the decision depends on the outcome of either a lottery or a contest (*aut sorte, aut certamine*; *Mon.* 2. 7. 9). In the last type of judgment, human competition is made the instrument of divine justice. The contestants appear to win by their own efforts, but in truth the victory is God's will. Dante distinguished two forms of judgment by contest, and these are the basis of his argument in the *Monarchia* and also of his division of the runners in *Inferno* xv–xvi:

> By contest the judgment of God is revealed in two ways: either as a result of the collision of forces, as it is through a combat [*duellum*] between pugilists, who are so called *duelliones*; or else as a result of the competition of many trying to gain some mark of distinction, as it is through a contest of athletes running for a prize [*ad bravium*].[9]
>
> (*Mon.* 2. 7. 9)

In one case, the antagonists fight one another; in the other, each pursues his goal independently of the other contestants. Dante is at pains to make this distinction clear, for he adds that it is fair to hinder (*impedire*) one's opponent in combat but not in a race.[10] His examples show that the duel admits of any number of paired combatants: Hercules vs. Antaeus, Aeneas vs. Turnus, the trios of the Horatii and the Curiatii, and even larger matched forces (2. 7. 10, 2. 10. 1–6). The duel is no ordinary war, however, because the champions have offered themselves out of a zeal for justice when all other means of settling the dispute have failed (2. 9), and because the parties they represent have agreed in advance to abide by the result. The duel, then, is a just war or its antecedent; and Dante proceeds to argue, quite unconvincingly, that Rome's Punic and Greek wars were in fact trials *per duellum*, which proves that her empire was won justly (2. 10. 7–11). However dubious his argument may be, it leaves no doubt that Dante associated the *duellum* with the medieval concept of the just war,[11] and as a corollary of this equation it would follow that the military of the just state would be its champions. Thus we have Dantesque authority for our previous assertion that the metaphor of the champions is an image appropriate to a military aristocracy.

It is equally certain that the *duelliones* of the *Monarchy* were in fact the basis of the *campion* metaphor in *Inferno* XVI. The duellist par excellence in the *Monarchia* is the pugilist, since boxing and wrestling are the most elemental forms of *collisio virium*; also the prize fighter, by the conventions of his sport (as Dante understood them), is expected to take advantage of his opponent. The noble trio of Florentine statesmen remind the poet of just such pugilists (*Inf.* XVI, 22–24): the correspondence between the two passages could hardly be more complete. Further, in the light of Dante's insistence that the duel serves justice and that duellists are the dispassionate and disinterested instruments of God, his comparison of the three factious Florentines to such champions becomes a profound irony which lays bare the nature of their fault. As has often been observed, the metaphors of the poem provide the reader with a commentary on the action whereby he can transcend the limited knowledge of the pilgrim and share in the perfected knowledge of the poet.[12]

Of the two forms of divine judgment revealed by means of a trial (*disceptatione mediante*) that are distinguished in *Monarchia* 2. 7–9, one served to define the sin of the statesmen. Can the other be identified with the sin of Brunetto Latini? If canto XV contains a metaphor based on "the competition of many trying to gain some mark of distinction," the principle that differentiates the sins of the runners can be established on the basis of internal evidence. The image of such a metaphor is clearly prescribed by the text of the *Monarchia*: the pugilistic contest has as its contrasting example the foot race—"pugna athletarum currentium ad bravium" (2. 7. 9). Indeed, although Dante framed his definition of the second type of contest in terms that, if taken figuratively, apply to forms of competition other than foot racing, he nonetheless used only foot races to illustrate the meaning of "contentio plurium ad aliquod signum prevalere conantium." Atalanta's contest with Hippomenes is his *locus classicus*; Euryalus' victory through foul play during the games in *Aeneid* 5. 315–49 raises an objection, which is surmounted by citing Chrysippus on stadium racing (*Mon.* 2. 7. 10, 12). If the scholars are to be compared to the second type of contestant in metaphoric terms that are the strict counterpart of the pugilist/statesman simile, then they can only be likened to runners in a race. And canto XV concludes with just such a metaphor, describing the departure of Brunetto:

Then he turned back, and seemed like one of those who run for the green cloth at Verona through the open field; and of them seemed he who wins, not he who loses.

Poi si rivolse, e parve di coloro
    che corrono a Verona il drappo verde
    per la campagna; e parve di costoro
quelli che vince, non colui che perde.

(Inf. xv, 121–24)

This metaphor is Dante's means of characterizing scholarship, in contrast to statesmanship, by reference back to the *Monarchia*. Scholarship is a race in pursuit of knowledge, wherein each participant concentrates on the common goal rather than on his relations with fellow scholars. Impersonal concurrence is the ideal condition of intellectual competition, as interpersonal conflict is of political life. The aspect of racing that is uppermost in Dante's mind in this connection is "the loneliness of the long-distance runner," for isolation is essential in a trial of individual merit. This concern explains his insistence that the racer, unlike the pugilist, must never hinder his rivals. Because the stress is on individual effort, the competitors need not even run simultaneously but may each try in turn to attain the goal. Thus, when Dante argues that Rome's empire was won by the "romanus populus cunctis athletizantibus pro imperio mundi" (*Mon.* 2. 8. 15, 2), he conceives her rivals to be, not the contemporary peoples that stood in her way, but rather the pre-Roman aspirants to world rule. Assyria, Egypt, Persia, and Macedon, each in its turn, strove for world empire, but Rome alone attained the prize. Similarly, each scholar seeks to surpass all past performances, while the politician seeks only to dominate his contemporaries. The metaphor of Verona's foot race, then, supports our view that the sin of Brunetto's band of scholars is professionally determined.

Still more important, the metaphor leads the reader to the key passage in the *Monarchy* that will elucidate the sin of the scholars, as it did that of the statesmen. Through this device the poet indicates the fatal aspect of scholarship: it is a solitary pursuit in which an individual by independent effort seeks to surpass the intellectual achievements of the past. This is only a clue, however, and not the answer itself. To discover how scholars have been damned by the spirit of emulation that is inherent in their profession, the reader could seek, with the aid of this principle, to understand the case histories presented in canto xv of the *Inferno*. But this task we have already accomplished, and we may therefore reflect instead on the larger significance of this imagery. At first, one is struck by the remarkable correspondence between *Inferno* xv–xvi and *Monarchia* 2. 7. A more penetrating examination will reveal one of those deliberate inconsistencies with which Dante teases the reader to pursue his thought to the end. The difficulty can readily be made apparent by a schematic presentation of the various forms of divine judgment upon human affairs that are set out in *Monarchia* 2. 7.[18]

Human reason can attain divine judgment upon human affairs

(I) through general laws that are manifest to human reason
    (A) in natural law
        and are accessible to unaided human reason
    (B) in scriptural law
        and are accessible to reason aided by faith
(II) through special grace, whereby divine judgments otherwise hidden to human reason are revealed
    (A) directly by God
        (1) of his own accord *(sponte)*
            (a) expressly
            (b) through a sign
        (2) in response to prayer
    (B) indirectly through a trial *(disceptatio)*
        (1) by lot *(sorte)*
        (2) by contest *(certamen)*
            (a) between forces opposed in combat
            (b) between competitors for some mark of distinction

The offenses punished on the burning sands are all perversions of the general laws that manifest divine judgment to human reason (I). For the most part the offenders violated natural law (I, A), though Mozzi, for whom faith was literally a profession, acted contrary to scriptural law as well (I, B). The difficulty is that the punishment does not seem to fit the crime, for the actions imposed on them by divine justice are images that exemplify modes of human contest (II, B, 2). A lesser poet than Dante would surely have derived their punishments from the examples given under (I) by the simple expedient of inversion: thus the offenders against (I, A) could be unjust warriors who refused to defend their city, whereas ones who refused to give the Lord his due could represent (I, B). Obviously, Dante's figure of perversion is more complex.

Before seeking some explanation of his seemingly displaced images, we may observe that the other branches of the schema are also reflected in our cantos, though faintly. Both kinds of simple revelation appear in the legend of the translation of Saint Zenobius, for the miraculous halt of his relics was a spontaneous act of God (II, A, 1), while their release came in response to Saint Andreas' prayer (II, A, 2). Even the trial by lot (II, B, 1) is not irrelevant, for Dante's example of the election of Matthias figures prominently in his concept of episcopal office.[14] None of these, of course, reflects the sins of the runners; on the contrary, they exemplify the proper attitude of the devout Christian. He has no difficulty in accepting God's direct intervention in human affairs (II, A, 1–2) and in ecclesiastical affairs (II, B, 1): it can be depended on because Christ promised that he would be with his Church even unto the end of the world.[15]

But what of the final category (II, B, 2), from which the motion images of *Inferno* xv and xvi are derived? Can man be certain who "won" the contest? In the *Monarchia*, wrestling and racing are images of human effort, directed respectively against other men and toward the attainment of some common goal. Certainly, battles are won and prizes gained, but God does not necessarily endorse every success. Might does not always make right. Only in certain contests, in which the issue depends upon divine intervention, can the result be considered as a judgment of God. These special cases Dante subsumes under the more general category of "trials" *("disceptationes")*, which are situations wherein man can recognize that the decisive factor is God. Thus, human will is eliminated by an obvious device in the casting of lots (II, B, 1), but the means of ascertaining God's judgment by the ways of contest (*certamen*; II, B, 2) are more subtle.

The first variety (II, B, 2, a) *balances* human forces by pairing evenly matched contestants in combat. This is suggested by Dante's classical examples, and it is confirmed by the conditions under which such contests were conducted in Tuscany during his lifetime.[16] Thus, a judicial duel does not test the prowess of the champions, since it must be determined *before* the duel begins that the forces about to be pitted against each other are in fact equal. In this case, therefore, man can perceive divine judgment only when he knows it to be the only decisive factor, *ceteris paribus*.

Markedly different are the conditions for the other form of contest (II, B, 2, b) between competitors for some mark of distinction. This type reveals which of the participants best performs the activity for which he is qualified by his nature. Attainment of a set goal confers the prize, which distinguishes the winner from the rest of mankind in this respect. But how can the judgment of God be made manifest by an individual who demonstrates his own *virtù*? That will be a recurrent question in this and the following chapter. A preliminary answer is suggested by Mozzi's association with the Sermon on the Mount, namely the *a fructibus* criterion, by which God's own are known by their fruits.[17] All the runners were, like Andrea, entrusted with certain talents, for the use of which they are held accountable in the sight of God. We have Christ's word that he shall recognize as his own only those who are good and faithful stewards and, moreover, that from their fruits they may also be recognized by their fellow men. Thus the image of the foot race does suit the sin of Brunetto's band of scholars who misused their talents, for it was by examining their fruits—that is, their lives and doctrines—that we were able to discover their sins. In effect, then, the scheme of *Monarchia* 2. 7 explains how the poet could identify sinners of this sort without presuming to usurp the divine prerogative of judgment, for Dante had but to report God's own judgment upon them, as it was revealed to him and to all men by the fruits of sin.

Now we are in a position to clarify the relationship of these contestants to the general laws by which God makes certain of his judgments manifest to human reason. The rationale of the imagery unfolds when we recall how the runners were motivated by a thirst for fame.[18] So intent were these men on success that they did not hesitate to substitute their own judgments for the divine judgments that are manifest to human reason as general laws (I). Though they might be applauded by those who were as blind as themselves, still their successes could only be accounted failures by the few whose reason had not been blinded to the significance of their evil fruits.

[167]

ECCLESIASTES AND THE *VELOCES ET FORTES*

Dantesque images often bear their own credentials in some reference by association to an authoritative source, and perhaps, as the title of this chapter hints, these fighters and racers may already have reminded my reader of a memorable verse from Ecclesiastes: "The race is not to the swift, nor the battle to the strong."[19] The immediate context is a discrete pair of verses (Eccles. 9:11–12):

> 11. I turned me to another thing, and I saw that under the sun, the race is not to the swift, nor the battle to the strong, nor bread to the wise, nor riches to the learned, nor favour to the skilful: but time and chance in all.

> 12. Man knoweth not his own end: but as fishes are taken with the hook, and as birds are caught with the snare, so men are taken in the evil time, when it shall suddenly come upon them.

> 11. Verti me ad aliud, et vidi sub sole, nec velocium esse cursum, nec fortium bellum, nec sapientium panem, nec doctorum divitias, nec artificum gratiam; sed tempus casumque in omnibus.

> 12. Nescit homo finem suum: sed sicut pisces capiuntur hamo, et sicut aves laqueo comprehenduntur, sic capiuntur homines in tempore malo, cum eis extemplo supervenerit.

"The swift and the strong," then, is a Biblical figure, and not only a Dantesque one, for man's inability to effect his own ends. Man's fate is determined ultimately by forces beyond his control. To the preacher this is evident because a man's natural endowments do not ensure success no matter how diligently they be exploited. Wisdom, learning, and skill pass unrecognized, just as strength and speed do not gain the victory.

"Nec velocium esse cursum, nec fortium bellum": the metaphoric actions of the runners acquire new meaning from this association, for both are fruitless actions. Brunetto would win the prize at Verona, but in Hell he runs to no goal: he has his reward. The *campioni* also habitually maneuver for an advantage over their fellows, though they never come to grips, and hence settle nothing by combat. Both *litterati* and *nobili* have habituated themselves to pointless contests that have already been decided, and this activity is its own reward.

As the *tinea* tag was a bookmark in the Sermon on the Mount, so the phrase *veloces et fortes* leads us to consider the short book of Ecclesiastes as a whole. Its message is quite in accord with the theme of *Inferno* xv–xvi, as can be shown by a brief analysis and several examples. Since the book is a disordered collection of aphorisms, the interpreter who seeks to determine the meaning of the work as a whole is always in danger of subsuming the proverbs under categories that are foreign to the author's intention. This pitfall yawns all the wider when one comes to Ecclesiastes, as we do, with some preconception of what might be found there. While it is always possible that Dante read his own ideas into the work and expected the interpreters of the *Commedia* to do likewise, I fear that my readers would in that case suspect that they heard my voice speaking through the mask of Dante. For their assurance and my own, I shall therefore rely on the understanding of an impartial interpreter, the *Encyclopaedia Britannica*.[20]

The appropriate article singles out some seven basic themes that run through Ecclesiastes' gnomic utterances. The first assures us that the work is entirely apposite to the sin of the runners: (1) "His fundamental proposition is that there is a fixed, unchangeable order in the world, a reign of inflexible law: . . . it is impossible to add to or take from the content of the world, impossible to change the nature of things, to effect any radical betterment of life." This contrast between natural order and human ignorance can be seen, for example, in these verses:

> 4. One generation passeth away, and another generation cometh: but the earth standeth for ever.
> 9. What is it that hath been? the same thing that shall be. What is it that hath been done? the same that shall be done.
> 10. Nothing under the sun is new, neither is any man able to say: Behold this is new: for it hath already gone before in the ages that were before us.

> 4. Generatio praeterit, et generatio advenit: terra autem in aeternum stat.
> 9. Quid est quod fuit? ipsum quod futurum est; quid est quod factum est? ipsum quod faciendum est.
> 10. Nihil sub sole novum, nec valet quisquam dicere: Ecce hoc recens est; iam enim praecessit in seculis, quae fuerunt ante nos.[21]

> (Eccles. 1:4, 9–10)

(2) Although man is not the Creator, he has been created with a curiosity that is vain, for he can never comprehend God's work:

> He hath made all things good in their time, and hath delivered the world to their consideration, so that man cannot find out the work which God hath made from the beginning to the end.

> Cuncta fecit bona in tempore suo, et mundum tradidit disputationi eorum, ut non inveniat homo opus, quod operatus est Deus ab initio usque ad finem.

> (Eccles. 3:11)

> And I understood that man can find no reason of all those works of God that are done under the sun: and the more he shall labour to seek, so much the less shall he find: yea, though the wise man shall say, that he knoweth it, he shall not be able to find it.

> Et intellexi, quod omnium operum Dei nullam possit homo invenire rationem eorum quae fiunt sub sole: et quanto plus laboraverit ad quaerendum, tanto minus inveniat: etiam si dixerit sapiens se nosse, non poterit reperire.

> (Eccles. 8:17)

24. I have tried all things in wisdom. I have said: I will be wise: and it departed farther from me,

25. Much more than it was: it is a great depth, who shall find it out?

26. I have surveyed all things with my mind, to know, and consider, and seek out wisdom and reason. . . .

30. Only this I have found, that God made man right, and he hath entangled himself with an infinity of questions. Who is as the wise man? and who hath known the resolution of the word?

24. Cuncta tentavi in sapientia. Dixi: Sapiens efficiar: et ipsa longius recessit a me.

25. Multo magis quam erat: et alta profunditas, quis inveniet eam?

26. Lustravi universa animo meo, ut scirem, et considerarem et quaererem sapientiam, et rationem: . . .

30. Solummodo hoc inveni, quod fecerit Deus hominem rectum, et ipse se infinitis miscuerit quaestionibus. Quis talis ut sapiens est? et quis cognovit solutionem verbi?[22]

(Eccles. 7:24–26a, 30)

Jerome's choice of words at the beginning and end of this catena makes the Sage's search appear more academic, or even scholastic, than the original. Where a modern translator simply says that God has "implanted ignorance in their mind," the Vulgate has it that "he gave over the world to their disputation."[23] Again, the sense of the passage Englished as "they have sought out many inventions" (or "contrivances" in another version),[24] was for Jerome that man "confused himself by infinite questions."[25] The correctness of the translation is no concern of ours, but the comparison does show that the Vulgate made Ecclesiastes seem to condemn in particular the scholastic compulsion to dispute endlessly. By our interpretation, these passages would apply especially to those who confused and blinded man the rational animal— "whom God made upright"—by bringing the manifest truths of natural law into question or even disrepute.[26]

(3) Man's inborn compulsion to grasp the incomprehensible is, for Koheleth, the height of human frustration; but more modest goals do not bring him satisfaction either, for he has found that in the end all human enterprise is vanity. This attitude we already know from his metaphor of the swift and strong; he rings many variations on the theme throughout the book, but the basic thesis is laid down in the prologue:

2. Vanity of vanities, said Ecclesiastes: vanity of vanities, and all is vanity.

3. What hath a man more of all his labour, that he taketh under the sun?

2. Vanitas vanitatum, dixit Ecclesiastes: vanitas vanitatum, et omnia vanitas.

3. Quid habet amplius homo de universo labore suo, quo laborat sub sole?

(Eccles. 4:2–3)

Among the variations, one is notable for the light that it sheds on another feature of the runners' punishment:

> As he came forth naked from his mother's womb, so shall he return, and shall take nothing away with him of his labour.

> Sicut egressus est nudus de utero matris suae, sic revertetur, et nihil auferet secum de labore suo.

(Eccles. 5:14)

Just so these *violenti* run naked as the day they were born, stripped of the symbols and tools of their various professions. In this connection it is perhaps not irrelevant that Brunetto's recommendation of his *Tresor* serves to remind the reader that death separates even the intellectual from the fruit of his labor: he must leave his writings behind him on earth.[27]

(4) Ecclesiastes posits a world governed by natural law, but as far as man can tell, the precepts of that law are physical rather than moral. Death is inevitable, and the sun also rises; yet the wicked flourish, and the just do not (e.g., Eccles. 8:14, 9:2). Ecclesiates' only explanation of what Dante would call the *occulta iudicia Dei* is that God sends both good and evil to every man, balancing the fortunes of each so that none can have just cause to complain against God.[28]

(5) Koheleth concludes that human life is not worth living, for man is no better than the animals, and it were best for him not to be born (e.g., Eccles. 4:2–3).

(6) This life is vanity, but after death there is not even that, for the dead know nothing at all. Hence he bitterly urges man to indulge in the vanity of licit pleasure and hard work while he can: "For neither work, nor reason, nor wisdom, nor knowledge shall be in hell, whither thou are hastening."[29]

(7) Probably the author of this gloomy philosophy saw God as an immeasurably remote creator and ordainer of the world. Indeed, he may have been under the influence of Greek, perhaps Epicurean, thought. Modern criticism has suspected that later editors attempted to ameliorate this unrelieved pessimism, notably by appending a more positive conclusion to the work:

> 12. More than these, my son, require not. Of making many books there is no end: and much study is an affliction of the flesh.

> 13. Let us all hear together the conclusion of the discourse. Fear God, and keep his commandments: for this is all man:

> 14. And all things that are done, God will bring into judgment for every error, whether it be good or evil.

> 12. His amplius, fili mi, ne requiras. Faciendi plures libros nullus est finis: frequensque meditatio, carnis afflictio est.

> 13. Finem loquendi pariter omnes audiamus. Deum time, et mandata eius observa: hoc est enim omnis homo:

> 14. Et cuncta, quae fiunt, adducet Deus in iudicium pro omni errato, sive bonum, sive malum illud sit.

(Eccles. 12:12–14)

Medieval critics recognized that the conclusion put the whole work in another light—Jerome indeed considered that the book would not have been received into the canon of Sacred Scripture otherwise[30]—but it was by that light that they read the rest of the book, and so must we, if we are to understand it as Dante did.

At the last minute the perspective has shifted, and we discover that for twelve hopeless chapters the world has been analyzed from the limited point of view of human reason. In the end, the would-be sage abandons his rational enterprise; the author confesses that there can be no conclusion to the book he set out to write; the Speaker—as our latest translators English "Koheleth"—at the last recommends silence. Having perceived the limitations of his race, the investigator realizes that he too is tarred by the same brush. His findings contradict his method. By an epistemological paradox, if reason denies its own efficacy, that conclusion itself must be suspect: reason cannot prove its own inefficacy. For Koheleth the outcome of his confusion is the religious solution of transcendance through self-negation. Having exhausted his faith in all human understanding, his own included, he affirms his faith in God and thus gains the certitude he otherwise had been unable to find. Aided by faith, man can learn from revelation that the universe is governed by a moral order, for Scripture contains both God's commandments and the assurance that He shall do justice to all who disobey.

The final conclusion supplies the antidote to the sin of the runners: the *uomo mondano* in a Christian society has blinded himself not only to the limitations of human reason but also to the means of transcending these limitations, which revelation affords. All the runners had attempted to improve upon God's handiwork that was manifest to them in the laws of nature and Scripture. In so many words, Ecclesiastes 7:14 had warned them that it was impossible for man to contest the explicit judgment of God: "Consider the works of God, that no man can correct whom he hath despised" ("Considera opera Dei, quod nemo possit corrigere quem ille despexerit"). Had they trusted in God's revelation to Koheleth, they would have been spared their pains, both temporal and eternal. From him, to summarize, they would have learned first that the truth attainable by human reason is limited and that it cannot bring the whole man to happiness; the final peripeteia, moreover, would turn them to revelation, by which, with the aid of faith, reason can extend the scope of its understanding sufficiently to attain eternal beatitude. In this connection it is noteworthy that there are no known pagans among the runners: all are members of Christian society who have had the opportunity to be saved.[31] Their first step away from God was the rejection of revelation as an aid to rational understanding.

A corollary of this interpretation brings out the essential irony of the literati. All believed themselves to be wise men, and yet they were in truth fools. In considering the case of Mozzi, we observed that he was popularly regarded as a fool because of his preaching, and Brunetto, in the poem, emphatically scorned him as such.[32] Although Brunetto correctly stated that all his band were condemned for the same sin, still he failed to recognize that he too was a fool. The *stultus/sapiens* contrast is one of the recurrent themes of Ecclesiastes,[33] and though the author repeatedly expresses contempt for fools, yet in the end he discovers that he is no better than a fool for his attempt to attain an understanding that surpassed his natural powers. Brunetto and the rest persisted in their folly to the end, and they went to their reward still thinking that they were truly wise. Their punishment is their crime: squinting and still confident of their wisdom, they eternally run as if in pursuit of a goal that in fact does not exist. *Vanitas vanitatum.*

SOLOMON'S REGAL PRUDENCE

If the race, then, is not to the swift nor the battle to the strong, to whom does the victory belong? We have already noted that Paradise contains counterparts to several of the runners, and therefore we have some reason to suspect that the metaphor of the *veloces et fortes* may itself be reflected in Heaven. If so, we must expect that the functions of the counterparts will correspond to the functions of their exemplars in the scheme of *Monarchia* 2. 7; they too will exemplify contests that reveal divine judgments, which otherwise would remain hidden to human reason. Further, it would be appropriate if these victors were closely associated with Koheleth himself. Let us accordingly look first for the author of Ecclesiastes, and then for echoes of his imagery.

To the modern Biblical critic, the identity of the author of Ecclesiastes has become a puzzle; but this problem did not trouble the medieval exegete, who accepted the book's own statement that the author was King Solomon (Eccles. 1:1, 12). Twice in the *Convivio* (2. 10. 10; 4. 2. 8) Dante himself did not hesitate to quote Ecclesiastes as the work of Solomon, whom he also names as the author of two other canonical books: Proverbs and the Song of Songs.[34] As the sponsal imagery of the latter has already proved no less relevant to our theme than has Ecclesiastes, it would seem that the reader of *Inferno* xv is referred to the common author by a convergence of cross references.

Once again the road leads to the heaven of the Sun, where we found the counterparts to Priscian and Francesco d'Accorso respectively in Donatus and Gratian, both of whom appear with Aquinas among the *spiriti sapienti* (*Par.* x-xiv). To some of these dozen spirits Dante devotes hardly a line, but on Solomon he lays particular and repeated stress. Aquinas introduces him as

> La quinta luce, ch'è tra noi più bella,
>   spira di tale amor, che tutto 'l mondo
>   là giù ne gola di saper novella:
> entro v'è l'alta mente u' sì profondo
>   saver fu messo, che, se 'l vero è vero,
>   a veder tanto non surse il secondo.
>
> (*Par.* x, 109–14)

The fifth light, which is the most beautiful among us, breathes from such a love that all the world below hungers for news of it; within it is the lofty mind to which was given wisdom so deep that, if the truth be true, there never arose a second of such wisdom.[35]

[173]

Later, almost the whole of canto xiii (35–142) is devoted to the Angelic Doctor's commentary on this description. Finally, with encouragement from Beatrice, the pilgrim elicits a lengthy explanation of the resurrection of the body from Solomon himself, "the most divine light of the lesser circle."[36]

We have been referred, then, to a major figure among the wise. Dante, through his spokesman Aquinas, is at great pains to tell us exactly why Solomon occupies a place of such prominence. This explanation constitutes Dante's final evaluation of man's intellectual endeavors. Whereas *Inferno* xv displayed the abuse of human reason, the figure of Solomon epitomizes its proper application to the affairs of this world. Moreover, to corroborate the interrelationship of his two treatments of the same theme, the poet integrated a reference to Ecclesiastes in Aquinas' exposition. This much, which shall suffice to illuminate Brunetto's band, can be established with relative ease; the greater task of elaborating the consequences in a reinterpretation of the heaven of the Sun cannot be attempted here.

When the pilgrim was told that there was never another man who saw so much as the wise spirit of the fifth light, he inwardly was amazed, because he recalled the orthodox view that there were but two perfect men—Adam and Christ, the second Adam. Reading his thoughts, Aquinas proceeded to show him how the two propositions could be reconciled by making a distinction. His basic premise is that the works of nature are invariably defective in some degree, unless they are perfected by grace (*Par.* xiii, 49–77). Human nature has only twice been so perfected, once in Adam and again in Christ (*Par.* xiii, 79–87). Thus the pilgrim had correctly understood that their perfection was unique; he had failed, however, to comprehend that the perfection Aquinas attributed to Solomon was of a different kind:

> Ma perché paia ben ciò che non pare,
>   pensa chi era, e la cagion che 'l mosse,
>   quando fu detto "Chiedi," a dimandare.
>
> Non ho parlato sì, che tu non posse
>   ben veder ch'el fu re, che chiese senno
>   acciò che re sufficïente fosse;
>
> non per sapere il numero in che enno
>   li motor di qua sù, o se *necesse*
>   con contingente mai *necesse* fenno;
>
> non *si est dare primum motum esse,*
>   o se del mezzo cerchio far si puote
>   trïangol sì ch'un retto non avesse.
>
> Onde, se ciò ch'io dissi e questo note,
>   regal prudenza è quel vedere impari
>   in che lo stral di mia intenzion percuote;
>
> e se al "surse" drizzi li occhi chiari,
>   vedrai aver solamente respetto
>   ai regi, che son molti, e buon ' son rari.

(Par. xiii, 91–108)

But, to make quite clear what is obscure to thee, think who he was and what moved him to his petition when he was bidden "Ask." I have not spoken so darkly but that thou canst see that he was a king, who asked for wisdom that he might be fit to be a king, not to know the number of the movers here above, nor if *necesse* with a contingent ever made *necesse*, nor *si est dare primum motum esse*, nor if a triangle can be made in the semicircle so that it has no right angle. Therefore, if thou note this along with what I said, [it follows that] regal prudence is that unmatched vision on which the arrow or my intention strikes; and if thou have careful regard to "arose" thou wilt see it to have sole reference to kings,—who are many, and the good ones rare.[37]

Three cantos earlier, Aquinas had identified Solomon by a Biblical allusion to 3 Kings 3:12: "if the truth be true, there never arose a second of such wisdom" (*Par.* x, 113–14). Now, without ever mentioning Solomon by name, he directs us to the same passage by making another allusion.[38] More of it is relevant than has been recognized, so I shall not abridge it:

5. And the Lord appeared to Solomon in a dream by night, saying: Ask what thou wilt that I should give thee.

6. And Solomon said: Thou hast shown great mercy to thy servant David my father, even as he walked before thee in truth, and justice, and an upright heart with thee: and thou hast kept thy great mercy for him, and hast given him a son to sit on his throne, as it is this day.

7. And now, O Lord God, thou hast made thy servant king instead of David my father: and I am but a child, and know not how to go out and come in.

8. And thy servant is in the midst of the people which thou hast chosen, an immense people, which cannot be numbered nor counted for multitude.

9. Give therefore to thy servant an understanding heart, to judge thy people, and discern between good and evil. For who shall be able to judge this people, thy people which is so numerous?

10. And the word was pleasing to the Lord that Solomon had asked such a thing.

11. And the Lord said to Solomon: Because thou hast asked this thing, and hast not asked for thyself long life or riches, nor the lives of thy enemies, but hast asked for thyself wisdom to discern judgment,

12. Behold, I have done for thee according to thy words, and have given thee a wise and understanding heart, insomuch that there hath been no one like thee before thee, nor shall arise after thee.

13. Yea and the things also which thou didst not ask, I have given thee: to wit, riches and glory, so that no one hath been like thee among the kings in all days heretofore.

14. And if thou wilt walk in my ways, and keep my precepts, and my commandments, as thy father walked, I will lengthen thy days.

15. And Solomon awaked, and perceived that it was a dream. . . .

(3 Kings 3:5–15)

Aquinas, it will be recalled, had prodded the pilgrim's understanding by posing a double question: "Think who he was and what moved him to his petition" (*Par.* XIII, 92). Forthwith he answered the first half: "He was a king, who asked for wisdom that he might be fit to be a king" (*Par.* XIII, 95–96). But what motivated Solomon? This second question, left unanswered in the *Commedia*, simply begs the reader to consult his Bible. Solomon, then a lad approaching puberty, had explained his predicament: "ego autem sum puer parvulus, et ignorans egressum et introitum meum" (3 Kings 3:7)—he was a child who did not know which way he was going; he lacked the requisite wisdom to govern his people, who were also the Lord's.

Why did Dante so forcibly draw our attention to the fact that Solomon was a child-king? Because the poet associated this fact with another tag, to which he attached certain concepts of kingship. He alluded to Eccles. 10:16: "Vae tibi, terra, cuius rex puer est!" ("Woe to thee, O land, when thy king is a child!").[39] In *Convivio* 4 this aphorism is twice quoted to illustrate the Dantesque conception of the philosopher-king. In the first instance it serves to summarize his conclusion that the authority of the philosopher and that of the emperor are not only mutually compatible but also ought to be conjoined, for each strengthens the other:

> And therefore it is written in the book of *Wisdom* [6:23], "Love the light of Wisdom, all ye who go before the people," which is as much as to say, let Philosophic be combined with Imperial authority for good and perfect government. O wretched men who at present bear rule; and O most wretched men who are subject to rule! For no philosophical authority is combined with your forms of government, whether by means of your own studies or by good advice; so that to all of you these words of the *Preacher* may be applied, "Woe to thee O land whose King is a child, and whose princes eat in the morning"; and to no country could the words which follow be applied: "Blessed is the land whose King is noble, and whose princes eat in due season, for their necessity and not for wantonness."[40]

He then proceeds to develop the main argument of the fourth tractate, that to be truly noble the emperor must be a philosopher—that is, a lover of wisdom. In *Convivio* 4. 16 he defines nobility as the perfection of nature in any thing and explains that it is most easily known by its fruits, which are the moral and intellectual virtues. To introduce the crux of the treatise, Dante reverts to the image of the boy-king, whom he now identifies as a figure of the man who is imperfect because he is deficient in virtues:

> I say, therefore, that if we would have regard to the common habit of speech, this word nobility signifies in each thing the perfection of the nature peculiar to it. Hence it is predicable not only of man, but also of all other things; for men apply the epithet noble to stones, plants, horses, falcons, whatever is seen to be perfect in its own proper nature. Therefore Solomon says in *Ecclesiastes*, "Blessed is the land whose King is noble," which is the same as to say, "whose King is perfect as regards the perfection of soul and of body"; and this he makes plain by what he says before when he affirms, "Woe to thee, O land, whose King is a child," that is, whose king is not

completely a man; and a man is a child not only by reason of his age, but by reason of disorderly ways and faults of life, as the Philosopher teaches us in the first book of the *Ethics*.[41]

Thus Aquinas' exhortation to consider the motive of Solomon's request for wisdom to rule has led us to the heart of *Convivio* 4. The two works are linked together by the allusion to Ecclesiastes, which, like a kingpin, further binds both passages to *Inferno* xv. Taken together, the three texts express Dante's doctrine of man's intellectual powers and their proper use. As the first two are primarily concerned with kingship, it might seem that their relation to the sin of Brunetto Latini is somewhat remote, but Aquinas' discourse on Solomon contains not only the clue that interrelates them but also comments on that relationship. His argument, which has been quoted above,[42] can be paraphrased thus: (1) To make clear that I did not mean that in this spirit, as in Adam or Christ, human nature had been perfected by grace, you have only to consider (a) who this spirit was in life and (b) the context of my earlier allusion to 3 Kings 3:5–15, where you should note especially the motive of his request. (2) You did in fact catch my allusion and thus at least know that he was a king and (3) that he asked only for such wisdom as was necessary to make him a perfect king. (4) He did not require knowledge of things that transcend human experience and are useless for the conduct of human affairs. (5) Hence it follows from what I originally said and from the explanations of it just given, that I meant that no one has been this man's equal in "regal prudence." (6) If you look carefully at the verb I chose, you will see that my original statement could in fact have had no other meaning, since *surse* could only refer to kings, of whom there are many, though few of them are good kings.

To understand this argument, one must bear in mind the anomalous circumstances of the occasion. Aquinas addresses himself to one who is already familiar with the work of the Angelic Doctor, and moreover to one whose thoughts are known to the saint. Hence if we wish to understand as the pilgrim did, we must place ourselves in his position of familiarity with much of the Thomistic corpus. Here the key lies in Thomas' reference to *prudenza*, which draws us to his extensive treatment of *prudentia* in the *Summa theologica*.[43] There we find that the prudence proper to one who rules a city or kingdom Thomas designates by the technical term *prudentia regnativa*, which I take to be equivalent to Dante's *regal prudenza*.[44] We need note only two features of this Thomistic virtue in order to interpret his argument in the *Comedy*. (1) Regnative prudence Thomas considers to be the highest and most perfect form of human prudence (II-II q.50 a.1). (2) The prudence of kings, like that of other men, is not a natural endowment. Instead, according to Aquinas, this virtue can be either (a) acquired by experience, over a long period of time and hence is found chiefly in old men, or (b) infused by grace (II-II q.47 a.14–15). With these theses in mind, we can now perceive how the pilgrim was expected to deduce from his introduction to the *quinta luce* that Solomon was not another *optimus homo* but rather the *optimus rex*.

Let us start from the beginning and reconstruct the train of thought by which the pilgrim could have anticipated the explanation that is finally given to him in *Paradiso* xiii. Originally he had Thomas' statement of *Paradiso* x, 109–14, which told him that the fifth light contained a high mind that had been given such profound wisdom *(saper)* that "to see so much another arose not." This opinion, Thomas had indicated, was based on revelation, and since it appears from his discourse in *Paradiso* xiii that Dante had in fact caught the allusion, we must assume that the pilgrim's problem was to reconcile the text of 3 Kings 3:5–15 with such objections as it suggested to him. The pilgrim, then, appears in the role of an objector in a Thomistic *quaestio*, where the respondent shows him how to overcome the difficulty. But let us instead follow the course that he should have taken unaided.

From the Biblical text, Dante the pilgrim knew that the virtue for which the *quinta luce* had no peer was not acquired but had been infused in him by God. Further, his text told him that God had told Solomon that in respect to that virtue "there hath been no one like thee before thee, nor shall arise after thee" (3 Kings 3:12). But what was that virtue? In the same verse God conferred on Solomon "a wise and understanding heart" ("cor sapiens et intelligens"), and this the pilgrim mistook to mean that Solomon excelled all other men in the two intellectual virtues of *sapientia* and *intelligentia*. Remembering that Adam and Christ were believed to have been perfect men, it seemed to him, since they must have had the perfection proper to Homo sapiens, that Solomon did indeed have a peer, both before and after him.

Here the pilgrim's deduction ceased, but Aquinas later indicated what the next step should have been. Having met an impasse, the interpreter should have returned to his text to see whether he had properly understood it. There he would have found the key in the word *"surge"* (or in the Vulgate, *"surrecturus sit"*). Basically, the verb denotes motion from a lower to a higher level. But neither Adam nor Christ could be said to have risen to their perfection: Christ was born perfect, while Adam was made perfect and then fell from that state. Thus, God would seem to have assured Solomon that no man could attain Solomon's perfection unless he had come into the world with it.

But this proposition in its turn deserves to be tested. Was not Aristotle, for example, Solomon's peer in wisdom and understanding? Was not Caesar a better general? When the interpreter realizes that many men have excelled Solomon in one respect or another, he will again return to his text to discover whether *cor sapiens et intelligens* is to be taken generally or whether some implicit qualification is to be understood. The context of verse 12 of course supplies the answer: it pleased God to grant Solomon's request for a *cor docile*, "to judge thy people, and discern between good and evil" (3 Kings 3:9). As Aquinas reminded the pilgrim, one must remember that Solomon was a child-king whose wish was to rule his people well. The infused wisdom of King Solomon, therefore, must be compared with that of other *kings*, "who are many, and the good ones rare" (*Par.* xiii, 108). In other words, it would be hard to find a better king than Solomon, though in other respects than kingship, some had equaled if not surpassed his understanding and wisdom.

Having answered Dante's question, we may go on to raise a difficulty of our own. It is clear that no king can hope to acquire regnative prudence equivalent to that which Solomon possessed by infusion. Does this imply that one cannot become a good king? and that man's natural powers are not sufficient to obtain the beatitude of this life? Such implications are contradicted by the conclusion of *Monarchia* 3, where we are assured that the *phylosophica documenta* contain all that is necessary to attain that end (*Mon.* 3. 15. 8–9). A solution is suggested by Thomas' treatment of the infusion of habits, especially those habits that are virtues. He explained that God, to manifest his power, sometimes infused "into men even those dispositions [*habitus*] which can be caused by natural power. Thus, for instance, he gave the Apostles knowledge of the Scriptures and of all languages, which men may acquire by study and custom, though not in so perfect a manner" (*S.T.* I-II q.51 a.4).[45] Further, one man can possess a virtue to a greater degree than another man:

> If, however, virtue is considered on the part of the subject who shares in it, then it may then be greater or less, either in relation to different times for the same person, or to different persons. One man is better disposed than another to attain to the mean of virtue set by right reason; and this from greater habituation, or better natural disposition, or a more discerning judgment of reason, or again a greater gift of grace, which is given to each one *according to the measure of the giving of Christ* [Eph. 4:7].
>
> On this point the Stoics erred, for they held that no man should be adjudged virtuous unless he were in the highest degree disposed to virtue. For the nature of virtue does not require that a man should reach the mean of right reason as though it were an indivisible point, as the Stoics thought; it is enough that he should be close to the mean, according to the teaching of the *Ethics* [2. 9; 1109b18]. Again, one indivisible mark is reached more nearly and more readily by one than another; as may also be seen when several archers aim at a fixed target.[46]
>
> (*S.T.* I-II q.66 a.1)

Since virtue is a habit for Thomas, both statements can be applied to regnative prudence, which is a species of the cardinal virtue of prudence. That virtue, Thomas taught, "is in us, not by nature, but by teaching and experience"; moreover, he insisted, the "prudence is rather in the old, not only because their natural disposition calms the movement of the sensitive passions, but also because of their long experience" (*S.T.* II-II q.47 a.15).[47]

Since experience increases prudence, it would therefore appear that no one lifetime would suffice for a man to acquire perfect prudence. The best that he might hope to attain would be experience of his own time and circumstances, which must necessarily be limited. To some degree he can transcend these limitations, as Dante suggests, either through study or by taking counsel with others more experienced and prudent than himself.[48] Since kingship is a practical art rather than a theoretical science, a king is judged to be good if he acts wisely and well in concrete situations; he has no need to know how to act in a situation he shall never face, though other kings under different circumstances may need the knowledge that he did not need. Thus a good king is one who is adequate to the circumstances of his reign; however varied these may be, he will never need to know how to deal with every possible problem of government. But that, I submit, is precisely the perfect regnative prudence that God gave to Solomon: the ability to judge wisely and justly on the basis of slight experience (and without recourse to the advice of others, it would seem) in every situation that would ever possibly confront any ruler whatsoever. Thus the regal wisdom of Solomon was far more than was necessary for the governance of his own kingdom, and for this reason, other rulers can acquire enough prudence to rule their kingdoms adequately and still never approach the superabundant royal wisdom of Solomon.

The prudence of Solomon Rex constitutes a very special case.[49] So special, indeed, that the reader may well wonder why Dante gave it such prominence. One reason, on which I can only touch in passing, may ultimately prove to be the best.[50] To understand what the character Aquinas meant requires an extensive knowledge of the teachings of the man himself. I think it more than likely that the poet used this device to refer the reader to the Thomistic corpus in general for an extended course of study, and perhaps more particularly to the *Theological Summa* and its second part. Although in the course of these essays the most fruitful discoveries have been made by following such promptings, I have in the present case attempted nothing more than a reconnaissance, partly because the explication of the *sapienti* of the heaven of the Sun is not the purpose of this study, and partly because such an excursus would be a major undertaking in itself, and one, moreover, for which many Dantists are better fitted than I am. There is, however, another reason, perhaps not unrelated to the first, that bears more directly on our theme. This may be seen by stating concisely what the pilgrim at length learned about the wisdom of Solomon: by a miracle, God made him a perfect king but not a perfect man. Again we have the familiar distinction between the office and the man. Just as the king can stand as a symbol of royal reason perfected by special grace, so Solomon the man could represent human reason seeking to acquire the intellectual virtues by the ordinary means available to mankind. The latter is of course precisely the role of Solomon-Koheleth, who found in the end that the wisest thing a man could do was to obey the laws of God. It is in this capacity that Solomon links the circles of the *violenti* and the *sapienti*.

Already we have seen that Koheleth differs from the runners in that he never opposes himself to God's laws, either natural or Scriptural. Here the wisdom of the child was superior to the blind folly of Brunetto and his learned companions. For the one request of the immature king was that he might be enabled through God's grace to rule the Lord's people with justice. His motto might well have been the one Dante placed in the heaven of Jupiter: "Diligite iustitiam qui iudicatis terram!" What motivated him was of course charity manifested as a love both of the people committed to his care and of justice.[51] Of this the poet was well aware, for Solomon's light "breathes from such a love that all the world below hungers for news of it" (*Par.* x, 110–11). Perhaps these words have several meanings, but one surely is that the world longs for a king who is motivated by a love like Solomon's.

The lack of this love, in the last analysis, lies at the root of the sin of the runners. As we have remarked repeatedly, a thirst for fame perverted Brunetto, Priscian, and Francesco; while Mozzi's stumbling block was avarice. All professed to serve society in their several ways; yet, in fact, they pursued their own selfish goals rather than the common welfare. They had been blinded, to employ Dante's favorite metaphor for their condition, by self-interest.

FRANCIS AND DOMINIC: CHAMPIONS IN HEAVEN

Starting from an analysis of the imagery of the runners, we passed via *Monarchia* 2. 7 to Dante's source in Ecclesiastes, whom we found to be the most discussed soul in the heaven of the Sun. My attempt to relate Solomon to the runners can doubtless be improved upon by one whose mastery of Thomism is greater than my own. I shall be content if my conclusions here are firm enough to pave the way for others; in particular I would hope to establish that a correspondence exists between Brunetto's band and the *sapienti*. Points of contact have already been found in Donatus, Gratian, and Solomon, but it remains for us to observe the most striking one of all—the correspondence between the images themselves.

If we had at our disposal a repertory of the images of the *Commedia*, the duplicate imagery of the two passages would no doubt have been observed long ago. As it is, a concordance provides the best approach.[52] Among the words that describe the runners metaphorically, one reappears only once in the *Commedia*. The three Florentines who form a *rota* remind the poet of *i campion* (*Inf.* xvi, 22), a term approximated but not repeated in the counterpart passage of *Monarchia* 2. 7. The word does reappear, however, in *Paradiso* xii, 44-45, where Saints Francis and Dominic are described as "*due campioni*, at whose deeds, at whose words the divided people rallied." Here, as before, *campione* is a key word around which an extended metaphor is built. This time the image is not acted out by the characters, but rather it forms part of a rhetorical figure employed by one of them, Bonaventure, as the leading theme in his account of the life of Saint Dominic (*Par.* xii, 31-105). It forms, of course, a companion piece to Thomas' life of Saint Francis (*Par.* xi, 43-117) and, like it, begins by stressing that both were sent by God to reform the Church at a critical time. Bonaventure chose to express this by a military metaphor, which the Franciscan first suggested in his opening sentence and then developed at length:

> . . . L'amor che mi fa bella
>   mi tragge a ragionar de l'altro duca
>   per cui del mio sì ben ci si favella.
>
> Degno è che, dov' è l'un, l'altro s'induca:
>   sì che, com' elli ad una militaro,
>   così la gloria loro insieme luca.
>
> L'essercito di Cristo, che sì caro
>   costò a rïarmar, dietro a la 'nsegna
>   si movea tardo, sospeccioso e raro,

quando lo 'mperador che sempre regna
>   provide a la milizia, ch'era in forse,
>   per sola grazia, non per esser degna;
e, come è detto, a sua sposa soccorse
>   con due campioni, al cui fare, al cui dire
>   lo popol disvïato si raccorse.

(Par. xii, 31–45)

The love that makes me fair draws me to speak of the other leader [Dominic], on whose behalf so much good is spoken here [by the Dominican Aquinas] of mine [Francis]; it is fitting that where the one is the other should be brought in, so that, as they fought for one end, their glory should shine together.

Christ's army, which cost so dear to rearm, was moving, slow, doubtful and few, behind the standard, when the Emperor who reigns eternally took thought for His soldiers in their peril—only of His grace, not for their deserving—and, as was said, succoured His bride by two champions at whose deeds and words the scattered people rallied.

The lines are filled with military terms, many of which recur in the poem; but some are basic to the metaphor, whereas others appear to elaborate the image but are not essential to the meaning. Thus the fundamental idea is that the Church militant *(la milizia; l'essercito di Cristo)* was in difficulty until encouraged by two champions sent from God. Bonaventure could have conveyed this idea without referring to the cost of rearmament or to the army's ensign; the *campioni*, however, are integral to the basic image, which indeed had been built up to the climactic presentation of Francis and Dominic in this role. The whole exordium, then, has the *campioni* at its core: they occupy the center of a stage filled with Christian soldiers. Thus the single word *campioni* here, as before, is the key word in a complex image that dominates its canto. Hence the repetition of this word, which is not found elsewhere in the poem, serves to link the two cantos together.

Once that connection has been recognized, the significance of the relation can be gathered by further comparison of the passages. The infernal champions had failed in life to fulfill their natural function as defenders of the secular order; opposed to them in heaven are champions of the Church, who through preaching and poverty reveal God's judgment on the progress of mankind toward the beatitude of the other life. There is, then, a double contrast between them and the *tre fiorentini*. The latter represent the perversion of a militia that is both literal and temporal, while the mendicant founders reform one that is spiritual and metaphorical. Moreover, the saints do not match their counterparts in *Monarchia* 2. 7, for their encounter with the enemy involves no *collisio virium*. This circumstance might perhaps be interpreted in a spiritual sense, did not Bonaventure's eulogy contain a still greater discrepancy with the schema of the *Monarchia*, which is concealed in the various epithets applied to the saint. One, "the amorous vassal" ("l'amoroso drudo"; *Par.* xii, 55), modulates the military theme into the feudal language of courtly love,

[182]

paralleling the *cortesia e valor* motif of *Inferno* XVI. Another represents him in a less noble relation to his master:

> Domenico fu detto; e io ne parlo
>   sì come de l'agricola che Cristo
>   elesse a l'orto suo per aiutarlo.
>
> (Par. XII, 70–72)

He was called Dominic, and I speak of him as of the labourer [*agricola*] whom Christ chose to help Him in His garden [*orto*].

Finally, these two themes are interwoven at the climactic moment of Dominic's career—the recognition of his order by the pope, to whom he applies "for leave to fight with the erring world for the seed of which twenty-four plants encircle thee."[53] Dominic's subsequent course resembles a mountain torrent that is driven against the thickets of heresy and at length is divided into many streams watering the Catholic garden (*Par.* XII, 97–105). Among these loosely related figures another epithet appears to be an intruder: he was

the loving liegeman of the Christian faith, the holy athlete, gracious to his own and pitiless to enemies.

> . . . l'amoroso drudo
>   de la fede cristiana, il santo atleta
>   benigno a' suoi e a' nemici crudo.
>
> (Par. XII, 55–57)

Within the context of the canto, the phrase *il santo atleta* seems to be unrelated to any of the other descriptions of Dominic; then when one recalls *i campion nudi e unti* of *Inferno* XVI, it, like *l'amoroso drudo*, seems on second thought to be a variation on Bonaventure's initial metaphor. Yet a further difficulty arises when one compares this image of Dominic the *campione-atleta* to the judgment schema of *Monarchia* 2. 7. There *athletae* designates the swift runners rather than the strong fighters, the *pugiles* whose actions are those of the three noble Florentines. By now alert to the significance of inconsistency in the poem, we can take the hint to press our comparisons further.

We have found traces of the imagery of both the swift and the strong in Bonaventure's life of Dominic; beside it the poet set Aquinas' life of Francis, giving every indication that the two were parallel lives. Does the companion piece then perhaps also draw on the same imagery? Undoubtedly, though less strikingly. Twice Aquinas uses images of the foot race, which we have already seen reflected in the canto of Brunetto Latini. In the paradigm of *Monarchia* 2. 7, divine judgment is revealed in this form: "ex contentione plurium ad aliquod signum prevalere conantium, sicut fit per pugnam athletarum currentium ad bravium." And Francis certainly does run: "for, still a youth, he ran into strife [*in guerra . . . corse*] with his father for a lady" whom no suitor had pursued for centuries.[54] Francis was united to his Lady Poverty, and the success of these lovers soon inspired others:

Their harmony and happy looks moved men to love and wonder and sweet contemplation and led them to holy thoughts, so that the venerable Bernard first went barefoot and ran after that great peace and, running, thought himself too slow [*corse e, correndo, li parve esser tardo*]. O wealth unknown and fruitful good! Barefoot goes Giles, barefoot goes Sylvester, after the bridegroom, so greatly does the bride delight them. Then that father and master went on his way with his lady and with that family which now was bound with the lowly cord. . . .

(Par. xi, 76–87)

At first glance, only the act of running relates this to the competition of Brunetto: he pursued fame as Francis did poverty. Significantly, the competitive element is completely absent; indeed this is stressed by Francis' curious conflict with his father. They were far from being competitors for the same prize: the friction between father and son arose because one pursued wealth and the other poverty; therefore the question was not which racer should prevail, but rather which race should be run. Again, since poverty, unlike property, knows no limit,[55] there is always more than enough for all who wish to be poor. Hence those who pursue Lady Poverty are not in competition but can proceed together in charity. Accordingly, Francis and his bride inspire emulation rather than envy; kindred spirits race to their side, but there is room for all in their company. Francis and his followers are united by the bonds of love; their relationship has as its model the family:

> Indi sen va quel padre e quel maestro
> con la sua donna e con quella famiglia
> che già legava l'umile capestro.[56]

(Par. xi, 85–87)

The image of the Franciscan *famiglia* recalls our introduction to Brunetto's band, whom the narrator refers to as "such a family" (*"cotal famiglia"*).[57] This coincidence suggests that the second and outer circle of spirits in the heaven of the Sun might correspond to the *schiera* of the literati, while the inner one, animated by the spirit of Dominic, would then be equated with the troop of the three Florentines.

Against this hypothesis Dante left clear indications: Gratian and Donatus, the most obvious counterparts of the literati, stand one on the inner and the other on the outer wheel of lights. Still more decisive is the poet's insistence that the twin images of the swift and the strong cannot be applied *respectively* to Francis and Dominic. Instead, as we have noted, they are *due campioni*; and they are also both equated to the swift as well. Francis, as we have seen, is described with the image of the runner; but Dominic too was called *il santo atleta*, which according to the terminology of the *Monarchia* makes him a racer no less than a pugilistic champion.

To these images we must add one more, that of the *rota*, or wheel. In Hell the strong form themselves into a wheel, but the swift do not; the spirits of the Sun, however, form two *rote* of twelve lights each, and the pilgrim glimpses yet a third one, whose lights seemed to him the "very sparkling of the Holy Ghost" (*Par.* xiv, 76). The first two "revolve in such a manner that the one goes first and the other

[184]

after,"[58] and from this detail it would seem that the two are interlinked so closely that their actions are coordinated to produce a single effect. The outer is identified with Francis and the inner with Dominic, the *due principi* of whom Thomas said:

> The one was all seraphic in ardor; the other, for wisdom, was on earth a splendor of cherubic light.[59]

> L'un fu tutto serafico in ardore;
>   l'altro per sapïenza in terra fue
>   di cherubica luce uno splendore.

(*Par.* xi, 37–39)

The two saints are in turn equated by Bonaventure with the two *rote* of the chariot of the Church (*Par.* xii, 106–11), which had figured prominently in the mystical procession through the Earthly Paradise. Let us not worry what these celestial *rote* signify; the image alone is enough to assure us that it is a symbol of coordinated effort. And in Heaven this image of cooperation embodies the essence of Francis and Dominic. In proportion to its importance, the image of the coordinated wheels dominates five cantos of the *Paradiso* and overshadows the image of the *veloces et fortes*. The figure of mistrust in the *Inferno* becomes in Paradise the symbol of coordination. In Hell, each scholar runs for himself, with personal rather than community goals in mind. The *rota* is appropriate, not to them, but to the politicians who were intent on devising a community, however perversely. In Dante's ideal state, the efforts of scholars and statesmen alike would be directed toward the common welfare of mankind, and hence the restriction of the *rota* image to the statesmen reflects the disordination of their unnatural efforts.

Of this, as of so much else, Brunetto Latini is the spokesman. When he sees the statesmen approach, he cries: "Gente vien con la quale esser non deggio" ("I ought not to be with the kind of people who are coming"; *Inf.* xv, 118). From this, commentators usually deduce that it is a law of Hell that the one band of runners cannot mix with the other, which is apparently true—but why? The obligation, I suggest, is the self-imposed pride of caste that causes the scholars to hold themselves aloof from those with whom they should work in close harmony. On earth they refused to pursue the common welfare of the community but instead ran off on a tangent in the name of scholarship; in Hell their habitual apartheid has become part of their punishment. For the same reason, the image of the swift and the strong has primary application to the perverted orders of scholars and statesmen, since the image is a double one, evoking two contests rather than one. In the natural polity, both should cooperate in leading mankind to its twofold beatitude. Instead, each order has become an end unto itself, for the scholar strives to surpass other scholars, and the statesman to dominate other statesmen. In Hell these divisions, ingrained by vicious habit, form an integral part of the punishment that fits the crime.

The image of the swift and the strong, which is literally true in Hell, persists in Heaven *only as a metaphor* or, rather, as two metaphors applied to the same persons from different points of view. Both Francis and Dominic worked toward the same end, the heavenly beatitude of mankind. Their common effort can be considered either as the pursuit of the good or as the struggle against evil, and hence, respectively, can be compared to a race or to a battle. Nonetheless the effort is made in common. Both Thomas and Bonaventure described this common cause at the commencement of their mendicant vitae, and by this device the poet could present the same object from two points of view. Thus the image that seemed part of objective reality in Hell now is seen to be nothing more than a manner of speaking: the race and the battle are one. Although there is but a single common end, yet the means by which it is obtained are diverse. Hence, the way of Francis is distinct from the way of Dominic: each formed his own *ordo* dedicated to preaching and poverty, which Thomas compares to the angelic orders (*Par.* xi, 37–39), but one stressed charity, and the other, wisdom. The two are closely related, for *sapientia* is the gift of the Holy Spirit that corresponds to the theological virtue of *caritas*, but nonetheless each is distinct.[60] Both saints are imbued with love and wisdom, though each has his characteristic stress. The poet conveys this complex interrelationship by interweaving his metaphors. Thus Francis "runs into war with his father," and Dominic is "the amorous vassal of the Christian faith."[61]

The image of the swift and the strong, therefore, is an image of disordered effort. Divers talents should be directed, not to divers ends, but to a common goal, the common welfare of mankind. The natural image of this coordinated effort is the two-wheeled vehicle that is moved in one direction by the cooperation of its twin *rote*.

[7]

Nomina sunt consequentia rerum

Images indicate most clearly how Dante related the perverse runners to their perfected counterparts in the heaven of the Sun; but the poet, like nature, was bountiful in his creation. Metaphor was not the only device at his disposal wherewith to establish the correspondence between the two passages. We have already discovered the significance that could attach to a name in the case of Andrea de' Mozzi,[1] and from the vantage point of the solar heaven, we are encouraged to scrutinize the names of the other characters for some hidden meaning.

Both Aquinas and Bonaventure teach the pilgrim that proper names provide a key to character. Thus, Bonaventure finds significance in the names of Dominic's parents as well as in the name Domenico itself. Similarly, Thomas had derived a presage of Francis' career from the name of his birthplace.[2] As Pézard remarked, these three glosses all exemplify Dante's conviction that proper names express the essence of the thing for which they stand.[3] To express this principle, Dante borrowed a maxim from civil law: "Nomina sunt consequentia rerum."[4]

In accordance with this dictum, that "names are the consequence of things," more than once in the *Comedy* nominal associations serve to indicate essential relations.[5] Yet to modern critics, such serious wordplay is somewhat embarrassing, and perhaps it is no wonder that such clues have not been pursued with enthusiasm. As a matter of personal taste, I, for one, would hesitate to construct an interpretation from such evidence. Although I think that the evidence of names has considerable value as a heuristic device, others may perhaps find such testimony convincing only when it corroborates what has previously been discerned by methods that are more credible to the modern mind. In either case, if we can transcend the limitations of our age and proceed in the spirit in which Dante worked, his meaning can, I believe, often be discovered, or at least elaborated, by reflecting upon his use of proper names. The canto of Brunetto Latini is particularly susceptible to this approach, as we are now in a position to appreciate.

FRANCESCO

The reader is advised in the heaven of the Sun to pay attention to the significance of names. That of Domenico was explained, but that of Francesco was not. Again our attention is captured by asymmetrical omission. Since Domenico has been explained by etymology to signify that the Lord would possess him completely, one is not surprised to find that the same method, when applied to the other, yields a correlative result.

Francesco's name is, of course, an Italian adjective meaning "French." The same meaning, however, is also conveyed by another Italian adjective, *franco*, which has other senses as well. Since the two adjectives overlap in meaning and are cognate in form, I suggest that Dante associated the name Francesco with some quality of character signified by *franco*. The latter has several senses, but within the context of the *Comedy* it would seem to signify one who is *free* rather than simply frank, for it is used twice in this sense and never in any other.[6] And "free" Francis certainly is in Aquinas' tale, for he is freed from his father to run after Lady Poverty, in whose company he wanders thereafter, free from the temporal concerns of this world.

This interpretation can be confirmed by comparison with his counterpart, Dominic. In name as in deed, they stress different means to the same end. As Francis feels freed from false values, so Dominic senses that the Lord dominates his life. The two states are of course reconciled into one by the Pauline paradox that Christ's "service is perfect freedom."[7]

If the significance of the name Francesco now is apparent, we must remember that Aquinas laid particular stress on the name of Francis' birthplace, and we must not forget that he is usually called Francis of Assisi—or in the Italian of the poem, Francesco d'Ascesi. Free association is not needed to find a counterpart to this name in the *Comedy*, because we already know that counterparts to the *sapienti* are to be found among the runners of *Inferno* xv.

That canto yields one name that is strikingly similar to Francesco d'Ascesi—Francesco d'Accorso. The resemblance can be heightened by discarding the modern apostrophes and capitals from the surnames: *dascesi/daccorso*. Further, although one hesitates to tamper with the text, it is worth pointing out that some of the oldest manuscripts read *dacorso*,[8] which form agrees with *dascesi* in having seven letters. There is no need to emend the text, however; for in the Tuscan dialect, the two forms are phonetically identical.[9] Thus the lawyer's name, as Dante pronounced it, becomes a perfect pun, since the sound could equally well be transcribed Francesco *da Corso*. Evidently his proper name conveys the accessory idea of a race or of running *(corso)*, and moreover it can be construed to mean "Frank-fit-for-running," or alternatively "characterized by running."

To grasp the full significance of this double entendre, we must remember that according to Dante's theory, character is reflected not only in baptismal names but also in patronymics. We need not imitate Bonaventure's analysis of the parentage of Dominic, however, because the *Glossa ordinaria* contains Accursius' own gloss on his name: "Instituo te heredem si imponas tibi nomen meum, scilicet Accursium, quod est honestum nomen, dictum quia *accurrit et succurrit* contra tenebras iuris civilis."[10] He "hastens and helps" against the obscurities of civil law, and both verbs have *curro* as their root.

As we know, Francesco d'Accorso owed everything to his father. The son followed his father throughout his life, and even in death he shared his father's tomb and reputation.[11] In this regard he presents a vivid contrast to Francesco d'Ascesi, "ché per tal donna, giovinetto, in guerra / del padre corse" (*Par.* XI, 58–59). One son ran his father's race after fame and fortune; the other "ran into conflict with his father" and freed himself to pursue poverty.

The relation between the two Franceschi is, I believe, in the strictest sense nominal. For was not the one the patron saint of the other? Certainly Francesco the jurist made his devotion to the Franciscans manifest, most notably by moving his father's remains from the Dominican convent in Bologna to the Franciscan cemetery, where the son had built their magnificent common mausoleum.[12] Christened Francesco, the lawyer's son might have followed the example of his patronal namesake and escaped from his father's influence. Instead, paternal influence predominated over patronal, and Francesco, perverted, became the reverse image of his saintly exemplar.

Saint Francis, then, stands in the special relation of patron saint to Francesco d'Accorso, just as Saint Andrew of Florence did to Mozzi. But we know that the legist has another counterpart among the *sapienti*, in the person of Gratian. The canonist also can be drawn into this pattern by the curious circumstance that in Dante's time his full name was mistakenly believed to have been *Francesco* Graziano.[13] Is it too much to suppose that Gratian's characteristic Dantesque attitude— that the jurisdiction of the clergy should be restricted to the forum of conscience—reflects its consequences in this name, the roots of which are, respectively, freedom and grace (*franco* and *grazia*)? If that seems too fanciful, the three Franceschi can be interpreted less imaginatively as representing three types of *professio*. The highest is that of d'Ascesi, who not only professed apostolic poverty himself but also founded an *ordo* in which others could follow his profession. At the other extreme stands the perverted profession of d'Accorso, made to the pope as a test of political loyalty, by which he betrayed the civil law that he professed to teach. Between them stands the third Francesco as a common denominator: his profession, like that of Francesco the sinner, is law, but he has gained salvation because he observed the distinction, essential for Dante, between the outer and inner forums.

ANDREA

The existence of this third Francesco suggests that other Andrews may be found as well, and in fact there are two more. Any Florentine could have recognized the first as our bishop's counterpart and first cousin, for he was the son of Rucco, the Mozzi suicide of *Inferno* XIII—"reverendus et religiosus vir dominus frater Andreas florentinus de Moczis, Ordinis Minorum, in provincia Tuscie inquisitor heretice pravitatis," as a notarial act of 1311 entitles him.[14] This other Andrea de' Mozzi was indeed a spirit of whom Folco could approve! His career began as a missionary to Tartary, whence he was sent as papal legate by Nicholas III in 1278. Old age did not cool his Franciscan ardor, for he climaxed his career by hunting down Tuscan heretics as a veritable Grand Inquisitor,[15] and in due course he was beatified for his zeal. To Dante, as to Folco, the contrast between the homonymous cousins was no doubt more edifying than it is to the modern reader, who in this respect, I should hope, falls short of the poet's ideal. Prejudice aside, the example of the Blessed Andrea de' Mozzi presents so evident a contrast to his relative in Hell that further comment is hardly required.

For the opposite reason, I shall be equally brief in noticing yet another Andrew who is of possible relevance to the bishop and his transmutation. During the years that Dante is thought to have studied at Bologna, the most quoted canonist of the first half of the fourteenth century had just begun his teaching career, and if (as I suspect) the poet had at least begun a course of canon law, very likely the lectures that he heard were given by Johannes Andreae.[16] In 1302 he lectured on the *Decretales*, and the next year on the *Decretum*; in the following year or so he composed his earliest and best-known work, the *Glossa ordinaria* to the *Liber Sextus* of Boniface VIII. His works are more compendious than original, for his method is to collect and report the opinions of his great predecessors, the Decretalists of the thirteenth century. If in one man, Dante wished to condemn all the works of the Decretalists, he could have found no better symbol than Johannes Andreae, whom contemporaries respected as the *fons et tuba iuris*. Since we have reason to believe that Andrea de' Mozzi is the poet's figure for all the damnable Decretalists, his name may hint that their living compendium may eventually run in Brunetto's band.

These two Andrews—the one undeniably relevant, and the other a tenuous plausibility—both were living in 1300. As such, they functioned, if at all, outside the poem and served to relate its characters to souls who were still living. To put it another way, their presence is at best peripheral: they appear, not on the stage, but amongst the audience, who may be prompted by the piece to wonder how the names of the living are shaping their ends. For such curiosity, the poem provides the antidote, which is administered by the same character that brought the significance of names to our attention. Aquinas, in his final words, cautions us not to imagine that the living can judge their neighbors: "Let not Dame Bertha and Master Martin, when they see one rob and another make an offering, think they see them within the divine counsel; for the one may rise and the other fall."[17] Therefore, it would be appropriate if the poet had evoked by name these two enigmatic Andrews simply to remind us that their future is no less ambiguous than their relation to the poem.

PRISCIAN

Of quite another order of certitude are the two remaining characters in *Inferno* xv, whose names we have yet to explain. Priscian presents no difficulty whatever, for the etymology of his name matches the sin that we have assigned to him. *Priscus* denotes that which belongs to former, primitive times: as a noun, *prisci* signifies the ancients themselves.[18] In grammar, it was Priscian's distinctive method to summon all the ancients to testify by example to the former usage of the Latin vocabulary.

Since this characteristic was the cause of his damnation, we could have no clearer proof that "Nomina sunt consequentia rerum."

BRUNETTO LATINI AND HIS COUNTERPARTS: WORKS

But what of Brunetto Latini? As yet we have found no counterpart for him in the poem, much less heard an echo of his name.[19] In view of the manifold correspondences between his canto and those of the *sapienti*, we may well search among them for some clue that will supply the deficiency. Ironically, the connection is formed by his precious book, which led to both his fame on earth and his infamy in Hell. It can be no coincidence that one of the *sapienti* owes his salvation to another book that is truly his treasure,[20] though he did not give it that proud title:

> L'altro ch'appresso addorna il nostro coro,
>   quel Pietro fu che con la poverella
>   offerse a Santa Chiesa suo tesoro.
>
> <div align="right">(<i>Par.</i> x, 106–8)</div>

The other who next adorns our choir was that Peter who, like the poor widow, offered his treasure to Holy Church.

This *tesoro* was the *Libri sententiarum*, written about 1152, which became the standard scholastic textbook of theology.[21] The author is identified in Heaven by the opening words of the prologue to his *Sentences*, so there can be little doubt that Dante has referred us to that passage. It remains to be seen whether it has any relevance to the sin of Brunetto Latini:

[1] Though poor and weak, I, like the widow, wish to contribute my mite to the Lord, and therefore I have presumed to attempt a work that is both difficult in itself and beyond my powers. For the completion of the work and the reward of my labors, I have placed my trust in the Good Samaritan, who not only left two coins for the care of him who was half alive, but also promised that if this were not enough he would make up the difference. The honesty of the undertaking attracted me, but the immense amount of work deterred me; I was encouraged by my desire to be of service but discouraged by my own inadequacy. [2] Zeal for the Church prevailed on me in the end to fortify our faith against the errors of carnal and bestial men, or rather to show the faint-hearted that it is already the tower of David fortified with shields. Hence I have done my best to expound the intricacies of theological questions and also to pass on what our limited intelligence understands about the sacraments of the Church. I have no valid right to resist the wishes of fellow scholars who have begged me in Christ's name that I serve their praiseworthy studies with both my tongue and pen [*lingua ac stylo*], since this my team is driven by the charity of Christ [*quas bigas in nobis agitat Christi caritas*].[22]

Next, the Lombard turns to face his opponents. A new fashion in theology has made his work necessary. Writing in about 1152, he complains that nowadays men study the Fathers only to contradict them. So intent are they on raising objections that they are not receptive to the truth when it is expounded to them. They cannot understand sound patristic doctrine, because their wills are not subject to reason. Moreover, they imagine that they have a method whereby they can arrive at truth without long study, though in fact it prevents them from grasping the truth and, still worse, often leads them into error. Such men, who would rather argue than understand, should be lawyers rather than scholars.

Although the Lombard mentions no names, it is clear that he, like Anselm of Bec, has faith in his authorities and seeks to understand them. His conservative attitude displays the old-fashioned motto "Fides quaerens intellectum." From this standpoint he views with alarm the success of Abelard's new critical theology, which proceeds dialectically by ferreting out the inconsistencies after the manner of *Sic et non* and then seeks to reconcile them with the aid of the newly sharpened tools of scholastic logic. Peter Lombard will fight fire with fire. He adopts the new instruments but announces that he will use them in the spirit of Anselm rather than of Abelard. Having clarified his intention, he next explains the purpose of his book:

[4] Because I wish to destroy the ungodly errors they have assembled and to shut them up (lest they be able to pour forth the poison of iniquity into others), and to raise up the lamp of truth upon a candelabrum, I by much labor and sweat and with God's help have compiled this volume from the witnesses of the truth established in eternity and have divided it into four books. [5] In them you will find the examples and doctrine of our elders. I have exposed therein the fraudulence of heretical doctrine by professing soundly the faith of the Lord. My approach has been to demonstrate the truth and never to imperil piety by professing anything uncertain. I have avoided extreme statements, preferring moderation in all things. If my own voice at any point sounds inadequate, it at least stays within the bounds set by the Fathers.

Peter Lombard's preface immediately suggests many contrasts with the Brunetto we have come to know; but the two are not strictly comparable, since we have not seen Brunetto's character reflected in the preface to his *Tresor*. Let us therefore lay Latini's text beside that of the Lombard and then compare the two:

> *This book is called the Treasury*
> *and speaks of the origin of all things.*
>
> This book is called the Treasury, for just as a lord who wishes to collect together in a small space things of the greatest value, not only for his enjoyment but also to increase his power and to assure his status in war and in peace, fulfills his intention by putting all the most costly things and the most precious jewels he can into his treasury; just so is the body of this book made up of wisdom [*sapience*], the essence of which has been as it were extracted from all the members of philosophy.[23]

Brunetto then extends his metaphor by comparing each of the three component parts of his book to one of the kinds of treasure that lords lay up for themselves. (1) His first part contains pure, abstract knowledge, which he describes simply as "the first science of philosophy, namely *theorika*." This he compares to ready cash which one keeps on hand to be expended for everyday necessities. "And just as without money there would be no medium for men to exchange their goods and services, so also we would not be able to understand other things plainly without the first part of this book." (2) "Precious stones, which give man pleasure and virtue," are like the treasure contained in the second part. These are ethics and logic, which tell man what he ought and ought not to do, and show him the reason why. (3) Ethics is, however, not the whole of applied philosophy *(pratike)*; the third part concerns politics, which for Brunetto includes rhetoric and is properly called *rectorique*.[24] Because this final treasure is the best of all, he likens it to pure gold, "for as gold surpasses all other metals, so the science of rhetoric and government is more noble than any other art in the world."

Having described his treasures, Brunetto explains why and how he has collected them. Such riches should not be given to a man unless he is adequate *(soufissables)* to them, and therefore Brunetto will entrust them only to a close and dear friend who, in his judgment, is worthy *(dignes)*:

> [5] And I do not say that the book was drawn from my own poor understanding or from my slight knowledge [*de mon povre sens ne de ma menue science*]; rather it was, like a comb of honey, collected from various flowers, for this book is compiled only from the wonderful sayings of the authors who, before our time, have treated of philosophy. Each of my authorities was a specialist in his own field, for men on earth cannot know philosophy in its entirety because it is the root from which grow all the sciences that man can know. Thus philosophy resembles a fountainhead from which many streams issue and flow away hither and yon, so that this man drinks from one stream and that man from another; but because the streams are distinct, although some drink more and some drink often, yet none can drink the fountain dry.
>
> [6] That is why Boethius in his *Consolation* says that he saw Philosophy in the form and dress of a woman who had the marvelous ability to grow, when she wished, so high that her head rose above the stars and the heavens[25] and she could see upstream and downstream according to law and according to truth.

Brunetto's preface accurately describes his work as an anthology of established authorities on various branches of philosophy. Whole chapters are transcribed or condensed from his sources, and often the chapter itself is a catena of quotations from famous writers, like an article in a modern dictionary of quotations, wherein are collected the opinions of famous authors on a given subject.[26] In essence, then, what Brunetto compiled was neither more nor less than a collection of expert opinions, which is to say *sententiae*.[27] The *Tresor*, therefore, invites comparison with Peter Lombard's *Libri sententiarum*, since both belong to the same literary genre. Although one deals with theology and the other with philosophy, the same method could be applied to both kinds of *documenta*. But in fact it was not. Instead, the two works represent two radically different approaches to similar, occasionally even the same, material. Indeed, the two methods yield results so divergent that they agree only in being collections of *sententiae*.

Brunetto correctly represents himself as the compiler and translator of an anthology. He has garnered the thoughts of others into his storehouse and is responsible only for their selection and arrangement. His work is encyclopedic in character, a compendium of the type known to the thirteenth century as a speculum;[28] and this is a fact of considerable significance when one recalls Dante's complaint against "nescio quod 'Speculum.'" Although Dante probably made use of such works himself on occasion, nonetheless he was positive that they were no substitute for the original sources.[29] But that is precisely what the *Tresor* pretends to be: the reader is told that the valuables of philosophy have been collected there. Presumably only worthless stuff has been left behind; certainly the reader is not encouraged to return to the sources and see for himself.

By contrast we have the Lombard's insistence that his sources be studied long and hard, and especially that they be understood. He would rather study the Fathers than argue about them. Basically the Master of the Sentences dislikes the dialectical approach which the imitators of Abelard have forced him to assume in defense of the faith, but he will make the best of a bad thing and exhibit the essential harmony of patristic doctrine. The *Sententiae* is a work designed to meet a specific need, not for a sourcebook, but for a systematic resolution of apparent difficulties. As such, it could serve as a companion to the student of patrology in his studies, rather than as a substitute for them.

To be sure, the Lombard wrote for a different audience than did Latini, but Dante will not accept this argument as an excuse for Brunetto's approach, for Alighieri himself undertook to expound philosophy in the vernacular for the layman. In his introduction to the *Convivio*, Dante took care to define both his audience and his approach as second best: the banquet will consist of crumbs from "that table where the bread of angels is eaten." Within the limitations of author and audience, the *Convivio* is a serious attempt to convey an understanding of philosophy. The opening words define its purpose: it will provide that knowledge which all men desire because as rational animals their ultimate happiness consists in the exercise of their noblest faculty, reason. In short, Dante would lead his readers to their temporal beatitude.

Judged by the model of the *Convivio*, Brunetto's *Tresor* appears to be a perverted work. Although it professes to teach philosophy, it in fact does nothing of the sort. We already know that its fundamental error lies in the intention of the work, which is to give practical instruction in how to be a podesta.[30] The illegitimate end has misshapen the means thereto. The civil servant judges and is judged by practical results. Brunetto promises to teach him all that one needs to know to be a successful rhetorician-ruler, which falls far short of the training of a philosopher-king. The *Tresor*'s preface takes a pragmatic view of theoretical knowledge: pure learning is the indispensable foundation for the high, practical arts. As a result of this inverted view, Brunetto ruthlessly omits all theoretical matters that have no practical application in his ethics and politics. By this principle of selection, conventional theology is substituted for metaphysics (*Tresor* 1. 6–18); Aristotelian physics and psychology are reduced to the doctrine of the four elements (1. 99–107); and natural history, stripped of all generalizations, becomes a simple bestiary (1. 130–99). The tendency to describe rather than explain leads Brunetto to include a small geographical gazetteer (*mapamunde*; 1. 121–24) and a very considerable epitome of world history (1. 19–98). Astronomy is perhaps the only theoretical science that Brunetto gives an acceptable summary of (1. 108–20), and Aristotle would have laughed aloud on being told that *theorika* includes domestic economy (1. 125–29).

Assuredly the book has a perennial appeal, and indeed its several parts had already withstood the test of time when Brunetto collected and translated them. Dante had no quarrel with honest encyclopedists: Isidore of Seville, the greatest of them all, has his place among the *sapienti* (*Par.* x, 131). What is reprehensible is Brunetto's misrepresentation of his material. The reader is promised the flowers of philosophy, culled from the best authorities; but what is he given? The wilted weeds cultivated by inferior and outdated authors, now pressed into the treasure book of Brunetto Latini. By educated standards then prevailing, this was no treasury of philosophy but was, rather, the thesaurus of a rhetorician, a commonplace book farced with decorative data wherewith the *dictator* could embellish his prose. As such, it would be eminently practical, for its aim was to provide the appearance of learning rather than true understanding. Then as now, an apposite quotation from a recognized authority lent weight to an argument, and the rhetorician did not need to burden either himself or his audience with philosophical explanations. Brunetto's goal, then, was to create a suitable impression, to gain the success of political rhetoric —in short, to attain *fama*.

Simply put, the fault of the *Tresor* is that it does not serve its ostensible purpose, which is to confer the riches of philosophy upon the reader. A true philosophic treasury would lead its readers to their temporal beatitude by perfecting them in the intellectual virtues. Far from assisting men to attain this goal, Brunetto assures them, as he did the pilgrim (*Inf.* xv, 119), that they need nothing more than what his *Treasury* can provide. Those who accept his teaching will, like Latini, assist the insubordinate cities of Italy in opposing the emperor. By so doing, they will deny to the rest of mankind that beatitude to which Brunetto has blinded these pseudo intellectuals.[31]

Certainly this interpretation will stir Brunetto's apologists—he has them still— into outraged protest. Is it not unfair to condemn a man for not imitating the *Convivio*, a book written after his death? Dante provided against this objection, as he did against similar ones that could be raised in behalf of the other characters.[32] Brunetto himself cites, at the end of his preface, the book that would have taught him how to present philosophy to the common man in the manner of the *Convivio*. This, of course, is the *Consolation of Philosophy*, which we can be sure is relevant because its author, Boethius, circles with Peter Lombard in the heaven of the Sun:

> Per vedere ogne ben dentro vi gode
> l'anima santa che 'l mondo fallace
> fa manifesto a chi di lei ben ode.

Lo corpo ond' ella fu cacciata giace
    giuso in Cieldauro; ed essa da martiro
    e da essilio venne a questa pace.

(Par. x, 124–29)

Within it [the eighth light] rejoices in the vision of all good the holy soul
who makes plain the world's deceitfulness to one that hears him rightly;
the body from which he was driven lies below in Cieldauro, and he came
from martyrdom and exile to this peace.

Brunetto cites no other philosopher in his preface, and thereby his very method
betrays him, for he has extracted Boethius' image of Philosophy without comprehending its meaning, much less the message of the whole work. For Brunetto takes
the lofty stature of Philosophia to mean that she can be incomprehensible, and he
cites it to excuse himself for presenting his reader with *disiecta membra.* The original sense, however, would seem to be that through philosophy man can understand
not only the familiar things of this world but also can rise to an understanding of
things heavenly and unseen.[33] Boethius' book itself condemns the sort of success
that Brunetto sought—fame through public service (*Consol. Philos.,* 2. 7)—and
instead teaches, as Dante did, that man's final beatitude and perfect good are one
and the same goal, namely the contemplation of God, the Greatest Good.[34]

    Brunetto and Boethius contrast as philosophers false and true. Although the
points of contact between them are susceptible of extensive elaboration, the details
would but bear out our analysis of Latini's philosophic fault. To one who is
familiar with their works, the contrast is indeed obvious, once it is pointed out.
The curious thing is that Dante did not lead us directly from one to the other;
instead he deliberately included Peter Lombard in the relationship. The reference
to the preface of the Lombard's *tesoro* caused us to consult its counterpart in
Brunetto's work, which in turn refers us back to Boethius, the Lombard's companion
in Heaven. The primary contrast is not the obvious one between philosophers but
rather some less evident difference between Ser Brunetto and the *Magister Sententiarum.* One would not have thought to compare them had not the poet himself
juxtaposed the two prefaces, but once they have been laid side by side, a whole
series of contrasts emerges.

    We have already noted the Lombard's conviction that an anthology of *sententiae*
is no substitute for a profound study of the *auctoritates.* Nor is his work anything
of the sort. He collects the opinions of the Fathers in the same spirit that Gratian
collected canons: in order to harmonize the apparently disharmonious. Unlike
Brunetto, who stresses the diversity of his subject and the impossibility of mastering
the whole of it, Pietro insists that there is but one *doctrina Christiana,* because the
Truth is One, and it is his enterprise to exhibit the unity of the parts and of the
whole. Above all, he desires to convey understanding rather than information, so
that men will understand the *documenta spiritualia* which can lead them to salvation. Brunetto, by contrast, does not urge or assist us to understand the *documenta
philosophica*; instead, he has plundered them for information that will serve his
own purpose, which is contrary to their teaching.

[196]

We could extend the catalogue of contrasts still further, but the point of this comparison does not require an accumulation of detail, since all the differences can be referred to a single cause, namely the author's intent. The Lombard himself plainly declares that both his tongue and his pen are guided by Christian charity: "lingua ac stylo. . . . Quas bigas in nobis agitat Christi caritas."[35] Thomas Aquinas, the most distinguished of all the Lombard's commentators, took him at his word and reduced all the motives mentioned in the opening paragraphs of the prologue to one form of charity or another. Love of God prompted Peter's zeal for His Church and his desire to be of assistance; also it made him long for divine reward and gave him trust in divine assistance. The same love caused him to love his neighbor as himself; and for this reason he acceded to the wishes of his colleagues who urged him to undertake the work that would profit their sacred studies.[36] Dante, it would seem, followed Thomas' interpretation of the prologue to the *Sentences*, and indeed in the *Comedy* he expresses it through the character Aquinas himself, by whom the Lombard is introduced as "that Peter who, like the poor widow, offered his treasure to Holy Church" (*Par.* x, 107–8). Peter's authorship, therefore, is compared to an act of charity in the most concrete sense—that of almsgiving.

The poet thus alerts us to the quality that informs the *Sentences* and makes that work a true treasure, in contradistinction to the misdirected assemblage of trivia that Brunetto gathered into his *Tresor*. The contrast recalls the thesaurus *topos* that contained the essence of Mozzi's fault: "Lay not up to yourselves treasures on earth . . . but lay up to yourselves treasures in heaven . . . for where thy treasure is, there is thy heart also."[37] Motivated by Christian charity, the Lombard placed his store in Heaven, which is to say that his scholarship was motivated by the desire to teach men how to achieve their ultimate beatitude in divine contemplation. By comparison, Brunetto's treasure is altogether on earth. Not only is its reward fame among men, but it positively obstructs the progress of mankind towards the twofold beatitude. Finally, to complete the parallel, Brunetto's gift of effective public speaking is appropriately corrupted by Mozzi the Moth. Who, then, are the thieves that break through and steal? Are they not the plagiarists who, like Brunetto, plunder the pantries (*armamentaria*) of the ancients for their borrowed finery?

The Lombard and his *tesoro*, then, afford the reader a specific instance of the effects of charity on scholarship. From the case of Solomon and the image of the runners, he can perceive in a general way that those who are violent against nature lack the essential virtue of charity, but their counterpart characters exemplify the course that would have led to eternal victory. Brunetto Latini has as his pacemakers Boethius and the Lombard. The poet's message is simplicity itself: if Brunetto had, like the Lombard, been motivated by love of God and neighbor, then his treasure of philosophy would have resembled that of Boethius.

BRUNETTO LATINI AND HIS COUNTERPARTS: NAMES

Brunetto, like the lesser characters of his canto, has his heavenly counterpart or, rather, counterparts, whose virtues correspond to his vices. To complete our inquiry we must now consider whether some further significance may lie concealed in the names of Brunetto and his alter egos. There is, at the least, the superficial correspondence between the initial letters of the name Brunetto Latini and those of Boethius and Lombardus, but this can hardly be more than an artificial device by which the poet reassures the reader that he has hit upon the characters equivalent to B. L. More essential is the sense of the name "Brunetto" itself, which literally signifies "one who is rather dark." Certainly this suits one who runs in the obscure half-light and who, moreover, half blinds himself by squinting. The light, of course, is that divine light which emanates from the Sun of Truth, of which the sun itself is the symbol throughout the *Comedy*.

Brunetto's Christian name certainly suggests the sinner we have come to know, and perhaps it also suggests a nuance that has not been sufficiently stressed before. Brunetto and his companions are not totally blind. Rather they squint, voluntarily excluding a portion of the light that is theirs by the bounty of nature, but only a portion. Likewise Brunetto is "a little dark," but not altogether so. In intellectual terms, I take this qualification to mean that he and his companions do not make full use of their rational powers; instead they limit their scope to a specialized subject, concentrating "like an old tailor on the eye of his needle" (*Inf.* xv, 21). The nuance that we must not miss is that their darkness is only relative: in fact, by excluding much of nature's light, they may see the object of their attention all the more clearly. Their mistake, then, would be to insist perversely that the world can only be seen in proper perspective from their *professional* point of view, as it were, through the eye of a needle.

Brunetto's baptismal name reflects his fault, but I can detect no echo of it in the names of his heavenly counterparts. Accordingly, the correspondence, if any, must be sought in his family name, "Latini," or as he himself on occasion wrote it, "Latino."[38] If the coordinate initials are any guide, its counterpart form will be Lombardo, as the "Pietro" of the poem would be known in Italian. But Pietro is not the only Lombardo in the poem, for more than once we have found our cantos elucidated by that Marco Lombardo who is placed in Purgatory halfway between Ser Brunetto and the Master of the Sentences. If the name Latino stands in any significant relation to Lombardo, then Marco too must be included in the pattern.

Juxtaposed, Latino and Lombardo can easily be related to one another. Who, after all, were the Latins and the Lombards? Both were peoples of Italy; one was subject to Rome, and the other subjected Rome. For Dante, "to call the Italians *Latini* and their homeland *Latium* indicated that they were subordinated to a world empire and yet at the same time were its heart."[39] In the poem, Brunetto is certainly conscious of his racial origins, so much so that he may rightly be regarded as a racist. He identifies himself and Dante with "the holy seed of those Romans who remained there when it became the nest of such wickedness" (*Inf.* xv, 76–78). But the place whereof he speaks is not Rome, not Italy, not the empire, but Florence, whose elite stock Brunetto identifies with the Roman or, more precisely, *Latin* colonists, as opposed to the Fiesolani, who emigrated to Florence from the nearby mountains.[40] Now, we already know that Brunetto Latini is in Hell because he had denied the allegiance that he and all Florentines owed to Rome, and had claimed instead that Florence was independent, under the rule of her insubordinate aristocracy. Therefore it is ironic, to say the least, that Brunetto should at the same time take conscious pride in his own Latino-Roman origins and those of his fellow traitors to Rome.[41]

Loyalty to Rome, it would appear, was not among the genetic gifts of Brunetto's *sementa santa*. The fate of both Lombardi augments the irony, for despite their unpromising racial origins, Marco is on his way to Heaven, and Pietro already is there. Moreover, Brunetto also has as his heavenly counterpart a Latin who was second to none in nobility: Anicius Manilius Severinus Boethius, whose exemplary loyalty to Rome's Church and empire led him to the martyrdom for which he is remembered in the poem. Boethius, the loyal Latin, then, reproaches Brunetto no less by his life than by his doctrine.

The presence of both Latin and Lombard in Heaven assures us that salvation is not racially determined. Simple Christian doctrine could hardly be interpreted otherwise, for one is saved or damned in the afterlife on the basis of individual acts, which are not racially determined. But absurdly, Brunetto in the *Comedy* appears to maintain the contrary, for he attributes virtue to the inheritors of *la sementa santa* and vice to another racial stock. In general, he warns Dante that the bestial Fiesolani have befouled Florence and consumed almost all the old stock of the holy Roman seed. Among the few survivors he counts Dante and presumably himself, but for the most part he takes the Florentine character to be that of the intrusive majority.

These general outlines are conveyed by metaphoric contrasts between bitter mountain sorbs and sweet figs, between filthy, omnivorous goats and the holy seed whose plants they devour. Brunetto does not neglect, however, to detail the nature of the Florentines' debased character: they are dominated by greed, envy, and pride; their city has become a nest of wickedness.[42] The word *malizia* decidedly suggests that their faults are of a moral order, and this is placed beyond doubt by imputing to them in particular three of the seven deadly sins: "avara, invidiosa e superba." This, then, is the essence of Brunetto's theory: race is a moral factor. One racial stock, he asserts, tends to vice, another to virtue.

Latini in the poem holds a racist theory of morality that is discredited by his own damnation, on the one hand, and by the salvation of the Lombardi and Boethius, the noble Latin, on the other. Since the contrast between Latins and Lombards is a racial one, it would seem plausible to suppose that Dante made Brunetto the spokesman for a racial theory that was not the poet's own. This can be readily verified from the *Commedia* itself, for Brunetto's explanation of the corruption of Florence is revised in Paradise, where the truth of the matter is stated by Cacciaguida:

> Sempre la confusion de le persone
>   principio fu del mal de la cittade,
>   come del vostro il cibo che s'appone;

> e cieco toro più avaccio cade
>> che cieco agnello; e molte volte taglia
>> più e meglio una che le cinque spade.

(Par. xvi, 67–72)

The mixture of peoples was ever the beginning of the city's ills, as food in excess is of the body's, and a blind bull falls more headlong than a blind lamb, and often one sword cuts more and better than five.

From the beginning, racism is ruled out; for the stress does not fall on families or peoples but on individual persons *(persone)*. Moreover, the three reasons are all based on *quantitative* considerations rather than on heritable moral qualities. Florence is dysfunctional because it has more persons than one community can absorb; its excessive size exaggerates its faults ("The bigger they are, the harder they fall"); sheer numbers are no substitute for quality and efficiency.[43]

Dante, then, rejected Brunetto's approach to Florentine moral decay, though on what grounds Cacciaguida does not say. For a critique of Brunetto's theory of heritable virtue, we must turn to the fourth tractate of the *Convivio*, the whole argument of which stands as a refutation of Brunetto's racism. Because the subject of *Convivio* 4 is nobility, the inquiry is chiefly directed toward familial rather than racial inheritance, but at the end of the treatise, Dante demonstrates that his arguments apply no less to race than to family. He had previously shown that true nobility is a quality of the soul that progeny cannot inherit from their progenitors. Since only individual persons have souls, it follows that the soulless family, race, stock, or line of descent—his term, *schiatta*, includes them all—cannot, strictly speaking, be called noble. Any collection of individuals can be loosely called noble, however, if men of noble soul predominate therein—that is, if they exceed the ignoble in number. "So in a noble family it would be possible for the good to die off one by one, and for the bad to be born into it to such an extent that it would change its name and deserve to be called not noble but vile."[44] Hence it is clear that Dante wholly dissociated himself from Brunetto's racism, not only as an explanation of the corruption of Florence, but also in principle.

If it were my intention here to explicate the heaven of the Sun, the consequences of the name Latini could lead us on to consider some of the most difficult Dantesque questions. Within the system of Alighieri's thought, the progression is swift and inevitable. To know why some souls are noble, one must understand human embryology and psychogenesis, which in turn requires a more general understanding of the operation of nature, of the generative process, and of its relation to its Creator and his grace. I suspect that Dante himself clearly recognized that the problem of race entailed the whole of his philosophy and theology, and I imagine that he therefore raised that question in connection with Brunetto in order to lead the reader to these twin studies wherein man learns the truth of nature and of her God. To understand Brunetto's damnation, however, we need only assure ourselves that his concept of *la semanta santa* was not the poet's. I shall therefore pass directly to Dante's conclusion without attempting to expound the arguments on which it is based. It is enough, I think, that one realize that the curious reader must inevitably retrace the steps from this conclusion back through the whole system of Dantesque philosophy and theology.

Dante's *sementa santa* is the nobility that God confers on such human embryos as are disposed by the workings of nature to receive the divine gift. To explain how the noble soul is formed, Dante offers a double explanation in *Convivio* 4. 21, "explaining it first after the natural fashion, and then after the theological fashion, which is to say the divine and spiritual fashion."[45] For the natural explanation he follows Aristotelian psychology, though it is noteworthy that he concedes that the views of other philosophers may also approximate the truth.[46] Among philosophers, the Peripatetic opinion enjoys a relative superiority, but even the best philosophic explanation can only approximate the truth somewhat more nearly than less satisfactory naturalistic accounts. To the philosopher—limited as he is, by his method, to unaided human reason—the divine activity of the human soul can never be fully comprehended, simply because God does not reveal himself fully in nature. Thus, after tracing the genesis of intelligence in the human embryo, much as he does in *Purgatorio* xxv,[47] Dante concludes: "And this is almost all that can be said by way of natural explanation."[48] For fuller comprehension, man must turn to the *documenta spiritualia*, which will teach him more perfectly what it is within man that enables him to be a good—that is to say, a noble—man:[49]

> By way of theological explanation it may be said that after the supreme Deity, that is, God, sees His creature made ready to receive of His kindness [*beneficio*], He bestows on it as much as the creature is prepared to receive of it. And since these gifts proceed from ineffable Caritas [*caritate*], and because Divine Caritas may be especially attributed to the Holy Spirit, hence it is that they are called "gifts of the Holy Spirit." [12] These gifts are seven according to the division made by the prophet Isaiah, namely, Wisdom, Understanding, Counsel, Strength, Knowledge, Piety, Fear of God. O goodly crop! O goodly and admirable seed! [*Oh buone biade, e buona e ammirabile sementa!*] O admirable and gracious Sower, who waits only for human nature to prepare the ground to be sown! How blessed are they who duly cultivate such seed![50]

Here, somewhat elliptically, Dante unveils his own version of *la sementa santa*. Unlike Brunetto's "holy seed," it is not the natural seed of one's progenitor but rather a benefit conferred on an individual by God himself. The benefit itself, the *buona e ammirabile sementa*, is never named; instead the seed is identified by its effects, the goodly crop *(buone biade)* of gifts of the Holy Spirit. This is not surprising, since Dante had earlier explained that it would be his method to define and discover the seed of nobility from its effects or fruits.[51] What then is the seed from which spring the seven gifts of the Holy Spirit? The commentators on this passage have long since observed that scholastic theology taught that all seven derived from a single source, the greatest of the theological virtues, charity.[52]

Convivio 4. 21, therefore, offers a double view of human nobility. The chapter illuminates the definition proposed by the text of the canzone upon which it comments: "Nobility is the seed of happiness placed by God in a well-disposed soul."[53] In effect, the chapter offers two glosses on *gentilezza*, the nobility of the human soul. Understood according to natural philosophy, it can be equated to *intelligenza*, the capacity to function as a rational animal.[54] Theologically speaking, however, nobility of soul consists in *caritate*.

We are here in the presence of a double truth that superimposes revelation upon reason to yield a higher understanding than is available to human reason alone. The highest, noblest operations of the human soul are those that most resemble God himself, who is both omniscient and omnibeneficent. To the extent that man possesses either love or wisdom, he approaches divinity. Thus, perhaps the simplest way to reconcile the several meanings of "the seed of happiness" would be to say that it represents man's capacity to be godlike. Certainly more complex explanations can be given, and Dante himself provided them in his philosophy and theology. Yet my point, as has been said, can be made from his conclusions, without reference to the underlying reasons. It is enough to know that, for Dante, nobility of soul consists no less in an innate capacity for charity than in a superior, inborn intelligence. This double truth must be learned from the coordinate *documenta* of revelation and of reason. Human reason alone cannot discover that human perfection consists in godlike love. The man of great intelligence who rejects the theological way of understanding will consequently not fully cultivate his God-given seed of happiness, for he will never come to realize that with his intelligence he was endowed with a concomitant measure of charity.

"How blest are they who duly cultivate such seed," Dante exclaims, and shortly thereafter he laments how numerous are those who do not.[55] Among the latter, must we not number Brunetto and his fellows, in whom we have already detected a signal lack of charity? Our study of the images keeps returning us, by a sort of spiral ascent, to this point: Brunetto had worldly knowledge, but he was deficient in charity. Now we can see more clearly, though not perfectly, why he deserves damnation therefor. As an intellectual, Latini rejected the full wisdom that revelation placed at his disposal. His great intellect presupposed an equal capacity for charity, which he, intent on his mundane goal of glory, refused to recognize. Guided by this misconception of his talent, Brunetto could not develop into a whole man; through his blindness, he became a lopsided intellectual. The effects of this overspecialization are already evident in his selective view of philosophy, which developed rhetoric at the expense of all other parts of science; and now it is clear that he wholly ignored the teaching of theology, from which he could have learned the full range of his gifts. As his epitaph we may suitably take the words of Saint Paul: "And if I should have prophecy and should know all mysteries, and all knowledge, and if I . . . have not charity, I am nothing."[56] This tragic waste is Brunetto's essential sin.

> Puossi far forza ne la deïtade,
>> col cor negando e bestemmiando quella,
>> e spregiando natura e sua bontade.[57]

(*Inf.* xi, 48–50)

[202]

Violence may be done to the Godhead by denying and blaspheming Him in the heart and by despising Nature and her bounty.

He denied the divine goodness that was his birthright; it would have been his salvation, had he not neglected it.[58]

BRUNETTO AND DANTE ON THE ORIGINS OF NOBILITY

As art follows nature, so Dante's fictions reflect historical fact: they are poetic images of their originals. This remarkable fidelity has enabled us in earlier essays to discover the sins of the runners from their biographies. Now that the evidence of the imagery has permitted us to refine those first conclusions, we should turn again and ask whether the historical Brunetto did in fact correspond to the character as he appears in the poem. For in the preceding section, we did not pause to inquire whether the author of the *Tresor* held the opinions that his shade in Hell expressed.

The comparison proves decidedly disconcerting, for we have no record that the historical Brunetto considered the mixture of races to be the cause of the moral corruption of Florence. Indeed, at the point in the *Tresor* where one might expect him to introduce this theory, he remarks instead that the planet Mars must be blamed for the prominence of strife in Florentine affairs.[59] To be sure, the two theories are not necessarily incompatible, but still one would have expected the poet to have his character adhere more closely to the opinions that Latini had published while living. Was this deviation perhaps intentional on the part of the poet? This suspicion grows with reading the *Tresor*, where one looks in vain for the theory that virtue is racially determined. The whole tirade against the Florentines appears to be not only uncharacteristic of the historical Brunetto but perhaps even contrary to the *Tresor*'s doctrine of virtue and nobility. What is more, the most recent study of Dante's debt to Brunetto concludes that it consisted precisely in the theory of true nobility!

Charles Davis' work has persuaded me that this was the debt acknowledged by Dante when he said that Brunetto had taught him "how man makes himself eternal" (*Inf.* xv, 85). We have already remarked, however, that Brunetto can hardly have taught Dante what the poet conceived to be the *whole* range of virtue, since man can be said to "eternize himself" only in respect to those pagan virtues that require no special grace.[60] But since we have found in the preceding section that, according to Dante's theory of nobility, the gifts of the Holy Spirit are, theologically speaking, the fruits of nobility, we must suspect that, although Dante may have begun with Brunetto's concept of nobility, still he learned from some other source how God makes man eternal. Thus the poem itself prepares us to expect that Brunetto was a formative influence on Dante's theory of nobility, but does so by a locution that immediately cautions us to determine not only the influence but also its extent.

Professor Davis has found convincing evidence of the influence.[61] Certainly Brunetto's own phrase in the *Tresor*—"those who delight in a noble lineage and boast of lofty ancestors"[62]—is echoed in the *Convivio*: "they who because they are of

famous and ancient lineage, and are descended from excellent forefathers. . . ."[63]
Other correspondences between the passages, however, may be derived from a
common source, namely the treatise *Moralium dogma philosophorum.* At any rate,
Dante and Brunetto are in substantial agreement that one whose ancestors were
noble can only be accounted so himself if, like his forebears, he too is virtuous.
Although we might discern some slight differences in point of view, none would
be conclusive, since neither passage gets to the root of the matter, which is the nature
of true nobility. Let us pass on, then, to compare our authors on this crucial issue.

Again, both the *Tresor* and the *Convivio* echo a common source, this time
William Perrault's *Summa virtutum ac vitiorum.* But in this case, Davis found no
evidence that the *Tresor* was Dante's immediate source. Since M. Corti had already
concluded from extensive comparison that Dante drew directly from Perrault,[64]
Professor Davis has suggested that Brunetto still might have recommended that
book to Dante. However he may have come to read Perrault's *Summa,* Dante
certainly drew from it an essential feature of his own theory of nobility, which
Brunetto had left there unused. This was Perrault's principle that "the nobility
of the soul ought to be regarded as twofold, derived from a natural disposition
towards virtue and the bestowal of that virtue by divine grace."[65] Dante made this
the keystone of his account of the genesis of human nobility (*Conv.* 4. 21), and we
have already seen that it stands as a reproach to the character Brunetto in the poem.

Significantly, the author of the *Tresor* did not appropriate Perrault's concept of
the double origin of nobility, and his reason is not far to seek: for Latini, the soul's
nobility was a product of nature but not of grace. He agreed with Perrault and
Dante that the noble soul was the result of its natural disposition towards virtue, but
Brunetto did not regard virtue as a gift of grace. Instead, true to his classical models,
he maintained that man could attain nobility by cultivating his natural powers.

The function of grace in Latini's system can be seen from his primary division
of the virtues into two classes—moral and contemplative (*Tresor* 2. 55), corresponding respectively to the four cardinal and the three theological virtues (2. 123). The
one he equates with the active life; the other, with the contemplative life. The
former "uses well worldly things" ("use bien les mondaines choses"), while the latter
renounces them for things celestial (2. 123. 2). Thus the theological virtues of faith,
hope, and charity are, for Brunetto, the "*iii. vertus contemplatives,*" which are proper
to holy men *(li saint home)* who have rejected the way of the world (2. 124). The
evangelical commandment enjoining poverty also pertains to the saints (2. 125).
This contemplative way is open only to a few through the grace of God (2. 123. 5).

Brunetto devotes but six short chapters to the contemplative way (2. 123–28),
for he and his audience are men of the world, who therefore are concerned only
with the moral virtues of the active life; and he accordingly treats these on a scale
commensurate with their relevance—in some sixty-seven chapters (2. 56–122). All
moral virtues are classified under one or another of the four cardinal virtues, namely,
prudence, temperance, fortitude, and justice. Thus, liberality is a species of justice,
and one of its subspecies is *charité* (2. 101–6). This Brunetto first identifies with the
Golden Rule, but as a moral virtue he soon equates it with the classical concept

of *amicitia*, to which all but the first of his six chapters on charity are devoted. Basically, Brunetto's theory of friendship is derived from classical sources, and though he is careful to adduce Christian authorities to the same effect, still the ethical doctrines they endorse remain essentially secular.

In *Convivio* 4. 22, Dante offers a division of virtue that is significantly different. He agrees with Brunetto that some virtues pertain to action and others to contemplation, and the former he also identifies as the four cardinal virtues. There, however, the resemblance ends. Action and contemplation are by no means two exclusive ways of life for Dante, but rather they are two ways in which any mind can be used, either with a practical or a speculative purpose (4. 22. 10–11). The latter consists "in reflecting on the works of God and of Nature"; it uses the intellect, which is the mind's most noble part; and as the noblest function possible to man on earth, the speculative life is man's highest beatitude and happiness this side of heaven (4. 22. 13–18).

The contrast between the *Convivio*'s concept of the *vita contemplativa* and that of the *Tresor* appears clearly in the virtues appropriate to it: they are theological for Brunetto, intellectual for Dante.[66] Emphatically, Dante insists that the noble soul will not be content with the life of action but will prefer the greater good of contemplation (*Conv.* 4. 22. 16). Moreover, every man can come to enjoy this intellectual life, for which he either has a natural aptitude or else can be fitted "by means of much training and cultivation" (4. 22. 12). Grace, then, is no more necessary for Dante's contemplative life than for his active life. Whereas Brunetto considers that the active life is the lot of most men, Dante admits no excuse for one who rests content with its imperfect form of virtue (4. 22. 12, 18).

What Dante has done, of course, is to substitute an Aristotelian view of contemplation for Brunetto's monastic one. At first glance it might seem that the Dantesque view is still more secular than that of the *Tresor*: but this is not so, for Perrault's principle enabled Dante to attribute every virtue to divine grace as well as to nature. Thus, man owes even his moral virtues to grace. Further, the twofold origin of nobility obviates Latini's dichotomy between things celestial and things mundane: instead, man becomes God-like through the proper use of the goods of this world.

Paradoxically, Brunetto both over- and underrated moral virtue. On the one hand, it was overvalued as the only possible goal for the greater part of mankind, thereby denying most men the full measure of happiness that is their birthright. On the other hand, Latini fell short of the mark by neglecting the role of grace in the formation of moral virtue. Brunetto would seem to have practiced what he preached, for Villani characterized him as an *uomo mondano*, an epithet that aptly described not only the author of the *Tresor* but also his friend for whom the book was intended.[67]

From the foregoing, it is easy to see that the conclusion we have just reached applies no less to the historical Brunetto than to the character in the poem. Both failed to appreciate that nobility springs as much from grace as from nature. But

[205]

this does not explain why the poet made the character Brunetto utter opinions that he apparently did not hold in life. Various explanations of this incongruity have been offered. Davis, for example, comments on *Inferno* xv, 55–78: "Dante thus makes Brunetto use the legend of the mixed population of Florence as a metaphor for a contemporary situation: for the contrast between those numerous citizens caught up in factional passion (the Fiesolans) and those few still attempting to promote the cause of order and civic unity (the Romans)."[68] In other words, Brunetto did not maintain that virtue was racially determined; instead, he used racial mixture as a metaphor for the mixture of vice and virtue.

If so, then it seems to me that Dante depicts this man as an offender against both rhetoric and philosophy, for as I understand Dante's concept of a metaphor,[69] it must be a true comparison based on a real similarity between the two terms. In false metaphor, art fails to follow nature, and thereby makes a statement that is both philosophically false and rhetorically wrong. If Latini was addicted to such frivolous comparisons, it would of course have been in character to have him commit such an error in the poem; and since the essence of the error consists in framing groundless fictions, one would hardly expect to find that error repeated in Brunetto's philosophical works.

Nonetheless, it still seems unfair to impute to him opinions that he did not hold. The incongruity between Brunetto in the poem and in history therefore seems to be susceptible of another interpretation. Like the imputation of sodomy, it *is* an incongruity, and as such, it stirs the observant reader to inquire why Brunetto's shade does not follow the *Tresor* more closely. And one discovers that Brunetto, like Dante, believed that nature does dispose a soul to virtue; and since one's natural parents are admittedly factors in the genetic process, it is not incorrect to say that race was for both men one of the factors, though not the only one, that predisposed man to virtue or to vice. Further, one learns that Brunetto, no less than Dante, maintained that a man of noble lineage could disgrace his stock by turning from virtue to vice. Hence Brunetto's racism in the poem proves to be compatible with the doctrine of the *Tresor*, provided it be understood with qualifications that are not to be found in the poem. Once we have been led, or misled, by his rhetoric to discover the convictions that he expressed while living, Latini appears condemned, ironically, by his own tirade, as we suspected from the Latini-Lombardi contrast that was our point of departure.

THE *SEMANTA SANTA* COMPLEX

"If you do not believe me, consider the ear of corn, for every plant is known by its seed" (*Purg.* xvi, 113–14). My argument, here as elsewhere in this and the preceding chapter, is intended, not to demonstrate, but to suggest, how Dante integrated the infernal runners into the structure of his poetry and thought. Those who wish greater certainty in these matters must pursue the poet's clues until every implication has been unfolded. And in the case of Brunetto, the thread of Ariadne has its beginning in the principle laid down by Marco Lombardo in *Purgatorio* XVI, 113–14:

> se non mi credi, pon mente a la spiga,
> ch'ogn' erba si conosce per lo seme.

To be sure, this is offered in explanation of the present wickedness of Italy (of which Brunetto is part); nonetheless the maxim is a general rule that must again recall to any Christian ear the Sermon on the Mount:

> By their fruits you shall know them. Do men gather grapes of thorns, or figs of thistles? Even so every good tree bringeth forth good fruit, and the evil tree bringeth forth evil fruit. A good tree cannot bring forth evil fruit, neither can an evil tree bring forth good fruit. Every tree that bringeth not forth good fruit, shall be cut down, and shall be cast into the fire. Wherefore by their fruits you shall know them.[70]

Dante himself laid down the same principle in its Biblical form as the touchstone by which one could discover true nobility:

> I say then that, inasmuch as in those things which are of a single species, such as are all men, their highest perfection cannot be defined by their essential constituents; it is meet to define and to ascertain it by means of their effects; and therefore we read in the Gospel of St. Matthew what Christ says, "Beware of false prophets, by their fruits ye shall know them," and we may ascertain the definition of which we are in quest [man's nobility] by the straight road, namely, by their fruits, which are the moral and intellectual virtues, of which this nobility of ours is the seed. . . .[71]
>
> (*Conv.* 4. 16. 9–10)

This passage of the *Convivio*, I believe, explains why in Marco's maxim the stress falls on seeds rather than on fruits. Good seeds can go bad, but bad ones cannot become good. What Marco seeks to prove is that the descendants of the good seeds that brought forth crops of virtue in Italy two generations earlier now produce nothing of the sort. The attributes of nobility—*valore e cortesia*—are no longer to be found in Italy, because the seeds have not been cultivated; instead the country has been plunged into civil war by the papacy's subversive attempt to substitute papal for imperial authority in temporal affairs.

Marco's maxim begs for explication, and materials for this abound in the heaven of the Sun. There the image of the seed is developed by generative imagery of every sort—fruits and seeds, plants, vines, saplings, as well as pastures, vineyards, gardens, and the workers therein.[72] This profusion of images, drawn from all things generated by the sun, culminates in Aquinas' exposition of the process by which all things are generated, man in particular.[73] Already in the poem the reader had learned the naturalistic explanation of human psychogenesis; now to this is added the theological explanation, for Aquinas coordinates in a single account the two explanations that were presented separately in *Convivio* 4. 21.

This discourse by Aquinas has long been recognized as the scholastic crux of the poem, as the text that determines the position Dante occupied in the scholastic spectrum of his day. To some, most notably Busnelli and Vandelli, he appears from this passage and its analogues in the *Convivio* to be an orthodox Thomist. This conclusion has been challenged and demolished in detail by the immense erudition of Bruno Nardi, seconded by a penetrating sally of Etienne Gilson against the vulnerable barbican thrown up by Mandonnet rather than against the ring wall erected by Busnelli and Vandelli. The victors, however, agree chiefly in denying Dante's exclusive Thomism, and Gilson has led many to doubt that the *Comedy* is based on any systematic philosophy.[74]

If Dante's interpreters were in agreement in their interpretation of the discourse of Dante's Thomas, no doubt the sin of Brunetto Latini could be tightly integrated into the whole system of Dantesque thought. Since there is no general agreement, however, I think the best course here is to indicate that the imagery of the poem links Brunetto to this crux by what may be called the *sementa santa* complex. The linkage is generally implicit in the Latin-Lombard opposition, but most particularly the link is formed by Marco, whose discourse, together with that of Statius,[75] expounds the Dantesque doctrine of psychogenesis in naturalistic terms. This connection is, as it were, a loose end in my account, a trail down which we have, at most, reconnoitered. Its present value, I feel, lies in the very fact that it is not integral to my interpretation, and I should hope that if my view of the so-called sodomites finds favor, this shall in turn cast light on other obscurities in the poem. First among them, at least in order of importance, would be the interpretation of the cantos of the Sun, and especially their "sematology." In sum, I profer the *sementa* complex as a new approach to an old problem.

[8]

The Image of Sodom:
Old Testament

But what about Sodom? This question, I fear, has been nagging not a few readers throughout my argument. At the outset we saw that the traditional interpretation of sodomy as the sin of the runners failed to explain their division into two mutually exclusive groups, and for that reason we embarked on the long search for another sense in which they could be said to have done violence to nature. Throughout, we have concentrated on the two bands of runners that Dante met and on the historical figures that ran in them; our purpose has been to define the sins of those bands through an examination of their known members. What we have arrived at, therefore, may be only a partial definition of the sin of the runners, since (as has been repeatedly stressed) we cannot be certain that there are not yet other bands running upon the sands. Quite possibly one such unnoticed band might contain genuine Sodomites, tainted with sexual violence against nature. On the literal level of interpretation, we can never know, at least not from what the pilgrim observed in the circle of the violent. Now that we are tolerably certain what the sins were that he saw punished there, however, we must not neglect to reconsider what Virgil meant when he said that the sin of this place "seals with its sign both Sodom and Cahors."[1]

If we accept the prevalent view that *Soddoma* in Virgil's phrase stands for the runners, it would follow that the sins we have assigned to them somehow left their mark on the Biblical city of Sodom. The preponderance of evidence now indicates that these sins were not sexual. We must accordingly ask whether it is still possible that the city of Sodom was an appropriate symbol for nonsexual violence against nature.

The question, like most we have posed, is essentially a historical question. I would hesitate to suggest that Dante assigned a private, idiosyncratic meaning to Sodom. Instead, we have every reason to expect that his meaning here, as elsewhere, was rooted deeply in tradition. Since the reference to Sodom is patently an allusion to the Bible, we cannot doubt that the basis for Dante's meaning is ultimately to be found in Sacred Scripture. Certainly the author of the *Monarchia* would adhere to the principle that the primary document of revelation was to be preferred before all secondary traditions derived therefrom. Almost every interpreter of the *Comedy* would agree with this principle; but in practice, Dantists of the past have searched no further in Scripture than Genesis 19 for the image of Sodom. The most successful and recent attempt to comprehend Dante's image of Sodom was made twenty-five years ago by André Pézard, and it is significant that his approach was not through Sacred Scripture but through patrology, where he perceived, as in a glass darkly, the Biblical Sodom.[2] Were he writing today, he would no doubt have profited from the renaissance in Biblical studies that has taught medievalists in general and Dantists in particular to read the Bible as Dante and his contemporaries did.[3]

One is now conscious that the significance of an event recorded in the Bible as history cannot be determined simply from that record, for its meaning often appeared only in subsequent revelation, and indeed the major *typoi* reverberate throughout the Bible. Thus, medieval interpreters, whose ears were attuned to these allegorical echoes, would not elucidate Adam's fall or Abraham's covenant from the account in Genesis alone, but rather in the light of the second Adam and the new covenant, together with all the intervening references that prefigured the type's emergent significance.

Could Sodom too be such a *typos*? Certainly it is a recurrent theme throughout the Bible, as reference to any concordance reveals.[4] Sodom is named in forty-eight verses of the Bible, twenty-four times in conjunction with Gomorrah, and occasionally with Seboim and Adamah, the other Cities of the Plain, as well. The book of Genesis contains less than half of these references (twenty); the remainder are divided between seven books of the Old Testament and seven of the New. Thus a preliminary reconnaissance indicates that at least the name of Sodom was echoed often in Holy Writ, and hence was an apt subject for typological interpreters.

"Lo minor giron suggella / del *segno* suo e Soddoma e Caorsa" (*Inf.* xi, 49–50): Dante's language itself suggests that the word Sodom possesses a certain significance. The insistence, verging on redundancy, that the cities are *sealed* with the *sign* of a certain sin fairly urges the reader to recognize that a significant allusion has been made and to follow it up. For the contemporary reader, the task set was a simple reference to the *sacra pagina* and its interpreters; for us, it is essentially a problem of historical research in the same authorities. Either way, there is a determinable, objective answer to the question, What did Sodom signify in Christian tradition circa 1300?

Some day, no doubt, the question will be fully answered by an exhaustive survey of every Biblical commentary, many of which are difficult of access because they exist only in manuscript or in rare early printed editions; this is particularly true of the scholastic commentators of the generations immediately preceding Dante.[5] The poet's own prejudices, however, render such an exhaustive search unnecessary for the present purpose. His reliance on the primary authority of Scripture itself enables us to secure at least an approximate answer from a survey of the Biblical references to Sodom. To control our own impressions of the Vulgate text, there is the *Glossa ordinaria* to the Bible, which Dante's contemporaries customarily took as their principal guide to the sacred text.[6] On crucial points, I have also consulted the authorities cited by the *Gloss*, notably Jerome and the Venerable Bede, since Dante particularly urged that works by the latter be not neglected and therefore must have accounted him among those trustworthy *hagiographi* whose works (*scripture doctorum*) he regarded as inspired by the Holy Spirit.[7] Beyond this point I have not pressed the search, for the simple reason that these authorities suffice to demonstrate that Sodom was not primarily a sexual image in Biblical tradition.

In presenting the evidence, I have thought it best to begin with Genesis and proceed text by text through first the Old and then the New Testament. Except for Genesis and Deuteronomy, the Old Testament texts will be presented in the order in which it now appears they were composed, chiefly to bring into relief the historical development of the Biblical concept of Sodom. In expounding the New Testament texts, the Gospels will be treated together, and the remainder grouped so that similar concepts can be treated together.

SODOM IN GENESIS

The destruction of Sodom and its sister cities was not an isolated event; to the contrary, it forms an integral part of the origins of Israel as recounted in Genesis. For medieval commentators, the events of Genesis possessed a special significance, for God's earliest contacts with man set the patterns for the future history of the race in general and for His chosen people in particular. The Venerable Bede, who was especially attracted to the historical allegory of Biblical types, produced a commentary on the opening chapters of Genesis, down to Abraham's repudiation of Ishmael in favor of Isaac (Gen. 12:10), apparently stopping in mid chapter because his repertory of prototypes was complete at that point.[8] They included the creation; the fall of man, with the consequent expulsion of Adam and Eve from the Terrestrial Paradise; the destruction of mankind by the waters of the Flood, excepting only the remnant saved in the ark with Noah, with whom God covenanted never again to destroy every living thing.

GENESIS 10: CITY, LAND, AND PEOPLE

Sodom is first mentioned in the catalogue of nations descended from Noah: "and the limits of Chanaan were from Sidon as one comes to Gerara even to Gaza, until thou enter Sodom and Gomorrha, and Adama, and Seboim even to Lesa."[9] These five cities, usually called the Cities of the Plain,[10] were therefore in the southeastern corner of the land of Canaan, the cursed grandson of Noah. As Canaanites, their inhabitants were doomed, by Noah's prophetic curse, to serve the Semites who were descended from his son Shem, notably the line of Abraham.[11] Thus, the destiny of all the characters in the drama of Sodom was already fixed before the cities were founded.

The ancestry of the citizens of the Plain marked their character in yet another way, for Canaan was the son of Ham (or Cham), who had brought the curse upon his son by looking on the drunken Noah as he slept naked.[12] Among the descendants of Ham, the catalogue of Genesis 10:6–32 includes not only the Canaanites of Syria but also, among others, the Egyptians (*Mesraim*; AV, Mizraim) and the Babylonians of lower Mesopotamia (*terra Sennar*; AV, Shinar). Hence the Hamites inhabited the old, established centers of civilization, whereas the less desirable lands bordering on the favored river valleys were relegated to the Semitic peoples. The more remote parts of the earth, the lands to the north of the Fertile Crescent and those overseas (*insulae gentium*), were peopled by Japheth, Noah's third son.[13] In Jewish thought, then, Sodom was literally related to the Hamites and their higher material culture, of which the city was the characteristic institution.

Sodom therefore was an apt symbol for any city, and its Hamitic affinity particularly suggested similitudes to Babylon and Egypt.[14] The comparison to Egypt was made in Genesis itself, and because the parallel is based not on race but on the fertile abundance of the lands irrigated respectively by the Nile and the Jordan, the two remain for future interpreters as examples of prosperity based on natural advantages. Genesis also offers an implicit parallel between Sodom and Babylonia, if, as Bede inferred, that was the site of the Tower of Babel,[15] the destruction of which—after a divine visitation like that made to Sodom[16]—is the only major event (apart from patriarchal history) that Genesis records between the Flood and the history of Sodom.

The fact, established by Genesis 10:19, that the Sodomites were generically Hamitic and specifically Canaanite, does not seem to have been significant to medieval Christian commentators. Nonetheless, these affinities may have influenced their concept of Sodom indirectly through the Biblical prophets, who, as we shall see, often recalled Sodom in connection with her surviving cousins and the way of life that the seed of Ham represented. But the attentive reader of the canto of the sodomites does not require the authority of exegetes to perceive that the Bible's first reference to Sodom bears a suspicious resemblance to Brunetto's view that vice is racially determined. That much is clear from a close and literal reading of the text of Genesis 9–10. Therefore we have reason to believe that the Biblical image of Sodom may correlate to the *sementa santa* complex, and thus would integrate with the other images of *Inferno* xv.

Sodom and the Origin of Israel

The narrative of Genesis traces the history of mankind down to the confusion of tongues after the postdiluvian dispersion of the children of Noah (Gen. 9:1–9). At that point the scope of the story narrows to focus on Abram-Abraham, whose biography occupies the next fifteen chapters (Gen. 11:10–25:8). The main theme, of course, is the origin of Israel, but interwoven with this as a subplot is the story of Abram's nephew Lot, who escapes the destruction of Sodom to found Israel's Semite neighbors, Ammon and Moab. Thus the decline and fall of Sodom cannot be understood, either literally or figuratively, apart from the career of Abraham. To recount so familiar a story might seem superfluous had Dantists of the past not consistently interpreted Sodom without reference to this necessary context. Critics recognize that a text does not speak for itself; similarly, one cannot assume that its context will be tacitly understood.

The links between Shem and Abram are recited as a long genealogy (Gen. 11:10–27), and a few more terse sentences establish the patriarch's circumstances at the moment that God called him to his historic role as founder of Israel. Abram has a childless wife, Sarai; with her and his father and Lot, his dead brother's son, he had emigrated from his birthplace in Mesopotamia, bound for the land of Canaan. Halfway around the Fertile Crescent they had stopped at Haran, where the father died (Gen. 11:28–32). At this juncture, God revealed to Abram that he would found a great people if he proceeded on into Canaan, and obedient to the divine command, Abram set out for the south with Lot, his nephew and coheir.[17] Living a nomadic life, they passed together into the promised land. Famine there caused them to continue on into Egypt, but a misadventure with the pharoah eventually returned them to Canaan, considerably enriched (Gen. 12). It is at this point that Sodom enters the story. Because of a dispute over pasturage in Canaan, which could not support the herds of both men (Gen. 13:6), Lot and Abram decided to part company, and Lot chose the then-fertile Jordan basin as his range (Gen. 13:5–9):

> Gen. 13:10. And Lot, lifting up his eyes, saw all the country about the Jordan, which was watered throughout, before the Lord destroyed Sodom and Gomorrha, as the paradise of the Lord, and like Egypt as one comes to Segor.
> 11. And Lot chose to himself the country about the Jordan, and he departed from the east: and they were separated one brother from the other.[18]
> 12. Abram dwelt in the land of Chanaan; and Lot abode in the towns that were about the Jordan, and dwelt in Sodom.
> 13. And the men of Sodom were very wicked, and sinners before the face of the Lord, beyond measure.

> Gen. 13:10. Elevatis itaque Lot oculis, vidit omnem circa regionem Jordanis, quae universa irrigabatur antequam subverteret Dominus Sodomam et Gomorrham, sicut paradisus Domini, et sicut Aegyptus venientibus in Segor.
> 11. Elegitque sibi Lot regionem circa Jordanem, et recessit ab oriente: divisique sunt alterutrum a fratre suo.
> 12. Abram habitavit in terra Chanaan: Lot vero moratus est in oppidis, quae erant circa Jordanem, et habitavit in Sodomis.
> 13. Homines autem Sodomitae pessimi erant, et peccatores coram Domino nimis.

Once again the family was divided, and as before, destiny did not rest on the branch that preferred the advantages of civilization, with lands made abundant by irrigation, to the austere simplicity imposed by the sparse, semiarid land of Canaan. Abram remains in the promised land, and the action of the next six chapters contrasts his growth in God's favor with the troubles experienced by Lot in his attempt to live righteously in an unjust society. Twice Lot's city is threatened with destruction, and both times Abram intervenes for Lot's sake, saving the whole society in the first instance, and in the second, only Lot and his family.

GENESIS 14–16: ABRAM AND SODOM

The first episode is a tale of kingdoms at war. The kings of Sodom and its sister cities of the Plain—Gomorrah, Adama, Seboim, and Segor—revolted against the king of Elam, Kedorlaomer (or Chodorlahomer), to whom they had been subject for twelve years. The Elamite came from the north with three allied kings and in a single campaign defeated the rebels and plundered both Sodom and Gomorrah, whose people—including Lot—he carried off as slaves, together with their goods. Abram, hearing the news, hastened to save his nephew. Accompanied by 3 neighboring chieftains and some 318 men of his own, the patriarch overtook the plunder-laden kings at the border; he not only recovered the booty in a night attack on the kings' camp at Dan, but also ensured their withdrawal by harassing the retreating army for several days until it had passed beyond Damascus (Gen. 14:13–16).

As the victorious rescuers neared home, they were met by Melchisedech (AV, Melchisidek), the priestly Canaanite king of Salem (or Jerusalem), to whom they apparently owed tribute, for he was given a tithe of their spoils. The king of Sodom, who had taken refuge near Jerusalem, also met Abram and his allies, to whom he offered all the recaptured goods as a reward, asking only that his captive people be restored to him. Abram responded that, though his allies might claim their shares, he himself would accept nothing more than what his men had consumed on the expedition, for he had sworn by God, "the possessor of heaven and earth," that he would take nothing that the Sodomites possessed, lest their king might say, "I have enriched Abram."[19]

Generosity is the keynote of Abram's actions in Genesis 14. He has no express command from God to save the persons and property of Lot and his neighbors without thought of reward. Nonetheless, these acts are pleasing to God, as is revealed immediately after the events. "Now when these things were done, the word of the Lord came to Abram by a vision, saying: Fear not, Abram, I am thy protector, and thy reward exceeding great" (Gen. 15:1). The reward, of course, consists in the gift of two sons, Ishmael and Isaac, who shall be given to the childless patriarch in his extreme old age, together with the promise that his posterity shall multiply greatly and eventually inherit the land of Canaan.

"Increase and multiply, and fill the earth" had been God's chief command to mankind after the Flood (Gen. 9:1), and as his reward for rescuing Lot and the Sodomites, Abram desires only that his efforts to produce offspring in accordance with God's command be blessed with fruition. God assures him that his wish shall be granted, and "Abram believed God, and it was reputed to him unto justice."[20] Moreover, Abram (like Solomon) is promised more than he requested, for he is told that his progeny shall inherit the land of Canaan, and this is confirmed by a prophetic sign and a vision (Gen. 15:7–21). Shortly thereafter his wish is granted when Hagar, his wife's maidservant, bears him his first son, Ishmael (Gen. 16).

Thus, in Genesis 14–16 we have a single episode in which Abram, without hope of reward, aids both his "brother" Lot[21] and his neighbors of Sodom, only to receive from God the gift of a son, Ishmael, as the reward for his piety.[22]

GENESIS 17–19: ABRAHAM AND SODOM

Nothing is recorded in Genesis about the twelve years between the birth of Ishmael and the beginning of the second episode, which culminates in the birth of Isaac (Gen. 21:1–8). The new train of events begins with another call to Abram: "I am the Almighty God: walk before me, and be perfect. And I will make my covenant between me and thee: and I will multiply thee exceedingly."[23] Abram, who up to this moment had pleased God in the order of nature, now is called to be perfected by grace. A greater destiny awaits him: he shall be "father of many nations," and accordingly his name henceforth shall be "Abraham." His descendants are to be a chosen people from whom nations and kings shall arise, and in token of this status, all males of Abraham's household and their descendants are to be artificially marked by circumcision. Finally, the patriarch is told that within the year his barren wife, Sarah, shall conceive a son, Isaac, from whose line nations shall come and kings of peoples, whereas Ishmael's line shall only increase and multiply to become a single nation (Gen. 17:1–21).

After this revelation, Abraham hastens to perform the circumcisions as commanded. The next three chapters narrate the subsequent events of the year before Isaac is born: the first two interrelate the destruction of Sodom with the new status of Abraham (Gen. 18–19). The conceptual contrast is simple enough: on the one hand, God singles out for perfection one people who in Abram have been proven worthy, while on the other hand, He destroys another people who in Sodom have been proven unworthy even of life. The two themes are integrated by the mission of three angels, who first visit Abraham and announce to him that Sarah is pregnant and that Sodom shall be destroyed (Gen. 18). Two of the angels then visit Sodom and, in consequence of their reception, destroy the city but rescue Lot, their host (Gen. 19). The two visits are clearly juxtaposed for the sake of contrast, in order to make the sin of Sodom stand out in relief.

The angels appear to Abraham before his tent in the Vale of Mambre, where he hastens to make them welcome with all the ceremonious hospitality of a pastoral people. After they have eaten the best he could provide, they foretell the birth of Isaac, and then begin their journey towards Sodom. Abraham accompanies them for a way and is told that Sodom is doomed.

> Gen. 18:17. And the Lord said: Can I hide from Abraham what I am about to do:
>
> 18. Seeing he shall become a great and mighty nation, and in him all the nations of the earth shall be blessed?
>
> 19. For I know that he will command his children, and his household after him to keep the way of the Lord, and do judgment and justice: that for Abraham's sake the Lord may bring to effect all the things he hath spoken unto him.

20. And the Lord said: The cry of Sodom and Gomorrha is multiplied, and their sin is become exceedingly grievous.

21. I will go down and see whether they have done according to the cry that is come to me: or whether it be not so, that I may know.

Gen. 18:17. Dixitque Dominus: Num celare potero Abraham quae gesturus sum:

18. Cum futurus sit in gentem magnam ac robustissimam, et benedicendae sint in illo omnes nationes terrae?

19. Scio enim quod praecepturus sit filiis suis, et domui suae post se, ut custodiant viam Domini, et faciant iudicium et iustitiam: ut adducat Dominus propter Abraham omnia quae locutus est ad eum.

20. Dixit itaque Dominus: Clamor Sodomorum et Gomorrhae multiplicatus est, et peccatum eorum aggravatum est nimis.

21. Descendam, et videbo utrum clamorem, qui venit ad me, opere compleverint: an non est ita, ut sciam.

After revealing their errand, the divine messengers depart for Sodom, leaving Abraham to commune with the Lord concerning this new turn of events.[24] Once again he intervenes to save the Sodomites, this time by prayer rather than by deeds, and the terms of his intercession, when taken in conjunction with the angelic message just preceding, provide the most explicit description in Genesis of the sin of Sodom:

Gen. 18:23b. Wilt thou destroy the just with the wicked? [Abraham asks, and then expands this theme:]

25. Far be it from thee to do this thing, and to slay the just with the wicked, and for the just to be in like case as the wicked, this is not beseeming thee: thou who judgest all the earth, wilt not make this judgment.

Gen. 18:23b. Numquid perdes iustum cum impio?

25. Absit a te, ut rem hanc facias, et occidas iustum cum impio, fiatque iustus sicut impius, non est hoc tuum: qui iudicas omnem terram, nequaquam facies iudicium hoc.

He does not plead for Lot but for all in Sodom who are just, urging that they should not be destroyed indiscriminately with the impious. The emphasis on justice is driven home by Abraham's progressive pleading that Sodom not be destroyed if the city contains fifty *iusti*, then forty-five, forty, thirty, twenty, and finally ten just persons (Gen. 18:23–33).

From Genesis 13:13 we already know that the Sodomites were the worst men (*homines . . . pessimi*) and that God regarded them as very great sinners (*peccatores . . . nimis*). Now, from Genesis 18:20, we learn that the complaint (*clamor*) against them has multiplied and that their sin has become very much more grievous (*peccatum eorum aggravatum est nimis*). Numerically, it should be noted from this last text, there is but one single sin of Sodom. Abraham identified it with impiety, and subsequent Biblical writers echo him. He does not define it except to oppose the impious to the just, but as he himself is the type of the just man, the angelic description of Abraham in Genesis 18:19b does, by contrast, indicate what constitutes righteousness: "to keep the way of the Lord, and do judgment and justice." I do not mean to invest these vague terms with a specific content, but rather to point out that some of them, such as *impius*, have that potential, which was to be realized elsewhere in the Bible, on the strength of this elastic terminology.

GENESIS 19: THE DESTRUCTION OF SODOM

While Abraham is interceding for Sodom, the angels are on their way to the city. At nightfall they find Lot sitting in the gate. Like Abraham, he urges hospitality upon them, and when they politely refuse, he persists, showing thereby that his invitation is no mere gesture.[25] Assured of Lot's good will, the angels enter his house, eat his bread, and thereby assume the special status of guest. The law of hospitality now obligates Lot, at all costs, to treat his guests honorably. Lot's mettle as a host soon is tried to the utmost, for all the men of Sodom come, demanding that he surrender the visitors "that we may know them" ("ut cognoscamus eos").[26]

Lot goes outside and reasons with the Sodomites. He reproves them, not for their sexual practices, but rather for directing these towards his guests. Instead he offers his virgin daughters, whom the Sodomites may abuse as they please *(abutimini eis sicut vobis placuerit)*. He pleads with them as a brother *(fratres mei)* that they forego the particular evil they have proposed *(nolite malum hoc facere)*. What he urgently desires is that they "do no evil to these men," and he explicitly states the reason why: "because they are come under the shadow of my roof" ("viris istis nihil mali faciatis, quia ingressi sunt sub umbra culminis mei").

Manifestly the point at issue between Lot and his fellow Sodomites is not their sexual mores but rather their obligations to strangers who have been accepted as guests! The Sodomites maintain that they are governed by no law other than their own custom, and Lot's appeal to the common law of hospitality especially outrages them. Who is Lot that he dare to question their customs? for in choosing to settle in their community, had he not tacitly approved of its customs? Because he now refuses to conform to their ways, the Sodomites think he deserves worse treatment than his visitors.

The angels, however, avert the assault of the Sodomites, first by returning Lot to the safety of the house, and secondly—a significant detail—by striking the Sodomites with blindness *(caecitate)*, so that they cannot find the way into the house. Having baffled the assault, the angels announce that the city must be destroyed, and they bid Lot to evacuate his household.

At this point we may well raise the question, Were the Sodomites to be punished for a sin that they had actually committed against the angels, or only for demonstrating their intent? If the former, then certainly their offense was not sexual. But lest my paraphrase be thought misleading, consider the passage in its entirety:

> Gen. 19:1. And the two angels came to Sodom in the evening, and Lot was sitting in the gate of the city. And seeing them, he rose up and went to meet them: and worshipped prostrate to the ground,
>
> 2. And said: I beseech you, my lords, turn in to the house of your

servant [*pueri*], and lodge there: wash your feet, and in the morning you shall go on your way. And they said: No, but we will abide in the street.

3. He pressed them very much to turn in unto him: and when they were come in to his house, he made them a feast, and baked unleavened bread and they ate:

4. But before they went to bed, the men of the city beset the house both young and old, all the people together.

5. And they called Lot, and said to him: Where are the men that came in to thee at night? bring them out hither that we may know them [*ut cognoscamus eos*]:

6. Lot went out to them, and shut the door after him, and said:

7. Do not so, I beseech you, my brethren [*fratres*], do not commit this evil [*malum*].

8. I have two daughters who as yet have not known man: I will bring them out to you, and abuse you [*abutimini*] them as it shall please you, so that you do no evil [*nihil mali*] to these men, because they are come in under the shadow of my roof.

9. But they said: Get thee back thither. And again: Thou camest in, said they, as a stranger, was it to be a judge? [*ut advena, numquid ut iudices*] therefore we will afflict thee more than them. And they pressed very violently upon Lot: and they were even at the point of breaking open the doors.

10. And behold the men [i.e., the angels] put out their hand, and drew in Lot unto them, and shut the door:

11. And them that were without, they struck with blindness [*caecitate*] from the least to the greatest, so that they could not find the door.

12. And they said to Lot: Hast thou here any of thine? son in law, or sons, or daughters, all that are thine bring them out of this city:

13. For we will destroy this place, because their cry [*clamor*] is grown loud before the Lord, who hath sent us to destroy them.

Gen. 19:1. Veneruntque duo angeli Sodomam vespere, et sedente Lot in foribus civitatis. Qui cum vidisset eos, surrexit, et ivit obviam eis: adoravitque pronus in terram,

2. Et dixit: Obsecro, domini, declinate in domum pueri vestri, et manete ibi: lavate pedes vestros, et mane proficiscemini in viam vestram. Qui dixerunt: Minime, sed in platea manebimus.

3. Compulit illos oppido ut diverterent ad eum: ingressisque domum illius fecit convivium, et coxit azyma: et comederunt.

4. Prius autem quam irent cubitum, viri civitatis vallaverunt domum a puero usque ad senem, omnis populus simul.

5. Vocaveruntque Lot, et dixerunt ei: Ubi sunt viri qui introierunt ad te nocte? educ illos huc, ut cognoscamus eos.

6. Egressus ad eos Lot, post tergum occludens ostium, ait:

7. Nolite, quaeso, fratres mei, nolite malum hoc facere.

8. Habeo duas filias, quae necdum cognoverunt virum: educam eas ad vos, et abutimini eis sicut vobis placuerit, dummodo viris istis nihil mali faciatis, quia ingressi sunt sub umbra culminis mei.

9. At illi dixerunt: Recede illuc. Et rursus: Ingressus es, inquiunt, ut advena; numquid ut iudices? te ergo ipsum magis quam hos affligemus. Vimque faciebant Lot vehementissime: iamque prope erat ut effringerent fores.

10. Et ecce miserunt manum viri, et introduxerunt ad se Lot, clauseruntque ostium:

11. Et eos, qui foris erant, percusserunt caecitate a minimo usque ad maximum, ita ut ostium invenire non possent.

12. Dixerunt autem ad Lot: Habes hic quempiam tuorum? generum, aut filios, aut filias, omnes, qui tui sunt, educ de urbe hac:

13. Delebimus enim locum istum, eo quod increverit clamor eorum coram Domino, qui misit nos ut perdamus illos.

Lot does not find it easy to abandon his chosen way of life, and the difficulties that attend his flight from the doomed city reflect the problems of disengagement. His sons-in-law refuse to take the threat of destruction seriously. When the angels urge Lot to leave, he delays until they take him in hand and lead him outside the city. Told to take to the hills, he pleads that he cannot survive in the wilderness and begs that one city be saved as his place of refuge. The incident gains significance by comparison to Abraham's prayer that the just be saved. Lot's request is, by contrast, selfish and, as it turns out, unnecessary; above all, it shows how attached he now is to city life. For his wife, this attachment proves fatal, because in disobedience to the angelic instructions, she looks back to see the destruction of Sodom and in consequence is turned into a statue of salt (Gen. 19:15–23, 26). All these details serve to stress Lot's involvement with the community of his choice: intermarriage with mocking infidels, a hesitant and forced departure from one city only to seek out another, and finally a wife who cannot put Sodom from her mind.

Lot's journey from Sodom to Segor (AV, Zoar) was made in great haste, between dawn and sunrise it would seem (Gen. 19:15, 23), and it does not appear that the refugees escaped with anything but their lives. In the disaster, Lot, who had chosen to exchange a pastoral life in Canaan for settlement in the garden city of Sodom, lost all that he had thought to gain. His urban life having vanished with the Cities of the Plain, Lot retreated to a cave in the mountains, where his two daughters contrived to beget sons by him—Ammon and Moab, who people the trans-Jordanian lands that bear their names (Gen. 19:30–38).

Thus, Lot's descendants returned to a way of life that was not too different from the one that they would have led had he elected to remain in Canaan. For Lot, Sodom was an urban interlude that taught him the dangers of city life. His salvation lay in his inability to accommodate himself completely to the conventions of the community in which he settled. He retained both his respect for the God of Abraham and for the customary generosity to travelers that was usual among Semitic peoples. Hence, implicit in the plot of Lot's history, there is a condemnation of the corrupting influence of urban life.

Abraham, not Lot, however, defines the sin of the Sodomites. Lot, in entertaining the angels, only echoes the hospitality that has already been shown to them by his uncle. Indeed, we are told that Lot was spared for Abraham's sake.[27] Sodom, in the Genesis narrative, stands opposed to Abraham and everything that he represents. This is perhaps the best key to the significance of the city for later Biblical writers and commentators.

We have noted how Genesis interweaves the fortunes of the pastoral patriarch with those of the Pentapolis. Each, by specific acts, exemplifies virtues or vices, but it is easier to perceive the acts than to identify the implicit moral qualities. Faith, hope, and charity can be discerned in Abraham's actions, especially charity toward kindred, neighbor, and stranger. Moreover, he displays piety, justice, and wisdom. Perhaps the opposing qualities can be imputed to the Sodomites, but a surer guide to their sin lies in the contrasts between their particular acts and those of Abraham.

Abram unselfishly aids the Sodomites in their distress, but they, in turn, are thoroughly xenophobic. Abram also respects the property of the Sodomites, who are strangers to him, whereas they respect not even the person of a stranger in their midst. Abraham welcomes strangers, as does Lot, but the citizens of Sodom assault travelers and compel them to conform to the customs of the place. God favors Abraham with visions, but His angels strike the Sodomites with blindness. As his reward, Abraham receives progeny and a promised land; the Sodomites are destroyed in their city, while their fertile land is rendered sterile. Fire, it should be noted, figures in both these transactions, for in token that Abraham's seed should possess the promised land, "a smoking furnace and a lamp of fire" passed between the divided portions of Abraham's sacrifice.[28] Both smoke and fire figure, of course, in the lurid destruction of Sodom:

> Gen. 19:24. And the Lord rained upon Sodom and Gomorrha brimstone and fire from the Lord out of heaven.
>
> 25. And he destroyed these cities, and all the country about, all the inhabitants of the cities, and all things that spring from the earth.
>
> 28. [Abraham] looked towards Sodom and Gomorrha, and the whole land of that country: and he saw the ashes rise up from the earth as the smoke of a furnace.[29]

Sex also has its place in these contrasts, but it is only one of several significant elements. As a patriarch, Abraham desires heirs, but he is no less concerned with their heritage, for his story is essentially the tale of how a clan settled in a new land. His success depends on the favor of a God who, as we know from the earlier chapters of Genesis, had created the world and all living things. To please this God, Abraham had to obey not only His particular commands but also His general injunctions to all mankind. Of these, the oldest was the command to Adam that he "increase and multiply, and fill the earth, and subdue it, and rule over . . . all living creatures" (Gen. 1:28). After the Flood, further precepts were added, which taught the sons of Noah respect for life in general and for human life in particular (Gen. 9:1-7).[30] For the loss of human life, God will hold every man and his brother responsible, not only the killer, "for man was made to the image of God."[31] This was an affirmative answer to the question of Cain: Yes, you *are* your brother's keeper (Gen. 4:9). The descendants of Noah, then, were bound not only to generate their kind but also to protect and to respect both life and humanity.

Implicit in this teaching is the concept that all men are brothers, and the point is indeed emphasized by the following genealogy, which traces all the races of man back to the three sons of Noah. Abraham, I would argue, was conscious of the brotherhood of man in his dealings with the Sodomites, whereas they recognized no obligations outside their own community. These, I conceive, are the fundamental faults of the Sodomites—that by their customary sexual abuse of strangers, they despised God in violating his two principal commandments to all men, and that by their perverse custom, they set themselves apart from the course of nature *and* from the rest of the human race.

In this view, the sin of Sodom implies a perversion of social, no less than sexual, intercourse. How closely the two are interrelated may be seen from further contrasts to Abraham. Obviously the patriarch strove to beget children, while the men of Sodom, whatever they meant to do with the manlike angels (*viri*; Gen. 9:5, 8) did not have procreation in mind, since Lot's daughters would not serve their purpose. Moreover, their custom is to have sexual knowledge of *strangers*, whereas Abraham knows only women of his own household. Further, the Sodomites are a multitude that desires to have a pair at their disposal,[32] which denies both terms of the natural sexual relation of one to one.

Even self-respecting homosexuals would find the idea of an orgy with a pair of strangers to be repugnant, for such an arrangement completely dehumanizes sex. Knowledge *(cognitio)* implies *awareness* of the object;[33] between individuals, the intimacy of sexual knowledge can be accompanied by mutual understanding and love, but this possibility is diminished by sex between strangers and does not exist for a multitude in relation to one common sex object, much less two. In short, the sexual mores of the Sodomites preclude the possibility of love through sex. Still worse, their determination to literally violate their victims—to have sexual knowledge without the consent of one party—further dehumanizes the relationship. Thus their sexual perversion appears to be but one expression of a more fundamental failure to recognize the brotherhood of all mankind, which is implicit in their common descent from Noah. Finally, their conduct implies that they take nature for granted and recognize no debt of gratitude to the Creator. Abraham, by contrast, piously recognized God working through nature when he named his firstborn son Ishmael—literally, "God heard"—who was the child of Hagar, a woman not past the age of childbearing.[34]

Before we turn to consider the long tradition of commentary on the Sodom story, I must acknowledge that I have myself been commenting on that story in the course of retelling it. This should not be surprising, since even paraphrase constitutes a commentary, but my conclusions, which are clearly interpretive in a broader sense, may prove a stumbling block to my reader unless their intent is explained. My interpretation of the Dantesque image of Sodom, it must be emphasized, will not be based on my reading of Genesis but rather on the authorities that

Dante recognized. Insofar as the text of Genesis is such an authority, my reader would ideally consult it for himself; but because its familiarity and apparent simplicity can be deceptive, I have thought it best to present a modern reading that takes into account the complexities that underlie, often tacitly, the observations of medieval commentators. Biblical scholars, who have no need of my analysis, may accordingly ignore it; other readers may at least be stimulated by my reading to undertake a close and comparative examination of the Vulgate text of Genesis 1–21. Their results may differ from my own, but I trust it will be apparent that the significance of Sodom within the context of Genesis is not necessarily limited to unnatural sexual intercourse. At this point I only wish that the reader be aware of the *range* of potential interpretations that are inherent in the Genesis story of Sodom. Whether Dante and his Biblical authorities recognized any or all of them remains to be seen.

SODOM IN RABBINIC TRADITION

In understanding the Old Testament, the place of pride surely belongs to the rabbinic tradition, since it often antedates the earliest Christian commentaries. A generation ago, however, few medievalists in the Latin Christian tradition would have thought to explicate the *Divine Comedy* from Jewish sources. But today the possibility of influence cannot be dismissed summarily, for we now know, chiefly from the work of Beryl Smalley, that in the thirteenth century, Christian Biblical scholars studied Hebrew even more than philosophers did Greek. Although the appropriation of Jewish learning lagged a generation or more behind the assimilation of Aristotle by the scholastics, the process was nearing completion during the years in which the *Comedy* was being written.[35] The ultimate tool that embodied the results of this spoiling of the Egyptians was the *Postilla* to Scripture by Nicholas of Lyra, Dante's close contemporary (ca. 1270–1340). As a commentator, Lyra's principal concern was to determine "the exact and literal sense," as opposed to the allegorical senses stressed by the earlier tradition of Christian commentary.[36]

Whether, and to what extent, Dante was influenced by the *Hebraica veritas* that fascinated his generation of Biblical scholars, is now, I think, an opportune question. Until it is answered, one cannot of course connect Dante's image of Sodom to rabbinic tradition with any degree of certitude. Nonetheless it must be said, and plainly, that the Talmudic interpretation of Sodom is especially congruent to the thought of *Inferno* xv.[37] It will be useful, therefore, to begin our survey of Biblical comment on Sodom with the Talmud, if only to show that a tradition did exist that is wholly consistent with my view of the cantos of the Sodomites. The similarity may perhaps stimulate others to determine whether a historical connection can be established between Dante and the Talmud.[38]

Chapter 11 of the tractate *Sanhedrin* enumerates those who shall not have a portion in the future world. The men of Sodom are included along with other groups drawn from Scripture, notably the generations of the Flood and of the

Dispersion (Gen. 6:3, 11:3–9).[39] The discussion of Sodom is self-contained and relatively brief, so it may be conveniently laid before the reader in somewhat abridged form, with my own observations interspersed. While following the order of the original, I have inserted topical headings (A–H) to ease the abrupt and initially puzzling transitions; further, to facilitate reference, the *sententiae* have been numbered serially (1–18).

i. Deductions from Scripture

A. MISHNAH: THE AFTERLIFE OF THE MEN OF SODOM

The Hebrew text of the tractate proper (Mishnah), which was compiled not long before A.D. 200, explains the main point concisely:

> 1. The men of Sodom have no portion in the future world, as it is written, but the men of Sodom were wicked and sinners before the Lord exceedingly [Gen. 13:13]: "wicked," in this world, and "sinners" in the world to come [i.e., their claim to a portion therein will not be admitted]; yet will they stand at judgment.

The dissenting opinion of Rabbi Nehemiah, that the Last Judgment will not affect them, is then reported and then answered: they will be adjudged unjust.

The rest is commentary. The Hebrew Mishnah is supplemented by the Aramaic Gemara (compiled in Babylonia between A.D. 200 and 400), which employs several distinct methods to elaborate the nature of the sin of Sodom: glosses on the key text cited in the Mishnah (B); parallel passages from Scripture that illustrate and elucidate the nature of the sin (C, D); and finally a collection of anecdotes that exemplify the sin through instances in concrete, though fictional, examples *(haggadoth)*.

B. GLOSSES ON GENESIS 13:13: THE SIN OF SODOM DEFINED

Three opinions are collected on the meaning of the Scriptural text alleged in the Mishnah.

The first sees no reference to particular sins but instead distinguishes between conduct in this world and status in the next:

> 2. Our Rabbis taught . . . *wicked*—in this world, and *sinners*—in respect of the world to come [i.e., they are excluded therefrom on account of sin].

The remaining two are variants of the same interpretation, and although laconic, after the manner of glosses, they compress into a word or so the essence of much thought. Both are remarkable in that they reduce the sin of Sodom to elements with which we are already familiar from the *Commedia*:

> 3. Rab Judah said: [They were]
> *wicked*—with their bodies [i.e., immoral] and
> *sinners*—with their money [i.e., uncharitable] . . . [3a].
> "*Before the Lord*" refers to blasphemy;
> "*exceedingly*"—that they intentionally sinned.

4. A Tanna taught:
> *Wicked*—with their money; and
> *sinners*—with their bodies . . . [4a].
> *Before the Lord*—this refers to blasphemy.
> *Exceedingly*—this refers to bloodshed. . . .

They are in complete agreement on blasphemy, the typical sin of Dante's violent against God, and further they agree that the Sodomites abused their wealth as well as their bodies. Both forms of abuse were expressly attributed to the Sodomites by Scripture (Gen. 19:5, and Ezech. 16:49), and hence the two terms require no justification. The rabbis' problem was rather to determine whether the blasphemous iniquity consisted in the abuse of body or of wealth, if not both, as would be consistent with the more cautious gloss of 2. The positive arguments, both based on scriptural allusion, were evidently not decisive, since all three interpretations were retained by the compiler. The respective explanations may be quoted to illustrate their reasoning on what is, for our inquiry, a crucial question:

> 3a. Rab Judah said: [They were] . . . "*Wicked*—with their bodies," as it is written, *How then can I do this great wickedness, and sin against God* [Gen. 39:9]? "And *sinners*—with their money," as it is written, *and it be sin unto thee* [Deut. 15:9].

Rab Judah quotes from two verses which in their original context refer to abuses similar to those for which the Sodomites were famous: In the first, Joseph repulses the adulterous advances made by the wife of his master, Potiphar:

> Gen. 39:9 (RSV). He [my master] is not greater in this house than I am; nor has he kept back anything from me except yourself, because you are his wife; how then can I do this great wickedness, and sin against God?

Because adultery, which is done with the body, is here expressly identified as "wickedness," Rab Judah concluded that Genesis 13:13 calls the Sodomites *wicked* because they sinned with their bodies. Likewise, a second passage permits him to describe them as "*sinners*—with their money":

> Deut. 15:9 (RSV). Take heed lest there be a base thought in your heart, and you say, "The seventh year, the year of release is near," and your eye be hostile to your poor brother, and you give him nothing, and he cry to the Lord against you, and it be sin in you.

The context of this verse (Deut. 15:1–11) first enjoins the sabbatical forgiveness of loans to brother Jews, though not to Gentiles, to whom the Jews may be creditors but not debtors. Moreover, it cautions that out of charity, loans should be made to poor brethren living in towns, to the extent of their needs. Thus usury, another of the Dantesque forms of violence against God, can be linked to Sodom. For Rab Judah, however, Deuteronomy 15:9 proves that it is *blasphemy* for a rich man not to aid the poor with his wealth. That verse warns the well-to-do not to refuse the request of "your poor brother," lest he "cry to the Lord against you" (as men did against Sodom), and "it be *SIN* unto you." Hence he concludes that the Sodomites, whom Genesis 13:13 calls "sinners before the Lord," committed blasphemy with their money (3).

The opinion of Rab Judah, a Palestinian rabbi contemporary with the Mishnah and often credited with its final redaction, was paired by the Babylonian compiler of the Gemara with the opinion of a tanna, that is, a "teacher" whose doctrines were current in Palestine in Rab Judah's time:

> 4a. A Tanna taught: . . . "*Wicked*—with their money," as it is written, *And thine eye be wicked against thy poor brother*; "and *sinners*—with their bodies," as it is written, *and I will sin against God*.

The tanna cleverly counters Rab Judah's interpretation by pointing out that the two texts he cited can more aptly be applied vice versa to Genesis 13:3. Rab Judah had failed to note that Deuteronomy 15:9 also uses the term "wicked" (RSV, "hostile") to describe the selfish outlook of the uncharitable miser, and consequently the "wicked" of Genesis 13:13 can equally well be identified as those who offended with their money. The tanna also points out that since Genesis 39:9 states that to commit adultery is to "sin against God," the "sinners before the Lord" (1) must consequently have sinned with their bodies.[40]

These two Palestinian interpretations neatly balance one another, and thus it would seem that the Babylonian rabbis recalled both opinions in their Gemara but prudently advocated a more general interpretation (2).

For Dantists, this intricate debate brings out a point that has hitherto eluded interpreters of the *violenti*. Although Dantology conventionally divides them into *bestemmiatori*, *sodomiti*, and *usurai*, yet the three categories are not necessarily distinct, since avaricious moneylenders appear, according to Deuteronomy 15:1–11, to be guilty not only of blasphemy but also of the sin of Sodom. It is an unsettling possibility that must not be forgotten when we come to assess the poet's image of Sodom.

C. ASSIMILATION: HAGIOGRAPHIC REFLECTIONS OF THE SINS OF SODOM

The rabbis, as we have seen, were certain from Ezechiel 16—a passage we have yet to consider in detail—that the Sodomites abused their wealth as well as their bodies. Although they recognized both aspects of the sin of Sodom, their commentary concentrates almost exclusively on the former, so that Sodom, in the rabbinic tradition, appears primarily as a type of the unjust society. Their method of explication, as should be evident from the glosses on Genesis 13:13, proceeded by assimilation: by which I mean that they enlarged their understanding of a passage by reading it in conjunction with texts that were *similar*. Parallelism, the mainstay of Hebrew prosody and rhetoric, most probably suggested this approach, as would appear from the emphasis laid upon purely verbal distinctions.

Not all books of Scripture had equal authority, however, for resemblances discovered in the Pentateuch or the Prophets were weightier than those observed in the other canonical books of Scripture, which collectively are called Ketubim, which is Hellenized as Hagiographa. Accordingly, in explicating the sin of Sodom, the

Gemara considered first the evidence of parallels from the books of the Mosaic Torah (B), and then, in a separate section (C), assembled similitudes found in the Hagiographa, placing the most significant of these deductions foremost:

> 5. Our Rabbis taught: The men of Sodom waxed haughty only on account of the good which the Holy One, blessed be He, had lavished upon them. What is written concerning them?—*As for the earth, out of it cometh bread: and under it is burned up as it were with fire. The stones of it are the place of sapphires: and it hath dust of gold. There is a path which no fowl knoweth, and which the vulture's eye hath not seen: The lion's whelps have not trodden it, nor the fierce lions passed by it* [Job 28:5–8]. They said: Since there cometh forth bread out of [our] earth, and it hath the dust of gold, why should we suffer wayfarers, who come to us only to deplete our wealth. Come, let us abolish the practice of travelling [lit., "cause the law of the foot to be forgotten"] in our land, as it is written, *The flood breaketh out from the inhabitants; they are forgotten of the foot; they are dried up, they are gone away from men* [Job 28:4].[41]

The Babylonian rabbis took it for granted that the Sodomites were, as Lot implied, breaking the unwritten laws of hospitality (Gen. 19:8), and here they explain the motives of the men of Sodom in the light of Job 28, where two notions that are distinct in Genesis occur in juxtaposition, thereby authorizing one to be interpreted as the cause of the other. The Sodomites' inhospitality is understood as a deliberate withdrawal from human society, which is accomplished by ignoring its common "law of the foot." Moreover, from the following verses, their motive appears to have been a sense of self-sufficiency based on the fertility and wealth of their land. This, then, elaborates on the view taken in 3 and 4 that the Sodomites did not use their wealth well.

The parallel that is here drawn between the Sodomites and Job 28 has an especial significance for *Inferno* xv, as will be evident if one reads that chapter in its entirety. Job's theme is that man, by his ingenious technology, can exploit the natural resources of the earth, but that only God possesses true wisdom and understanding, so that, for man, wisdom is the fear of the Lord, and understanding is the avoidance of evil.[42]

6. The Gemara then reports other similitudes to the crimes of Sodom, which are drawn from Job and the Psalms. Several of these concern envious men who use their cunning to rob the wealthy; others detail various forms of social injustice that men do openly, though Job is sure that God will eventually punish them: they leave the naked unclothed, steal from orphans, and take advantage of widows by making loans on ruinous terms; they remove landmarks and join others' flocks to their own.[43] Careful exegesis could justify the attribution of each of these verses to Sodom, but their collective significance is more to our point. In the main, they link Sodom to the unjust society that is lamented in Job 24. One verse of the context deserves quotation: "If the morning suddenly appear, it is to them the shadow of death: and they walk in darkness as if it were in light."[44] Job has already equated

light with the Lord, and darkness with evildoing (24:13–16); so the sense is that the wicked do evil as if it were the will of the Lord, but his coming would be their undoing. The paradoxical pretense that dark is light serves to summarize, if not to generalize, the concrete cases that Job had previously enumerated; and to the rabbinic commentators it apparently also enucleated the essential sin of the Sodomites, for the remainder of their comment (D–G = 7–18) illustrates the sin of Sodom with anecdotes, all of which embody Job's principle.

ii. Haggadoth

Up to this point, the Talmudic commentary has drawn on Scripture to explain the sin of Sodom. Progressively, the nature of that sin has been elaborated from analogous passages, and these cumulative conclusions may here be conveniently summarized, since the remainder of the comment merely applies these deductions. The sin of Sodom, then, involves blasphemy; it was done "with their money" as well as "with their bodies," but stress is laid chiefly on the former aspect. The wealth of Sodom led its men to alienate their community from the rest of mankind, for whose common principles of justice the Sodomites substituted their own arbitrary injunctions. Theirs is accordingly the type of the unjust society, in which men condone, or even prescribe, conduct that is contrary to natural justice. To reasonable men, their premise that justice is a matter of convention cannot but seem an absurd paradox, for only the Sodomites cannot see that injustice can never be just.

The rabbis illustrated their scriptural deductions by stories or anecdotes, called haggadoth, in which the tractate *Sanhedrin* is particularly rich. Those that are told about the men of Sodom depict a moral world turned upside down. The Gemara's compiler grouped them into three general categories: (D) the rules of Sodom, containing examples of the sort of laws and customs by which the Sodomites might have agreed to do injustice to one another; (E) the judgments of Sodom, in which four principles that subvert justice are personified as the appointed judges in Sodom, whose decisions reflect their combined effect. The remaining *exempla*, grouped under (F), concern Sodom's mistreatment of aliens, who include the poor as well as travelers, since the poor man is by definition foreign to the affluent society of Sodom (cf. 16). Except for the last haggada (18), the rabbis used the anecdotal method, not to develop their understanding of Sodom, but only to exemplify it; and hence these anecdotes will principally serve to reinforce our view of the rabbinic image of Sodom. It should be added that these fictional examples are enlivened by pendent tales, in which a commonsense person, usually Abraham's steward Eliezer, comes to Sodom and turns the Sodomites' injustice back upon its perpetrators. These episodes serve to contrast the folly of the Sodomites with the common sense to which they are blind; for brevity I have omitted them.

D. THE RULES OF SODOM

They [the Sodomites] ruled:

7. He who has [only] one ox must tend [all the oxen of the town] for one day; but he who has none must tend [them] two days. . . .

8. [Likewise, they ruled,] He who crosses with the ferry must pay one *zuz* [for the privilege], but he who does not, [entering by another way] must give two.

9. If one had rows of bricks every person came and took one, saying "I have taken only one."

10. If one spread out garlic or onions [to dry them], every person came and took one, saying, "I have taken only one."

E. THE JUDGMENTS OF SODOM

There were four judges in Sodom . . . [named Liar, Awful Liar, Forger, and Perverter of Justice].

11. Now, if a man assaulted his neighbour's wife and bruised her, they would say [to the husband], "Give her to him, that she may become pregnant for thee."

12. If one cut off the ear of his neighbour's ass, they would order, "Give it to him until it grows again."

13. If one wounded his neighbour they would say to him [the victim], "Give him a fee for bleeding thee."

14. He who crossed over with the ferry had to pay four *zuzim*, whilst he who crossed through the water had to pay eight. . . [cf. 8, above].

F. THE STRANGER IN SODOM

15. Now, they had beds upon which travellers slept. If he [the guest] was too long, they shortened him [by lopping off his feet]; if too short, they stretched him out. . . .

16. If a poor man happened to come there, every resident gave him a *denar*, upon which he wrote his name, but no bread was given him. When he died, each came and took back his.

17. They made this agreement amongst themselves: whoever invites a man [a stranger] to a feast shall be stripped of his garment. . . .

18. A certain maiden gave some bread to a poor man, [hiding it] in a pitcher. On the matter becoming known, they daubed her with honey and placed her on the parapet of the wall, and the bees came and consumed her. Thus it is written, *And the Lord said, The cry of Sodom and Gomorrah, because it is great* ["rabbah" in Hebrew; Gen. 18:20]: whereon Rab Judah commented in Rab's name: On account of the maiden [*ribah*—a play on *rabbah*].

iii. Midrash

To confirm the view of Sodom's sin that is found in the Babylonian Talmud, we may turn briefly to the *Bereshith Rabbah*, a running commentary on Genesis that was largely compiled in Palestine at about the same time.[45] As the work proceeds verse by verse, many aspects of the Sodom story are discussed here that were not treated in the Talmud, but the nature of Sodom's sin receives far less attention. The *locus classicus* here, as in the Talmud, is Genesis 13:13. The brief commentary may be quoted in its entirety:

Rabbi said: There was no city more wicked than Sodom: when a man was evil he was called a Sodomite; and there was no nation more cruel than the Amorites; when a man was cruel he was called an Amorite.

R. Issi said: There was no city [in the Plain] better than Sodom, for Lot searched through all the cities of the plain and found none like Sodom. Thus these people were the best of all, yet, *The men of Sodom were wicked and sinners* [Gen. 13:13]—they were *wicked* to each other; *sinners* in adultery; *against the Lord* in idolatry; while *exceedingly* refers to bloodshed.[46]

This resembles most closely the view of the tanna reported in the Talmud (3, above). Wickedness "with their money" here is generalized as mutual injustice, which accords with the conclusions of the Talmudic analysis. The sin of their bodies, by contrast, is more narrowly interpreted as adultery, and similarly, idolatry is specified instead of blasphemy in general. These differences amount to variations on a theme with which we are already familiar, and it would obscure the basic agreement of the rabbinic tradition to dwell further upon relatively slight shifts in emphasis. The outstanding feature remains the insistence that the Sodomites sinned together as a community, by committing injustice against one another, against the rest of mankind, and against God. The midrashic *Bereshith* diverges, to be sure, from the analysis of the Talmud in many particulars but not in basic conception.[47]

BEDE ON GENESIS

If Dante profited from the rabbinic tradition, he gave his readers no hint that they should follow his footsteps. Instead, as we have already observed, on several occasions Dante does particularly commend the Venerable Bede among patristic writers. It is true that other Christian commentaries on Genesis were more widely known in the thirteenth century, but they offer little explication of the sin of Sodom,[48] whereas Bede offers an extended analysis that may well have suggested the *Comedy's* image of Sodom. Bede states this view in generalized form at the first mention of the sinfulness of Sodom, and subsequently he qualifies it in connection with other passages. The basic thesis deserves quotation in full:

[The writer of Genesis] praises the fertility of the land and notes at the same time the impiety of its inhabitants, that they might be understood to deserve greater damnation because they turned God's greatest presents not to the fruit of piety but to the increase of luxury.

Tacitly this passage also praises the blessed Lot because, although he lived in the same land among such people, yet he was in no way able to be corrupted from the integrity of his purity, neither by the abundance of rich soil nor by the example of his coinhabitants.

The sins to which the Sodomites were subject—except that unspeakable one recorded below [Gen. 19:4–11]—are sufficiently expounded by the prophet Ezekiel, who said, speaking to Jerusalem: "Behold this was the iniquity of Sodom thy sister, pride, fulness of bread, and abundance, and the idleness of her, and of her daughters: and they did not put forth their hand to the needy, and to the poor. And they were lifted up, and committed abominations before me" [Ezech. 16:49–50]. Lot himself was free from all of these faults, as is evident from the text of Genesis, for we are told there that he received the angels with hospitality and was seized by them from the impious infatuation of the Sodomites.

This interpretation is confirmed by the opinion of the Apostle Peter, who wrote: "And [God] delivered just Lot, oppressed by the injustice and lewd conversation of the wicked. For in sight and in hearing he was just: dwelling among them, who from day to day vexed the just soul with unjust works" [2 Pet. 2:7–8]. Could one whom the apostle described by the word "just" have failed in any respect to be good and worthy? To his pure eyes and ears the sight and sound of his neighbors' misdeeds could only have been torment and affliction. What did those present hear about such a man if not that he had a reputation for justice [*fama iustitiae*]?[49]

Like the rabbis before him, Bede—under the influence of Ezekiel—stressed the social injustice of the Sodomites as a community. Their attack on the angels he considered to be a sin of another kind, presumably sexual, which in itself would not account for the severity of Sodom's punishment. He identified the aggravating factor as the misuse of material prosperity, particularly the environmental gifts of nature. Both in the abuse of their resources and of their guests, the Sodomites were *unjust*, in contrast to Lot, who would not have been just had he been subject to either of their sins. Moreover, the injustice of Sodom also constituted *impiety*. The relation between the two aspects of their sin can be inferred from the opening statement: piety consists in the proper use of God's gifts; impiety, in their malversation to *luxuria*. The favored possessor evidently can convert only a just portion to his own use: God intended the surplus for others; to ignore this divine intention and selfishly to retain all the benefits is unjust to the less fortunate and is impious because contrary to God's will.

How, one might ask, could the Sodomites be expected to know that they were not using their natural gifts as God intended? One explanation, which I adopted in my earlier exposition,[50] sees them as obligated by the Noachic laws, which were delivered to all mankind after the Flood. Bede, however, finds a more immediate explanation within the Sodom story itself. At the time that Lot went to dwell in the Pentapolis, the inhabitants were already "very wicked, and sinners before the face of the Lord, beyond measure" (Gen. 13:13). Therefore, Bede argues, their defeat by King Chodorlahomor, coupled with their rescue by Abram, was God's way of calling them to repentance. In both cases, victory went to the weaker force: the five kings of the Plain were defeated by the four kings of the North, but the victors were in turn vanquished by Abram's tiny force of 318 men.[51] Such unlikely triumphs against odds teach man to trust, not in his own power, but in God, who gives the victory. But this lesson was lost on the Sodomites, who not only persisted in their evil ways but actually grew worse (Gen. 18:20).

The model for their conduct should have been Lot, for whose sake they had been rescued: "He faithfully served God among them . . . so they might learn from the example of him by whom and through whom they were saved by the grace of God." Their failure to do so established a precedent for divine vengeance. The Flood had come without warning, but the men of Sodom were the first to be given an opportunity to repent before being punished. Ever since Sodom, God has followed the same pattern of reproof followed by retribution upon the impenitent. Thus, for Bede, the sin of Sodom culminated in their inability to comprehend what Dante termed a manifest judgment of God. Hence Bede takes them as the prototype of impiety, which is compounded of ingratitude and incorrigibility. God "shall not cease to consume such men and the world, which is their state, since everywhere men who persist in being not only ungrateful for gifts from on high but also insensible to punishment, are suddenly carried off to eternal ruin by the whirlwind soon after their trial."[52]

Bede does not doubt that the Sodomites were homosexuals, but he thinks it far worse that they were so far from being ashamed of their vice that they both practiced it openly and forced others to join them. Intrinsically, homosexuality is a shameful act *(turpitudo)* that the males of Sodom practiced together as a group with no thought of modesty *(absque respectu pudoris)*. Still worse, they did so in the presence of guests and strangers, whom—and this was worst of all—they forced to participate in this heinous and outrageous immorality *(sceleribus atque suis facinoribus)*.[53]

The sexual sin of Sodom, then, is not simple homosexuality but that sin twice compounded. According to Bede, the sexual Sodomite performs his crimes publicly en masse and, moreover, forces outsiders to participate in his orgies. Since Bede attaches no special significance to the sexual aspect of Sodom's crimes, it would seem that he subsumed them under his previous general definition of the sin of Sodom. Sodomy, then, is not distinct from man's other wilful abuses of the gifts of God, whether these are conferred through the regular course of nature or as a special act of grace. Sodom rejected both, and hence was guilty of impious injustice. For Bede, the city typifies any and all such impieties, and not simply, or even especially, unnatural sex. In accordance with his concept of sodomy as impiety in general, Bede takes Sodom's destruction by fire as a prefiguration of the penalty that is to be inflicted at the Last Judgment on "all the impious" ("omnes impii").[54]

Up to this point, we have concentrated on the story of Sodom in Genesis, which for all commentary on Sodom must be the beginning and the end: the beginning because all subsequent allusions descend from this source; the end because it is the logical place for commentators to present their general interpretations distilled from a comparative analysis of all allusions in the Bible to Sodom. This approach, then, has afforded us the most general view of the Biblical significance of Sodom. To complete it, we must not neglect the rest of Scripture, however, for medieval men interpreted Genesis in accord with the inspired understanding expressed in other books of the Bible. Each of these in turn was read with the aid of Christian commentators, whose patristic authority was weighty if not revealed.

We must now turn to these Biblical passages that are complementary to Genesis, beginning with Deuteronomy; thence passing to Amos, the earliest of the prophets; and then progressing chronologically through the Bible to the book of Revelation. Our survey shall be cursory, for we wish to review the materials for the history of an idea, rather than actually to write that history.

At the least, such a rapid review should suffice to demonstrate to Dantists that, for Biblical writers, the sexual aspect of the Sodom story was not paramount. Instead, Biblical writers develop other possibilities that are inherent in the account of Genesis, including not a few themes that we have already encountered in connection with *Inferno* xv. In the Bible itself these themes have little apparent unity save that they all are analogies suggested by the pages of Genesis. Christian commentators, however, by reading the Old Testament in the light of the New, were able to reduce these disparate themes to an allegorical interpretation of Sodom that is strikingly consistent with our interpretation of Dante's violent against nature. From a wealth of patristic comment, therefore, I shall report only such commentaries as contribute to an understanding of the Dantesque image of Sodom. The parade of authorities will necessarily be long, but as they pass in review, the recurrence of now-familiar themes may perhaps convey to the reader, better than any other form of demonstration, the fact that the diverse themes of *Inferno* xv are united in Christian Biblical commentary by the master image of Sodom.

DEUTERONOMY 29: *ABSCONDITA MANIFESTA*

Since any allusion to Sodom refers back to Genesis, every analogy to Sodom contains an implicit interpretation of the Bible's first book. One, however, takes precedence over all others; for Deuteronomy, the last book of the Pentateuch, purports to be the authoritative clarification of the covenant as revealed through Moses. Since medieval men accepted it at face value, we who are attempting to reconstitute their Biblical image of Sodom must do likewise.[55]

According to Deuteronomy, Moses collected in this book the revelations he had received at the end of his life, when, after forty years of wandering in the wilderness, the Israelites came to Moab and were about to enter the promised land of Canaan. At that crucial juncture, the covenant was renewed by the whole people, and the obligations implicit in their earlier agreement were now made explicit in practical terms and were reinforced by an impressive array of blessings and curses that spelled out the consequences of their future conduct. All these are summarized by Moses towards the end of the book in a lengthy description of the fate that awaits Israel as a whole if the people do not keep the covenant.

> Deut. 29:22. And the following generation shall say, and the children that shall be born hereafter, and the strangers that shall come from afar, seeing the plagues of that land and the evils wherewith the Lord hath afflicted it,
>
> 23. Burning it with brimstone, and the heat of salt, so that it cannot be

sown any more, nor any green thing grow therein, after the example of the destruction of Sodom and Gomorrha, Adama and Seboim, which the Lord destroyed in his wrath and indignation [*Sulphure et salis ardore comburens, ita ut ultra non seratur, nec virens quippiam germinet, in exemplum subversionis Sodomae et Gomorrhae, Adamae et Seboim, quas subvertit Dominus in ira et furore suo*].

24. And all the nations shall say: "Why hath the Lord done thus to this land? what meaneth this exceeding great heat of his wrath?"

25. And they shall answer: Because they forsook the covenant of the Lord, which he made with their fathers, when he brought them out of the land of Egypt:

26. And they have served strange gods, and adored them, whom they knew not, and for whom they had not been assigned:

27. Therefore the wrath of the Lord was kindled against this land, to bring upon it all the curses that are written in this volume:

28. And he hath cast them out of their land, in anger and in wrath, and in very great indignation, and hath thrown them into a strange land, as it is seen this day.

29. Secret things to the Lord our God: things that are manifest, to us and to our children forever, that we may do all the words of this law [*Abscondita Domino Deo nostro, quae manifesta sunt nobis et filiis nostris usque in sempiternum, ut faciamus universa verba legis huius*].

In Genesis, God had cast Sodom down at the same time that he prepared to raise Israel up. Since these actions were, respectively, the penalty for unrighteousness and the reward for righteousness, one might infer that if Israel ceased to be righteous, she would receive the punishment of Sodom; but in Genesis the threat is only implicit. Here in Deuteronomy, however, Moses reveals that such is indeed the inference to be drawn from the two juxtaposed events in Genesis.

To the inhabitants of Sodom, the calamity appeared as an unintelligible, perhaps even wholly irrational, disaster. Lot learned from the angels that God was the cause, but he could only guess the reason for the divine wrath, because, to men, God's motives are hidden (*abscondita*) unless He chooses to reveal them. God did so to Abraham, who learned that justice motivated the Lord to avenge the injustice done by the men of Sodom. Thus, in the scheme of *Monarchia* 2. 6, God spontaneously revealed his hidden judgment to Abraham.[56] Moreover, through Moses in Deuteronomy, God explains why these things had been made manifest to Abraham and his posterity forever: "that we may do all the words of this law" ("ut faciamus universa verba legis huius").

This, then, is God's own commentary on the significance of Sodom in Genesis: the cause of its destruction was revealed to Israel as a warning to abide forever by the *whole* of divine law. Hence only an ignorant or perverse medieval exegete would have dared to maintain that Sodom signified nothing but sexual perversion, for this narrow interpretation would have contradicted the positive teaching of revelation. God intended Sodom as an example to his people that would deter their departure from any divine law whatsoever.

[233]

In Deuteronomy, the curse of Sodom affects only the promised land, which shall be rendered infertile as a sign that the Lord has punished his people, while the people, like Lot, shall not be destroyed but only expelled. Furthermore, the effects are not necessarily permanent, since the next chapter promises repatriation of the repentant (Deut. 30:1–10). Deuteronomy thus maintains the recurrent distinction made in Genesis between the seed of Abraham and the land in which it shall be planted. The prophets will ring many variations on this fertility imagery, which we have already found associated with the theme of Sodom in the *Comedy*.

DEUTERONOMY 32: THE *POMA SODOMITICA* OF ISRAEL'S ENEMIES

After the covenant had been renewed, Deuteronomy continues, Moses committed the Second Law to writing and then concluded his ministry with a final charge that is embodied in the Song of Moses. This warning to observe the Law he recited "in the hearing of the whole assembly of Israel," but significantly, it was addressed especially to the leaders of Israel, to the *maiores atque doctores*. "For I know that, after my death," he explained, "you will do wickedly, and will quickly turn aside from the way that I have commanded you" (Deut. 31:24–30). In the same spirit, we shall find that the prophets hold the leaders of Israel particularly responsible for the observance of the Law, and hence for the sin of Sodom.

The canticle, or psalm, of Moses contrasts the fidelity of God with the infidelity of His people. The theme of Sodom appears here in connection, not with Israel, but with her enemies. They can triumph over Israel only if God wills it to punish the sins of His people:

> Deut. 32:31. For our God is not as their gods: our enemies themselves are judges.
> 32. Their vines are of the vineyard of Sodom, and of the suburbs of Gomorrha: their grapes are grapes of gall, and their clusters most bitter.
> 33. Their wine is the gall of dragons, and the venom of asps, which is incurable.

> Deut. 32:31. Non enim est Deus noster ut dii eorum: et inimici nostri sunt iudices.
> 32. De vinea Sodomorum, vinea eorum, et de suburbanis Gomorrhae: uva eorum uva fellis, et botri amarissimi.
> 33. Fel draconum vinum eorum, et venenum aspidum insanabile.

The fruit of the enemies of God is likened to the proverbially deceptive fruits of Sodom and Gomorrah, which Augustine described as "*poma* that contain an interior of ashes within a deceptively ripe skin."[57] The canticle, however, ascribes more than ashes to the fruit of Sodom: their grapes are bitter as gall, and the wine they yield is the most potent of poisons. Human works, the poet seems to say, may appear fair, but without divine favor they are worthless and will be fatal if not discarded. The message will be often repeated more explicitly by the prophets, but the metaphor is unique in Scripture, and indeed it alludes to a tradition that is better known from extra-Biblical sources.[58]

Although grapes are clearly intended by Deuteronomy, the Augustinian tradition is less precise, for "*poma*" can refer to the fruit on any tree or bush. Thus it is possible that these *poma Sodomitica* suggested to Dante the bittersweet-fruit imagery in the cantos of the Sodomites. Brunetto compares the good and bad elements in Florence to a "sweet fig" and "bitter sorb-apples,"[59] and the same bitter/sweet contrast describes the pilgrim's mission: "I am leaving the gall and going on for the sweet fruits" ("Lascio lo fele e vo per dolci pomi"; *Inf.* xvi, 61). The latter line, in particular, may allude by verbal echo to the *uva fellis* of Deuteronomy 32:32, in which case Rusticucci's misunderstanding gains new point, for he has failed to grasp a reference to his own sin.[60]

Elsewhere in the Bible, as earlier in Deuteronomy, the land of Sodom is represented as a sterile and infertile waste. Such descriptions must be read with the fruit of Sodom in mind, for although some plants can still flourish on the blighted land, nevertheless they are worthless, so the net effect is sterility, understood as the incapacity to produce anything beneficial. Though medieval exegetes develop this concept of relative infertility in connection with other Sodom analogies, the *poma Sodomitica* symbolize it better than do other Biblical images.[61]

In the Old Testament, two types of analogies to Sodom appear—one to Israel and the other to the Gentiles—which may conveniently be denoted Sodom:Israel and Sodom:Gentiles. The former, we have seen, was a revealed relationship; the latter is less clear in Deuteronomy, at least in the Vulgate. Are all Gentiles to be compared to Sodomites? Only, it would appear, those who are the enemies of Israel and trust in false gods. More specifically (though obscurely) it is said that "our enemies themselves are judges," which recently has been rendered "in themselves they are mere fools" (NEB), that is, they judge by their own standards rather than by God's. At the least, the Song of Moses suggests that the sin of Sodom is prevalent among the Gentiles and is associated with a failure to recognize the true God. To discover what obligations bind even the Gentiles, we must turn to the prophets.

AMOS 4:11: THE SODOMY OF DISOBEDIENT JEWS AND HERETICS

God, speaking through Amos, reminds a complacent and prosperous Israel that it has recently received, but has ignored, signs of divine displeasure. The specific signs are all natural disasters—famine, drought, blight, locusts, and a plague among the army (Amos 4:6–10). The list concludes with the following verse, which does not seem to refer to any particular event but instead summarizes the effect of all the previous afflictions:

> Amos 4:11. Subverti vos, sicut subvertit Deus Sodomam et Gomorrham, et facti estis quasi torris raptus ab incendio: et non redistis ad me, dicit Dominus.

> Amos 4:11 (RSV). I overthrew [some of] you, as when God overthrew Sodom and Gomorrah, and you were as a brand plucked out of the burning; yet you did not return to me, says the Lord.

Amos very likely had in mind the subversion of Sodom by the kings of the North, but Jerome seized upon the firebrand and identified it with the destruction of Sodom by fire. In Jerome's view, Lot represents the Sodomite who was saved, though in the process he lost not only his property but also part of his body (i.e., his wife). Invoking 1 Cor. 3:14–15,[62] Jerome takes Lot's case to signify the "extreme remedy of the Ten Tribes, and of heretics, and of all sinners," who at the Last Judgment will be purged by fire of their evil works but will escape with their lives. He is particularly insistent that Israel and heretics in general resemble Sodom and Gomorrah in their works, and although these are not specified here, Jerome elaborates on them elsewhere.[63]

OSEE 11:8–9: SODOM THE HERESIARCH OF UNJUST CITIES

8. How shall I deal with thee, O Ephraim, shall I protect thee, O Israel? how shall I make thee as Adama, shall I set thee as Seboim? my heart is turned within me, my repentance is stirred up.

9. I will not execute the fierceness of my wrath: I will not return to destroy Ephraim: because I am God, and not man: the holy one in the midst of thee, and I will not enter into the city.

8. Quomodo dabo te, Ephraim? protegam te, Israel? quomodo dabo te sicut Adama, ponam te ut Seboim? Conversum est in me cor meum, pariter conturbata est poenitudo mea.

9. Non faciam furorem irae meae: non convertar ut disperdam Ephraim: quoniam Deus ego, et non homo: in medio tui sanctus, et non ingrediar civitatem.

Hosea, who was nearly contemporary with Amos, reproaches Ephraim, the Northern Kingdom, which was his home, and the rest of Israel as well. God has redeemed them from slavery in Egypt and has established them as prosperous nations. Now they are ungrateful and honor foreign gods. For this they deserve the fate of the Pentapolis; nevertheless, God will not judge and punish them by the unjust standards of human civil justice, but rather he will temper his justice with mercy and not destroy them utterly.

Jerome, whose commentary at this point is extensive, sees the reference to Adama and Seboim as a threat of total destruction.[64] At the literal level he expounds the distinction between divine and human law as the quality of mercy, which is lacking in the retributive justice of civil law:

The holy one in the midst of thee, and I will not enter into the city, which is to say: I am not one of those who inhabit cities, who live by human laws, who approve of cruel justice, for whom the greatest right is the greatest malice; for my law and my justice is to save those who correct their ways.[65]

Thus, the five Cities of the Plain represent communities whose human laws do not correspond to the law of God, and Jerome, perhaps faintly echoing here the rabbinic tradition of his Palestinian neighbors and masters, brings out the paradox of unjust justice: "ius summum summa malitia est."

Disobedience to divine law is, for Jerome, the essential sin of Sodom, and hence

[236]

allegorically the Pentapolis again signifies either Israel disinherited or Christianity perverted by heretics. These allegories suggest to Jerome that the sin of Sodom and Gomorrah is greater than that of their sister cities, since Hosea compares the lesser cities to Israel as a whole and to Ephraim, whereas Scripture elsewhere identifies Sodom and Gomorrah with Judah, the elite of Israel. Thus Jerome infers that Sodom and Gomorrah can signify ecclesiastics who lead laymen into doctrinal error: they represent "the servant who knows the will of his lord." Read as a figure of heresy, the passage is an assurance that God will not enter into "the false councils and cities of heretics" but will welcome the faithful who leave to join him outside the perverted community.[66]

ISAIAS 1:4–10: THE SCRIBES AND PHARISEES AS PRINCES OF SODOM

The Great Prophet compared the afflictions of Judah and Jerusalem to the devastation of Sodom and Gomorrah, his recurrent image for total destruction. Their common sin is blasphemy, and for this they shall be as a city that is laid waste by fire:

Isa. 1:4. Woe to the sinful nation, a people laden with iniquity, a wicked seed, ungracious children: they have forsaken the Lord, they have blasphemed the Holy One of Israel, they are gone away backwards.

5. For what shall I strike you any more, you that increase transgression? the whole head is sick, and the whole heart is sad.

6. From the sole of the foot unto the top of the head, there is no soundness therein: wounds and bruises and swelling sores: they are not bound up, nor dressed, nor fomented with oil.

7. Your land is desolate, your cities are burnt with fire: your country strangers devour before your face, and it shall be desolate as when wasted by enemies.

8. And the daughter of Sion shall be left as a covert in a vineyard, and as a lodge in a garden of cucumbers, and as a city that is laid waste.

9. Except the Lord of hosts had left us seed, we had been as Sodom, and we should have been like to Gomorrha.

10. Hear the word of the Lord, ye rulers of Sodom, give ear to the law of our God, ye people of Gomorrha.

Isa. 1:4. Vae genti peccatrici, populo gravi iniquitate, semini nequam, filiis sceleratis: dereliquerunt Dominum, blasphemaverunt sanctum Israel, abalienati sunt retrorsum.

5. Super quo percutiam vos ultra, addentes praevaricationem? omne caput languidum, et omne cor moerens.

6. A planta pedis usque ad verticem, non est in eo sanitas: vulnus, et livor, et plaga tumens, non est circumligata, nec curata medicamine, neque fota oleo.

7. Terra vestra deserta, civitates vestrae succensae igni: regionem vestram coram vobis alieni devorant, et desolabitur sicut in vastitate hostili.

8. Et derelinquetur filia Sion ut umbraculum in vinea, et sicut tugurium in cucumerario, et sicut civitas quae vastatur.

9. Nisi Dominus exercituum reliquisset nobis semen, quasi Sodoma fuissemus, et quasi Gomorrha similes essemus.

10. Audite verbum Domini, principes Sodomorum, percipite auribus legem Dei nostri, populus Gomorrhae.

In successive verses, Isaiah draws two analogies to the Pentapolis. In the first (verse 9), Sodom and Gomorrah typify the total destruction which would have been Israel's fate had not God "left us seed." This contrast is followed by a comparison: Israel resembles the blighted cities in her sin, the implication being that she consequently does deserve the punishment that she will not get because of God's mercy. Furthermore, the prophet identifies Sodom with Israel's leaders (*principes*) and Gomorrah with her people (*populus*). Thus, with Isaiah, Sodom symbolized those persons who led God's people to blaspheme their benefactor—which is precisely the sin of the runners.

In his commentary, Jerome enlarges upon this interpretation. The "wicked seed" (verse 4), his gloss argues, does not refer to a people wicked by nature, but to a good seed gone bad. Literally this people can be understood only to be Israel,

> who first [verse 2] are called the sons of the Lord because of the good he has done to them [*per beneficium*]; afterwards [verse 4] they may be called sons of iniquity for their vice. Or, since later in that verse they are called *abalienati*, they might by analogy be called "sons perverting" [*corrumpentes*], i.e. διαφθείροντες, who by their vice shall have lost the good of nature.[67]

The phrase "the whole head is sick, and the whole heart is sad" (verse 5) indicates to Jerome that an unhealthy head causes the whole body to suffer, whether it be the body natural or the body politic. "And by the metaphor, Isaiah teaches that health is in no part from the principal men [*principes*] down to the lowest classes, from the teachers [*doctores*] down to the unlearned commons, but they all consent with equal ardor in impiety."[68]

Jerome has a surprise in store for the reader who might suppose that Isaiah was warning his people of the imminent Babylonian captivity. The prophecy, we are assured, was not fulfilled until the time of the Romans, when the greater part of the Jews rejected Christ, leaving only a remnant in the Apostles, who were the seed that disseminated the Gospel throughout the world.[69] Accordingly, for Jerome the *literal* sense of the prophecy in verse 10 must speak "to the scribes and Pharisees, and to the people who shouted 'Crucify him, crucify him.'" Hence it was the mob at Christ's Passion that Isaiah likened to the *populus Gomorrhae*, while the *principes Sodomorum* he compared to the scribes and Pharisees who led them. The comparison cost the prophet his life, Jerome adds, for "the Hebrews say that Isaiah was killed for two reasons, because he called them the chiefs of the Sodomites and the populace of Gomorrah" and because he claimed to have seen God.[70]

ISAIAS 3:1–12: THE VISION OF THE *PUERI PRINCIPES*

Koheleth found in the child-king the image of misgovernment, and we have seen Solomon praised in Paradise for sparing his people this calamity. Isaiah predicts that just such a fate shall reduce the kingdom of Judah to an anarchy comparable to Sodom. The crucial factor in the impending disintegration will be the loss of the key men of the kingdom—the swift and the strong—whom the Lord shall take away. Their places shall be filled by boy-leaders, who will have only their inexperience and their womenfolk to guide them:

Isa. 3:1. For behold the sovereign the Lord of hosts shall take away from Jerusalem, and from Juda the valiant and the strong, the whole strength of bread, and the whole strength of water.

2. The strong man, and the man of war, the judge, and the prophet, and the cunning man, and the ancient.

3. The captain over fifty, and the honourable in countenance, and the counsellor, and the architect, and the skilful in eloquent speech.

4. And I will give children to be their princes, and the effeminate shall rule over them.

5. And the people shall rush one upon another, and every man against his neighbour: the child shall make a tumult against the ancient, and the base against the honourable.

6. For a man shall take hold of his brother, one of the house of his father, saying: Thou hast a garment, be thou our ruler, and let this ruin be under thy hand.

7. In that day he shall answer, saying: I am no healer, and in my house there is no bread, nor clothing: make me not ruler of the people.

8. For Jerusalem is ruined, and Juda is fallen: because their tongue, and their devices are against the Lord, to provoke the eyes of his majesty.

9. The shew of their countenance hath answered them: and they have proclaimed abroad their sin as Sodom, and they have not hid it: woe to their souls, for evils are rendered to them.

10. Say to the just man that it is well, for he shall eat the fruit of his doings.

11. Woe to the wicked unto evil: for the reward of his hands shall be given him.

12. As for my people, their oppressors have stripped them, and women have ruled over them. O my people, they that call thee blessed, the same deceive thee, and destroy the way of thy steps.

Isa. 3:1. Ecce enim dominator Dominus exercituum auferet a Jerusalem et a Juda validum et fortem, omne robur panis, et omne robur aquae:

2. Fortem, et virum bellatorem, iudicem, et prophetam, et ariolum, et senem:

3. Principem super quinquaginta, et honorabilem vultu, et consiliarium, et sapientem de architectis, et prudentem eloquii mystici.

4. Et dabo pueros principes eorum, et effeminati dominabuntur eis.

5. Et irruet populus, vir ad virum, et unusquisque ad proximum suum: tumultuabitur puer contra senem, et ignobilis contra nobilem.

6. Apprehendet enim vir fratrem suum domesticum patris sui: Vestimentum tibi est, princeps esto noster, ruina autem haec sub manu tua.

7. Respondebit in die illa, dicens: Non sum medicus, et in domo mea non est panis, neque vestimentum: nolite constituere me principem populi.

8. Ruit enim Jerusalem, et Judas concidit: quia lingua eorum et adinventiones eorum contra Dominum, ut provocarent oculos maiestatis eius.

9. Agnitio vultus eorum respondit eis: et peccatum suum quasi Sodoma praedicaverunt, nec absconderunt: vae animae eorum, quoniam reddita sunt eis mala.

10. Dicite iusto quoniam bene, quoniam fructum adinventionum suarum comedet.

11. Vae impio in malum: retributio enim manuum eius fiet ei.

12. Populum meum exactores sui spoliaverunt, et mulieres dominatae sunt eis. Populus meus, qui te beatum dicunt, ipsi te decipiunt, et viam gressuum tuorum dissipant.

This conjunction of our major themes invites comment while the text is still before us, for this passage may well have inspired the imagery of *Inferno* xiv–xvi. Certainly Isaiah divides the leaders of his community into two elites—one military, the other intellectual—and the parallel structure of verses 2 and 3 emphasizes the contrast between the two groups. These *principes* are the key men who make their society effective and strong (*validum et fortem*, verse 1). The prophet predicts that the Lord shall strike these chief men down, for reasons that are not immediately apparent. Moreover, the prophecy continues, he shall send boys to replace the competent men he has removed (verse 4). The result will be anarchy, for without strong and competent leaders, the people break the bonds of society: man against man, each against his neighbor, young against old, ignoble against noble (verse 5). There shall be no respect for humanity or community, none for age or rank; in short, all the natural distinctions that form the basis of social order will cease to be recognized. These four severed relationships have as their consequence the lawless society of which Sodom is the type in the Talmud. The same symptoms are attributed in the *Comedy* to the city of Florence and the kingdom of Italy by Cacciaguida and Marco Lombardo respectively.

Once authority has been undermined, leadership will become an impossible burden that men will avoid. The point is made dramatically: one of the *pueri principes*, the heir to his father's position, presses the mantle of leadership upon his disinherited younger brother, who disqualifies himself, arguing that he lacks the skill to cure a sick society, and who moreover disclaims all responsibility, since it was not he who had inherited his father's office and wealth (verses 6 and 7).[71]

And why will this all happen? Because the city of Jerusalem and the kingdom of Judah have offended the majesty of God and, more specifically, "because their tongue, and their devices [*adinventiones*] are against the Lord." Moreover, the leaders commit their blasphemy openly and, like the Sodomites, make no effort to conceal their sin. Thus the sin does not, properly speaking, involve fraud. Instead, the whole people are implicated in it, if only by tacit consent. Therefore, Isaiah aptly describes the failure of leadership that was the sin of the runners.

But to what extent does the sin of Isaiah's *principes* coincide with that of the men of Sodom? The text appears to compare Judah to Sodom in one respect only, namely the shameless publicity with which God's will was contravened. Any

Biblical student in Dante's time, however, would understand from the *Glossa ordinaria* that the sin Isaiah imputed to Judah was analogous in all its essential features to that of Sodom, and moreover the *Gloss* would refer him to Jerome's commentary, of which it was at this point but an abstract.[72]

Jerome's equation is simplicity itself: the *principes Sodomorum* of Isaias 1:10 are the *pueri principes* of 3:4, who are understood literally to be the scribes and Pharisees of the rejected Jews. Accordingly, for Jerome, Isaias 3:1-12 describes the causes and effects of the disinheritance of Old Israel. Some, he admits, refer the prophecy to Israel's subjection to either the Babylonians or the Romans, but it is better referred to the Passion, in conformity with the view taken of the first two books, since it is certain that after the killing of Christ "all graces and gifts were taken from the Jews."[73]

Jerome's commentary on our passage works out this thesis in detail by demonstrating that the loss of God's *gratiae et donationes* affected the Jews in just the manner that Isaiah had prophesied. The first approach is necessarily indirect, and somewhat tedious, as he must show that the Jews now lack all the competent personnel listed in verses 2 and 3. We shall note only his conclusions, which are recapitulated as he turns to expound, at verse 4, his concept of the *pueri principes*:

> Suddenly God speaks through the prophet in his own person and says, "I shall give them boys as their princes." Just as, because of the injuries done to me, I in my wrath took back the good things which I had given, so now I shall give evils instead. I took the elder and the captain, and the admirable counsellor and wise architect and prudent auditor and the rest. In place of these I shall give boys for leaders.[74]

The term *pueri principes*, Jerome explains, should not be taken literally, since it is a metaphor for incompetence, as in the proverb, "Woe to thee, O land, when thy king is a child, . . . Blessed is the land, whose king is noble" (Eccles. 10:16-17). Mature behavior is not so much the result of age as of wisdom. Thus Scripture says that Solomon's son followed the counsels of youth, though he was over forty when he became king. Solomon himsef, however, is not called a youth *(iuvenis)* when he was king at the age of twelve, because he had wisdom: "for he was great of heart and had as much wisdom as there is sand [*arena*] on the shores of the sea."[75] Just as God had given Solomon wisdom, so, the implication is, he withheld it from the leaders of the Former Israel.

Effeminati—Deliciis affluentes.—The prophet extends the metaphor of the puerile princes by adding that they shall be dominated by *thalulim*. This Hebrew word puzzled Jerome; he consulted several Greek translations, and finally adopted that of Aquila, whose ἐναλλάκτας he approximated by *effeminati*. Literally the Hebrew word means "babyish things,"[76] and hence Isaiah really meant that the juvenile rulers shall be dominated by their immature values, or as the most recent English translation more elegantly has it, "mere boys . . . shall govern as the fancy takes them" (NEB). The other Greek translation, which Jerome rejected in the Vulgate, does in fact come close to Isaiah's meaning, for the Septuagint had personified these fancies or deceptions of childhood as "deceivers" (ἐμπαῖκται), though the Greek word has the primary sense of "mockers." Jerome reports this alternate translation in his commentary and nicely expresses the twofold sense of the Greek with the Latin *illusores*.[77]

Why Jerome as a translator preferred *effeminati* to the more correct *illusores* is a moot question. What is important is that as a commentator, he stressed the correct sense, which he derived from the Septuagint, and converted the *effeminati* of his Vulgate into a personification of excessive sensuality, or even self-indulgence. These exegetical gymnastics must be followed in detail, for they provide our most explicit assurance that the sin of Sodom in Christian allegory does not refer to homosexuality:

> "*And effeminates shall dominate them.*" The Hebrew word *thalulim* was translated *illusores* by the Septuagint and Theodotion, and by Aquila as ἐναλλάκτας, i.e. "those who (ex)change themselves and practice shameful alterations [*vices*]" which are the kind of things we read in the book of Judges [19:1–28] concerning the Levite's concubine at Gibeah. If we regard the patriarchs of the Jews as effeminate youths or boys and thus "sporting themselves to excess [*deliciis affluentes*]," we shall find the prophecy to be fulfilled. *Illusores* we can refer to the rabbis [*magistri*] of the people of Israel, "who devour God's people as they eat bread" [Ps. 13:4], who interpret sacred scripture perversely, and who mock [*illudunt*] the disciples' folly.[78]

Jerome begins with a tacit admission that *effeminati* fails to render the general and even nonsexual sense of Aquila's Greek, which can be applied to both parties to any exchange, or to one who diverts something from one use to another.[79] As a translator, Jerome had narrowed the meaning to one specific form of exchange, namely a sexual one in which males assume a female role; as a commentator, he widens the sense to include those men who have relations indiscriminately with either sex as the opportunity presents itself.

Jerome accomplishes this shift by citing the men of Gibeah as an example of sexual exchange or alteration. Like the men of Sodom, they demanded a male guest for their pleasure, but having been given the Levite's mistress instead, they raped her to death. This is not to say that Jerome imputes bisexuality to the apostate patriarchs of the Jews. They can be said to resemble effeminate boys or young men in only one respect, namely that both enjoy sensual pleasures in abundance.[80] What form the unbridled lust of the rabbinate takes, Jerome does not immediately specify, but a few verses later it eventually comes out when he explains how the *pueri principes* of the Jews can be said to be dominated by women (*mulieres*, verse 12): "because they do all things out of lust [*libido*] and are given to voluptuousness."[81]

Jerome, who was notoriously obsessed with celibacy, would seem here to be reproving the rabbis, who customarily were married, for being insensible to the virtues of virginity for both sexes—an ideal of which Jerome was the first influential advocate among the Latins. From the ascetic point of view, marital bliss is no less abundant in delights than the sex life of bisexual teenagers or the lustful indifference of the men of Gibeah.

To accommodate *effeminati/mulieres* to the immature leaders he had in mind, Jerome passed from one extreme to the other. Whereas the *effeminati* of the translation had been unduly specific, the *deliciis affluentes* of the commentary is more general than Jerome had perhaps intended. The delights that Jerome had in mind were all sexual, but *deliciae* can signify any form of pleasure, especially of the senses, and, by extension, of the mind as well. Similarly, *libido* can refer to inordinate desire of any sort.

Thus, by a roundabout route, Jerome discovered that inordinate pursuit of selfish pleasure characterizes the sin of Sodom. This is a very general concept, which in the framework of the *Inferno* embraces all the sins that are being punished in Circles I–VII. Violence is only the lowest and worst of these sins, for cannot all the forms of excessive and perverted love be characterized as *deliciis affluentes*? Hence, by Jerome's reasoning, the words of Isaiah could be applied indifferently to all of Dante's sinners, from those in Limbo on down to the usurers who are perched on the edge of the *alto burrato* (*Inf.* XVI, 114): "et effeminati dominabuntur eis." In sum, although the runners are *effeminati* in this Hieronymic sense, the trait is not peculiar to their sin of Sodom but rather is shared with half of Hell.

Sodomitica peccata.—Jerome is at no loss to identify the sin of Sodom. His definition begins at verse 8; at that point the prophet, who for seven verses has been dealing with the effects of the sin, "returns to the causes of their impiety." Isaiah plainly declares that the leaders of the city and kingdom are rendered impotent "because their tongues, and their devices [*adinventiones*] are against the Lord." Somewhat more darkly, he adds "to provoke the eyes of his majesty" (Isaias 3:8). "Because they blasphemed against the Lord," Jerome adds in explanation, and he identifies this blasphemy with what was said and done by the Jews at the Crucifixion. The people cried, "Away with him; away with him; crucify him"; while their leaders, the chief priests *(pontifices)* denied their true Lord, saying, "We have no king but Caesar" (John 19:15).

The following verse explains why the leaders are called princes of Sodom for their part in this blasphemy. Like the Sodomites at Lot's door, "they proclaimed their sin publicly and were not ashamed to blaspheme. . . . Whence they who had the sodomitic sin are called princes of the sodomites."[82] Here, then, is at least part of Jerome's definition of the *sodomiticum peccatum*: blasphemy expressed publicly and without shame.

The definition is not yet complete, however, for the next pair of verses (10, 11) gives specific content to the general impiety of blasphemy. Again, the Septuagint version[83] supplies Jerome with the definitive sense in which the passage is to be understood: "Woe unto their souls for it is against themselves [*contra semetipsos*] they have taken the worst counsel, saying, 'Let us bind the just man, since he is of no use to us' [cf. Wisd. 2:12]; and thus they shall eat the fruit of their works."[84] For Jerome, the just man par excellence was of course Christ, and rejection of Him

[243]

was the worst possible act, and thus this reference provides the clearest indication of the precise nature of the offense of the Pharisees and scribes. Moreover, it forms an integral part of the sin of Sodom, and indeed constitutes the essential act, as may be seen even more clearly from Jerome's general statement of his thesis: the princes of the Sodomites can be identified with the scribes and Pharisees because Isaiah prophesied that they, like Sodom, would publicly manifest their iniquity (Isaias 3:9) and that their decision to "bind the just man" would be not only the worst posssible one but also *contra semetipsos*.[85] Thus we can be sure that, for Jerome, the sin of Sodom consisted basically in a rejection of divine justice, personified in the case of the Jews by the just man whom they denied.

Exactores populi Dei.—Having determined the immediate cause of Israel's impotence, Jerome goes on at Isaias 3:12 to delineate the underlying motives of the scribes and Pharisees, which rendered them incapable of recognizing the Messiah. One, as we already know, was their attachment to a luxurious way of life, for which they are here called *mulieres*; but in this the leaders were not to be distinguished from their followers. A distinction is drawn between the people and their leaders, however, in the opening words of the verse: "Populum meum exactores sui spoliaverunt" ("As for my people, their *exactores* have stripped them").

Now an *exactor* is by definition one who forces others to fulfill their obligations. He can be a demanding public official, such as a supervisor of public works or a collector of taxes; he can also be one who exercises private rights—for example, an exacting overseer of workers or an insistent collector of debts. Although many may find it burdensome to fulfill their obligations, still the term by itself does not necessarily connote oppression but does stress the determination to exact all that is rightfully due.

Very probably Isaiah had in mind a specific form of exaction, namely usury. In this sense the verse recently has been Englished thus: "Money-lenders strip my people bare, and usurers lord it over them" (NEB). Jerome's Masoretic text read "and they are dominated by *nashim*," which he, following the Greek of Symmachus, literally translated *mulieres*. Other Greek translators, apparently working from a pre-Masoretic Hebrew text, read there instead a word that Theodotion translated literally as "usurers" and that the Septuagint and Aquila rendered more broadly as "those who demand back." Jerome faithfully reports their variants, for which he offers as Latin equivalents the words *feneratores* and *exactores* respectively. Thus, although usury plays no part in Jerome's interpretation of the passage, any medieval reader could discover from his commentary that Jerome's version of Isaias 3:12 could legitimately be altered to mean that exacting rulers will *in turn* be dominated by usurers: "Populum meum exactores sui spoliaverunt, et <feneratores> dominatae eis." Jerome rejected *feneratores,* because in his interpretation the prophecy had to apply literally to the Passion:

> The prophecy, however, speaks against the scribes and Pharisees, who denied the Son of God for the sake of filthy lucre so they might receive tithes and first fruits. And it does not call them masters, scribes, and

[244]

teachers, but rather *exactores*, who equate profit with piety. And they not only devour widows' houses (as the Apostle says) but the whole people. They are called *exactores* because they exact money from the unwilling.[86]

Illusores.—Fiscal exactions were only one sign that the leaders of Israel were false. More fundamental was their failure to provide spiritual leadership, as the conclusion of Isaias 3:12 suggested to Jerome: "O my people, they that call thee blessed, the same deceive thee, and destroy the way of thy steps." To explicate this, Jerome returns to verse 4, which now he will read with the Septuagint: "Et *illusores* dominabuntur eis." Just as he has taken *effeminati* and *mulieres* to be the personifications of abstract qualities that dominate the leaders, so also they can be said to be dominated by *illusio*, by deception or by a penchant for mockery. Thus the leaders deceive the people because they themselves are deceived.

This can be seen from the examples of rabbinical *illusiones* that Jerome gave at verse 4. "*Illusores* we can refer to the rabbis [*magistri*] of the people of Israel, 'who devour God's people as they eat bread' [Ps. 13:4], who interpret sacred Scripture perversely, and who mock [*illudunt*] the disciples' folly."[87] All three are effects of intellectual arrogance, based on the *stultitia/sapientia* paradox. This is most easily seen in the last case, wherein the rabbis consider themselves wise and the Disciples foolish, when in fact the reverse is true. The same false sense of their own wisdom leads them to interpret Scripture perversely and to oppress their people so completely that, as Psalm 13 declares, faith in God is man's only hope for justice.

Why are they blind to the truth? For the same reason that they are *exactores*. Jerome discovers the common cause in a verse concerning the judges and magistrates of Israel, which is found in Deuteronomy 16:19: "Thou shalt not accept person nor gifts: for gifts blind the eyes of the wise, and change the words of the just." Once again, avarice is the root of all evil. Having discovered the intimate connection between exaction and illusion, Jerome interweaves the two themes to portray the characteristic feature of false and foolish leadership, from which he deduces the contrary virtues of the wise and true religious leader:

[Isaiah] called the scribes and pharisees *exactores*, not *magistri*; and above [verse 4] he called them *illusores*, who are guided by the profit motive [*propter munera*], which blinds the eyes even of the wise. For this reason they not only fail to rebuke sinners among the people, but they lavish praise on riches and advantages [*compendia*]. These sinners they call blessed, and pillars of the house of God, and all the other things flatterers usually say. Therefore the true teacher of the Church [*doctor ecclesiasticus*] is he who does just the opposite: he moves to tears, not laughter; he rebukes sinners; he calls no man blessed or happy. . . . *Exactores*, however, pervert and disorder the way of the Lord because they have the key of knowledge [*clavis scientiae*]. That way they neither enter themselves nor do they permit the people to enter therein. Instead they cause the people to lose the way of truth, which says in the Gospel, "I am the way and life and truth."[88]

The first twelve verses of Isaias 3 have yielded an abundant harvest on Jerome's threshing floor. They foretell how the leaders of the Jews shall have perverted Israel into another Sodom. As this is the literal meaning for Jerome, the pattern of events can apply to the New Israel of Christianity in all three spiritual senses of Scripture—allegorical, moral, and anagogic. In other words, Jerome has shown how God's people once were misled to commit the sin of Sodom, and his account of the process can be applied to any future Christian society.

Before we plunge again into the labyrinth of exegesis, it may be well to recapitulate, in generalized form, Jerome's prognosis: the just society has committed the keys of knowledge to an intellectual elite who interpret God's law to their ignorant people. Cupidity, especially avarice, blinds the understanding of this elite, so they no longer understand the law of God as it is contained in Scripture. In their blindness, these intellectuals imagine that they still have understanding, and accordingly they teach and practice their own perverse inventions as God's law. As a result, society is turned upside down, because injustice reigns under the name of justice. Eventually such leaders will bring destruction upon themselves and upon the whole community, which they have taught to blaspheme against its Lord, his justice, and themselves.

The pattern corresponds in every particular to what we have already identified as the sin of the runners. Although it brings perhaps unexpected confirmation to our theory, there is little need to dwell upon each point of contact. Rather, I must stress the value of the pattern as a whole, for here the sins of the runners are reduced to a single sin, blasphemy, which in turn is identified as the sin of Sodom. As our survey progresses, we shall find some passages that link sodomy to blasphemy and others that characterize the sin of Sodom and its consequences. But nowhere will all these features be drawn together into a single, articulated configuration as in Isaias 3. In consequence, this chapter provides for us the framework that integrates the Biblical Sodom references into a unified conceptual complex. The close correspondence between this pattern and the one we have independently derived from an analysis of *Inferno* xv strongly suggests that the Hieronymic interpretation of Isaias 3 provided Dante with the conceptual model for *Inferno* xv and its adjacent cantos. This hypothesis affords the means whereby the divers themes and images that we have discerned can be drawn together and correlated by the master image of Sodom. Before this can be attempted, however, we must round out our view of the Biblical image of Sodom from the rest of Holy Writ.

ISAIAS 13:19–22: *BABYLON GLORIOSA, CONFUSIO MUNDI*

Sodom and Gomorrah reappear in Isaias 13 as symbols of the total destruction of a city and its people. The prophet foretells that the Medes shall subvert Babylon, just as the Lord overthrew Sodom and Gomorrah. There follow three verses in which he stresses that the desolation shall be complete and permanent:

> Isa. 13:19. And that Babylon, glorious among kingdoms, the famous pride of the Chaldeans, shall be even as the Lord destroyed Sodom and Gomorrha.
> 20. It shall no more be inhabited for ever, and it shall not be founded unto generation and generation: neither shall the Arabian pitch his tents there, nor shall shepherds rest there.

21. But wild beasts shall rest there, and their houses shall be filled with serpents, and ostriches shall dwell there, and the hairy ones shall dance there:

22. And owls shall answer one another there, in the houses thereof, and sirens in the temples of pleasure.

Isa. 13:19. Et crit Babylon illa gloriosa in regnis, inclyta superbia Chaldaeorum, sicut subvertit Dominus Sodomam et Gomorrham.

20. Non habitabitur usque in finem, et non fundabitur usque ad generationem, et generationem: nec ponet ibi tentoria Arabs, nec pastores requiescent ibi.

21. Sed requiescent ibi bestiae, et replebuntur domus eorum draconibus: et habitabunt ibi struthiones, et pilosi saltabunt ibi:

22. Et respondebunt ibi ululae in aedibus eius, et sirenes in delubris voluptatis.

The text itself enlarges the theme of Sodom in only one obvious respect: the Sodom-like city is characterized as "glorious among kingdoms" and as the "famous pride" of her people. Since we have found that our runners were obsessed far more by *fama* than by *avaritia*, we might hope to find this aspect of their sin developed in the commentary. Jerome does not disappoint us: this also he reduces to the sin of the scribes and Pharisees.

Babylon, for Jerome, symbolizes the forces of this world that pervert God's people. Babel, its Hebrew name, means "confusion." Just as the tower built there brought confusion to human speech, so Babylon represents the corrupt world *(mundus)* that confounds not only the speech but also the minds and works of all men. Its king, Nebuchadnezzar, who in his pride stood against God *(contra Dominum superbiens)*, signifies the prince of this world, Satan himself.[89]

Satan's subjects, the Babylonians, are those "who are confused in mind." Their sin coincides with that of the runners, for they excel in worldly eloquence and wisdom *(eloquentiae et sapientia saecularis)*. The day of reckoning that was foretold by the prophet Isaiah can refer to any confrontation in which they are confounded by those who know and speak the truth, though their ultimate confusion shall be the destruction of the world itself. In the prophecy, their nemesis is represented by the Medes, who shall call them to account *(mensura)* and shall repay each according to his works. Then the Babylonians "shall receive neither the beauty of eloquence nor the sharpness of intellect [*acumen ingenii*] on which they prided themselves." Instead, their offspring, who are the sons of heretics, and of all who are deceived," shall be killed by the "testimony of the Scriptures."[90]

Babylon shall be turned into the city of confusion by those who use rightly the gifts that are abused there. The eloquence of the Babylonians shall be matched by the discourse of preachers *(ecclesiasticus sermo)*, and their teaching shall be countered by the doctrine of the Savior *(doctrina Salvatoris)*. Thus confounded, the heretics constitute a Synagogue of Satan—which may be compared to the devastated ruins of Sodom and Gomorrah—where the hairy ones dance and sirens sing. The dancers signify the doctrines of the Babylonians, which are false as the words of Esau the Hairy *(pilosus)*;[91] the sirens represent their fatal eloquence, which lures souls to destruction.[92]

A Babylonian captivity takes place whenever God's people become captivated by worldly words and wisdom, but not the least of these enslavements would be the captivity of Old Israel, from which only the Christian remnant escaped to found the New Israel. Babylon, then, is not a symbol of a human community, as are Jerusalem and Sodom, but rather of a *moral state* or status, namely confusion, to which men, or communities of men, can be subjected. Babylon represents "this world" under the Satanic empire of Evil. Sodom, then, is not Babylon; rather, it is a society of men that is governed by confused principles of polity, or more concretely, by the *principes Sodomorum*—individual men who are not the trustworthy authorities that they and their followers believe them to be, because they are confused in mind.

SOPHONIAS 2: MOAB AND AMMON REVERT TO SODOMY : HERESY

The first prophets had used the example of Sodom to warn Israel. Isaiah used their comparison, and to it he added another that was also to become a prophetic *topos*, namely the analogy between Sodom and the enemies of Israel. Both applications were developed by three prophets who flourished in the second half of the century that extended from the death of Isaiah down to the fall of Jerusalem (687–587 B.C.). Zephaniah, Jeremiah, and Ezekiel compose the trio, to which modern Biblical scholarship recognizes that the book of Deuteronomy, compiled in 621, was contemporary. The two traditional analogies to Sodom—Sodom:Israel and Sodom: Gentiles—were both developed ever more explicitly under the rising pressure of events. The weakness of Judah and the strength of her enemies were the twin concerns of these prophets, who reduced both effects to a single cause—namely, Israel's disobedience, which led her to resemble her enemies, so that Sodom's fate suited them all.

Both Zephaniah and Jeremiah began their ministries at about the same time, early in the 620s, but the former lasted hardly a decade, ending before Deuteronomy was issued in 621; whereas the career of Jeremiah was longer by forty years, ceasing in the early years of the Exile with the Lamentations that tradition ascribes to him. Both these prophets bear the impress of Isaiah, whom they followed after half a century of prophetic silence, and so it is not surprising that Sodom appears in the prophecies of Zephaniah as a variation on a theme by Isaiah. Not long after 630, Zephaniah (Hellenized by the Septuagint as Sophonias) foretold the approach of doom for Judah and her oppressive neighbors in the form of an unnamed conqueror from the north. Among the nations who are warned appear Moab and Ammon, the descendants of Lot's daughters:

> Soph. 2:8. I have heard the reproach of Moab, and the blasphemies of the children of Ammon, with which they reproached my people, and have magnified themselves upon their borders.
>
> 9. Therefore as I live, saith the Lord of hosts the God of Israel, Moab shall be as Sodom, and the children of Ammon as Gomorrha, the dryness of thorns, and heaps of salt, and a desert even forever: the remnant of my

people shall make a spoil of them, and the residue of my nation shall possess them.

10. This shall befall them for their pride: because they have blasphemed, and have been magnified against the people of the Lord of hosts.

11. The Lord shall be terrible upon them, and shall consume all the gods of the earth: and they shall adore him every man from his own place, all the islands of the Gentiles.

Soph. 2:8. Audivi opprobrium Moab, et blasphemias filiorum Ammon: quae exprobraverunt populo meo, et magnificati sunt super terminos eorum.

9. Propterea vivo ego, dicit Dominus exercituum Deus Israel, quia Moab ut Sodoma erit, et filii Ammon quasi Gomorrha, siccitas spinarum, et acervi salis, et desertum usque in aeternum: reliquiae populi mei diripient eos, et residui gentis meae possidebunt illos.

10. Hoc eis eveniet pro superbia sua: quia blasphemaverunt, et magnificati sunt super populum Domini exercituum.

11. Horribilis Dominus super eos, et attenuabit omnes deos terrae: et adorabunt eum viri de loco suo, omnes insulae gentium.

Isaiah's Sodom:Gentiles theme is varied by a novel application to the descendants of those who escaped from Sodom on her day of wrath. They thus occupy an intermediate position between the people of Israel, who are dedicated to do the will of their Lord, and the other nations, who are wholly ignorant of him. If Lot's descendants have departed from the righteousness of their father, it presumably shall be worse for them than for those nations who have less reason to know the ways of justice. In particular, they have forgotten their ancestral ties to Abraham's seed and now honor neither Lot's choice of the Transjordan nor the God who protected them. Thus, it seems appropriate to me that the prophet should liken Moab and Ammon to Sodom and Gomorrah, so that by this allusion they might be reminded of Lot's heritage and therefore repent.

Jerome perceived this relationship, of course, and makes it the basis of a curious interpretation to which he devotes an unusually long comment of some six pages.[93] The first half attempts to explain why the fate of Sodom did not in historical fact befall Moab and Ammon for their part in the destruction of Jerusalem. Since the post-Exilic remnant did not plunder and possess them as prophesied, the rabbis (according to Jerome) refer the fulfillment of the prophecy to the coming of the Messiah. Jerome retorts that instead it must be taken as a parable, which he deduces from inconsistencies that would result from a literal-historical interpretation. Consequently, Moab and Ammon must be interpreted spiritually as "*magistri* who teach opinions contrary to the Church," to which they are related as Moab and Ammon were to Israel:

Do you wonder how to interpret spiritually the reproaches of Moab and the insults of the sons of Ammon, that they cast at God's people? Consider how heretics behave toward the Church and you will see the answer. On the one hand they congratulate themselves on their dialectic and rhetoric and all of their sophistic dogmas; while on the other they condemn the Church's lack of culture, and because they consider the Christian mysteries to be unworthy of what they idolize, they despise these holy things and hold them to be worthless.[94]

To this he appends a few words of explanation that illuminate the Hieronymic view of the sin of Sodom. Moab and Ammon are not likened to Sodom and Gomorrah because their ancestors once lived there, as some have thought, but rather "they are lumped with Sodom and Gomorrah because they blasphemed God's people and acted against Israel, and so they shall be obliterated as the others were before them, and shall have in them no vestige of verdure or life."[95]

Blasphemy, then, is reckoned as the sin of Sodom! And most particularly that form of blasphemy that oppresses the Lord's people. We should not be surprised, he adds, to find such a crime imputed to heretics, since Isaiah's *principes Sodomorum* signify "ecclesiastics who do not observe the mandates of God and departed from his precepts."[96] For Jerome, then, sodomy is not peculiar to heretics; it is imputed to anyone who sets himself against God. Presently Jerome will refine this concept in his commentary on Jeremiah, but at this point his definition consists of examples. Some, which we have already discussed, exemplify the sin of Sodom; others illustrate the sins of Moab and Ammon, which are listed most fully in Jerome's concluding summary:

> And accordingly Moab and Ammon . . . who set themselves against the knowledge of the Lord, who blasphemed the people of God, and said many insulting things of them, and who wished to enlarge their boundaries into the land of the Church and to possess the people of God, they shall be deserted and destroyed; and the remnant of the people of God, i.e. ecclesiastics learned in the Sacred Scriptures, shall tear them to pieces, and the rest of the Lord's people shall possess them; and this shall happen to them in return for the insults they hurled and because they magnified themselves against the Lord omnipotent.[97]

JEREMIAS 50: VARIATION ON A THEME OF ISAIAH

About a century after Isaiah, the prophet Jeremiah (fl. 600 B.C.) echoed his great predecessor's image of the desolation of Sodom, which was to be the fate of Babylon:

> Jer. 50:39. Therefore shall dragons dwell there with the fig fauns: and ostriches shall dwell therein, and it shall be no more inhabited for ever, neither shall it be built up from generation to generation.
>
> 40. As the Lord overthrew Sodom and Gomorrha, and their neighbour cities, saith the Lord: no man shall dwell there, neither shall the son of man inhabit it.

> Jer. 50:39. Propterea habitabunt dracones cum faunis ficariis: et habitabunt in ea struthiones: et non inhabitabitur ultra usque in sempiternum, nec extruetur usque ad generationem et generationem [cf. Isa. 13:21].
>
> 40. Sicut subvertit Dominus Sodomam et Gomorrham, et vicinas eius, ait Dominus: non habitabit ibi vir, et non incolet eam filius hominis [cf. Jer. 49:18].

[250]

This, though the least and last of Jeremiah's prophetic references to Sodom, does aptly bring out the influence that Isaiah exercised on his successor. As a prophet, Jeremiah uses the image of Sodom much as Isaiah had done, although he introduces significant variations on the original theme. This basic similarity appears most clearly in the commentators, who uniformly understand that Jeremiah compared the fate of Sodom to that of *heretics*. They offer no comment on the present passage, probably because none was necessary, since both verses are quotations that presumably retain their original meaning. Death cut short Jerome's commentary on Jeremiah at chapter 32, but since he connects heresy with Sodom in the completed portion, we may safely suppose that he would have developed the theme here as he did in explanation of the analoguous verse in Isaias.

JEREMIAS 49: EDOMITES AS HERETICS

Since Jeremiah denounces Edom in the same words that he next applies to Babylon, it is not surprising that both are taken to have the same meaning.

> Jer. 49:17. And Edom shall be desolate: every one that shall pass by it, shall be astonished, and shall hiss at all its plagues.
> 18. As Sodom was overthrown and Gomorrha, and the neighbours thereof, saith the Lord: there shall not a man dwell there, and there shall no son of man inhabit it [cf. Jer. 50:40].
> 19. Behold one shall come up as a lion from the swelling [*superbia*] of the Jordan, against the strong and beautiful: . . . who is that shepherd that can withstand my countenance?

> Jer. 49:17. Et erit Idumaea deserta: omnis qui transibit per eam, stupebit, et sibilabit super omnes plagas eius.
> 18. Sicut subversa est Sodoma, et Gomorrha, et vicinae eius, ait Dominus: non habitabit ibi vir, et non incolet eam filius hominis.
> 19. Ecce quasi leo ascendet de superbia Jordanis ad pulcritudinem robustam . . . et quis est iste pastor, qui resistat vultui meo?

Edom, the neighbor and "brother" of Judah, was comparable to Babylon, because Edom also held part of the kingdom captive, having occupied southern Judah in 587 B.C.[98] Although Jerome's commentary does not extend to this chapter, the standard medieval commentary by Rabanus Maurus interpreted the passage much as Jerome had analogous texts. The *Glossa ordinaria* omitted Rabanus' comments on the first two verses, but repeated his full gloss on the third (Jer. 49:19). The Lord shall castigate the perfidy and envy of Edom just as he did the pride of the Jews, whom the prophet refers to as the river Jordan. "Similarly both heretics and enemies of the Church of God shall not escape torments appropriate to their iniquitous deeds and dogmas."[99]

Dante's knowledge of Rabanus most probably extended beyond the *Glossa ordinaria*, however, since the abbot of Fulda is placed among the *sapienti* in the heaven of the Sun (*Par.* XII, 139: "Rabano è qui"). Therefore, it is not inappropriate for us to include his comment, which the *Gloss* omitted. Edom he identifies as the conciliabules of heretics or the blasphemies of the Jews, both of which shall cease on the Day of Wrath, when they and their adherents shall be silenced forever. Moreover, their punishment shall be like that of Sodom and Gomorrah: "He shall rain fire and brimstone upon sinners, and storms of winds shall be the portion of their cup."[100]

JEREMIAS 23: THE PROPHETS OF JERUSALEM *QUASI SODOMA*

Just as Jeremiah followed Isaiah in taking Sodom as the image of the desolation that awaited Israel's external oppressors, so also he applied the image still more forcefully to the forces of oppression within the Jewish community. Unlike Isaiah, he does not lump all leaders together as *principes* in a single denunciation; instead, Jeremiah distinguishes temporal from spiritual leadership, and accordingly denounces in parallel first the kings and then the prophets of Judah (Jer. 22–23). The kings are castigated as unjust rulers (Jer. 21:11–30), and Jeremiah foretells that in their place the Lord "will raise up to David a just branch: and a king shall reign, and shall be wise: and shall execute judgment and justice in the earth" (23:5b, cf. 23:1–8). Next he turns to the spiritual leaders of the nation, the prophets and priests (*propheta et sacerdotes,* 23:11), but concentrates on the former, perhaps because they had appeared in Isaiah's catalogue of *principes* (Isaias 3:2). The prophets of Samaria were bad enough—they prophesied in the name of Baal and led the people of Israel astray—but the prophets of Jerusalem are worse.

> Jer. 23:14. And I have seen the likeness of adulterers, and the way of lying in the prophets of Jerusalem: and they strengthened the hands of the wicked, that no man should return from his evil doings: they are all become unto me as Sodom, and the inhabitants thereof as Gomorrha.

> Jer. 23:14. Et in prophetis Jerusalem vidi similitudinem adulterantium, et iter mendacii: et confortaverunt manus pessimorum, ut non converteretur unusquisque a malitia sua: facti sunt mihi omnes ut Sodoma, et habitatores eius quasi Gomorrha.

Here, as in Isaias 1 and 3, it is only because Israel has sinned that she can be compared to Sodom; hence the passage bears directly on our principal interest, the sin of Sodom. Even more clearly than in Isaias, the sin of Sodom is associated with the leaders of Israel, while her people are likened to Gomorrah. Thus we can say that Sodom in the Bible, as in the *Comedy*, is the image of a perverse elite.

Jeremiah sharpens the Isaian image in other pertinent respects as well. We have already noted the distinction that he made between kings and prophets: these he would seem to equate respectively with Judah and Jerusalem, whom Isaiah addressed jointly. With Jeremiah, then, Jerusalem becomes the image of the City of God, the spiritual community of God's people, as opposed to their civil society. The leaders of this spiritual society are not primarily priests, functionaries whose capacity is (ad)ministrative; but rather, they are prophets, the men of vision whose specific function is to know and speak forth the will of the Lord.

Jeremiah describes the sin of the prophets indirectly, with a simile: he sees in them the likeness *(similitudo)* of "adulterants" and liars. Because the *adulterantes* are paired with liars, they must be understood primarily as counterfeiters, falsifiers, those who "give a foreign nature to a thing,"[101] in short, as adulterators rather than as adulterers. What they have debased is of course their sacred trust, the Word of God. And how? "They strengthened the hands of the wicked [*pessimorum*], that no man should return from his evil doings [*ut non converteretur unusquisque a malitia sua*]." Their prophecies support just such men as were citizens of Sodom: "Homines autem Sodomitae pessimi erant" (Gen. 13:13). This unholy alliance gives full rein to evil, so that none is restrained or turned aside from the headlong course of evildoing. The prophets who lend aid and comfort to the *pessimi* participate in their sin and therefore are stained with the same sin: "They are all become unto me as Sodom."

To enlarge further on Jeremiah's concept of social evil would needlessly carry us far afield in search of a definition of the sin of Sodom that can be supplied more explicitly by Ezekiel. Jeremiah's contribution to the image of Sodom lies in his unambiguous equation of sodomy with false prophecy. The latter theme is developed at length in chapter 23, so vividly and so clearly that a summary is no substitute for the impression of the full passage, although several key verses can convey the essence.

They are "the prophets that prophesy lies, and that prophesy the delusions of their own heart."[102] Moreover, their falsehoods and illusions have corrupted Israel, "for from the prophets of Jerusalem corruption is gone forth into all the land."[103] Next comes a solemn injunction: "Thus saith the Lord of hosts: Hearken not to the words of the prophets that prophesy to you, and deceive you: they speak a vision of their own heart, and not out of the mouth of the Lord."[104] Such is the message, which can be accommodated all the more easily to Brunetto's band because Latini himself assumes the role of a prophet *(vates)* in the action of the canto.[105]

Hidden among Jeremiah's many incisive images, however, lies one of Dante's bookmarks, those unmistakable echoes that assure us that we have hit upon a key passage: "Because the land is full of adulterers, because the land hath mourned by reason of cursing, the fields of the desert are dried up: and their course is become evil, and their strength unlike."[106] Here are the swift and the strong—perverted: "factus est cursus eorum malus, et fortitudo eorum dissimilis!" The *veloces* run an evil course, while the strength of the *fortes* is no longer what once it was. Rather than hazard a guess as to the meaning, let us accept the interpretation of Jerome, whose commentary happily included this chapter.

Jerome on Jer. 23: *Doctores contra Deum.*—Literally, we are to understand that "sterility of the fruits of the earth is the consequence of adultery and cursing (or of superfluous oaths), which is to say perjury." Allegorically, however, since the land of Judah signifies the congregation of believers, the sense is that "in the churches there is sterility of virtues and of God's gift because of adultery and mendacity or perjury."[107]

Thus their "dissimilar fortitude" signifies sterility in a twofold sense: on the one hand, to the natural fruits of the earth; and on the other, to human virtues and divine gifts. The second sense not only corresponds to the withdrawal of God's "graces and gifts," which for Jerome was the meaning of the metaphor of the *pueri principes*,[108] but it also resembles the confusion that he imputed to mundane rhetoric and worldly wisdom.[109] Jerome, then, sees three consequences to the misuse of God-given powers: sterility, confusion, withdrawal. That they are three interrelated aspects of a single process can be seen from his explication of the false prophets denounced by Jeremiah.

"And I have seen folly in the prophets of Samaria: they prophesied in Baal, and deceived my people Israel" (Jer. 23:13). These Samaritans are taken allegorically by Jerome to signify "heretics and all who disseminate knowledge falsely so called." Because they are Samaritans who are alien to Israel, these prophets typify manifest heretics who are outside the Church. Heresy, however, is not only found openly "in the conciliabules of heretics"; it also can be held covertly, and perhaps inadvertently, by false teachers of the Church *(doctores ecclesiae)*. According to Jerome, the prophets of Jerusalem whom Jeremiah denounced typify these erroneous authorities. The prophet's description of the Samaritans suggests to Jerome a simple definition of heresy, which serves to distinguish not only between false and true prophets, but also between the very truth or falsity of their inspirations, their virtues, and their wisdom:

> Now whatever the prophets of Samaria say, they prophesy in Baal, which is to say an idol consecrated to demons. Similarly, whatever heretics say, either within the Church or outside, in order to subvert the people "Israel," who already "had seen God," is inspired by demons. Whence Jeremiah significantly says "and in the prophets of Samaria I have seen folly"; for they have not him of whom it is said, *"Christus dei virtus et dei sapientia."*
>
> [At 23:14] Jeremiah says, in effect, "These things are found not only in the conciliabules of heretics, but also in the prophets of Jerusalem, i.e. the doctors of the Church. I have seen them do likewise (or horrible things) by adulterating the word of God and by entering into the way of liars; for they acquire the errors of heretics; they comfort the hand of evil men [*pessimi*], whose bad deeds they add thereby to their own crimes; and they lead to perdition those whom they ought to correct. Let not those who act thus judge themselves to be unpunished! for they and those whom they support shall be like Sodom, and all who dwell with them and do not withdraw from such company shall be like Gomorrah."[110]

The key to the passage lies in the text alleged by Jerome—1 Corinthians 1:17–31—where Paul most completely develops the *stultitia/sapientia* paradox. It is an important passage, to which we must return; but the point for Jerome's argument is Paul's insistence that the Gospel of Christ crucified is the strength and wisdom of Christians, even though that Gospel and those who preach it may appear weak and foolish by the standards of this world. Thus the word of God becomes the Christian standard by which truth and falsity are to be judged. Whatever contradicts the truth of revelation, this Christians must consider to be mere human weakness and folly compared to the strength and wisdom of God. Hence the faithful Christian can readily detect a false doctrine by comparing it to the truth of Scripture. It makes no difference whether he who holds this *doctrina pessima* is a prophet of Samaria or of Jerusalem, for heresy is heresy if it contradicts the word of God.

Paul's contrast was between the wisdom and the virtue of this world as opposed to the wisdom and virtue of God. The Samaritans—who have never seen God, since they are not of Israel—obviously rely on the power of this world. Since Baal is an idol consecrated to demons, Jerome infers that anything said by the prophets of Samaria is inspired by demons; moreover, anything spoken by the prophets of Jerusalem that conflicts with revelation must likewise be imputed to demons, even though it is spoken in the name of God. Both groups of prophets commit the sin of heresy by teaching false doctrine, but the sin is compounded by those within the Church who claim to speak in the name of God.

These distinctions Jerome relates with great precision to the sin of Sodom. All the *doctores contra Deum* shall be like Sodom, whether they claimed divine authority for their teaching or not; whereas their followers shall all be like Gomorrah.

Erunt quasi Sodoma! the resemblance lies in the future, which is to say that their teaching shall not bear the fruit of salvation, either for themselves or for their followers. Such doctrines are the seeds by which the sterile plant can be known, in Marco Lombardo's metaphor. If a doubtful doctrine contradicts revelation, the Christian may be sure not only that the doctrine is sterile but also that its invention and dissemination have been a waste of man's God-given powers, which, as long as they are employed against God, may equally be said to be sterile.

Indeed, when man applies his *virtù* and *ingegno* to deny *Christus Dei virtus et Dei sapientia* (1 Cor. 1:24), then his virtue becomes vice, his wisdom folly. To be sure, neither his eloquence nor his wit is impaired; rather, they are misdirected, turned away from God, perverted to do the work of the devil, and, in a word, *confusi*—both confused and confounded. Thus Jerome can say that all who oppose the truth of revelation belong to Babylon, the city of confusion, for they are inspired by the Father of Lies. Or again, that they resemble Sodom the Sterile, inasmuch as their talents are wasted. Since the virtue, or *virtus*, of human power consists in using that power to perform its proper function, he who attempts to use a power improperly for some other purpose will of necessity be deprived of the benefit of its proper use or virtue. Similarly, God's gifts, when misused, turn from assets into liabilities, as more shall be demanded from the steward to whom much has been entrusted.

EZECHIEL 16: *ECCE HAEC FUIT INIQUITAS SODOMAE*

The ministry of the prophet Ezekiel began in 593 B.C., less than a decade before the fall of Jerusalem, and continued in exile long after that catastrophe. His earliest oracles (chaps. 1–24) were Israel's last call to repentance before the Day of the Lord, and in them the cumulative message of his predecessors is brought into focus with a clarity born of urgency. In the face of impending doom, the sin of Jerusalem seemed greater than ever before; indeed, it loomed so large that its enormity made the sin of Sodom seem slight by comparison.

In the successive prophecies of Amos, Hosea, Isaiah, and Jeremiah, not to mention Deuteronomy, the sin of Sodom had been held up to Israel as the supreme example of iniquity, which was repaid by the heaviest punishment. The comparison to Jerusalem had been implicit in the juxtaposition of Melchizedek—the just king of (Jeru)Salem—and the unjust king of Sodom (Genesis 14). God himself had revealed in Deuteronomy that Sodom had been intended as an example to Israel, and the prophets had not been slow to develop the comparison. Amos and Hosea had threatened their kingdoms with the fate of the Pentapolis, but Isaiah was the first to introduce Jerusalem into the comparison, perhaps to symbolize the leadership of Judah. With Jeremiah the comparison became more specific, for it was the prophets of Jerusalem, not the kings of Judah, who were *quasi Sodoma*. Interpreting this passage, perhaps with the benefit of hindsight, Jerome could extract the implication that the sin of Jerusalem's prophets was *worse* than that of Sodom, since they compounded the latter with their own.[111] Ezekiel, however, was the first to weigh the sins of Jerusalem and Sodom, the first to declare flatly that the sins of Jerusalem were greater in number and worse in kind than those of her sister Sodom.

This exaggeration suitably stressed the gravity of Jerusalem's precarious situation, but it carried with it the difficult consequence that justice required that the punishment must suit the crime. Was Jerusalem then to become an eternal waste like Sodom? Ezekiel announces another solution, which has unexpected consequences for Sodom: the Lord shall temper his justice with mercy. Both Jerusalem and Sodom shall be saved, and Samaria as well! The germ of this surprising revelation probably is to be traced back to Deuteronomy 30, where it is foretold that the curse of Sodom shall be removed from the land of Israel, and its people shall be repatriated if they repent; but Ezekiel is the first to hold out hope for Sodom itself.

To render this comparison and his prediction plausible, Ezekiel has recourse to definition. For the first and only time in Scripture, the sin of Sodom is identified in terms of concrete acts, rather than in generic terms such as blasphemy or impiety. We have already encountered that definition, notably in Bede's exposition of Genesis, but its importance for the *Comedy* must now be stressed. For medieval commentators, there was but one complete and authoritative definition of the sin of Sodom, and that was to be found in the divinely inspired words of Ezekiel 16:49-50. Let us read them in context and then consult the commentators on this cardinal passage.

The whole of Ezechiel 16 is an allegory in which God reproaches Jerusalem, his unfaithful wife *(uxor)*. Born a foundling in Canaan, she was unwanted by her Amorite and Hittite parents, but the Lord raised her up and took her to wife, so that she entered into the covenant by marriage. Her Lord endowed her lavishly with gold, silver, jewels, and rich clothing, but trusting in her beauty and secure in her prosperity, Jerusalem became an unfaithful wife.

Her offenses were many, but it is stressed that in every one she wasted her precious endowment and abused her prosperity. Much of her wealth she devoted to idolatry, even her own children, who were offered as blood sacrifices although they were her Lord's most precious gift. Further, she was a wanton woman—"nymphomaniac" is the right word today—who was worse than either the adulteress or the prostitute in that she not only took lovers promiscuously but even paid for their services (Ezech. 16:1–34).

Personification requires extensive sexual imagery; but in fact, sex is the least of the crimes signified by the allegory, and indeed it is only a component feature of the idolatry. The adultery is altogether allegorical; it refers to intercourse, both political and commercial, with foreign nations. Far more essential, as the sequel shows, is the theme of prosperity perverted.

The harlot Jerusalem shall be punished by the loss of all her goods: she shall be stripped naked before her lovers; and thus deprived of her resources and pride, she shall be forgiven but not reendowed (Ezech. 16:35–43). There the allegorical narrative ends, and the rest of the chapter contains the Lord's long rebuke of his unfaithful wife:

> Ezech 16:44. Behold every one that useth a common proverb, shall use this against thee, saying: As the mother was, so also is her daughter.
> 45. Thou art thy mother's daughter, that cast off her husband, and her children: and thou art the sister of thy sisters, who cast off their husbands, and their children: your mother was a Cethite [Hittite], and your father an Amorrhite.
> 46. And thy elder sister is Samaria, she and her daughters that dwell at thy left hand: and thy younger sister that dwelleth at thy right hand is Sodom, and her daughters.
> 47. But neither hast thou walked in their ways, nor hast thou done a little less than they according to their wickednesses: thou hast done almost more wicked things than they in all thy ways.
> 48. As I live, saith the Lord God, thy sister Sodom herself and her daughters, have not done as thou hast done, and thy daughters.
> 49. Behold this was the iniquity of Sodom thy sister, pride, fulness of bread, and abundance, and the idleness of her, and of her daughters: and they did not put forth their hand to the needy, and to the poor.
> 50. And they were lifted up, and committed abominations before me: and I took them away as thou hast seen.
> 51. And Samaria committed not half thy sins: but thou hast surpassed them with thy crimes, and hast justified thy sisters by all thy abominations which thou hast done.
> 52. Therefore do thou also bear thy confusion, thou that hast surpassed thy sisters with thy sins, doing more wickedly than they: for they are justified above thee, therefore be thou also confounded, and bear thy shame, thou that hast justified thy sisters.
> 53. And I will bring back and restore them by bringing back Sodom, with her daughters, and by bringing back Samaria, and her daughters: and I will bring those that return of thee in the midst of them.
> 54. That thou mayest bear thy shame, and mayest be confounded in all that thou hast done, comforting them.
> 55. And thy sister Sodom and her daughters shall return to their ancient state: and Samaria and her daughters shall return to their ancient state: and thou and thy daughters shall return to your ancient state.

56. And Sodom thy sister was not heard of in thy mouth, in the day of thy pride,

57. Before thy malice was laid open: as it is at this time, making thee a reproach of the daughters of Syria, and of all the daughters of Palestine round about thee, that encompass thee on all sides.

58. Thou hast borne thy wickedness, and thy disgrace, saith the Lord God.

59. For thus saith the Lord God: I will deal with thee, as thou hast despised the oath, in breaking the covenant:

60. And I will remember my covenant with thee in the days of thy youth: and I will establish with thee an everlasting covenant.

61. And thou shalt remember thy ways, and be ashamed: when thou shalt receive thy sisters, thy elder and thy younger: and I will give them to thee for daughters, but not by thy covenant.

62. And I will establish my covenant with thee: and thou shalt know that I am the Lord,

63. That thou mayest remember, and be confounded, and mayest no more open thy mouth because of thy confusion, when I shall be pacified toward thee for all that thou hast done, saith the Lord God.

The passage is not only the longest scriptural allusion to Sodom, but also the most definitive. As might be expected, Jerome's commentary rises to the occasion both in quality and quantity. In fourteen pages,[112] he draws together many of the themes that he has developed in other connections, so that we can at last see the relationship between natural law and the sin of Sodom.

The argument can be reduced to three propositions: (1) Sodom represents the Gentiles, as opposed to God's people, both present and past, namely Jerusalem and Samaria. (2) All three have committed the sin of impiety by forgetting their debt to God, though not all in the same degree. The Gentiles are bad, because their deformed human nature does not recognize that the benefits of nature, which they abuse, have been bestowed upon them by their Creator. Heretics are worse, because they once recognized the truth and then relapsed into the ignorance of the Gentiles. Worst of all are impious churchmen, because their impieties are committed in God's name. (3) Ezekiel's prophecy has been fulfilled because all three kinds of impiety have been redeemed by Christ; and in particular, the Gentiles, who are blinded by original sin, can have their human nature reformed by grace.

To trace the course of the exposition verse by verse would add little to our understanding of Sodom. Let us therefore sketch the bulk of Jerome's argument and fill in only those details that relate directly to Sodom.

Whom do the three sisters of the allegory personify? Samaria is easily identified as the northern kingdom of Israel, and Jerusalem as the southern kingdom of Judah. But how can Sodom, which is mentioned in the Bible before Jerusalem, be said nonetheless to be *younger*? The Sodom that was destroyed in Genesis, Jerome argues, did not exist in the time of Ezekiel, and hence it must not be taken literally but instead represents generally "the crowd of nations" (*gentium turba*).[113] "Further, according to the tropological sense, Samaria and Sodom, i.e. heretics and heathens [*ethnici*], often commit lighter offenses than those who are represented by Jerusalem, i.e. churchmen [*ecclesiastici*]."[114] Thus Ezekiel foresees at verse 53 that the impious heathen shall be restored first, because their impiety is lesser than that of heretics and churchmen.[115] How, then, are the heathen impious? Theirs is the sin of Sodom, which God, speaking in his own person, defines in Ezech. 16:48–50:

> 48. Vivo ego, dicit Dominus Deus, quia non fecit Sodoma soror tua ipsa, et filiae eius, sicut fecisti tu, et filiae tuae.
> 49. Ecce haec fuit iniquitas Sodomae sororis tuae, superbia, saturitas panis et abundantia, et otium ipsius, et filiarum eius: et manum egeno et pauperi non porrigebant.
> 50. Et elevatae sunt, et fecerunt abominationes coram me: et abstuli eas sicut vidisti.[116]

Vivo ego.—Only God is not subject to death and hence only He can say "I live" without qualification. This implies, as Jerome proves by many citations, that God is the creator and sustainer of the world, the source of all life and all good things.

Superbia.—All men would recognize their debt to God were it not for the sin of pride, which was the especial sin of the devil and hence the first of all sins. As the basic element in Sodom's sin, pride is accordingly named first in the definition.[117] Among other examples of such sodomitic pride, Jerome cites the boast of the king of Assyria: "For he hath said: By the strength of my own hand I have done it, and by my own wisdom I have understood."[118] *"Fortitudinem faciam et sapientiam intelligentiae!"* This boast is the specific sin of pride that applies to the swift and the strong in particular: it confirms beyond doubt that theirs is the sin of Sodom.

If pride is the seed of this evil, prosperity is the seedbed in which it grows. The image of the *seminarium* is Jerome's, though he found the relationship in the Septuagint, where he read, "pride *in* fullness of bread and *in* abundance."[119] Thus it is the pride born in prosperity "whose seedbed is fullness of bread, and abundance of all things, and idleness, or, as the Septuagint translated this last term, 'affluence of pleasures' and of luxury."[120] In the domestic allegory of Ezechiel 16, the Lord's unfaithful queen, Jerusalem, had wasted the treasures with which she had been adorned. The endowments of her younger sister Sodoma are of a more humble order—"fullness of bread, abundance, and idleness"—but they, too, are wasted, for Sodoma and her imitators do not use their surplus to aid those who are less fortunate, but consume or dissipate their advantages. Since the allegory represents Sodoma as a housewife, the advantages attributed to her are appropriately of a domestic order, but Jerome's reference to the Assyrian boast reminds us that these can stand for the more manly gifts of nature as well—for strength and the wisdom of understanding.

Dei oblivio.—Jerome formulates his final interpretation of Sodom's sin thus in a single sentence: "The sodomitic sin is pride, fullness, abundance of all things, leisure and pleasure; and in consequence God is forgotten because man regards his present advantages as perpetual and imagines that his necessities shall never be lacking."[121] In short, it is the error of Sodom to take all of Creation for granted.

The whole of mankind are the beneficiaries of nature, and thus the Psalmist bade "all the earth": "know ye that the Lord he is God: he made us, and not we ourselves."[122]

Later the text enables Jerome to bring pagan learning into relation with Sodoma, who in Ezekiel's allegory signified literally the crowd of nations *(gentium turba)* around Israel, or tropologically the unconverted pagans *(ethnici)*. Eventually two groups of Israel's neighbor nations appear in the allegory—the daughters of Syria and of Palestine (Ezech. 16:57)—and according to Jerome, they personify, respectively, pagan philosophers and other Gentiles who err in many and diverse opinions. Other nations could presumably signify still other forms of the sin of Sodom, but here, as before, it would seem that intellectual pride is the highest form of impious ingratitude.[123]

Sodoma restituta.—Throughout his exposition, Jerome has refused to identify the allegorical Sodoma with the ruins of the city in Genesis, but his reason only becomes fully apparent at the end of the passage, where he must explain in what sense Sodoma will be restored. There he flatly denies the rabbinic interpretation that "in the thousand-year reign of the Messiah, the Pentapolis will be restored to its former state, in which it resembled God's paradise and the land of Egypt." The Jews do not realize, of course, that the Messiah has already come, and consequently that the whole of Ezekiel's prophecy is fulfilled by Christianity "and is being fulfilled daily. Sodom is returned to its former state when the Gentile is restored to his former nature and the impious soul comprehends the Creator." Likewise, Samaria will be restored as heretics relinquish their errors; and when all mankind is reconciled in the Church, Jerusalem itself, "the vision of peace," will have regained its pristine state.[124]

Sodomy among the Gentiles, then, is clearly the product of original sin: since Eden, human nature has been deformed so that it cannot comprehend its Creator. This explains in large part why pride born of prosperity is a far graver offense for the baptized than for the heathen, who know not what they do.

LAMENTATIONS 4: JERUSALEM COMPOUNDS THE SIN OF SODOM

"Quomodo sedet sola civitas plena populo! facta est quasi vidua domina gentium":[125] these opening words of Jeremiah's Lamentations, or *Threni*, are Dante's most famous Biblical reminiscence; they appear twice in his works to express utmost desolation. In the *Vita nuova* they are placed at the head of chapter 28 to announce the death of Beatrice (1290), and two chapters later we are told that they were the incipit of a Latin letter "written to the princes of the earth" concerning the condition of the desolate city that her departure left "as if a widow, dispoiled of all dignity."[126] Although no such letter is extant, these very words do appear as the *initium* of Dante's *Epistle* xi, *Cardinalibus Italicis*, which laments the desolation of *Roma vidua et deserta* as Jeremiah mourned the sorry state of Jerusalem. The letter urges that the cardinals console the Roman church, which the death of Clement V has widowed (1314), by electing a suitable successor. Their choice can also effect a return of the papacy to the city of Rome, which is presently abandoned by the curia in preference for Avignon, and moreover it can provide relief "for the whole city [of God] now in pilgrimage on earth" (§ 26), the misgovernment of which is in fact the major theme of the letter.[127]

Only a most audacious Dantist would venture to maintain that the *Vita nuova* does in fact refer to the letter addressed to the Italian cardinals twenty-four years after the death of Beatrice de' Bardi, nee Portinari.[128] Nor does the present case require such heterodoxy, for it is certain that Dante (whether twice or once) assumed the epistolary role of Jeremiah to lament the sorry state of a city which, like Jerusalem, was desolate. One wonders whether the allusion implies an extended analogy between Dante's message and that of the prophet, but such an excursus must not detain us. Suffice it to note that the analogy would place Dante's "*sanctam Ierusalem velut exstinctam*"[129] in a remarkable relation to Sodom, for the prophet said of Jerusalem:

> Lam. 4:6. And the iniquity of the daughter of my people is made greater than the sin of Sodom, which was overthrown in a moment, and hands took nothing in her.

> Lam. 4:6. Et maior effecta est iniquitas filiae populi mei peccato Sodomorum, quae subversa est in momento, et non ceperunt in ea manus.

The passage occurs early in the dirge recalling the horrors of the siege of Jerusalem and its sack by the Babylonians in 587/586 B.C. On the principle that the punishment fits the crime, Jeremiah suggests that the sin of Jerusalem must have been greater than that of Sodom, since the punishment of Sodom was effected, without humiliation, by an instantaneous *coup de grâce*.[130] Jerusalem's Day of Wrath had confirmed the novel assertion made by Ezekiel that Sodom's sin was the lesser.

The cause of Judah's downfall was also more sharply apparent after the event. The poet of the fourth threnody declares plainly that Jerusalem was destroyed

> Lam. 4:13. For the sins of her prophets, and the iniquities of her priests, that have shed the blood of the just in the midst of her.
> 14. They have wandered as blind men in the streets, they were defiled with blood: and when they could not help walking in it, they held up their skirts.[131]

The blame is laid squarely and solely on the spiritual leaders of the nation, the prophets and priests who had already been singled out in the prophecies of Jeremiah. Once again their sin is connected with the oppression of the just man, which here becomes still more abominable because by this act a priest would make himself ritually unclean and hence incapable of fulfilling his office. The image may well have been meant to convey the compound nature of their offense, which was Sodom-like in its oppression of the just, but worse because it was committed by those who were most bound to avoid and prevent such acts. Once again, those who commit the sin of Sodom are described as blind men *(caeci)*.

In the *Glossa ordinaria*, Dante would have found the vivid analogy that Paschasius Radbertus drew between the unjust society of Sodom and that of Christendom under the successors of Charlemagne. Even in this condensed version of the *Gloss*, the poet could perceive that his own complaints against the declining thirteenth century described the sin of Sodom, though the guilt of God's people was greater than that of the pagan Sodomites:

> Allegorically, "*Maior est*" etc. [Lam. 4:6] is spoken by the Church, which bewails the sins of the people as if they were greater than the sins of the men of Sodom. For does it not seem to us today that faith and justice may have vanished from the earth? We can discern no trace of humanity or kindness. Instead, discord and greed consume the world, as does the voracious flame of wrath and envy. The Church is plundered by violence and fraud, the poor are stripped to the bone. Already thorns fill the world's neglected lands. Lawful rights are considered nonsense; between things divine and human, between things licit and illicit, confusion reigns. In short, the innumerable evils are accumulating daily. Therefore our iniquity is "greater" than that of those who never knew the way of truth, and hence Sodom, "which was overthrown in a moment," deserved the lesser punishment.[132]

The Book of Wisdom: Links with Philosophy and Law

With the Lamentation for Jerusalem, the image of Sodom was complete in the Hebrew Hagiographa, though not in Jewish thought. We have already seen what significance Sodom assumed in rabbinical interpretation in the first centuries of the Christian era, and we are all but ready to trace the course of its development in the other major branch, the New Testament. Yet in between the two Testaments lies the Apocrypha, one of whose deuterocanonical books Dante particularly favored and occasionally cited as "*il Libro di Sapienza*."[133] Dante, doubtless warned by Jerome, was careful not to ascribe this Book of Wisdom to Solomon.[134] Yet, although Wisdom was not one of the four and twenty books of the Old Testament canon that are represented by as many elders in the mystical procession,[135] Dante was nonetheless certain that the work was inspired by the Holy Spirit.[136]

The so-called Wisdom of Solomon exists only in Greek, forming part of the Septuagint. Probably the book was the work of an Alexandrian Jew, as its characteristic conflation of Jewish religion with Greek philosophy suggests. The date of composition, which remains a matter of conjecture, may be as late as A.D. 40, though the range of earlier possibilities extends across the first two centuries before Christ.[137] Thus, Wisdom was written some four to six centuries after the last reference to Sodom in the Hebrew canon of Scripture.

What attracted the author of Wisdom to a theme that had gone so long neglected? The very title of his book suggests an answer: it vindicates the *sapientia* of the just against the *stultitia* of the unjust. In part conceived as an antidote to the pessimism of Ecclesiastes, the book affirms that God emanates his wisdom to men, who if they receive her, can avoid human folly. Since Sodom was the stock example in the Law and the prophets for the human community that departed from divine law, it fitted the author's theme admirably.

The pseudo-Solomon, however, is more rabbi than prophet: Sodom for him is a matter of fact, complete with explicit interpretations that in all likelihood reflect a long tradition of exegesis. A didactic clarity informs his work to our advantage, for here no poetic mystery shrouds the image of Sodom: in Wisdom the significance lies on the surface.

WISDOM 10: *INSIPIENTES IGNORARENT BONA*

The second half of Wisdom traces the effects of divine wisdom acting in the history of Israel, and almost at once we are told what wisdom did for Lot:

> Wisd. 10:6. She delivered the just man who fled from the wicked that were perishing, when the fire came down upon Pentapolis:
>
> 7. Whose land for a testimony of their wickedness is desolate, and smoketh to this day, and the trees bear fruits that ripen not, and a standing pillar of salt is a monument of an incredulous soul.
>
> 8. For regarding not wisdom, they did not only slip in this, that they were ignorant of good things, but they left also unto men a memorial of their folly, so that in the things in which they sinned, they could not so much as lie hid.
>
> 9. But wisdom hath delivered from sorrow them that attend upon her.

> Wisd. 10:6. Haec iustum a pereuntibus impiis liberavit fugientem, descendente igne in Pentapolim:
>
> 7. Quibus in testimonium nequitiae fumigabunda constat deserta terra, et incerto tempore fructus habentes arbores, et incredibilis animae memoria stans figmentum salis.
>
> 8. Sapientiam enim praetereuntes, non tantum in hoc lapsi sunt ut ignorarent bona, sed et insipientiae suae reliquerunt hominibus memoriam, ut in his, quae peccaverunt, nec latere potuissent.
>
> 9. Sapientia autem hos, qui se observant, a doloribus liberavit.

Apologetic in purpose, the passage stresses the testimonia that would corroborate the account of Genesis for a Greek rationalist. But along with the smoking desert, the blighted trees, and the pillar of salt, the author has tucked in a definition of Sodom's sin that is more concise than Ezekiel's and more explicit than any text of the Hebrew Bible. The men of Sodom took no notice of wisdom. As a result of this oversight, "they were ignorant of good things," which is to say they were senseless, unwise fools *(insipientes)*.[138]

The generality of the formulation is remarkable, for there is no middle ground between wisdom and folly, between good and evil. The Platonic conviction that the Good is indivisible has been integrated with the Hebraic conception of the Law, any infraction of which constitutes an intolerable breach of contract. Moreover, and most important for the Dantesque concept of Sodom, the crucial factor that determines ethical conduct is now conceived to be knowledge rather than will. Epistemology posed no problem for Israel, for revelation declared all that a Jew needed to know; rather the question was whether or not he would will to obey the Law. The Greek philosopher, however, had no such revelation, and therefore he had to discover his ethical standards through reason. Once these were known, ethics presented no further problem, at least for those philosophers who agreed with Socrates that "virtue is knowledge," that "virtue is indivisible," and that "nobody errs willingly."[139] To a Hellenizing Jew, such as the author of Wisdom, this Platonic view of ethics solved the age-old problem of Israel, for one had but to realize that true wisdom was contained in revelation, and one had attained the knowledge that was virtue. The true philosopher, "the lover of wisdom," found the object of his affection in the *sophia-sapientia* revealed in the Bible.

In these terms, the decisive difference between the wise man and the fool is that the sage recognizes that only God can be said to be truly wise, and therefore human reason must accept its limitations and be guided by revealed wisdom. Thus the Book of Wisdom says that the men of Sodom lapsed into folly simply by taking no notice of wisdom. That oversight deprived them ipso facto of all moral direction: *ut ignorarent bona.*

In this sapiential view, the sin of Sodom is conceived essentially as an assertion of man's intellectual independence from God. The foolish philosophers of Sodom place their trust in human reason, whereas Lot accepts as his guide the wisdom sent from God.

If we had not read the prophets in the light of Jerome's commentary, the extent to which the image of Sodom has been Hellenized in Wisdom would be more readily perceptible. As it is, we are already accustomed to Sodom as a figure of false philosophy.[140] Among the sources of revelation, Wisdom alone makes the connection explicit. If, as I suspect, Dante took Scripture as his guide in constructing the *Comedy*, then Wisdom more than any other book would justify his use of Sodom as an image of intellectual perversion.

Of this I can offer no more convincing evidence than the use that Dante made throughout his works of the *Libro di Sapienza*. Six verses are quoted by our poet, and another is paraphrased. They constitute our only positive indication of what aspects of the book most interested Dante. Collected into a catena, they display the principal relations between Sodom and wisdom that we earlier discovered through an analysis of imagery. For once I shall trust my sources to speak for themselves,[141] at least for the moment:

> And thy wisdom with thee, which knoweth thy works, which then also was present when thou madest the world.[142]
>
> For the spirit of the Lord hath filled the whole world.[143]
>
> For she is the brightness of eternal light, and the unspotted mirror of God's majesty, and the image of his goodness.[144]
>
> For she is an infinite treasure to men! which they that use, become the friends of God.[145]
>
> For he that rejecteth wisdom, and teaching is unhappy: and their hope is vain, and their labours without fruit, and their works unprofitable.[146]
>
> Love justice, you that are the judges of the earth.[147]
>
> Love the light of wisdom, all ye that bear rule over peoples.[148]

WISDOM 19: EGYPT AND SODOM—COMPARATIVE INHOSPITALITY

The image of Sodom passed out of prophetic fashion with the end of the Jewish monarchy, probably because Israel now had, in the overthrow of Jerusalem, a more powerful example of divine vengeance on a perverse community. Ezekiel had claimed that the sin of Jerusalem was greater than that of Sodom, and the subsequent destruction of Jerusalem had demonstrated that in fact Sodom's sin was the lesser (Lam. 4:6). In Wisdom, the image of Sodom undergoes a similar depreciation in the Sodom:Gentiles analogy, in order to heighten the sin of Egypt, the immediate oppressor of Wisdom's Alexandrian author. In the closing chapters (16–19) he recalls how God had dealt with the injustices of Egypt in sacred history, and in the final chapter he compares the inhospitality of the Egyptians in Exodus unfavorably to that of the Sodomites:

> Wisd. 19:13. For they exercised a more detestable inhospitality than any: others indeed received not strangers unknown to them, but these brought their guests into bondage that had deserved well of them.
>
> 14. And not only so, but in another respect also they were worse: for the others against their will received the strangers.
>
> 15. But these grievously afflicted them whom they had received with joy, and who lived under the same laws.
>
> 16. But they were struck with blindness: as those others were at the doors of the just man, when they were covered with sudden darkness, and every one sought the passage of his own door.

> Wisd. 19:13. Etenim detestabiliorum inhospitalitatem instituerunt: alii quidem ignotos non recipiebant advenas, alii autem bonos hospites in servitutem redigebant.
>
> 14. Et non solum haec, sed et alius quidam respectus illorum erat: quoniam inviti recipiebant extraneos.
>
> 15. Qui autem cum laetitia receperunt hos qui eisdem usi erant iustitiis, saevissimis afflixerunt doloribus.
>
> 16. Percussi sunt autem caecitate: sicut illi in foribus iusti, cum subitaneis cooperti essent tenebris, unusquisque transitum ostii sui quaerebat.

Although Sodom is not mentioned by name, the allusion to the blindness with which the Sodomites were afflicted (verse 16, cf. Gen. 19:11) makes the analogy unmistakable. The Sodomites here appear as a xenophobic people that mistreated those whom they did not know, whom they had not invited to enter their community, and who did not share their standards of justice. Certainly the writer of Wisdom regarded these actions as offenses, since he goes on to observe their punishment. To be sure, he has singled out those misdeeds of Sodom that resemble the inhospitality of Egypt, but it is nonetheless significant that he recognized the nonsexual aspect of their misconduct. One particular is especially noteworthy: apparently he conceived of Sodom as a community living under a common law that did not extend equal justice to aliens. This conception of Sodom as a community of law reappears in the Talmud, where that law is identified as a paradoxical *ius iniustum*. One suspects that Wisdom here reflects the same tradition of commentary at an earlier stage in its development.

To Dante the text could suggest that the men of Sodom were a law unto themselves. Just as the previous passage placed Sodom in relation to philosophy, so this links the city to law. The professions of the literati of *Inferno* xv, therefore, are suggested by Wisdom's image of Sodom.

[9]

The Image of Sodom:
New Testament

Jesus Christ took up the weakened image of Sodom where the prophets had left it, and he applied it in fresh comparisons which, although they are indebted to the contemporary rabbinic interpretation, nonetheless place the city of Lot in a new perspective. Jesus employed the image on three separate occasions, always with reference to the fate of Sodom on the Day of Judgment. While there is no record of any earlier interest in the eschatology of Sodom, it can hardly be a coincidence that the Talmud displays the same concern, and indeed the Last Judgment provided the occasion for the whole discussion of Sodom in the tractate *Sanhedrin*.[1] Since the Talmud digests several centuries of rabbinic discussion in Palestine, it is altogether likely that in Jesus' time Jewish exegetes were already debating whether "the men of Sodom had a portion in the future world," and whether "they shall stand at judgment." Jesus stated no opinion on the former question, but assumed an affirmative answer to the latter. That affirmation was made explicit in the next century by Rabbi Nehemiah, whose opinion on this was to be the prevailing one in the Mishna. Another indication that Jesus was in contact with contemporary rabbinic thought is that for him Sodom was an image of inhospitality, as it had been in the Book of Wisdom.[2]

Christ's distinctive message—the Gospel—acquires a new dimension from its background of a long and living tradition of the Law, the prophets, and their interpreters; but this historical dimension only heightens its impact, causing the Good News to stand out from its background as in a stereopticon. For it was not the Noachic or Mosaic Law toward which Christ's latter-day sodomites were inhospitable: rather, the Gospel itself was what they rejected—and the incarnate Word that bore it to mankind.

MATTHEW 10: REJECTING THE GOSPEL—A SIN GREATER THAN SODOM'S

Christ began his ministry as a personal one, but eventually he dispatched other ministers to spread his Gospel—first twelve, and then seventy-two, according to Luke.[3] Mark and Matthew report only the mission of the Twelve, but they are exhorted, in Matthew's account, with part of the speech that is addressed in Luke to the Seventy-two.[4] Whether in fact the words were addressed to one or the other mission or to both need not concern us, for in any case they manifestly express Christ's attitude towards those who rejected his Gospel:

> Matt. 10:14. And whosoever shall not receive you, nor hear your words: going forth out of that house or city shake off the dust from your feet.
> 15. Amen I say to you, it shall be more tolerable for the land of Sodom and Gomorrha in the day of judgment, than for that city.

> Matt. 10:14. Et quicumque non receperit vos, neque audierit sermones vestros: exeuntes foras de domo, vel civitate, excutite pulverem de pedibus vestris.
> 15. Amen dico vobis: Tolerabilius erit terrae Sodomorum et Gomorrhaeorum in die iudicii, quam illi civitati.

These words were spoken soon after Christ had himself experienced the shock of rejection when, having returned to evangelize his native Nazareth, an outraged mob had tried to lynch him.[5] Confident that he was the fulfillment of the Law and the prophets, Jesus chose the image of Sodom to express both the nature and the extent of the guilt incurred by those who rejected him. Since the Twelve were told in no uncertain terms to limit their ministry to "the lost sheep of the house of Israel" (Matt. 10:5–6), Sodom in Christ's analogy was being compared, not to the Gentiles, but only to the Jews. Moreover, the comparison was of the distinctive type in which Israel's sin is said to be *greater* than that of Sodom. As we know, this amplification (auxesis) by comparison occurs only in Ezechiel and Lamentation 4, immediately before and after the destruction of Jerusalem. The new formulation substituted for Jerusalem any city of Israel that again rejected God by failing to hear and obey the fulfillment of the Law and the prophets in the message of the Messiah. A new Day of the Lord was at hand! The Apostles should not dwell among the unjust, as Lot had done, but must hasten on; for the Son of Man would arrive before they had visited the last city of Israel (Matt. 10:23).

Thus Christ himself took the sin of Sodom to typify blindness to his Gospel: and hence Dante extracted the essence of the sodomy of the runners—for each was a false *Christian* who rejected revelation as the guide to human reason.[6]

MATTHEW 11: JESUS:LOT AND CAPERNAUM:SODOM

In Matthew's next episode, which constitutes the whole of chapter 11, Christ again draws an analogy to Sodom, which lays a still heavier burden of guilt on those cities of Galilee that fail to respond to the Gospel. The context here is important, because the image of Sodom is associated in this sermon with two of its Dantesque companions—*violentia* and *sapientia*. An inquiry from John the Baptist prompted Christ to proclaim publicly that John was the promised forerunner who heralded the advent of the Messiah.[7] Two remarks in this discourse relate to the theme of the swift and the strong:

> Matt. 11:12. And from the days of John the Baptist until now, the kingdom of heaven suffereth violence, and the violent bear it away

13. For all the prophets and the law prophesied until John:

14. And if you will receive it, he is Elias that is to come.

15. He that hath ears to hear, let him hear.

19b. And wisdom is justified by her children.

Matt. 11:12. A diebus autem Joannis Baptistae usque nunc, regnum caelorum vim patitur, et violenti rapiunt illud.

13. Omnes enim prophetae et lex, usque ad Joannem, prophetaverunt:

14. Et si vultis recipere, ipse est Elias, qui venturus est.

15. Qui habet aures audiendi, audiat.

19b. Et iustificata est sapientia a filiis suis.

According to Jerome, the violence of Matthew 11:12 is directed against nature but not against God, for it represents man's strenuous effort to attain salvation by means of a virtue that he does not possess through human nature.[8] Consequently it appears that *violentia contra naturam* is not necessarily *violentia contra Deum*. The context suggests that revelation is man's surest means to distinguish licit from illicit violence against nature, though after the event, perhaps too late, results will also prove the wisdom of his course. More concretely, the wisdom of the Gospel teaches man how he ought to govern his own human nature and direct his efforts towards God. In short, the penitence that John preached required forceful self-control:[9]

Matt. 11:20. Then began he to upbraid the cities wherein were done the most of his miracles, for that they had not done penance.

21. Woe to thee, Corozain, woe to thee, Bethsaida: for if in Tyre and Sidon had been wrought the miracles that have been wrought in you, they had long ago done penance in sackcloth and ashes.

22. But I say unto you, it shall be more tolerable for Tyre and Sidon in the day of judgment, than for you.

23. And thou Capharnaum, shalt thou be exalted up to heaven? thou shall go down even unto hell. For if in Sodom had been wrought the miracles that have been wrought in thee, perhaps it had remained unto this day.

24. But I say unto you, that it shall be more tolerable for the land of Sodom in the day of judgment, than for thee.

25. At that time Jesus answered and said: I confess to thee, O Father, Lord of heaven and earth, because thou hast hid these things from the wise and prudent, and hast revealed them to little ones.

Matt. 11:20. Tunc coepit exprobrare civitatibus, in quibus factae sunt plurimae virtutes eius, quia non egissent poenitentiam.

21. Vae tibi, Corozain; vae tibi, Bethsaida: quia, si in Tyro et Sidone factae essent virtutes quae factae sunt in vobis, olim in cilicio et cinere poenitentiam egissent.

22. Verumtamen dico vobis: Tyro et Sidoni remissius erit in die iudicii, quam vobis.

23. Et tu, Capharnaum, numquid usque in caelum exaltaberis? usque in infernum descendes, quia, si in Sodomis factae fuissent virtutes quae factae sunt in te, forte mansissent usque in hanc diem.

[269]

24. Verumtamen dico vobis, quia terrae Sodomorum remissius erit in die iudicii, quam tibi.

25. In illo tempore respondens Jesus, dixit: Confiteor tibi, Pater, Domine caeli et terrae, quia abscondisti haec a sapientibus et prudentibus, et revelasti ea parvulis.

Had Sodom and Gomorrah heard the Gospel, possibly they might have repented, which is to say they might have resisted the perverse inclinations of their corrupt human nature. Such resistance would be an act of licit violence; paradoxically, to do otherwise would be an act of illicit violence to the true nature of man.

Though such an argument seems to be implicit in the discourse of Matthew 11, let us be cautious and insist only that the *ipsissima verba* of Christ here associate Sodom with both *violentia* and *sapientia*. More important is the Sodom analogy itself, on which the *Glossa ordinaria* makes this comment to Matthew 11:23:

> Have you [Capharnaum] not been made famous by my presence and the miracles I have done in you? And have you not resisted most proudly [*superbissime*] against my preaching? In Capharnaum, the name of which means "city most beautiful," the faithlessness [*perfidia*] of Jerusalem is condemned, of whom it is said "Your sister Sodom is justified from you," i.e. in comparison with her who was not corrected by Lot's example, you have always been ungrateful [*ingrata*] for the words and miracles of the Son of God.[10]

The *Gloss* not only understands this to be the counterpart of one of the analogies that exaggerate the sin of Jerusalem by comparison with Sodom, but it also infers that Capernaum therefore stands for Jerusalem. This reduction confirms the view that we took of the Sodom analogy in Matthew 10, and permits the glossator to nuance the image of Sodom in several respects.

His first point is simple but nonetheless noteworthy: the sin of Sodom involves *ingratitude*. Certainly this has been implicit all along, but here it is put into a word: *ingrata*. The other point brought out by the gloss is one we have already encountered in Bede's interpretation of Genesis,[11] namely that Lot was given to Sodom as a model of the just man. The glossator therefore suggests, I think rightly, that Christ was comparing himself to Lot. What the commentator, in his preoccupation with allegory, does not apparently recognize is that the literal application to Capernaum is both more apt and more vivid than the one he offers. For as Matthew tells us elsewhere, Jesus' ministry began when, "leaving the city Nazareth, he came and dwelt in Capharnaum" (4:13a). Like Lot, then, Jesus came as an alien to dwell in a sinful city, which, like Sodom, failed to profit from the example of a just man in its midst.[12] Because the terms in this analogy to Sodom are all concrete, its configuration expresses, more clearly than any other, Christ's own typology of rejection:[13]

Sodom : Lot :: Capernaum : Jesus

The prophets before him had made Sodom a type of rejection in the Old Testament typology; but Christ himself, not some ingenious medieval exegete, drew the analogy that gave Sodom the same significance in Christian typology. Jesus was beyond doubt the founder of Christian typology, "the science of history's relations to its fulfilment in Christ"; and to belabor the obvious, the foundation that he laid was his own typology.[14] All of which is an erudite way of saying that a Christian is surely bound to place the authority of Christ above that of all others, at the very least as an interpreter of the Bible, and consequently the Lord's interpretation(s) of Sodom will, for his followers, take precedence over all others. What I am suggesting is simply that Dante's image of Sodom is based on what was for him the highest authority, namely the express word of Christ. Indeed, I should not be surprised if the whole structure of the *Comedy* proved to have the Gospel as its basis, though I am arguing here only the case of Sodom. All the evidence is not yet in, but when the time comes for our summation, we shall see whether Christ's application of the Sodom *topos* can be taken as the paradigm for the image of Sodom both in the Bible and the *Comedy*.

LUKE 10: A SUPERIMPOSED IMAGE—*PLUS PETENT AB EO*

The two analogies to Sodom that, according to Matthew, were occasioned by the dispatch of the Twelve and by the inquiry of John the Baptist, are used together in Luke on yet a third occasion, the dispatch of the Seventy-two (10:1–16), which bears a certain resemblance to each of the other events. In most respects, the commission to the Twelve is repeated to the Seventy-two disciples, but in one particular, their intended purpose, the latter resemble John the Baptist. They, too, were Christ's forerunners, quite literally so, for "he sent them two and two before his face into every city and place whither he himself was to come" (verse 1). Jesus counseled them much as he had the Apostles, concluding his charge with these words:

> Luke 10:10. But into whatsoever city you enter, and they receive you not, going forth into the streets thereof, say:
> 11. Even the very dust of your city that cleaveth to us, we wipe off against you. Yet know this, that the kingdom of God is at hand.
> 12. I say to you, it shall be more tolerable at that day for Sodom, than for that city [Dico vobis, quia Sodomis in die illa remissius erit, quam illi civitati; cf. Matt. 10:15, 11:24].
> 13. Woe to thee, Corozain, woe to thee, Bethsaida. For if in Tyre and Sidon had been wrought the mighty works that have been wrought in you, they would have done penance long ago, sitting in sackcloth and ashes.
> 14. But it shall be more tolerable for Tyre and Sidon at the judgment, than for you.
> 15. And thou, Capharnaum, which art exalted unto heaven, thou shalt be thrust down to hell [Et tu, Capharnaum, usque ad caelum exaltata, usque ad infernum demergeris; cf. Matt. 11:23].
> 16. He that heareth you, heareth me; and he that despiseth you, despiseth me; and he that despiseth me, despiseth him that sent me.

Sodom, it will be observed, appears without Gomorrah, and is not compared to Capernaum. Since textual criticism of the Bible is no part of our Dantesque concern, we must take this conjunction at face value as an indication that Sodom, for Jesus, typified any city that was not disposed to receive either himself or his message. The *Glossa ordinaria* relates Sodom to this concept of Christian office:

> Although the Sodomites were being consumed by vice and were inhospitable, yet no guests such as the Apostles were found among them, as were the prophets among the Jews. Although Lot was just when he was with them, still he neither taught anything nor performed any miracles. And for that reason "to whomsoever much is given, of him much shall be required" [Luke 12:48b] and "the mighty shall be mightily tormented" [Wisd. 6:7].

Because Jesus applied Sodom to the mission of the Seventy-two, he authorized the application of the image to all Christians whose function it is to serve as a liaison between God and his people. To them, special powers are given, just as the Seventy-two found that "devils also are subject to us in thy name" (Luke 10:17). Significantly for our theme, Christ replied, "But yet rejoice not in this, that spirits are subject unto you; but rejoice in this, that your names are written in heaven" (Luke 10:20). Salvation must be their final goal; the powers given to them by God are incidental, though such power must be used with humility.[15]

Further, the powers committed by Christ must be used with charity, as the *Glossa ordinaria* deduces from the fact that the Seventy-two were sent out in *pairs*, "two by two," like the angels sent to Sodom. "By sending them out in pairs, he indicated that no one ought to undertake the office of preaching who does not have charity toward the other."[16] This quality we found stressed in the blessed runners, but conspicuously absent in Bishop Mozzi, who preached for his own salvation and quarreled incessantly with his subordinates.[17]

The superior material advantages with which Sodom had been endowed made it a type of the advantaged city, though not the highest type, since spiritual benefits bring greater responsibility than material ones. There is a twofold application of this principle to the infernal runners, for more had been given to them than to Sodom in two respects: first, because their prosperity was a nobility of mind and *ordo*; secondly, because they lived under the New Dispensation as leaders of God's people. They stand to Sodom as heretics and/or ecclesiastics stand to pagan philosophers in Jerome's Old Testament tropologies: the basic sin of Sodom has been compounded by the addition of greater benefits and, in consequence, greater responsibilities. Yet, in both cases, Sodom remains the basic type, which is to say its mark is set on the aggravated, compound form of the vice no less than on the simple, typical sin of Sodom.

LUKE 17: THE PROSPERITY OF SODOM

The three preceding passages all present essentially the same image of Sodom as the type of those who accept benefits from God but reject the duties that these benefits entail. Because Jesus used the image to prepare his missionaries, the stress was on rejection; but, because their mission was directed to the cities of Israel, the element of divine favor was also implicit. Towards the end of Christ's ministry, as he journeyed to its climax in Jerusalem, he made a second analogy to Sodom in which the emphasis is reversed. The Sodomites are depicted as enjoying the special benefits conferred on them by God, even as divine justice overtakes them for their ingratitude. Luke alone includes the image among the analogies to the "days of the Son of man" (17:26) that accompany Christ's description of his Second Coming, the so-called "synoptic Apocalypse":[18]

> Luke 17:26. And as it came to pass in the days of Noe, so shall it be also in the days of the Son of man.
> 27. They did eat and drink, they married wives, and were given in marriage, until the day that Noe entered into the ark: and the flood came and destroyed them all.
> 28. Likewise as it came to pass, in the days of Lot: they did eat and drink, they bought and sold, they planted and built.
> 29. And in the day that Lot went out of Sodom, it rained fire and brimstone from heaven, and destroyed them all.
> 30. Even thus shall it be in the day when the Son of man shall be revealed.
> 31. In that hour, he that shall be on the housetop, and his goods in the house, let him not go down to take them away: and he that shall be in the field, in like manner, let him not return back.
> 32. Remember Lot's wife.

> Luke 17:27. Edebant, et bibebant; uxores ducebant, et dabantur ad nuptias, usque in diem qua intravit Noe in arcam: et venit deluvium, et perdidit omnes.
> 28. Similiter sicut factum est in diebus Lot: Edebant, et bibebant: emebant, et vendebant: plantabant, et aedificabant;
> 29. Qua die autem exiit Lot a Sodomis, pluit ignem et sulphur de caelo, et omnes perdidit:
> 30. Secundum haec erit qua die Filius hominis revelabitur.
> 31. In illa hora qui fuerit in tecto, et vasa eius in domo, ne descendat tollere illa; et qui in agro, similiter non redeat retro.
> 32. Memores estote uxoris Lot.

The antediluvian men have only one pair of activities in common with the men of Sodom: "they did eat and drink." Marriage appears as the peculiar concern of men before the Flood—"they married wives, and were given in marriage"—for the simple reason that Genesis tells us nothing more specific about their activities.[19] With this clue, it is not hard to see that some of the activities especially attributed to Sodom are also derived from Genesis, which praises the fertility of the land and mentions both the gate of Sodom, where Lot sat, and his house, with its solid doors and protective roof.[20] Hence "they planted and built," but whence is it said "they bought and sold?" One might infer as much from the fact that Sodom was a city, but I think it far more likely that Jesus echoes here the rabbinic interpretation that the men of Sodom "sinned with their money."[21] Either way, the important point is that Jesus characterized the preoccupations of Sodom as agriculture, building, and commerce. In a word, the men of Sodom were civilized.

There is no suggestion that any of these activities are in themselves bad. Quite to the contrary, we are told in subsequent verses that at the Second Coming, some who do these things shall be saved and others damned.[22] The moral drawn by the *Glossa ordinaria* is that such benefits are licit when used in moderation.[23] The text itself suggests a stronger interpretation: "Remember Lot's wife." These activities are a means to an end, not an end in themselves. When the Son of Man comes, his followers must give no thought to their goods or their cities (Luke 17:31), for such attachments shall prove fatal to them, as they did to Lot's wife. Sodom here is the image of a community in which the just and unjust alike exploit their natural advantages: the danger lies again in *oblivio Dei*.

ROMANS 9: JUSTIFICATION THROUGH FAITH

In the epistles of Paul, the image of Sodom appears only in a quotation from Isaiah 1:9, where it is said that Israel shall not be totally destroyed as were Sodom and Gomorrah, because a remnant shall be left. Jerome, it will be recalled, insisted that this prophecy referred to the Christian remnant of Old Israel that did not reject Christ.[24] Jerome's interpretation was nothing if not orthodox, for Paul had fully developed this exposition of Isaiah in his epistle to the Romans, to whom he explained the historical place of the Jews in God's plan for the salvation of mankind. God had always reserved the right to confer his benefits as he chose. All that he promised Israel was that a remnant of Abraham's physical seed should be saved, as indeed it was in those Jews who believed in Christ:

> Romans 9:27. And Isaias crieth out concerning Israel: "If the number of the children of Israel be as the sand of the sea, a remnant shall be saved.
>
> 28. For he shall finish his word, and cut it short in justice; because a short word shall the Lord make upon the earth" [Isa. 10:22].
>
> 29. And as Isaias foretold: "Unless the Lord of Sabaoth had left us a seed, we had been made as Sodom, and we had been like unto Gomorrha" [Isa. 1:9].
>
> 30. What then shall we say? That the Gentiles, who followed not after justice, have attained to justice, even the justice that is of faith.
>
> 31. But Israel, by following after the law of justice, is not come unto the law of justice.
>
> 32. Why so? Because they sought it not by faith, but as it were of works. For they stumbled at the stumblingstone.
>
> 33. As it is written: "Behold I lay in Sion a stumblingstone and a rock of scandal; and whosoever believeth in him shall not be confounded" [Isa. 7:14, 28:16; cf. 1 Pet. 2:6].

The stone, of course, was Christ; and the supreme test of the Jews was whether they could believe that he was the Messiah. Faith in Christ was the criterion that distinguished the just from the unjust of Israel. Paul's description of those that rejected Christ characterizes to perfection the sin of the runners:

> For I bear them witness, that they have a zeal of God, but not according to knowledge. For they, now knowing the justice of God, and seeking to establish their own, have not submitted themselves to the justice of God. For the end of the law is Christ, unto justice to every one that believeth.[25]

Paul provides the finishing touch in the following chapter, where he says of the incredulous Jews: "and the rest have been blinded [*excaecati*]."[26] It is precisely in this respect, the *Glossa ordinaria* points out, that Isaiah's prophecy has been fulfilled and they have "been made as Sodom."[27]

THE EPISTLE OF JUDE: *SEMETIPSOS PASCENTES*

Israel had become the Christian Church. In consequence of this Pauline doctrine, all that was said of Israel in the Old Testament might be understood now to apply to Christianity. Thus the Church became the second term in the analogy Sodom:Israel, and the resultant tropology of Sodomites as heretics within or without the Church we already know from Jerome. Once again, however, he followed exegetical precedents established in the New Testament canon, for the Apostolic age was already troubled by the false prophets against whom Christ had warned in the Sermon on the Mount.[28]

Two of the Catholic Epistles warn against these pseudo prophets and compare their offenses to the sin of Sodom, just as the prophets had identified it with the perverted leadership of Old Israel. The brief epistle of Jude is wholly devoted to the theme, which is still further developed in the second epistle-general of Peter. Modern critics are inclined to accept the former at face value, as the work of that obscure apostle Jude, the brother of James, but find it "virtually impossible to hold that St. Peter was the author" of the latter, not least of all because of its borrowings from Jude.[29] Thus, if we were patrologists, we would cherish Jude and slight the pseudo Peter, but as we are Dantologists, the stress must be reversed; accordingly, I shall consider Jude's epistle briefly and then hasten on to the Prince of the Apostles:

> Jude 3b. [He writes] to beseech you to contend earnestly for the faith once delivered to the saints.
>
> 4. For certain men are secretly entered in, (who were written of long ago unto this judgment,) ungodly men [*impii*], turning the grace of our Lord God into riotousness [*luxuria*], and denying the only sovereign Ruler, and our Lord Jesus Christ.
>
> 5. I will therefore admonish you, though ye once knew all things, that Jesus, having saved the people out of the land of Egypt, did afterwards destroy them that believed not:
>
> 6. And the angels who kept not their principality, but forsook their own habitation, he hath reserved under darkness in everlasting chains, unto the judgment of the great day.
>
> 7. As Sodom and Gomorrha, and the neighbouring cities, in like manner, having given themselves to fornication, and going after other flesh, were made an example, suffering the punishment of eternal fire.
>
> 8. In like manner these men also defile the flesh, and despise dominion, and blaspheme majesty.
>
> 9. When Michael the archangel, disputing with the devil, contended about the body of Moses, he durst not bring against him the judgment of railing speech [*blasphemiae*], but said: The Lord command thee.
>
> 10. But these men blaspheme whatever things they know not: and what

things soever they naturally know, like dumb beasts, in these they are corrupted.

Jude 3b. [Scribat] deprecans supercertari semel traditae sanctis fidei.

4. Subintroierunt enim quidam homines (qui olim praescripti sunt in hoc iudicium) impii, Dei nostri gratiam transferentes in luxuriam, et solum dominatorem et Dominum nostrum Jesum Christum negantes.

5. Commonere autem vos volo, scientes semel omnia, quoniam Jesus populum de terra Aegypti salvans, secundo eos qui non crediderunt, perdidit:

6. Angelos vero, qui non servaverunt suum principatum, sed dereliquerunt suum domicilium, in iudicium magni diei, vinculis aeternis sub caligine reservavit.

7. Sicut Sodoma, et Gomorrha, et finitimae civitates simili modo exfornicatae, et abeuntes post carnem alteram, factae sunt exemplum, ignis aeterni poenam sustinentes.

8. Similiter et hi carnem quidem maculant, dominationem autem spernunt, maiestatem autem blasphemant.

9. Cum Michael archangelus cum diabolo disputans altercaretur de Moysi corpore, non est ausus iudicium inferre blasphemiae, sed dixit: Imperet tibi Dominus.

10. Hi autem, quaecumque quidem ignorant, blasphemant: quaecumque autem naturaliter, tanquam muta animalia, norunt, in his corrumpuntur.

Once again impiety and blasphemy are committed by men who place human reason in opposition to the authority of revelation. Jude writes, above all, to preserve the purity of the faith (Jude 3b) against men who would pervert the Gospel of Christ. Because the Gospel has freed them from the strict observance of the Old Law, certain converts have attempted to turn their liberty into license.[30] Jude does not specify what the nature of their offense was, but he does make it clear that they have disobeyed the Gospel because they do not understand it. They are "worldly people, devoid of the Spirit";[31] and consequently they do not speak with the Spirit, but instead have only natural knowledge, "like dumb beasts" (*"tanquam muta animalia"*). Their blasphemy consists in substituting their merely human understanding for the perfect understanding that is born of faith (10).[32] Like the archangel Michael in the legend, God's representatives should deliver His word and not blasphemously substitute their own (9). In short, the Christian must have faith that the Bible means what it says; for to reason away the truths of revelation constitutes not only disobedience but also blasphemy. Jude brings out the consequences of such folly by three examples, of which the *Glossa ordinaria* offers this explanation:

As an example of the damnation of those who deny the only authority [verse 4], he had recalled the ruin of both the unfaithful people [in verse 5] and of the angels who raised themselves against God [verse 6]; now he also gives an example of the penalties of those who turn the Lord's grace into luxury, namely the burning of the men of Sodom [verse 7].[33]

Sodom, then, here typifies the punishment of those who rationalize revelation be-

[276]

cause they lack faith. Jude adds a string of similes to characterize them, several of which are apposite images of the perverted swift and strong. "They are shepherds who take care only of themselves [*semetipsos pascentes*]. They are . . . trees that in season bear no fruit, dead twice over and pulled up by the roots."[34]

2 PETER: *INDOCTI ET INSTABILES DEPRAVANT . . . SCRIPTURAS*

Peter is as plain as Jude was obscure. His argument is summarized thus by the *Glossa ordinaria*: "Through faith Simon Peter declares to this world that the wise are dead, and by the same light he shows more clearly the extent of their piety."[35] Three chapters develop the argument: (1) tells the faithful how to use properly the gifts they have received from God; (2) describes those pseudo prophets who attempt to pervert the faithful; and (3) assures the faithful that these false prophets will be confounded on Judgment Day.

Almost the whole epistle has relevance to the sin of the runners, and because it represents the opinion of the first pope, the reader of the *Comedy* can detect a special irony in its message. To bring this out in every detail, however, would require a commentary whose length would be greater than its value. I shall therefore recommend the entire letter to the interested reader, but here shall attempt only to relate its fundamental doctrines to the offense of the *cherci e litterati grandi*. Even so, the relevant passages are long, and accordingly let us not confront them en bloc but rather proceed by easy stages:

2 Pet. 1:1. Simon Peter, servant and apostle of Jesus Christ, to them that have obtained equal faith with us in the justice of our God and Saviour Jesus Christ.

2. Grace to you and peace be accomplished in the knowledge of God and of Christ Jesus our Lord:

3. As all things of his divine power which appertain to life and godliness, are given us, through the knowledge of him who hath called us by his own proper glory and virtue.

4. By whom he hath given us most great and precious promises: that by these you may be made partakers of the divine nature: flying the corruption of that concupiscence which is in the world.

5. And you, employing all care, minister in your faith, virtue; and in virtue, knowledge;

6. And in knowledge, abstinence; and in abstinence, patience; and in patience, godliness;

7. And in godliness, love of brotherhood; and in love of brotherhood, charity.

8. For if these things be with you and abound, they will make you to be neither empty nor unfruitful in the knowledge of our Lord Jesus Christ.

9. For he that hath not these things with him, is blind, and groping, having forgotten that he was purged from his old sins.

10. Wherefore, brethren, labour the more, that by good works you may make sure your calling and election. For doing these things, you shall not sin at any time.

2 Pet. 1:1. Simon Petrus, servus et apostolus Jesu Christi, iis qui coaequalem nobiscum sortiti sunt fidem in iustitia Dei nostri et Salvatoris Jesu Christi.

2. Gratia vobis et pax adimpleatur in cognitione Dei et Christi Jesu Domini nostri:

3. Quomodo omnia nobis divinae virtutis suae, quae ad vitam et pietatem donata sunt, per cognitionem eius qui vocavit nos propria gloria et virtute,

4. Per quem maxima et pretiosa nobis promissa donavit: ut per haec efficiamini divinae consortes naturae: fugientes eius, quae in mundo est, concupiscentiae corruptionem.

5. Vos autem curam omnem subinferentes, ministrate in fide vestra virtutem, in virtute autem scientiam,

6. In scientia autem abstinentiam, in abstinentia autem patientiam, in patientia autem pietatem,

7. In pietate autem amorem fraternitatis, in amore autem fraternitatis charitatem.

8. Haec enim si vobiscum adsint, et superent; non vacuos, nec sine fructu vos constituent in Domini nostri Jesu Christi cognitione.

9. Cui enim non praesto sunt haec, caecus est, et manu tentans, oblivionem accipiens purgationis veterum suorum delictorum.

10. Quapropter, fratres, magis satagite, ut per bona opera certam vestram vocationem et electionem faciatis: haec enim facientes, non peccabitis aliquando.

As in Jude, faith is the primary concept. As in Paul, it is a faith that brings justification. The gloss to 2 Peter 1:1 explains that "this justice is not found by human prudence, neither is it taught by legal institution, but our Saviour shows it in the Gospel: 'Unless your justice abound more than that of the scribes and Pharisees, you shall not enter into the kingdom of heaven.' "[36]

Peter addresses those who already have faith, and he begins by assuring them that because they have faith, God will enable them to know Him better. They need not worry about their weaknesses if only they are strong in faith, for God from his own virtue shall give them whatever virtues are necessary for life and piety. These virtues he then lists in a progressive series, starting with faith. He who has faith should try to give it effect by seeking virtue or goodness (*virtus, arete*). Next he should seek to acquire knowledge (*scientia, gnosis*), which in turn will lead successively to abstinence, patience, piety, brotherly love, and, finally, *caritas (agape)*.

Fides, virtus, scientia: The order of the first three is important, for knowledge springs from virtue, which in turn is founded on faith.[37] Without faith, one cannot receive the gift of knowledge, or any of the other six. And conversely, one who lacks these qualities "is blind and groping" (*"caecus est, et manu tentans"*). Faith without good works, then, is dead; but a living faith receives from God the ability to do right and avoid evil. Or, to paraphrase Peter more closely, God promises the faithful those gifts which enable them to share in the divine nature and to escape the concupiscence of this world.

Peter speaks plainly, as was said earlier, but only, I must explain, when he emerges from the thicket of theological abstractions and descends to concrete cases. Like Jude, Peter asserts the primacy of faith against those who cannot accept revelation without first rationalizing it. Since he is about to die, he wishes to affirm the literal truth of the Gospel (1:13–21). He has not followed "learned fables" ("*doctas fabulas*," 16) in teaching them, for as an eyewitness of the Transfiguration he heard the Father acknowledge the Son with the injunction, "Hear ye him." And this is the practical application of the foregoing exhortation to faith:

> 2 Pet. 1:19. And we have the more firm prophetical word: whereunto you do well to attend, as to a light that shineth in a dark place, until the day dawn, and the day star arise in your hearts:
> 20. Understanding this first, that no prophecy of scripture is made by private interpretation.
> 21. For prophecy came not by the will of man at any time: but the holy men of God spoke, inspired by the Holy Ghost.

> 2 Pet. 1:19. Et habemus firmiorem propheticum sermonem: cui bene facitis attendentes, quasi lucernae lucenti in caliginoso loco, donec dies elucescat, et lucifer oriatur in cordibus vestris:
> 20. Hoc primum intelligentes, quod omnis prophetia Scripturae propria interpretatione non fit.
> 21. Non enim voluntate humana allata est aliquando prophetia: sed Spiritu sancto inspirati, locuti sunt sancti Dei homines.

This Peter is a fundamentalist! In practice, the primary object of faith is the revealed truth found in Scripture. Further, one part of that faith is to accept the truth of Scripture whole, for, as Bede explains, "These things are said lest anyone expound the Scriptures as he wishes."[38] Repeatedly we have found that Sodom is a Biblical type of those who reject revelation and pervert it with rationalization. Peter invokes the traditional image in the same connection, but the words of the first bishop of Rome apply most particularly to the teachers of a Christian society:

> 2 Pet. 2:1. But there were also false prophets [*pseudoprophetae*] among the people, even as there shall be among you lying teachers [*magistri mendaces*], who shall bring in sects of perdition, and deny the Lord who bought them: bringing upon themselves swift destruction.
> 2. And many shall follow their riotousnesses [*luxurias*], through whom the way of truth shall be evil spoken of.
> 3. And through covetousness [*avaritia*] shall they with feigned words make merchandise of you. Whose judgment now of a long time lingereth not, and their perdition slumbereth not.
> 4. For if God spared not the angels that sinned, but delivered them, drawn down by infernal ropes to the lower hell, unto torments, to be reserved unto judgment:
> 5. And spared not the original world, but preserved Noe, the eighth

person, the preacher of justice, bringing in the flood upon the world of the ungodly.

6. And reducing the cities of the Sodomites, and of the Gomorrhites, into ashes, condemned them to be overthrown, making them an example to those that should after act wickedly.

7. And delivered just Lot, oppressed by the injustice [*iniuria*] and lewd conversation [*luxuriosa conversatione*] of the wicked.

8. For in sight and hearing he was just: dwelling among them, who from day to day vexed the just soul with unjust works.

9. The Lord knoweth how to deliver the godly from temptation, but to reserve the unjust unto the day of judgment to be tormented.

2 Pet. 2:1. Fuerunt vero et pseudoprophetae in populo, sicut et in vobis erunt magistri mendaces, qui introducent sectas perditionis, et eum, qui emit eos, Dominum negant, superducentes sibi celerem perditionem.

2. Et multi sequentur eorum luxurias, per quos via veritatis blasphemabitur:

3. Et in avaritia fictis verbis de vobis negotiabuntur: quibus iudicium iam olim non cessat, et perditio eorum non dormitat.

4. Si enim Deus angelis peccantibus non pepercit, sed rudentibus inferni detractos in tartarum tradidit cruciandos, in iudicium reservari.

5. Et originali mundo non pepercit, sed octavum Noe iustitiae praeconem custodivit, diluvium mundo impiorum inducens.

6. Et civitates Sodomorum et Gomorrhaeorum in cinerem redigens, eversione damnavit: exemplum eorum qui impie acturi sunt, ponens:

7. Et iustum Lot oppressum a nefandorum iniuria ac luxuriosa conversatione eripuit:

8. Aspectu enim, et auditu iustus erat: habitans apud eos qui de die in diem animam iustam iniquis operibus cruciabant.

9. Novit Dominus pios de tentatione eripere; iniquos vero in diem iudicii reservare cruciandos.

Christendom shall be troubled by "lying teachers" *("magistri mendaces")* just as Israel was misled by pseudo prophets who were not "inspired by the Holy Ghost" but prophesied instead "by private interpretation" (1:20–21, 2:1). These mendacious masters, the *Gloss* explains, "deny their Redeemer, or they preach not what the truth shows but what they themselves invent."[39] These doctors stray from Christ, the way of truth, whose word should be their law, and therefore they follow their own pleasure as interpreters, and hence are guilty of "riotousness" *("luxuria,"* 2:2, 7).[40] Their sin is often compared to sexual pleasure, because both indulge the concupiscence of the natural man (cf. 2 Pet. 1:4), but obviously the powers that run riot in exegesis are not sexual but rational. By not subjecting their reason to revelation, by not having faith in the explicit truth of Scripture, they adulterate the Word of God (cf. 2 Pet. 2:12–14).

Et in avaritia fictis verbis de vobis negotiabuntur. One might suppose from the sexual imagery that the false teaching benefited its inventors by permitting them to indulge in illicit forms of sexual gratification; but in fact, Peter indicates plainly enough that their perverted words served, not their lust, but their avarice. For it will be out of avarice that those teachers will use their lies to exploit the faithful (2 Pet. 2:3a). Peter reiterates this charge even more clearly a few verses later: "Leaving the right way they have gone astray, having followed the way of Balaam of Bosor, who loved the wages of iniquity."[41] Since the promise of a substantial honorarium tempted Balaam to misuse his prophetic gifts,[42] the allusion is clearly to financial gain. But because Balaam obeyed God, he was prevented from his folly (*insipientia*), and consequently he typifies the motive rather than the punishment.

More than anything else, however, Peter wishes to impress upon the faithful that perverters of Scripture shall be punished. The punishment will not come until the Day of Judgment (2:9), as he explains in detail in the final chapter, but their punishment is prefigured by God's treatment of similar offenses in the past. Peter adduces the three *exempla* that Christ himself gave of the separation of the just from the unjust:[43] the punishment of the rebellious angels, of the generation of the Flood, and of the Pentapolis (2:4–9). The example of Sodom particularly relates to the Day of Judgment, because the Lord shall then destroy the world with fire as he had formerly done with water.[44] Thus the *Gloss* states that "the fire which once punished the Sodomites signifies that the impious shall suffer without end."[45] For Peter, therefore, Sodom is the image of that conflagration which shall consume the perverters of Scripture.

Lest there be any doubt that this epistle is specifically directed against those who misinterpret the Holy Writ, Peter concludes his letter with a most particular warning:

> 2 Pet. 3:14. Wherefore, dearly beloved, waiting for these [last] things, be diligent that you may be found before him unspotted and blameless in peace,
> 15. And account the longsuffering of our Lord, salvation; as also our most dear brother Paul, according to the wisdom [*sapientiam*] given him, hath written to you:
> 16. As also in all his epistles, speaking in them of these things; in which are certain things hard to be understood, which the unlearned and unstable wrest [*indocti et instabiles depravant*], as they do also the other scriptures, to their own destruction.
> 17. You therefore, brethren, knowing these things before, take heed, lest being led aside by the error of the unwise [*insipientium*], you fall from your own steadfastness.

APOCALYPSE 11: JERUSALEM, SODOM, AND EGYPT

At the end of the mystical procession, Dante saw "an old man come behind all the rest, alone, sleeping, with visage keen."[46] This singular book, the Apocalypse of John the Apostle, draws up at the rear of our procession of Biblical authorities as well; its image of Sodom follows likewise in their footsteps. The reference occurs in a section devoted to the fate of Jerusalem in the last days (10:1–11:13), just before the seventh and final trumpet of doom is sounded (11:15–19).[47]

A mighty angel tells John to take the measurements of the temple of God, but not of the outer court of the Gentiles, for they shall oppress the holy city for forty-two months (= 3½ years = 1,277½ days), during which time two witnesses sent from heaven with miraculous powers shall prophesy for 1,260 days. Towards the end of the period, both prophets shall be killed by "the beast that ascendeth out of the abyss" (Apoc. 11:7); for three days and a half their bodies shall lie unburied in the streets of the city, while "they that dwell upon the earth" (11:10) are rejoicing to be rid of these prophets who have tormented them. Then the pair shall be resurrected and, in the presence of their enemies, shall ascend into heaven: whereupon a great earthquake shall destroy a tenth of the city and the names of seven thousand men as well, filling the remainder with fear and respect for God. Directly after this episode, the seventh trumpet sounds, proclaiming the Day of Judgment.

John never names the great and holy city—site of the temple and scene of the witnesses' passion—that is finally decimated by earthquake, but its identity is conveyed by this verse:

> Apoc. 11:8. And their bodies shall lie in the streets of the great city, which is called spiritually, Sodom and Egypt, where their Lord also was crucified.

> Apoc. 11:8. Et corpora eorum iacebunt in plateis civitatis magnae, quae vocatur spiritualiter Sodoma, et Aegyptus, ubi et Dominus eorum crucifixus est.

To explicate this verse, let us depend upon the standard scholastic apparatus to the Bible, namely the *Glossa ordinaria*, which offers, all told, eight glosses, seven of which are interlinear and one marginal (s.v. "Aegyptus"):

> *iacebunt*: ut quicumque viderint timeant eis conformari.
> *civitatis*: Hierusalem.
> *magne*: olim in virtutibus nunc in malicia.
> *Sodoma*: i.e. muta: quia nemo predicabit spiritualiter.
> *Aegyptus*: i.e. tenebrosa sine cognitione Dei.
> *Dominus*: Christus.
> *eorum*: Helie et Enoch.
> *crucifixus*: contradicendo veritati.[48]

The sense of these comments can best be grasped by integrating them with the text of the verse, thus: "And their bodies shall lie, *so that whoever saw would fear to imitate them*, in the streets of the city *Jerusalem*, great *formerly in virtues but now in malice*, which is called spiritually, Sodom, *i.e. 'mute,' because no one shall preach spiritually*, and Egypt, *i.e. 'shadowy,' without cognition of God*, where *Christ*, their Lord, *i.e. of Elijah and Enoch*, was also crucified *by contradicting the truth*."

The *civitas magna*, therefore, is Jerusalem, not taken absolutely, however, but with an important qualification: this is *Hierusalem perfida, Hierusalem incredula*, the city that deserves to be compared to Sodom and Egypt because its great virtues have been replaced by malice. Like the other cities that Christ himself compared to Sodom, its sin consists in "contradicting the truth." The glossator, it will be noted, takes the Crucifixion not as a reference to a single historical event in a geographical place, but as the type par excellence of the rejection of Christ. Thus, any city that rejects Christ might be called Jerusalem, as was Capernaum by the *Glossa ordinaria*.[49]

Whatever the city may be called, it is another name for Israel: and so it was used by Isaiah, Jeremiah, Ezekiel, and Christ himself. Further, since the Apocalypse refers to a time when Israel has become the Church, it would seem that the glossator understands that New Israel shall reject Christ even as Old Israel had done. Certainly he identifies this city with a corrupt Church, for when preaching comes to lack spiritual content, what but the Church itself can be said to be "mute"?

The *Glossa ordinaria* has only told us what we might have readily deduced from the Apocalypsist's plain indication that the *civitas magna* was to be understood as the second term in the traditional analogy Sodom:Jerusalem. Other commentators arrived at substantially the same conclusion, though often expressing it in other terms. Nicholas of Lyra, for example, identified the great city as the *congregatio fidelium*;[50] while the Venerable Bede explained that the witnesses' testimony came to an end, not because they had nothing more to say, but rather because when faced by the Beast, "the Church was then believed to have been forsaken by the grace of virtues." After the death of the witnesses, he calls the Sodom-like city both the *civitas impiorum* and the *civitas diaboli*,[51] which indeed a false church would become ipso facto.[52]

If we took the trouble to trace the image of Egypt through the Bible as we have done that of Sodom, no doubt we could grasp with equal ease the other spiritual identity of the *civitas magna*. The opening verses of the passage enable us to approximate the answer, however:

> Apoc. 11:1. And there was given me a reed like unto a rod: and it was said to me: Arise, and measure the temple of God, and the altar and them that adore therein.
> 2. But the court, which is without the temple, cast out, and measure it not: because it is given unto the Gentiles, and the holy city they shall tread under foot two and forty months.

> Apoc. 11:1. Et datus est mihi calamus similis virgae, et dictum est mihi: Surge, et metire templum Dei, et altare, et adorantes in eo:
> 2. Atrium autem, quod est foris templum, eiice foras, et ne metiaris illud: quoniam datum est gentibus, et civitatem sanctam calcabunt mensibus quadraginta duobus.

The *Glossa ordinaria* explains that the holy city is "the Church, congregated for living justly and imbued with virtues"; the temple is Christ himself, and the true believers are those adoring within the temple; whereas the atrium represents "false Christians, who pretend to be part of the Church but deny it by their deeds."[53] They are said to be "given to the Gentiles," an interlinear gloss adds, because "they have become like the Gentiles," who in turn are positively identified as oppressors of the Church.

Thus John is sent to preach, but only to the true Christians who abide in Christ;

the false ones he is to treat as non-Christians.[54] Hence it is clear that the City-Church contains both true and false Christians, but the latter should be reckoned as non-Christians, which is precisely what John does in verse 8 when he compares the pseudo church to Egypt.

"*Egypt*: i.e. 'dark,' without cognition of God," explained the *Glossa ordinaria*. This simple comment could no doubt be justified by a massive survey of Biblical texts, but Dante has saved his readers the trouble by expounding to Can Grande the verse beginning *In exitu Israel de Aegypto*. "Literally the Bible land that held Israel captive, Egypt allegorically signifies the captivity from which Christ redeemed mankind; morally, it is 'the sorrow and misery of sin' from which the soul is converted to a state of grace; and anagogically, Egypt represents 'the bondage of the corruption of this world' from which the sanctified soul passes to 'the liberty of everlasting glory.' "[55] Any of Dante's three "mystical" senses could describe "the great city, which is called spiritually, Sodom and Egypt, where their Lord also was crucified." Call it whatever name you will, it is the State of Sin. Whether *Sodoma caeca*, or *Aegyptus tenebrosa*, or *Hierusalem incredula*, the spiritual city-state is the same.

Dante's verse raises an instructive objection. Earlier we argued that since the *civitas magna* was the Church, a fortiori it was the New Israel; but that leads to the apparently paradoxical position that Israel spiritually is to be called Egypt. The obvious answer, of course, is that when Israel deserves to be called Egypt, she is no longer Israel but "like unto the Gentiles." The *Glossa ordinaria* may have had a still more pointed reversal of roles in mind, however, when it glossed *Aegyptus* as "*sine cognitione Dei*." For this stands in perfect opposition to the interpretation that Jerome gave to the name Israel: "Israel is to see God, or a man or mind seeing God."[56] This meaning, which admirably suits Dante's exposition, reminds us again that *Nomina sunt consequentia rerum*. Once Israel ceases to see God, she ceases to be Israel and properly should be called Egypt. Or, alternatively, Sodom can be interpreted as "blindness."[57]

Jerusalem and Israel, then, are pseudonyms for the corrupt City-Church that properly, according to its nature, deserves the name Sodom or Egypt. I must point out in passing that for the interpretation of the *Commedia*, this conclusion has consequences that far exceed the scope of the present study. For Dantists have long debated the significance of Apocalyptic symbols in the *Comedy*, not least of which is the Great Whore of Babylon, the *magna meretrix* associated with the simoniac popes of *Inferno* XIX, and presumably the *puttana* of *Purgatorio* XXXII as well.[58] If her *civitas magna* is Rome, then she would represent the *ecclesia Romana*—or rather, in each case, the corrupt form thereof. Because Dante simply appropriated the symbols from the Apocalypse, the great question has been, What was his exegesis of John's vision? In search of his source, scholars for over two generations past have pored through the expositions of Joachim of Flora (d. ca. 1202) and of those who developed his interpretation in the next century, notably Peter John Olivi and Ubertino da Casale.[59] Since Joachim appears among the *spiriti sapienti*, with the assurance that he was "endowed with the spirit of prophecy" (*Par.* XII, 140), his opinions at least deserve special consideration, though other expositors of the Apocalypse who are with him in the heaven of the Sun have perhaps been relatively neglected—Bede, Rabanus, and Richard of Saint Victor.[60] Nonetheless, I have purposely avoided these guides to the Apocalypse in the hope that a more modest approach through the *Glossa ordinaria* might establish the significance of at least one of Dante's Apocalyptic images, that of Sodom. The results may well help to clarify Dante's relation to Joachim, for we have been able to establish the identification of the *civitas magna* as the pseudo church without recourse to Joachite exegesis. The Apocalypsist himself had alluded to the spiritual significance of Sodom as something that was already known to his readers, and indeed it was fixed by the many Sodom:Israel analogies scattered throughout Scripture. The *Glossa ordinaria* grasped his meaning well enough, and so, I suspect, did both Dante and Joachim, if not every medieval exegete. Thus the Apocalyptic image of Sodom can, I believe, provide a firm point of departure for the interpretation of other, related Apocalyptic symbols, such as the *magna meretrix*, which Dante employs. The next step requires parallel studies of other Biblical images, notably Babylon and the *meretrix*, and I suspect that their meaning, like that of Sodom, can be deduced from Scripture and the Biblical commentators whom Dante commended to us. In short, the case of Sodom suggests that *Dante derived not only his images, but also their significance directly from Scripture!*[61]

THE HEBREW NAMES *SODOMA* AND *GOMORRHA*

The medieval exegete had yet another resource for determining the Biblical image of Sodom, and we must not neglect to consult it. This was Jerome's *Liber interpretationis Hebraicorum nominum*, which provided translations, or rather interpretations, of those words for the most part proper names—that the Vulgate text transliterated but did not translate. The work was intended as a supplement to the then-standard Hebrew-Greek lexicons of Philo Judaeus and Origen, which were difficult to consult because of the diversity of transliterated forms. Jerome's solution was to group together all the Hebrew names from each book of the Bible, so that they formed short lists, which could be scanned quickly. The system also permitted Jerome to alter the meaning to suit the context, which gives the work a character that is more exegetical than lexical. Thus no two of his six definitions of *Sodoma (-is)* are quite the same; while *Gomorra* has two definitions, one of which is repeated thrice. The Old Testament significance of both terms was apparently considered to be constant, for each is defined only at its first occurrence in Genesis. In the New Testament, however, where Jerome's translations are, he tells us, original, the coverage is more systematic.[62] One meaning is given at Luke for all the Gospels, and a separate definition is made for the Apocalypse and for each of the epistles.

Although we might have considered each of these interpretations in relation to the passage that it glosses, this would have been deceptive, because the definitions in Genesis and Luke extend respectively over the rest of the Old Testament and the Gospels. Therefore it has seemed better to reserve them for separate consideration here, which will not only permit comparison but also can serve as a retrospect on the Biblical image of these sister cities. Since the definitions are brief, they can conveniently be compared in tabular form:

SODOMA[a]

in:	interpretatur:	
GENESIS:	*pecus silens,* vel *caecitas,* sive similitudo eorum.	
LUKE:	*pastio silens,* vel declinatio eorum, aut *fulva.*	
ROMANS:[b]	*pecus tacens,* sive *sterilis*	aut *fulva.*
JUDE:	*pecus tacens.*	
2 PET.:[c]	*tacentibus,*	aut *fulvis.*
APOC.:	*pecori tacenti.*	

GOMORRA[d]

in:	interpretatur:
GENESIS:	*populi timor,* sive *seditio.*
ROMANS JUDE 2 PET.	*populi timor,* sive *caecitas.*

[a] Jerome, *Liber interpretationis Hebraicorum nominum,* ed. CCL, 72:71, 142, 151, 153, 160 (italics and punctuation supplied).
[b] Transposed from the original order: "Sodoma pecus tacens sive fulva vel sterilis."
[c] Transposed from: "Sodomis fulvis aut tacentibus"; for all other entries, the headword is *Sodoma.*
[d] *CCL,* 72:66, 150, 151, 152.

In each case, comparison shows that there is a single constant meaning that we may take to be the literal sense: Sodom is regularly associated with the state of "being silent" (*"silens," "tacens"*), and Gomorrah with "fear of people." The former casts new light on the interpretation of Apocalypse 11:8, for it shows that the glossator extracted the essence of the name when he glossed Sodoma *"i.e. muta"*[63] because the pseudo church did not preach spiritually. That special sense of being silent pertains only to the Apocalypse, and accordingly it appears that the context determines the respect in which Sodom can be said to be taciturn. Here Jerome's variant senses offer some assistance, though much is still left to the ingenuity of the interpreter. In effect, this is the raw material from which interpretations are made, and consequently there is no determinate application.

Take *Sodoma fulva* for example. Why should Sodom appropriately be colored deep yellow? Was it because Sodom, like Israel under Solomon, had commercial prosperity, which the golden color of his throne symbolized?[64] Or because Sodom was reduced to a sterile wasteland in which the predominant color was that of sand?[65] Or because all that glitters is not gold? There is no single answer, only potentialities, none of which in this case seems to have struck the fancy of any interpreter whom we have encountered.

By contrast, *Sodoma caeca* is a recurrent image, suggested no doubt by the blindness with which the Sodomites were stricken in Genesis 19:11. Had some text described anything to do with Sodom as tawny yellow, probably *fulva* too would have become an integral part of the image of Sodom.

It is hard to see why *Sodoma sterilis* is suggested only for Romans, since it suits well the sense in which Sodom appears in the Old Testament as an image of the wasted land; indeed the passage in Romans quotes just such a passage (Isa. 1:9), which suggests that had Jerome reworked the Old Testament definitions, he would have added this meaning.

Blindness and sterility are aspects under which we have often seen Sodom, both in the Bible and in the *Comedy*. Less familiar, and therefore more suggestive, is Jerome's insistence that Sodom resembles a herd of domestic animals.[66] The beasts are usually livestock: cattle, properly speaking, sheep, goats, asses, horses, but also swine, bees, and even fish. Since Jerome took *Sodoma* in Luke as a reference to the land rather than the people of Sodom, and then rendered it accordingly as *pastio*, "a pasture," we may infer that he conceived *Sodoma pecus* as essentially a *pastoral* image. The people of Sodom are a flock that is dependent on God, just as domesticated animals are on man.[67] It is because they are well cared for that they are silent, grazing in satisfaction and not calling on their pastor, for whom they have no need at the moment. In Luke, the image is altered slightly, for the pasture is silent as they are feeding. Were men dumb animals, the Good Shephrd could expect no more of them, though the psalmist bids even them to praise their Creator: "Praise the Lord . . . : Beasts and all cattle."[68] Yet, when applied to men, *pecus* is an abusive term that contemptuously reproaches brutish human ignorance, stupidity, or base behavior of any sort.[69] Thus, Sodom signifies a human community whose members descend to the level of irrational beasts while prospering under God's providence; taking prosperity for granted, they live for the moment and call on their benefactor only in adversity.[70]

The image of Gomorrah complements that of Sodom by putting the offense in human terms. Scripture abounds in reminders that men should live in fear of the Lord God (*timor Dei, timor Domini*), yet Gomorrah lives in fear of the people. Hence the city represents blindness to the true source of authority. Individuals show this misplaced respect by conforming to the unjust practices of their community; leaders, by making a god of popularity, as for example the preachers whom Beatrice reproved.[71] It is not part of the Dantesque image of Sodom, for the poet expressly eliminated it by conjoining Sodom, not with Gomorrah, as in the Biblical phrase, but with Cahors: *Soddoma e Caorsa* (*Inf.* XI, 50).

POSTSCRIPT

After chapters 8 and 9 had been written, I discovered that the same ground had already been surveyed from a different point of view by Derrick S. Bailey, *Homosexuality and the Western Christian Tradition* (London, 1955). His principal thesis is that English laws against homosexuality are unnecessarily harsh because they are founded on a misconception of the sin of Sodom. Using the fruits of modern Biblical scholarship, he traces the sexualization of the image of Sodom in three stages: (1) In Genesis 19 the Sodom story is ambiguous, because in the Old Testament the verb *yada'* ("to know"), which commonly means "to get acquainted with," does by exception denote coition, though never clearly homosexual intercourse. As an alternative to the homosexual interpretation of Genesis 19:5, Dr. Bailey suggests that the citizens of Sodom were angry because Lot, a resident alien (*gēr*), had arrogated to himself their right to examine visitors and judge whether to let them stay in the city (p. 4). Sex enters the story only when Lot offers his daughters as a bribe to appease the mob (p. 6). The Biblical tradition of Sodom, which we have followed in detail, Bailey passes over with few words: "The Old Testament depicts Sodom as a symbol of utter destruction, and its sin as one of such magnitude and scandal as to merit exemplary punishment, but nowhere does it identify that sin explicitly with the practice of homosexuality. . . . The witness of the Old Testament is maintained in the Apocrypha, where three passages tell only of the folly, pride, and inhospitality of the Sodomites" (pp. 9–10).

(2) The sexual interpretation of the sin of Sodom first appears in two pseudepigraphic works composed by Palestinian Jews at the end of the second century B.C. The Sodomites' wish to "know" the angels was linked by both these writers with the sin of the "sons of God" who copulated with human women in Genesis 6:1–4. The link is that in both cases a sexual union between *angels* and men "changed the order of their nature." The disparity between the two orders is the heart of the offense, but nonetheless a sexual element had been introduced, though not necessarily a homosexual one. This interpretation, which is most clearly reflected in the *Book of Jubilees* 16:5–6 and the *Testament of Naphtali* 3:4–5, was adopted in the New Testament, notably in Jude 6–7, followed by 2 Peter 2:4, 6–8, with "a perceptible emphasis upon its homosexual implications" (pp. 11–18).

(3) It was Philo Judaeus (died about A.D. 50), however, who first "expressly associates Sodom with homosexual practices" (p. 21). He reflects a view that was popular among Jews of his century, although rabbinical exegetes generally avoided it. Philo was followed by many Christian Fathers, beginning with Clement of Alexandria and Tertullian, and including Augustine and Gregory (p. 25); their reading of Genesis 19 is echoed by Justinian in *Novellae* 77 and 141.

Here Dr. Bailey leaves the image of Sodom and goes on to trace the actual attitudes towards homosexuality that are expressed in the Bible, Roman law, the medieval Church, and English law. Clearly, his study complements my own: he shows how Sodom came to be associated with sex, whereas I show what the Biblical image was before it acquired homosexual connotations. Although those connotations do appear in Jude 7, still I would stress the possibility that Jude may be using the image of Sodom as it was used by Christ and the prophets, namely as a symbol of rebellion against God's law.

Once the significance of Sodom as a symbol in the Bible has been grasped, I think the specific nature of Sodom's offense makes little difference to the interpretation of Dante's *Inferno*. The main question for Dantists ought not to be what particular sins were committed at Sodom; instead, they should concentrate on the *significance* of those sins in order to explicate *Inferno* xi, 49–50: "Lo minor giron *suggella* / del *segno* suo e Soddoma e Caorsa." It would be otherwise were the ring sealed with the sin of Sodom, but the text states that it is Sodom *and* Cahors that are imprinted with a common significance, which implies a category more general than their several sins. The interpreter's problem is where to seek out that significance. In Dante's day there was, in fact, a link between the two cities, for both sodomites and usurers were termed *bougres* by the French: "usuarii, quos Franci Bugeros vulgariter appellant," wrote Matthew Paris.[72] If this association underlies Dante's coupling of Sodom and Cahors, ironically it serves to dispel the suspicion of homosexuality, which Sodom mentioned alone might suggest, for surely no one could seriously imagine that all usurers were homosexuals; hence the term *bougres* must apply to them in some wider sense, and by implication we are invited to consider the sin of the runners as signifying something other than sexual sodomy. Thus, yet another clue could have led us to the point where we began chapter 8. Either way, the search for the significance of Sodom must lead ultimately back to the Bible, wherein we now know Sodom possessed a symbolic significance to which the specific nature of its sins, sexual or otherwise, was not essential.

[10]

The Sin of the Runners

Ars brevis, historia longa est. It is the burden of the historical critic that he must travel a long, rugged route to collect the components of a poetic image. Perhaps it is some consolation to believe that the poet too had traveled this way before us, but we must marvel the more at his art, which fitted the multiplex Biblical image of Sodom into the complex structure of his vast poem. I shall not attempt to explain how it was done: it will be enough if we grasp what he meant. To do this, let us again assume the role of the contemporary reader. He has discovered many things already in this book, and now in search of the image of Sodom, he has returned to his Vulgate text, surrounded and interlineated by the *Glossa ordinaria*; we have had him read something also of Bede and a great deal of Jerome. Has he found in revelation and its recommended interpreters any reason to doubt what his reason had already discovered in the poem?

At least this reader can be certain that he was justified in rejecting a homosexual interpretation of *Inferno* xv–xvi, and thus his reading of the poem is confirmed against the vulgar misreading of his less perceptive contemporaries. Still, he wishes now that his search had begun with the Bible, rather than ended with it, and he resolves hereafter to profit from the poet's counsel and let his own reason be guided by revelation, if only in the interpretation of the poem. He may begin at once, for the mass of Biblical Sodom imagery that has been garnered contains more than the reader had expected. He was looking for a Sodom image that corresponded to the sin of the runners, and though the Bible often reflects that, yet Sodom proved to be the image of their infernal neighbors as well—particularly of blasphemers, but occasionally of usurers, not to mention heretics. If Dante's image of Sodom is Biblical, the reader had best return to canto xi and reconsider yet again Virgil's explanation of the sins that are punished in "the smallest ring" that is the circle of the violent.

VIRGIL'S DESCRIPTION: VIOLENCE TO THE THINGS OF GOD

Rereading Virgil's description of the sin of the burning sands in context assures us that this third ring is devoted to those who "use force against God" ("A Dio . . . far forza"; *Inf.* xi, 31–32), as the preceding two were assigned to those who did violence (*forza = vis*) to their neighbors and to themselves respectively. Further, like the other forms of violence, the offense can be committed *in se* or *in re*—that is, against the person or against the things that are his (xi, 32). Holding this firmly in mind, together with what we now know of Sodom, let us reread Virgil's description:

> Puossi far forza ne la deïtade,
>> col cor negando e bestemmiando quella,
>> e spregiando natura e sua bontade;
> e però lo minor giron suggella
>> del segno suo e Soddoma e Caorsa
>> e chi, spregiando Dio col cor, favella.

One can do violence to the deity with heart negating and blaspheming it, and disdaining nature and its goodness; and hence the smallest ring seals with its sign both Sodom and Cahors and him who, disdaining God with heart, speaks.[1]

(*Inf.* xi, 46–51)

Each of the two tercets that form the sentence contains a distinct thought, as the editor's semicolon indicates. The first three lines explain how violence can be done to the deity; the last three explain, as a consequence of that generalization, what sins are punished in the ring of the violent against God. We have, then, *two* ostensive statements, each followed by a list. As both halves treat the same subject, one might reasonably expect to find parallels between them, as indeed appears to be the case when the two clauses are placed side by side:

Puossi far
forza ne la deïtade, ... e però lo minor giron
                                       suggella del segno suo

  (*A*) col cor
      negando e bestemmiando   e (*b*) Soddoma e Caorsa
      quella,

                                     e (*a*) qui,
e (*B*) spregiando   spregiando
    natura e sua bontade;   Dio
                                      col cor,
                                        favella.

Virgil has already explained that each form of violence has two subdivisions, *in se* and *in re*; further, he promised to make plain how this scheme worked out in each *giron* (*Inf.* xi, 33). Since the promise was carried out in the descriptions of the first two *gironi*, we have every expectation that the same distinction should appear in the description of the third ring as well.

In the first clause, the two elements are easily discerned: violence can be done to God (*A*) by negating and blaspheming the deity, and (*B*) by scorning nature and her goodness. The only problem is whether the words *col cor* are to be construed with both phrases or only with the first, but this can be resolved once we have similarly divided the second clause.

The smallest ring seals with its sign two distinct classes of objects: (*a*) any *person* who, despising God in his heart, speaks; and (*b*) the *cities* Sodom and Cahors. Do either of these correspond to Virgil's distinction between actions *in personam* and *in rem suam*?[2] Obviously *a* does, for it has only God as its object. By elimination, therefore, we must identify the violent against God *in re* with Sodom and Cahors (*b*).

The four phrases accordingly are reduced to two pairs that stand in the familiar rhetorical relation of chiasmus, since $A = a$ and $B = b$. The pair *Aa* is further linked together by the rhyme *quella-favella*. There can be no doubt that in the second clause the phrase *col cor* has no relation to *b*, for it is neatly boxed within its clause, *a*.

Another, possibly important, inference emerges by reading the pair *Aa* together: *spregiando* is a synonym for *negando e bestemmiando*! Since *spregiando* also describes the offense *in re* (*B*), can we reverse the equation and say that "disdaining nature and its goodness" amounts to "negating and blaspheming"? Inasmuch as we are not speaking of two different actions, but rather a *single kind of action* directed against *two distinct objects*—God and his things—it seems only reasonable to assume that the various verbs and verb phrases describing that single action should be equivalent. Thus:

> *far forza ne la deïtade* (to do violence to the deity)
> = *negando e bestemmiando* (denying/negating and blaspheming)
> = *spregiando* (disdaining/despising)

Now, to what sin or sins does this scheme refer? The appearance of *spregiando* in both *Aa* and *Bb* authorizes us to say that the sin in general is doing violence to deity by *disdaining* either God's person or the things of God. To give it a name, let us exercise supreme caution and take the poet at his word, *spregiando*: "disdain" is the generic name. By the same literalistic approach, we can be certain that the species *Aa* consists of "negating and blaspheming" God *in personam*. This, as I think every one agrees, is exemplified by Capaneus in the poem. Can we say that he does both? Although his group is commonly called the *bestemmiatori*,[3] one can argue, as A. Masseron appears to have done,[4] that *blasphemia* is an offense peculiar to the Judeo-Christian tradition, whereas Capaneus was a pagan. So it may have appeared to Dante, for he probably knew well enough that *blasphemia* was a word that had been introduced into Latin by patristic authors, though he may not have known that it originated as a pagan Greek term for profane speech, βλασφημία.[5] Still, since he related the verbs conjunctively, not disjunctively (*negando e bestemmiando*), I think it more likely that Dante admitted the possibility of pagan blasphemy. Indeed, his choice of the pagan Capaneus to illustrate the sin most probably serves to define Dante's use of blasphemy in this broader sense.

Probably no one will quarrel over this fine distinction unless I follow A. Pézard in his attempt to extend blasphemy to cover the sin of Brunetto's band.[6]

Inasmuch as we have found blasphemy connected with the Biblical image of Sodom, I have been strongly tempted to do so, but have hesitated for two reasons: first, as critics of Pézard agreed almost unanimously, the text will not quite bear that interpretation;[7] and secondly, the logic of my approach would require that it cover *all* the sins in group *Bb*, which would involve further complications in explaining the sins of not only the three Florentines but also the usurers as blasphemous. Therefore, I shall propose a far simpler solution that will have the double advantage of adhering to the text with literal tenacity and of granting Professor Masseron the perfectly pagan sin required.

What, then, do we know of the species *Bb*? Specifically, it consists in *spregiando*, not God himself, but "the things of God" *("le cose di Dio")*, to rephrase Virgil's division of the sins: "A Dio, a sé, al prossimo si pòne / far forza, dico in loro e in los cose" *(Inf.* xi, 31–32). Further, the object is defined as "nature and its goodness,"[8] and finally, the offense is typified by Sodom and Cahors. My argument is simplicity itself: Is there an offense known to both classical and Christian thought such that it literally consists in doing *violence to the things of God*? Both Roman law and Catholic theology recognize just such a crime. Its name is sacrilege.

AQUINAS ON SACRILEGE

Sacrilegium, as both Aquinas and the medieval legists recognized, originally referred to the theft from a temple of things that were consecrated to divine service *(furtum sacrorum).* Under the Dominate, however, the term came by extension to cover neglect or violation of the commands of the *divinus imperator,*[9] with the result that this was the standard medieval definition: "They commit sacrilege who through ignorance confound or through negligence violate and offend the sanctity of a divine law."[10]

The medieval Romanists of Bologna extended this definition still further to embrace the commandments of the Gospel *(lex Evangelica),*[11] so that all who erred in some article of faith were held to be guilty of the civil crime of sacrilege.[12]

The glossators understood that sacrilege proper involved actual theft, and hence they glossed the extended senses as *quasi sacrilegium.*[13] Hence, in essence, sacrilege was committed, not by simply "breaking a law," but rather by violating and offending its *sanctity*, especially when the violator *(sacrilegus)*, like a thief, appropriated the holy thing to himself.

It should be evident enough that this corresponds exactly to the Biblical image of that sodomy by which man usurps the authority of the divine legislator by perverse interpretation of God-given law, but the *Code* offers other instances of sacrilege that are none the less fitting to the runners: "It is not proper to take exception to the principal judge, for it is equivalent to sacrilege to doubt whether he whom the emperor selected may be worthy."[14] The *casus* understands this to mean that no one without the express permission of the prince shall question the authority of any provincial governor or civil magistrate whom the emperor has appointed.[15] Thus it is sacrilege even to question the authority of imperial appointees, much less that of the emperor himself: which, as we have said, is precisely the offense of the three Florentine Guelfs, not to mention Messer Brunetto.

Further, it is sacrilege for any man to hold administrative office in his own province without an imperial dispensation.[16] For two reasons, the gloss explains: "Because they do many things as favors, and because 'No man is a prophet in his own country.' "[17] Here, too, Brunetto and the other Florentine statesmen have been at fault.

Aquinas, in his theology, established the crime of sacrilege as a sin. Starting from Isidore's etymology—"sacrilegus dicitur, ab eo quod sacra legit"—he concluded that "whatever pertains to irreverence for sacred things, pertains to injury of God, and is to be considered as sacrilege."[18] Like the lawyers, Saint Thomas also recognized the extended senses of the term: "Through a certain extension of the word, that which pertains to irreverence for the prince, namely to dispute whether his judgment should be followed, is called sacrilege by a certain similarity."[19] In like manner, "that which is done in injury of the Christian people, namely that infidels be placed in authority over it, pertains to the irreverence for a sacred thing: hence it is reasonably called sacrilege."[20]

Moreover, sacrilege is a specific sin, as Damascene recognized by his statement: "When the purple is made the royal vestment, it is honored and glorified; and if anyone dishonors this, he is condemned to death." Thomas continues: "as if acting against the king; so also if anyone violate a sacred thing, by this very fact he acts against reverence for God, and thus he sins through irreligiosity."[21]

Most especially relevant to the runners, however, is Thomas' interpretation of the Roman definition of sacrilege which he found in Gratian. The objection was raised:

> It seems that sacrilege is not a special sin. For Gratian says, "They commit sacrilege who through ignorance sin against the sanctity of the law or violate it and offend by their negligence." But every sin does this, for, as Augustine says, "sin is a word or deed or desire against the law of God." Therefore, sacrilege is a sort of general sinfulness.[22]

To which Thomas responded:

> People sin against the sanctity of divine law when they assail it, as heretics and blasphemers do. By disbelieving God they commit the sin of denying faith; by twisting the words of his law they commit the sin of sacrilege.[23]

THE RUNNERS AS PERVERTERS OF DIVINE LAW

Divinae legis verba pervertunt, sacrilegium incurrunt! Precisely the Biblical image of Sodom:Israel. Thanks to Thomas' distinction, we can perceive the difference between blasphemy and sacrilege, and thereby be sure that we have hit exactly upon the sin of the runners. For the runners whom we know did not attack the law of God directly: rather, they perverted it, "spregiando natura e sua bontade" (*Inf.* xi,

48). Now we know that for Dante, all of natural law forms part of divine law;[24] so it follows that the violations of natural law that we have established for Brunetto, Priscian, Francesco d'Accorso, and Andrea de' Mozzi all constitute offenses against the divine law a fortiori. Since these violations all involved a perverse interpretation of the law of nature, they qualify as sacrilege under either the Thomistic or the Romanistic definition.

The sacrilege of the three Florentines and their band of runners is even more evident. As leaders of the Guelfs, they denied by word and deed the sacrosanct authority of the emperor. This crime, Thomas would agree with the glossators, deserves the name of sacrilege.

Dante himself, speaking through Virgil, argued the case against the usurer, who gains his livelihood neither from nature nor from her follower, art. The law he perverts, however, is not to be found either in Roman law or in the *documenta philosophica*; it is not discoverable by unaided human reason. Instead,

> if thou recall to mind Genesis near the beginning, it behooves mankind to gain their livelihood and their advancement.

> . . . se tu ti rechi a mente
> lo Genesì dal principio, convene
> prender sua vita e avanzar la gente

(Inf. xi, 106–8)

Thus the divine law they have violated is one that is given in revelation and otherwise is unavailable to human reason. Since the sin of Cahors is based on Holy Scripture, it is possible that the same source has also revealed the sin of Sodom; and inasmuch as Sodom itself is to be found in "Genesis near the beginning," we could have used the *documenta spiritualia* to justify the condemnation of the swift and the strong. No doubt we could draw new arguments from the Bible to buttress the naturalistic reasons that have already been advanced; but the results would not be much different, except perhaps in the case of Priscian.[25]

In fact, the sins of Brunetto's band, though comprised in the Biblical image of Sodom, played a relatively minor part. The predominant image of sodomy in the Bible was rather that form of sacrilege which Aquinas defined as "perverting the words of God's law." Of this, Mozzi the preacher was palpably guilty, but Brunetto and the other runners that he named were not expositors of Sacred Scripture *ex professo*. Rather, they were Christians who paid lip service to revelation and ignored it, preferring instead to rely on their own ingenious reason. The results of their rationalism contradicted the divine law: through criminal neglect they violated and offended its sanctity. Guilty though they were of sacrilege, theirs was not the worst kind.

Dante himself defined this *summum facinus*, the "crime unsurpassed," against which he inveighs so eloquently in *Monarchia* 3. 4. Our publicist in his preceding chapter had excluded from the arena those opponents who were either ignorant of the *documenta* or incapable of understanding them.[26] Now he turns to those remaining opponents who are versed in theology and philosophy; for them he defines the proper method of interpreting the truth of revelation. Long though the passage is, there is no shorter way of concluding our argument:

[6] In order to appreciate this refutation and the following ones better, the point to bear in mind is that errors concerning the mystical sense may be committed in two ways: either by looking for it where it does not exist, or by interpreting it as it ought not to be interpreted.

[7] Referring to the first, Augustine in his *De Civitate Dei* says: "Not every happening that is recorded need be taken as significant, for even those not significant may be included for the sake of those which are. Only the ploughshare actually cleaves the soil, but the other parts of the plough are also necessary for this to happen."

[8] Referring to the second, the same Doctor in his *Doctrina Christiana* says of the person who tries to give the Scriptures a sense different from that intended by the writer: "He makes the same mistake as a person who leaves the main road and then only after a long detour reaches the place to which the road was leading"; and he adds: "This must be pointed out to him in case this habit of deviating leads him to take the wrong road or go off at a tangent."

[9] Then he indicates the reason why this is to be avoided in dealing with the Scriptures: "Faith will waver if the authority of the sacred Scriptures is shaken."

[10] But I say that if a person makes such mistakes through ignorance he should be firmly corrected and then pardoned, just as one pardons a person who fears a lion in the clouds. With those who deliberately commit such errors, however, there is no other course but to treat them as one would treat tyrants who do not maintain the constitution [*iura*] for the common benefit but try to pervert it for their own ends.

[11] What an unsurpassed crime [*O summum facinus*]—though it were committed only in dreams—to abuse the intention of the Holy Spirit! It is not against Moses that they are sinning, nor against David, nor Job, nor Matthew, nor Paul, but against the Holy Spirit speaking through them. For although those who write down the divine word are many they all do so at the dictation of the one God who has condescended to display His good pleasure towards us by employing the pens of many people.[27]

Clearly the *summum facinus* is sacrilege. For, as Aquinas wrote, "ex hoc vero quod divinae legis verba pervertunt, sacrilegium incurrunt." In the scheme of Dante's Hell, then, those who committed this "unsurpassed crime" belong in Brunetto's band. They, more than anyone else, are signified by the Biblical image of Sodom. They are not philosophers or pagan *magistri*, but are the scribes and Pharisees of Israel, both Old and New—that is, *viri ecclesiastici*, aberrant doctors of the Church, mendacious Christian *magistri*, pseudo prophets—all of them abusers of the intention of the Holy Spirit, perverters of the divine *iura*.

Is Mozzi their only representative? Brunetto did not name him, and there were yet others whom he hesitated to name, not out of scorn but from a higher motive: "of the rest it will be more creditable to be silent" ("de li altri fia laudabile tacerci"; *Inf.* xv, 104). One such perverter of Scripture we have already detected because he was implicated by the transfer of Bishop Mozzi. Moreover, this pope, by perverting Scripture, did indeed subvert the constitutional *iura* of the Church, making a tyrant of the *vicarius Christi*. And of such men, Dante, like Brunetto, thought it laudable to be silent.[28] Their identity is known to us by a single instance; but *par excellence*, Innocent III, whom the Decretalists recognized as the father of their new legal system, typifies the breed. They are popes who by virtue of their supposed vicarial plenitude of power claim to interpret Scripture in Christ's name. These perverse popes utter no word of blasphemy against God directly; their violence has the same object as the sin of the simonists—*le cose di Dio* (*Inf.* xix, 2). It is no accident, I submit, that "the things of God" is but a paraphrase of Virgil's very words that define violence against God *in re*: "A Dio, a sé, al prossimo si pòne / far forza, dico in loro e in lor cose" (*Inf.* xi, 31–32).

HOMOSEXUALITY AS LUST

Violence done to the things of God is sacrilege. Does this definition admit the possibility of a band of homosexuals running on the burning sands? Aquinas subsumes unnatural sexual vices under the deadly sin of lust *(luxuria, lussuria)* in *Summa theologica* II-II q.154 a.11. The article immediately preceding he devotes to the relevant question, "Whether sacrilege can be a species of lust?" The Angelic Doctor replies in the affirmative with the following argument:

> On the contrary, Augustine says that "if it is wicked, through covetousness, to go beyond one's earthly bounds, how much more wicked is it through venereal lust to transgress the bounds of morals!" Now to go beyond one's earthly bounds in sacred matters is a sin of sacrilege. Therefore it is likewise a sin of sacrilege to overthrow the bounds of morals through venereal desire in sacred matters. But venereal desire pertains to lust. Therefore sacrilege is a species of lust.
>
> I answer that, as stated above, the act of a virtue or vice, that is directed to the end of another virtue or vice, assumes the latter's species: thus, theft committed for the sake of adultery, passes into the species of adultery. Now it is evident that as Augustine states (*De virgin.* 8), the observance of chastity, by being directed to the worship of God, becomes an act of religion, as in the case of those who vow and keep chastity. Wherefore it is manifest that lust also, by violating something pertaining to the worship of God, belongs to the species of sacrilege: and in this way sacrilege may be accounted a species of lust.[29]

The same principle would presumably permit an unnatural sexual act to be subsumed under sacrilege, *provided* that the sex act violated a consecrated person, place, or thing, not for the sake of lust, but for the sake of irreligion, that is, sacrilege.[30] We cannot, therefore, categorically exclude sexual sodomy from punishment under the rain of fire, but we can be sure that such acts of desecration would be punished there by reason of their intentional irreligion, not qua unnatural sex. Such acts would, in any case, be exceedingly rare, though I may suggest that Dante did in fact have one of that species in mind. As we have seen, the archetype of the virgin consecrated to Christ is his Bride the Church; and consequently, one who presumed to substitute himself for the Bridegroom would be guilty of this form of sacrilege, since carnal lust would be out of the question. Once again the third Innocent is guilty.

As for the conventional, lustful devotees of unnatural sex whose only thought is to enhance their own sensual luxury, we now know where to find them in Dante's *Inferno*: driven before the hellish storm that torments carnal sinners "who subject reason to desire" up in the second circle (*Inf.* v, 28–51). Lest there be any doubt, we find chief among these *lussuriosi* is Queen Semiramis, "who was so corrupted by licentious vice that she made lust lawful in her law to take away the scandal into which she was brought" (*Inf.* v, 52–60). According to Aquinas, *vitium contra naturam* is a species of lust, and thus it would follow that this pagan ruler was not, in Dante's estimation, obligated to abstain from lust by any divine law, or else she would surely run with the sacrilegious under the rain of fire. It would seem, therefore, that the men of Sodom were equally innocent of sacrilege, at least before their rescue by Abram from the kings of the North signified to them that God favored Lot and his uncle, who were given to them as an example. In general, the case of Semiramis exonerates from sacrilege those not in the Judeo-Christian tradition whose lust drove them to sexual practices *contra naturam*. It does not, however, excuse their lust, which is punished with that of Francesca and Paolo in the circle of luxury.

This explains why some of those who are being purged of the sin of lust in Purgatory cry out "Sodom and Gomorrah!" while others say "Pasiphae enters the cow that the bull may run to her lust":

> sopragridar ciascuna s'affatica:
> la nova gente: "Soddoma e Gomorra";
>   e l'altra: "Ne la vacca entra Pasife,
>   perché 'l torello a sua lussuria corra."
>
> (*Purg.* xxvi, 39–42)

Both forms of unnatural vice are just where Thomas put them, with the mortal sin of lust. Thus Dante assured the attentive reader that by no means did he condone unnatural sex, whether homosexuality or bestiality; but at the same time he made it plain that such sins, for Christians as well as for pagans like Semiramis, were a species of lust but not of sacrilege. Thus Dante cannot be accused of undermining morality by failing to indicate the nature and eternal consequences of the vice against nature that is commonly called sodomy.

Against this interpretation, some will doubtless object that the sin of Semiramis does not belong in either of the bands of the unnaturally lustful in Purgatory, since her incest was no more the sin of Sodom than of Pasiphae. The obvious response is that Dante described her sin in general terms that were appropriate to the other species of unnatural lust as well as to her own particular form. But for those who will not credit reason unsupported by authority, I have a variant of the Semiramis legend that may establish the connection. On the eve of the Reformation, a humanistic lawyer offered Semiramis as an example of sodomy: "Legitur etiam, quod Semiramis Regina, quae Babilonicam urbem fieri fecit tantae fuit libidinis, et spurcitiae, ut non modo filium proprium sed *etiam equum usque ad coitum amaverit.*"[31] If Dante, too, had read somewhere that the queen "had even loved a horse all the way to coition," there would be no doubt that her vice was the Dantesque companion to that of Sodom and Gomorrah. Those who feel that the matter is indeed crucial may care to determine whether or not Dante might have known this uncommon variation on the medieval Semiramis legend.[32] Whatever the answer, however, it will not alter the fact that the poet did frame his definition of her sin so broadly that it can include not only incest but also bestiality and homosexuality. Whether Semiramis' legendary perversions assumed one form or many is, I would insist, irrelevant. The point is rather that, according to Dante's definition, these unnatural sexual acts are punished as lust.

SODOMY IN THE CONTEXT OF AUGUSTINE'S *CONFESSIONS*, BOOK 3

Our overworked contemporary reader may be permitted one afterthought. He came to the *Comedy* thinking that he knew very well what sodomy was. Only through an arduous and unwonted trek through the *Textus Biblie cum Glosa ordinaria* did he discover that in revelation and its patristic interpreters, sex was the least of Sodom's sins. Will he not wonder how he and the Christian culture of which we suppose him to be an educated product had acquired this lopsided—nay, perverse— image of Sodom? And to probe still deeper, why, out of all the heinous offenses against natural law, did one trivial and relatively harmless one preempt the very name *vitium contra naturam*? Now he knows what to tell a society that trivializes thus the laws of nature: "You hypocrite! First take the plank out of your own eye, and then you will see clearly to take the speck out of your brother's."[33] Were the enlightened reader a Marsiglio of Padua, or even a historian, he might make it his life work to answer this truly significant question. But let us have him seek an immediate answer that may have been the poet's own, for we have by no means exhausted the richness of this canto, nor ever can.

Granted, men of Dante's generation snickered at the name of Sodom and associated it with only the lustful species of unnatural vice. Who would our curious reader suspect had given it this narrow sense? If Dante has taught him anything, it is that he should suspect the worst of the canon lawyers. And thus he will consult Gratian's *Decretum* and there find his answer. In the course of an inquiry into fornication, the *Magister Decretorum* cited three canons, entitled:

> *Minus est secundum naturam coire, quam contra naturam delinquere.*
> *Graviora sunt flagicia, que contra naturam probantur.*
> *Turpior et flagitiosior est usus contra naturam, quam fornicationis vel adulterii.*[34]

The first, an excerpt from Ambrose, assures us that Lot offered his daughters for natural intercourse, which was less sinful than what was proposed by his neighbors, who are unnamed.[35] The last, incorrectly ascribed to Augustine, also makes no mention of Sodom,[36] the name of which appears only in the third canon, a quotation from Augustine's *Confessions*:

> Those crimes which be against nature are to be everywhere and at all times both detested and punished; such as those of the men of Sodom were: which should all nations commit, they should stand all guilty of the same crime, by the law of God, which hath not so made men, that they should this way use one another. For even that society which should be betwixt God and us, is then violated, when the same nature of which He is author, is polluted by the preposterousness of lust.[37]

As it stands in Gratian, this extract indicates that sodomites belong with the lustful pagan Semiramis. But by the same token it represents Sodom as the image of unnatural lust, *and nothing more*. Is Augustine then the originator of the exclusively sexual image of Sodom? To judge from Gratian, yes; but to judge from the context of *Confessions* 3, emphatically, No!

Since our trecento critic has by now learned that Dantesque allusions are to be understood with reference to the original context, he will soon be rereading the *Confessions*, where he will discover, as we can too, that Augustine's third book is neither more nor less than a treatise on the sin of the runners. The contrast between the extract read in and out of context sufficiently answers the question that sent him to Gratian. Sodom was reduced to insignificance by those canonists who used Gratian's concordance as an authority in itself. The antidote, recommended by Peter Lombard against similarly opportunistic theologians, was a lifetime of patristic study of the *auctoritates*. Augustine himself has the same message if we but read him.

Those who are familiar with the *Confessions* need read no further in my book, while those who require an explanation might do better to spend an hour over the text of *Confessions* 3 than to bear with me to the end. Yet, lest there be some who do not read those pages as I have done, I must make my case explicit by rehearsing Augustine's argument chapter by chapter. Let it also stand as the summary of the argument of this my book and, I submit, of *Inferno* xv as well.

(3. 1. 1) The third book of the *Confessions* is devoted to the problem of intellectual blindness, into which state Augustine passed during his first years of higher education at Carthage: "To Carthage then I came, where there sang all around me in my ears a cauldron of unholy loves."[38] These *flagitiosi amores* were the source of the disorders that were overcome only by his conversion. They are compared to, and include, sexual lust, but these corrupt forms of love extend to the more subtle snares of a university community: the theater and other diversions, professional growth and associates, and, especially for the budding intellectual, the attractions of rationalized religion. One after another, these things seduced Augustine between his seventeenth and nineteenth years because, as he tells us at the outset, "I hated security": that is, the *securitas* that came to him with conversion.[39] "For I continued without all appetite towards incorruptible nourishments, not because I was already

full, but the more empty, the more queasy stomached" ("sed quo inanior, fasti-diosior").

Naturally he longed to love but did not realize that all love must be ordained to God. Instead he sought those unholy loves with which Carthage seethed: first of all, human love, beginning with innocent friendship (*amicitia*), which was presently defiled by lust.

(3. 2. 2–4) Item: from passion he passed to compassion, seeking to experience vicariously, as an empathic spectator, the human passions that were simulated in the theater. There the sentiment of sorrow could be experienced with pleasure rather than pain. But it is unnatural to love what is painful, and hence he declares his vicarious enjoyment of the suffering of stage lovers to be a perversion of *amicitia* and in fact a form of sodomy.[40]

(3. 3. 5) Item: sacrilege. In a church during divine service, he did something—unspecified—out of "sacrilegious curiosity" ("*sacrilega curiositate*"). (3. 3. 6) Item: *caecitas mentis*. In preparation for a forensic career (*fora litigiosa*), he studied rhetoric, was eminently successful, and became swollen with pride: "Tanta est caecitas hominum de caecitate etiam gloriantium."[41] Only an immodest modesty kept him from overtly making fun of the ignorant (*ignoti*), although he confesses that he condoned those who did, namely the elitist clique who proudly called themselves "destroyers" ("*eversores*").

(3. 4. 7–8) In addition to these unholy loves, he found another that was, ulti-mately, to lead him to salvation. In his nineteenth year,[42] Augustine was converted to philosophy by reading Cicero's *Hortensius*. In retrospect, he saw that the desire he had conceived therefrom for "the immortality of wisdom" ("*inmortalitas sapientiae*") turned him toward the source of all wisdom. Augustine later reflected that he might have been more cautious had he known the inspired advice of Paul: "Beware lest any man cheat you by philosophy, and vain deceit; according to the tradition of men, according to the elements of the world, and not according to Christ: for in him dwelleth all the fulness of the Godhead corporeally."[43] Fortunately the *Hor-tensius* had affected Augustine only to wisdom in general: "This it was that so delighted me in that exhortation, that it did not engage me to this or that sect, but left me free to love, and seek, and obtain, and hold, and embrace Wisdom itself, whatever it was."[44]

Resolved to pursue wisdom, young Augustine knew well enough where to look for it. He had noted one defect in the *Hortensius*: that the name of Christ was not there, which his mother Monica had taught him so to cherish "that what book soever was without that Name, though never so learned, politely and truly penned, did not altogether take my approbation."[45]

(3. 5. 9) *Itaque*: "And thus," he adds directly, "I resolved to bend my studies towards the Holy Scriptures, that I might see what they were."[46] All that has preceded contributes to our understanding of this confrontation, the pivotal event of the book. Though turned by Cicero towards a holy love of wisdom, and though predisposed by childhood training to seek it in revelation, yet professional pride proved to be the young rhetorician's stumbling block:

> For when I attentively read these Scriptures, I thought not then so of them, as I now speak; but they seemed to me far unworthy to be compared to the stateliness of the Ciceronian eloquence. For my swelling pride soared above the temper of their style, nor was my sharp wit able to pierce into their sense. In truth, however, the greatness of Scripture would be apparent to children, but I disdained to be as a child [*parvulus*], and swollen with pride, I took my self to be a great man [*grandis*].[47]

Scripture, he explained, is a veiled mystery that neither the proud nor the immature mind can comprehend: its truth is accessible only to the humble mind, which is made lofty thereby. "And I was not so fitted at that time, as to pierce into the sense, or stoop my neck to its coming."[48]

(3. 6. 10) *Itaque*: "And thus," he pursues the chain of consequences, "I fell upon a sect of men proudly ploughing the wrong way" ("*homines superbe delirantes*"). These were veritable pseudo prophets, Manichaeans who were forever speaking of Christ and of Truth: "but they spake falsehood, not of thee only (who truly art the Truth itself) but also of the elements of this world, thy creatures, concerning which I out of love for thee ought to have neglected even the philosophers who speak truly."[49]

(3. 6. 11) The second state of this man was worse than the first, for he had not believed the fables of the rhetoricians which he deserted in search of wisdom, but his professional pride had now led him to believe the fantastic natural theology of the Manichaeans. "Alas, alas! by what steps was I brought to the very bottom of hell, toiling and turmoiling through want of Truth, since I sought after Thee, my God, . . . not according to the understanding of the mind, wherein Thou made me to excel the beasts, but according to the sense of the flesh."[50] "*Quibus gradibus deductus in profunda inferi!*" The descent through lust down to sacrilege and thence to the depths of Hell will ultimately lead Augustine to God, by stages through which the pilgrim Dante passed also.

To impress upon us the character of the state into which he had fallen, Augustine reverts to sexual imagery: "I chanced upon that bold woman, who knows nothing, that riddle of Solomon, sitting at the door of her house, and saying: Eat ye bread of secrecies willingly, and drink ye stolen waters which are sweet. She seduced me, because she found my soul outdoors, dwelling in the eye of my flesh, and chewing the cud by myself, upon such baits as I had devoured through that eye."[51] The passage alludes to Proverbs 7, where Solomon exhorts his son to love Sapientia as his sister. Both Dante and Augustine take the passage as an exhortation to *amicitia sapientiae*, as they interpret *philosophia* = *philo* + *sophia*.[52] Solomon's son is further cautioned to avoid the company of a wanton woman who walks the streets by night, seducing young men. The identity of this slut is not immediately disclosed, because Solomon has announced his intention to teach through riddles: "A wise man shall hear and shall be wiser: and he that understandeth, shall possess governments. He shall understand a parable, and the interpretation, the words of the wise, and their mysterious sayings."[53] Presently, however, she is described again in terms, echoed by Augustine, that hint broadly at her name:

Prov. 9:10. The fear of the Lord is the beginning of wisdom: and the knowledge of the holy is prudence.

11. For by me [Wisdom herself is speaking] shall thy days be multiplied, and years of life shall be added to thee.

12. If thou be wise, thou shalt be so to thyself: and if a scorner, thou alone shalt bear the evil.

13. A foolish woman and clamorous, and full of allurements, and knowing nothing at all,

14. Sat at the door of her house, upon a seat, in a high place of the city,

15. To call them that pass by the way, and go on their journey:

16. He that is a little one, let him turn to me. And to the fool she said:

17. Stolen waters are sweeter, and hidden bread is more pleasant.

18. And he did not know that giants are there, and that her guests are in the depths of hell.[54]

(3. 7. 12) In the next sentence, Augustine himself hints at her identity: "For I knew not that other [Sapientia], which truly is; and I was, as it were, in some subtle way persuaded to give my consent to those foolish deceivers [stultis deceptoribus], when they put their questions to me." What he lacked was the mainstay that Scripture could have provided, for "I was altogether ignorant how rightly in the Scriptures we may be said to be made after the image of God."[55] What then does the *mulier stulta* represent? Certainly she is the opposite of Sapientia, or better, of the revealed wisdom of Holy Scripture. As she personified the opposite of Wisdom, we may simply call her Folly (*Stultitia*); but as Augustine had a special sort of wisdom in mind, so its opposite must be a *specific* form of folly. Hence the *Glossa ordinaria* tells us that the foolish woman impersonates *heresy*: she is the whore Haeresis, who "often calls catholics to perfidy."[56]

(3. 7. 13) At this point, in the middle of his discussion of the Manichaeans, Augustine interrupts his loose narrative to declare more fully how revelation might have aided his reason.[57] The excursus begins with a single, inordinately long periodic sentence that announces the thesis:

> Nor knew I that true inward righteousness, which judgeth not according to custom, but out of the most rightful law of God Almighty, whereby the ways of places and times were disposed, according to those times and places; itself meantime being the same always and everywhere, not one thing in one place, and another in another; according to which Abraham, and Isaac, and Jacob, and Moses, and David, were righteous, and all those commended by the mouth of God; but were judged unrighteous by inexpert men [*imperitis*], judging out of man's day, and measuring by their own petty habits, the moral habits of the whole human race.[58]

By many examples he shows that circumstances alter cases, and then he asks: "Is Justice therefore various or mutable? No; but the times rather, which justice governs, are not like one another; for they are times."[59]

But human life is too short, Augustine argues, for men to acquire expert understanding of the affairs of more than a few nations and centuries at best, and since it is experience that teaches man prudence, no man can judge as prudently as does God in His omniscience. He has but one standard of justice, but we lack the experience to understand how it applies to circumstances of which we have only partial and imperfect knowledge.

(3. 7. 14) As a poet, Augustine confesses, he should have realized that there is but one art of justice, just as there is but one of poetry. But he was then blind, and hence he did not hesitate to condemn the prophets and patriarchs of the Bible for doing and saying what God had commanded them, whenever this seemed unjust to Augustine.

(3. 8. 15) The remedy, of course, is faith. This, the crucial argument of book 3, Augustine develops in chapter 8. The answer is apparent from the first lines: "Can it at any time or place be an unjust thing for a man to love God with all his heart, with all his soul, and with all his mind; and his neighbour as himself?" Directly follows the passage on sodomy that is extracted in Gratian, but here it is bound to the preceding statement with another significant *itaque*.[60]

The sin of Sodom pollutes with lust our friendship with God and with his wisdom, because it is contrary to the *ratio* and *natura* of man, in which God is reflected and hence is repudiated whenever violence is done to man's raison d'être. Augustine begins with the sin of Sodom, because he had never doubted that homosexual intercourse is repugnant to human nature and reason; therefore God's judgment on Sodom was one that he had never questioned. In his argument, it functions as an absolute: a self-evident sin, relative to neither time nor place nor person, since reason alone can perceive the intent of nature without any special revelation from God. Yet it is for Augustine, as for Dante, an instance of lust—the simplest of sins—which for Augustine at least, led to all the rest.

In contrast to sexual sodomy, which is always wrong, there are, at the other extreme, offenses that are purely matters of human convention. Some are mere matters of custom, to which one nonetheless is in duty bound to conform because human communities are formed by participation. The supreme social convention is the understanding that the ruler is to be obeyed, and therefore the prince can alter the customs of the community by legislation, since his prerogative takes precedence over all other social conventions. God, however, takes precedence over all other rulers, for he is the ruler of all creatures (*regnator universae creaturae*), and thus, like lesser rulers, the Almighty from time to time issues special decrees by revelation which no human law can contradict with justice.

Hence it appears that Sodom in Augustine's exposition represents the most fundamental form of human defiance to divine law. In other words, the Augustinian image of Sodom coincides with the Biblical tradition, in which it consistently signified man's rejection of the law of God.

(3. 8. 16) Since the human community is itself founded on the law of nature, which is in turn a form of divine law, it follows that God is the ultimate source of all justice. Having explained this, Augustine goes on to anatomize the ways in which man transgresses the law of God, which he expounds in terms of the Ten

Commandments. Next he turns from the crime to its punishment, asking why God punishes men for offenses that cannot conceivably harm him:

> But Thou avengest what men commit against themselves, seeing also when they sin against Thee, they act impiously against their own souls, and iniquity gives itself the lie, by corrupting and perverting their nature, which Thou hast created and ordained, or by an immoderate use of things allowed, or in burning in things unallowed, to that use which is against nature.[61]

The list goes on, but the point is sufficiently made: *all* sins abuse the Creator in his creatures; and although Augustine does not say so, his point of departure, the fundamental, self-evident sin of Sodom, aptly typifies this his conclusion.

(3. 9. 17) One can be wrong, even a lawbreaker, and still not sin, for not every offense falls under Augustine's definition. Only what offends either God or "the bond of society" *("sociale consortium")* must be accounted a sin. Only God knows whether the greater part of human laws are just or not, and he, like a schoolmaster who encourages the learner, corrects only the worst mistakes and lets the lesser ones pass as *peccata proficientium.* Human justice, then, will always be imperfect and uncertain. That being the case, there is only one safe rule—serve God: for "that society of men is a just society, which serves thee."[62]

(3. 10. 18) "I myslf being at that time ignorant of these things, derided heartily those holy servants and prophets of thine. And what gained I by scorning them, but that myself should in the meantime be scorned by thee, being sensibly and by little and little drawn on to these toys."[63] Thus he concludes the excursus on justice and returns to the philosophical errors of the Manichaeans, namely the theory of light metabolism. Brief and inconsequential though the matter may be, it serves to emphasize man's dependence on God, even in matters of natural philosophy. Blinded by professional pride, Augustine had rejected Scripture and thus had cut himself adrift from the one absolute standard that is available to human reason.

(3. 11. 19–20) The treatise does not close without foreshadowing the eventual solution to Augustine's *caecitas mentis.* His mother, Monica, dreamed that while she stood sorrowing on a wooden rule *(regula lignea)*, she was told that presently her son should join her, as indeed we find him after his conversion nine years later, "standing upon the same rule of faith."[64]

(3. 12. 21) But how shall he attain to faith? An experienced bishop refused Monica's plea to reason with her son, for he understood

> that I was as yet unripe for instruction [*indocilem*], being puffed up with the novelty of that heresy, and that I had already troubled divers unskilful persons with captious questions, as she had told them. "But let him alone a while," said he, "only pray to God for him; he will of himself find by reading [*ipse legendo*] his own mistake, and how great his impiety is."[65]

EPILOGUE

No one, I trust, shall be fatuous enough to characterize the present work as an attempt to "rehabilitate" Brunetto Latini and his fellow runners. Far from it, I have laden them with what was, in Dante's eyes, a far more grievous sin, for which I have no more relish than he. That scholars for generations have not seen it should come as no surprise: the sin itself has bred our *caecitas mentis*.[66] For is not mental blindness the occupational hazard of our profession? Surely Dante hoped to jar his learned contemporaries into deep reflection by the outrageous implication that honorable persons of unblemished reputation were apparently homosexuals. Instead, his admirers took his teasing innuendo for the gospel truth: ironically, for the Gospel itself would have told them the truth of the matter. And we believed them because they were contemporary sources, or nearly so.

I accuse myself, for I am but describing the weakness of my own academic calling. To the benevolent reader, I must disclaim any special insight that led me to these discoveries. Rather, it has been, as I am sure the poet intended it to be, a thoroughly humiliating experience that brought into question every value by which I live. As a token of that humility, I may conclude at the point where I truly began—not twenty-odd years ago when I first found the canto of Brunetto Latini a mysterious disappointment, devoid of any anticipated sensationalism—but rather a night some ten years ago, when my wife sought to draw me from my study of the *Comedy* with this suggestive jibe: "Dante must have a place in Hell for scholars like you." I think I have found it.

Notes

For a list of abbreviations and special forms of reference, see above, pp. xv–xx.

CHAPTER 1

1. André Pézard is a distinguished exception: his Sorbonne dissertation, *Dante sous la pluie de feu (Enfer, chant xv)*, Etudes de philosophie médiévale, no. 40 (Paris, 1950), strives with ingenuity and erudition to reverse the verdict of sodomy, marshaling historical and philological evidence for 408 dense pages in support of the thesis that the sin was blasphemy. The crux of this interpretation is the alleged blasphemy of Brunetto, which consisted in his international glorification of French, to him a foreign language, at the expense of Italian, his God-given mother tongue (p. 95). Although the thesis itself has found little acceptance, the book remains a mine of insights and evidence, which have saved me much effort and spared my readers many notes as long as this one. My own views, however, were formed before reading the book. Pézard's approach differs from mine in that he does not seek a sin common to *all* the runners; rather, in his view, the nobles of *Inf.* xvi remain sodomites. For further criticism of Pézard, consult the reviews cited by E. Esposito, *Gli studi danteschi dal 1950 al 1964* (Rome, 1965), p. 251. Against these hostile critics, Pézard reaffirmed his thesis in *Cahiers du sud,* an. 38, no. 308 (1951), pp. 35–38. In contrast to the reactionary tone of most reviewers, L. Portier accepted the need for reinterpretation but suggested essential modifications in Pézard's approach: *Revue des études italiennes*, n.s. 1 (1954): 5–19. This perceptive discussion anticipated my own line of argument without pursuing it. Pézard in his book gives a conspectus of previous interpretations (pp. 29–57) and a copious bibliography, now updated by Esposito for *Inf.* xv at pp. 249–51.

2. F. Mazzoni typifies the consensus on *Inf.* xi, 46–51: "la chiara precisazione" of the passage places the sin of the runners beyond question: *Studi danteschi* 30 (1951): 278–84, esp. 282.

3. D. L. Sayers, trans., *The Comedy of Dante Alighieri the Florentine* (New York, 1963), 1:165; who further observes, "Their perpetual fruitless running forms a parallel, on a lower level, to the aimless drifting of the Lustful in Canto v."

4. *Inf.* xv, 106–8. The key word is *tutti*: it indicates that the three terms of the

description each apply to *all* members of the band without exception. Three statements can be made in consequence: (a) All in Brunetto's troop were clerks, broadly speaking. Pézard argues for this translation of *cherci* (p. 78 n.3) but on dubious grounds: *sages clercs* in his example I take to be ecclesiastics, in contrast to lay *philosophes* (Brunetto's *Tresor* 1. 1. 2). (b) All were also men of letters (*litterati*), or more precisely, of *Latin* letters, since little or no Latin made the *illiteratus,* even though he could both read and write in his vernacular: see H. Wieruszowski, "Brunetto Latini als Lehrer Dantes und der Florentiner," *Archivio italiano per la storia della pietà* 2 (1959): 171–98, at pp. 187–88. All were "litterati *grandi*" in the sense that each had risen to a position of prominence in a profession for which Latin was the basic requirement (notary, grammarian, lawyer, bishop). (c) None were *obscure* men; rather all were "of great fame." Since Brunetto had earlier used *fama* to signify an infamous reputation (*Inf.* xv, 67), his definition can properly include even Bishop Mozzi. For the early commentators on these lines, see Pézard, pp. 32–33. Cf. the variant "e litterati *tutti* e" (ed. Petrocchi, 2:255 in apparatus).

5. *Inf.* xv, 115–18 (Temple translation, rev.).

6. Biographical details and sources conveniently given by Toynbee-Singleton, s.vv. "Aldobrandi, Tegghiaio," "Borsiere, Guiglielmo," "Guido Guerra," and "Iacopo Rusticucci."

7. Pézard reviews the various explanations for the division into two bands and argues that it is not based on profession (p. 69 n.3; cf. p. 79) but on distinct crimes which have appropriate punishments (p. 296 n.5).

8. H. Oelsner, ed., *Inferno,* p. 167 at xv, 109.

9. Ernst R. Curtius, *European Literature and the Latin Middle Ages,* trans. W. R. Trask, Bollingen Series, no. 36 (London, 1953), p. 43 n.22. See below, n. 29, chap. 2.

10. J. Ciardi, trans., *Inferno* (New York, 1954), pp. 147–48; Pézard, p. 22, cf. pp. 17, 133–35, 203, for Brunetto, Priscian, Mozzi; Scartazzini-Vandelli[19] at xv, 22, xvi, 38, 40, 43, for Brunetto and the nobles.

11. A similar attempt to disquiet the reader has been discerned by D. J. Donno, "Dante's Argenti: Episode and Function," *Speculum* 40 (1965): 611–25, esp. 622–24. See also Pézard, pp. 23–24.

12. Dante's surprise at finding Brunetto among the supposed sodomites has puzzled the commentators, for either Dante the pilgrim did know that he was guilty and should not have been surprised, or else the poet did not know and therefore placed him there unjustly. The dilemma has been ingeniously evaded by supposing that Dante did not know in 1300, the ideal date of the poem, but discovered Brunetto's sin before the *Inferno* was written (1310–14): M. Scherillo, *Alcuni capitoli della biografia di Dante* (Turin, 1896), p. 136; quoted by Scartazzini-Vandelli[19] at *Inf.* xv, 30. See Pézard, chap. 2 and esp. p. 59 n.1.

13. After posing the riddle of the DXV, Beatrice added: "And perhaps my dark tale, like Themis and the Sphinx, persuades thee less because, in their fashion, it clouds thy mind" (*Purg.* xxxiii, 46–48). Then, when the pilgrim asked " 'but why do your longed-for words fly so far above my sight that the more it strives the more it loses them?' 'So that you mayst know,' she said, 'that school which thou hast followed and see if its teaching can follow my words and see your way to be as far from God's way as the heaven that spins highest is parted from the earth' " (*Purg.* xxxiii, 82–90, trans. Sinclair).

14. As he has Marco Lombardo exclaim: "Brother, the world is blind and indeed thou comest from it" (*Purg.* XVI, 65–66, trans. Sinclair).

15. Etienne Gilson, *Dante et la philosophie,* Etudes de philosophie médiévale, vol. 28 (Paris, 1939); published in English as *Dante the Philosopher,* trans. D. Moore (New York, 1949; facsimile reprint 1963 under the title *Dante and Philosophy*). Although the translation is cited here, the pagination approximates the original within two or three pages. The analysis of *Mon.* 3. 15 below should be read in the context of his full exposition of the *Convivio* and *Monarchia* (chaps. 2 and 3, pp. 83–224). While my reading of the passage follows Gilson closely, it seeks to avoid the controversial aspects of his interpretation, which are not essential to the present argument. See the review by B. Nardi, "Dante e la filosofia," *Studi danteschi* 24 (1940): 5–42, esp. § 3; cf. below, nn. 20, 21 of this chap.

16. *Mon.* 3. 15, ed. Ricci (1965). Useful commentary by G. Vinay, ed., *Monarchia* (Florence, 1950), pp. 279–89; expounded by Gilson, *Dante,* pp. 191–201; see also Edward Williamson, "De beatitudine huius vite," *Annual Report of the Dante Society* 76 (1958): 1–22.

17. Thus Gilson, *Dante,* p. 197, without textual authority for the term *virtutes naturales.*

18. Gilson, *Dante,* pp. 134–35, 144.

19. *Mon.* 3. 15. 9: "Has igitur conclusiones et media, licet ostensa sint nobis hec ab humana ratione que per phylosophos tota nobis innotuit, hec a Spiritu Sancto qui per prophetas et agiographos, qui per coecternum sibi Dei filium Iesum Cristum et per eius discipulos supernaturalem veritatem ac nobis necessariam revelavit, humana cupiditas postergaret nisi homines, tanquam equi, sua bestialitate vagantes 'in camo et freno' [Ps. 31:9] compescerentur in via."

20. On the relationship between the *imperiatus* and *papatus* in *Mon.* 3. 15, see M. Maccarrone, "Il terzo libro della *Monarchia,*" § 6, *Studi danteschi* 33 (1955): 112–42.

21. Gilson, *Dante,* pp. 142–51; quoted from p. 150. The essential dualism of the *Monarchia* is not endangered by attributing to philosophy an authority distinct from that of the emperor and pope, as Ernst Kantorowicz supposed: *The King's Two Bodies* (Princeton, 1957), pp. 460–62. Quite rightly he castigated Gilson (p. 190) for applying *Mon.* 3. 11. 9 ("non potest dici quod alterum subalternetur alteri") to the *optimus homo* as well as to pope and emperor. This minor slip does not, however, invalidate Gilson's exposition of the chapter (pp. 189–91), for the *optimus homo* is not an authority in the same sense that the emperor and pope are: the former rules man by virtue of the *substantia humanae naturae,* the latter pair by virtue of their respective *relationes dominationis et paternitatis.* Thus Kantorowicz's schematic representation of the relationship among the three authorities (n.31) is only a more graphic expression of the distinction between substance and relation in Gilson's *original* diagram (p. 190). The authority of philosophy is not exercised by an officer but by the *philosophica documenta* of *Mon.* 3. 15. 9–10. That their authority guides the emperor but is distinct from his own is certain from *Conv.* 4. 4–6, esp. 4. 6. 17 (cf. Busnelli-Vandelli, 2:68 n.10). Although the authority of philosophy is distinct from that of government, both serve the same natural end— the temporal happiness of mankind: "opus fuit homini ... Imperatore, qui secundum phylosophica documenta genus humanum ad temporalem felicitatem dirigeret" (*Mon.* 3. 15. 10). By thus coordinating the two authorities towards a single goal in

the natural order, the independence of each is assured without creating a third human goal by which the teleological dualism of the *Monarchia* would be impaired.

22. To Pézard's 1950 bibliography, add now that of E. Esposito, *Studi danteschi dal 1950 al 1964*, pp. 251–55.

23. The opposition of the two pairs of virtues and vices was remarked by Scartazzini-Vandelli[6] (1911) at *Inf.* xvi, 74. *Cortesia e valor* were the two ennobling virtues proper to the knight. Writing of *cortesia* in *Conv.* 2. 10. 8, Dante declared that this virtue is no longer characteristic of the courtly society after which it was named: "ne le corti anticamente le vertudi e li belli costumi s'usavano, sì come oggi s'usa lo contrario...." The interrelated decline of Florence, her nobles, and their virtues as a recurrent Dantesque concept can be traced conveniently in the apparatus of *La Divina Commedia*, ed. N. Sapegno, in *La letteratura italiana, Storia e testi*, vol. 4 (Milan-Naples, [1957]), starting at *Inf.* xvi, 67–69, 74. Note especially the identification of knightly virtues at *Purg.* xvi, 115.

24. F. Schevill, *History of Florence* (New York, 1936; facsimile reprints in 1961 and 1963 under the title *Medieval and Renaissance Florence*), pp. 128–32. Two of the trio—Guido Guerra and Tegghiaio Aldobrandi degli Adimari—play leading roles in G. Villani's account of the deliberations preceding the battle: *Cronica* 6.77; see 78–81 for the engagement and its aftermath.

25. On the Guelf restoration of Easter 1267, see Schevill, *History of Florence*, pp. 138–39, 144; G. Villani, *Cronica* 7. 13–15.

26. They were particularly apt to represent the spirit of partisan strife *within* Florence, because in no other regard were any of them notably men of strife and contention. Guido, though a man of war, was the most notable supporter of Tegghiaio's peace policy on the eve of the Montaperti disaster in 1260 (G. Villani, *Cronica* 6. 77). Tegghiaio and Rusticucci have been described as "campioni di pace" for their joint efforts as peacemakers in 1237 between Volterra and San Gimignano; and indeed both appear to have been moderate partisans before their exile in 1260: see P. Santini, "Sui fiorentini 'che fur sì degni,'" *Studi danteschi* 6 (1923): 25–44, at pp. 31–40.

27. C. W. Previté-Orton, *A History of Europe from 1198 to 1378*, 3d ed. (London, 1951), p. 100. Schevill, *Florence*, pp. 157–60; G. Villani, *Cronica* 7. 131–32, 8. 1, linking Campaldino to the Ordinances; C. C. Bayley, *War and Society in Renaissance Florence* (Toronto, 1961), pp. 3–4.

28. Rusticucci complained that his proud wife was the principal cause of his damnation: "e certo / la fiera moglie più ch'altro mi nuoce" (*Inf.* xvi, 44–45). The trecento commentators, having assumed that Rusticucci was a sodomite, conjectured variously how a wife who was *fiera* might have driven him to such a vice. Some took her to be a person of changeable and displeasing disposition: "diversa e malvagia moglie" (Lana); "diversa e spiacevole tanto" (Anonimo Fiorentino). Others supposed her to have had a violent temper: "ferocissima mulier" (Pietro di Dante); "mulierem ferocem" (Benvenuto). Boccaccio reported that others said she was a frivolous woman who took up every new fashion: "una donna tanto ritrosa e tanto perversa, e di sí nuovi costumi e maniere, come assai spesso ne veggiamo, che in alcuno atto con lei non si poteva né stare né vivere...." All that the commentators can agree on is that Rusticucci found her company unbearable and hence turned to sodomy. That these comments represent nothing more than speculation is suggested by the divergent line adopted in the *Ottimo* by Lancia, who took the wife to be a metaphor

for Rusticucci's perversion, an interpretation also advanced by the Pseudo-Boccaccio. Obviously one cannot expound the verse until it is first determined whether Rusticucci was or was not married. And if married, did his wife have a noble family origin of which to be proud? Or if a commoner, was she a social climber? or affected, as Boccaccio might suggest, to the new, ignoble element within the Guelf party? Or again, if Rusticucci proved to have had no wife, one might pursue Lancia's line of reasoning and understand Jacopo as one who was "married to his party." In any case, the character of Rusticucci's wife could have made him an ardent Guelf as readily as a sodomite, if not more so. But it would be idle to elaborate, as the commentators appear to have done, without more substantial information. Of Rusticucci's domestic affairs, it is recorded that the house in which he lived was owned, and perhaps occupied, jointly by his nephews; it was destroyed by vindictive Ghibellines during his exile (Santini, "Sui fiorentini," p. 32 n.1).

29. The foregoing is not objective history but an *expositio ad mentem Dantis*. For a perceptive analysis of Dante's civic milieu, see M. B. Becker, "Dante and His Literary Contemporaries as Political Men," *Speculum* 41 (1966): 665–80, and "A Study in Political Failure: The Florentine Magnates, 1280–1343," *Mediaeval Studies* 27 (1965): 246–308.

30. Sapegno and Scartazzini-Vandelli[19], both at *Inf.* xv, 55; Pézard, pp. 126–27; and H. Wieruszowski, "Brunetto Latini," pp. 173, 185.

31. Helene Wieruszowski argues persuasively (pp. 186–89) from the evidence of Brunetto's *Sommetta*, a small collection of Italian epistolary forms which she has identified and edited (pp. 193–98), that he lectured publicly at Florence on rhetoric and politics. This removes the traditional objection to a literal interpretation of Dante's indications (*Inf.* xv, 84–85, 97) that Brunetto was his teacher, which can now be understood to refer either to public lectures or to private tuition (pp. 172–73). Charles T. Davis has argued that the relationship was informal but the influence nonetheless profound: "Brunetto Latini and Dante," *Studi medievali*, 3d ser., vol. 8, no. 1 (1967), pp. 421 50, esp. pp. 441 ff. Pézard lists Brunetto's older biographers; most recent is Bianca Ceva, *Brunetto Latini: L'uomo e l'opera* (Milan-Naples, 1965).

32. Sapegno, at *Inf.* xv, 85.

33. Brunetto Latini, *Li livres dou tresor*, ed. F. J. Carmody, University of California Publications in Modern Philology, vol. 22 (Berkeley, 1948).

34. *Tresor*, ed. Carmody, pp. xxii–xxxii.

35. Or in his decision to write in French, for him an alien vernacular, as Pézard maintains: p. 94; elaborated in two chapters on "La question de la langue," pp. 92–130.

36. Cf. Pézard, App. 1 "Rhetor, rector, dictator," pp. 329–31.

37. *Tresor* 3. 73. 6, ed. Carmody, p. 392: "l'autre est en Ytaile, que li citain et li borgois et li communité des viles eslisent lor poesté et lor signour tel comme il quident qu'il soit plus proufitables au commun preu de la vile et de tous lor subtés." Cf. Ceva, *Brunetto Latini*, pp. 155–56.

38. Thus Carmody, ed., *Tresor*, pp. xxxi–xxxii. Ceva, after an extended analysis (pp. 161–83) of the three comparable manuals extant, reluctantly agrees (p. 185). On the office of podesta, see Schevill, *Florence*, p. 91, and monographs cited by Ceva.

39. *Cronica* 8. 10: "Nel detto anno 1294 morì in Firenze uno valente cittadino il quale ebbe nome ser Brunetto Latini, il quale fu gran filosofo, e fu sommo maestro in rettorica, tanto in bene sapere dire come in bene dittare. E fu quegli che

spuose la Rettorica di Tullio, e fece il buono e utile libro detto Tesoro, e il Tesoretto, e la chiave del Tesoro, e più altri libri in filosofia, e de' vizi e di virtù, e fu dittatore del nostro comune. Fu mondano uomo, ma di lui avemo fatta menzione, perocch'egli fu cominciatore e maestro in digrossare i Fiorentini, e farli scorti in bene parlare, e in sapere guidare e reggere la nostra repubblica secondo la politica." Text in *Cronica di Giovanni Villani*, ed. F. G. Dragomanni, Collezione di storici e cronisti italiani editi ed inediti, vols. 1–4 (Florence, 1844–45), 2:17; my trans. Earlier Villani describes him as "ser Brunetto Latini, uomo di grande senno e authoritade" (6. 73) and lists him among the Guelf exiles of 1260 (6. 79).

40. Davis, "Brunetto Latini," pp. 421–50, esp. pp. 424–31.

41. Ibid., p. 427.

42. Ibid., pp. 428–29.

43. Ibid., pp. 424–29.

44. Toynbee-Singleton, s.v. "Cicero," for references.

45. Davis, "Brunetto Latini," pp. 444–45, 449–50.

46. Ibid., p. 449: "Dante seems to have conceived his own function in terms of a wider application of the activities of virtuous rhetoricians like Cicero and Brunetto."

47. Brunetto Latini, *Rettorica*, ed. F. Maggini (Florence, 1915), p. 8; trans. Davis, "Brunetto Latini," pp. 427–28: "And there (in the *De Inventione*) where he (Cicero) says ... 'our commune,' I read 'Rome,' since Tully was a citizen of Rome.... Perhaps he calls her 'our commune' because Rome is the head of the world and the commune of everyone." Davis himself interprets Brunetto's loyalty to Rome in terms of culture rather than of politics: Brunetto's "patriotism was one of the strongest influences on his life. He attempted to place it in the context of the cultural heritage of Rome, which he called 'the commune of everyone'" (p. 434).

48. Quoted by A. Passerin d'Entrèves, *Dante as a Political Thinker* (Oxford, 1952), p. 22, with this note (p. 104): "The draft of the Florentine protest against the demand of an oath of fealty to Rudolph of Habsburg can be read in Kern, *Acta Imperii, Angliae et Franciae, ab A. 1267 ad A. 1312* (Tübingen, 1911), p. 12, no. 21 *a*. The words I have quoted should be compared to the answer given to the summons of Henry VII, as quoted by Compagni (*Cron. Fior.*, III): 'fu loro risposto per parte della Signoria da messer Betto Brunelleschi, che mai per niuno signore i Fiorentini inchinarono le corna.'" On the circumstances in 1281, see R. Davidsohn, *Storia di Firenze* (Florence, 1957), 3:261–62, under the rubric "Le richieste del cancelliere aulico" (by which it can be readily identified in the original *Geschichte*, bk. 2, pt. 2, chap. 9). The incident is reported by G. Villani, *Cronica* 7. 78.

49. "Certainly he was the leading *dittatore*, or rhetorician, of his commune...." Thus Davis ("Brunetto Latini," p. 432) concludes his summary of Brunetto's official career (1254–94), based on D. Marzi, *La cancelleria della repubblica fiorentina* (Rocca San Casciano, 1910), pp. 43, 56–57; to which add pp. 16–18 (from 1273 Brunetto Latini was entitled "notary and scribe of the council of the commune") and pp. 35–47, on Latini as "Cancelliere Dettatore" or "Dettatore e Cancelliere," where it is concluded that Villani called him chancellor only by analogy because such was his function. Indeed, Villani applied *dittatore* only to Brunetto Latini and to Pier della Vigna ("il buono Dittatore," *Cronica* 6. 22), from which Marzi infers that the chronicler reserved the term for the head of a staff of notaries, a quasi chancellor distinguished by his own skill in the *ars dictaminis* (p. 22). Dante

juxtaposed the two men in adjacent *gironi,* perhaps to suggest that Brunetto's sin, like Vigna's, was a consequence of his professional career. Cf. Davis, "Brunetto Latini," p. 433.

50. Davis feels "that no certain product of his activity as a *dittatore* has been preserved" (p. 433). That depends on the order of certainty one requires. Davidsohn and Maggini inferred that Brunetto had composed Florence's official apologia for her execution of the Ghibelline abbot of Vallombrosa (ibid., n.50). Who *else* would have drafted so important a document?

51. *Ep.* v, 20, trans. Toynbee (*Ep.* v, 7), p. 61: "nolite, velut ignari, decipere vosmetipsos [Jer. 37:8], tanquam somniantes, in cordibus et dicentes: 'Dominum non habemus' [1 Kings 22:17; Ps. 13:1, 52:1]."

52. *Ep.* vi, 6–8, trans. Toynbee (*Ep.* vi, 2), pp. 77–78: "An ignoratis, amentes et discoli [1 Peter 2:18], publica iura cum sola temporis terminatione finiri, et nullius prescriptionis calculo fore obnoxia? Nempe legum sanctiones alme declarant, et humana ratio percontando decernit, publica rerum dominia, quantalibet diuturnitate neglecta, nunquam posse vanescere vel abstenuata conquiri; nam quod ad omnium cedit utilitatem, sine omnium detrimento interire non potest, vel etiam infirmari; et hoc Deus et natura non vult, et mortalium penitus abhorreret adsensus. Quid, fatua tali oppinione summota, tanquam alteri Babilonii [Gen. 11:4], pium deserentes imperium nova regna temptatis, ut alia sit Florentina civilitas, alia sit Romana?"

53. See above, especially chap. 7, where Brunetto's shortcomings as a philosopher shall become more apparent.

CHAPTER 2

1. To the Florentines he wrote: "Does the dread of the second death not haunt you, seeing that you first and you alone, shrinking from the yoke of liberty, have murmured against the glory of the Roman Emperor, the king of the earth, and minister of God; and under cover of prescriptive right, refusing the duty of submission due to him, have chosen rather to rise up in the madness of rebellion?" *Ep.* vi, 5, trans. Toynbee (*Ep.* vi, 2), p. 77; cf. p. 68. See above, chap. 1, at n. 52.

2. *Epistola ad Canem Grandem* xiii, 33 (ed. Toynbee, x, 11): "status animarum post mortem."

3. The foundations for the present essay were laid by A. Pézard, not only by his study of Priscian and other grammarians appearing in the *Commedia* (pp. 133–72), but also by his brilliant discussion of "La question de la langue" (pp. 92–130), much of which can be applied to my Priscian no less than to his Brunetto.

4. *Inf.* xv, 109. See above, chap. 1, at nn. 8–9.

5. See above, n. 4, chap. 1.

6. One early commentator identified the city and status of all the characters in the Canto except Priscian, whose name he evidently took to be self-explanatory: *Chiose alla cantica dell' Inferno di Dante Alighieri scritte da Jacopo Alighieri,* ed. Jarro [G. Piccini] (Florence, 1915), p. 95. The specification that "tutti fur ... di gran fama" (*Inf.* xv, 106–7) disqualifies the obscure "magister Prisianus" (*sic*) whom Bolognese documents entitled "doctor gramatice" in 1291 and "repetitor gramatice" in 1294: see F. Filipini, "Il grammatico Prisciano nell'Inferno dantesco," *Archiginnasio: Bullettino della Biblioteca communale di Bologna* 12 (1917): 23–31; and

review by A. Aruch in *Bullettino della Società dantesca italiana*, n.s. 24 (1917): 184–85.

7. Alain de Lille, *Anticlaudianus* 2. 8. 16–18: "nomenque sibi speciale meretur, / Ut [Donatus] non grammaticus dicatur: at emphasis ipsam / Grammaticam vocat hunc, signans sub nomine numen" (ed. Migne, *PL*, 210:508). Thus Matthew Paris praises the learning of Johannes de Cella, abbot of St. Albans, 1195–1214, who "cum virilis esset aetatis, in Grammatica Priscianus, in Metrico Ovidius, in Physica censeri potuit Galenus." *Gesta abbatum*, in *Chronica monasterii s. Albani*, ed. H. T. Riley, Rolls Series, no. 28, vol. 4, pt. 1 (1867), p. 217. Cf. Pézard, p. 135.

8. For Priscian's life, reputation, and Dantology, see Pézard, pp. 133–37. A convenient notice printing the early commentators: Toynbee-Singleton, s.v. "Prisciano." The best biography is now R. Helm's article "Priscianus," in *Pauly's Realencyclopädie der classischen Altertumswissenschaft*, vol. 22, pt. 2 (Stuttgart, 1954), cols. 2328–46.

9. On Donatus, see Pézard, pp. 164–69; Toynbee-Singleton, s.v. "Donato"; and now G. Brugnoli, in *Enciclopedia dantesca*, vol. 2 (Rome, 1970), s.v. "Donato." Grammatical studies in the age of Donatus are aptly characterized by H. I. Marrou, *Saint Augustin et la fin de la culture antique*, BEFAR[1], no. 145 (Paris, 1938), pp. 11–15.

10. *Par.* xii, 137–38. As the basis for all further learning, grammar was the first of the seven liberal arts. This traditional primacy was maintained by Dante in *Conv.* 2. 13. 10.

11. "*Dottori*" was Scartazzini's preferred term, which Vandelli discarded for "*Sapienti*": cf. the heading to *Par.* x–xiv in Scartazzini-Vandelli[5] (1907), and in Scartazzini-Vandelli[19] (1965).

12. By Aquinas and Bonaventure: *Par.* xi, 43–139, xii, 46–126. See E. Gilson, *Dante and Philosophy* (New York, 1963; see above, n. 15, chap. 1), pp. 242–53.

13. Aquinas is cited for this interpretation of the two angelic orders by Scartazzini-Vandelli[19] at *Par.* xi, 37–39: "Seraphim interpretatur ardentes ... et sic patet quod ... Seraphim denominetur ab ardore charitatis. .... Cherubin interpretatur plenitudo scientiae ... et sic patet quod Cherubin denominetur a scientia" (*S.T.* I q.63 a.7).

14. Donatus and Priscian are paired as typical grammarians by Isidore: "De incongruitate vero grammaticae locutionis, quae in Veteri Testamento reputatur, vel Novo, respondemus, verba coelestis oraculi non subiacent Prisciani regulis, vel Donati, et quamvis sit analogia scienda, usus prae omnibus aemulandus est": *Ep.* vii, 9, ed. Migne, *PL*, 83:907; cited by Pézard, p. 157.

15. *Prisciani grammatici Caesariensis Institutionum grammaticarum libri XVIII*, ed. M. Hertz, in *Grammatici latini*, ed. H. Keil, vol. 2 (Leipzig, 1855), pp. 1–597; vol. 3 (1859), pp. 1–105, 106–377.

16. *Donati de partibus orationis Ars minor* and *Donati grammatici urbis Romae Ars grammatica*, ed. H. Keil, in his *Grammatici latini*, vol. 4 (1864), pp. 355–66, 367–402.

17. C. E. Bennett, *New Latin Grammar*, 3d ed. (Boston, 1918), p. iv: from the preface to the 1st ed. (1894).

18. Bks. 17–18. Pézard, pp. 136 n, 138 n.

19. *Historische Grammatik der lateinischen Sprache*, ed. G. Landgraf (Leipzig, 1894–1903). Though incomplete, it covers in 958 pages the subjects treated by Priscian in 974 pages. The Leumann-Hofmann *Lateinische Grammatik*, Müller's Handbuch

der Altertumswissenschaft (Munich, 1928; vol. 1, reprinted 1963; vol. 2, revised by Szantyr, 1965), is somewhat longer (1,186 pages of text).

20. On Dante's theory of language, see A. Marigo, ed., *De vulgari eloquentia*, 3d ed. (Florence, 1957), pp. lvi–xcix, with appendix reporting later studies, 1938–54 (pp. 359–76). Succinct and suggestive is Grayson's essay, "'*Nobilior est vulgaris*': Latin and Vernacular in Dante's Thought," in *Centenary Essays on Dante by Members of the Oxford Dante Society* (Oxford, 1965), pp. 54–76.

21. *De vulg. eloq.* 1. 1. 2–3 (trans. Temple Classics): "vulgarem locutionem asserimus, quam sine omni regula nutricem imitantes accipimus. Est et inde alia locutio secundaria nobis, quam Romani gramaticam vocaverunt ... ad habitum vero huius pauci perveniunt, quia non nisi per spatium temporis et studii assiduitatem regulamur et doctrinamur in illa."

22. *De vulg. eloq.* 1. 9. 10–11 (trans. Temple Classics): "Si ergo per eandem gentem sermo variatur, ut dictum est, successive per tempora, nec stare ullo modo potest, necesse est ut disiunctim abmotimque morantibus varie varietur, ceu varie variantur mores et habitus, qui nec natura nec consortio confirmantur, sed humanis beneplacitis localique congruitate nascuntur. [11] Hinc moti sunt inventores gramatice facultatis; que quidem gramatica nichil aliud est quam quedam inalterabilis locutionis idemptitas diversis temporibus atque locis. Hec cum de comuni consensu multarum gentium fuerit regulata, nulli singulari arbitrio videtur obnoxia, et per consequens nec variabilis esse potest. Adinvenerunt ergo illam, ne propter variationem sermonis arbitrio singularium fluitantis, vel nullo modo vel saltim imperfecte antiquorum actingeremus autoritates et gesta, sive illorum quos a nobis locorum diversitas facit esse diversos."

23. The *auctoritates* for Dante presumably include not only theological and philosophical writers but also poets. See *De vulg. eloq.*, ed. Marigo, p. 73 n.63b, at 1. 9. 11; see also 2. 10. 5.

24. Classical grammarians gave little guidance on mood and tense, which were learned by imitating model authors: see *De vulg. eloq.*, ed. Marigo, p. 310; cf. pp. 301–2.

25. For Pézard, Grecophilia is both the root of Priscian's preciosity and the essence of his perversity, which has political as well as philological manifestations (pp. 138–50). To me this seems only incidental, since a dysfunctional grammar can be elaborated without reference to foreign models, as was Greek grammar itself. Priscian indisputably was influenced by the Greeks, and this may well have heightened Dante's distaste for him, since Grecophobia was common enough in the medieval Latin West, but *Graecismus* constitutes no more than the occasion of his sin, which could have been committed against grammar in quite other ways.

26. *Conv.* 1. 9. 2–3 (trans. Jackson): "tanto sono pronti ad avarizia, che da ogni nobilitade d'animo li rimuove, la quale massimamente desidera questo cibo. E a vituperio di loro dico che non si deono chiamare litterati, però che non acquistano la lettera per lo suo uso, ma in quanto per quella guadagnano denari o dignitate; sì come non si dee chiamare citarista chi tiene la cetera in casa per prestarla per prezzo, e non per usarla per sonare." Dante's view of the role of grammar might well be elucidated by Aquinas' discussion of the *artes operativae*, cited at this passage by Busnelli-Vandelli, 1:57, at 1. 9. 3. For analogous reproaches to other professions see *Conv.* 3. 11. 10 and 4. 27. 8 (legists, physicians, most religious).

27. In Keil, *Grammatici latini*, 2:1–2: Ep. ad Iulianum 1–4. For a literal yet readable

[317]

translation, I am indebted to the kindness and skill ot Prof. David F. Heimann, University of Colorado. Pézard translated only part of the passage "en simplifiant son style, dont les périodes sentent parfois trop le rhéteur" (pp. 137–38).

28. See the Index Scriptorum in Keil, *Grammatici latini*, 3:529 ff., s.vv. "Apollonius," "Aristarchus," "artium auctores," "Caper," "Didymus," "Donatus," "grammatici," "Herodianus," "Probus," "*Rhetor*," "Seruius," "Victor," etc.

29. In Keil, *Grammatici latini*, 2:2–3 (Ep., § 4): "tibi ergo hoc opus devoveo, omnis eloquentiae praesul, ut quantamcumque mihi deus annuerit suscepti laboris gloriam, te comite quasi sole quodam dilucidius crescat." This expression of pride was considered to be Priscian's tragic flaw long before Dante. It provided Alain de Lille (d. 1202) with the motive for Priscian's supposed apostasy (*Anticlaudianus* 2. 8. 28–30, ed. Migne, *PL*, 210:508). Alain explicitly recognized the greatness of the *Institutes* (ibid., lines 31–33) but deplored its turgid style and lengthy digressions (ibid., lines 24–27). Such, at least, is my understanding of his obscure remarks: see E. R. Curtius, *European Literature and the Latin Middle Ages,* trans. W. R. Trask, Bollingen Series, no. 36 (London, 1953), p. 43 n, and Pézard, pp. 134, 137, 165. Although Alain de Lille, like Dante, preferred Donatus above Priscian (*Anticlaudianus* 2. 8. 12–18; cf. above, n. 7 of this chap.), the contrast must have been commonly observed; hence no direct influence can be inferred. The lexicographer Huguccio of Pisa stated that Priscian followed his patron Julian into apostasy ("legamus eum fuisse sacerdotem, sed amore Iuliani postea apostatasse"), and G. Schizzerotto has recently proposed that Dante misunderstood him to mean *amore carnale*: "Uguccione da Pisa, Dante e la colpa di Prisciano," *Studi danteschi* 43 (1966): 79–83.

30. This attitude seems justified by Cecil Grayson's success in reconciling most of Dante's thought on these matters in his essay " '*Nobilior est vulgaris,*' " pp. 54–76. The one passage that he accounted irreconcilable (*Conv.* 1. 5. 7–10) might be integrated with the others by the line of argument suggested below in n. 44 of this chap.

31. Horace *De arte poetica* 70–72: "multa renascentur quae iam cecidere, cadentque / quae nunc sunt in honore vocabula, si volet usus, / quem penes arbitrium est et ius et norma loquendi."

32. *Conv.* 2. 13. 9–10 (trans. Jackson, p. 107) and commentary by Busnelli-Vandelli, 1:194–96.

33. Busnelli-Vandelli, 1:194–95 n.7, quoting Averroës.

34. Sinclair's translation.—*Nota bene*: Dante likened the sin of Brunetto Latini to the building of Babel: see above, n. 52, chap. 1; cf. *Ep.*, ed. Toynbee, p. 68 n.8: "By *Babylonii* here Dante evidently means the builders of the Tower of Babel; cf. *Gen.* xi.4: 'Venite, faciamus nobis civitatem et turrim....'" The association has significant Biblical roots, for Dante reckoned the Fall, the Flood, and the Confusion of Tongues to be the results of mankind's first three rebellions against God (*De vulg. eloq.* 1. 7. 1–4), to which series Genesis next adds the destruction of Sodom (see above, chap. 8).

35. *De vulg. eloq.* 1. 3 argues that speech is a necessary consequence of human nature: as man is rational, he requires a means of communicating concepts; as he is corporeal, the concepts must be communicated in a sensible medium. Cf. *Conv.* 3. 7. 8.

36. *De vulg. eloq.* 1. 5. 1: "Opinantes . . . rationabiliter dicimus ipsum loquentem primum, mox postquam afflatus est ab animante Virtute, incunctanter fuisse locutum."

37. The argument is stated more explicitly in *De vulg. eloq.* 1. 9. 6 and is explained help-fully by Marigo's commentary (pp. 67–69). In that passage, Dante made an exception for Hebrew because he was then of the opinion that it was the original and natural language of man, which had been corrupted and lost through sin at the Babelic Confusion of Tongues. But in *Par.* xxvi, 124–38, he simplified his theory by discarding the idea of an unalterable and natural primeval language. Instead, *all* human speech is subject to change, including the Adamic tongue, which is no longer identified with Hebrew. See also P. Damon, "Adam on the Primal Language: 'Paradiso' 26.124," *Italica* 38 (1961): 60–62.

38. The influence of the heavens on human minds was acknowledged in *Conv.* 4. 2. 6–10, but was not there related to linguistic change.

39. Sinclair's translation. Cf. Horace *De arte poetica* 60–62: "ut silvae foliis pronos mutantur in annos, / prima cadunt; ita verborum vetus interit aetas, / et iuvenum ritu florent modo nata vigentque." The passage in which Horace justified the coinage of new words (lines 46–72) was evidently for Dante the *locus classicus* that supported his own view, for he alleged it explicitly in *Conv.* 2. 13. 10 (see above, nn. 31, 32 of this chap.) and echoes it here in the same connection.

40. *De vulg. eloq.* 1. 9. 11. Cf. *Conv.* 1. 5. 7: "lo latino è perpetuo e non corruttibile, e lo volgare è non stabile e corruttibile."

41. *De vulg. eloq.* 1. 10. 1: "gramatice positores inveniuntur accepisse *sic* adverbium affirmandi. . . ." Marigo, ed., *De vulg. eloq.*, p. 75, draws the analogy to the *ponitori* of the *Convivio.*

42. *Conv.* 1. 8. 4 (trans. Jackson): "E ancora: dare a molti è impossibile sanza dare a uno, acciò che uno in molti sia inchiuso, ma dare a uno si può bene, sanza dare a molti. Però chi giova a molti fa l'uno bene e l'altro; chi giova a uno, fa pur un bene; onde vedemo li ponitori de le leggi massimamente pur a li più comuni beni tenere confissi li occhi, quelle componendo." Busnelli-Vandelli, 1:48 n.8, illustrates the passage with citations to civil law, Aquinas, and *Mon.* 1. 14. 5, 2. 5. 2.

43. Thus Marigo, who sees a distinction between *inventores* and *positores,* ed. *De vulg. eloq.*, pp. 72–75.

44. Such would seem to be the suggestion of *De vulg. eloq.* 2. 1. 1: "prosaycantes ab avientibus [= poetis] magis accipiunt, et quia quod avietum est prosaycantibus permanere videtur exemplar, et non e converso (que quendam videntur prebere primatum)." If this were true, then it might be argued that by providing Italian with model works of poetry and prose, Dante the artist was consciously working to stabilize and standardize a vernacular which before his time had been "fashioned at pleasure" (*Conv.* 1. 5. 8): "volgare, lo quale a piacimento artificiato si transmuta"). *De vulg. eloq.* 2 was certainly intended to place the writing of canzoni beyond the "pleasure" of incapable poets (e.g., 2. 1. 4, 2. 4. 4).

45. The foundation for such a study is laid by Marigo's appendix "La Latinità del Trattato" and glossary (pp. 299–335).

CHAPTER 3

1. Petrocchi's new text places the semicolon after *anche* in the last line; I have accord-ingly altered Sinclair's translation. On the punctuation of verse 110, see Petrocchi's edition (2:255).

2. See above, n. 4, chap. 1.

3. *Inf.* xv, 110–14. We shall return to Brunetto's scorn for Mozzi in chap. 4, above.

4. St. Accursius, a disciple of St. Francis' who was martyred in Morocco in 1220, attests its use as a personal name: *Lexikon für Theologie und Kirche*, 2d ed., vol. 1 (1957), p. 105, s.v. "Accursius, St."

5. *Dizionario biografico degli italiani* (hereafter cited as *Diz. biog. ital.*), vol. 1 (Rome, 1960), pp. 116–21, s.v. "Accorso." Most recently the Glossator has been confused with his son by the *Enciclopedia cattolica* (1949) and the *New Catholic Encyclopedia* (1967). Other postwar reference works are listed by P. Fiorelli, "Minima de Accursiis," *Annali di storia del diritto* 2 (1958): 345–59, at p. 357 n.79.

6. Fascimile in M. Sarti and M. Fattorini, *De claris archigymnasii Bononiensis professoribus,* 2d ed. by C. Albicini and C. Malagola (Bologna, 1888–96), 1:160.

7. Pézard, pp. 174–75. Fiorelli, "Minima," traces the false date (p. 350 n.22) and rejects Pézard's interpretation (p. 358 n.80) with the approval of F. Mazzoni in *Studi danteschi* 38 (1961): 359.

8. F. Fiorelli, "Accorso da Reggio," *Diz. biog. ital.*, 1:121–22.

9. Sarti, *De claris,* 1:199. Filippo Villani (fl. 1364–1404) dates his death 1309: *Liber de civitatis Florentiae famosis civibus,* ed. G. C. Galletti (Florence, 1847), p. 23; F. Villani, *Le vite d'uomini illustri fiorentini,* trans. and ed. G. Mazzuchelli, Collezione di storici e cronisti italiani editi ed inediti, vol. 7 (Florence, 1847), p. 25. Mazzuchelli demonstrates the impossibility of this (n. 80, pp. 93–94); cf. his *Scrittori d'Italia,* vol. 1, pt. 1 (Brescia, 1753), p. 90 n.10.

10. *Comedia di Dante degli Allagherii col commento di Jacopo della Lana bolognese,* ed. L. Scarabelli, 2d ed. (Bologna, 1866–67), 1:285, at *Inf.* xv, 110.

11. "Accursius excellentissimus legum doctor fuit natione florentinus.... Ipse ... glossavit leges.... Franciscus filius Accursii primogenitus fuit etiam famosissimus doctor legum...." *Benevenuti de Rambaldis de Imola comentum super Dantis Aldigherij Comoediam,* ed. J. P. Lacaita, vol. 1 (Florence, 1887), pp. 522–23. On his Bolognese career, see L. Paoletti, "Benvenuto da Imola," *Diz. biog. ital.,* vol. 8 (Rome, 1966), pp. 691–94.

12. Unless otherwise stated, my account is based on Sarti, *De claris,* 1:193–203, which in turn supplied most of the materials for the notice by F. C. von Savigny, *Geschichte des römischen Rechts im Mittelalter,* 2d ed., vol. 5 (Heidelberg, 1850), pp. 306–22. Other general accounts, such as that of Mazzuchelli (above, n. 9 of this chap.) add little save confusion. Works treating special aspects of Francis' career will be cited in their place.

13. See below, n. 21 of this chap.

14. Fiorelli, *Diz. biog. ital.,* 1:120.

15. Sarti, *De claris,* 1:159; G. Gozzadini, "Il palazzo detto di Accursio," *Atti e memorie della R. Deputazione di storia patria per le provincie di Romagna,* 3d ser. 1 (1883): 425–50, at p. 429.

16. Fiorelli, *Diz. biog. Ital.,* 1:118: "che costituisce la più importante raccolta privata di libri giuridici che si conosca per il Medioevo." See H. U. Kantorowicz, "Accursio e la sua biblioteca," *Rivista di storia del diritto italiano* 2 (1929): 35–62, 193–212: his critics are summarized and reinforced by Fiorelli, "Minima," pp. 350 ff.; cf. *Diz. biog. Ital.,* 1:117–20.

17. Gozzadini, "Palazzo," p. 435 n.3. The Glossator's second wife was also named Aichina (*Diz. biog. Ital.*, 1:117), which may indicate an alliance with the same clan.

18. E. Martène and U. Durand, eds., *Veterum scriptorum et monumentorum historicorum, dogmaticorum, moralium amplissima collectio*, vol. 2 (Paris, 1724), col. 1173. Cf. Sarti, *De claris*, 1:163.

19. Gozzadini, "Palazzo," pp. 430–32.

20. Sarti, *De claris*, 2:88; cf. below, nn. 93, 94, of this chap.

21. "Francesco d'Accorso fu giudice in legge valentissimo, e chiosò tutt' i libri di legge, e fu bolognese...." *Chiose anonime alla prima cantica della Divina Commedia di un contemporaneo del poeta*, ed. F. Selmi (Turin, 1865), p. 88.

22. Sarti, *De claris*, 1:202 n. 1, quoted below, n. 114 of this chap.

23. Révigny taught at Orléans, and Meijers apparently assumes that the incident took place there (3:94; cf. p. 84), which is the more likely because Toulouse only became a center of legal studies after 1280: E. M. Meijers, *Etudes d'histoire du droit*, ed. R. Feenstra and H. F. W. D. Fischer, vol. 3 (Leiden, 1959), pp. 174, 182.

24. *Cinus in Codicem et aliquot titulos primi Pandectorum tomi* (Frankfurt, 1578), fol. 460^{rv}; Bartolus, *Commentaria in Codicem* (Lyons, 1552), fol. 85^v. Both quoted with secondary references by G. L. Haskins, "Three English Documents Relating to Francis Accursius," *Law Quarterly Review* 54 (1938): 87–94, at p. 88 nn. 10, 11. On his opponent, see now Meijers, *Etudes*, 3:59–80, and above, n. 23 of this chap.

25. Savigny, *Geschichte des römischen Rechts*, 5:316–22.

26. Sarti, *De claris*, 1:202 nn.5, 6.

27. *Le novelle antiche*, ed. G. Biagi (Florence, 1880), no. 81, pp. 84–85; quoted here from *Novellino e conti del duecento*, ed. S. Lo Nigro (Turin, 1963), no. 50, pp. 132–33 (on the date, see p. 9 n.1). "Maestro Francesco, figliuolo del maestro Accorso de la città di Bologna, quando ritornò d'Inghilterra, dove era stato longamente, fece una così fatta proposta dinanzi al Comune di Bologna, e disse:—Un padre d'una famiglia si partìo di suo paese per povertade, e lasciò i suoi figliuoli e andonne in lontana provincia. Stando un tempo, ed elli vide uomini di sua terra. L'amore de' figliuoli lo strinse a domandare di loro. E quelli rispuosero: 'Messere, vostri figliuoli hanno guadagnato, e sono molto ricchi.' Allora udendo così, propuosesi di ritornare. Tornò in sua terra; trovò li figliuoli ricchi. Adomandoe a' suoi figliuoli che 'l rimettessero in su le possessioni, sì come padre e signore. I figliuoli negaro, dicendo così: 'Padre, noi il ci avemo guadagnato, non ci hai che fare': sì che ne nacque piato. Onde la legge volle che 'l padre fosse al postutto signore di ciò ch'aveano guadagnato i figiuoli. E così adomando io al Comune di Bologna che le possessioni de' miei figliuoli siano a mia signoria: cioè de' miei scolari, li quali sono gran maestri divenuti, e hanno molto guadagnato poi ch'io mi parti' da loro. Placcia al Comune di Bologna, poi ch'io sono tornato, ch'io sia signore e padre, sì come comanda la legge che parla del padre de la famiglia."

28. "Francisco, Juris Civilis Doctori, civi bononiensi. Gratum est nobis..." (Orvieto, 13 Aug. 1291). Text in Sarti, *De claris*, 2:70, from collection of extracts concerning Bologna from Vatican documents made by order of Benedict XIV, now in the university library at Bologna: see G. Del Giudice, *Carlo Troya: Vita pubblica e privata, studi, opere* (Naples, 1899), pp. 30–31. Summaries in *Les registres de Nicolas IV*, ed. E. Langlois, BEFAR^2, no. 5 (Paris, 1886–93), 2:796, no. 5907; A. Potthast, *Regesta pontificum Romanorum* (Berlin, 1874–75), no. 23808.

29. The will, dated 19 May 1293, printed by Sarti, *De claris*, 2:70–75.

30. For these see Haskins, "Three English Documents," p. 90 n.29.

31. G. Post, "Masters' Salaries and Student-Fees in the Mediaeval Universities," *Speculum* 7 (1932): 181–98; "Philosophantes and Philosophi in Roman and Canon Law," *Archives d'histoire doctrinale et littéraire du Moyen Age*, vol. 21, an. 29 (1955; an. 1954), pp. 135–38; (with K. Giocarinis and R. Kay), "The Medieval Heritage of a Humanistic Ideal," *Traditio* 11 (1955): 195–234.

32. The following paragraph is based on the texts and citations collected by Post in "Medieval Heritage," pp. 206–7; interpretation of them, especially the last point, is my own.

33. *Casus* to *Dig*. 50. 13. 1.

34. Post, "Medieval Heritage," pp. 206–7. The honorarium "debet dari pro facultate et dignitate donantis ..., et etiam eius cui donatur" (*Gl. ord.* to *Dig*. 50. 13. 15, ad v. *honor,* quoted by Post in n. 37, p. 207).

35. This distinction undermines the argument of Pézard in *Dante sous la pluie de feu,* pp. 173–84, which is based on supposed blasphemies discerned in the *Gl. ord.*

36. Giocarinis, in Post, "Medieval Heritage," pp. 215, 219–23.

37. Moreover, the law of nature obligates the son to honor and reverence his parents for what they have given him, which can never be repaid; the student is similarly obligated to his teachers (Post, "Medieval Heritage," p. 223). Francis, who stood in both relations to the Glossator, assumed to himself the honors due Accursius, thereby disparaging his parent.

38. *Novellino*, ed. Lo Nigro, p. 132 (see above, n. 27 of this chap.).

39. See above, n. 24 of this chap.

40. What is known of Francis' English career is conveniently summarized by A. B. Emden, *A Biographical Register of the University of Oxford to A.D. 1500*, vol. 1 (Oxford, 1957), pp. 9–10. My account is again based on Sarti, *De claris*, 1:193–203, supplemented by G. L. Haskins, "Three English Documents"; also his "Francis Accursius: A New Document," *Speculum* 13 (1938): 76–77; and (with Ernst H. Kantorowicz), "A Diplomatic Mission of Francis Accursius and His Oration before Pope Nicholas III," *English Historical Review* 58 (1943): 424–47. Cf. the light sketch by W. Senior, "Accursius and His Son Franciscus," *Law Quarterly Review* 51 (1935): 513–16.

41. Thus Sarti, *De claris*, 1:195–96; Savigny, *Geschichte des römischen Rechts*, 5:308–9; Haskins, "Three English Documents," p. 87.

42. *Calendar of the Patent Rolls Preserved in the Public Record Office: Edward I, A.D. 1272–1281* (London, 1901), p. 299 (hereafter cited as *Cal. Pat. Rolls, 1272–1281*). On 24 Jan. 1279, the king's Lucchese bankers were ordered to pay Francis, who was then in Rome, "100*l.* for Michaelmas term, 6 Edward I. [1278] of his yearly fee which he receives for his maintenance in the king's service." Haskins took this semiannual payment to be the whole of his yearly salary ("Three English Documents," p. 89).

43. *Cal. Pat. Rolls, 1272–1281*, pp. 168, 269, for the constable, Anthony Bek. The keeper of Dover Castle received £300 to support both himself and the chaplains, servants, watchmen, and a carpenter who resided there (p. 299). The barons of the exchequer received 20 marks annually (p. 295); "Master Angelus de Urbe, king's clerk and advocate at the court of Rome," 50 marks per annum in lieu of an

ecclesiastical benefice worth 80 (p. 274); the papal notary "Master Berard de Neapoli, king's clerk," was given a fee of 80 marks (p. 336), which, since a mark is two-thirds of a pound sterling, amounts to £53. 2s. 6d.

44. Ibid., p. 460 (Westminster, 27 Oct. 1281).

45. F. Pellegrini, "Il Serventese dei Lambertazzi e dei Geremei," *Atti e memorie della R. Deputazione di storia patria per le provincie di Romagna*, 3d ser. 9 (1891): 22–71, 181–224; 10 (1892): 95–140; at 10: 182–85.

46. On Edward's movements, see F. M. Powicke, *King Henry III and the Lord Edward*, vol. 2 (Oxford, 1947), pp. 606, 612; W. Hunt, "Edward I," in *Dictionary of National Biography*, vol. 17 (1889), pp. 14–38, at p. 22 (hereafter cited as *DNB*); H. Gough, *Itinerary of King Edward the First throughout His Reign, A.D. 1272–1307* (Paisley, Scotland, 1900), 1:ii–iii, 17–38.

47. *Corpus chronicorum Bononiensium*, ed. A. Sorbelli, in *RIS²*, tome 18, pt. 1, vol. 2 (Città di Castello, 1910–38), pp. 186–88 (hereafter cited as *Corpus chron. Bonon.*). Cronaca A: "E quello anno [1273] Bolognisi assediono Forlì apresso Sam Varano. E misser Odorido re d'Inghilterra passò per mezo el canpo cum la soa gente che tornava d'oltra mare e fé multi cavalieri in el dicto canpo, li nomi di quali son quisti...." Cronaca B: "*De alchune discordie fate in Bologna e de la guerra fata a' Forlovixi*. 1273.—In Bologna fuo grandissima sedicione e grandissimo rumore el quale fuo cominciamento della destrucione de Bologna.... la parte di Ieremii obtenne che ll'exercito de Bologna andasse a campo a Forlìo contra el volere della parte di Lambertacii. Et così, essendo posto el campo intorno Forlìo, advenne che ... Odovardo re de Anglia retornava dalla Terra Sancta de Yerusalem e passando per Italia pervenne al campo de' Bolognexi e udite le casone de quella guerra, tractoe asai de compore pace tra loro, ma non possendo loro pacificare, andoe al suo viazo. El quale Odovardo re fece molti cavallieri bolognixi nel dicto campo. El quale exercito destrusse tuto el contado de Forlìo."

48. *Petri Cantinelli Chronicon*, ed. F. Torraca, in *RIS²*, tome 28, pt. 2 (Città di Castello, 1902), p. 16: "Et tunc transivit per dictum exercitum dominus Odoardus et uxor eius, qui voluit facere concordiam, et non potuit. Et fecit in ipso exercitu multos milites novos, et etiam in civitate Faventie et Bononie." Ibid., p. 11: "Hoc anno, de mense madii, comune Bononie fecit exercitum super civitatem Forlivii, et duravit per sex septimanas. Et dominus Hodoardus rex Anglorum, rediens de ultra mare, venit per illud exercitum, et in eo multos milites novos fecit de pluribus civitatibus, Bononie et Romaniole, et voluit conponere inter comune Bononie et comune Forlivii, sed non potuit; non tamen hoc stetit per comune Forlivii, neque per partem Lanbertaciorum, sed pars Geremiorum noluit pacem facere...."

49. *Chronica fratris Salimbene*, ed. O. Holder-Egger, in *MGH, Scriptores*, vol. 32 (1905–13), p. 489, lines 27–29.

50. *DNB*, 17:22.

51. Powicke, *King Henry III*, 2:613–16.

52. Ibid., 2:614–15.

53. "Edwardus recessit a curia, cui communitates civitatum Tusciae et Italiae cum magno tripudio tubis ductilibus obviarunt, communiter proclamantes, 'Vivat imperator Edwardus.'" *Flores historiarum*, ed. H. R. Luard, Rolls ser., no. 95, vol. 3 (London, 1890), p. 30. According to the same source, the Milanese pressed gifts upon him:

"Mediolanenses ei munera optulerunt, equos electos, coopertos sclavoniis de scarleto, quos illis cogentibus, invitus recepit."

54. T. Rymer, *Foedera*, 4th ed., vol. 1, pt. 1 (London, 1816), p. 511. Among the *praesentes*: "domini Francisco domini Acursii legum professore de Bononia."

55. Ibid., p. 516.

56. *Cal. Pat. Rolls, 1272–1281*, p. 79.

57. Ibid., p. 94; Rymer, *Foedera*, vol. 1, pt. 2 (London, 1816), pp. 524–25.

58. On the case, see E. C. Lodge, *Gascony under English Rule* (London, 1926), pp. 60–61. Although Gaston's case appears to have been a purely feudal one, it is not unlikely that Edward was already using arguments from Roman law to counter French feudal law, as he certainly did later in his reign. As early as 1286, Edward's lawyers cited Roman law and the Italian *Libri feudorum* to prove that Aquitaine was not a fief of the French crown. See P. Chaplais, "English Arguments Concerning the Feudal Status of Aquitaine in the Fourteenth Century," *Bulletin of the Institute of Historical Research* 21 (1946–48): 203–13, esp. 208–9; cf. G. P. Cuttino, "Historical Revision: The Causes of the Hundred Years War," *Speculum* 31 (1956): 471 n.46. In the Great Cause of 1291–92, Edward's extraordinary tribunal entertained Bruce's Roman-law arguments but eventually deemed them inapplicable: B. C. Keeney, "The Medieval Idea of the State: The Great Cause," *University of Toronto Law Journal* 8 (1949): 48–71, at pp. 60–61. This ad hoc judicial body may have been "modeled on the Roman *judicium centumvirale*" (p. 53. n.11); curiously, its official reporters were notaries-apostolic (pp. 50 n.3 and 60 n.33). Gascon feudal law is cited by the Accursian *Gl. ord.* at one point, which just possibly might be an addition by the Glossator's son: *Dig.* 1. 18. 3, ad vv. *praeses. privatus est*: "Vascones ... dicunt se non teneri sub rege Angliae, nisi ipse sit in Vasconia: alias nolunt ei servire: sed dicunt eum privatum: et non esse eorum regem." For commentary, see J. W. Perrin, *Legatus in Roman Law and the Legists* (Ph.D. diss. in history, University of Wisconsin, Madison, 1964, available as no. 64–13914 from University Microfilms, Ann Arbor, Mich.), p. 151, at n.44.

59. Sarti, *De claris*, 1:196 n.1. He connects Francis' departure with the impending civil war (§ 4, p. 195); Savigny, *Geschichte des römischen Rechts*, 5:310 n, reports it as Sarti's opinion.

60. Sarti quotes the contract (*De claris*, 1:204 n.1); Savigny, *Geschichte des römischen Rechts*, 5:309.

61. In a petition to the Bologna city council, dated 1288, William alleged himself "a tempore primorum rumorum stetisse ad confinia ultra montes ad viginti dietas et ultra a civitate Bononiae" (Sarti, *De claris*, 1:207 n.3). Before leaving, he had attempted to secure his goods against confiscation by conveying them to his Geremeid father-in-law, but the fraud having been discovered, he lost everything (ibid., n. 2). William apparently followed his brother to France, for he too taught at Orléans (Meijers, *Etudes*, 3:94).

62. *Corpus chron. Bonon.*, ed. Sorbelli, tome 18, pt. 1, vol. 2, p. 189, Cronaca B: "Del comenciamento della destrucione de Bologna" (but see sub an. 1273, quoted above, n. 47 of this chap.). The *Serventese*, ed. Pellegrini, begins: "Hoc est principium destructionis civitatis Bononie" (edition cited above, in n. 45 of this chap., 9:196).

63. Torraca, in his edition of *Petri Cantinelli Chronicon*, p. 17 n.1, collects the evidence on the duration of the conflict.

64. On Francis' children, see Sarti, *De claris*, 1:197–98.

65. Receipts in Sarti, *De claris*, 1:197 n.7. Francis deposited both sums, "apud Londram vel apud Parixius," with Jacobus Agolante, who appears on the patent rolls as Jacobus Agolantis (or Aguilanti) of Pistoia: *Cal. Pat. Rolls, 1272–1281*, pp. 91, 214. One receipt states that the payment was made in Bologna by his compatriot "domino Forixio de Pistorio." Edward later used one Lupus de Pistoria to transmit Francis' retainer to Bologna in 1290: *Calendar of the Patent Rolls Preserved in the Public Record Office: Edward I, A.D. 1281–1292* (London, 1893), p. 364 (hereafter cited as *Cal. Pat. Rolls, 1281–1292*).

66. *Cal. Pat. Rolls, 1272–1281*, p. 127.

67. *The Liber epistolaris of Richard de Bury*, ed. N. Denholm-Young, Roxeburghe Club (Oxford, 1950), p. 62, no. 125. Also less correctly printed with commentary by G. L. Haskins, "Francis Accursius," pp. 76–77. Both editors date the letter ca. 1274 or 1275, but since the king had offered to bear the expense of Aichina's trip, the sums she received from her husband would not seem to have been for that purpose, being (as Savigny observed, *Geschichte des römischen Rechts*, 5:310 n) far more than such a journey would require. The invitation would accordingly seem to have been extended in 1275, no earlier than the support payment in April and no later than the provision for housing in December.

68. *Calendar of the Close Rolls Preserved in the Public Record Office: Edward I, A.D. 1272–1279* (London, 1900), p. 296 (hereafter cited as *Cal. Close Rolls, 1272–1279*): "To John son of Nigel, keeper of the forest of Bernewode. Order to cause Sir Francis de Bonon' legum professori to have two young bucks and four young does for the present year, four live hares and six live rabbits to be placed in the king's garden at Oxford, as the king has enjoined upon Francis by word of mouth" (6 June 1276).

69. *Cal. Pat. Rolls, 1272–1281*, p. 177 (18 May 1276); cf. *Cal. Close Rolls, 1272–1279*, p. 289 (20 May to the sheriff).

70. Emden, *Biographical Register*, 1:10; Haskins, "Three English Documents," p. 91.

71. Great Britain, Record Commission, *Parliamentary Writs*, ed. F. Palgrave, vol. 1 (London, 1827), p. 6; W. Stubbs, *The Constitutional History of England*, 3d ed., vol. 2 (Oxford, 1883), p. 273.

72. *Statutes of the Realm*, vol. 1 (London, 1810), p. 42; Stubbs, *Constitutional History*, 2:275.

73. *Calendar of the Close Rolls Preserved in the Public Record Office: Edward I, A.D. 1279–1288* (London, 1902), p. 5 (20 Jan. 1280; hereafter cited as *Cal. Close Rolls, 1279–1288*).

74. Rymer, *Foedera*, vol. 1, pt. 2, p. 598: "omnia consilla et secreta sua, michi revelata et revelanda, fideliter celabo."

75. That Francis was considered to be one of the king's *clerici* appears from an order issued to pay the travel expenses of the Roman mission in 1278 "dilecto clerico nostro domino Francisco Accursii et sociis suis nunciis nostris" (Rymer, *Foedera*, vol. 1, pt. 2, p. 562). Tentatively, I would suggest that Francis was retained to complete the work of Henry de Bracton (d. 1268). Certainly the treatise *De legibus et consuetudinibus Angliae* was heavily revised by a redactor working between 1272 and 1277, during just those years when Francis was so mysteriously and lucratively employed in England. Moreover, as S. E. Thorne has recently pointed out, the

treatise abounds with errors in English law, which surely must be the work of the redactor; one would expect as much from Francis. Civil law is also slightly misquoted, as if from memory, and now it appears to pervade the work. Further, I am not sure that any of it can safely be attributed to Bracton himself. At least one cannot maintain that the legal maxim *Volenti non fit iniuria* proves, because used by Bracton, that he studied under William of Drogheda: Bracton, *On the Laws and Customs of England*, ed. and trans. S. E. Thorne, 2 vols. (Cambridge, Mass., 1968), 1:xxxviii. In fact this *regula* was not original with Drogheda but is rather a commonplace apparently based on *Dig.* 47. 10. 1. 5 and formulated in the *Gl. ord.* ad *Dig.* 47. 10. 17. pr., ad vv. *Iniuriarum actio*. In short, it is not impossible that Francis *alone* was responsible for the Romanist elements in "Bracton." To test this hypothesis, one would have to compare the text of *De legibus* closely with the apparatus to the *Corpus iuris civilis,* and especially with Francis' signed *casus*. Needless to add, such a work would be far greater than the present one, and hardly less controversial. Hence this note but points the way. On Bracton's redactor, see Thorne's introduction to Bracton, *On the Laws*, 1:xxxii–xlviii, esp. xl, xlvii; 2:vi.

76. Haskins-Kantorowicz, "Diplomatic Mission," pp. 426–33, on the *ars arengandi*.

77. Ibid., p. 424 n.1; cf. above, n. 43 of this chap.

78. C. V. Langlois, "Nova Curie," *Revue historique* 87 (1905): 55–79, at p. 66. Francis' own report *suo domino* follows.

79. Ibid., p. 65: "dominus Franciscus, quo diligentiorem in iniuncto sibi negocio nullus usquam invenit, secundum quod per relatum cardinalium de hiis que ante adventum meum gesta fuerant et postea occulata fide inveni...."

80. Pellegrini, "Serventese," 9:62–65. Some of the Accursii fought on the Lambertazzi side: *Corpus chron. Bonon.*, ed. Sorbelli, 2:203, 205.

81. *Inf.* xxxii, 122–23; cf. Toynbee-Singleton, pp. 599–600.

82. Pellegrini, "Serventese," 10:102–23, lines 392–712.

83. Rymer, *Foedera,* vol. 1, pt. 2, p. 598.

84. *Cal. Pat. Rolls, 1272–1281*, p. 460 (27 Oct. 1281).

85. *Cal. Close Rolls, 1279–1288*, pp. 133, 135.

86. Sarti, *De claris*, 1:198 n.3.

87. Ibid., n. 6, "Ex libris Bannit. et Confinat. an. MCCLXXXII scriptis." The documents cited by Sarti are now in the Archivio di Stato di Bologna and for the most part can readily be identified in the "Inventario dell' Archivio del Comune" published by his editor, C. Malagola, in *Atti e memorie della R. Deputazione di storia patria per le provincie di Romagna*, 3d ser. 1 (1882–83): 183–220.

88. Sarti, *De claris*, 1:199 n.1. The extent of this commitment can be seen in the text of such an oath preserved by William Durandus, *Speculum iudiciale* (Rome, 1474), lib. iv, de feudis, § 2, no. 73; reprinted by G. Fasoli in *Archivio storico italiano* 91 (1933): 68–69: "quando primo civitas Bononie et provincia Romandiole ad Ecclesiam romanam pervenerunt [July 1278] ... sacramentum fidelitatis a baronibus et a sindacis omnium universitatum in generalibus parlamentis nec non a singularibus personis recipimus sub hac forma: 'Iuro quod ab hac hora in antea fidelis et hobediens ero B. Petro, principi apostolorum et vobis, sanctissime pater domino Nicolao Papae III, vestrisque successoribus canonice intrantibus, sanctaeque apostolice romanae Ecclesiae. Non ero in consilio aut consensu vel facto quod vitam perdatis seu membrum, aut capiamini mala captione; consilium quod mihi credituri estis per

vos, aut per nuncios vestros sive per litteras, ad vestrum damnum me sciente nemini pandam. Et si scivero fieri vel tractari aliquid quod sit in vestrum vel Ecclesie predicte damnum, impediam, et si impedire non potero, illud vobis et ipse ecclesie significare curabo. Papatum romanum et regalia sancti Petri, iura et iurisdictiones vestras et successorum vestrorum singulorum ac romanae Ecclesiae, tam in civitate eiusque territorio et districtu quam alibi ubicumque existentia adiutor ero vobis et ipsis successoribus ac Ecclesie ad retinendum, defendendum, recuperandum, et recuperata manutenendo contra omnem hominem.' " Durandus doubtless received the oath (*recipimus*) as a member of Cardinal Latino's legation (see below, nn. 65, 66, 73 of chap. 4).

89. "Predicta vero locum non habeant nec tangant in personam domini Francisci domini Acursii." Statute of Saturday, 1 July 1284, in the municipal code of 1288, Lib. ii, 8, ed. G. Fasoli and P. Sella, *Statuti di Bologna dell' anno 1288*, vol. 1, Studi e testi, no. 73 (Vatican, 1937), pp. 58–60; Francis at p. 59, line 35. Sarti (*De claris,* 1:199 n.3) dates Francis' exemption 5 July but cites the same source.

90. Sarti, *De claris*, 1:199 n.2, "Ex lib. Reformat." an. 1286. According to the law of 1 July 1284, reconciled Lambertazzi were defined as "illi qui iuraverunt partem ecclesie et Ieremiensium" (Fasoli-Sella, *Statuti di Bologna*, p. 59, lines 29–30).

91. The principals are named by Sarti, *De claris*, 1:199–200. As far as I know, the political connotations of these matches have escaped notice. For the party loyalties of the various families, I have consulted the lists in the *Corpus chron. Bonon.*, ed. Sorbelli, 2:202–3; these and variant lists are also printed by Pellegrini, "Serventese," vol. 10, apps. 1–5. The lists all purport to represent the division of loyalties at the time of the second expulsion (Dec. 1279).

92. The surname of Dotta's husband—Deuteclerius de Logliano (Sarti, *De claris*, 1:200) —appears on the Ghibelline lists of 1279 as (Qui) Da Logliano or Quelli da Loyano: so identified in Sorbelli's index, *Corpus chron. Bonon.*, 2:726, s.v. "Loiani." The husband was named after his ancestor Detiglerio, who died in 1251 (ibid., p. 131). The Guelf branch originated in 1276, when Ubaldino da Loiano sold the family castle to the Geremei and joined them (ibid., pp. 192–96).

93. Sarti, *De claris*, 1:201; document printed at 2:88–89; cf. above, n. 20 of this chap.

94. Sarti, *De claris*, 2:88: "Item, considerantes quante utilitatis et honoris sunt et fuerunt perpetuo et erunt deinceps, Domino concedente, scolares et studium scolarium Communi et populo bononiensibus, et nolentes propter modicam gratiam ab eis per Rectores universitatis scolarium postulatam, indignationem aliquam ipsos scolares assumere posse rationabiliter contra dictum populum et comune, set petitioni ipsorum dominorum Rectorum reverentiam et honorem, qui tot eorum posse, procuraverunt et procurant retinere studium et scolares in civitate Bononie, cuius petitionis tenor talis est: . . . ."

95. *Mon.* 3. 15. 10. See above, chap. 1, at n. 15 ff.

96. *Conv.* 4. 9. 8: "E con ciò sia cosa che in tutte queste volontarie operazioni sia equitade alcuna da conservare e iniquitade da fuggire (la quale equitade per due cagioni si può perdere, o per non sapere quale essa si sia o per non volere quella seguitare), trovata fu la ragione scritta, e per mostrarla e per comandarla."

97. *Conv.* 4. 9. 9: "A questa scrivere, mostrare e comandare, è questo officiale posto di cui si parla, cioè lo Imperadore. . . ." On the meaning of *scrivere, mostrarla, e comandare,* see Busnelli-Vandelli, *Conv.*, 2:100 n.4.

98. *Conv.* 4. 4. 7 (trans. Temple Classics): "E questo officio per eccellenza Imperio è chiamato, sanza nulla addizione, però che esso è di tutti li altri comandamenti comandamento. E così chi a questo officio è posto è chiamato Imperadore, però che di tutti li comandamenti elli è comandatore, e quello che esso dice a tutti è legge, e per tutti dee essere obedito, e ogni altro comandamento da quello di costui prendere vigore e autoritade."

99. *Conv.* 4. 9. 8. Dante himself identified his source: "è scritto nel principio del Vecchio Digesto" (*Dig.* 1. 1. 1. 1).

100. *Conv.* 4. 12. 9–10 (trans. Temple Classics): "E che altro intende di meditare l'una e l'altra Ragione, Canonica dico e Civile, tanto quanto a riparare a la cupiditade che, raunando ricchezze, cresce? Certo assai lo manifesta e l'una e l'altra Ragione, se li loro cominciamenti, dico de la loro scrittura, si leggono." Appropriate references, cited by Busnelli-Vandelli, are found in *Dig.* 1. 1. 1. 1 (cf. 3) and in the proems to the *Institutes* and the *Decretals of Gregory IX*. On the meaning of *ragione scritta*, see A. Passerin d'Entrèves, *Dante as a Political Thinker* (Oxford, 1952), pp. 80–82.

101. *Inf.* i, 124; the speaker is Virgil.

102. *Mon.* 3. 15. 10: "summo Pontifice, qui secundum revelata humanum genus perduceret ad vitam ecternam."

103. *Mon.* 3. 15. 9: "Has igitur conclusiones et media ... ostensa sint nobis ... a Spiritu Sancto qui per prophetas et agiographos, qui per coecternum sibi Dei filium Iesum Cristum et per eius discipulos supernaturalem veritatem ac nobis necessariam revelavit...."

104. *Mon.* 3. 15. 8: "Nam ... venimus ... ad secundam [beatitudinem = conclusionem] vero per documenta spiritualia que humanam rationem transcendunt, dummodo illa sequamur secundum virtutes theologicas operando, fidem spem scilicet et karitatem."

105. *Mon.* 3. 15. 11: "Et cum ad hunc portum vel nulli vel pauci, et hii cum difficultate nimia, pervenire possint, nisi sedatis fluctibus blande cupiditatis genus humanum liberum in pacis tranquillitate quiescat, hoc est illud signum ad quod maxime debet intendere curator orbis, qui dicitur romanus Princeps, ut scilicet in areola ista mortalium libere cum pace vivatur."

106. R. Naz, "For," in his *Dictionnaire de droit canonique*, vol. 5 (Paris, 1953), pp. 871–73.

107. "Perchè Dante colloca in Paradiso il fondatore della scienza del Diritto canonico," *Atti della Accademia nazionale dei Lincei, Rendiconti della classe di scienze morali, storiche e filologiche*, 6th ser. 2 (1926): 65–149. Approved by P. Fournier, *Revue historique de droit français et étranger*, 4th ser. 6 (1927): 565–68; defended by F. Ruffini, *Studi danteschi* 13 (1928): 119–25. Cf. Pézard, p. 192.

108. Gratian's *Decretum*, Causa 33, questio 3, is disproportionately long and in effect constitutes a separate treatise, as the title, *Tractatus de poenitentia*, indicates (ed. Friedberg, 1:1159–1247).

109. The two forums hardly figure in recent discussions of medieval religio-political concepts; instead, much is heard of two related distinctions, the *corpus mysticum/iuridicum* and the *potestas ordinis/iurisdictionis*: e.g., E. H. Kantorowicz, *The King's Two Bodies* (Princeton, N.J., 1957), pp. 194–206; M. Wilks, *The Problem of Sovereignty in the Later Middle Ages* (Cambridge, Eng., 1963), pp. 368–94. Wilks notes what may be an important clue for Dantists: "Nearly all the writers who

deal with the distinction between jurisdictional and sacerdotal powers were either Frenchmen or products of the Parisian schools" (p. 377 n.2).

110. *Mon.* 2. 9. 20. Commentators frequently assert that this apostrophe is addressed to *Decretalistae,* but surely it is no less applicable to *Legistae,* since it is specifically directed against *iuristae* and we have just seen that Dante includes both laws within *ius* (see above, n. 100 of this chap.).

111. Savigny, *Geschichte des römischen Rechts,* 5:316–22; on the last two, see above, nn. 76–79 of this chap.

112. M. Chiaudano, "Dante e il diritto romano," *Giornale dantesco* 20 (1912): 37–56, 94–119, argued that Dante's references were derived for the most part from Aquinas. In at least one instance, however, it would seem that he quoted the *Digestum vetus* directly: *Conv.* 4. 9. 8 (see above, n. 99 of this chap.); cf. Busnelli-Vandelli, 2:100. His debts to the *Glossa ordinaria* are largely unexplored, but one now celebrated—the maxim *Nomina sunt consequentia rerum*—was discovered simultaneously by Nardi and Pézard (see Pézard, p. 355 n.3).

113. Dante's academic career is largely a matter of inference, but a persuasive case for his rhetorical studies at Bologna is made by A. Marigo, ed., *De vulg. eloq.,* pp. xxiv–xxvi.

114. "Francisci scientia inter alios lucet velut sol, splendet velut luna et gemma, cuius mores radiant velut sydera, cuius doctrina crescit sicut pluvia, cuius eloquium fluit ut ros, quasi imber super herbam et quasi stillae super gramina et cuius fama et gesta magnifica divulgantur a cardine ortus solis usque ad limites orbis terrae." Quoted from his *Prooemium commentarii ad artem notarilem* by Sarti, *De claris,* 1:202 n.1. On Boattieri, see Haskins-Kantorowicz, "Diplomatic Mission," p. 430.

115. On the MSS and *ars arengandi,* see Haskins-Kantorowicz, "Diplomatic Mission," pp. 426–31.

116. Ibid., pp. 440–47: "Incipit arenga domini Francisci filii condam domini Accursii doctoris legum coram domino papa pro rege Anglie in curia romana." Citations refer to the 31 *sectiones* supplied by the editors.

117. Ibid., pp. 430–33. The genre is represented in the next generation by the famous opinion delivered in consistory by Cardinal Matthew of Aquasparta to the envoys of Philip the Fair in defense of the policies of Boniface VIII (June 1302): ed. [P. Dupuy], *Histoire du différend d'entre le pape Boniface VIII et Philippes le Bel roy de France* (Paris, 1655), Preuves, pp. 73–77.

118. H. Walther, ed., *Proverbia sententiaeque latinitatis medii aevi: Lateinische Sprichwörter und Sentenzen des Mittelalters in alphabetischer Anordnung,* Carmina medii aevi posterioris latina no. 2, vol. 5 (Göttingen, 1967), p. 919, no. 34182.

119. E. Auerbach, "Figura," *Archivum Romanicum* 22 (1938): 436–89, reprinted in his *Neue Dantestudien,* Istanbuler Schriften no. 5 (Istanbul, 1944), pp. 11–71; English translation in his *Scenes from the Drama of European Literature: Six Essays* (New York, 1959), pp. 11–76. Also, for specific *figurae* in the *Commedia,* his *Typologische Motive in der mittelalterlichen Literatur,* Schriften und Vorträge des Petrarca-Instituts Köln no. 2 (Krefeld, 1953).

120. *Arenga,* § 6: "Dictus enim populus magnifice deum coluit eumque honoravit . . . ; patet etiam in aliis donariis a dicto populo ad opus sanctuarii atque ministeriorum collatis in tantum, ut Moysi diceretur: 'plus offert populus quam necessarium sit,' ut hec leguntur in Exodo xxxvi. capitulo [verse 5] et in sequentibus capitulis usque

ad eius finem [38:33] et in parabolis primo et ultimo capitulo." The last reference, which baffled the editors, is probably to 2 Paralipomena 1:1, 36:23.

121. *Arenga*, § 10: "In donationibus, in ecclesiis earumque ministris iuris civilis regulas non observant neque consuetudines gentium aliarum, quibus in talibus denarius pro marcha videtur, sed <illa> imperiali auctoritate utuntur, in qua pro mensura optima immensitas approbatur." At the editors' suggestion, I insert *illa* to improve the sense, which the allegations cited in the notes (see below, nn. 122–24 of this chap.) place beyond doubt.

122. *Cod.* 1. 2. 19: "sin vero amplioris quantitatis donatio sit, excepta scilicet imperiali donatione, non aliter valeat, nisi actis intimata fuerit." *Corpus iuris civilis*, vol. 2: *Codex Iustinianus*, ed. P. Krueger (Berlin, 1880), p. 16. Cf. *Cod.* 8. 53. 35. 5d (p. 365).

123. *Cod.* 1. 2. 19 gl. ad vv. *imperiali donatione*: "nam imperator potest plus dare piis locis ultra quingentos solidos sine actis, ut in [*Nov.* 7. 2. 1]."

124. *Nov.* 7. 2. 1. *Corpus iuris civilis*: vol. 3, *Novellae*, ed. R. Schoell and W. Kroll (Berlin, 1895), p. 53, lines 17–22; quoted in the medieval Latin translation of the Greek original.

125. The editors, having not located this reference, declared that "the allusions are obscure" (p. 442 n.7).

126. Other peoples, he seems to say, have raised the value of Justinian's limit by customarily computing each denarius of the 500 solidi as a mark (§ 10 and above, n. 121 of this chap.).

127. G. Post, *Studies in Medieval Legal Thought* (Princeton, N.J., 1964), p. 374 n.16. Both kings and emperors act in concert with their *proceres* (pp. 390, 470).

128. Baldus de Ubaldis, *In libros codicem commentaria* (Venice, 1586), at *Cod.* 10. 1, no. 12: "quia princeps repraesentat illum populum, et ille populus Imperium, etiam mortuo principe"; quoted by Kantorowicz, *King's Two Bodies*, p. 179 n.275.

129. Post, "Rex Imperator," in *Studies*, pp. 453–82, at p. 481.

130. Ibid., pp. 472–74; above, n. 24 of this chap.

131. Meijers, *Etudes d'histoire du droit*, 3:117–18.

132. Post, *Studies*, pp. 455–56, for Cino and the glossators.

133. E.g., see above, n. 121 of this chap. Cino certainly connected *Cod.* 1. 2. 19 *Illud* with *Nov.* 7, for he comments at the former: "Ista est bona lex ad quam oppono duobus modis, et primo opponitur quod possit donari ultra 500 aureos Auth. de non alienando. §. sinimus col. 2 [*Nov.* 7. 2. 1]; respon. ibi loquitur in principe cuius immensitas est mensura ut in Auth. de non ali. re. ec. §. ultimo [idem]." *Cyni Pistoriensis in Codicem ... commentaria* (Turin, 1964, reprinting ed. of Frankfurt a/M., 1578), fol. 10A.

134. *Arenga*, §§ 11–12: "Qualiter autem deo et eius vicario eiusque fratribus [Anglicani] obedientes extiterint et existant, ex fama, visu et operibus comprobatur. Quante enim devotionis bone memorie rex Henricus extiterit ... in romana ecclesia eiusque nuntiis venerandis, ... cuius vestigia iure successorio in eius filium sunt transfusa. [12] In eo etenim est ... versus romanam ecclesiam et eius nuntios obed<i>entia. ..."

135. *Arenga*, § 13: "Cunctus populus autem anglicanus tam clericorum quam laycorum, qualiter deo et eius vicario obedientes existant tum in decimis persolvendis, tum in litteris romane ecclesie exequendis, tum in clericis honorandis et maxime extraneis

fere de omnibus terris constitutis et eorum licet absentium iuribus conservandis, satis ex paucitate super hoc vobis conquerentium declaratur."

136. *Arenga*, § 14: "Veniunt itaque filii anglicani ad vos, sancte pater, significatum non immerito nomine Samuelis."

137. After listing the seven points of resemblance (§§ 14–20), the thesis is stated: "Que omnia in vestra sanctitate conveniunt plus quam in Petri aliquo successore."

138. *Arenga*, § 19: "Sexto legitur, quod [Samuel] dilectus a deo fuit et sacerdos summus et renovavit imperium et inunxit principes in gente sua; et sic summus tum in consecrando <et> oleum infundendo, ut in x. capitulo primi regum...." Applied to Nicholas in § 24: "ob que tamquam deo dilectum in summum sacerdotem vos assumptum extitisse apparet, principes inungendo, cardinales et prelatos creando...."

139. *Mon.* 3. 6. 1–3: "De lictera vero primi libri *Regum* assumunt etiam creationem et depositionem Saulis, et dicunt quod Saul rex intronizatus fuit et de trono depositus per Samuelem, qui vice Dei de precepto fungebatur, ut in Lictera patet. Et ex hoc arguunt quod, quemadmodum ille Dei vicarius auctoritatem habuit dandi et tollendi regimen temporale et in alium transferendi, sic et nunc Dei vicarius, Ecclesie universalis antistes, auctoritatem habet dandi et tollendi et etiam transferendi sceptrum regiminis temporalis.... Et ad hoc dicendum per interemptionem eius quod dicunt Samuelem Dei vicarium, quia non ut vicarius sed ut legatus spetialis ad hoc, sive nuntius portans mandatum Domini expressum, hoc fecit...."

140. *Mon.* 3. 6. 4–6: "Unde sciendum quod aliud est esse vicarium, aliud est esse nuntium sive ministrum.... Nam vicarius est cui iurisdictio cum lege vel cum arbitrio commissa est; et ideo intra terminos iurisdictionis commisse de lege vel de arbitrio potest agere circa aliquid, quod dominus omnino ignorat. Nuntius autem non potest in quantum nuntius; sed quemadmodum malleus in sola virtute fabri operatur, sic et nuntius in solo arbitrio eius qui mictit illum. Non igitur sequitur, si Deus per nuntium Samuelem fecit hoc, quod vicarius Dei hoc facere possit. Multa enim Deus per angelos fecit et facit et facturus est que vicarius Dei, Petri successor, facere non posset."

141. *Mon.* 3. 4. 1: "Isti vero ad quos erit tota disputatio sequens [sc. *Mon.* 3. 4–13], asserentes auctoritatem Imperii ab auctoritate Ecclesie dependere velut artifex inferior dependet ab architecto...."

142. D. E. Queller, *The Office of Ambassador in the Middle Ages* (Princeton, N.J., 1967), pp. 57–59. I am further indebted to Prof. Queller for personal communications clarifying the technical import of Dante's terminology. See also the gloss signed by Accursius in the *glossa ordinaria* to *Dig.* 3. 3. 1. 1 ad vv. *Sed verius*: "Sed differunt in officio exequendo, nam procurator unius rei in sua persona concipit contractum ... sed nuncius eius in persona domini, ut vendis illi domino...."

143. *Arenga*, § 20: "Item septimo legitur, quod in lege domini et in fide domini sive christiana iudicavit congregationem...."

144. *Arenga*, § 25: "Iudicatis etiam congregationem, id est gentem humanam, in lege domini et in fide divina, decretando contra infideles et decretantibus aliis adiutor astando, iudicem [*var.* radicem] in istis partibus extirpando, quod, etsi per alios extitit, attemptatum effectum non potuit statuisse." The editors found that "this passage, too, is anything but clear." To extract some sense from the clause "quod

... statuisse," I have preferred the variant *iudicem* to their *radicem* (p. 446, variant *t*) and have placed a comma before, rather than after, *attemptatum*.

145. Hostiensis (Henry of Susa), *Lectura*, at X 4. 17. 13 *Per venerabilem* ad vv. *certis causis inspectis temporalem iurisdictionem exercemus*: "Puta quando requirimur et alii non preiudicamus . . . et propter defectum iustitie ius reddimus etiam in temporalibus, et in causa miserabilium personarum; . . . et vacante regno vel imperio; . . . et ratione cuiuslibet peccati notorii et iuramenti; . . . et ratione connexitatis, et ratione diversarum opinionum ut sequitur; et ubicunque dominus iniuste tractat hominem suum vel iniuste iudicat et ubicunque civitas iudice caret; et si recusetur iudex ordinarius ut suspectus. Nam et hi quattuor premissi casibus etiam secundum leges imperatoris communes sunt omnibus episcopis per suas civitates et dyoceses, ut in [*Nov.* 86. 1. 4. 7]...." For commentary, see J. A. Watt, "The Theory of Papal Monarchy in the Thirteenth Century," *Traditio* 20 (1964): 179–317, esp. 281–92 (quotation at p. 290). On *Per venerabilem*, see also B. Tierney, " 'Tria quippe distinguit iudicia . . .,' " *Speculum* 37 (1962): 48–59, esp. 51–53.

146. *Nov.* 86, cited by Hostiensis in the preceding note. The title conveys its import: "Ut differentes iudices audire interpellantium allegationes cogantur ab episcopis hoc agere; et ut quando in suspicionem habuerint iudicem, pariter audiat causam et civitatis episcopus; et de cautela quam oportet omnino episcopum agere" (ed. Schoell-Kroll, p. 419).

147. Pézard, pp. 185–200.

148. *Par.* x, 104–5; cf. xii, 137–38 (Donatus).

149. See above, n. 107 of this chap. Although Dante does not echo the passage, doubtless he knew that the *Digestum vetus* declared that jurists were the priesthood of the law, for he cites the *locus* in another connection (see above, n. 99 of this chap.).

150. Notably Raimondo de Peñafort: see S. Kuttner, "Zur Entstehungsgeschichte der Summa de casibus poenitentiae des hl. Raymund von Penyafort," *Zeitschrift der Savigny-Stiftung für Rechtsgeschichte, Kanonistische Abteilung* 39 (1953): 419–34.

151. Sarti, *De claris*, 1:199: "Ac paucos post menses ipse quoque, cum Aichinam uxorem amisisset, alteram duxit, Remgardam Papazzonis Aldigherii ferrariensis filiam, quae annis multis Rigutio Galluccio, ex primariis urbis nostrae civibus, nupta fuerat." The source is not stated; Savigny accepts the statement (*Geschichte des römischen Rechts,* 5:313).

152. See Toynbee-Singleton, s.v. "Alighieri." The connection with Francesco d'Accorso has, I believe, passed unobserved.

153. Ibid., table 22 and s.v. "Cacciaguida." *Par.* xv, 137–38: "Mia donna venne a me di val di Pado; e quindi il sopranome tuo si feo."

CHAPTER 4

1. See above, chap. 1, at n. 29 ff.

2. Scartazzini-Vandelli[19], p. 123 at *Inf.* xv, 111: "*tigna*: malattia schifosa, col cui nome è designato quel sozzo peccatore."

3. *Dizionario della lingua italiana*, ed. N. Tommaseo and B. Bellini, vol. 4 (Turin, 1879), p. 1464, s.v. "tigna"; *The Cambridge Italian Dictionary*, ed. B. Reynolds, vol. 1 (1962), p. 815, s.v. "tigna." See also s.v. "tinea" in Lewis-Short; in C. Du Fresne sieur du Cange, *Glossarium ad scriptores mediae et infimae Latinitatis,*

ed. L. Favre, 10 vols. (Paris, 1883–87); and in *Webster's New International Dictionary of the English Language,* 2d ed. (Springfield, Mass., 1934). *Tigna* is Englished as "scurf" by Carlyle-Wicksteed, Sinclair, and Singleton.

4. *Commedia,* ed. Petrocchi, 2:255, at *Inf.* xv, 110: "A questa scelta non m'induce soltanto la mera attestazione dei codici nel senso prescelto dal canone d'edizione, ma una migliore efficacia nel separare, pur all'interno della stessa *masnada,* due *litterati grandi,* come Prisciano e Francesco di Accursio, da un personaggio assai minore per prestigio di cultura, e soltanto uomo di chiesa, e, per di più, l'unico dannato tra i violenti contro natura che subisca il sarcasmo del poeta (fra tre grandi letterati: Brunetto, Prisciano e Francesco, e tre eminenti gentiluomini: Guerra, Aldobrandi e Rusticucci)."

5. *Urkundenlehre,* 2d pt.: *Papsturkunden* by L. Schmitz-Kallenberg, Grundriss der Geschichtswissenschaft, ed. A. Meister, vol. 1, pt. 2 (Leipzig-Berlin: Teubner, 1913), p. 67.

6. *Dictionnaire de droit canonique,* ed. R. Naz, vol. 7 (Paris, 1965), pp. 1320–25, s.vv. "Translation" and "Translation d'office." See also above, chap. 5. The Italian *trasmutare* happily conflates the two Latin verbs that designate this act: e.g., Gratian, *Decretum,* C.7 q.1 c.34: "Petrus . . . est translatus Romam. . . . Eusebius . . . mutatus est in Alexandriam" (ed. Friedberg, 1:579).

7. [Graziolo de' Bambaglioli (*ante* 1324)], *Il commento più antico . . . dell' Inferno di Dante,* ed. A. Fiammazzo (Udine, 1892), p. 70: "dicit etiam quod hic punitur quidam Episcopus florentinus qui transitus [*var.* translatus] fuit a servo servorum—hoc est a summo pontifice—de episcopato florentinum in episcopatum vicentinum—Et hoc est quod dicit textus—*fu trasmutato darno in bachillone*—qui arnus est flumen transiens per medium Civitatis Florentie—Bachillone est flumen vicentie—per que flumina auctor significat Civitates istas—alia per se patent."

    Comedia di Dante degli Allagherii col commento di Jacopo della Lana [1323 ✕ 1328] *bolognese,* ed. L. Scarabelli, 2d ed. (Bologna, 1866), 1:286: "Questo fu vescovo di Firenze, e tramutato in vescovo di Vicenza per lo *Servo dei servi,* cioè per lo papa che si scrive: *Servus Dei servorum,* e fu simile sodomita. Per Arno intende Firenze, per Bacchiglione intende Vicenza."

8. *Inf.* xv, 106–7: "tutti fur cherci / e litterati grandi e di gran fama." On the meaning of *cherci* in this context, see above, n. 4, chap. 1. Quite possibly Dante may have known the passage in the *Magnae derivationes* of Huguccio of Pisa wherein Priscian is said (falsely) to have been a priest ("legamus eum fuisse sacerdotem"): G. Schizzerotto, "Uguccione da Pisa, Dante e la colpa di Prisciano," *Studi danteschi* 43 (1966): 79–83.

9. *Chiose alla cantica dell' Inferno di Dante Alighieri scritte da Jacopo Alighieri,* ed. Jarro [G. Piccini] (Florence, 1915), p. 95: "vescovo Andrea de' Mozzi di Firenze, il quale essendo pastore della detta città, per cotal vizio dal papa nel vescovado di Vicenza fu trasmutato, il cui fiume così Bacchiglione è chiamato, come Arno quel di Firenze, nel quale finalmente morta sua lussuria rimase."

    Guido da Pisa, quoted by G. Biagi, *La Divina Commedia nella figurazione artistica e nel secolare commento: Inferno* (Turin, 1924), p. 413a: "tertius est quidam episcopus florentinus qui vocabatur Andrea de Moçis, qui a domino papa fuit translatus de episcopatu Florentie in episcopatum Vicentie." Cf. E. Palandri,

"Il vescovo Andrea de' Mozzi nella storia e nella leggenda dantesca," *Giornale dantesco* 32 (1931): 91–118, at 106 n.59.

The exception is Selmi's Anonymous, who nonetheless associates the Mozzi family with the passage: "E que' che fu trasmutato d'Arno in Bachiglione fu, a cui papa Inocenzio avia data una chiesa molto ricca in Firenze, in su l'Arno. Il detto papa il trasmutò, e diegli una chiesa a Vincenza. E questo procacciaro i Mozzi suoi consorti, per levarsi dinanzi il vituperio suo della soddomia per non vederlo ogni dì." *Chiose anonime alla prima cantica della Divina Commedia di un contemporaneo del poeta*, ed. F. Selmi (Turin, 1865), pp. 88–89.

10. Although not a few of his successors were removed to obscure sees, none went to Vicenza. In 1524, however, Cardinal Niccolò Ridolfi, a notable Medicean pluralist, added both sees to his collection of bishoprics: *Enciclopedia cattolica*, vol. 10 (1953), col. 890. For a conspectus of the bishops of Vicenza, see P. B. Gams, *Series episcoporum ecclesiae catholicae* (Regensburg, 1873), p. 807.

11. E. Palandri, "Il vescovo Andrea de' Mozzi nella storia e nella leggenda dantesca," *Giornale dantesco* 32 (1931): 91–118.

12. R. Davidsohn, *Geschichte von Florenz*, vol. 2 (Berlin, 1908), index, s.v. "Mozzi"; notably, vol. 2, pt. 1, p. 441, and vol. 2, pt. 2, pp. 450–54.

13. G. Villani, *Cronica* 5. 39, lists them among the nobles "che a quello tempo [1215] furono e divennero guelfi in Firenze"; they are grouped with two other banking houses: "i Frescobaldi, i Bardi, é Mozzi, ma di piccolo comminciamento," in contrast to the older families previously named.

14. Palandri, "Il vescovo Andrea de' Mozzi," p. 102 n.48. Andrea's uncle Jacopo and his brother Tommaso bore the title *cavaliere* (ibid., p. 94 n.7).

15. Ibid., p. 94 nn.4, 5.

16. On the importance of the papacy in the rise of Florentine banking, see Davidsohn, *Geschichte von Florenz*, vol. 2, pt. 1, pp. 438–39, and his *Forschungen zur Geschichte von Florenz*, vol. 4 (Berlin, 1908), pp. 281–94; also F. Schevill, *History of Florence* (New York, 1936), pp. 135–36, 295–96.

17. This in itself is a fact of considerable interest for Dantists, as it may serve to identify him as the anonymous Florentine suicide who appears in *Inf.* xiii, 130–51. See my article "Rucco di Cambio de' Mozzi in France and England," *Studi danteschi* 47 (1970): 49–57.

18. *Calendar of the Patent Rolls Preserved in the Public Record Office: Henry III, 1247–1258* (London, 1908), pp. 498, 515–16 (an. 1256).

19. Davidsohn, *Geschichte von Florenz*, vol. 2, pt. 1, p. 552.

20. E. Masi, "Fra savi e mercanti suicidi del tempo di Dante," *Giornale dantesco* 39 (1936): 199–238, brackets the failure between 1300 and 1303 (pp. 206–8).

21. Davidsohn, *Geschichte von Florenz*, vol. 2, pt. 2, pp. 90, 93, 96; Palandri, "Il vescovo Andrea de' Mozzi," p. 96.

22. Davidsohn, *Geschichte von Florenz*, vol. 2, pt. 2, p. 159; Schevill, *History of Florence*, pp. 149–50.

23. G. Villani, *Cronica* 8. 40, 43, 49. Palandri, "Il vescovo Andrea de' Mozzi," p. 117 n.109, citing the chronicle of Dino Compagni. Pietro da Piperino also headquartered his Tuscan legation there in 1296: Davidsohn, *Geschichte von Florenz,* 3:33–34.

24. Davidsohn, *Geschichte von Florenz*, vol. 2, pt. 2, p. 232.

25. Ibid., p. 550.

26. Ibid., p. 233, citing the manuscript register of Martin IV: Archivio segreto vaticano, Serie generale de' regestri, vol. 42, f. 35 (21 Sept. 1282).

27. Ibid., p. 263.

28. Ibid., p. 335, citing *Les registres de Nicolas IV*, ed. E. Langlois, BEFAR², no. 5 (Paris, 1886–93), nos. 7215–19, 7108–12 (an. 1288–89).

29. Davidsohn, *Geschichte von Florenz*, vol. 2, pt. 2, p. 107: "wir nennen sie, weil diese Männer offenbar die Oligarchie bildeten, die dermalen die Stadt unter dem Deckmantel unerschütterlicher guelfischer Gesinnung zu eigenem Nutzen regierte." Strictly speaking, under the Guelf commune of 1267–80 *nobile* was an outmoded concept, while the designation *magnate* was not yet in use, at least as a juridical concept. Thus under the *Primo Popolo* the Mozzi were indistinguishable in legal status from other families formerly reckoned as noble, many of which were after 1280 accounted among the *popolani* rather than the *magnati*. See N. Ottokar, *Il comune di Firenze alla fine del Dugento*, 2d ed. (Turin, 1962), p. 38.

30. M. Becker, "A Study in Political Failure: The Florentine Magnates, 1280–1343," *Mediaeval Studies* 27 (1965): 246–308, especially 263–66.

31. *La cronaca di Dino Compagni*, ed. I. Del Lungo, RIS², vol. 9, pt. 2 (Città di Castello, 1907–16), p. 141: "e sbandi e confinò . . . messer Vanni de' Mozzi."

32. Davidsohn, *Geschichte von Florenz*, vol. 2, pt. 2, pp. 552 ff. The Tommaso-Vanni partnership is documented by their accounts for the years 1300–1303, cited by Masi, "Fra savi," p. 206 n.6.

33. The efforts of the two great rival magnate-banking families—the Bardi and the Mozzi—to ally in the face of the Ordinances (29 May 1295), indicate the concern of the whole Mozzi clan. The connection, if any, of these events to the mission of Vanni at the curia on behalf of the commune (20 Apr. 1295) is not clear. Davidsohn, *Geschichte von Florenz*, vol. 2, pt. 2, pp. 548–49. Cf. Palandri, "Il vescovo Andrea de' Mozzi," p. 118 n.114.

34. Masi, "Fra savi," p. 208 n.17: "Il bando di Vanni, se non provocò, certo aggravò il disastro."

35. Ibid., pp. 207–10.

36. In February 1301, Mozzi agents collected the proceeds of a crusading tenth in England for Boniface. W. E. Lunt, *Financial Relations of the Papacy with England to 1327*, Mediaeval Academy of America Publication no. 33 (Cambridge, Mass., 1939), p. 344 n.4.

37. W. H. Bliss, ed., *Calendar of Entries in the Papal Registers Relating to Great Britain and Ireland: Papal Letters*, vol. 1, *A.D. 1198–1304* (London, 1893), p. 245 (hereafter cited as *Cal. Papal Letters*). *Les registres d'Innocent IV*, ed. E. Berger, BEFAR², no. 1 (Paris, 1884–1921), no. 3874 (11 Apr. 1248).

38. Dated 13 Mar. 1254: Bliss, *Cal. Papal Letters*, 1:298.

39. Lunt, *Financial Relations*, p. 648: "Item, pro decima ecclesie Sancti Botulfi Lincolniensis diocesis cuius rector est magister Andreas Spiliati xxii li." And 5 items later: "Item, pro decima ecclesie de Reylega [Rayleigh] Londoniensis diocesis cuius rector est Andreas Spiliati iiii li." On the collection, see ibid., pp. 332–33. The taxes were a sexennial tenth granted at the Council of Lyons in 1274 for the crusade; the figure in the 1283 accounting presumably represents 60 percent of the value of the benefice, being a tenth of six years' income. In *The Valuation of Norwich*, ed. W. E. Lunt (Oxford, 1926), made in 1254, the estimated value of the church

of Rayleigh was 24s. (p. 341), and St. Botolph's Boston was valued at 10 marks directly after a severe flood, which may have caused it to be undervalued (p. 248). The diocese of Lincoln in general was underassessed in 1254; the assessment made in 1276 for the tax that Andrea paid more closely approximated the true value, to the dismay of the clergy (p. 155). The valuation of Norwich also noted that the abbot of York paid 100s. for St. Botolph's, which perhaps explains how Andrea received the benefice, since Innocent's letter of 1254 was directed to one "Master Innocent, papal writer, canon of Trani, living in England," who in other transactions was the curia's agent in the area of York (Bliss, *Cal. Papal Letters*, 1:258, 395).

40. G. Barraclough, *Papal Provisions* (Oxford, 1935), pp. 39–42, 55–56, 152; for other factors, see pp. 96, 109–10.

41. On Florentine merchants at Boston in the mid-thirteenth century, see F. M. Powicke, *King Henry III and the Lord Edward* (Oxford, 1947), 1:314–15. The Mozzi connection could be traced in the Close Rolls (see my article cited above, in n. 17 of this chap.).

42. E.g., Powicke, *King Henry III*, 1:277–89. English antipapalism in the thirteenth century was incisively delineated by A. L. Smith, *Church and State in the Middle Ages* (Oxford, 1913), especially lecture 4. Barraclough, in his *Papal Provisions,* sought to moderate the conclusions that have frequently been drawn from these expressions. Note that the principal complainant against Italians in English benefices was Robert Grosseteste, bishop of Lincoln, 1235–53: both time and place coincide with Andrea's richest English living (Smith, *Church and State,* lecture 3; Barraclough, *Papal Provisions*, pp. 13, 166–71).

43. Davidsohn, *Geschichte von Florenz*, vol. 2, pt. 1, p. 441; followed uncritically by Palandri, "Il vescovo Andrea de' Mozzi," p. 95, despite his discovery that Andrea was in Italy in 1251 (n. 14), whereas Davidsohn declares "wir finden Andrea de' Mozzi von 1248 bis 1256 in England ansässig."

44. E.g., for "Stephen, a scholar, son of James de Ponte, Roman citizen," on 25 Sept. 1250 (Bliss, *Cal. Papal Letters*, 1:272) and another on 4 June 1251 (ibid., p. 273). The abbot of Dunfermlin, to whom Innocent's original mandate for Andrea was addressed, received another on 19 Feb. 1246 to provide a benefice of 20 marks in Scotland for "Peter, son of Ingembald, a Roman citizen" (ibid., p. 225). The mandate in favor of Andrea is not extant, but most probably it was issued at the same time, as his claims arising from the abbot's provision were heard in the curia hardly more than two years later (20 Mar. 1248, mentioned in *Reg. Innoc. IV,* no. 3874; see above, n. 37 of this chap.).

45. Palandri, "Il vescovo Andrea de' Mozzi," p. 96 n.14: "Venerabili Capitulo Florentino. Al. domini papae capellanus, bononiensis et florentinus canonicus, et Andreas Spiliati, eiusdem ecclesie florentine canonicus, salutem et prosperis successibus habundare. Evidenter didicimus dominum Accursum a summo pontifice litteras impetrasse pro G. suo nato in canonica florentina, et assensum et consensum domini Io. flor. electi habuisse . . . quas litteras vidimus et legimus bullatas bulla summi pontificis et eiusdem domini electi sigilli munimine roboratas. . . ."

46. Palandri, "Il vescovo Andrea de' Mozzi," p. 95 n.13.

47. M. Sarti and M. Fattorini, *De claris archigymnasii Bononiensis professoribus*, 2d ed. by C. Albicini and C. Malagola (Bologna, 1888–96), 1:206 n.9. His putative date of birth is computed to be 1246 by subtracting 25 years from the date of his earliest

extant public act (1271). Accepted by F. C. von Savigny, *Geschichte des römischen Rechts im Mittelalter,* 2d ed., vol. 5 (Heidelberg, 1850), p. 331.

48. Thus Davidsohn, *Geschichte von Florenz,* vol. 2, pt. 1, p. 441 n (*"mag. Andreas, Sohn des Spiliatus Cambii civis Flor."*) from Reg. 24, fol. 154ᵛ. Cf. *Les registres d'Alexandre IV,* ed. C. Bourel de la Roncière et al., BEFAR², no. 15 (Paris, 1895–1959), nos. 1065, 1250 (both "canonicus Florentinus," not seen). In ibid., no. 2911 (20 June 1259), he acts as *"auditor"* of a lawsuit and is styled "magistro Andrea Spiliati, subdiacono et capellano apostolico," from which it would appear he was one of the papal chaplains who served as *auditores causarum,* i.e. *juges d'instruction.* Later the same year, however, he witnessed a sentence of Riccardo Annibaldi, cardinal-deacon of Sant' Angelo and abbot of Monte Cassino (no. 2958, 12 Aug. 1259).

49. P. Herde, *Beiträge zum päpstlichen Kanzlei- und Urkundenwesen im dreizehnten Jahrhundert,* 2d ed., Münchener historische Studien, Abteilung geschichtl. Hilfswissenschaften, no. 1 (Kallmünz, 1967), pp. 46–47.

50. Palandri, "Il vescovo Andrea de' Mozzi," p. 95 n.11.

51. Three cases in 1264, all subdelegated to him by Cardinal Riccardo: *Les registres d'Urbain IV,* ed. J. Guiraud, BEFAR², no. 13 (Paris, 1899–1958), nos. 1010–11 (6 Mar.), 1073–74 (31 May), 2493 (13 Feb.); also mentioned in no. 1197 (7 Jan. 1264). Cf. Bliss, *Cal. Papal Letters,* 1:406 (2 May 1264).

52. Similarly, Pope Martin IV, who was Andrea's contemporary, owed his education to the patronage of the French crown; as cardinal, the curia chiefly employed him as legate to France: for effective liaison Rome relied on the rapport arising from ambivalent loyalties. See my "Martin IV and the Fugitive Bishop of Bayeux," *Speculum* 40 (1965): 460–83, esp. p. 3 nn.3–5.

53. E.g., *Reg. Urb. IV,* nos. 518, 520 (13 Jan. 1264). Another hint as to his curial functions appears shortly after his last recorded judicial work. On 21 June 1265, he witnessed at Rome the investiture of Charles of Anjou as Roman senator: *Les registres de Clément IV,* ed. E. Jordan, BEFAR², no. 11 (Paris, 1893–1945), no. 411 ("coram discretis viris magistris … et Andrea de Spiliato, domini pape capellanie"). During the second half of 1265, Charles negotiated heavy loans with Florentine banks: S. Runciman, *The Sicilian Vespers* (Baltimore, Md., 1960), p. 103.

54. J. Lami, *Sanctae ecclesiae Florentinae monumenta,* vol. 2 (Florence, 1758), col. 935b (25 June 1273; hereafter cited as *Monumenta*); cf. Palandri, "Il vescovo Andrea de' Mozzi," p. 98 n.25. At least one clerk of the papal chancery ascribed the hospitality of the Palazzo Mozzi to Andrea rather than to Tommaso, witness a document dated 14 July 1273 at "Florentie in palatio domini Andree de Spillato, ubi tunc summus pontifex residebat" (Davidsohn, *Forschungen,* 4:222).

55. On Latino's legation: R. Davidsohn, "Der Friede des Kardinals Latino (1280)," *Forschungen,* 4:226–58; Davidsohn, *Geschichte von Florenz,* vol. 2, pt. 2, pp. 152–75; G. Fasoli, "La pace del 1279 tra i partiti bolognesi," *Archivio storico italiano* 91 (1933): 49–75, esp. 53–57; Schevill, *History of Florence,* pp. 149–50.

56. See above, chap. 3, at nn. 75–80.

57. Nicholas' master plan is a problem in itself. See, in addition to the citations in note 55 of this chapter, the contrasting interpretations of Runciman, *Sicilian Vespers,* pp. 202–5, and of H. K. Mann and J. Hollnsteiner, *Lives of the Popes in the Middle Ages,* vol. 16 (London, 1932), pp. 105–27, esp. 125 n.5.

58. Latino was thus foremost among the cubs that the she-bear's son so avidly advanced,

as Nicholas describes his notorious nepotism at *Inf.* xix, 70–72: "e veramente fui figliuol de l'orsa, / cupido sì per avanzar li orsatti, / che sù l'avere e qui me misi in borsa." On Latino's career (d. 1294): Davidsohn, *Forschungen*, 4:233–35; *Geschichte von Florenz*, vol. 2, pt. 1, p. 243, and vol. 2, pt. 2, p. 150. *Enciclopedia italiana*, vol. 22 (Rome, 1934), p. 4, s.v. "Malebranca."

59. *Les registres de Nicolas III*, ed. J. Gay and S. Vitte, BEFAR², no. 14 (Paris, 1898–1938), no. 344 (25 Sept. 1278): letters of legation for Tuscany, Città di Castello (at the headwaters of the Tiber), Romagna, and the March of Treviso, plus the ecclesiastical provinces of Ravenna and Aquileia, which overlap the civil boundaries of the commission. See also Davidsohn, *Forschungen*, 4:233, 236.

60. Davidsohn, *Forschungen,* 4:236.

61. Ibid., p. 239; Palandri, "Il vescovo Andrea de' Mozzi," p. 97 n.19: a sum is paid for Andrea by a prior who was styled "gerens vice domini et magistri Andree Spigliati de Mozzis, delegati venerabilis fratris Latini, legati domini pape in Thuscia et alibi" (16 Mar. 1279).

62. Davidsohn, *Forschungen*, vol. 2 (Berlin, 1900), p. 214, no. 1588: "domino Andree Spiliato, subdelegato fratris Latini legati summi pontificis."

63. Davidsohn, *Forschungen*, 4:239: "Andreas Spiliatus subdelegatus et nuntius venerabilis patris fratris Latini cardinalis Hostiensis et Velletrensis episcopi" was seeking to collect imperial tolls at San Miniato. Cf. Palandri, "Il vescovo Andrea de' Mozzi," p. 97 n.19.

64. Documents dated 9 Oct. 1279, the day after his arrival, at "Florentie, in palatio domini Thome de Mozzis" (Davidsohn, *Forschungen*, 4:241) and 5 Apr. 1280 "in palatio domini Thome de Mozzis ... in quo moratur dominus legatus" (Palandri, "Il vescovo Andrea de' Mozzi," p. 97, at n. 22).

65. Davidsohn, *Geschichte von Florenz*, vol. 2, pt. 2, pp. 165–70, and *Forschungen,* 4:247–48.

66. Davidsohn, *Geschichte von Florenz*, vol. 2, pt. 2, p. 175.

67. Davidsohn, *Forschungen*, 2:217, no. 1613; 4:255. The acts of the legation dated 1281 that Palandri cites from Salvini both belong to 1280, under which year they were used by Davidsohn, *Forschungen*, 4:248; cf. Palandri, "Il vescovo Andrea de' Mozzi," p. 98, at n. 23.

68. *Bullarium Franciscanum,* ed. J. H. Sbaralea, vol. 3 (Rome, 1765), p. 481 "Ex Vatic. Reges. Pontif. epist. 111. tom. 2. anni ɪ.": "ad dilectum filium magistrum Andream Spiliati canonicum Cameracen. cappellanum nostrum, de cuius fidelitate, ac experta bonitate confidimus, nostrae mentis aciem convertentes; rectoriam Campaniae, ac Maritimae praedictarum [*sc.* provinciarum] auctoritate Apostolica in spiritualibus, et temporalibus, ipsi duximus committendam...." I have not been able to locate the letter in *Registres de Martin IV*, ed. F. Olivier-Martin et al., BEFAR², no. 16 (Paris, 1901–35). Another of Latino's aides was similarly posted: see below, note 73 of this chapter. An instrument of sale executed by Andrea as rector was confirmed on 4 Dec. 1291: *Reg. Nic. IV,* no. 6418. D. P. Waley, *The Papal State in the Thirteenth Century* (London, 1961), documents Andrea as rector between 7 Nov. 1283 and 18 Mar. 1284 (p. 308, no. 20); a new rector was in office on 15 Oct. 1284 (no. 21).

69. Bull quoted above, in n. 68 of this chap.

70. Davidsohn, *Geschichte von Florenz*, vol. 2, pt. 2, p. 302.

71. See above, chap. 4, at nn. 24–29.

72. *Les registres d'Honorius IV*, ed. M. Prou, BEFAR², no. 7 (Paris, 1886–88), no. 500; C. Eubel, *Hierarchia Catholica Medii Aevi*, vol. 1, 2d ed. (Münster, 1913), p. 250. The dangers faced by a headless church were represented to the pope in 1281 by a French council: see my article "An Episcopal Petition from the Province of Rouen, 1281," *Church History* 34 (1965): 294–305.

73. E.g., his colleague in Latino's legation, William Durandus, Sr. (see above, chap. 4, at n. 65), who continued his curial career as governor of various of the papal states until his consecration as bishop of Mende in Oct. 1286. See L. Falletti, "Guillaume Durand," *Dictionnaire de droit canonique*, vol. 5 (1953), cols. 1014–75, esp. 1020–25.

74. *Reg. Hon. IV*, no. 700; Palandri, "Il vescovo Andrea de' Mozzi," p. 99 n.28 (original). The consecration was performed at the curia, not by the pope, but, as was usual, by the bishop of Ostia, namely the same Latino on whose staff Andrea had served (ibid.; for similar consecrations, see index to *Reg. Hon. IV*, s.v. "Latinus," e.g., nos. 500, 522). According to Palandri, Salvini thought that the consecration took place at Florence, where he supposed Latino still was legate (p. 99 n.29).

75. See above, chap. 4, at n. 7 ff.

76. Palandri, "Il vescovo Andrea de' Mozzi," p. 98.

77. Gams, *Series episcoporum*, p. 747.

78. Palandri, "Il vescovo Andrea de' Mozzi," pp. 99–100 nn.32–36. His "L'archivio vescovile di Firenze: Appunti storici e inventario sommario del materiale più antico," *Rivista delle biblioteche e degli archivi*, n.s. 4 (1926): 167–200 and *169–*191 (page numbers repeated by error), lists three surviving items that attest to Mozzi's methodical enterprise: (1) The *Memoriale reddituum et iuramentorum* prepared in 1287 by Mozzi's order. The chartulary formerly compiled by Bishop Ardingo was recopied and brought up to date by the addition of charters from the intervening years. This contains oaths of fealty sworn to the bishop by viscounts and other vassals, with similar proofs of the temporal rights exercised during the preceding half century by the bishop over "castles, lands, possessions, and places pertaining to the bishopric of Florence." The collection survives as copied into a larger register, the *Bullettone*, ca. 1322–23 (pp. 187–88). (2) In Dec. 1288 and Jan. 1289, Mozzi caused every legal obligation to the bishopric to be formally recognized in a notarial act. In 1292, some 180 such acts were transcribed into a register of *Recognitiones*, which is extant (pp. 194–95). (3) On 27 Apr. 1289, the same notary who had collected these recognitions notarized a quire containing summary versions of a third of them, which was apparently intended to form part of a larger volume (pp. *177–*178).

79. Davidsohn, *Geschichte von Florenz*, vol. 2, pt. 2, pp. 450–54; and E. Sanesi, "Del trasferimento di messer Andrea dei Mozzi da Firenze a Vicenza," *Studi danteschi* 22(1938): 115–22; "Un ricorso del capitolo fiorentino alla signoria alla fine del sec. XIII," *Rivista storica degli archivi toscani* 3 (1931): 141–61; and "Maestro Perfetto da Castelfiorentino, canonico di S. Reparata," *Miscellanea storica della Valdelsa* 39 [1931]: 144–51.

80. Sanesi, "Trasferimento," prints this extract from the original in the capitular archives (pp. 119–20): "Canon ille quem fecit episcopus non habet ius aliquod et in hoc concordant omnes sapientes de Curia et reputaverunt nos minus sapientes, quia quilibet deberet scire hoc.... Si est ita sicut ponitis casum, non potest nos

cogere ad solvendum decimam impositionis.... Omnes maiores curiae sentiunt contra episcopum et super hoc allegantur multa iura quae vobis mictam cito." Another extract, ibid., p. 122. The writer, Cambio delle Panche (or di Sesto), was not only a canon of Santa Reparata in Florence but also a master of canon law (titled *magister* in a doc. of 1298: Lami, *Monumenta*, 3:1668a).

81. Lami, *Monumenta*, 2:1139b; Davidsohn, *Geschichte von Florenz*, vol. 2, pt. 2, pp. 452–54. For the following events, see Sanesi, "Ricorso del capitolo," pp. 141–61. The vacancy, undated by Sanesi (p. 142), was caused by the election of Lotterio (Lotherius), archdeacon of Florence, to the see of Faenza on 18 Aug. 1287: Gams, *Series episcoporum*, p. 688; repeated by Eubel, *Hierarchia Catholica*, 1:246.

82. Lami, *Monumenta*, 2:1140b.

83. Sanesi, "Trasferimento," pp. 116–18. Tebaldo's letters are dated *sine anno* 15 and 26 March, but the year can be supplied from internal evidence unnoticed by the editor: "die *veneris* xxiiii marzii" (p. 117). During the reign of Nicholas IV, Friday fell on 24 March only once, in 1290. Tebaldo assumed that the chapter knew his business and accordingly refers only to specific points: witnesses are urgently requested to appear again in Rome in the matter of the church of St. Andrea. Also he transmitted to the pope an account of the bishop's deeds (*opera episcopi*) written by the abbot of San Miniato al Monte, whose grievances are otherwise unknown (ibid., p. 117; cf. commentary at pp. 118–19).

84. Ibid., p. 118: "Sciatis quod episcopus procurat ampliare iurisdictionem suam in quantum potest. Sed non credo quod papa faciat sibi aliquid super hoc et super ea quae a<u>divit de eo maxime propter iniurias et afflictiones quas ipse infert clericis."

85. Ibid., pp. 116–17: "Episcopus vadit ad cardinales et ad alios dominos de curia et dicunt capellani cardinalium quod cardinales non vident eum alacri facie. Et dicunt omnino florentini qui sunt in curia et viderunt episcopum quod videtur totus stupefactus."

86. Ibid., pp. 117–18: "Episcopus fecit unum ensenium papae ... et unum ecum [= equum] praesentavit domino Benedicto sed ipse non recepit eum." Sanesi (p. 121) takes *ecum* to be the antecedent of *eum*; in that sense, the usual verb would be *accepit*.

87. Ibid., p. 117: "Et die veneris xxiiii marzii ego eram ad domum domini Iacobi et episcopus venit ibidem et multum respexit obliquo oculo me sed tunc non potui loqui cum domino Iacobo quia erant cum eo in camera iii cardinales." Sanesi gives the encounter a different twist: "Qui nella Curia incontra il suo arciprete, che sa lì presente contro di sè, e lo guarda a lungo di mal'occhio" (p. 119).

88. Ibid., p. 117: "Ego procuro cum domino Iacobo de Columna qui est alter papa in quantum possum quod ipse stet apud papam quod inquiratur contra episcopum officio papae. Et dominus [*sic*] Nepoleone vidi et dixit mihi quod faceret hoc et etiam ipse dominus Nepoleone dixit quod loqueret cum domino Iacobo super hoc."

89. *Reg. Nic. IV*, no. 4037 (21 Jan. 1291). Davidsohn, *Geschichte von Florenz*, vol. 2, pt. 2, p. 450, assumes that the excommunication mandate, addressed to the abbots of Santa Trinità and Badia di Ripoli, was executed; echoed by Palandri, "Il vescovo Andrea de' Mozzi," pp. 100–101 n.40. The mandate provided for a month's delay before execution.

90. Document dated 11 Sept. 1291, edited by Lami, *Monumenta*, 2:1139a–40b. Sanesi,

"Ricorso," p. 142, prints extracts from the copy in the Spogli Strozzi (Archivio di Stato di Firenze, MS. 510, p. 238). See also Davidsohn, *Geschichte von Florenz,* vol. 2, pt. 2, p. 450.

91. Sanesi, "Ricorso," p. 152.

92. Ibid., p. 143; cf. Lami, *Monumenta,* 2:1026a: "praepositura Florentina vacante, et ipse Dominus Andreas episcopus vice. . . ."

93. Sanesi, "Ricorso," p. 143; document edited by Lami, *Monumenta,* 2:1025–26. For details on a violent partisan of the bishop during the conflict of 1293–96, see Sanesi, "Maestro Perfetto," pp. 144–51.

94. Sanesi, "Ricorso," pp. 159–60: ". . . Episcopus Florentinus facit istam novitatem . . . videlicet quod mandavit preposito ut deberet sibi et familie sue parare prandium cum volebat venire et visitare prepositum et canonicos quod de iure facere non debet et nullus episcopus florentinus unquam fecit unde post primam et secundam appelationem legiptime [*sic*] interpositas super predictis suspendit predictum prepositum ab amministratione prepositure et eum excommunicavit et mandavit denuntiari excommunicatum per omnes ecclesias civitatis florentie et fecit sibi porrigi articulos super quibus dicit se velle inquirere contra eum et deponere a prepositura et etiam mandavit sibi preposito et domino Gualtero de Ponturme, quod deberent sibi episcopo ostendere qualiter sint canonici et qualiter tenent prebendas in ecclesia memorata volens eos super hoc indebite et contra iustitiam vexare et molestare. . ." (*Ricorso del Capitolo*).

95. Ibid., p. 154.

96. Ibid., pp. 158–61, prints both the *Ricorso del Capitolo* and the *Intimazioni della Signoria.*

97. The date of the Signoria's *Intimazioni* is admittedly obscure. The date here proposed is a full year later than that suggested by Sanesi, who had miscalculated his *terminus ante.* He argued quite correctly that the document was issued when Aldobrandino still occupied the office of treasurer, since the first article of the ordinances requires that the capitular statutes be turned over to the *distributores* by him or by whoever had them: "per dominum Ildebrandum de Cavalcantibus, si habet vel per quemcumque alium qui haberet" (Sanesi, "Ricorso," p. 160). Aldobrandino lost both his office and his place in the chapter, to which he owed the title *dominus,* by contracting a marriage: "de thesauraria ecclesiae Florentinae vacantis per matrimonium contractum, ut dicitur, per Aldobrandinum Domini Manetti de Cavalcantibus de Florentia olim dictae ecclesiae Florentinae thesaurarium . . ." (Lami, *Monumenta,* 3:1669a; document dated 4 Mar. 1297). Sanesi failed, however, to date this event correctly. He gives the date on which the new treasurer, Giovanni di Angiolino Ma(l)chiavelli, was admitted to office as 18 Jan. 1296. His source is more precise: "anno Incarnationis 1296. Ind. 10. die 18. Ianuarii" (ibid., 1667b). Since 1297 was the year of the *tenth* indiction, the event must be dated o.s. 1296/1297 n.s. This conclusion is supported by a series of documents wherein the new treasurer was recognized by various canons (*recipitur*) successively on 24 Jan. 1296 o.s. and 4 Apr., 19 May, 28 Nov., and 17 Dec. 1297 o.s. (ibid., 1667b–68a). Sanesi's date of Jan. 1296 n.s. is in fact impossible, since the new treasurer was provided by the papal legate in Tuscany, Pietro da Piperino, cardinal-deacon of S. Maria Nuova, who only arrived in Florence in mid July 1296 (ibid., 1669a; Davidsohn, *Geschichte von Florenz,* 3:33–34); he had been commissioned as

legate on 20 Apr. 1296: *Les registres de Boniface VIII,* ed. G. Digard et al., BEFAR[2], no. 4 (Paris, 1884–1935), no. 1599.

Thus the *terminus ante* for the *Intimazioni* is no later than 11 Jan. 1297 n.s., a year later than Sanesi had supposed. The *terminus post,* as Sanesi recognized, is early 1295, when Tebaldo became the chapter's provost ("Ricorso," p. 145). Moreover, internal evidence indicates that the ordinances were issued in the spring, for the decrees were to be put into effect "incontinenter et sine mora ante festum beati Zenobii" ("Ricorso," p. 160), and consequently must have been issued not long before the feast of San Zanobi, which was celebrated on 25 May and was a red-letter day in the Florentine calendar: see Davidsohn, *Geschichte von Florenz,* vol. 4, pt. 3, p. 101, and the Florntine calendar described by V. Leroquais, *Les bréviaires manuscrits des bibliothèques publiques de France,* vol. 2 (Paris, 1934), p. 435; cf. below, n. 136 of this chap.

Hence it is possible that the *Intimazioni* were, as Sanesi thought most probable, issued in the spring of 1295 ("Ricorso," pp. 155–56). But this would require us to believe that the whole dispute between the bishop and the new provost took place during a few months early in 1295, which hardly corresponds to the usual pace of medieval litigation. The new *terminus ante* of Jan. 1297 permits us to suppose that the end of the case came more plausibly a year later, in the spring of 1296. This later date has a decisive advantage over the other, in that it falls *after* the bishop's transfer to Vicenza on 13 Sept. 1295, which would explain why the ordinances ignored the last article of the petition: his removal rendered it irrelevant.

98. *Reg. Bonif. VIII,* no. 406, incipit *Ecclesiarum omnium.* For full text of the formula, see the edition of *Reg.* no. 66 cited in A. Potthast, *Regesta pontificum Romanorum* (Berlin, 1874–75), no. 24051. The date of *Reg.* no. 406 ("id. septembris") is misprinted as 17 Sept. by Palandri, "Il vescovo Andrea de' Mozzi," p. 102 (but given correctly at p. 114 n.95) and as 27 Sept. by Sanesi, "Ricorso," p. 155.

99. Pietro Saraceno, bishop of Vicenza 1237–95, died after 16 June but before 18 Aug., according to F. Lampertico, whose evidence I have not seen: "Dei fatti d'arme combattuti al palude e del vescovo Andrea de' Mozzi," in *Dante e Vicenza* (Vicenza, 1865), pp. 42–87 (only pp. 62–71 concern Mozzi), at p. 65. Eubel, however, gives the *terminus post* as 16 July (*Hierarchia Catholica,* 1:526). On the erroneous assertion that Andrea vacated his Florentine see as early as July 1294, see R. Davidsohn, *Storia di Firenze,* vol. 3 (Florence, 1957), p. 606 n.1, the last three sentences of which are an addition to the original (Davidsohn, *Geschichte von Florenz,* vol. 2, pt. 2, p. 454).

100. *Reg. Bonif. VIII,* ep. 438, incipit *Romanus pontifex.* Orvieto waited over seven months for a replacement: ibid., ep. 1029 (an. 2, ep. 145), 24 Apr. 1296; Eubel, *Hierarchia Catholica,* 1:260.

101. Lampertico, "Fatti d'arme," pp. 68–69.

102. Authorities have long differed on the date of Mozzi's death in 1296. I have followed *Reg. Bonif. VIII,* where the see of Vicenza is stated to have been vacated by his death "circa principium septembris" (no. 1412, editor's minute; cf. Lampertico, "Fatti d'arme," p. 66 n). Lampertico, however, from evidence not available to me, stated that the precise date was 28 Aug. 1296 (p. 66); and thus Scartazzini-Vandelli[19],

p. 123; cf. Palandri, "Il vescovo Andrea de' Mozzi," p. 112 n.85. Mozzi's *acta* dated Mar. 1296 (above, n. 100 of this chap.) rule out the death date Feb. 1296 given by F. Ughelli, *Italia sacra*, 2d ed., rev. N. Coleti, vol. 5 (Venice, 1720), p. 1057; followed by Toynbee-Singleton, p. 37. The death is dated Apr. 1296 by Gams, *Series episcoporum*, p. 807; 28 Apr. by Eubel, *Hierarchia Catholica*, 1:526; followed by Davidsohn, *Geschichte von Florenz*, vol. 2, pt. 2, p. 454.

103. *Reg. Bonif. VIII*, no. 1387. Despite Boniface's reservation (no. 1412), the Vicenza chapter had elected its own candidate, and the patriarch of Aquileia had confirmed this choice; but Boniface on 18 Oct. 1296 ordered both patriarch and intruder to be summoned to his presence (no. 1382). The pope's will prevailed, and eventually the bishopric went to Rainaldus (no. 2611).

104. Palandri, "Il vescovo Andrea de' Mozzi," p. 102.

105. Ibid., p. 100 n.39 (13 Dec. 1308).

106. Davidsohn, *Geschichte von Florenz*, vol. 2, pt. 1, p. 441.

107. Palandri, "Il vescovo Andrea de' Mozzi," p. 100: "In vece è storicamente certo che, impetuoso ed imperioso per natura, avvilì e compromise, più d'una volta, la sua autorità di pastore."

108. See above, chap. 4, at n. 3.

109. The principal references are collected by A. Passerin d'Entrèves, *Dante as a Political Thinker* (Oxford, 1952), p. 69.

110. Trans. Sinclair, altered.

111. *Ep.* xi (ed. Toynbee, *Ep.* viii); dated "shortly after the death of Clement V, in May or June 1314" by Passerin d'Entrèves, *Dante as a Political Thinker*, p. 61; cf. Colin Hardie's chronological note to *Monarchy and Three Political Letters*, trans. D. Nicholl, Library of Ideas (London, 1954), p. 121.

112. *Ep.* xi, 13–16 (trans. Toynbee, *Ep.* viii, 6–7, p. 145, with commentary on pp. 133–35): "6. Non itaque videor quemquam exacerbasse ad iurgia; quin potius confusionis ruborem et in vobis et aliis, nomine solo archimandritis, per orbem dumtaxat pudor eradicatus non sit totaliter, accendisse, cum de tot pastorio officium usurpantibus, de tot ovibus, et si non abactis, neglectis tamen et incustoditis in pascuis, una sola vox, sola pia, et hec privata, in matris Ecclesie quasi funere audiatur. 7. Quidni? Cupiditatem unusquisque sibi duxit in uxorem, quemadmodum et vos, que nunquam pietatis et equitatis, ut caritas, sed semper impietatis et iniquitatis est genetrix. A, mater piissima, sponsa Christi, que in aqua et Spiritu generas tibi filios ad ruborem! Non caritas, non Astrea, sed filie sanguisuge facte sunt tibi nurus; que quales pariant tibi fetus, preter Lunensem pontificem omnes alii contestantur. Iacet Gregorius tuus in telis aranearum; iacet Ambrosius in neglectis clericorum latibulis; iacet Augustinus adiectus, Dionysius, Damascenus et Beda; et nescio quod 'Speculum,' Innocentium, et Ostiensem declamant. Cur non? Illi Deum querebant, ut finem et optimum; isti census et beneficia consequntur."

113. The Speculator identified by Toynbee, *Ep.*, p. 135 n.4; also in Toynbee-Singleton, p. 588, s.v. "Speculum iuris." See above, nn. 65, 73, of this chap., for Durandus.

114. *Par.* ix, 127–38 (trans. Sinclair). In passing I may observe that this passage introduces the themes of the complaints to follow: Folco, the master of *constructio*, fitly serves to introduce the thesis concisely.

115. Vita in Toynbee-Singleton, s.v. "Folco" (p. 286), with bibliography, to which add G. Bertoni, *Cinque letture dantesche* (Modena, 1933), pp. 103–11, and items in *Diction-*

naire des lettres françaises, ed. G. Grente et al.: [vol. 1] *Le Moyen âge*, ed. R. Bossuat et al. (Paris, 1964).

116. *De vulg. eloq.* 2. 6. 5–6 (trans. Temple Classics): "Est et sapidus et venustus etiam et excelsus, qui est dictatorum illustrium. . . . Hunc gradum constructionis excellentissimum nominamus. . . ."

117. Eubel, *Hierarchia Catholica*, 1:488 (dates), based on Gams, *Series episcoporum*, p. 638. His predecessor, Raimundus de Rabastencs, bishop 1202–5, was deposed.

118. "L'evesque de Tholosa Folquets cel de Maselha, / Que degus de bontat ab el no s'aparelha." Quoted by Toynbee-Singleton, p. 286 (verses 1026–27).

119. See above, pp. 87–94.

120. [Il Falso Boccaccio], *Chiose sopra Dante*, [ed. Lord Vernon] (Florence, 1846), p. 129: "epuoi intendere ogni prelato percostui perche illoro molto regnia questo vizio." Cf. Palandri, "Il vescovo Andrea de' Mozzi," p. 107 n.65.

121. Falso Boccaccio, *Chiose*, p. 128: "ilprimo fu umonacho chebbenome presciano effu appostata eperquesto sipuol intendere ogni maestro edottore." The vice of the place is identified with reference to Brunetto: "maestro didante mapur mostra cheditalvizio cioe disoddomito eglifosse pecchatore" (p. 126).

122. See above, chap. 4, at n. 8 ff.

123. The epithet was applied to Latini by G. Villani, *Cronica* 8. 10 (cf. above, n. 39, chap. 1).

124. See above, n. 111 of this chap.

125. Palandri, "Il vescovo Andrea de' Mozzi," p. 111; cf. pp. 106–11.

126. *Chiose anonime*, ed. Selmi, p. 89: "E questo procacciaro i Mozzi suoi consorti, per levarsi dinanzi il vituperio suo della soddomia per non vederlo ogni dì."

127. G. Boccaccio, *Il comento alla Divina Commedia*, ed. D. Guerri, vol. 3, Scrittori d'Italia vol. 86 (Bari, 1918), p. 204: "Dicesi costui essere stato un messer Andrea de' Mozzi, vescovo di Firenze, il quale e per questa miseria [see p. 203], nella quale forse era disonesto peccatore, e per molte altre sue sciocchezze che di lui si raccontano nel vulgo; per opera di messer Tommaso de' Mozzi, suo fratello, il quale era onorevole cavaliere e grande nel cospetto del papa, per levar dinanzi dagli occhi suoi e de' suoi cittadini tanta abominazione, fu permutato dal papa, di vescovo di Firenze, in vescovo di Vicenza."

128. See L. Paoletti, "Benvenuto da Imola," *Dizionario biografico degli italiani,* vol. 8 (Rome, 1966), pp. 691–94, with copious bibliography.

129. A = Ashburnham MS. 839, f. 40v, ed. M. Barbi, "La lettura di Benvenuto da Imola e i suoi rapporti con altri commenti," *Studi danteschi* 18 (1934): 79–98, at pp. 96–97 (with parallel passages from the commentary of Giovanni da Serravalle); cf. *Studi danteschi* 16 (1932): 137–56.

130. B = *Benevenuti de Rambaldis de Imola comentum super Dantis Aldigherij Comoediam*, ed. J. P. Lacaita, vol. 1 (Florence, 1887), pp. 524–25, ad *Inf.* xv, 110–14.

131. References hereafter are to my improvised sigla and section numbers (A, 2; B, 3); editions cited in the two preceding notes.

132. Or, rather, nothing reliable, for he does attribute the transfer erroneously to Pope Nicholas III, probably because his Florentine informant associated Andrea with the pope whom he served in Latino's legation—certainly his most significant role in the history of the city. Somehow the brother's name also became Nicholas (A, 6),

though this was brought into conformity with Boccaccio and genealogy in the B version.

It is easy to see how Benvenuto rendered Boccaccio's *messer* as *dominus* (A, 6; B, 7), but how the *onorevole cavaliere* became progressively *doctor magnus* (A, 6) and *magnus iurista* (B, 7) is less evident. Perhaps Benvenuto's notes from Boccaccio's lecture styled him only *dominus*, which Benvenuto later mistook in the academic sense most familiar to him at Bologna, but more probably the reference originally was to Andrea's legal learning but was transferred to Tommaso because the bishop's legendary character made it seem incredible.

133. Palandri, "Il vescovo Andrea de' Mozzi," p. 106.

134. See above, n. 105 of this chap.

135. *Commento alla Divina Commedia d'Anonimo Fiorentino del secolo XIV*, ed. P. Fanfani, vol. 1 (Bologna, 1866), pp. 361–62: "Fu costui messer Andrea de' Mozzi vescovo di Firenze, il quale fu per questo peccato disonestissimo, et ancora oltre a questo di poco senno: et non stava contento di tenere occulto il suo difetto et il suo poco senno, anzi ogni di volea predicare al popolo, dicendo parole sciocche et dilavate: onde il Papa, sentendo la sua misera vita, gli tolse il vescovado di Firenze ... et fecelo vescovo di Vicenze.... Et parve che'l Papa questo facesse a' prieghi del fratello, che fu valente cavaliere et d' assai."

136. D. Moreni, *Mores et consuetudines ecclesiae Florentinae* (Florence, 1794), pp. 20, 48, 53; cf. Davidsohn, *Geschichte von Florenz*, vol. 4, pt. 3, p. 64 n. 4. On the feast of Saint Zanobius, see above, n. 97 of this chap.

137. See above, nn. 112, 114 of this chap.

138. Ezech. 33:7–9; a doublet that is substantially the same occurs at Ezech. 3:17–19.

139. Jerome, *Commentarii in Ezechielem*, ed. *CCL*, 75:468–69 (ed. Migne, *PL*, 25:318–19): "Speculator terrae Iudaeae, vel rex potest intelligi, vel propheta; speculator autem ecclesiae, vel episcopus, vel presbyter, qui a populo electus est et, scripturarum lectione, cognoscens et praevidens quae futura sint, annuntiet populo et corrigat delinquentem. Unde magnopere formidandum est, ne ad hoc officium accedamus indigni, et assumpti a populo, negligentiae nos demus atque desidiae, et, quod his peius est, deliciis ventrique et otio servientes, honorem nos accepisse putemus, non ministerium." Cf. comm. ad Ezech. 3:17–19, ed. Migne, *PL*, 25:39.

140. Augustine, Serm. 339, §§ 2, 4, ed. Migne, *PL*, 38:1480–82. The Maurist text in Migne is a fragment of a longer sermon (Frangipani 2), ed. C. Lambot in *Stromata patristica et mediaevalia*, vol. 1 (Utrecht, 1950), according to Dekkers, nos. 284, 287.

141. The treasonous sense of *prodidit* is suggested by the context, for technically in Roman law, a *proditor* was a military spy or scout (*explorator* = *speculator*, the "watchman" of the traditional English translation), "who betrayed military secrets to the enemy," a capital offense. See Berger, s.vv. "Proditor" and "Explorare."

142. Gregory the Great, *Homiliae in Ezechielem* (Dekkers, no. 1710) 1. 11. 9, ad Ezech. 3:18; ed. Migne, *PL*, 76:909: "In quibus verbis quid nobis notandum est, quid sollicite cogitandum, nisi quia nec subjectus ex culpa praepositi moritur, nec praepositus sine culpa est quando verba vitae non audiens, ex sua culpa moritur subjectus? Inpio etenim mors debetur, sed ei a speculatore via vitae nuntianda est, et eius impietas increpanda. Si vero speculator taceat, ipse impius in iniquitate sua morietur, quia impietatis eius meritum fuit, ut dignus non esset ad quem speculatoris sermo fieret. Sed sanguinem eius Dominus de manu speculatoris requirit, quia ipse

hunc occidit, quia eum tacendo morti prodidit. In quibus utrisque pensandum est quantum sibi connexa sunt peccata subditorum atque praepositorum, quia ubi subiectus ex sua culpa moritur, ibi is qui praeest, quoniam tacuit, reus mortis tenetur. Pensate ergo, fratres charissimi, pensate, quia et quod nos digni pastores non sumus etiam ex vestra culpa est, quibus tales praelati sumus. Et si quando vos ad iniquitatem defluitis, etiam ex nostro hoc reatu est, quos obsistentes atque reclamantes in pravis desideriis non habetis. Vobis ergo et nobis parcitis, si a pravo opere cessatis. Vobis et nobis parcimus, quando hoc quod displicet non tacemus."

143. "Tua lingua clavis est regni caelorum; quapropter numquam a bonis sileat, numquam ab ammonitionibus cesset." Alcuin, *Ep.* 267 (an. 804, perhaps to Arno, archbishop of Salzburg), ed. E. Dümmler, *MGH, Epistolae aevi Carolini*, vol. 4 (Berlin, 1895), pp. 425–26.

144. Gratian, *Decretum* D.88 c.6, ed. Friedberg, 1:307–9: "Episcopus nullam rei familiaris curam ad se revocet, sed lectioni et orationi et verbo predicationis tantummodo vacet."

145. The *Edictum* appears in its original, shorter form in all three recensions of the Roman Pontifical, ed. M. Andrieu, *Le Pontifical romain au moyen-âge*, Studi e testi nos. 86–88. The full text is printed only in the edition of the earliest, quoted below: (1) *Pontificale Romanum saeculi XII*, Ordo xi = Studi e testi no. 86 (1938), pp. 152–54. Most probably Mozzi used the compilation in the revised form most common in his century: (2) *Pontificale secundum consuetudinem et usum Romanae Curiae*, Ordo xii = Studi e testi no. 87 (1940), p. 369. Since the third major recension of the Roman Pontifical was made by William Durandus (see above, n. 73 of this chap.) between 1292 and 1295, it is hardly possible that Mozzi was influenced by it, though it would of course reflect views closest to his own: (3) *Pontificale Guillielmi Durandi*, Ordo xv = Studi e testi no. 88 (1940), p. 393, with a new and more descriptive title composed by Durandus: *Edictum quod metropolitanus tradit scriptum consecrato.*

146. The earliest copy of the original version of the *Edictum* follows the episcopal consecration ordo in a collection of ordines from Besançon, written ca. 1000 (London, British Museum, MS. Add. 15222). This original version was already expanded when the *Edictum* was inserted into the *Pontificale Romano-Germanicum*, which was compiled at Mainz between 950 and 964 (Ordo lxvi). See *Le Pontifical romano-germanique du dixième siècle*, ed. C. Vogel and R. Elze, vol. 1 = Studi e testi no. 226 (1963), pp. 231–40.

147. *Pont. Rom. saec. XII*, Ordo xi, 1, ed. Andrieu, p. 152: "scias te maximum pondus suscepisse laboris, quod est sarcina regiminis animarum et commodis deservire multorum omniumque fieri minimum atque ministrum et, pro credito tibi talento, in die divini examinis redditurum rationem."

148. Ibid., § 5, p. 153: "Praedicationi insta; verbum Dei plebi tibi commissae affluenter melliflueque atque distincte, in quantum rore coelesti perfusus fueris, praedicare non desinas."

149. See above, pp. 000.

150. *Par.* xvii, 138–42, trans. Sinclair.

151. See above, n. 114 of this chap. Note that in *Ep.* xi, 16 (see above, n. 112 of this chap.), addressed to the Italian cardinals, "Gregorius tuus" is contrasted to "Ambrosius in neglectis clericorum latibulis," suggesting that the prelates could especially profit from Gregory, while Ambrose is pertinent to the clergy in general, as indeed his *De*

officiis ministrorum (Dekkers, no. 114) decidedly was. Thus Dante's reference to Gregory would seem to indicate the *Regula pastoralis* specifically.

152. Alcuin, *Ep.* 116 (an. 796, to Archbishop Eanbald II of York), ed. Dümmler, *MGH, Epist.*, 4:171: "Numquam a sanctae praedicationis verbo lingua sileat, numquam a bono opere manus torpescat; et quocumque vadas, liber sancti Gregorii pastoralis tecum pergat. Sepius illum legas et relegas, quatenus te ipsum et tuum opus cognoscas in illo; ut, qualiter vivere vel docere debeas, ante oculos habeas. Speculum est enim pontificalis vitae et medicina contra singula diabolicae fraudis vulnera."

Cf. *Ep.* 124 (an. 797, to Higbald, bishop of Lindisfarne), ibid., p. 182: "Lege saepius, obsecro, beati Gregorii praedicatoris nostri libellum de pastorali cura, ut in eo periculum sacerdotalis officii agnoscas et bene operantis servi mercedem non obliviscaris. Iste liber tuis saepius inhereat manibus, illius sensus tuae firmiter infigantur memoriae; ut scias, qualiter quisque ad sacerdotalem honorem accedere, et accedens quanta consideratione se ipsum circumspicere debeat; et quibus exemplis vivere necesse sit; et quanta intentione praedicare iubeatur. Et quid cui personę conveniat maxima discretione descripsit."

153. The Maurist edition of the *Regula pastoralis* (Dekkers, no. 1712) in Migne, *PL,* 77:10–128; pt. 3, entitled *Qualiter rector bene vivens debeat docere et admonere subditos,* covers cols. 49–126. Translations quoted below are by J. Barmby, in *A Select Library of Nicene and Post-Nicene Fathers of the Christian Church,* 2d ser., ed. P. Schaff and H. Wace, vol. 12, pt. 2 (New York, 1895), pp. 1–72. Useful notes in the somewhat freer translation by Henry Davis in the series "Ancient Christian Writers," no. 11 (Westminster, Md., 1950).

154. *Reg. past.* 1. proem, ed. Migne, *PL,* 77:13: "Pastoralis curae me pondera . . . quae . . . praesentis libri stylo exprimo de eorum gravedine omne quod penso, ut et haec qui vacat, incaute non expetat; et qui incaute expetiit, adeptum se esse pertimescat."

155. Idem: "Sed quia sunt plerique mihi imperitia similes, qui dum metiri se nesciunt, quae non didicerint docere concupiscunt; qui pondus magisterii tanto levius aestimant, quanto vim magnitudinis illius ignorant; ab ipso libri huius reprehendantur exordio; ut quia indocti ac praecipites doctrinae arcem tenere appetunt, a praecipitationis suae ausibus in ipsa locutionis nostrae ianua repellantur."

156. *Reg. past.* 1. 11, ed. Migne, *PL,* 77:25–26. Gregory links it with *impetigo,* which he considers to be a condition that does not itch. He contrasts it to a scabrous condition that continually does itch because the heat of the body is drawn out to the skin. To Gregory, this chronic itch signifies unrestrained lust (*luxuria*), because voluptuous thoughts are generated in the heart and can be either expressed in action or repressed by an act of will. The impulses, he explains, are only human, but it is the work of the devil when one follows them: "Iugem vero habet scabiem, cui carnis petulantia sine cessatione dominatur. In scabie etenim fervor viscerum ad cutem trahitur, per quam recte luxuria designatur, quia si cordis tentatio usque ad operationem prosilit, nimirum fervor intimus usque ad cutis scabiem prorumpit; et foris iam corpus sauciat, quia dum in cogitatione voluptas non reprimitur, etiam in actione dominatur. Quasi enim cutis pruriginem Paulus curabat abstergere, cum dicebat: 'Tentatio vos non apprehendat, nisi humana' [1 Cor. 10:13]; ac si aperte diceret: Humanum quidem est tentationem in corde perpeti, daemoniacum vero est in tentationis certamine et in operatione superari. Impetiginem quoque habet in corpore, quisquis avaritia vastatur in mente: quae si in parvis non compescitur, nimirum sine mensura

dilatatur. Impetigo quippe sine dolore corpus occupat, et absque occupati taedio excrescens membrorum decorem foedat, quia et avaritia capti animum dum quasi delectat, exulcerat; dum adipiscenda quaeque cogitationi obiicit, ad inimicitias accendit, et dolorem in vulnere non facit, quia aestuanti animo ex culpa abundantiam promittit. Sed decor membrorum peditur, quia aliarum quoque virtutum per hanc pulcritudo depravatur; et quasi totum corpus exasperat, quia per universa vitia animum supplantat, Paulo attestante qui ait: 'Radix omnium malorum est cupiditas' [1 Tim. 6:10]."

Those who would interpret Mozzi's crime as sodomy might well argue that Brunetto's epithet *tigna* (see above, chap. 4, at n. 2) corresponds to this scabrous itch rather than to Gregory's painless *impetigo*. Certainly the gnawing sensation of an itch gave Latin *tinea* its medieval medical sense (see above, n. 3 of this chap.), which the Italian *tigna* retained. *Jugis scabies,* then, might be equated to *tigna,* but there the similarity ends, since *scabies* for Gregory signified a *natural* lust (*luxuria*), such as is punished in the circle of the *lussuriosi* (*Inf.* v, 28–142), while Mozzi is guilty of some violence *against* nature.

Gregory's itchless *impetigo* is clearly not the itchy *impetigo contagiosa* of modern medicine but simply a rash or eruption, in which general sense the word was used in both ancient and medieval Latin, as well as in Italian: see respectively s.vv. "impetigo" and "impetig(g)ine" in lexicons cited above, in n. 3 of this chap.

Forensic medicine somewhat clarifies the distinction between the two conditions. The *Glossa ordinaria* to *Dig.* 21. 1. 6. 1 glosses *impetiginosum* "id est lenticulis, ut ita dicam, plenum." The glossator would seem to agree with Gregory's aetiology of the itch, for at *Dig.* 21. 1. 3 he glossed *pruriginosi* "id est scabiosi, qui ardorem carnis patiuntur." Apparently the Bolognese lawyer regarded this *vitium corporale* as a natural condition (see ibid., ad v. *muti*), rather than as a *morbus*, which Roman law defined as a "habitum cuiusque corporis contra naturam, qui usum eius ad id facit deteriorem" (*Dig.* 21. 1. 1. 7). Hence it would seem that both pope and lawyer drew on a medical tradition that regarded scabrous itch as the natural effect of a certain type of physical constitution. This would explain why Gregory thought the *iugis scabies* was appropriate to signify the inborn impulse to lust: both are *vitia naturalia*, neither of which could be aptly applied to the unnatural vice of Andrea de' Mozzi.

157. D.49 c.1, ed. Friedberg, 1:175–77.

158. See above, n. 142 of this chap.

159. *Reg. past.* 3, proem, ed. Migne, *PL*, 77:49: "Pro qualitate igitur audientium formari debet sermo doctorum, ut et ad sua singulis congruat, et tamen a communis aedificationis arte nunquam recedat. Quid enim sunt intentae mentes auditorum, nisi ut ita dixerim, quaedam in cithara tensiones stratae chordarum? quas tangendi artifex, ut non sibimetipsi dissimile canticum faciat, dissimiliter pulsat. Et idcirco chordae consonam modulationem reddunt, quia uno quidem plectro, sed non uno impulsu feriuntur. Unde et doctor quisque, ut in una cunctos virtute charitatis aedificet, ex una doctrina, non una eademque exhortatione tangere corda audientium debet."

160. *Reg. past.* 3. 18, ed. Migne, *PL*, 77:79–80: "Illis [pertinacibus] dicendum est quod plus de se quam sunt sentiunt, et idcirco alienis consiliis non acquiescunt.... Illis dicendum est quia nisi meliores se caeteris aestimarent, nequaquam cunctorum

consilia suae deliberationi postponerent.... Illis per Paulum dicitur: 'Nolite prudentes esse apud vosmetipsos' [Rom. 12:16].... Pertinacia quippe ex superbia ... generatur. Admonendi igitur sunt pertinaces, ut elationem suae cogitationis agnoscant, et semetipsos vincere studeant; ne dum rectis aliorum suasionibus foris superari despiciunt, intus a superbia captivi teneantur."

161. *Reg. past.* 3. 36, ed. Migne, *PL*, 77:121: "et tanta arte vox temperanda est, ut cum diversa sint auditorum vitia, et singulis inveniatur congrua, et tamen sibimetipsi non sit diversa; ut inter passiones medias uno quidem ductu transeat, sed more bicipitis gladii tumores cogitationum carnalium ex diverso latere incidat, quatenus sic superbis praedicetur humilitas, ut tamen timidis non augeatur metus, sic timidis infundatur auctoritas, ut tamen superbis non crescat effrenatio."

162. *Reg. past.* 3. 39, ed. Migne, *PL*, 77:124 (I have altered Barmby's translation and supplied section numbers): *"Quod infirmis mentibus omnino non debent alta praedicari.* [1] Sciendum vero est praedicatori, ut auditoris sui animum ultra vires non trahat, ne, ut ita dicam, dum plus quam valet tenditur, mentis chorda rumpatur. Alta enim quaeque debent multis audientibus contegi, et vix paucis aperiri. [2] Hinc namque per semetipsam Veritas dicit: 'Quis putas est fidelis dispensator et prudens, quem constituit dominus super familiam suam, ut det illis in tempore tritici mensuram?' [Matt. 24:45; Luke 12:42]. Per mensuram quippe tritici exprimitur modus verbi, ne cum angusto cordi incapabile aliquid tribuitur, extra fundatur.... [4] Hinc Moyses a secreto Dei exiens, coruscantem coram populo faciem velat [Exod. 34:33, 35], quia nimirum turbis claritatis intimae arcana non indicat. [5] Hinc per eum divina voce praecipitur [Exod. 21:33, 34], ut is qui cisternam foderit, si operire neglexerit, corruente in ea bove vel asino, pretium reddat; quia ad alta scientiae fluenta perveniens, cum haec apud bruta audientium corda non contegit, poenae reus addicitur, si per verba eius in scandalum, sive munda sive immunda mens capiatur. [6] ... qui recte praedicat, obscuris adhuc cordibus aperta clamat, nil de occultis mysteriis indicat, ut tunc subtiliora quaeque de coelestibus audiant, cum luci veritatis appropinquant."

163. The Gregorian exposition of Ezech. 3:18 explains why: see above, n. 142 of this chap.

164. See above, § 1 in n. 162 of this chap.

165. See above, n. 159 of this chap.

166. Terence *Eunuchus* 2. 3. 20; Cicero *In Verrem* 1. 3: "quo animum *intendat,* facile perspicio." See Lewis-Short, s.v. "intendo."

167. Lewis-Short, s.v. "nervus" II.

168. Pézard, pp. 203–18.

169. Both Latin *nervus* and Italian *nervo* are singular when related to the *topos* of the *arcus* but plural in relation to that of the cithara. Examples s.v. "nervus" in Lewis-Short and s.v. "nervo" in *Vocabulario degli Accademici della Crusca*, 5th ed., vol. 11, pt. 1 (Florence, 1914), p. 114.

170. *Reg. past.* 3. 2, ed. Migne, *PL*, 77:53: "cum Saulem spiritus adversus invaderet, apprehensa David cithara, eius vesaniam sedabat [1 Kings 18:10].... quia cum sensus potentum per elationem in furorem vertitur, dignum est ut ad salutem mentis quasi dulcedine citharae, locutionis nostrae tranquillitate revocetur."

171. Pézard has collected and classified Dante's tension metaphors on pp. 206–9; our key text he relegated to note 2, p. 209.

172. *De vulg. eloq.* 2. 4. 9: "prius Elicone potatus, tensis fidibus ad supremum, secure

plectrum tum movere incipiat." Marigo notes here that Rajna obscured the sense of the passage by emending *ad supremum*, on which all MSS agree, to *adsumptum*. Lewis-Short, s.v. "fides²" II, equates *fides*, a musical string, with *nervus* and *chorda*.

173. See Marigo's translation: "invenzione espressa in versi secondo [arte] retorica e musicale" (*De vulg. eloq.*, p. 189). My understanding of the whole chapter has largely been guided by his commentary.

174. *De vulg. eloq.* 2. 4. 4 (trans. Temple Classics): "Ante omnia ergo dicimus unumquenque debere materie pondus propriis humeris coequare, ne forte humerorum nimio gravata virtute in cenum cespitare necesse sit. Hoc est quod magister noster Oratius precipit, cum in principio poetrie 'Sumite materiam [vestris, qui scribitis, aequam viribus]' dicit."

175. *De vulg. eloq.* 2. 4: "9. Caveat ergo quilibet et discernat ea que dicimus; et quando hec tria pure cantare intendit, vel que ad ea directe ac pure secuntur, prius Elicone potatus, tensis fidibus ad supremum, secure plectrum tum movere incipiat. 10. Sed cautionem atque discretionem hanc accipere, sicut decet, hoc opus et labor est, quoniam nunquam sine strenuitate ingenii et artis assiduitate scientiarumque habitu fieri potest. Et hii sunt quos poeta Eneidorum sexto Dei dilectos et ab ardente virtute sublimatos ad ethera deorumque filios vocat, quanquam figurate loquatur. 11. Et ideo confutetur illorum stultitia, qui arte scientiaque immunes, de solo ingenio confidentes, ad summa summe canenda prorumpunt; et a tanta presumptuositate desistant, et si anseres natura vel desidia sunt, nolint astripetam aquilam imitari." I have altered Howell's Temple Classics translation (p. 79), notably by rendering *strenuitate ingenii* as "a vigorous intellect" rather than "strenuous efforts of genius"; Marigo has "ingegno animoso." Why "intellect" is preferable to "genius" will become evident as my argument progresses.

176. See above, chap. 4, at n. 134 ff.

177. *Aeneid* 6. 126–31, trans. J. W. Mackail, *Virgil's Works*, Modern Library (New York, 1950), p. 107: "easy is the descent into hell; all night and day the gate of dark Dis stands open; but to recall thy steps and issue to upper air, this is the task, this the burden. Some few of gods' lineage have availed, such as Jupiter's gracious favor or virtue's ardor has upborne to heaven."

178. Pézard, pp. 215, 219. For this theme, fundamental in his argument, see "Index des noms," s.v. "blasphème."

179. Trans. Sinclair.

180. Trans. Sinclair.

181. *Conv.* 1. 1. 19: "Li quali priego tutti che se lo convivio non fosse tanto splendido quanto conviene a la sua grida, che non al mio volere, ma a la mia facultade imputino ogni difetto; però che la mia voglia di compita e cara liberalitate è qui seguace."

182. See above, chap. 1, text following n. 30.

183. *Li livres dou tresor de Brunetto Latini* (3. 1. 10, 12–13), ed. F. J. Carmody, University of California Publications in Modern Philology, vol. 22 (Berkeley, 1948), pp. 318–19: "10. Or est il dont prové que la science de rectorique n'est pas dou tout aquise par nature ou par us mais par ensegnement et par art, por quoi je di que chascuns doit estudiier son engien a savoir le.... 12. Neporquant dist li proverbes que noureture passe nature; car selonc ce que nous trovons en la premiere et en la seconde partie de cest livre, l'ame de tous homes est bone naturelement, mais ele mue sa

nature por la mauvaisté dou cors en quoi ele maint enclose, autresi com le vin ki enpire por la malvaistié du vaissel. Et quant li cors est de bone nature, il conorte s'ame et aide a sa bonté, et lors li valent ars et us. Car art li ensegne le commandement ki a ce covient, et us le fait prest et apert et esmolut a l'oevre. 13. Et pour ce vieut li mestres ramentevoir a son ami le riule et l'ensengnement de l'art de rectorique ki mout li aideront a la soutillece ki est en lui par sa bone nature."

184. If Boccaccio was reliably informed that Mozzi suffered from the gout, then by Brunetto's theory that physical defect could explain the aging bishop's immunity to art and experience alike. See *Tresor* 3. 1. 12, quoted above, n. 183 of this chap. Boccaccio wrote: "Era questo vescovo sconciamente gottoso, in quanto che, per difetto degli omóri corrotti, tutti i nervi della persona gli s'erano rattrappati, come in assai gottosi veggiamo, e nelle mani e ne' piedi; e cosí per questa parte del corpo, cioè per li nervi, intende tutto il corpo, il quale morendo lasciò in Vicenza" (*Il comento alla Divina Commedia*, ed. Guerri, 3:204). As the Anonimo Fiorentino remarked, the interpretation is vitiated by the fact that gout does not draw out the sinews but contracts them: "però ch' elli fu gottoso, pare che alcuno voglia dire che l'Auttore intese per questo i mal protesi nervi; ma questo non è protendere, ma è ristrignere et ratrappare i nervi; ma protendere è di cosa che si stenda innanzi" (*Commento alla Divina Commedia*, ed. Fanfani, 1:362); cf. Pézard, p. 205. Though the interpretation is certainly wrong, still it would hardly have occurred to Boccaccio had he not considered Mozzi's gout to be an established fact.

185. On *habitus*, see *De vulg. eloq.*, ed. Marigo, p. 196.

186. *Tresor* 2. 73. 5, ed. Carmody, p. 251: "Tuilles dit, chascuns doit metre s'entente as choses a quoi il est covenables; et ja soit ce que autre chose li seroit millour et plus honorable, toutefoies doit il amesurer ses estuides selonc sa riule. Raison comment: s'il est fiebles de son cors et il ait bon engien et vive memore, ne sive pas chevalerie mais l'estuide de letre et de clergie. Car nus ne doit aler contre nature ne sivre çou k'il ne puet consivre; mais se besoigne nos fait meller as choses ki n'apartient a nostre engin, nous devons curer ke nous les fachons beles sans laidece ou a poi de deshonour, ne nous ne devons pas tant efforcier les biens ki ne nous sont doné comme de fuir les visces." Cf. Cicero *De officiis* 1. 31.

187. See above, chap. 1, at n. 30.

188. An alternative, and equally asexual, interpretation of *li mal protesi nervi* is suggested by Cassiodorus' commentary on the Easter Psalm 56 (AV 57), *Ne disperdas*, verse 9 (verse 12 in ed. Migne, *PL*, 70:404): "*Exsurge, gloria mea; exsurge, psalterium et cithara.... Cithara* vero gloriosam significat passionem, quae tensis nervis dinumeratioque ossibus, virtutem patientiae intellectuali quodam carmine personabat." ("*Cithara* signifies the glorious passion, which, with stretched sinews and numbered bones [Ps. 21:18], loudly proclaimed the virtue of patient suffering, by a kind of song that was intellectual.") Both harp and bow have been studied as symbols of the Crucifixion by F. P. Pickering, most recently in his *Literature and Art in the Middle Ages* (London, 1970), pp. 285–307 (p. 292 for the passage quoted above); see also his index, s.vv. "Cithara" and "Harp." This art historian says that the harp "was the most influential of all the many medieval symbols of the Crucifixion" (p. 301). If Mozzi's ill-stretched sinews derive from this tradition, then the bishop should be compared to Christ in his ministry.

CHAPTER 5

1. See above, n. 127 of chap. 4.
2. See above, chap. 4, at n. 131 (A, 7; B, 7).
3. See above, n. 136 of chap. 4.
4. See above, n. 126 of chap. 4.
5. R. Davidsohn, *Geschichte von Florenz*, vol. 2, pt. 2 (Berlin, 1908), p. 414 n.1.
6. For examples from an earlier period, see the appendix to my note "Rucco di Cambio de' Mozzi in France and England," *Studi danteschi* 47 (1970): 49–57.
7. Davidsohn, *Geschichte von Florenz*, vol. 2, pt. 2, p. 550 n.1.
8. E. Palandri, "Il vescovo Andrea de' Mozzi nella storia e nella leggenda dantesca," *Giornale dantesco* 32 (1931): 91–118, at pp. 115–18. Cf. above, chap. 4, at n. 125 ff.
9. See above, n. 85 of chap. 4.
10. E. Sanesi, "Del trasferimento di messer Andrea dei Mozzi da Firenze a Vicenza," *Studi danteschi* 22 (1938): 115–22, at p. 121.
11. Davidsohn observed that deposition would have been the canonical penalty for a bishop who was a notorious sodomite (*Geschichte von Florenz*, vol. 2, pt. 2, p. 454 n.1). Palandri agrees ("Il vescovo Andrea de' Mozzi," p. 113 n.91) that this disproves the commentator's charge of sodomy. In view of the papal *plenitudo potestatis* and Boniface's unparalleled exercise of it, the assumption that he did not let circumstances alter cases is, I think, unwarranted.
12. See above, n. 84 of chap. 4.
13. See above, chap. 4, at n. 131 (A, 6 and 7). Sanesi has perceived the slightest hint of scandal (*maldicenza*), which, he tentatively suggested, might be related to Dante's condemnation. He printed an extract from one of the reports to the Florentine chapter from its proctor in Rome, Cambio delle Panche (or di Sesto), written about 1290 (see above, n. 10 of this chap.): "Unum volo tangere. Credo quod episcopus habet ad praesens arduiora facere quam si<n>t fori nostri non scribere plus; propter malas linguas. Adhuc super praedictis claribus vobis scribam" ("One thing I wish to mention. I believe that the bishop has more difficult things to do at present than might be of our court, not to write more because of bad tongues. Besides I shall write to you more clearly about the aforesaid matters"; my trans. and emendation of text in Sanesi, "Trasferimento," p. 122). This passage is open to less lurid interpretations: the proctor may have feared that the bishop's adherents in the chapter would relay the information back to him—*malas linguas* being thus hostile rather than defamatory—or judging from the last remark, he may merely have been using innuendo to justify to his principals a prolonged stay at the curia. Most likely he was withholding the sort of observations about the disposition of certain *curiales* to the bishop that Tebaldo did report not long afterward (see above, chap. 4, at nn. 80–87).
14. *Inf.* xxvii, 67–129.
15. *Par.* xxvii, 22–24.
16. To study six dozen cases individually would necessitate a monograph in itself, and perhaps a deceptive one, for translation was not an isolated phenomenon but rather an integral part of the growing system by which Rome came to control the appointment of bishops. Its workings for an important sector of the Church have been studied for the period 1198–1303 with particular reference to France: B. A.

Pocquet du Haut-Jussé, "Le second différend entre Boniface VIII et Philippe le Bel: Note sur l'une de ses causes," in *Mélanges Albert Dufourcq: Etudes d'histoire religieuse* (Paris, 1932), pp. 73–108, especially 90–104; based on data derived from Eubel. "La conclusion de cette trop longue statistique n'est guère contestable. Il est manifeste que Boniface VIII a fait des provisions apostoliques un usage tout à fait hors de proportion avec les habitudes de ses prédécesseurs. . . . En somme, bien avant la réserve des bénéfices majeurs prononcée par Grégoire XI, Boniface VIII, et il est le premier pape à en avoir agi ainsi, disposa en fait de la plupart des sièges épiscopaux de la France" (pp. 103–4). I doubt that Dante had either the data or the temperament to perceive this unobtrusive policy, which indeed has not been apparent to most modern students. Still historians no less than Dantists might consider Pocquet's hint that the trend culminating in Boniface was inaugurated by his immediate predecessor among Dante's simoniacal popes, namely Nicholas III (p. 98).

17. On the date of composition of *Inf.* xv (1307 × 1313), see U. Cosmo, *Guida a Dante*, 2d ed., Maestri e compagni, no. 4 (Florence, 1962), pp. 148–50.

18. Abuse: "Everything which is contrary to good order established by usage," or "departure from use; immoderate or improper use." *Black's Law Dictionary*, ed. H. C. Black, 4th ed. (St. Paul, Minn., 1951), p. 24.

19. Italian sees were affected by all sixteen translations enregistered during the first year of Boniface VIII: thirteen were both from and to an Italian see; of the remainder, one was *from*, both the others *to* Italian sees. As the letters were not entered by date, their numbers are here given in chronological order to exhibit Andrea's place in the series (tenth). *Les registres de Boniface VIII,* ed. G. Digard et al., BEFAR², no. 4 (Paris, 1884–1935), nos. 980 (cf. 99), 67, 64, 66, 76, 79, 68, 329, 261 (cf. 260), 331, 406 (Andrea to Vicenza), 438 (Franciscus to Florence), 398, 425, 586, 584. Significantly, the chancery at this time did not distinguish translation from other forms of episcopal nomination but applied the same repertory of form letters to all indifferently.

20. *Inf.* xix, 53–57 (Boniface), 79–87 (Clement).

21. In *Purg.* xx, 85–93, as Dante deplores the outrage at Anagni to the papal office, his words echo a devotional poem, "Stava la Vergin," that Boniface himself had composed: R. Artinian, "Dante's Parody of Boniface VIII," *Dante Studies* 85 (1967): 71–74.

22. The evolution of the complex of ideas clustered around the office/man distinction has been anatomized by E. Kantorowicz in *The King's Two Bodies* (Princeton, N.J., 1957). On the papal theorists, see especially M. Wilks, *The Problem of Sovereignty in the Later Middle Ages: The Papal Monarchy with Augustinus Triumphus and the Publicists* (Cambridge, Eng., 1963).

23. S. Kuttner, "The Father of the Science of Canon Law," *Jurist* 1 (1941): 2–19, at p. 15. Another magisterial estimate by G. Le Bras, *Institutions ecclésiastiques de la Chrétienté médiéval*, in *Histoire de l'Eglise,* ed. A. Fliche et al., vol. 12, pt. 1 (Paris, 1959), pp. 50–55. The sources and plan of the *Decretum* are described by J. Rambaud-Buhot in *Histoire du droit et des institutions de l'Eglise en Occident*, ed. G. Le Bras, vol. 7 (Paris, 1965), pp. 52–129.

24. The others are Honorius III, Gregory IX, Urban IV, Clement IV, Gregory X, Hadrian V (cf. *Purg.* xix, 79 ff.), and Martin IV—for a total of nine out of eighteen. Perhaps also Alexander IV, Nicholas III, and Honorius IV might qualify. Based

mainly on notices by H. K. Mann, *Lives of the Popes in the Middle Ages,* vols. 13–17 (London, 1925–32).

25. The acts of general councils also supplied a small yet important fraction of new canons. For definitions of "decretal," see Le Bras, *Institutions ecclésiastiques,* p. 56 n.2, especially Kuttner's definition: "toute réponse papale à une consultation canonique, tout mandat judiciaire avec ou sans nomination de juges délégués au cas d'appel ou *provocatio* au pape."

26. *Mon.* 3. 3. 4–5 (trans. Nicholl): "hic litigium causa ignorantiae sit magis. Hominibus nanque, rationis intuitu voluntatem prevolantibus hoc sepe contingit: ut, male affecti, lumine rationis postposito, affectu quasi ceci trahantur et pertinaciter suam denegent cecitatem. Unde fit persepe quod non solum falsitas patrocinium habeat, sed—ut plerique—de suis terminis egredientes per aliena castra discurrant; ubi nichil intelligentes, ipsi nichil intelliguntur: et sic provocant quosdam ad iram, quosdam ad dedignationem, nonnullos ad risum."

27. *Mon.* 3. 3. 6–9 (trans. Nicholl, altered): "Igitur contra veritatem que queritur tria hominum genera maxime colluctantur. Summus nanque Pontifex, domini nostri Iesu Cristi vicarius et Petri successor, cui non quicquid Cristo sed quicquid Petro debemus, zelo fortasse clavium, necnon alii gregum cristianorum pastores, et alii quos credo zelo solo matris Ecclesie promoveri, veritati quam ostensurus sum de zelo forsan—ut dixi—non de superbia contradicunt. Quidam vero alii, quorum obstinata cupiditas lumen rationis extinxit—et dum ex patre dyabolo sunt, Ecclesie se filios esse dicunt.... Sunt etiam tertii—quos decretalistas vocant—qui, theologie ac phylosophie cuiuslibet inscii et expertes, suis decretalibus—quas profecto venerandas existimo—tota intentione innixi, de illarum prevalentia—credo—sperantes, Imperio derogant."

28. Cf. *Inf.* xix, 100–103 (trans. Sinclair): "And were it not that reverence for the supreme keys which thou didst hold in the glad life still forbids it to me, I should use yet harder words." He stops short of a direct attack on the office, contenting himself with invective against the man and the like of him.

29. *Mon.* 3. 3. 17–18 (trans. Nicholl): "Hiis itaque sic exclusis, excludendi sunt alii qui, corvorum plumis operti, oves albas in grege Domini se iactant. Hii sunt impietatis filii qui, ut flagitia sua exequi possint, matrem prostituunt, fratres expellunt, et denique iudicem habere nolunt. Nam cur ad eos ratio quereretur, cum sua cupiditate detenti principia non viderent? Quapropter cum solis concertatio restat qui, aliquali zelo erga matrem Ecclesiam ducti, ipsam que queritur veritatem ignorant...."

30. They are usually identified as secular princes by their claim to be "*filios ... Ecclesie*" (§ 8) independent of the empire (*iudicem habere nolunt*; § 17), e.g., by Vinay, ed. *Monarchia,* p. 204. The curiously mixed metaphor of sheep in crows' feathers confirms this: they are those who disguise themselves in false plumage as the imperial eagle.

31. *Mon.* 3. 15. 9 (trans. Nicholl, p. 93). The *Decretales* does collect conciliar canons but none concern episcopal translation: see Lib. i, tit. 7, in the several decretal collections cited below, n. 47 of this chap.

32. *Mon.* 3. 15. 10 (trans. Nicholl, p. 93).

33. Gratian never intended his collection to be a substitute for Scripture. The canons supplement rather than incorporate Biblical law, as appears from the fact that the Bible is not among the *fontes* of the *Decretum.* Consequently, one who would consult

the authorities whom Dante recognized would consult *both* Gratian and the Bible, as we shall in due course.

34. Basic bibliography in Cross, *ODCC,* pp. 493–94.

35. In general, see L. Ober, "Die Translation der Bischöfe im Altertum," *Archiv für katholisches Kirchenrecht* 88 (1908): 209–29, 441–65, 625–48, and 89 (1909): 3–33. Broad, thorough, but controversial is J. P. Pozzi, "Le fondement historique et juridique de la translation des évêques depuis les premiers documents du droit canonique au Décret de Gratien" (unpubl. diss., Faculté de droit, Université de Paris, 1953). More briefly, H. Feine, *Kirchliche Rechtsgeschichte,* 3d ed., vol. 1 (Weimar, 1955), pp. 109–10, 302. For episcopal translation as a factor in the diffusion of the Pseudo-Isidorean *Decretals* in Italy, see Pozzi's dissertation: *"De episcoporum transmigratione et quod non temere judicentur regule quadraginta quattuor": Libellus ex tomo XVIII Vallicelliano editur, in<t>roductione historico-iuridica auctus* (Pontificia Universitas Lateranensis, Institutum Utriusque Juris: Rome, 1959).

36. Gratian, *Decretum* C.7 q.1 c.19, ed. Friedberg, 1:576: "Non oportet episcopum vel reliquos ordines de civitate ad civitatem migrare; non episcopus, non presbiter, non diaconus transeat. Si quis autem post diffinitionem sancti et magni concilii tale quid agere temptaverit, et se huiusmodi negotio mancipaverit, hoc factum prorsus in irritum ducatur, et restituatur ecclesiae, cuius fuit episcopus, aut presbiter, aut diaconus ordinatus." Original Greek text of Nicaea I, c.15, ed. H. T. Bruns, *Canones apostolorum et conciliorum saeculorum IV. V. VI. VII.,* Bibliotheca ecclesiastica, ed. A. Neander, no. 1, 2 vols. (Berlin, 1839), 1:18.

On the early history of *translatio,* see esp. J. Gaudemet, *L'Eglise dans l'Empire romain (IVe–Ve siècles),* in *Histoire du droit et des institutions de l'Eglise en Occident,* ed. G. Le Bras, vol. 3 (Paris, 1958), pp. 356–63.

37. On this aspect of translation, see Kantorowicz, *King's Two Bodies,* pp. 212–18, esp. n. 61.

38. *Ep.* 209. 7 n.42, ed. *CSEL* 57:350–51; cf. Gaudemet, *L'Eglise,* p. 361 n.6.

39. *Ep.* 65. 5, ed. *CSEL* 54:621–23; cf. Gaudemet, *L'Eglise,* p. 361, at n. 8.

40. *Statuta Ecclesiae antiqua* c.27, ed. Bruns, *Canones,* 1:144: "Ut episcopus de loco ignobili ad nobilem per ambitionem non transeat, nec quisquam inferioris ordinis clericus. Sane si id utilitas ecclesiae fiendum poposcerit, decreto pro eo clericorum et laicorum episcopis porrecto <per sententiam> synodi transferatur, nihilominus alio in loco eius episcopo subrogato. . . ." On the emendation, see Gaudemet, *L'Eglise,* p. 361 n.8; in Gratian (C.7 q.1 c.37, ed. Friedberg, 1:580–81) the reading is "in presentiam."

41. Letters ascribed to Popes Anterus (§ 2) and Pelagius II, ed. P. Hinschius, *Decretales Pseudo-Isidorianae* (Leipzig, 1863), pp. 152, 726.

42. Gratian, *Decretum* C.7 q.1 c.34 *Mutaciones,* ed. Friedberg, 1:579, where the addition is rejected by the *correctores Romani* of 1582. For pseudo-Pelagius, see ibid., c.35 *Scias.*

43. *Decretum* C.7 q.1 cc.19–39, ed. Friedberg, 1:576–81.

44. Gratian C.7 q.1 c.26, ed. Friedberg, 1:577: "Propter eos episcopos sive clericos, qui de civitate ad civitatem transeunt, placuit diffinitiones datas a sanctis Patribus habere propriam firmitatem." For original, Conc. Chalcedon. 451 c.5, ed. Bruns, *Canones,* 1:27.

45. Gratian C.7 q.1 c.20, ed. Friedberg, 1:576: a certain truant bishop is to be imprisoned in a monastery if he refuses to reside in his see.

46. *Mon.* 3. 13. 3 (trans. Nicholl): "Unde, cum Ecclesia non sit effectus nature, sed Dei . . . manifestum est quod ei natura legem non dedit."

47. See the decretal collections that constitute the *Corpus iuris canonici*, ed. E. Friedberg, vol. 2: *Decretalium collectiones* (Leipzig, 1881); X 1. 7 on cols. 96–100. In subsequent decretal collections, all of which employ the Gregorian framework of *libri* and *tituli*, the section *De translatione episcopi* (1. 7) is vacant. Two post-Gregorian compilations were published in Dante's time: The *Liber Sextus* by Boniface VIII (1298) and the *Clementinae* by Clement V (posthumously promulgated in 1317, well after the completion of the *Inferno*). On dates, see A. M. Stickler, *Historia iuris canonici latini*, vol. 1 (Turin, 1950), pp. 260, 267; cf. 251–57 for intermediate collections, 1234–98.

48. By Bernard of Parma, ca. 1241, with author's additions to 1266.

49. *Compilatio tertia* 1. 5. 3, ed. E. Friedberg, *Quinque compilationes antiquae* (Leipzig, 1882), p. 106. The compilation was made at the curia and was transmitted by Innocent to Bologna in 1210 for use "tam in iudiciis quam in scholis" (ibid., p. 105). Since the four translation decretals comprising X 1. 7 originally appeared in the *Compilatio tertia* under the title *De translatione episcopi et electi* (1. 5), the Gregorian selection and arrangement was in fact Innocent's own. However, as the *Compilatio tertia* purports to be an accurate transcript of the Vatican register (ed. Friedberg, p. 105), while the compiler of the Gregorian *Decretals* was authorized to eliminate superfluous matter ("resecatis superfluis," ed. Friedberg, 2:3–4), probably Innocent did not authorize the decidedly tendentious textual alterations, notably "spirituale foedus coniugii, quod est inter episcopum et [eius] ecclesiam" (ibid., 2:100, in X 1. 7. 4; see below, n. 61 of this chap.), though to be certain of this, one would have to consult the unedited text of the *Compilatio tertia*.

50. Le Bras, *Institutions ecclésiastiques*, p. 315.

51. X 1. 7. 1, *Cum ex illo* (17 March 1198), ed. Friedberg, 2:96: "Cum ex illo generali privilegio, quod beato Petro et per eum ecclesiae Romanae Dominus noster indulsit, canonica postmodum manaverint instituta, continentia maiores ecclesiae causas ad sedem apostolicam perferendas, ac per hoc translationes episcoporum, et sedium mutationes ad summum apostolicae sedis antistitem de iure pertineant, nec super his quicquam praeter eius assensum debeat immutari: miramur. . . ." For the original form of the letter, which was revised for insertion in the *Decretales*, see *Die Register Innocenz' III*, ed. O. Hageneder and A. Haidacher, vol. 1 (Graz-Cologne, 1964), pp. 77–78, no. 50.

52. X 1. 7. 1, *Gl. ord.*, ad vv. *Instituta continentia*, ed. Lyons, 1548: "quia quaestio religionis et fidei ad Petrum tantum referenda est."

53. X 1. 7. 1, *Gl. ord.*, ad v. *pertineant*.

54. X 1. 7. 1, *Gl. ord.*, ad v. *privilegio*: "quo videlicet praetulit eam cunctis ecclesiis [D.21 c.1–2] et in hoc differt a papatu imperium: quia imperator habet suam iurisdictionem a populo [*Inst.* 1. 2. 6, *Cod.* 1. 17. 1. 7; *Nov.* 6 pr.], ubi dicitur quod ab eodem principio sunt, sed Romana ecclesia voce domini tantum praelata est, ut hic et [D.12 c.2]." On *Nov.* 6, see below, n. 155 of this chap.

55. On the canonistic interpretation of the passage in Innocent's day, see Brian Tierney, *Foundations of the Conciliar Theory: The Contribution of the Medieval Canonists from Gratian to the Great Schism*, Cambridge Studies in Medieval Life and

Thought, n.s., vol. 4 (Cambridge, Eng., 1955), pp. 25–29 (and pp. 30–36 on the next verse, "Et tibi dabo claves regni caelorum").

56. X 1. 7. 3, *Quanto personam* (21 Aug. 1198), ed. Friedberg, 2:99; cf. Hageneder-Haidacher, *Register Innocenz' III*, 1:495–98, no. 335: "Ipse [episcopus] ... auctoritate propria se transtulit, non attendens, quod Veritas in evangelio protestatur: 'Quos Deus coniunxit homo non separet.' Potestatem transferendi pontifices ita sibi retinuit Dominus et magister, quod soli beato Petro vicario suo, et per ipsum successoribus suis, speciali privilegio tribuit et concessit, sicut testatur antiquitas, cui decreta Patrum sanxerunt reverentiam exhibendam, et evidenter asserunt sacrorum canonum sanctiones. Non enim homo, sed Deus separat, quos Romanus Pontifex, qui non puri hominis, sed veri Dei vicem gerit in terris, ecclesiarum necessitate vel utilitate pensata, non humana, sed divina potius auctoritate dissolvit."

57. See above, n. 42 of this chap.

58. X 1. 7. 2, *Inter corporalia* (21 Jan. 1199), ed. Friedberg, 2:97; cf. Hageneder-Haidacher, *Register Innocenz' III*, 1:766–69, no. 530: "Inter corporalia et spiritualia eam cognovimus esse differentiam, quod corporalia facilius destruuntur quam construantur, spiritualia vero facilius construuntur quam destruantur. Unde iuxta canonicas sanctiones episcopus solus honorem dare potest, solus auferre non potest. Episcopi quoque a metropolitanis suis munus consecrationis accipiunt, qui tamen non possunt nisi per Romanum Pontificem condemnari. Cum ergo fortius sit spirituale vinculum quam carnale, dubitari non debet, quin omnipotens Deus spirituale coniugium, quod est inter episcopum et ecclesiam, suo tantum iudicio reservaverit dissolvendum, qui dissolutionem etiam carnalis coniugii, quod est inter virum et feminam, suo tantum iudicio reservavit, praecipiens, ut quos Deus coniunxit homo non separet. Non enim humana, sed potius divina potestate coniugium spirituale dissolvitur cum per translationem, depositionem, aut cessionem auctoritate Romani Pontificis, quem constat esse vicarium Iesu Christi, episcopus ab ecclesia removetur: et ideo tria haec, quae praemisimus, non tam constitutione canonica, quam institutione divina soli sunt Romano Pontifici reservata."

59. This formulation worried the canonists of the mid-thirteenth century. Bernard of Parma glosses *fortius* "id est dignus, quoniam carnale in veritate fortius est." This opinion of the *Gl. ord.* is echoed by Innocent IV, *Commentaria* on X 1. 7, while Hostiensis, *Summa aurea* on X 1. 7, no. 5, accepts *fortius* with many qualifications. See J. Trummer, "Mystisches im alten Kirchenrecht: Die geistige Ehe zwischen Bischof und Diözese," *Österreichisches Archiv für Kirchenrecht* 2 (1951): 62–75, at 67 n.22.

60. E.g., Trummer, "Mystiches," p. 67; R. L. Benson, *The Bishop-Elect: A Study in Medieval Ecclesiastical Office* (Princeton, N.J., 1968), pp. 146–49.

61. X 1. 7. 4 *Licet in tantum* (26 Jan. 1200), ed. Friedberg, 2:100: "Sicut legitimi matrimonii vinculum, quod est inter virum et uxorem, homo dissolvere nequit, Domino dicente in evangelio: 'Quos Deus coniunxit, homo non separet,' sic et spirituale foedus coniugii, quod est inter episcopum et ecclesiam, quod in electione initiatum, ratum in confirmatione, et in consecratione intelligitur consummatum, sine illius auctoritate solvi non potest, qui successor est Petri et vicarius Iesu Christi."

62. At least Maccarrone noted no others: *Vicarius Christi: Storia del titolo papale*, Lateranum, n.s., an. 18, nos. 1–4 (Rome, 1952), pp. 100, 103. But many twelfth-

century papal letters are as yet unedited, while most of the others are scattered in many publications.

63. Maccarrone, *Vicarius Christi*, p. 109; J. A. Watt, "The Use of the Term 'Plenitudo Potestatis' by Hostiensis," *Proceedings of the Second International Congress of Medieval Canon Law*, ed. S. Kuttner and J. J. Ryan, Monumenta Iuris Canonici, C.1 (Vatican City, 1965), pp. 161–87; App. A (pp. 175–77) for Innocent's use of *plenitudo potestatis* (vicar in nos. 4, 9).

64. J. A. Watt, "The Theory of Papal Monarchy in the Thirteenth Century: The Contribution of the Canonists," *Traditio* 20 (1964): 179–317, at p. 260: "With Innocent III the term [*plenitudo potestatis*] acquired its final standing: it was he who set the formal seal of official approval on it.... There was little, if anything, however, about his use of the term which was intrinsically new."

65. *Summa*, on X 5. 7, § 1, "Innocentius pater iuris"; 5. 39, § 12, "pater iuris canonici, divini et humani"; 5. 3, § 10. Quoted by Watt, "Theory of Papal Monarchy," p. 189.

66. Kantorowicz, *King's Two Bodies*, p. 90. Tierney, *Foundations*, p. 259, stresses Innocent's originality.

67. Maccarrone's *Vicarius Christi* is the fundamental work. This outline, which is largely limited to the history of the literal term (p. 10), pretends neither to pursue in detail the same idea expressed in other terminology nor to place that idea in relation to other ideas. The former line has since been pursued by Kantorowicz in *The King's Two Bodies* (see p. 89 n.8), and the latter, for Dante's generation at least, by Wilks, *Problem of Sovereignty*, pt. 4 (pp. 331–407).

68. Ignatius of Antioch, *Ep. ad Manesian*. 3. 1–2, ed. F. X. Funk, p. 232; cited by Maccarrone, *Vicarius Christi*, p. 22. On Cyprian, see ibid., pp. 28–29.

69. Maccarrone, *Vicarius Christi*, pp. 36–41; cf. Kantorowicz, *King's Two Bodies*, p. 91 n.12. To Ambrosiaster are also attributed the pseudo-Augustinian *Quaestiones veteris et novi testamenti*. See Dekkers, nos. 184–88.

70. Maccarrone, *Vicarius Christi*, pp. 45–55. This account of the *vicarius Christi* concept during the first five Christian centuries is based on Maccarrone's data and general conclusions; his attempts to establish a logical connection between the vicarial concept and terminology, on the one hand, and the primacy of Peter, on the other, belong to apologetic theology rather than to history. He cites many instances in which early authors seem to apply the term *vicarius Christi* to the pope, but his examples can all be interpreted in the generic, episcopal sense that is attested by contemporary usage, rather than in the specifically primatial one for which he argues. The curial preference for the *vicarius Petri* formula strongly suggests to me that *vicarius Christi* was unsuitable because its connotations were more general.

71. Kantorowicz, *King's Two Bodies*, p. 90 n.9.

72. Maccarrone, *Vicarius Christi*, pp. 70–72. Thus the *vice Dei* formula was applied to a pope as early as 862 (four centuries before *Quanto personam*) by Anastasius Bibliothecarius, who informed Pope Nicholas I that "vicem namque in terris possides Dei."

73. Kantorowicz, *King's Two Bodies*, pp. 89–91; see note 12 for a case where Gratian edited out a statement that all kings are vicars of God.

74. C.33 q.5 c.13, 19, ed. Friedberg, 1:1254–56 (both Ambrosiaster).

75. Gratian, *De poen*. D.3 c.35, ed. Friedberg, 1:1222: "Christus vicarios suos in ecclesia constituit," taken to refer to *sacerdotes* by *Gl. ord.* and Huguccio (quoted by

Maccarrone, *Vicarius Christi*, p. 106), who takes C.1 q.1 c.86 in the same sense (see above, chap. 5, at n. 96).

76. Maccarrone, *Vicarius Christi,* pp. 96–98, citing *Ep.* 251, ed. Migne, *PL*, 182:451c.

77. *De consideratione ad Eugenium papam*, ed. J. Leclercq and H. M. Rochais, *S. Bernardi Opera*, vol. 3 (Rome, 1963), pp. 393–493. Book 2 begins with reflections on the failure of the Second Crusade (siege of Damascus raised 28 July 1148), and book 3 was written during 1152 (ibid., p. 381).

78. *De consid.* 2. 8. 15–16, ed. Leclercq-Rochais, 3:423–24: "15. Age, indagemus adhuc diligentius quis sis, quam geras videlicet pro tempore personam in Ecclesia Dei. Quis es? Sacerdos magnus, summus Pontifex. Tu princeps episcoporum, tu heres Apostolorum, tu primatu Abel, gubernatu Noe, patriarchatu Abraham, ordine Melchisedech, dignitate Aaron, auctoritate Moyses, iudicatu Samuel, potestate Petrus, unctione Christus. Tu es cui claves traditae, cui oves creditae sunt. Sunt quidem et alii caeli ianitores et gregum pastores; sed tu, tanto gloriosius quanto et differentius, utrumque prae ceteris nomen hereditasti. Habent illi sibi assignatos greges, singuli singulos; tibi universi crediti, uni unus. Nec modo ovium, sed et pastorum tu unus omnium pastor. Unde id probem quaeris? Ex verbo Domini. Cui enim, non dico episcoporum, sed etiam Apostolorum sic absolute et indiscrete totae commissae sunt oves? 'Si me amas, Petre, pasce oves meas' [John 21:17]. Illius vel illius populos civitatis, aut regionis, aut certe regni? 'Oves meas,' inquit. Cui non planum, non dedignasse aliquas, sed assignasse omnes? Nihil excipitur, ubi distinguitur nihil. Et forte praesentes ceteri condiscipuli erant, cum, committens uni, unitatem omnibus commendaret in uno grege et uno pastore, secundum illud: 'Una est columba mea, formosa mea, perfecta mea' [Cant. 6:8; the Vulgate omits 'formosa mea']. Ubi unitas, ibi perfectio. Reliqui numeri perfectionem non habent, sed divisionem, recedentes ab unitate. Inde est quod alii singuli singulas sortiti sunt plebes, scientes sacramentum. Denique Iacobus, qui videbatur columna Ecclesiae, una contentus est Ierosolyma, Petro universitatem cedens. Pulchre vero ibi positus est suscitare semen defuncti fratris, ubi occisus est ille, nam dictus est frater Domini. Porro cedente Domini fratre, quis se alter ingerat Petri praerogativae? 16. Ergo, iuxta canones tuos, alii in partem sollicitudinis, tu in plenitudinem potestatis vocatus est. Aliorum potestas certis artatur limitibus; tua extenditur et in ipsos, qui potestatem super alios acceperunt. Nonne, si causa exstiterit, tu episcopo caelum claudere, tu ipsum ab episcopatu deponere, etiam et tradere Satanae potes? Stat ergo inconcussum privilegium tuum tibi, tam in datis clavibus quam in ovibus commendatis. Accipe aliud, quod nihilominus praerogativam confirmat tibi. Discipuli navigabant, et Dominus apparebat in littore, quodque iucundius erant: in corpore redivivo. Sciens Petrus quia Dominus est, in mare se misit, et sic venit ad ipsum, aliis navigio pervenientibus. Quid istud? Nempe signum singularis pontificii Petri, per quod non navem unam, ut ceteri quique suam, sed saeculum ipsum susceperit gubernandum. Mare enim saeculum est; naves, Ecclesiae. Inde est quod altera vice instar Domini gradiens super aquas [Matt. 14:29], unicum se Christi vicarium designavit, qui non uni populo, sed cunctis praeesse deberet: siquidem aquae multae, populi multi. Ita, cum quisque ceterorum habeat suam, tibi una commissa est grandissima navis, facta ex omnibus ipsa universalis Ecclesia, toto orbe diffusa."

79. For previous interpretations of *De consid.* 2. 8, see Elizabeth Kennan, "The 'De consideratione' of St. Bernard of Clairvaux and the Papacy in the Mid-Twelfth

Century: A Review of Scholarship," *Traditio* 23 (1967): 73–115, at pp. 95–97. She concludes: "The *plenitudo potestatis*, then, indicates monarchical rule over the ecclesiastical hierarchy and, probably, final jurisdiction over all legal disputes involving 'spiritual' questions" (p. 97). She does not, however, connect this with the papal vicariate, which she treats elsewhere (p. 82).

80. Bernard, *Ep.* 131. 2 to the Milanese, ed. Migne, *PL*, 182:286–87: "Sed dicit aliquis: Debitam ei reverentiam exhibebo, et nihil amplius. Esto, fac quod dicis; quia si exhibeas debitam, et omnimodam. Plenitudo siquidem potestatis super universas orbis Ecclesias, singulari praerogativa apostolicae Sedi donata est. Qui igitur huic potestati resistit, Dei ordinationi resistit. Potest, si utile iudicaverit, novos ordinare episcopatus, ubi hactenus non fuerunt. Potest eos qui sunt, alios deprimere, alios sublimare, prout ratio sibi dictaverit, ita ut de episcopis creare archiepiscopos liceat, et e converso, si necesse visum fuerit. Potest a finibus terrae sublimes quascunque personas ecclesiasticas evocare, et cogere ad suam praesentiam, non semel aut bis, sed quoties expedire videbit. Porro in promptu est ei omnem ulcisci inobedientiam, si quis forte reluctari conatus fuerit. Denique probasti et tu." He elaborates one of these examples in *De consid.* 3. 4. 14, ed. Leclercq-Rochais, 3:442: "Subtrahuntur abbates episcopis, episcopi archiepiscopis, archiepiscopi patriarchis sive primatibus. Bonane species haec? Mirum si excusari queat vel opus. Sic factitando probatis vos habere plenitudinem potestatis, sed iustitiae forte non ita. Facitis hoc, quia potestis; sed utrum et debeatis, quaestio est."

81. March 1147 to May 1148: Mann, *Lives of the Popes*, vol. 9 (London, 1925), pp. 187–99.

82. Anselm of Havelberg, *Dialogi* 3. 10, ed. Migne, *PL*, 188:1222a: "Fateor quoniam non super solum Petrum, verum etiam super omnes apostolos Spiritus sanctus descendit, nec soli Petro, sed et aliis omnibus dictum est: 'Accipite Spiritum sanctum; quorum remiseritis peccata, remittuntur eis; et quorum retinueritis, retenta sunt' [John 20:23]. Verumtamen specialiter ad Petrum sermonem hunc dirigens, et eum tanquam ianitorem coeli constituens, ait: 'Et tibi dabo claves regni coelorum' [Matt. 16:19]. Et rursum: 'Pasce,' inquit, 'oves meas' [John 21:17]." On Anselm (d. 1158), see *Repertorium fontium historiae medii aevi*, vol. 2 (Rome, 1967), p. 367.

83. *Dialogi* 3. 10, ed. Migne, *PL*, 188:1223: "Quocirca nulli fidelium convenit aliquatenus dubitare, seu in quaestionem ponere, sed firmissime tenere, quod Petrus a Domino princeps apostolorum sit constitutus. Quemadmodum autem solus Romanus pontifex vice Petri vicem gerit Christi, ita sane caeteri episcopi vicem gerunt apostolorum sub Christo, et vice Christi sub Petro, et vice Petri sub pontifice Romano eius vicario: nec in hoc aliquatenus derogatur alicui apostolorum, si unicuique humiliter suum attribuitur officium." Cf. Maccarrone, *Vicarius Christi*, p. 98.

84. *Dialogi* 3. 11, ed. Migne, *PL*, 188:1223: "Nechites archiepiscopus Nicomediae dixit: 'Potest esse quod dicis. Caeterum paulo ante dixisti. . . .'"

85. Maccarrone, *Vicarius Christi*, p. 97 n.47, citing Migne, *PL*, 183:77a, 177b, 299d, 567a.

86. *Dialogus de pontificatu sanctae Romanae ecclesiae*, ed. H. Boehmer, *MGH, Libelli de lite imperatorum et pontificum saec. xi et xii, conscripti*, vol. 3 (Hanover, 1897), pp. 526–46, at p. 529. Cf. Maccarrone, *Vicarius Christi*, p. 101. From his citations, the author appears to be professionally trained in both Roman and canon law. The question, "Why did Rahewin stop writing the Gesta Frederici?" has recently been answered twice in the *English Historical Review* 83 (1968): 294–303, and 84

(1969): 771–79. In passing I may suggest a third possibility: that Rahewin dropped the *Gesta* in order to take up the *Dialogus*.

87. Cant. 6:8: "Una est columba mea, perfecta mea, una est matris suae." Cf. above, n. 78 of this chap.

88. *Ottonis et Rahewini Gesta Friderici I Imperatoris* 1. 65, ed. *MGH, Scriptores rerum Germanicarum*, 3d. ed. by B. de Simson (Hanover-Leipzig, 1912), p. 93. Gerhoh of Reichersberg, in the adjacent province of Salzburg, used Bernard's *De consideratione* as early as 1155, three years before Otto's death: *De consid.*, ed. Leclercq-Rochais, 3:385. Gerhoh himself mentions the vicar of Christ once: *De investigatione Antichristi* (1161 × 1163), ed. *MGH, Libelli de lite*, 3:325: "Nunc vir [Gregory VII] mulieris huius [*sc.* Ecclesiae] Christus per suum vicarium, Petri successorem ... quid gesserit." For Gerhoh, the pope was usually the *vicarius Petri* and once God's vicegerent ("in terris vicem gerere," ed. Migne, *PL*, 194:39). Cited by Maccarrone, *Vicarius Christi*, p. 102, who notes that Gerhoh's doctrine of the *corpus mysticum* resembles that of Anselm of Havelberg.

89. *Dialogus*, ed. Boehmer, p. 528 n.9 and the *apparatus fontium* for passages found in Gratian.

90. *Summa Reginensis*, quoted by Maccarrone, *Vicarius Christi*, p. 107 (see below, n. 98 of this chap.). Cf. Bernard's use of *toto orbe* in conjunction with Peter's unique vicariate, at the end of n. 78 of this chap. John of Sutri is identified by Maccarrone, *Vicarius Christi*, p. 107 n.90, citing J. M. Brixius, *Die Mitglieder des Kardinalkollegiums von 1130–1181* (Berlin, 1912), p. 59; see also Watt, "Theory of Papal Monarchy," p. 210 n.48.

91. Maccarrone, *Vicarius Christi*, pp. 101–5.

92. Ibid., p. 104; cf. p. 106 n.86.

93. Ibid., p. 100, citing *Ep.* 575 (1153), ed. Migne, *PL*, 180:1589 (Jaffé-Loewenfeld, *Regesta pontificum romanorum*, no. 9714).

94. Maccarrone, *Vicarius Christi*, p. 103.

95. See above, n. 56 of this chap.

96. Huguccio, *Summa super Decreto*, on C.33 q.5 c.19, ad vv. *ante iudicem Domini* (MS. Vat. lat. 2280, f. 317ra, as quoted by Maccarrone, *Vicarius Christi*, p. 106): "Ubi ergo sunt illi qui dicunt quod solus papa est vicarius Christi? Quoad plenitudinem potestatis verum est, alias autem quilibet sacerdos est vicarius Christi et Petri, argumentum hic et I q.i Non quales [C.1 q.1 c.86]." Cf. Kantorowicz, *King's Two Bodies*, p. 91.

97. *Gl. ord.*, on C.33 q.5 c.19 *Mulier* (ed. Friedberg, 1:1255), ad v. *Episcopus*: "id est quilibet sacerdos." A similar gloss appeared earlier in the *Glossa Palatina* (ca. 1214, by Laurentius Hispanus), reported by Maccarrone, *Vicarius Christi*, p. 107.

98. *Summa Reginensis* (1192), on C.33 q.5 c.19 (Vat. MS. Reg. lat. 1061, f. 44rb in fine): "Episcopus: id est presbiter ... quia personam habet Christi. Argumentum contra illos qui dicunt solum papam esse vicarium Christi. Nam quilibet sacerdos est vicarius Christi et Petri, ut I q.I. Non quales. Dicebat cardinalis Sanctorum Johannis et Pauli quod inde papa dicitur Christi vicarius, quia Jesus Christus praeest toto orbi ita et papa." Quoted by Maccarrone, *Vicarius Christi*, p. 107; and more fully by A. M. Stickler, "Decretisti bolognesi dimenticati," *Studia Gratiana* 3 (1955): 377–410, at p. 393, cf. p. 408. On the cardinal, see above, n. 90 of this chap.

99. Maccarrone himself searched extensively in Huguccio: see his *Chiesa e stato*

nella dottrina di papa Innocenzo III, Lateranum, n.s., an. 6, nos. 3, 4 (Rome, 1940), pp. 68–78. Stickler communicated the reference in the *Summa Reginensis* to him (Maccarrone, *Vicarius Christi*, p. 107 n.89). Maccarrone did not explore the earlier Decretists (*Vicarius Christi*, p. 106 n.86).

100. *De sacro altaris mysterio* 1. 8, ed. Migne, *PL*, 217:778–79: "Verumtamen et maiores et minores sacerdotes communiter in quibusdam vices gerunt summi pontificis, id est Christi, dum pro peccatis obsecrant et peccatores per poenitentiam reconciliant." Cf. Maccarrone, *Vicarius Christi*, p. 110, who takes the qualification to be original with Innocent.

101. Probably *quoad plenitudinem potestatis*: cf. his *Sermo II in consecratione pontifices* (22 Feb. 1199), ed. Migne, *PL*, 217:665b: "Nam caeteri vocati sunt in partem sollicitudinis, solus autem Petrus assumptus est in plenitudinem potestatis."

102. Watt, "Theory of Papal Monarchy," pp. 259–60, quoting Huguccio on D.17 c.3, ad vv. *Huic soli sedi concessa*: "hec autem multa sunt, scilicet episcoporum depositio, ut [C.3 q.6 c.7]; episcoporum abrenunciatio, ut [C.7 q.1 c.9]; episcoporum mutacio, ut [C.7 q.1 c.34 *Mutaciones*]." The Decretist development of *plenitudo potestatis* has most completely been traced by Watt, "Theory of Papal Monarchy," pp. 250–60. See also his summary in "Use of Term 'Plenitudo Potestatis,'" pp. 164–65, with bibliography cited at p. 162 n.4; and Tierney, *Foundations*, pp. 143–46.

103. Watt, "Theory of Papal Monarchy," p. 260 n.34; cf. p. 253.

104. Tierney, *Foundations*, p. 146.

105. Hostiensis, *Summa*, on X 1. 32, § 3, quoted below, n. 124 of this chap.

106. See above, n. 51 of this chap. In some papal lists, Peter was said to have been Antiochene by birth ("natione anthiocenus"): See G. Barraclough, *The Medieval Papacy* (New York, 1968), frontispiece. Marsiglio of Padua argued that Antioch, as Peter's first see, had a better title to world primacy than had Rome: *Defensor pacis* 2. 16. 15 ff.

107. The Decretalists would seem to have recognized the importance of the *locus*, for it became their *locus classicus* for the enumeration of *causae maiores*: Gl. ord., on X 1. 7. 1, ad v. *pertineant*.

108. See above, nn. 37, 39 of this chap.

109. 1 Tim. 3:2a: "Oportet ergo episcopum irreprehensibilem esse, unius uxoris virum." Cf. Titus 1:6. So used by Jerome, *Ep. 50 ad Oceanum, de unius uxoris viro*, cited by Trummer, "Mystisches," p. 64 n.8.

110. Ordo xxxvb. 35 (saec. x), ed. M. Andrieu, *Les ordines romani du haut moyen-âge*, vol. 4, Spicilegium sacrum Lovaniense, no. 28 (Louvain, 1956), p. 108: "Accipe anulum, fidei scilicet signaculum, quatinus sponsam, Dei sanctam videlicet ecclesiam, intemerata fide ornatus, illibate custodias." Trans. Benson, *Bishop-Elect*, p. 123, together with other liturgical and theological examples of the bishop's *matrimonium spirituale* in the eleventh and twelfth centuries. Also Kantorowicz, *King's Two Bodies*, pp. 212–18, esp. n.61.

111. Gratian, C.7 q.1 c.1–11, esp. c.6 and c.11, ed. Friedberg, 1:566–71.

112. Benson, *Bishop-Elect*, chap. 5, pp. 116–49, esp. p. 124.

113. Ibid., pp. 144–49.

114. Because Huguccio's *Summa* has not yet been published, it is difficult to ascertain the extent of his influence on Innocent except at particular points. Huguccio's general theory of the Church—as distinct from his views on the relation between Church

and State—deserves further attention; whether he, like Innocent, there emphasized the bishop's role as *sponsus ecclesiae*, I do not know. Tierney, *Foundations*, passim, quotes Huguccio.

115. *De quadripartita specie nuptiarum; Sermo III, in consecratione pontificis* (22 Feb. 1199); and *De sacro altaris mysterio* 1. 60; ed. Migne, *PL*, 217:921–68, 659–66, 796. Trummer, "Mystisches," p. 67, at n. 21, recognizes the theme as a distinctive Innocentian stress, on which see now Connie M. Munk, "A Study of Pope Innocent III's Treatise *De quadripartita specie nuptiarum*" (Ph.D. diss., University of Kansas, 1975).

116. "Huius autem Domini et magistri omnium magisterium sancti patres diligentius attendentes maiores ecclesie causas, utpote cessiones episcoporum et sedium translationes, sine apostolice sedis licentia fieri vetuerunt, ut ea que sola obtinet plenitudinem potestatis de his disponeret nec liceret alicui de episcopatu ad episcopatum sine ipsius auctoritate transire." Watt, "Use of Term 'Plenitudo Potestatis,'" p. 177 (App. A.11), quoting *Collectio Rainerii Ponposiani* 5. 2, ed. Migne, *PL*, 216:1198 (no. 16).

117. Maccarrone, *Vicarius Christi*, p. 110 n.9, citing L. Billot, *De ecclesiae sacramentis*, vol. 2 (Rome, 1931), p. 427.

118. I follow here Tierney's interpretation of this much-misunderstood decretal, in his "'Tria quippe distinguit iudicia . . .' A Note on Innocent III's Decretal *Per venerabilem*," *Speculum* 37 (1962): 48–59.

119. The significance of both passages is appreciated by Tierney, "Tria quippe," pp. 56 n.24, and 58.

120. Innocent III, *Sermo II in consecratione pontificis maximi*, ed. Migne, *PL*, 217:658: "profecto vicarius Iesu Christi, successor Petri, Christus Domini, Deus Pharaonis: inter Deum et hominem medius constitutus, citra Deum, sed ultra hominem: minor Deo, sed maior homine: qui de omnibus iudicat, et a nemine iudicatur: Apostoli voce pronuntians, 'qui me iudicat, Dominus est' [1 Cor. 4:4]." See Watt, "Theory of Papal Monarchy," pp. 261–62.

121. Watt, "Theory of Papal Monarchy," pp. 243–47.

122. Ibid., p. 276. Quoted by Hostiensis, *Summa*, on X 2. 2, § 10 (Watt, "Use of Term 'Plenitudo Potestatis,'" p. 182, in App. B.42): "Quid si rex vel alius princeps qui superiorem non habet mortuus est, vel in reddenda iustitia negligens reperitur? Respondeo, tunc dicendum est idem, quod in iurisdictione succedit. . . . Sed si principatus non tenetur ab eo, non facit hoc de iure communi, sed de plenitudine potestatis quam habet quia vicarius Iesu Christi, supra, ti. i. Novit [2. 1. 13] § i. versi. non enim, et sequenti."

123. Hostiensis, *Lectura*, on X 4. 14, § 4, ad v. *non separet*, quoted by Watt, "Use of Term 'Plenitudo Potestatis,'" pp. 185–86, in App. B.58: "Iesus Christus reliquit vicarium suum generale<m> beatum Petrum et successores suos. . . . nec facit hoc homo sed deus, id est, vicarius veri dei cui hanc potestatem dedit" (my emendation).

124. Hostiensis, *Summa*, on X 1. 32, § 3, quoted by Watt, "Use of Term 'Plenitudo Potestatis,'" p. 179, in App. B.10 (allegations here omitted): "Plenusque vicarius extat: quamvis enim quilibet episcopus dici possit vicarius Iesu Christi ... est tamen particularis; sed papa est vicarius generalis, unde omnia gerit de omnibus prout placet, iudicat et disponit ...; plenus, id est, habens plenitudinem potestatis,

ad quam vocatus est, alii vero in partem sollicitudinis ...: ideo breviter dic, quod dummodo contra fidem non veniat, in omnibus et per omnia potest facere et dicere quicquid placet, auferendo etiam ius suum cui vult; quia nec aliquis audet ei dicere, cur ita facis? ... et omne ius tollere, et de iure supra ius dispensare ... quia veri Dei vicem gerit in terris [X 1. 7. 2–3] ...: licet autem hoc possit, caveat quod non peccet...."

125. On this see Watt, "Use of Term 'Plenitudo Potestatis,' " pp. 166–67; Tierney, *Foundations*, p. 147.

126. Hostiensis, *Summa*, on X 1. 8, § 2, quoted by Watt, "Use of Term 'Plenitudo Potestatis,' " p. 178, in App. B.5.

127. Innocent III, not without humor, remarked "etsi locum Dei teneamus in terris, non tamen de occultis potuimus divinare": X 3. 12. un. (an. 1198), ed. Friedberg, 2:512.

128. This contrast between dualism and hierocracy has been much discussed in the past generation. In stressing the contrast, I follow the view sketched by Tierney, "Tria quippe," pp. 55–59, as elaborated by Watt, "Theory of Papal Monarchy," pp. 199 ff., esp. pp. 307–8.

129. See above, chap. 3, at nn. 138–42 (*Mon. 3. 6*).

130. *Mon.* 3. 7. 4–5 (trans. Nicholl): "Et si quis instaret de vicarii equivalentia, inutilis est instantia; quia nullus vicariatus, sive divinus sive humanus, equivalere potest principali auctoritati: quod patet de levi. Nam scimus quod successor Petri non equivalet divine auctoritati, saltem in operatione nature: non enim posset facere terram ascendere sursum, nec ignem descendere deorsum per offitium sibi commissum." See Wilks, *Problem of Sovereignty*, p. 371, and Tancred, in *Gl. ord.*, on X 1. 7. 1, for occasional claims that the pope did in some way have power over nature. The problem was chiefly discussed in connection with the papal power of dispensation (Tierney, *Foundations*, pp. 89–90).

131. See above, chap. 5, at nn. 26–32 (*Mon. 3. 3*).

132. Matt. 20:30. Mark 12:25: "Cum enim a mortuis resurrexerint, neque nubent, neque nubentur, sed sunt sicut angeli in caelis" ("For when they shall rise again from the dead, they shall neither marry, nor be married, but are as the angels in heaven"). Luke 20:34–36: "Et ait illis Jesus: Filii huius seculi nubunt, et traduntur ad nuptias: Illi vero qui digni habebuntur seculo illo, et resurrectione ex mortuis, neque nubent, neque ducent uxores: Neque enim ultra mori poterunt: aequales enim angelis sunt, et filii sunt Dei, cum sint filii resurrectionis" ("And Jesus said to them: The children of this world marry, and are given in marriage: But they that shall be accounted worthy of that world, and of the resurrection from the dead, shall neither be married, nor take wives. Neither can they die any more: for they are equal to the angels, and are the children of God, being the children of the resurrection").

133. Sapegno, p. 665, glosses: "fu sposo della Chiesa; cioè pontefice."

134. Sinclair's trans. In verse 111, I have replaced his "bridegroom" with "husband," which is a more accurate translation of "marito." *Marito*, be it noted, is a Roman-law term that is "mentioned specifically in connection with adultery when the accusation of the wife is made by the husband *iure mariti*." Berger, p. 530, s.vv. "Ius mariti." Further, the husband who does not divorce an adulterous wife is himself liable to

prosecution as a pander (*leno*). Huguccio, and after him Innocent III and the Decretalists, did interpret spiritual *sponsalia* in terms of Roman law.

135. E.g., Sapegno, p. 226.

136. Sapegno states that the waters "che per san Giovanni erano le nazioni dominate politicamente dall'Impero, per Dante sono i popoli sottomessi spiritualmente al Chiesa" (p. 226).

137. C. Davis, *Dante and the Idea of Rome* (Oxford, 1957), pp. 223, 225.

138. Ibid., pp. 223–27.

139. Tierney, *Foundations*, pp. 36–46. Pier Giovanni Olivi interpreted Babylon as the Roman church in the extended sense, according to the papal commissioners who examined his *Postilla in Apocalipsim* in 1319 and found that "in toto isto tractatu per Babylonem ipse intelligit Ecclesiam Romanam et universalem ei obedientem, quam nos Ecclesiam catholicam appellamus" (Davis, *Dante*, p. 211).

140. E.g., Wilks, *Problem of Sovereignty*, pp. 36, 39–40, 375 n.2, 288, 492 n.2; and *Liber Sextus* 1. 6. 3. 4, ed. Friedberg, 2:948 (Gregory X in the Second Council of Lyons, 1274, c.2 *Ubi periculum*: "idoneo celeriter eidem [universalis] ecclesiae sponso dato").

141. Wilks, *Problem of Sovereignty*, pp. 396–97; cf. p. 362.

142. In passing we may note that this case is typical of the poet's dialectical strategy. He presents the reader with an apparent contradiction, the resolution of which leads to deeper understanding. The discovery that the papal spouse is the Roman church would seem to stress the point that the pope is essentially a *Roman* official, the spiritual leader of Rome's city and world.

143. Thus Scartazzini-Vandelli[19], p. 149, and Sapegno, p. 217, both at *Inf.* XIX, 1–4. The latter identifies *le cose di Dio* as "le cariche spirituali" and explains that simoniacs traffic in "le cose sacre (i beni spirituali e gli uffici ecclesiastici)"; the former simply gloss: "*le cose di Dio*, cioè i beni spirituali e gli uffizi ecclesiastici."

144. Acts 8:9–24.

145. *Inf.* XIX, 94–96, referring to Acts 1:15–26.

146. The emperor is represented as wedded both to Italia (*Ep.* v, 2) and to Roma (*Purg.* VI, 112–14); similarly the king of France is his kingdom's spouse, according to *Purg.* XX, 58–59, where Hugh Capet says "ch'a la *corona vedova* promossa / la testa di mio figlio fu." The Crown as *sponsa* I take to symbolize the kingdom. In medieval usage the meanings largely overlapped: see Kantorowicz, *King's Two Bodies*, chap. 7, sect. 2 "The Crown as Fiction," esp. pp. 336–42, 353, 363. Note that the change of dynasty "widowed" the Crown, whereas in dynastic succession "the king never dies," since "father and son are one according to the fiction of the law" (ibid., p. 338; cf. chap. 7, sect. 1). On the matrimonial metaphor in medieval political theology in general, see ibid., chap. 5, esp. pp. 212–23.

147. *Mon.* 3. 14. 1: "sed virtus auctorizandi regnum nostre mortalitatis est contra naturam Ecclesie: ergo non est de numero virtutum suarum."

148. *Mon.* 3. 14. 6 (trans. Nicholl, p. 90, altered): "Quod non sic intelligendum est ac si Cristus, qui Deus est, non sit dominus regni huius; cum Psalmista dicat 'quoniam ipsius est mare, et ipse fecit illud, et aridam fundaverunt manus eius'; sed quia, ut exemplar Ecclesie, regni huius curam non habebat."

149. As Dante, at *Mon.* 3. 8. 11, promised to prove.

150. See above, nn. 95–109 of chap. 3.

151. One might at this point object that Dante does recognize the pope's power to dispense and commute vows at *Par.* v, 34–84. Beatrice there explains to the pilgrim that once God has accepted a human commitment, a convenant is created that "is not cancelled if not carried out" ("non si cancella / se non servata"; *Par.* v, 46–47). This contract cannot be terminated, even by the pope. At most he can relax the obligation of the vow, so that although the obligation itself continues to exist, the terms need not be carried out (dispensation); he can also alter the terms (commutation). In all this, as is commonly recognized, Dante was closely following Aquinas, *S.T.* II-II q.88 a.10.

Undoubtedly, then, Dante acknowledged the papal power to grant dispensations from, and commutation of, vows. Did this constitute an exercise of jurisdiction in the external forum? Most medieval writers would answer in the affirmative, but I think that Dante disagreed. He equates the power of dispensation and commutation with the power of Peter's keys (*Par.* v, 56–57), which he twice identifies in the *Comedy* as the power exercised in the internal forum. When Boniface VIII encouraged Guido da Montefeltro to sin with the certainty that he would be absolved from his guilt through the power of the papal keys, it was the sacrament of penance that was being abused (*Inf.* xxvii, 103–5). Again, the angel at the gate of Purgatory held the keys from Peter and functioned as the pilgrim's father confessor (*Purg.* ix, 117–29; Sapegno, pp. 498–99). Since the *Comedy* shows us two cases in which the keys represent the powers exercised in the sacrament of penance, I think it likely that the third instance of the powers of the keys is likewise to be understood as a case of conscience.

152. *Cod.* 9. 29. 1 (Edict of Thessalonica). *Cod.* 1. 8. 1 condemns a specific form of sacrilege. With particular reference to the papacy, *Cod.* 1. 3. 30. 5 likens simony to the higher forms of treason ("ad instar publici criminis et laesae maiestatis") and imposes the penalty of deposition on the guilty cleric, on the analogy of the death penalty for treason. Could this Roman cognizance of simony explain why Dante's diatribe against simony seemed pleasing to Virgil (*Inf.* xix, 121–23)? The *Gl. ord.*, on *Cod.* 1. 3. 30, ad v. *Quantum (quisque mereatur)*, comments: "hoc est, eligendus cuius sit meriti, cuius sit bonitatis." Since *bontate* (*Inf.* xix, 2) is likewise the essential qualification for ecclesiastical office in Dante's definition (see above, n.143 of this chap.), a link between the passages is not impossible, though on the face of it, the thought would seem to be a commonplace.

153. *Gl. ord.*, on *Cod.* 9. 29. 1, ad v. *ommittunt*: "Errando in articulis fidei, vel rebaptizando per errorem vel negligentiam"; and ad v. *committunt*: the offender is one "qui non obedit legi evangelii."

154. *Nov.* 131. 1. On the reception of early ecclesiastical law into Roman law, see Gaudemet, *L'Eglise*, pp. 18–20.

155. *Nov.* 6. praef., ed. Schöll-Kroll, p. 36: "Nos igitur maximam habemus sollicitudinem circa vera dei dogmata et circa sacerdotum honestatem...." Cf. *Cod.* 1. 3. 54. pr., and Feine, *Kirchliche Rechtsgeschichte*, 1:69.

156. Although translation of bishops was not claimed as an imperial prerogative in Roman law, Frederick Barbarossa did excercise the right, probably by virtue of the imperial *plenitudo potestatis*, which he invoked to justify his direct appointment of bishops. See Benson, *Bishop-Elect*, p. 286 nn. 9–10.

157. *Conv.* 3. 12. 14.

158. *Purg.* xvi, 52–63.

159. *Mon.* 3. 3. 5.

160. See above, chap. 4, at nn. 45–69.

161. Matt. 6:19–20: "Lay not up to yourselves treasures on earth: where the rust, and moth consume, and where thieves break through and steal. But lay up to yourselves treasures in heaven: where neither the rust nor moth doth consume, and where thieves do not break through, nor steal."

162. See above, chap. 4, at n. 3.

163. Matt. 6:21: "Ubi enim est thesaurus tuus, ibi est et cor tuum."

164. E.g., the treatise *Oculus pastoralis sive Libellus erudiens futurum rectorem populorum*, ed. L. A. Muratori, in his *Antiquitates Italicae Medii Aevi*, vol. 4 (Milan, 1741), pp. 95 ff.; cf. F. J. Carmody, ed., *Li livres dou tresor de Brunetto Latini*, University of California Publications in Modern Philology, vol. 22 (Berkeley and Los Angeles, 1948), p. xxxi n.5: Brunetto probably drew on the same source used by the *Oculus pastoralis* (but see above, n. 38 of chap. 1).

165. Matt. 6:22–23: "Lucerna corporis tui est oculus tuus. Si oculus tuus fuerit simplex, totum corpus tuum lucidum erit. Si autem oculus tuus fuerit nequam, totum corpus tuum tenebrosum erit. Si ergo lumen quod in te est tenebrae sunt, ipsae tenebrae quantae erunt?"

166. Matt. 6:24: "Nemo potest duobus dominis servire: aut enim unum odio habebit, et alterum diliget: aut unum sustinebit, et alterum contemnet. Non potestis Deo servire et mammonae."

167. *Mon.* 3. 15. 10.

168. Matt. 6:26–30.

169. Benvenuto played on Mozzi's surname in another connection: "Ad cuius cognitionem volo te scire cum non *modico* risu, quod iste spiritus fuit civis florentinus, natus de Modiis...." *Comentum super Dantis Aldigherij Comoediam*, ed. J. P. Lacaita, vol. 1 (Florence, 1887), p. 524. Further possibilities are offered by the meanings "due measure; a measure which is not to be exceeded, a bound, limit, end, restriction" (Lewis-Short, s.v. "modus"), which have an ironic fitness for one whose sin consisted in transgressing the limits both of his natural capacities and of the natural order.

170. Matt. 7:15–16: "Attendite a falsis prophetis, qui veniunt ad vos in vestimentis ovium, intrinsecus autem sunt lupi rapaces: a fructibus eorum cognoscetis eos." On the *pastore-lupo*, see above, chap. 4, at n. 110 ff.

171. For Dante's use of the *a fructibus* criterion (Matt. 7:20), see *Mon.* 3. 3. 13 and above, chap. 5, after n. 28.

172. Matt. 7:19: "Omnis arbor, quae non facit fructum bonum, exciditur, et in ignem mittitur."

173. *Mon.* 3. 10. 7 (trans. Nicholl): "Nam Ecclesie fundamentum Cristus est; unde Apostolus *ad Corinthios*: 'Fundamentum aliud nemo potest ponere preter id quod positum est, quod est Cristus Iesus' [1 Cor. 3:11]. Ipse est petra super quam hedificata est Ecclesia." Thus indirectly does he comment on the Petrine locus, "super hanc petram aedificabo Ecclesiam meam" (Matt. 16:18).

174. *Inf.* xv, 117, "sabbione"; *Inf.* xvi, 28, "loco sollo."

175. Originally to be said directly after the consecration of a bishop: see *Pontificale G. Durandi* 1. 14. 63, ed. M. Andrieu, *Le Pontifical romain au moyen-âge*, vol. 3,

Studi e testi, vol. 88 (Vatican, 1940), p. 391. In the *Missale Romanum* it appears as the collect of the masses *In die creationis et coronationis papae et in eorum dierum anniversario* and *In anniversario electionis et consecrationis episcopi.*

176. *Mon.* 3. 15. 7; see esp. above, chap. 1.

177. See above, chap. 3, at n. 100.

178. See above, nn. 95–109 of chap. 3.

179. A sharp contrast was drawn by Marjorie Reeves, "Marsiglio of Padua and Dante Alighieri," in *Trends in Medieval Political Thought*, ed. B. Smalley (Oxford, 1965), pp. 86–104. The similarities seem more striking to the most recent commentator, J. Quillet, *La philosophie politique de Marsile de Padoue* (Paris, 1970); see also the review of her earlier work by C. T. Davis in *Studi medievali*, 3d ser. 9 (1968): 1225–26.

180. See above, n. 4 of chap. 1.

181. According to Huguccio, Priscian was actually a priest (*sacerdos*): see above, n. 29 of chap. 2. Francesco d'Accorso, by virtue of his profession as a Roman lawyer, was also traditionally accounted a member of a sacerdotal *ordo*: *Dig.* 1. 1. 1. 1, "Cuius merito quis nos sacerdotes appellet" (ed. Mommsen, p. 1); cf. Pézard, pp. 176–77.

182. See above, "Brunetto's Riddle" in chap. 4, pp. 68–71.

183. See above, nn. 97, 136 of chap. 4.

184. On the occasion, see E. Gibbon, *History of the Decline and Fall of the Roman Empire*, chap. 30, ed. J. B. Bury, 10th ed., vol. 3 (London, 1944), pp. 263–67, and App. 17; Davidsohn, *Geschichte von Florenz*, vol. 1 (1896), pp. 26–28, 36–37.

185. *Acta sanctorum*, ed. J. Bolland et al., Feb., vol. 3, 3d ed. (Paris and Rome, 1865), pp. 666–68, "De S. Andrea episcopo Florentino in Etruria, commentarius historicus," by G. Henschenius (1658). Cf. *Bibliotheca hagiographica latina antiquae et mediae aetatis*, vol. 1 (Brussels, 1898), no. 1314. The Bollandists distinguished the fourth-century Andreas from the homonymous bishop of Florence A.D. 873–97, who was more notable for the privileges he received from Emperor Charles the Fat than for his sanctity (Davidsohn, *Geschichte von Florenz*, 1:87–88). P. B. Gams tentatively lists a second *Saint* Andrew, bishop of Florence ca. 428, whose obit (26 Feb.) the Bollandists had taken to be that of Andreas I: *Series episcoporum ecclesiae catholicae*, vol. 1 (Regensburg, 1873), p. 747. Obviously, for the understanding of Dante, only the legend is a relevant datum.

186. See above, pp. 101–6.

CHAPTER 6

1. *Inf.* xv, 67; *Purg.* xvi, 66; cf. *Mon.* 3. 3. 4.

2. Note also the distinction between the *transmutatio naturalis* and *innaturalis*: see R. J. Deferrari, *A Latin-English Dictionary of St. Thomas Aquinas* (Boston, 1960), s.v. "transmutatio." The *potestas vicaria* was in fact often taken to confer the power to work miracles. See M. Wilks, *The Problem of Sovereignty in the Later Middle Ages* (Cambridge, Eng., 1963), p. 371. The opinion there attributed to Johannes Andreae (n. 4) is in fact that of Tancred, adapted by Bernard of Parma in the *Glossa ordinaria* on X 1. 7. 3: see J. A. Watt, "The Theory of Papal Monarchy in the Thirteenth Century: The Contribution of the Canonists,"

Traditio 20 (1964): 179–317, at pp. 262–63, esp. n. 42. This in turn may cast some light on Dante's supposed Nominalism, on which see R. Hollander, *Allegory in Dante's Commedia* (Princeton, N.J., 1969), p. 55 n.45.

3. To which I proposed a solution in "Dante's Razor and Gratian's D.XV," a paper presented at the Conference on Medieval Studies, Kalamazoo, Michigan, in May 1971.

4. E.g., Cino's doctrine that the emperor as the author of law is *natura naturata*. See B. Tierney, "Natura id est deus: A Case of Juristic Pantheism?" *Journal of the History of Ideas* 24 (1963): 307–22, at p. 319.

5. A. Passerin d'Entrèves, *Dante as a Political Thinker* (Oxford, 1952), pp. 4–7; cf. pp. 73–74.

6. Which is to say that the poet *follows* God's footsteps—nature and revelation. This does not necessarily make him either a prophet or even a *scriba Dei*, but only a poet whose art consists in the creation of verbal images that reflect the Word as it is manifest to man. How the *Comedy* was modeled on the Bible is best suggested by A. C. Charity, *Events and Their Afterlife* (Cambridge, Eng., 1966). Cf. his conclusion (p. 257): "the content and proportions of ... this study are not intended to represent the view that the *Divine Comedy* of Dante should or could constitute a third 'Testament,' such as that to which the Abbot Joachim of Fiore had looked forward. But these proportions did imply, and now the contents have I hope confirmed, ... that the *Divine Comedy*'s use and understanding of typology has a kind of continuity, if not identity, with the use and understanding of typology in the Bible...."

7. The bees of *Inf.* xvi, 1–3, like those of *Purg.* xviii, 58–59 and *Par.* xxxi, 7–9, have long been recognized as an image of human society: e.g., by G. B. Zoppi, *Gli animali nella Divina Commedia* (Venice, 1892; offprint from *L'Alighieri*, vols. 2 and 3), pp. 86–87.

8. Pézard, p. 297 n.

9. *Mon.* 2. 7. 9: "Certamine vero dupliciter Dei iudicium aperitur: vel ex collisione virium, sicut fit per duellum pugilum, qui duelliones etiam vocantur, vel ex contentione plurium ad aliquod signum prevalere conantium, sicut fit per pugnam athletarum currentium ad bravium" (my trans.). For the meaning of *bravium*, see G. Vinay, ed., *Monarchia* (Florence, 1950), p. 7 n.15, at 1. 1. 5.

10. *Mon.* 2. 7. 11: "Similiter et latere non debet quoniam in hiis duobus decertandi generibus ita se habet res, ut in altero sine iniuria decertantes impedire se possint, puta duelliones, in altero vero non; non enim athlete impedimento in alterutrum uti debent...."

11. On the *bellum iustum,* consult Gaines Post, *Studies in Medieval Legal Thought* (Princeton, N.J., 1964), index, s.v. "Just"; and E. Kantorowicz, *The King's Two Bodies* (Princeton, N.J., 1957), s.v. "War." The definitive monograph is now Frederick H. Russell, *The Just War in the Middle Ages,* Cambridge Studies in Medieval Life and Thought, 3d ser., vol. 8 (Cambridge, Eng., 1975).

12. A. Sacchetto, "Le chant des trois florentins," *Annales du Centre universitaire méditerranéen* 6 (1952–53): 117–81, at pp. 172–73. Also D. J. Donno, review in *Speculum* 42 (1967): 139.

13. *Mon.* 2. 7. 1–10: "Ad bene quoque venandum veritatem quesiti scire oportet quod divinum iudicium in rebus quandoque hominibus est manifestum, quandoque occultum.

[I] Et manifestum potest esse dupliciter: ratione scilicet et fide. [A] Nam quedam iudicia Dei sunt ad que humana ratio propriis pedibus pertingere potest, sicut ad hoc: quod homo pro salute patrie seipsum exponat; nam si pars debet se exponere pro salute totius, cum homo sit pars quedam civitatis, ut per Phylosophum patet in suis *Politicis,* homo pro patria debet exponere seipsum, tanquam minus bonum pro meliori. Unde Phylosophus *ad Nicomacum*: 'Amabile quidem enim et uni soli, melius et divinius vero genti et civitati.' Et hoc iudicium Dei est; aliter humana ratio in sua rectitudine non sequeretur nature intentionem: quod est inpossibile.

[B] Quedam etiam iudicia Dei sunt, ad que etsi humana ratio ex propriis pertingere nequit, elevatur tamen ad illa cum adiutorio fidei eorum que in Sacris Licteris nobis dicta sunt, sicut ad hoc: quod nemo, quantumcunque moralibus et intellectualibus virtutibus et secundum habitum et secundum operationem perfectus, absque fide salvari potest, dato quod nunquam aliquid de Cristo audiverit. Nam hoc ratio humana per se iustum intueri non potest, fide tamen adiuta potest. Scriptum est enim *ad Hebreos*: 'Inpossibile est sine fide placere Deo'; et in *Levitico*: 'Homo quilibet de domo Israel, qui occiderit bovem aut ovem aut capram in castris vel extra castra et non obtulerit ad hostium tabernaculi oblationem Domino, sanguinis reus erit.' Hostium tabernaculi Cristum figurat, qui est hostium conclavis ecterni, ut ex evangelio elici potest: occisio animalium operationes humanas.

[II] Occultum vero est iudicium Dei ad quod humana ratio nec lege nature nec lege Scripture, sed de gratia spetiali quandoque pertingit; quod fit pluribus modis: quandoque simplici revelatione, quandoque revelatione disceptatione quadam mediante.

[A] Simplici revelatione dupliciter: aut sponte Dei, aut oratione impetrante; [1] sponte Dei dupliciter: aut expresse, aut per signum; [a] expresse, sicut revelatum fuit iudicium Samueli contra Saulem; [b] per signum, sicut Pharaoni revelatum fuit per signa quod Deus iudicaverat de liberatione filiorum Israel. [2] Oratione impetrante, quod sciebant qui dicebant secundo *Paralipomenon*: 'Cum ignoremus quid agere debeamus, hoc solum habemus residui: quod oculos nostros ad Te dirigamus.'

[B] Disceptatione vero mediante dupliciter: aut sorte, aut certamine; 'certare' etenim ab eo quod est 'certum facere' dictum est. [1] Sorte quidem Dei iudicium quandoque revelatur hominibus, ut patet in substitutione Matthie in *Actibus Apostolorum*. [2] Certamine vero dupliciter Dei iudicium aperitur: [a] vel ex collisione virium, sicut fit per duellum pugilum, qui duelliones etiam vocantur, [b] vel ex contentione plurium ad aliquod signum prevalere conantium, sicut fit per pugnam athletarum currentium ad bravium.

14. See above, n. 145 of chap. 5.
15. Matt. 28:20, taken in *Mon.* 3. 3. 13 to prove that Christ's continuing presence gives the principal councils of the Church the authority of divine revelation. See above, chap. 5, at n. 28 ff.
16. R. Davidsohn, "I campioni nudi ed unti," *Bullettino della Società dantesca italiana,* n.s. 7 (1899–1900): 39–43; and "I campioni 'nudi ed unti' (*Inf.* xvi, 19)," ibid. 9 (1901–2): 185–87. Judicial duels, Davidsohn shows, persisted in Tuscany as a civil procedure among laymen for over a century after clerics were forbidden to participate (conc. Lateran. IV 1215 c.18 = X 3. 50. 9). Two chosen champions were matched,

anointed, and pitted against one another in a circle (*cerchium*): to that extent the Tuscan *duellum* of Dante's day is reflected in the poem.

17. See above, n. 171 of chap. 5.
18. See above, chap. 1, at n. 22 (*tre Fiorentini*) and at n. 30 (Brunetto); chap. 2, at n. 29 (Priscian); chap. 3, at n. 19 (Francesco); and chap. 4, at n. 187 (on Mozzi's infamy).
19. The association, which first alerted me to the significance of Dante's Biblical echoes, I owe to the spontaneous wit of my friend Richard Earl Fauber.
20. C. H. Toy, "Ecclesiastes," in *Encyclopaedia Britannica*, 11th ed., vol. 8 (1910), pp. 849–53. I follow Toy's exposition chiefly because its numbered points provide a convenient framework; his interpretation, which I paraphrase, largely agrees in substance with the excellent, conservative reading offered by M. Leahy, "Ecclesiastes," in *A Catholic Commentary on Holy Scripture*, ed. B. Orchard et al. (London, 1953), pp. 489–95.
21. Eccles. 1:4, 9–10; the intervening verses develop the theme. See also Eccles. 3:1–11, 14–15; 7:13; 8:5–9.
22. Eccles. 7:24–26a, 30 (AV, Eccles. 7:23–25, 29; 8:1).
23. Eccles. 3:11; trans. in *The Bible: An American Translation*, ed. J. M. Powis Smith and E. J. Goodspeed (Chicago, 1935); the Vulgate text is "et mundum tradidit disputationi eorum" (my trans. of Vulgate). See Toy's discussion of this difficult passage.
24. AV and Smith-Goodspeed translations respectively at Eccles. 7:29 (verse 30 in Vulgate).
25. Eccles. 7:30: "fecerit Deus hominem rectum, et ipse se infinitis miscuerit quaestionibus" (my trans. of Vulgate).
26. Brunetto, both in the poem and in life, practiced astrology in an attempt to comprehend and control human affairs (see above, note 27 of chap. 1, for refs.). The Roman-law prohibition against "the practice of astrology as a profession (*exercitio professio*) for the prediction of future events" could justify Dante's disapproval; for him I gather that astrology was one of the *arcana imperii* (cf. *Mon.* 3. 15. 12). Quotation from Berger, p. 368, s.v. "Astrologi."
27. Another parallel suggests the device of inversion, "the world turned upside down," by which Dante dramatized the perversions of the runners. In the same manner, Ecclesiastes complains that he has seen fools given precedence over the wealthy, and servants going on horseback while princes travel by foot (10: 6–7).
28. Eccles. 7:15: "In die bona fruere bonis, et malam diem praecave; sicut enim hanc, sic et illam fecit Deus, ut non inveniat homo contra eum iustas querimonias."
29. Eccles. 8:15 9:10b (last quoted): "quia nec opus, nec ratio, nec sapientia, nec scientia erunt apud inferos, quo tu properas."
30. *Commentarius in Ecclesiasten* (Dekkers, no. 583) at Eccles. 12:13–14, ed. Migne, *PL*, 23:1116; new ed. by M. Adriaen in *CCL*, vol. 72 (1959), p. 360. Note also that Jerome's interpretation of verse 12 anticipates Dante's Razor (see above, chap. 5, at n. 28): "Exceptis his verbis quae ab uno pastore sunt data et concilio atque consensu prolata sapientium, nihil facias, nihil tibi vindices; maiorum sequere vestigia ab eorum auctoritate non discrepes. Alioquin, quaerenti multa, infinitus librorum numerus occurret, qui te pertrahat ad errorem et legentem frustra faciat laborare. Vel certe docet brevitati studendum et sensus magis sectandos esse quam

verba, adversus philosophos et saeculi huius doctores, qui suorum dogmatum falsitates conantur asserere varietate ac multiplicatione sermonum. Contra scriptura divina brevi circulo coartata est et quantum dilatatur in sententiis, tantum in sermone constringitur. Quia consummatum breviatumque sermonem fecit Dominus super terram et verbum eius iuxta est in ore nostro, et in corde nostro" (ed. Adriaen, *CCL,* 72:359). We shall return to these themes in connection with the image of Sodom: see above, chaps. 8, 9.

31. Cf. *Mon.* 2. 7. 4–6; see above, n. 13 of this chap., where the Latin text is quoted under [B].

32. See above, at n. 131 of chap. 4 and the last section of that chapter.

33. Eccles. 5:3(4); 7:5–6; 10:1–3, 12–15. Toy notes their stylistic similarity to the *stultus* aphorisms in Proverbs.

34. Liber Proverbiorum: *Conv.* 3. 11. 12; 3. 14. 7; 3. 15. 16, 18; 4. 5. 2; 4. 7. 9, 13; 4. 15. 13; 4. 24. 14, 16; 4. 25. 2; *Mon.* 3. 1. 3. Canticum canticorum: *Conv.* 2. 5. 5; 2. 14. 20.

35. Sinclair's trans.; last word altered from "vision" to "wisdom."

36. *Par.* xiv, 3–60; "la luce più dia / del minor cerchio" (34–35) speaks 37 ff.

37. Sinclair's trans.; "royal wisdom" altered to "regal prudence" (verse 104).

38. Both allusions correctly identified by Dante's commentators, e.g., Sapegno at *Par.* x, 113–14 and xiii, 91–93.

39. Cf. Eccles. 4:13: "Melior est puer pauper et sapiens, rege sene et stulto, qui nescit praevidere in posterum." The wise boy here is opposed to the old fool, but the addition of a third contrast between pauper and king renders it inapplicable to the case of Solomon.

40. *Conv.* 4. 6. 18–19 (trans. Jackson); cf. Busnelli-Vandelli, 2:68–69.

41. *Conv.* 4. 16. 4–5 (trans. Jackson); cf. Busnelli-Vandelli, 2:198–99.

42. *Par.* xiii, 91–108, quoted above, chap. 6, at n. 40.

43. *S.T.* II-II q.47–56. For what follows I am indebted to Prof. Jan Rogozinski and his unpublished essay "Natural Law and Prudence: An Inquiry into the Nature and Function of Human Reason in the Political Theory of St. Thomas Aquinas."

44. *S.T.* II-II q.48 un. ad 1, and esp. q.50 a.1. In favor of this interpretation is Dante's use of *regalis* = "royal" in *De vulg. eloq.* 1. 12. 4 (*regale solium erat Sicilia*) and the English translation of Aquinas' term suggested by Deferrari, *Latin-English Dictionary of Aquinas,* s.v. "prudentia" (j), *regnativa* = "regal or executive prudence." Less obvious as a possibility is another Thomistic term of art: *prudentia regitiva* (ibid., [k], and *S.T.* II-II q.50; cf. q.47 a.10–11), which signifies the prudence by which one rules either oneself or a multitude. If this were the meaning of *regal prudenza,* then the understanding of *surse* would be absolutely essential to establish that the regnative subspecies of regitive prudence was intended. I think it more likely that (5) concludes Thomas' explanation, with the revelation that *prudentia regnativa* was the virtue he had in mind; then he goes on to explain in (6) that this would have appeared from his original statement if Dante had observed the implications of *surse.*

45. Blackfriars' trans., 22:65.

46. Ibid., 23:201.

47. English Dominican trans. (1918), pp. 26–27.

48. *Conv.* 4. 6. 19, quoted above, n. 40 of this chap.

49. Contemplated fleetingly, I believe, by Thomas in *S.T.* I-II q.63 a.4 ad 3.

50. But see below, n. 58 of chap. 10.

51. According to Aquinas, prudence cannot be infused unless charity is already present in the subject: *S.T.* I-II q.65 a.2.

52. In this case *A Concordance to the Divine Comedy of Dante Alighieri*, ed. E. H. Wilkins and T. G. Bergin (Cambridge, Mass., 1965).

53. *Par.* xii, 94–96: "ma contro al mondo errante / licenza di combatter per lo seme / del qual ti fascian ventiquattro piante."

54. *Par.* xi, 58–59: "ché per tal donna, giovinetto, in guerra / del padre corse...."

55. Aristotle *Politica* 1. 9. 13 (1257b25 ff.); cf. Virgil's distinction between temporal and spiritual goods in *Purg.* xv, 61–75.

56. "Then that father and master went on his way with his lady and with that family which now was bound with the lowly cord" (trans. Sinclair). I think it likely that the *capestro* does in fact signify this bond of mutual, familial charity; thus its temporal counterpart, the *corda* of *Inf.* xvi, 106, would correspond to the bonds of mutual trust or good will that justify all civil associations: in short, the *bona fides* of the Roman law. For a persuasive and far more radical interpretation, see the forthcoming essay by John F. McGovern, "The Conquest of Geryon," *Studies in Medieval Culture* 6–7 (1976): 129–34. An additional clue, relevant to the sponsal theme, is the etymological link between *incestus* and *cestus*, noted by the Parma editor of Thomas' *Opera*: "Alii volunt sic dici a cesto, hoc est cingulo, quod in honestiis nuptiis nova uxor marito tradebat: hinc consuetum vocari nuptias incestas, quae sine cesto fiunt. De quo ritu Catullus carm. xi et lxvii" (ed. Parma, 3:519 n, at *S.T.* II-II q.154 a.9).

57. *Inf.* xv, 22; cf. *Par.* xii, 115: "La sua famiglia."

58. *Par.* xiii, 17–18: "e amendue girarsi per maniera / che l'uno andasse al primo e l'altro al poi."

59. Cf. above, n. 13 of chap. 2.

60. *S.T.* II-II q.45; cf. I-II q.68 a.4, 5, 8.

61. *Par.* xi, 58–59; xii, 55–56.

CHAPTER 7

1. See above, at the end of chap. 5.

2. *Par.* xii, 79–81, 58–60, 67–69; xi, 49–54. The *Ottimo* already appreciated the pun *Assisi-Ascesi* = *montai*. Further, *oriente*, with its echo of Luke 1:78 ("Visitavit nos oriens ex alto"), completes the image of Francis-Christ as the rising sun, which is obviously proper to this heaven. The implications have been obscured, perhaps, by taking the Latin counterpart of *montai* to be simply *ascendere* (Sapegno, at *Par.* xi, 53). More appropriately it could be rendered by *surgere*, and thus linked first to Aquinas' keyword *surse* (*Par.* x, 114, xiii, 106) and thence to Solomon's discourse on re-surrection (*Par.* xiv, 19–33).

3. Pézard, App. 5, pp. 355–64, at p. 361.

4. *Vita nuova* 13. 4; ultimately from *Inst.* 2. 7. 3; cf. Pézard, pp. 356–57. As noted above (n. 112 of chap. 3), this source was identified independently by Pézard (p. 355 n.3) and by Bruno Nardi, *Dante e la cultura medievale* (Bari, 1942), pp. 152–55.

5. Pézard, p. 364 n.1: the Eliseo-Ulisse complex perhaps connects *Inf.* xxvi, 34–39, and *Par.* xv, 136, even more intimately than Pézard suggests (p. 364 n.1).

6. *Inf.* ii, 132; xxvii, 54.

7. The phrase quoted (*cui servire, regnare est*) appears in the *Missa pro pace* of the *Missale Romanum*; the translation is that of the *Book of Common Prayer*, where it occurs in the Collect for Peace of the Office for Morning Prayer. On the Pauline paradox, which the phrase expresses aptly, see *A Theological Word Book of the Bible*, ed. A. Richardson (New York, 1951), p. 87, s.v. "Free."

8. Petrocchi's Ash(burnham 828), Laur(renziana 40 22 [corr. to *daccorso*]), Mad(rid 10186), and Si(viglia 7 540 = Bambaglioli).

9. "In Tusc[an] speech a consonant following *da* is doubled: e.g., 'da capo' is pronounced 'daccapo.'" *The Cambridge Italian Dictionary*, ed. Barbara Reynolds, vol. 1 (Cambridge, Eng., 1962), p. 213, s.v. "da" ad fin.

10. *Dig.* 26. 1. 63. 10, *Gl. ord.* ad v. *conditio*; quoted by Pézard, p. 356.

11. See above, chap. 3.

12. See above, n. 19 of chap. 3.

13. This pseudo fact is widely repeated, e.g., *Encyclopaedia Britannica*, 11th ed., vol. 12 (1910), p. 378, s.v. "Gratianus, Franciscus"; and Toynbee-Singleton, p. 331. No comment in J. F. von Schulte, *Die Geschichte der Quellen und Literatur des canonischen Rechts von Gratian bis auf die Gegenwart*, vol. 1 (Stuttgart, 1875), pp. 46–48. Probably its mediate source is Sarti's notice on Gratian (*De claris*, 1:260 ff.), of which Schulte says: "Seine Ausführungen machen ein Eingehen auf Märchen und falsche Nachrichten überflüssig" (p. 47 n.3).

14. E. Palandri, "Il vescovo Andrea de' Mozzi nella storia e nella leggenda dantesca," *Giornale dantesco* 32 (1931): 91–118, at pp. 94–95 n.8.

15. Perhaps the fact that he was a Franciscan further integrates him into the onomastic symbolism of *Inferno* xv. But such possibilities can be multiplied at a dizzy rate: for example, the perverse pastor of Florence had as his immediate successor Bishop Monaldeschi, baptized Francesco (see above, chap. 4, at n. 100).

16. Schulte, *Geschichte der Quellen*, vol. 2 (Stuttgart, 1877), pp. 205–29. On Dante at Bologna, see above, n. 113 of chap. 3.

17. *Par.* xiii, 139–42 (trans. Sinclair).

18. Priscian, however, glossed his name thus: "Excipiuntur ab 'humo' 'humanus' et 'mundo' 'mundanus' et 'priscus Priscianus,' sed hoc magis a Priscio videtur esse derivatum; nam quod a Taurominio 'Taurominitanus' dicimus, sequimur Graecos, qui 'Taurominites' dicunt. Gentilia enim apud Graecos in 'τηs' desinentia mutata 'es' in a accipiunt 'nus,' cum in hanc formam veniunt: 'Μητροπολίτηs Metropolitanus,' 'Νεαπολίτηs Neapolitanus.'" *Institutiones*, ed. H. Keil, *Grammatici latini*, vol. 2 (Leipzig, 1855), p. 79.

19. Mozzi's connection with the legation of Cardinal *Latino* Malabrancha (see above, n. 58 of chap. 4) is a faint possibility in which some might detect a significant undertone.

20. *Par.* x, 106–8 (Sinclair's trans.). The correspondence of the two titles is noted by Toynbee-Singleton, s.v. "Tesoro"; for the author, see ibid., s.v. "Pietro²."

21. P. Delhaye, *Pierre Lombard: Sa vie, ses oeuvres, sa morale*, in Publications de l'Institut d'études médiévales à Montréal: Conférence Albert-le-Grand, 1960 (Paris, 1961). Also J. de Ghellinck, "Pierre Lombard," *Dictionnaire de théologie catholique*, vol. 12, pt. 2 (Paris, 1935), pp. 1941–2019. On his subsequent influence, M. D.

Chenu, *Toward Understanding Saint Thomas*, trans. A. M. Landry and D. Hughes (Chicago, 1964), pp. 264–72.

22. *Petri Lombardi Libri IV sententiarum*, 2 vols., 2d ed. (Quaracchi, 1916), 1:1–3; older ed. in Migne, *PL*, 192:521–22. For convenient reference, I have numbered the paragraphs of the Quaracchi edition; also I summarize its *apparatus fontium*:

"[1] Cupientes aliquid de penuria ac tenuitate nostra cum paupercula in gazophylacium Domini mittere [cf. Luke 21:2], ardua scandere, opus ultra vires nostras agere praesumsimus, consummationis fiduciam laborisque mercedem in Samaritano [cf. Luke 10:35] statuentes, qui, prolatis in curationem semivivi duobus denariis, supereroganti cuncta reddere professus est. Delectat nos veritas pollicentis, sed terret immensitas laboris; desiderium hortatur proficiendi, sed dehortatur infirmitas deficiendi, quam vincit zelus domus Dei. [2] 'Quo inardescentes, fidem nostram adversus errores carnalium atque animalium hominum' [Augustine, *De trinitate* 3. 1] Davidicae turris clypeis munire vel potius munitam ostendere ac theologicarum inquisitionum abdita aperire nec non et sacramentorum ecclesiasticorum pro modulo intelligentiae nostrae notitiam tradere studuimus, 'non valentes studiosorum fratrum votis iure resistere, eorum in Christo laudabilibus studiis lingua ac stilo nos servire flagitantium. Quas bigas in nobis agitat Christi caritas' [ibid.]. [3] 'Quamvis non ambigamus, omnem humani eloquii sermonem calumniae atque contradictioni aemulorum semper fuisse obnoxium, quia, dissentientibus voluntatum motibus, dissentiens quoque fit animorum sensus,' 'ut, cum omne dictum veri ratione perfectum sit, tamen, dum aliud aliis aut videtur aut complacet, veritati vel non intellectae vel offendenti impietatis error obnitatur, ac voluntatis invidia resultet,' 'quam *Deus huius saeculi operatur* in illis *diffidentiae filiis* [2 Cor. 4:4 and Eph. 2:2], qui non rationi voluntatem subiiciunt nec doctrinae studium impendunt, sed his quae somniarunt sapientiae verba coaptare nituntur, non veri, sed placiti rationem sectantes, quos iniqua voluntas non ad intelligentiam veritatis, sed ad defensionem placentium incitat, non desiderantes doceri veritatem, sed ab ea *ad fabulas convertentes auditum* [2 Tim. 4:4]; quorum professio est magis placita quam docenda conquirere, nec docenda desiderare, sed desideratis doctrinam coaptare. *Habent rationem sapientiae in superstitione* [Col. 2:23]: quia fidei defectionem sequitur hypocrisis mendax, ut sit vel in verbis pietas, quam amiserit conscientia, ipsamque simulatam pietatem omni verborum mendacio impiam reddunt, falsae doctrinae institutis fidei sanctitatem corrumpere molientes, auriumque pruriginem sub novello sui desiderii dogmate aliis ingerentes, qui contentioni studentes contra veritatem sine foedere bellant.' 'Inter veri namque assertionem et placiti defensionem pertinax pugna est, dum se et veritas tenet, et se voluntas erroris tuetur.' [§ 3 adapted from Hilary, *De trinitate* 10. 1–2.] [4] Horum igitur Deo odibilem ecclesiam evertere atque ora oppilare, ne virus nequitiae in alios effundere queant, et lucernam veritatis in candelabro exaltare volentes [cf. Matt. 5:15], in labore multo ac sudore volumen, Deo praestante, compegimus ex testimoniis veritatis in aeternum fundatis, in quatuor libris distinctum. [5] In quo maiorum exempla doctrinamque reperies, in quo per dominicae fidei sinceram professionem vipereae doctrinae fraudulentiam prodidimus, aditum demonstrandae veritatis complexi nec periculo impiae professionis inserti, temperato inter utrumque moderamine utentes. Sicubi vero parum vox nostra insonuit, non a paternis discessit limitibus. [6] 'Non igitur debet hic labor cuiquam pigro vel multum docto videri superfluus, cum multis impigris multisque indoctis, inter quos etiam et mihi, sit necessarius' [Augustine, *De trin.* 3. 1], brevi volumine complicans Patrum sententias, appositis eorum testimoniis, ut non sit necesse quaerenti librorum numerositatem evolvere, cui brevitas collecta quod quaeritur offert sine labore. In hoc autem tractatu non solum pium lectorem, sed etiam liberum correctorem desidero, maxime ubi profunda versatur veritatis quaestio, quae utinam tot haberet inventores, quot habet contradictores [cf. ibid., 2]. [7] Ut autem quod quaeritur facilius occurrat, titulos, quibus singulorum librorum capitula distinguuntur, praemisimus."

23. *Li livres dou tresor de Brunetto Latini*, ed. F. J. Carmody, University of California Publications in Modern Philology, vol. 22 (Berkeley and Los Angeles, 1948), pp. 17–18: 1. 1. *"Cis livres est apielés Tresors et parole de la naissance de toutes coses.* [1] Cis livres est apielés Tresors. Car si come li sires ki vuet en petit lieu amasser cose de grandisme vaillance, non pas pour son delit solement, mes pour acroistre son pooir et pour aseurer son estat en guerre et en pais, i met les plus chieres choses et les plus precieus joiaus k'il puet selonc sa bonne entencion; tout autresi est li cors de cest livre compilés de sapience, si come celui ki est estrais de tous les membres de philosophie en une sonme briement. Et la premiere parties de cest tresor est autresi comme de deniers contans, pour despendre tousjours es coses besoignables; c'est a dire k'ele traite dou comencement du siecle, et de l'ancieneté des vielles istores et de l'establissement dou monde et de la nature de toutes coses en some. [2] Et çou apertient a la premiere science de philosophie, c'est a theorika, selonc ce ke li livres parole ci aprés. Et si come sans deniers n'aroit nule moieneté entre les oevres des gens, ki adreçast les uns contre les autres, autresi ne puet nus hons savoir des autres cose plainement s'il ne set ceste premiere partie du livre. [3] La second partie ki traite des vices et des viertus est de precieuses pieres, ki donent a home delit et vertu, c'est a dire quex coses on doit faire et quels non, et moustre la raison pour quoi; et çou apiertient a la seconde et a la tierce partie de philosophie, c'est a pratike et a logike. [4] La tierce partie du tresor est de fin or, c'est a dire k'ele ensegne a home parler selonc la doctrine de retorike, et coment li sires doit governer ses gens ki souz li sont, meismement selonc les us as ytaliens; et tout ce apertient a la seconde sience de philosophie, c'est pratike. Car si comme li ors sormonte toutes manieres de metal, autresi est la sience de bien parler et de governer gens plus noble de nul art du monde. Et por ce ke li tresors ki ci est ne doit pas iestre donés se a home non ki soit souffissables a si haute richece, la baillerai jou a toi biaus dous amis, car tu en ies bien dignes selonc mon jugement. [5] Et si ne di je pas que le livre soit estrais de mon povre sens ne de ma [me]nue science; mais il ert ausi comme une bresche de miel coillie de diverses flours, car cist livres est compilés seulement des mervilleus dis des autours ki devant nostre tans ont traitié de philosophie, cascuns selonc çou k'il en savoit partie; car toute ne la puet savoir hons terriens, pour çou ke philosophie est la rachine de qui croissent toutes les siences ke hom puet savoir, tot autresi comme une vive fontaine dont maint ruissiel issent et decourent ça et la, si ke li un boivent de l'une et li autre de l'autre; mais c'est diversement, car li un en boivent plus et li autre mains, sans estancier la fontaine. [6] Pour çou dist Boesces el livre de la Consolation que il le vit en samblance de dame, en tel abit et en si trés mervilleuse poissance qu'ele croissoit quant

il li plaisoit, tant ke son chief montoit sor les estoiles et sour le ciel, et porveoit amont et aval selonc droit et selonc verité. . . ."

24. See above, chaps. 1 and 5.

25. *Consol. Philos.* 1. 1. 2, the only source for the preface identified in Carmody's apparatus.

26. E.g., the passages quoted above in chap. 5.

27. Aquinas, *Scriptum super libros Sententiarum*, Prologus (ed. Parma, 6:5): "Sententia, secundum Avicenna, est definitiva et certissima conceptio." The *Sententiae* of Isidore of Seville contributed heavily to the *Tresor*.

28. Carmody compares it to those of Vincent of Beauvais and Roger Bacon (*Tresor*, p. xxiii). Cf. above, chap. 1, at n. 33.

29. *Ep.* xi, 16 (ed. Toynbee, *Ep.* viii, 7): "Iacet Gregorius tuus in telis aranearum; iacet Ambrosius in neglectis clericorum latibulis; iacet Augustinus abiectus, Dionysius, Damascenus et Beda; et nescio quod 'Speculum,' Innocentium, et Ostiensem declamant." Toynbee thought that a legal speculum was intended, specifically that of William Durandus (ad loc., and Toynbee-Singleton, s.v. "Speculum iuris"). But would one who had mastered the legal works of Innocent IV and Hostiensis rely on such a work for his legal knowledge? Instead would he not substitute something like the doctrinal and moral *Specula* of Vincent of Beauvais for the theological authors that Dante feels are neglected?

30. See above, chap. 1, after n. 35.

31. This follows from the argument of *Mon.* 1. 4–5, that mankind requires universal peace to achieve happiness, and that it is the office of the emperor to preserve that peace.

32. E.g., Mozzi knew Gregory through Gratian: see above, n. 157 of chap. 4.

33. Boethius, *Philosophiae consolatio* 1. 1. 1–2, ed. L. Bieler, *CCL*, vol. 94 (Turnhout, 1957), p. 2: "mulier . . . statura discretionis ambiguae. Nam nunc quidem ad communem sese hominum mensuram cohibebat, nunc vero pulsare caelum summi verticis cacumine videbatur; quae cum altius caput extulisset ipsum etiam caelum penetrabat respicientiumque hominum frustrabatur intuitum." On the interpretation of the commonplace, the editor cites F. Klingner, *De Boethii Consolatione Philosophiae*, Philologische Untersuchungen, vol. 27 (Berlin, 1921), pp. 113 ff.

34. *Consol. Philos.* 3. 9–12. As is well known, there are many parallels between Dante and Boethius: see, e.g., Toynbee-Singleton, s.v. "Boezio."

35. See above, § 2 of n. 22 of this chap.: the Lombard is quoting Augustine *De trinitate* 3. 1.

36. Aquinas *Scriptum super libros Sententiarum*, Prologus (ed. Parma, 6:3): "Huic operi Magister prooemium praemittit, in quo tria facit. Primo reddit auditorem benevolum. . . . Benevolum reddit assignando causas moventes ipsum ad compilationem huius operis, ex quibus ostenditur affectus ipsius in Deum et proximum. Sunt autem tres causae moventes. Prima sumitur ex parte sui, scilicet desiderium proficiendi in Ecclesia; secunda ex parte Dei, scilicet promissio mercedis et auxilii; tertia ex parte proximi, scilicet instantia precum sociorum. E contra sunt tres causae retrahentes. Prima ex parte sui, defectus ingenii et scientiae; secunda ex parte operis, altitudo materiae et magnitudo laboris; tertia ex parte proximi, invidorum contradictio. Harum autem causarum moventium duae primae insinuant caritatem in Deum, tertia in proximum."

37. Matt. 6:19–21. See above, chap. 5, at n. 161 ff.

38. See Toynbee-Singleton, p. 116, s.v. "Brunetto Latino."

39. C. T. Davis, *Dante and the Idea of Rome* (Oxford, 1957), p. 109.

40. According to G. Villani, Florence was founded ca. 72 B.C. by Latin veterans of the Roman siege of Fiesole. The colony was first called "Little Rome" and "was peopled by the best of Rome, and the most capable, sent by the senate in due proportion from each division of Rome, chosen by lot from the inhabitants; and they admitted among their number those Fiesolans which desired there to dwell and abide" (*Cronica* 1. 38, trans. Rose E. Selfe). Brunetto's *Tresor* (1. 37. 2) summarizes this tradition: "Aprés ce assegerent li romain la cité de Fiesle, tant k'il le venkirent et misent en sa subjection; et lors firent il enmi les plains ki est au pié des hautes montaignes u cele cités seoit une autre cité, ki ore est apelle Florence" (ed. Carmody, p. 45). Brunetto goes on to remark that the influence of the planet Mars accounts for the prominence of war and discord in the affairs of Florence: "De ce doit maistre Brunet Latin savoir la verité, car il en est nés, et si estoit en exil lors k'il compli cest livre por achoison de la guerre as florentins" (*Tresor* 1. 37. 3).

41. Perhaps this sense of racial superiority based on Roman origins justified the rejection of the rule of the empire that, as Brunetto the historian stresses, had passed successively into the hands of the Franks, the Lombards, and the Germans: *Tresor* 1. 89–93 (ed. Carmody, pp. 70–75).

42. *Inf.* xv, 68: "gent' è avara, invidiosa e superba"; "il nido di malizia tanta" (xv, 78).

43. Two tercets diagnose the ills of the American megalopolis better than ten thousand sociologists. The concept, of course, derives from Aristotle *Politics* 7. 4. 3–8 (1326a9–1326b25).

44. *Conv.* 4. 29. 3, 8–11 (quotation at end, trans. Jackson). Cf. 4. 20. 5: " 'l divino seme non cade in ischiatta, cioè in istirpe, ma cade ne le singolari persone, e, sì come di sotto si proverà, la stirpe non fa le singolari persone nobili, ma le singolari persone fanno nobile la stirpe." Again the quantitative factor stressed by Cacciaguida predominates.

45. *Conv.* 4. 21. 1 (my trans.): "Acciò che più perfettamente s'abbia conoscenza de la umana bontade, secondo che in noi è principio di tutto bene, la quale nobilitade si chiama, da chiarire è in questo speziale capitolo come questa bontade discende in noi; e prima per modo naturale, e poi per modo teologico, cioè divino e spirituale."

46. *Conv.* 4. 21. 3.

47. *Purg.* xxv, 61–75.

48. *Conv.* 4. 21. 10 (trans. Jackson): "E quasi questo è tutto ciò che per via naturale dicere si puote."

49. I paraphrase Dante's program, quoted above, n. 45 of this chap.

50. *Conv.* 4. 21. 11–12 (trans. Jackson, altered): "Per via teologica si può dire che, poi che la somma deitade, cioè Dio, vede apparecchiata la sua creatura a ricevere de suo beneficio, tanto largamente in quella ne mette quanto apparecchiata è a ricever<n>e. E però che da ineffabile caritate vegnono questi doni, e la divina caritate sia appropriata a lo Spirito Santo, quindi è che chiamati sono doni di Spirito Santo. [12] Li quali, secondo che li distingue Isaia profeta, sono sette, cioè Sapienza, Intelletto, Consiglio, Fortezza, Scienza, Pietade e Timore di Dio. Oh buone biade, e buona e ammirabile sementa! e oh ammirabile e benigno seminatore, che non attende

se non che la natura umana li apparecchi la terra a seminare! e beati quelli che tale sementa coltivano come si conviene!"

51. *Conv.* 4. 16. 9–10.

52. Busnelli-Vandelli, 2:263 n.2: "Le 'buone biade,' sono i doni, sorti dalla sementa della carità, infusa con la grazia abituale dallo Spirito Santo."

53. "Che seme di felicità sia costa [gentilezza], / messo da Dio ne l'anima ben posta." Text and translation in K. Foster and P. Boyde, *Dante's Lyric Poetry* (Oxford, 1967), 1:137 (no. 69. 119–20 = Barbi no. 82), with commentary at 2:223–25.

54. For the term *intelligenze*, see *Conv.* 4. 21. 8 and Busnelli-Vandelli, 2:259 n.1.

55. *Conv.* 4. 21. 12; 4. 22. 12: "Così fossero tanti quelli di <f>atto che s'insetassero, quanti sono quelli che da la buona radice si lasciano disviare!"

56. 1 Cor. 13:2: "Et si habuero prophetiam, et noverim mysteria omnia, et omnem scientiam: et si habuero omnem fidem ita ut montes transferam, charitatem autem non habuero, nihil sum."

57. This passage is explicated above, in chap. 10.

58. This interpretation does not depend (as some have thought) on Vandelli's emendation of *Inf.* xi, 50. By Dante's theory of psychogenesis, it is nature that determines how much of divine *bontade* each individual soul shall receive. Hence the noble soul is an effect of nature, and the failure to cultivate it constitutes a denial of the goodness of *both* God and nature. On the disputed passage, see Petrocchi, 2:181.

59. See above, n. 40 of this chap.

60. See above, chap. 1, text before n. 32.

61. Charles T. Davis, "Brunetto Latini and Dante," *Studi medievali*, 3d ser., vol. 8, pt. 1 (1967), pp. 421–50, at pp. 434–39.

62. *Tresor* 2. 114. 2, ed. Carmody, p. 295: "Et cil ki se delitent en noblesce de lignie, et ki se vantent de haut antecessours, s'il ne font les vertueuses oevres, il ne pensent bien que li los de lor parens torne plus a lor honte que a lors pris."

63. *Conv.* 4. 29. 1: "coloro che, per essere di famose e antiche generazioni e per essere discesi di padri eccellenti, credono essere nobili, nobilitade non avendo in loro."

64. M. Corti, "Le fonti del *Fiore di virtù* e la teoria della 'nobilità' nel Duecento," *Giornale storico della letterature italiana* 136 (1959): 1–82, at p. 77.

65. Davis, "Brunetto Latini," p. 437.

66. *Conv.* 4. 22. 18. Nowhere does Dante list the intellectual virtues, though he does state that he does not number prudence among them (*Conv.* 4. 17. 8). Probably he would have recognized the three that Aquinas placed foremost—*sapientia, intellectus, scientia* (*S.T.* I-II q.57 a.2).

67. G. Villani, *Cronica* 8. 10 (see above, n. 39 of chap. 1). Cf. *Tresor* 2. 123. 2–3.

68. Davis, "Brunetto Latini," p. 443.

69. See above, n. 119 of chap. 3.

70. Matt. 7:16–20: "A fructibus eorum cognoscetis eos. Numquid colligunt de spinis uvas, aut de tribulis ficus? Sic omnis arbor bona fructus bonos facit: mala autem arbor malos fructus facit. Non potest arbor bona malos fructus facere: neque arbor mala bonos fructus facere. Omnis arbor, quae non facit fructum bonum, excidetur, et in ignem mittetur. Igitur ex fructibus eorum cognoscetis eos."

71. *Conv.* 4. 16. 9–10: "Dico adunque che, con ciò sia cosa che in quelle cose che sono d'una spezie, sì come sono tutti li uomini, non si può per li principii essenziali la loro ottima perfezione diffinire, conviensi quella e diffinire e conoscere per li loro

effetti. [10] E però si legge nel Vangelio di santo Matteo—quando dice Cristo: 'Guardatevi da li falsi profeti'—: 'A li frutti loro conoscerete quelli.' E per lo cammino diritto è da vedere questa diffinizione, che cercando si vae per li frutti: che sono morali vertù e intellettuali, de le quali essa nostra nobilitade è seme...."

72. *Par.* x, 91–92; xi, 105, 124–32, 137; xii, 65–66, 82–86, 95–96, 103–5; xiii, 34–39.

73. *Par.* xiii, 52–78.

74. E. Gilson, *Dante and Philosophy* (New York, 1963), p. 281: "Dante's work does not constitute a system, but is the dialectical and lyrical expression of all his loyalties."

75. *Purg.* xxv, 37–75.

CHAPTER 8

1. *Inf.* xi, 49–50.

2. Pézard, pp. 294–312.

3. For literary critics, the seminal work has been H. de Lubac, *Exégèse médiévale: Les quatre sens de l'Ecriture*, 4 vols. (Paris, 1959–1964). Blending the spirit and methods of Biblical exegesis, both medieval and modern, A. C. Charity has pointed the way to a deeper reading of the *Comedy* in *Events and Their Afterlife: The Dialectics of Christian Typology in the Bible and Dante* (Cambridge, Eng., 1966). Most recently, Robert Hollander has used typology, in his *Allegory in Dante's Commedia* (Princeton, N.J., 1969), to refine the approach to Dantesque allegory that was pioneered by Erich Auerbach and by Charles Singleton.

4. I have relied chiefly on the *Concordantiarum universae Scripturae sacrae thesaurus*, ed. E. Peultier et al., 2d ed. (Paris, 1939), controlled by the *Analytical Concordance to the Bible*, by Robert Young, 4th ed. (Edinburgh, 1881). This method is by no means anachronistic, for Dante had exactly the same means at his disposal if he chose to explore the Biblical usage of a Latin word. All the references to Sodom discussed above, chaps. 8 and 9, can be found in the great Dominican concordance to the Vulgate compiled in 1230 under the direction of Hugh of Saint-Cher, which was frequently printed: my copy is the *Sacrorum Bibliorum Vulgatae editionis concordantiae Hugonis cardinalis ordinis praedicatorum*, rev. F. Lucas [1617] and H. Phalesius (Venice, 1719). See Cross, *ODCC*, s.v. "Concordance," with bibliography.

5. A repertory of these commentators exists in F. Stegmüller, *Repertorium Biblicum Medii Aevi*, 7 vols. (Madrid, 1950–1961). The best sketch of their discipline is Beryl Smalley, *The Study of the Bible in the Middle Ages*, 2d ed. (New York, 1952).

6. On the authorship of the twelfth-century *Glossa ordinaria* (or *interlinearis*), see Stegmüller, *Repertorium*, vol. 2 (1950), nos. 2582–85. The marginal portions (wrongly attributed to Walafrid Strabo), ed. Migne, *PL*, vols. 113, 114, in abridged form, omitting certain books, notably Ezechiel. As an example of the regular use of the *Gl. ord.* in the exposition of Biblical texts by one close to Dante in culture as well as in time and place, see Marsiglio of Padua, *Defensor pacis*, ed. R. Scholz, in *MGH, Fontes iuris Germanici antiqui*, [no. 7] (Hanover, 1932–33), p. 633, s.v. "Glossa."

7. *Ep.* xi, 7: "iacet Augustinus adiectus, Dionysius, Damascenus et Beda"; cf. *Mon.* 3. 3. 13 and 3. 15. 9. He is among the *spiriti sapienti* (*Par.* x, 131). In Dante's day, Bede was known almost exclusively for his Biblical commentaries, which are

notable for their allegorizing. See, in general, M. L. W. Laistner, *Thought and Letters in Western Europe, A.D. 500 to 900*, 2d ed. (London, 1957), pp. 158–64.

8. On his reasons, see C. W. Jones, ed., *Libri quatuor in principium Genesis usque ad nativitatem Isaac et eiectionem Ismahelis adnotationum*, ed. CCL, vol. 118A, p. x.

9. Gen. 10:19: "Factique sunt termini Chanaan venientibus a Sidone Geraram usque Gazam, donec ingrediaris Sodomam et Gomorrham, et Adamam, et Seboim usque Lesa."

10. The Biblical text nowhere explicitly states that they were located on a plain, and indeed some commentators place them in the valley of Siddim (Gen. 14:8, 10 = Vulg. *vallis silvestris*). In Genesis their territory is *"omnem circa regionem Jordanis"* (Gen. 13:10, cf. 19:25, 28–29). Probably they were located in the shallow basin that now forms the southern bay of the Dead Sea. Very likely their region was conceived as a plain in contrast to the surrounding mountains, to which Lot eventually fled (Gen. 19:17, 19, 30). The *Gl. ord.* assures us that "haec enim regio plana erat et campestris [cf. the vale of Siddim-*silvestris*], et irrigata Jordane fluente, sicut Aegyptus Nilo" (on Gen. 13:10, ed. Migne, *PL*, 113:118).

11. Gen. 9:25–27.

12. Gen. 9:20–24.

13. The distribution of Noah's descendents is commonly mapped: e.g., Hammond's *Atlas of the Bible Lands* (Maplewood, N.J., 1959), p. B-4. Or *The Macmillan Bible Atlas*, ed. Y. Aharoni and M. Avi-Yonah (New York, 1968), map 15.

14. On Sodom as the exemplification of the evil city, see A. Richardson, ed., *A Theological Word Book of the Bible* (New York, 1951), p. 49, s.v. "City." Though Egypt is hardly a city, as a symbol of civilization it is likened to cities in Biblical usage, most explicitly in Apoc. 11:8 (see above, chap. 9).

15. Bede, on Gen. 11:8–9, ed. *CCL*, 118A:156–57. Gen. 10:5 names Babylon as one of the cities *in terra Sennaar;* Gen. 11:2 locates the Tower in the same land.

16. Cf. Gen. 11:7 and 18:21.

17. Lot's other uncle, Na(c)hor, settled in Haran, as appears from Gen. 24:10 and 29:4–5.

18. Augustine explained that in the Bible any male relatives can be called brothers. *Locutiones in Heptateuchum,* Genesis 43, ed. J. Fraipont, *CCL,* vol. 33 (Turnhout, 1958), p. 385: *"Quoniam homines fratres nos sumus* [Gen. 13:18]. Abraham dicit ad Lot: unde intelligitur morem esse scripturae ita loqui, ut fratres appellentur unius cognationis, etiamsi gradu sanguinis differant, ut alter sit in superiore, alter in inferiore, sicut hoc loco; nam patruus eius erat Abraham."

19. Gen. 14:22–23: "Qui respondit [Abram] ei [regi Sodomorum]: Levo manum meam ad Dominum Deum excelsum possessorem caeli et terrae, Quod a filo subtegminis usque ad corrigiam caligae, non accipiam ex omnibus quae tua sunt, ne dicas: Ego ditavi Abram."

20. Gen. 15:6: "Credidit Abram Deo, et reputatum est illi ad iustitiam."

21. So called in Gen. 14:16; see above, n. 18 of this chap.

22. Significantly, Ishmael is a "natural" son; cf. Gal. 4:23.

23. Gen. 17:1b–2: "Ego Deus omnipotens: ambula coram me, et esto perfectus. Ponamque foedus meum inter me et te, et multiplicabo te vehementer nimis."

24. Since only two angels arrive in Sodom, it is often assumed that one remained behind to continue the conversation with Abraham, though the text merely states that "they turned themselves from thence, and went their way to Sodom: But

Abraham as yet stood before the Lord" ("Converteruntque se inde, et abierunt Sodomam: Abraham vero adhuc stabat coram Domino"; Gen. 18:22).

25. Such reluctance would seem to be urbane manners: compare Abraham's dialogue with the Hittites in Gen. 23:3–16.

26. Gen. 19:5. The verb (*yada'*) is faithfully translated by the Vulgate and Douay versions: it can refer indifferently to knowledge of any sort, though sexual knowledge is implied in this context by Lot's offer of his daughters as substitutes (Gen. 19:8). Cf. NEB: "so that we can have intercourse with them" (Gen. 19:5).

27. Gen. 19:29: "Now when God destroyed the cities of that country, remembering Abraham [*recordatus Abrahae*], he delivered Lot out of the destruction of the cities wherein he had dwelt."

28. Gen. 15:17: "Cum ergo occubuisset sol, facta est caligo tenebrosa, et apparuit clibanus fumans, et lampas ignis transiens inter divisiones illas."

29. Gen. 19:24–25, 28: "Igitur Dominus pluit super Sodomam et Gomorrham sulphur et ignem a Domino de caelo: Et subvertit civitates has, et omnem circa regionem, universos habitatores urbium, et cuncta terrae virentia.... [Abraham] Intuitus est Sodomam et Gomorrham, et universam terram regionis illius: viditque ascendentem favillam de terra quasi fornacis fumum."

30. Antediluvian "iniquity" has been interpreted as "violence" by the translators of the English AV, RSV, and most recently NEB (Gen. 6:11, 13).

31. Gen. 9:5–6: "Sanguinem enim animarum vestrarum requiram de manu cunctarum bestiarum: et de manu hominis, de manu viri, et fratris eius requiram animam hominis. Quicumque effuderit humanum sanguinem, fundetur sanguis illius: ad imaginem quippe Dei factus est homo."

32. The *pair* may have been more significant than the gender, since Lot thought that a pair of the opposite sex might serve as a substitute.

33. "*Cognitio* ... is the ability, found in all living beings except plants, of receiving the form of things other than self without losing self-identity, because they possess formally or eminently a sensitive soul." R. J. Deferrari, *A Latin-English Dictionary of St. Thomas Aquinas* (Boston, 1960), s.v. "Cognitio (1)."

34. See above, n. 22 of this chap.

35. Smalley, *Study of the Bible*, chap. 6, esp. pp. 329–55, stopping just short of Nicholas of Lyra.

36. Notice with bibliography in Cross, *ODCC*, p. 957. Nicholas became a regent master at Paris in 1308.

37. Since this discovery was made after the foregoing chapters had been written, my interpretation did not benefit from rabbinic tradition. I am indebted to the kindness and learning of Rabbi Arthur Neulander of New York City for referring me to the passages cited below from the Talmud and Midrash.

38. It is noteworthy that the Talmud treats the sin of Sodom in the tractate *Sanhedrin*, which particularly attracted medieval Christian scholars because it describes the judicial system under which Jesus was tried. In the sixteenth century, Reuchlin could find no other treatise of the Talmud in Europe. See *The Babylonian Talmud, Seder Nezikin*, ed. I. Epstein, vol. 3, *Sanhedrin*, trans. J. Shachter and H. Freedman (London: Soncino Press, 1935), p. xii. Mishnah, on fol. 107b–108a; Gemara, on fol. 109ab (pp. 737–38, 749–52). The [bracketed] interpolations that are glosses have, for the most part, been supplied by the editor and translator.

39. The classification is systematic: any individual, for specified manifestations of heterodoxy; then seven specific individuals—three kings, four commoners—named in Scripture (*Sanhedrin*, pp. 601–3 ff.); six groups, also from Scripture: the generations of the Flood and of the Dispersion, the men of Sodom; and from Num. 14 and 16, the spies, the generation of the Wilderness, and the congregation of Korah (pp. 737–39 ff.); plus a seventh group, the ten tribes excluded from Palestine (pp. 759 ff.); and finally the inhabitants of any seduced city (pp. 765 ff.).

40. The tanna goes on to do Rab Judah one better by finding a specific act which according to Scripture was done "exceedingly": "Moreover, Manasseh shed innocent blood exceedingly" (4 Kings 21:16). Rab Judah had merely asserted without explanation "*exceedingly*—that they intentionally sinned" (no. 3).

41. *Sanhedrin*, fol. 109a (trans., p. 749).

42. It may be recalled that Job 28 inspired one of Augustine's most eloquent arguments for the divine origin of the human soul (*Confessions* 10. 6).

43. Ps. 62:4, 69:7; Job 24:16, 10, 7, 6, 2, 21:32. In passing, we may recall that Dante takes the violation of boundaries and of flocks as metaphors of the runners' sins. Cf. Job 24:2 ("Alii terminos transtulerunt, diripuerunt greges, et paverunt eos") with chaps. 4 and 5 of this book. *Mon.* 3. 3. 5 may recall verse 6 ("Agrum non suum demetunt").

44. Job 24:17: "Si subito apparuerit aurora, arbitrantur umbram mortis: et sic in tenebris quasi in luce ambulant."

45. The work comprises the first part of the *Midrash Rabbah, Translated into English*, ed. H. Freedman and M. Simon, 13 vols. (London: Soncino Press, 1939 ff.), where it appears under the title *Genesis* (vols. 1 and 2). Relevant to Sodom are the commentaries on Genesis 13:8–17 and 18:20–19:29, in *Bereshith Rabbah*, chaps. 41:6–10 and 49:5–51:6 (trans., 1:336–39, 424–27). On the work, see Freedman's introduction (1:xxvi–xxix). Midrashic material was being used by Christian commentators in the thirteenth century (e.g., William of Auvergne) and even more extensively by Nicholas of Lyra in the fourteenth (ibid., pp. xx–xxi).

46. *Bereshith Rabbah* 41:7, in *Midrash Rabbah*, trans. Freedman, 1:338.

47. Further points of comparison: the clamor of Sodom is again the cry of a maiden executed for her charity (ibid., p. 424; cf. above, p. 228, no. 18); the Sodomites counterfeit righteousness (ibid., p. 428; cf. above, p. 226, no. 6, and p. 228, no. 11, the Judge Forger); the judges are five—False-Principles, Lying-Speech, Cad, Justice-Perverter, and Man-Flayer—with Lot at their head (ibid., p. 436; cf. above, p. 228, no. 11). At Gen. 19:9, Lot is supposed to have challenged a particular rule of Sodom: "The Sodomites made an agreement among themselves that whenever a stranger visited them they should force him to sodomy and rob him of his money" (ibid., p. 438). To explain how Lot could be said to have dwelt in all the cities destroyed, it is suggested that "he lent money on interest there" (ibid., p. 447).

48. At Gen. 13:13, the *Gl. ord.*, ad vv. *coram domino*, remarks only "cui crimen puniendum committitur: nam et hominibus manifestum crimen, sed non puniendum" (ed. Migne, *PL*, 113:118). Judging from the *fontes* identified in Migne's edition, the *Gl. ord.* does not seem to have drawn on Bede *In principium Genesis*. Bede's principal authorities do not comment on the sin of Sodom: e.g., Jerome *Hebraicae quaestiones in libro Geneseos*, ed. *CCL*, 72:17; Augustine *Quaestiones in Heptateuchum*, Genesis, 27 (ed. *CCL*, 33:11).

49. Bede, on Gen. 13:10–14, ed. *CCL*, 118A:178–79: "Fertilitatem terrae laudat, simul et incolarum notat impietatem, ut eo maiori damnatione digni esse intellegantur, quod maxima Dei munera non ad fructum pietatis sed ad incrementum vertere luxuriae. Ubi etiam tacite laudibus beati Loth additur quia in ipsa terra inter ipsos degens indigenas, neque ubertate soli divitis, neque exemplo cohabitantium potuit ullatenus a suae puritatis integritate corrumpi. Quibus autem peccatis Sodomitae fuerint subiugati, excepto illo infando quod in sequentibus scriptura commemorat. Iezechiel propheta sufficienter exponit, loquens ad Hierusalem, 'Ecce haec ... coram me' [Ezech. 16:49–50, quoted above, p. 259]. A quibus omnibus immunem fuisse beatum Loth, et textus sacrae historiae testatur. Quem angelos hospitio recepisse, ac per eos a pereuntibus impiis ereptum esse declarat; et sententia beati Petri apostoli probat, qua dicitur, 'Et iustum Loth oppressum a nefandorum iniuria et conversatione eruit. Aspectu enim et auditu iustus erat, habitans apud eos qui de die in diem animam iustam iniquis operibus cruciabant' [2 Pet. 2:7–8]. Quid enim boni meriti ei deesse poterat, qui iustus apostolica voce astruitur? In quo praesentes non nisi iustitiae famam audire valebant, cuius oculis et auribus mundis audita ac visa proximorum facinora non nisi cruciatus et afflictio erant?"

50. See above, chap. 8, at n. 30 ff.

51. The *Glossa ordinaria* interprets the whole episode as an allegory in which five kings represent the five senses, which are overcome by four personified vices, only to be saved by the intervention of the four contrary virtues, namely Abram and his three allies. *Gl. ord.*, on Gen. 14:1–17, ed. Migne, *PL*, 113:119–20.

52. Bede, on Gen. 14:1–2, ed. *CCL*, 118A:182–83: "Non est autem putandum haec sacrae auctorem scripturae historici tantum studii gratia memoriae mandasse, et non intuitu potius commendandae nobis gratiae celestis; docet namque nos per victoriam Abrae, qua tantos reges cum paucis superavit, quae sit virtus fidei qua erat ipse munitus; quanta gratia benedictionis divinae, qua erat praeditus—quia modo per eandem fidem sancti postmodum nascituri, devicturi regna, operaturi iustitiam, adepturi essent promissiones. Sed et alia permagna neque ullatenus praetereunda causa est, quorum pugna regum et Sodomorum primo fuga ac post ereptio scriberetur, quos etiam in sequentibus celesti ira penitus constat esse subversos. Videns quippe eorum scelera, Deus primo haec caede hostili et captivitate corripuit; sed mox per fidelem suum famulum ab eadem eos captivitate cum omnibus quae erant capta eripuit. Et hoc ob gratiam beati Loth, qui inter eos fideliter Deo servivit, ut tali dono divinae protectionis adiuti ac liberati de malis, discerent et ipsi relictis erroribus Deo servire eiusque ad bona opera sequeretur exemplum a quo et per quem Dei sunt gratia salvati. Verum quia nec ipsi, nec correptionibus divinis, nec donis a sua iniquitate voluere corrigi, quin potius priscae scelera pravitatis recentibus cotidie accumulaverunt flagitiis, restabat ut ira celesti perpetuo damnarentur. Cuius correptionis ac punitionis ordo usque hodie, immo usque in finem seculi, erga impios et peccatores eodem modo agi non desinit, cum hi qui nec beneficiis, nec flagellis celestibus curant emendari, postmodum celesti ultione damnantur. Tali et ipse mundus statum suum sine fine consumet, dum homines per orbem universum et ad dona superna ingrati et ad flagella insensibiles perdurantes, subito novissimi examinis turbine ad aeternum rapiuntur interitum."

53. Bede, on Gen. 19:4–5, ed. *CCL*, 118A:221–22: "Hoc est quod propheta Esaias de populo Israhel supra modum peccante ait, 'Peccatum suum sicut Sodoma praedi-

caverunt nec absconderunt' [Isa. 3:9]. 'Peccatum' quippe 'suum' sicut Sodomitae 'praedicaverunt nec absconderunt,' cum absque respectu pudoris alicuius omnes a puerili aetate usque ad ultimam senectutem masculi in masculos turpitudinem operari solebant, adeo ut ne hospitibus quidem ac peregrinis sua scelera abscondere, sed et hos vim inferendo suis similes facere sceleribus atque suis facinoribus implicare contenderent. Quod vero furentibus eis in tale flagitium patrandum dicit inter alia Loth: [quotes Gen. 19:8, where Lot offers his daughters, and adds Augustine's comment that he is not to be imitated]."

54. Bede, on Gen. 19:17, ed. *CCL*, 118A:223–24: "Generaliter quidem incendium et perditio Sodomorum, de qua ereptus est Loth, poenam ultimae districtionis designat, quando, completa in fine seculi summa electorum, omnes impii aeterno rapiuntur in ignem, Domino exponente qui ait: 'Similiter sicut factum est in diebus Loth ...' [Luke 17:28–30, and also Jude 7]. Potest autem idem ignis sodomiticus etiam flammas vitiorum quibus in hac vita reprobi uruntur, atque ad sempiternum praeparantur incendium, non inconvenienter insinuare. Qui cum nunc in concupiscentiis terrenis carnisque inlecebris ardere non cessant, tunc igne ultionis ardere numquam desistent. [Cites Luke 17:31–32, "remember Lot's wife," in support.]"

55. Modern Biblical scholarship usually identifies Deuteronomy with "the book of the law" discovered at the Jerusalem Temple in 621 B.C., in the reign of King Josiah (4 Kings 22:8), whose reform program it reflects. Presumably, existing Mosaic traditions were compiled by the reformers in the Book of the Second Law, and thus it is possible that Deuteronomy does in fact preserve the earliest treatment of the Sodom theme outside Genesis. If so, however, this material had its greatest impact on Josiah's generation, since Zephaniah and Jeremiah, the two contemporary prophets whose ministries antedate the discovery of Deuteronomy by a decade, more or less, both make much the same use of the theme of Sodom.

56. Cf. above, chap. 6, at n. 13.

57. Augustine *De civitate Dei* 21. 8. 93–103, ed. *CCL*, 48:773: "Terra Sodomorum non fuit utique ut nunc est, sed iacebat simili ceteris facie eademque vel etiam uberiore fecunditate pollebat; nam Dei paradiso in divinis eloquiis comparata est [Gen. 13:10]. Haec postea quam tacta de caelo est, sicut illorum quoque adtestatur historia [Tacitus *Hist.* 5. 7] et nunc ab eis qui veniunt ad loca illa conspicitur, prodigiosa fuligine horrori est et poma eius interiorem favillam mendaci superficie maturitatis includunt. Ecce non erat talis, et talis est. Ecce a conditore naturarum natura eius in hanc foedissimam diversitatem mirabili mutatione conversa est; et quod post tam longum accidit tempus, tam longo tempore perseverat."

58. These *poma sodomitica* are a botanical problem in themselves, to which my colleague Jerry Stannard plans to devote a study.

59. *Inf.* xv, 65–66: "li lazzi sorbi ... dolce fico."

60. See above, chap. 1, at nn. 20, 21.

61. Since Augustine contrasts the present state of Sodom to its former condition, which was comparable to the Terrestrial Paradise (see above, n. 57 of this chap.), one is tempted to see the deceptive *poma* as the degenerate counterpart of the fruit of that more famous tree, the *"lignum ... scientiae boni et mali"* (Gen. 2:9b), in which case they might aptly be taken as a figure of false knowledge of good and evil.

62. 1 Cor. 3 should be read as a whole, with the sin of the runners in mind: The Corinthians are God's temple, founded by Paul on grace and built up by his

successors. All those who try to build the temple will gain eternal life, even though they build poorly, but those who destroy the temple will themselves be destroyed. The building standards are not those of this world, "for the wisdom of this world is folly in God's sight" (NEB, verse 19). Verses 16–17 have often been taken out of context as a warning against abuse of the natural body: "Know you not, that you are the temple of God, and that the Spirit of God dwelleth in you? But if any man violate the temple of God, him shall God destroy. For the temple of God is holy, which you are."

63. Jerome, on Amos 4:11, ed. *CCL*, 76:267–68: "Extrema medicina est, et decem tribuum, et haereticorum, et omnium peccatorum, ut postquam mortem miserit in via Aegypti, ... et nec sic quidem ad eum reversi fuerint, subvertat eos sicut subvertit Deus Sodomam et Gomorrham; et cum subversi fuerint, ob similitudinem criminum Sodomae et Gomorrhae, pessimaque in eis aedificia divinus ignis exusserit, ipsi liberentur quasi torris raptus de incendio. Et quomodo Lot, Sodoma pereunte, servatus est, amittens substantiam et partem corporis sui, quam intellegimus uxorem, sic isti omnes Sodomorum divitias amittentes evadant nudi, iuxta illud quod in apostolo legimus: 'Si cuius opus manserit quod superaedificavit, mercedem accipiet; si cuius autem opus arserit, detrimentum patietur, ipse autem salvus erit, sic tamen quasi per ignem' [1 Cor. 3:14–15]. Qui ergo salvatur per ignem, quasi torris de incendio rapitur.... Igitur et Israel et cuncti haeretici, quia habebant opera Sodomae et Gomorrhae, subvertuntur ut Sodoma et Gomorrha, ut quasi torris raptus de incendio liberentur. Et hoc est quod in propheta legimus: 'Restituetur Sodoma in antiquum' [Ezech. 16:55], ut qui suo vitio Sodomitis est, postquam in eo Sodomae opera arserint, in antiquum restituatur statum."

64. Jerome, on Osee 11:8–9, ed. *CCL*, 76:126: "*Quid tibi faciam, Ephraim?*... Sicut Adama et Seboim ponam te, quae duae sunt quinque urbium, sicut in Genesi [10:19] legimus.... Ponam itaque et vertam te in solitudinem, et delebo usque ad cineres ac favillas, sicut delevi Adama et Seboim...."

65. Ibid., p. 127: "*In medio tui sanctus et non ingrediar civitatem*, hoc est: non sum unus de his, qui in urbibus habitant, qui humanis legibus vivunt, qui crudelitatem arbitrantur iustitiam, quibus ius summum summa malitia est; mea autem lex meaque iustitia est salvare correctos...."

66. Ibid., pp. 127–28: "Notandum quoque quod ubi contra Iudam dicitur, id est populum Dei, non Adama ponitur et Seboim, sed Sodoma et Gomorrha [e.g., Isa. 1:10; Matt. 10:14–15; Ezech. 16:52].... Datur ergo nobis suspicio, quod Sodoma et Gomorrha principes fuerint in peccato, et Adama et Seboim earum exempla sectatae sint, quod 'potentes potenter tormenta patiantur' [Wisd. 6:7]; et servus qui scit voluntatem domini sui, et non facit eam, vapulet multis. Unde et ecclesiastici viri, si iisdem quibus haeretici sceleribus continentur, nequaquam Adamae et Seboim, quae inferiores sunt, sed Sodomae et Gomorrhae, quae maiorum criminum esse dicuntur cruciatibus subiacebunt. Ad haereticos quoque deceptumque ab eis populum loquitur Dominus, quod nisi egerint paenitentiam, ponantur sicut Adama et Seboim, ut nullam spem habeant salutis.... Et quia sanctus sum, propterea non ingrediar civitatem, id est conciliabula et urbes haereticorum. Foras exeuntes de urbibus suis, libenter recipio, in civitates eorum non ingrediar.... Hebraei autem ex persona Dei ita edisserunt: Non te derelinquam, non ibo ad aliam gentem; nec ingrediar alteram civitatem."

67. Jerome, on Isa. 1:4, ed. *CCL*, 73:10: "In quarto [verso] quasi in excessibus gentem increpat peccatricem et populum plenum vel gravem iniquitate. Non quo alia sit gens et alius populus, ut quidam putant, sed ipse Israel et gens appellatur et populus, et filii scelerati, sive iniqui, ut qui primum per beneficium filii appellati sunt Domini, postea vitio suo vocarentur filii iniquitatis. Sive ut reliqui consona voce dixerunt filii corrumpentes, id est διαφθείροντες, qui naturae bonum suo vitio perdiderunt."

68. Jerome, on Isa. 1:5, ed. *CCL*, 73:11: "Cum igitur caput doluerit, omnia membra debilia sunt. Et per metaphoram docet, quod a principibus usque ad extremam plebem, a doctoribus usque ad imperitum vulgus in nullo sit sanitas; sed omnes in impietate pari ardore consentiant."

69. Jerome, on Isa. 1:8, ed. *CCL*, 73:14.

70. Jerome, on Isa. 1:10, ed. *CCL*, 73:15–16: "Salvis factis reliquiis per apostolos populi Israel, ad scribas et pharisaeos et populum succlamantem: 'Crucifige, crucifige talem' [John 19:6].... Aiunt Hebraei ob duas causas Esaiam interfectum, quod principes Sodomorum et populum Gomorrhae eos appellaverit...." The editor tentatively identifies the source as the *Martyrium Esaiae* (*Ascensio Esaiae* 5), and cites E. Tisserant, *Ascension d'Isaïe* (Paris, 1909), pp. 67 ff., and Origen *In Esaiam*, hom. 1, ed. Baehrens, p. 247.

71. Note that office here is symbolized by a *vestimentum*. Since Dante's cord now appears to be just such a symbol (see above, n. 56 of chap. 6), this passage suggests that it stands to the swift and the strong as the *vestimentum* does to the *pueri principes*: i.e., it represents the *officia* that preserve the *ordo* of the just society; with them vanish all restraints, so society without justice degenerates into a den of thieves (cf. Augustine *De civitate Dei* 4. 4).

72. See *Gl. ord.*, on Isa. 3, ed. Migne, *PL*, 113:1238–40.

73. Jerome, on Isa. 3:1, ed. *CCL*, 73:41: "Quod sequitur, de captivitate ventura, quam alii ad Babylonios, alii referunt ad Romanos. Sed melius est, ut supra diximus, cuncta referri ad dominicam passionem. Post interfectionem quippe illius, omnes gratiae et donationes sublatae sunt a Iudaeis."

74. Jerome, on Isa. 3:4, ed. *CCL*, 73:47: "Subito Deus loquitur per prophetam ex persona sua et dicit: 'Dabo pueros principes eorum'; sublatis enim his quae ante donaveram et quasi bona iratus abstuleram, nunc e contrario dabo mala. Tuli senem et quinquagenarium, et admirabilem consiliarium et sapientem architectum et prudentem auditorem et cetera. Pro his dabo pueros principes."

75. Jerome, on Isa. 3:4, ed. *CCL*, 73:48: "Talis [as in Eccles. 10:16] fuit rex iuvenis Roboam filius Salomonis, qui secutus est iuvenum consilia. Non quod aetate esset iuvenis, sed sapientia [3 Kings 12:6–16]. Alioquin quadraginta et amplius annorum regnum accepisse narratur. Et e contrario Salomon duodecim annorum erat quando suscepit imperium et quia habebat sapientiam, propterea non est appellatus iuvenis. Erat enim in eo latitudo cordis, et amplitudo sapientiae quanta arena est in maris litoribus."

76. Cf. the "childish things" of 1 Cor. 13:11 (AV); Jerome renders τὰ τοῦ νηπίου as *quae erant parvuli*.

77. Though *illusores* in classical usage meant only "mockers," for the Latin Fathers it had the secondary sense of "deceivers" or "imposters." Thus Jerome translated Isa. 66:4 and Ps. 27:7; cf. Augustine *Ep.* 237. 9, where *illusor* is opposed to *veritatis doctor*. Ambrose, Leo I, and Gregory I give a similar sense to *illusio*: A.

Blaise, *Dictionnaire latin-français des auteurs chrétiens* (Paris, 1954), s.vv. "illusio," "illusor."

78. Jerome, on Isa. 3:4, ed. *CCL*, 73:48–49: *"Et effeminati dominabuntur eis.* Pro quo in Hebraeo scriptum est thalulim, quos LXX et Theodotio illusores interpretati sunt, Aquila ἐαλλάκτας, qui se mutent et turpitudinis exerceant vices. Quales in Iudicum libro [19:1–28] super concubina levitae in Gabaa legimus. Consideremus patriarchas Iudaeorum, et iuvenes sive pueros effeminatosque ac deliciis affluentes [2 Pet. 2:13], et impletam prophetiam esse cernemus. Possumus illusores dicere et magistros populi Israel, qui devorant populum Dei sicut escam panis, et perverse scripturas sanctas interpretantur illuduntque stultitiae discipulorum."

79. Aquila, who "did not shrink from perpetrating the most appalling outrages to the whole essence of the Greek language," had already departed from classical usage in giving the term the sense of "wantons" or "perverts": Liddell-Scott, s.v. "ἐαλλάκτης"; cf. "ἐαλλακτικός" (Deut. 20:14). On Aquila, see *Septuaginta*, ed. A. Rahlfs (8vo, Stuttgart, 1935), pp. xxiv–xxvii; p. xxiv quoted above.

80. The reason that he can apply the phrase *deliciis affluentes* to the *pueri principes Sodomorum* would seem to be that he assimilates them to the *pseudoprophetae*, to whom the phrase originally referred (2 Pet. 2:1, 13). As we shall see, both Peter and Jerome identify false prophets to Christendom with the sin of Sodom.

81. Jerome, on Isa. 3:12, ed. *CCL*, 73:52: "mulieres, quia propter libidinem omnia faciant, et sint dediti voluptatibus."

82. Jerome, on Isa. 3:8–9, ed. *CCL*, 73:51: "Causasque reddit impietatis eorum, quia contra Dominum blasphemaverunt, atque dixerunt: 'Tolle, tolle, crucifige talem, non habemus regem nisi Caesarem' [John 19:15]. Et clementissimum Deum furore linguae suae ad amaritudinem provocaverunt 'agnitioque vultus eorum respondebit eis,' id est: sua recepere peccata, sive ut Septuaginta transtulerunt: 'Confusio vultus eorum restitit eis,' id est: ante oculos suos propria semper habuere delicta. Et quomodo Sodomitae cum omni libertate peccantes et ne pudorem quidem ullum habentes in scelere, dixerunt ad Lot: 'Educ foras viros, ut concumbamus cum eis.' Sic et isti publice proclamantes, suum praedicavere peccatum, nec ullam in blasphemando habuere verecundiam.... Unde et principes appellantur Sodomorum, qui Sodomitica habuere peccata."

83. The reason that Jerome's commentary so often follows the Septuagint rather than the Vulgate text is simply that he plagiarized from earlier Greek commentators (e.g., Origen, Eusebius). On Jerome's sources, see *CCL*, 73:v–vi, with bibliography.

84. Jerome, on Isa. 3:10–11, ed. *CCL*, 73:51–52: "'Vae animae eorum, quoniam cogitaverunt, consilium pessimum contra semetipsos, dicentes: Alligemus iustum, quoniam inutilis est nobis; itaque fructus operum suorum comedent.'"

85. Jerome, on Isa. 1:10, ed. *CCL*, 73:15: "Propheticus sermo ... vocat eos [scribas et pharisaeos et populum] principes Sodomorum et populum Gomorrhae, iuxta illud quod in consequentibus legimus: 'Iniquitatem suam sicut Sodoma annuntiaverunt et ostenderunt. Vae animae eorum, quia cogitaverunt consilium pessimum contra semetipsos, dicentes: Alligemus iustum, quoniam inutilis est nobis' [Isa. 3:9]. Ergo propterea principes vocantur Sodomorum et populus Gomorrhae, quia cogitaverunt consilium pessimum et alligaverunt iustum atque dixerunt: 'Non habemus regem nisi Caesarem' [John 19:15]." The thesis is restated at the beginning of Book 2 of Jerome's commentary (ed. *CCL*, 73:41).

86. Jerome, on Isa. 3:12, ed. *CCL*, 73:52: "Pro mulieribus, quas solus interpretatus est Symmachus, et Hebraice dicuntur nasim, Aquila et LXX transtulerunt ἀπαιτοῦντας, qui significant exactores, Theodotio δανειστὰς, id est feneratores. Loquitur autem sermo propheticus contra scribas et pharisaeos, qui turpis lucri gratia, ut acciperent decimas et primitias, Dei Filium negaverunt. Et non eos vocat magistros, scribas atque doctores, sed exactores, qui quaestum putant esse pietatem; et devorant, non (iuxta apostolum) domos tantum viduarum, sed universum populum; ... exactores appellat, ut ab invitis pecuniam videantur exigere...."

87. See above, nn. 77, 78, of this chap.

88. Jerome, on Isa. 3:12, ed. *CCL*, 73:52–53: "Scribas et pharisaeos exactores appellaverat, non magistros; et supra illusores, qui propter munera, quae excaecant oculos etiam sapientium, non solum peccatores in populo non corripiebant, sed pro divitiis atque compendiis efferebant laudibus, beatos vocantes, et columnas domus Dei, et cetera quae solent adulatores dicere. *Ille est ergo doctor ecclesiasticus, qui lacrimas, non risum, movet, qui corripit peccatores, qui nullum beatum, nullum dicit esse felicem.... Exactores autem perverterunt atque turbaverunt viam Domini, ut habentes clavem scientiae, nec ipsi intrarent nec populum intrare paterentur; sed facerent eos perdere viam veritatis, quae loquitur in evangelio: 'Ego sum via, et vita, et veritas' [John 14:6]." **Gl. ord.* begins at this point.

89. Jerome, on Isa. 13:1, ed. *CCL*, 73:224: "Et quia Babylon, quae Hebraice dicitur Babel, interpretatur confusio, eo quod ibi aedificantium turrim sermo confusus est, spiritaliter mundus iste intellegitur, qui in maligno positus est, et non solum linguas, sed opera singulorum mentesque confundit. Huius Babylonis rex est verus Nabuchodonosor, contra Dominum superbiens ... [sc. Satan]. Denique in consequentibus nequaquam contra Babylonem, sed contra orbem terrarum comminatio est.... Ex quibus probatur, omnia quae dicuntur contra Babylonem, ad mundi huius confusionem et interitum pertinere." Jerome regularly equates Babylon with confusion, though the context can modify the concept. His *Liber interpretationibus Hebraicorum nominum* (ed. *CCL*, vol. 72) translates "Babylon vel Babel confusio" in Genesis; simply "Bablyon confusio" in Joshua, Psalms, and presumably other OT contexts; but "Babylon confusio vel [sive] translatio" in Peter and the Apocalypse (pp. 62, 90, 119, 150, 159).

90. Jerome, on Isa. 13:17–18, ed. *CCL*, 73:233.

91. Geryon "had two paws hairy to the armpits" ("due branche avea pilose infin l'ascelle"; *Inf.* xvii, 13). Jerome was not sure what *pilosi* might be (he-goats in NEB) but did not neglect to note the possibilities inherent in an alternate translation, *onocentauri*: "Porro onocentauri nomen, ex asinis centaurisque compositum, videtur mihi significare eos, qui ex parte aliquid humanum sapiunt; et rursum voluptatibus et caeno turpitudinis abducuntur ad vitia." Jerome, on Isa. 13:21, ed. *CCL*, 73:235.

92. Jerome, on Isa. 13:19–22, ed. *CCL*, 73:236: "Hoc quoque considerandum, quod postquam ecclesiasticus sermo et doctrina Salvatoris urbem confusionis everterit, ita ut Sodomae et Gomorrae comparetur; non habitetur a sanctis viris, nec pastores requiescant in ea, qui Christi gregem pascere consueverant; sed e contrario requiescant ibi bestiae et dracones, et struthiones et pilosi saltent in ea. Quidquid enim haeretici loquuntur in synagogis satanae, non est doctrina Domini, sed ululatus daemonum et pilosorum, quos imitabatur Esau. Et sirenae requiescent in delubris voluptatis, quae dulci et mortifero carmine animas pertrahunt in profundum, ut

saeviente naufragio, a lupis et canibus devorentur."

93. Jerome, on Soph. 2:8–11, ed. *CCL*, 76A:682–88.

94. Jerome, on Soph. 2:8–9, ed. *CCL*, 76A:686–87: "Vide haereticos in dialectica sibi et rhetorica et omnium sophismatum dogmatibus applaudentes, contemnere Ecclesiae rusticitatem, et quasi indignam mysteriis suis, quae sibi quasi idola confinxerunt, despicere, et habere pro nihilo, et non quaeres quae sint opprobria Moab, et contumeliae filiorum Ammon, in quibus exprobraverunt populo Dei."

95. Jerome, on Soph. 2:8–9, ed. *CCL*, 76A:687: "Sicut Sodoma et Gomorrha erunt, videntur quidem sibi in eo quod gentiles non sunt, exisse de Sodomis et Gomorrhis, sed quia blasphemant populum Dei, et contra Israel faciunt, in Sodomam reputabuntur et Gomorrham; et ita delebuntur ut illae deletae sunt ante, nullum in se habentes vestigium viroris et vitae."

96. Ibid.: "Nec mirum si hoc de haereticis intellegamus, quod reputentur quasi Sodoma et Gomorrha, cum etiam ad ecclesiasticos, qui Dei non observavere mandata, et egressi sunt a praeceptis eius, dicatur per Esaiam [1:10]."

97. Ibid., p. 688: "Et Moab igitur, et Ammon et Damascus, qui sese adversus Domini scientiam paraverunt, et blasphemaverunt populum Dei, et dixerunt in eum plurimas contumelias, et voluerunt dilatare terminos suos in terra Ecclesiae, et populum Dei possidere, desertae erunt et destructae, et reliqui de populo Dei, hoc est viri ecclesiastici in scripturis dominicis eruditi diripient eos, et residui gentis dominicae possidebunt eos, et hoc eis erit pro contumelia, qua exprobaverunt et magnificati sunt contra Dominum omnipotentem."

98. Cf. Lam. 4:21–22, Ezech. 25:12–14, Abdias 1–9; cf. Deut. 23:7–8.

99. Rabanus Maurus, *Expositio super Ieremiam* 15, on Jer. 49:17–19, ed. Migne, *PL*, 111:1132–33: "Erit ergo in die furoris Domini conciliabulum haereticorum, sive Iudaeorum blasphemantium desertum, quia nunquam postea habebunt potestatem congregare concilium malignantium. Omnisque, qui transierit per eam, stupebit, et sibilabit super omnes plagas eius. Quia supplicia eorum, quae sustinebunt pro impietatibus suis formidini et pavori valde digna erunt. Quoniam, sicut Sodomam et Gomorrham sulphur et ignis incendit, et in aeternam solitudinem redigit, ita et 'super peccatores pluit ignis et sulphur, et spiritus procellarum pars calicis eorum' [Ps. 10:7]." All this the *Gl. ord.* omits, but it incorporates the whole commentary on verse 19 (ed. Migne, *PL*, 114:56): "Igitur sicut Dominus castigavit superbiam Iudaeorum, quos Iordanis nomine notat: ita etiam et Idumaeorum perfidiam atque invidiam, quam exercuerant contra fratres suos, per ministros irae suae plena vindicta corripiet, nec est ullus qui eius consilio ac voluntati resistere possit. Similiter et haeretici et hostes Ecclesiae Dei non evadent tormenta, iniquis operibus et dogmatibus suis condigna."

100. The resemblance to Jerome, on Jer. 23:14 (see below, n. 110 of this chap.), is unmistakable.

101. Lewis-Short, s.v. "adultero" ii.

102. Jer. 23:26: "Usquequo istud est in corde prophetarum vaticinantium mendacium, et prophetantium seductiones cordis sui?"

103. Jer. 23:15b: "A prophetis enim Ierusalem, egressa est pollutio super omnem terram."

104. Jer. 23:16: "Haec dicit Dominus exercituum: Nolite audire verba prophetarum, qui prophetant vobis, et decipiunt vos: visionem cordis sui loquuntur, non de ore Domini."

105. *Inf.* xv, 70–72.

106. Jer. 23:10: "Quia adulteris repleta est terra, quia a facie maledictionis luxit terra, arefacta sunt arva deserti: factus est cursus eorum malus, et fortitudo eorum dissimilis."

107. Jerome, on Jer. 23:10, ed. *CCL*, 74:218–19: "Redditque causas, quod propter adulteria et maledicta sive superfluum iuramentum, immo periuria, frugum sterilitas consecuta sit. Quicquid de terra Iudaea iuxta litteram intellegis, refer ad congregationem credentium, quoniam propter adulteria et mendacia sive periuria virtutum et donationem dei sterilitas in ecclesiis sit."

108. See above, n. 73 of this chap.

109. See above, chap. 8, after n. 89.

110. Jerome, on Jer. 23:13–14, ed. *CCL*, 74:220: "'Et in prophetis Samariae vidi stultitiam'—sive 'iniquitatem'—; 'prophetabant in Bahal et decipiebant populum meum Israhel.' Ego prophetas Samariae iuxta mysticos intellectus proprie hereticos dici puto et omnes, qui iactant falsi nominis scientiam [1 Tim. 6:20]. *Quomodo autem prophetae Samariae, quicquid loquebantur, prophetabant in Bahal, idolo videlicet daemonibus consecrato, sic heretici, quicquid loquuntur in ecclesia sive extra ecclesiam, ut supplantent populum 'Israhel,' qui prius 'cernebat deum,' loquuntur in daemonibus;* unde et significanter ait: 'et in prophetis Samariae vidi stultitiam'; non enim habent eum, de quo dicitur: 'Christus dei virtus et dei sapientia' [1 Cor. 1:24]." On Jer. 23:14: "'Et in prophetis Hierusalem vidi similitudinem'—sive 'horribilia'—'adulterium et iter mendacii; et confortaverunt manus pessimorum, ut non converteretur unusquisque a malitia sua'—sive 'a via sua pessima'—; 'facti sunt mihi omnes Sodoma et habitatores eius quasi Gomorra.' 'Non solum,' inquit, 'in hereticorum conciliabulis haec reperta sunt, sed in prophetis quoque Hierusalem, id est doctoribus ecclesiae, vidi similia sive horribilia adulterantium verbum dei et ingredientium per viam mendacii, ut hereticorum fallaciis adquiescerent et confortarent manus pessimorum eorumque mala suis sceleribus adiungerent et, quos corrigere debuerant, ducerent in interitum. Qui hoc fecerint, non se aestiment inpunitos! Erunt enim et ipsi et hi, quibus favent, quasi Sodoma omnesque, qui habitant cum eis nec recedunt a talibus, quasi Gomorra'...." The *Gl. ord.* applies the passage marked (*—*) to the next verse, Jer. 23:14 (ed. Migne, *PL*, 114:38).

111. See above, n. 110 of this chap.: "Suis sceleribus adiungerent."

112. Jerome, on Ezech. 16:44–63, ed. *CCL*, 75:201–14.

113. Jerome, on Ezech. 16:46, ed. *CCL*, 75:203: "Dicitur ... et minor ac iunior Sodoma quae refertur ad gentium turbam; alioquin eo tempore Sodoma non erat quae prius quam in scripturis legamus Hierusalem, cum Gomorrha, Adama et Seboim, divino fuerat igne deleta."

114. Ibid.: "Porro, secundum tropologiam, Samaria et Sodoma, id est haeretici et ethnici, saepe leviora committunt quam ii qui putantur Hierusalem, hoc est ecclesiastici."

115. Jerome, on Ezech. 16:53, ed. *CCL*, 75:209: "Cui enim dubium, quin inter tres peccatores, immo impios, gentilem, haereticum, ecclesiasticum, multo maioribus poenis dignus sit, qui maioris fuerit dignitatis?"

116. In addition to the Vulgate, Jerome also draws on his Latin version of the Septuagint (the phrase in [brackets] he identifies as an interpolation of the Greek translators):

" 'Vivo ego, dicit Adonai Dominus, si fecit Sodoma soror tua, haec et filiae eius, sicut fecisti tu et filiae tuae. Verumtamen fuit iniquitas Sodomae sororis tuae superbia in saturitate panum et in abundantia. Deliciis affluebat ipsa et filiae eius [hoc habebat ipsa et filiae eius]: et manum pauperis et egeni non assumebat; et gloriabantur magnifice et fecerunt iniquitates in conspectu meo, et abstuli eas sicut vidisti.' " Jerome, on Ezech. 16:48–51, ed. *CCL*, 75:204–5. To regain the ambiguity of the Greek, remove all punctuation between *Verumtamen* and the interpolation: cf. *Septuaginta*, ed. Rahlfs. Jerome rendered ἐσπατάλων, "they were living luxuriously," by *deliciis affluebat* [sic] here but not elsewhere: cf. 1 Tim. 5:6 and James 5:5; cf. above, n. 80 of this chap.

117. Jerome, on Ezech. 16:48–51, ed. *CCL*, 75:205: "Iste igitur qui iurat et loquitur: 'Vivo ego, dicit Dominus,' describens Sodomae et filiarum eius scelera, primam superbiam posuit proprie diaboli, primumque peccatum...."

118. Isa. 10:13a: "Dixit enim: In fortitudine manus meae feci, et in sapientia mea intellexi" in the Vulgate; Jerome, however, is translating the Septuagint version: " 'Dixerat enim: Fortitudinem faciam et sapientiam intelligentiae' " (ed. *CCL*, 75: 205).

119. The prepositions were supplied by the Septuagint translators (or by the pre-Masoretic Hebrew text from which they worked), but the resultant phrase is probably to be construed with the following verb, as in Rahlfs' text: Ezech. 16:49a πλὴν τοῦτο τὸ ἀνόμημα Σοδομων τῆς ἀδελφῆς σου, ὑπερηφανία · ἐν πλησμονῇ ἄρτων καὶ ἐν εὐθηνίᾳ <οἴνου> ἐσπατάλων αὐτὴ καὶ αἱ θυγατέρες αὐτῆς · Literally, "But yet this was the lawlessness of Sodom your sister, pride: in fullness of bread and in abundance of wine they-were-living-luxuriously, she and her daughters." Since Jerome's Latin version of the Septuagint can be so construed (cf. above, n. 116 of this chap.), its punctuation may be the work of a later hand. I have enclosed in <angle brackets> the word omitted in the Septuagint recension that Jerome used, as in MS. Vat. gr. 1209.

120. Jerome, on Ezech. 16:48–51, ed. *CCL*, 75:206: "[Superbia] cuius seminarium est saturitas panis et rerum omnium abundantia et otium, sive, ut Septuaginta transtulerunt, deliciarum luxuriaeque opulentia...."

121. Ibid.: "Superbia, saturitas, rerum omnium abundantia, otium et deliciae, peccatum sodomiticum est, et propter hoc sequitur Dei oblivio, quae praesentia bona putat esse perpetua et numquam sibi necessariis indigendum."

122. Ps. 99:2–3: "Jubilate Deo, omnis terra: ... Scitote quoniam Dominus ipse est Deus: ipse fecit nos, et non ipsi nos...."

123. Jerome, on Ezech. 16:56–58, ed. *CCL*, 75:212–13: " 'Syria' hebraeo sermone dicitur 'aram' quae interpretatur 'sublimitas'; et iuxta explanationem illius loci Esaiae prophetae in quo Aram et Ephraim consentiunt contra Iudam et Hierusalem [Isa. 7:1–2, 9:20], ethnicorum arguta sapientia et quae sibi sublimitatem scientiae repromittat, in cuncta malitia haereticorum, impugnat Iudam, in quo vera confessio est, et non potest praevalere; hic quoque eadem arrogantia Syriae, id est philosophorum, cum filiabus alienigenarum in quibus multiplex diversorum in gentibus dogmatum error ostenditur, illudit Hierusalem, et opprobrio habet eam, cuius vitiis superata est."

124. Jerome, on Ezech. 16:55, ed. *CCL*, 75:210–11: "Iudaei inter ceteras fabulas et interminabiles genealogias et deliramenta quae fingunt, etiam hoc somniant: in

adventu Christi sui, quem nos scimus antichristum, et in mille annorum regnum Sodomam restituendam in antiquum statum, ita ut sit quasi paradisus Dei et quasi terra Aegypti, et Samariam pristinam recipere felicitatem ... Hierusalem quoque tunc esse fabricandam.... Nos autem horum perfectam scientiam, Dei iudicio relinquentes, immo liquido confitentes, post secundum adventum Domini Salvatoris, nihil humile, nihil futurum esse terrenum, sed regna caelestia quae primum in evangelio promittuntur, hoc dicimus: quod in ecclesiae statu cuncta completa sint et cotidie compleantur. Sodoma revertitur in antiquum statum, quando naturae suae reddita gentilis prius, et impia anima intellegit Creatorem. Samaria recipit antiquam beatitudinem, haereticorum, errore contempto, et iuncta doctrinae et fidei christianae. Cumque illae reversae fuerint, et Hierusalem, 'visio pacis' quae interpretatur ecclesia, revertetur in pristinum statum ... et revertetur cum filiabus suis, quae in toto orbe dispersae sunt; de quo plenius in Esaiae explanationibus disseruimus."

125. Jer. 1:1: "How doth the city sit solitary that was full of people! how is the mistress of the gentiles become as a widow...."

126. *La vita nuova di Dante Alighieri con il commento di Tommaso Casini*, 3d ed. by L. Pietrobono (Florence, n.d. [1922, 1968 reprint]), p. 106 (chap. 30): "Poi che fue partita da questo secolo, rimase tutta la sopradetta cittade quasi vedova dispogliata da ogni dignitade; onde io, ancora lagrimando in questa desolata cittade, scrissi a li principi de la terra alquanto de la sua condizione, pigliando quello cominciamento de Geremia profeta che dice: *Quomodo sedet sola civitas*."

127. *Ep.* xi, 3, 26 (viii, 2, 11, ed. Toynbee).

128. E.g., *Vita nuova* 30. 1, ed. Casini-Pietrobono, note on pp. 106–7. Suggestive of a less literal interpretation are the observations of C. S. Singleton, *An Essay on the* Vita nuova (Cambridge, Mass., 1958), pp. 23, 86, 125.

129. *Ep.* xi, 2 (viii, 1, ed. Toynbee): "holy Jerusalem as it were extinct."

130. The style of the five Lamentations differs sufficiently from that of the prophet Jeremiah to make their traditional ascription to him appear "improbable." *The Oxford Annotated Bible* (RSV), ed. H. G. May and B. M. Metzger (New York, 1962), p. 991.

131. Lam. 4:13–14: "Propter peccata prophetarum eius, et iniquitates sacerdotum eius, qui effuderunt in medio eius sanguinem iustorum. Erraverunt caeci in plateis, polluti sunt in sanguine: cumque non possent, tenuerunt lacinias suas."

132. *Gl. ord.*, on Lam. 4:6, ed. Lyons, 1520, vol. 4, fol. 196g: "Allegorice. *Maior est* etc. Plangit ecclesia peccata populi quasi maiora peccatis Sodomorum: Videmus enim quod fides et iusticia terram reliquerint, humanitas et benignitas nulla sit; discordia et concupiscentia orbem incendunt; et irae et invidiae flamma vorax; rapinis et fraudibus ecclesia populatur; pauperes exossantur; iam terrarum orbis vepribus incultus iacet; legum iura pro fabulis habentur; divina et humana fasque nefasque confunduntur; quotidie innumera mala cumulantur. *Maior* ergo iniquitas nostra quam eorum qui viam veritatis non agnoverint; et ideo minora supplicia meruerunt quae in momento subversa est." The original, again as long, ed. Migne, *PL*, 120:1212–13. The *Glossa interlinearis* to Lam. 4:6 (ed. Lyons, 1520) reduces the interpretation to its essentials in two opposed phrases: for *populi dei* read "sanctorum patrum," and note that the Sodomites were neither aware of God nor had his Law: "*Sodomorum* qui sine lege et noticia dei."

133. Toynbee-Singleton (pp. 560–61) list five citations in the *Convivio*, two in *Ep.* XI (XIII, ed. Toynbee), and *Par.* XVIII, 91, 93 (Wisd. 1:1).

134. *Conv.* 3. 15. 15. Cf. Jerome, "Prologus Galeatus" to the Vulgate (ed. Vercellone, p. xii): "quidquid extra hos [libros vigintiquatuor, sc. Veteris Testamenti] est, inter apocrypha esse ponendum. Igitur sapientia quae vulgo Salomonis inscribitur, et [alia] . . . non sunt in canone."

135. *Purg.* XXXII, 83; cf. Toynbee-Singleton, pp. 527, 556.

136. *Ep.* XIII, 6 (x, 2, ed. Toynbee): "Quod si cuiquam quod asseritur nunc videretur indignum, Spiritum Sanctum audiat . . . ; nam in Sapientia de sapientia legitur . . ." (cf. below, n. 145 of this chap.).

137. Cross, *ODCC*, p. 1471.

138. The Douay version weakly conveys the force of the result clause "ut ignorarent bona" (Wisd. 10:8). Cf. NEB: "Wisdom they ignored, and they suffered for it, *losing the power to recognize what is good* and leaving by their lives a momument of folly, such that their enormities can never be forgotten."

139. Cf. W. Jaeger, *Paideia: The Ideals of Greek Culture*, trans. G. Highet, vol. 2 (New York, 1944), p. 67, at n. 174.

140. See Jerome on Isa. 13:19–22 and on Ezech. 16:57 (see above, pp. 247–48 and 260).

141. A consideration of the context of each quotation would of course yield a more precise indication of its significance for Dante.

142. Wisd. 9:9a: "Et tecum sapientia tua, quae novit opera tua, quae et affuit tunc cum orbem terrarum faceres." Paraphrased in *Conv.* 3. 15. 15: "Con lei [sapienza] Iddio cominciò lo mondo. . . . Ciò è a dire che nel divino pensiero, ch'è esso intelletto, essa era quando lo mondo fece. . . ."

143. Wisd. 1:7a: "Quoniam spiritus Domini replevit orbem terrarum." Cf. *Ep.* XIII, 62 (*Kani Grandi*; *Ep.* x, 22, ed. Toynbee): "Et Sapientia dicit quod 'Spiritus . . . terrarum.' "

144. Wisd. 7:26: "Candor est enim lucis aeternae, et speculum sine macula Dei maiestatis, et imago bonitatis illius." *Conv.* 3. 15. 5: "E però si legge nel libro allegato di Sapienza, di lei parlando: 'Essa è candore de la etterna luce e specchio sanza macula de la maestà di Dio.' "

145. Wisd. 7:14a: "Infinitus enim thesaurus est hominibus: quo qui usi sunt, participes facti sunt amicitiae Dei." Cf. *Ep.* XIII, 6 (*Kani Grandi*; *Ep.* x, 2, ed. Toynbee): "nam in Sapientia de sapientia legitur 'quoniam [*sic*] infinitus . . . Dei.' " Note the relevance to the *Tresor* motif (see above, chap. 7, at n. 21 ff.).

146. Wisd. 3:11: "Sapientiam enim, et disciplinam qui abiicit, infelix est: et vacua est spes illorum, et labores sine fructu, et inutilia opera eorum." *Conv.* 3. 15. 5: "E però si dice nel libro di Sapienza: 'Chi gitta via la sapienza e la dottrina, è infelice.' " To convey Dante's sense of the passage, I have substituted "teaching" for the ambiguous "discipline" of the Douay version.

147. Wisd. 1:1a: "Diligite iustitiam, qui iudicatis terram." *Par.* XVIII, 91, 93.

148. Wisd. 6:23: "Diligite lumen sapientiae, omnes qui praeestis populis." *Conv.* 4. 6. 18 (cf. 4. 16. 1): "E però si scrive in quello di Sapienza: 'Amate lo lume de la sapienza, voi tutti che siete dinanzi a' populi.' "

CHAPTER 9

1. See above, chap. 8, after n. 38.

2. See above, chap. 8, after n. 148.

3. Luke 9:1–5 (the Twelve) and 10:1–12 (the Seventy-two).

4. Mark 6:6b–11; Matt. 9:35–10:1, 5–16.

5. Luke 4:16–30; Mark 6:1–6; Matt. 13:53–58.

6. Jerome, on Matt. 10:15, ed. *CCL*, 77:68: "Si tolerabilius erit terrae Sodomorum et Gomorraeorum quam illi civitati quae non receperit evangelium; et idcirco tolerabilius, quia Sodomis et Gomorris non fuit praedicatum, huic autem praedicatum sit et tamen non receperit evangelium; ergo et inter peccatores diversa supplicia sunt." For the Gospels, Dante's contemporaries had a more ample anthology of patristic commentary than the *Glossa ordinaria* in the *Catena aurea in quatuor Evangelia*, compiled by Aquinas. Marsiglio of Padua, for example, appears to have drawn all his Evangelical exegesis from this source, or so it would seem from the *apparatus fontium* to R. Scholz's ed. of the *Defensor pacis* (*MGH, Fontes iuris Germanici antiqui*, [no. 7] [1932–33]), cf. Index 4, *Bibelzitate*. Accordingly, I shall regularly supply references to it and identify its authorities, but shall not attempt to report or discuss any but their most pertinent comments. (Parenthetical references to the Parma edition of Aquinas' *Opera omnia*, vols. 11 and 12, 1860–62 = New York reprint by Musurgia, ed. V. J. Bourke, 1949). Thus, at this point: Aquinas, *Catena aurea*, on Matt. 10:11–15, § 4 (ed. Parma, 11:132–33), for Jerome, Remigius. No comment in *Gl. ord.* (ed. Migne, *PL*, 114:118).

7. Since John the Baptist was Christ's forerunner ("qui praeparabit viam tuam ante te," Matt. 11:10, quoting Mal. 3:1), he can perhaps be related to the other Dantesque runners discussed above in chap. 6, and especially to Dominic, whose mother's name was Giovanna (*Par.* xii, 80). Cf. *Vita nuova* 24. 3–4, where Dante explains that another Giovanna was called "Primaverra" because her namesake, Giovanni Battista, was Christ's precursor.

8. Jerome, on Matt. 11:12, ed. *CCL*, 77:80: "Si primus Johannes ut supra diximus paenitentiam populis nuntiavit dicens: 'Paenitentiam agite, adpropinquavit enim regnum caelorum,' consequenter a diebus illius 'regnum caelorum vim patitur, et violenti diripiunt illud.' Grandis est enim violentia in terra nos esse generatos et caelorum sedem quaerere possidere per virtutem quod non tenuimus per naturam." Cf. *Catena aurea*, on Matt. 10, § 5 (ed. Parma, 11:144), and *Gl. ord.* (ed. Migne, *PL*, 114:121). NEB offers this as an alternate version of Matt. 11:12b: 'The kingdom of Heaven has been forcing its way forward, and men of force are seizing it." ἡ βασιλεία τῶν οὐρανῶν βιάζεται, καὶ βιασταὶ ἁρπάζουσιν αὐτήν (NT, ed. B. F. Westcott and F. J. Hort).

9. Matt. 11:12 was spoken at a time when Christ's Kingdom was already being filled. "And this by dint of earnest effort ('violence') for indeed it is a kingdom which yields only to attack by storm. It is possible to understand the 'violence' and the 'bearing away' in a hostile sense," but that seems improbable, according to *A Catholic Commentary on Holy Scripture*, ed. B. Orchard et al. (London, 1953), p. 871.

10. *Gl. ord.*, on Matt. 11:23, ed. Migne, *PL*, 114:122: "*Nunquid usque in coelum exaltaberis?* Nonne tu es quae fama hospitii mei, et signorum in te factorum famosa efficeris, et contra praedicationem meam superbissime restitisti? Capharnaum interpretatur 'villa pulcherrima,' in qua condemnatur perfida Ierusalem, cui dicitur: 'Iustificata est Sodoma soror tua ex te' [Ezech. 16:52], id est, ex tui comparatione cum illa,

quae non est exemplo Loth correcta, tu Filii Dei verbis et miraculis semper exstitisti ingrata." The comment is a variant on Jerome, on Matt. 11:23, ed. *CCL*, 77:85: "In Capharnaum autem, quae interpretatur villa pulcherrima, condemnatur *incredula* Hierusalem cui dicitur per Hiezechielem: 'Justificata est Sodoma ex te.'" See also Aquinas, *Catena aurea*, on Matt. 11:20–24, § 7 (ed. Parma, 11:146–47), for Jerome, Remigius, Chrysostom, and Augustine.

11. See above, n. 49 of chap. 8.

12. The geographical relation of Capernaum to Christ's ministry in Galilee is well brought out in *The Macmillan Bible Atlas*, ed. Y. Aharoni and M. Avi-Yonah (New York, 1968), maps 228 and 231. Probably the Sermon on the Mount was preached there to its citizens.

13. On the "typology of rejection" and its connection with Matt. 11:21–24, see A. C. Charity, *Events and Their Afterlife* (Cambridge, Eng., 1966), pp. 148–49.

14. On the definition of typology, see ibid., pp. 1 ff.

15. Cf. the maxim "Scientia donum dei est, unde vendi non potest" which was linked to Christ's charge to the Twelve ("Gratis accepistis, gratis date ...") in "The Patristic and Medieval Tradition of Commentary on Matthew 10.8–10," pt. 3 of "The Medieval Heritage of a Humanistic Ideal," by Gaines Post, K. Giocarinis, and R. Kay, *Traditio* 11 (1955): 195–234, at pp. 224–31. Cf. above, chap. 3, at n. 32 ff.

16. *Gl. ord.*, on Luke 10:1, ed. Migne, *PL*, 114:284: "Per hoc quod binos mittit, innuitur quod nemo praedicationis officium debet suscipere, qui erga alium charitatem non habet."

17. *Gl. ord.*, on Luke 10:12, ed. Migne, *PL*, 114:285: "*Quia Sodomis in die illa.* Sodomitae, etsi in vitiis exardebant, et inhospitales erant, tamen apud illos nulli hospites tales quales apud Iudaeos prophetae, quales apostoli reperti sunt. Loth inter eos etsi iustus, non tamen aliquid docuit, nulla signa fecit. Et ideo 'cui multum donatum est, multum ab eo quaeritur,' et 'potentes potenter tormenta patientur' [Wisd. 6:7]." The view, here compressed into two citations, is developed at greater length in the *Catena aurea*, on Matt. 10–11 (see above, nn. 6, 8, 10 of this chap.).

18. Sodom does not appear in the parallel passage, Matt. 24:28, 37–41. Cf. *Synopse der drei ersten Evangelien*, ed. A. Huck, 2d ed. (Freiburg i.B., 1898), pp. 139–40. The synoptic Apocalypse proper comprises Mark 13:5–32; Matt. 24:4–36; Luke 21:8–33, 17:20–25 (ibid., pp. 135–39).

19. Gen. 6:1–2, 4: "And after that men began to be multiplied upon the earth, and daughters were born to them, the sons of God seeing the daughters of men, that they were fair, took to themselves wives of all which they chose.... Now giants were upon the earth in those days. For after the sons of God went in to the daughters of men, and they brought forth children, these are the mighty men of old, men of renown."

20. Gen. 13:10, 19:1, 4, 8, 9.

21. See above, chap. 8, no. (3) after n. 39.

22. Luke 17:34–35: "I say to you: in that night there shall be two men in one bed; the one shall be taken, and the other shall be left. Two women shall be grinding together: the one shall be taken, and the other shall be left: two men shall be in the field; the one shall be taken, and the other shall be left."

23. *Gl. ord.*, on Luke 17:27, ed. Migne, *PL*, 114:320–21: "*Edebant.* Non connubia vel alimenta damnantur, cum in his successionis, in illis naturae posita sint subsidia,

sed immoderatus licitorum usus arguitur. Quia enim his se totos dando, Dei iudicia contemnebant, igne vel aqua perierunt."

24. See above, chap. 8, at nn. 68–73.

25. Rom. 10:2–4: "Testimonium enim perhibeo illis quod aemulationem Dei habent, sed non secundum scientiam. Ignorantes enim iustitiam Dei, et suam quaerentes statuere, iustitiae Dei non sunt subiecti. Finis enim legis, Christus, ad iustitiam omni credenti."

26. Rom. 11:7b: "Ceteri vero excaecati sunt."

27. *Gl. ord.*, on Rom. 9:29, ed. Migne, *PL*, 114:502–3: *"Nisi Dominus sabaoth.* Dominus fecit verbum, quod tam necessarium erat, quod nisi esset semen, id est verbum, etc. Vel per semen intelliguntur reliquiae salvandae, id est apostoli et alii boni, et nisi per illas praedicatum esset verbum Dei, gentes periissent. Et hoc est: Nisi Dominus exercituum, quando alios *excaecavit*, reliquisset nobis, id est ad nostram utilitatem, semen, id est apostolos, de quibus seges Christi crevit." Cf. Isa. 1:9.

28. Matt. 7:15. Cf. above, n. 170 of chap. 5.

29. Cross, *ODCC*, pp. 1051, 750.

30. *Gl. ord.*, on Jude 4, ed. Migne, *PL*, 114:707: *"Gratiam transferentes.* Duritiam et districtionem legis: quae dicit oculum pro oculo, dentem pro dente, temperat gratia Evangelii, in quo purgantur scelera commissa per poenitentiam, et eleemosynae fructus. Sed hanc gratiam transferunt impii in luxuriam qui nunc tanto licentius peccant, quanto minus vident se asperitate legis de facinoribus examinari."

31. Jude 19 (RSV): "animales, Spiritum non habentes."

32. *Gl. ord.*, on Jude 5, ed. Migne, *PL*, 114:707: *"Omnia.* Arcana fidei, et non habetis opus, recentia quasi sanctiora a novis audire magistris, id est: Perfecte scitis omnia quae scienda sunt de fide, et ideo non est opus ut audiatis illos."

33. *Gl. ord.*, on Jude 7, ed. Migne, *PL*, 114:707–8: "Dederat exemplum damnationis eorum qui solum dominatorem negant: commemorato interitu infidelis populi vel angelorum erigentium se contra Deum, dat etiam exemplum poenae illorum qui Domini gratiam transferunt in luxuriam, commemorans incendium Sodomorum."

34. Jude 12 (NEB): "Hii sunt ... semet ipsos pascentes ... arbores autumnales, infructuosae, bis mortuae, eradicatae...."

35. *Gl. ord.*, on 2 Pet., init., ed. Migne, *PL*, 114:689: *"Argumentum.* Simon Petrus per fidem huic mundo sapientes mortuos esse declarat, eisdemque pietatis quanta sit magnitudo luce ipsa clarius manifestat."

36. *Gl. ord.*, on 2 Pet. 1:1, ed. Migne, *PL*, 114:689: "Hanc iustitiam non humana prudentia reperit, nec legis institutio docuit, sed noster Salvator in Evangelio ostendit: 'Nisi abundaverit iustitia vestra plus quam scribarum et Pharisaeorum, non intrabitis in regnum caelorum' [Matt. 5:20]." Based on Bede.

37. Cf. the relation of these three discussed above in chap. 8 in connection with the Book of Wisdom.

38. *Gl. ord.*, on 2 Pet. 1:21, ed. Migne, *PL*, 114:691: "Haec ideo dicuntur, ne quis ad libitum suum Scripturas exponat." Cf. Bede, on 2 Pet. 1:21, ed. Migne, *PL*, 93:73.

39. *Gl. ord.*, on 2 Pet. 2:1, ed. Migne, *PL*, 114:691: *"Perditionem.* Merito perditionem sibi inducunt, qui Redemptorem suum negant, vel non qualem veritas ostendit, sed qualem sibi ipsi fingunt, praedicant. Et propterea alieni a Redemptore, nil certius quam foveam expectant."

40. Cf. above, chap. 8, at nn. 76–88, and below, chap. 10, "Homosexuality as Lust."

41. 2 Pet. 2:15: "Derelinquentes rectam viam erraverunt, secuti viam Balaam ex Bosor, qui mercedem iniquitatis amavit."

42. Num. 22–24, esp. 22:7, 17–18.

43. Luke 17; cf. above, n. 23 of this chap.

44. 2 Pet. 3:5–7. Since Peter's opponents are said to be ignorant of this, their doctrinal error appears to have been a denial that the world would end. Cf. *Gl. ord.*, on 2 Pet. 3:5, ed. Migne, *PL*, 114:691 (Bede).

45. *Gl. ord.*, on 2 Pet. 2:6, ed. Migne, *PL*, 114:692: "Ignis qui Sodomitas semel punivit, significat quod impii sine fine sunt passuri."

46. *Purg.* xxix, 144. For the less probable identifications advanced by the trecento commentators, see Sapegno, p. 732.

47. On stylistic grounds, Apoc. 11:1–13 is generally considered to have been borrowed from an earlier work, or rather works, as 11:3–13 seems to be a fragment distinct from the first two verses: *Encyclopaedia Britannica*, 11th ed., vol. 23 (1911), p. 217. In general, see also Cross, *ODCC*, pp. 1161–62.

48. *Textus Biblie*, vol. 6 (Lyons, 1520), fol. 256ra.

49. *Gl. ord.*, on Matt. 11:23 (see above, n. 10 of this chap.).

50. Nicholas of Lyra, *Postilla litteralis*, on Apoc. 11:8, ed. *Textus Biblie*, 6:255h: "*In plateis*: id est in fidelium congregationem: que tunc erat valde magna."

51. Bede *Explanatio Apocalypsis* 2. 11, ed. Migne, *PL*, 93:163–64: "[7] *Cum finierint testimonium suum*, utique illud quod perhibent usque ad revelationem bestiae, quae cordibus emersura est impiorum. Non quod tunc eodem testimonio non nitantur hosti fortiter resistendo, sed quod tunc Ecclesia virtutum gratia destituenda credatur, adversario palam signis mendacii coruscante.... [8] *Et iacebunt corpora eorum in plateis civitatis magnae*. Si me, inquit, persecuti sunt, et vos persequentur. Non est ergo mirum si civitas impiorum, quae Dominum crucifigere non timuit, servos quoque ipsius ludibrio habeat etiam occisos.... [13] *Et illa hora factus est terrae motus magnus*, etc. Incumbente terrore iudicii, omnis diaboli civitas super arenam condita cum omnibus aedificatoribus suis corruet...."

52. See Jerome, above, chap. 8, at n. 110 ff.

53. *Gl. ord.*, on Apoc. 11:2, ed. Migne, *PL*, 114:730 = *Textus Biblie*, 6:256a: "*Atrium*. Id est falsos Christianos, qui se Ecclesiam simulant, sed factis abnegant. *Civitatem sanctam*. Id est Ecclesiam ad iuste vivendum congregatam, et virtutibus imbutam persequentur...."

54. *Textus Biblie*, 6:256a: "*Surge*: Erige ad praedicandum. *Templum*: i.e. Christum. *Eiice*: Excommunicando ostende te esse foris. *Metiaris*: Omnino subtrahe praedicationem. *Datum*: i.e. conformes facti sunt gentilibus. *Calcabunt*: et ipsi gentiles."

55. *Ep.* xiii, 21 (*Ep.* x, 7, ed. Toynbee): "'In exitu Israel de Egipto, domus Iacob de populo barbaro, facta est Iudea sanctificatio eius, Israel potestas eius' [Ps. 113/ 114:1–2]. Nam si ad literam solam inspiciamus, significatur nobis exitus filiorum Israel de Egipto, tempore Moysis; si ad allegoriam, nobis significatur nostra redemptio facta per Christum; si ad moralem sensum, significatur nobis conversio anime de luctu et miseria peccati ad statum gratie; si ad anagogicum, significatur exitus anime sancte ab huius corruptionis servitute ad eterne glorie libertatem."

56. Jerome, *Liber interpretationis Hebraicorum nominum*, Exodus, s.v. "Israhel," ed. *CCL*, 72:75: "Israhel est videre deum sive vir aut mens videns deum."

57. See above, chap. 9, after n. 65. Note also that *cognitio Dei* is the fundamental goal

in 2 Pet., where *cognitio* is used five times: 1:2, 3, 8; 2:20; 3:18. For Sodom:Egypt, see Gen. 13:10 and Wisd. 19:13–16.

58. See above, chap. 5, "Pope as Spouse."

59. There is a convenient survey of the question in C. T. Davis, *Dante and the Idea of Rome* (Oxford, 1957), Note B: "Influence upon Dante of the Doctrines of the Joachites and Spiritual Franciscans," pp. 239–43; also chap. 3, esp. pp. 197–216. Toynbee-Singleton, s.v. "Giovacchino."

60. On Bede, see above, n. 7 of chap. 8; on the others, see Davis, *Dante and the Idea of Rome*, p. 203.

61. Tradition may account for other supposedly Joachite elements as well. Francis and Dominic, our types of the properly swift and strong, were identified by Ubertino da Casale with the two witnesses of Apoc. 11: "In typo Helie et Enoch Franciscus et Dominicus singulariter claruerunt" (Davis, *Dante and the Idea of Rome*, pp. 215–16). Traditionally, the *testes* typified all preachers of the Gospel, and even the anti-Joachite interpretation of the conservative Franciscan Nicholas of Lyra describes them in terms similar to those that Dante applied to the mendicant founders (*Par.* XI, 37–39): the Apocalypse compares them to two olive trees "propter plenitudinem pietatis" and to two candelabra "propter ardorem charitatis" (*Postilla litteralis,* on Apoc. 11:4, ed. *Textus Biblie,* 6:256). Further, Nicholas notes in his *Postilla moralis* (ibid.) that like the Seventy-two sent forth by Christ, the *testes* are paired; accordingly, to the latter he extends Gregory's exposition of the former: the preachers are paired to signify that the Gospel must be preached in a spirit of charity. Gregory, *Homiliae XL in Evangelia* 1. 17. 1, on Luke 10:1–9, ed. Migne, *PL,* 76:1139. So, I might add, were the angels at Sodom, who stand to Christ's missionaries as Christ stands to Lot (see above, chap. 9, at n. 13).

62. Jerome, *Liber interpretationis Hebraicorum nominum*, Praefatio, ed. *CCL,* 72:59–60.

63. See above, chap. 9, at n. 48.

64. *Fulva* appears in the Vulgate only in this connection: "Salomon thronum ... vestivit ... auro fulvo" (3 Kings 10:18). Cf. Virgil *Aeneid* 7. 274.

65. Virgil *Aeneid* 12. 741, where "the shards [of Turnus' sword] lie glittering on the yellow sand—*fulva resplendent* fragmina harena."

66. The classical distinction between *pecus, pecudis* (f.), "a head of cattle," and *pecus, pecoris* (n.), "a herd of cattle," was rare in Jerome's Latin, where the neuter form has both senses. The feminine form appears thrice in the Vulgate: Gen. 9:10, Tob. 10:10, Bar. 3:32; the neuter occurs about six dozen times. With occasional exceptions (Salvian, Ennodius), Jerome's usage is typical of early Christian Latin: see A. Blaise, *Dictionnaire latin-français des auteurs chrétiens* (Paris, 1954), s.v. "Pecus I–II."

67. Cf. *greges pecorum*, Joel 1:18; cf. Mich. 5:8.

68. Ps. 148:7, 10: "Laudate Dominum.... Bestiae, et universa pecora."

69. Lewis-Short, s.v. "Pecus," 1.ii.A, 2.ii.

70. This pastoral image of Sodom provides yet another point of contact with the heaven of the Sun, where Aquinas relates the story of Francis to illustrate why he had said that he "was of the holy flock that Dominic leads on the path where there is good feeding" (*Par.* x, 94–96). Cf. *Par.* XI, 25, 123–29, where two derivatives of *pecus* describe the Franciscans as their founder's *peculio* (123) and as his *pecore* (127).

71. See above, chap. 4, after n. 179.

72. Derrick S. Bailey, *Homosexuality and the Western Christian Tradition* (London, 1955), p. 141.

CHAPTER 10

1. *Inf.* xi, 46–51, ed. Petrocchi, 2:181–82 (my translation).

2. On this distinction in Roman law, see Berger, p. 346, s.vv. "Actio in personam."

3. E.g., Toynbee-Singleton, s.v. "Bestemiatori," and Scartazzini-Vandelli[19], p. 107.

4. A. Masseron, "Brunetto Latini réhabilité?" *Lettres romanes* 5 (1951): 99–128, 187–98, at p. 190: "Encore que l'ordonnance morale de l'enfer 'dantesque' soit, comme on le sait, aristotélique, contrairement à l'ordonnance morale du purgatoire, strictement théologique, il n'en rest pas moins que tous les damnés sans exception se sont rendus coupables de péchés, expressément, formellement condemnés par la morale catholique."

5. Lewis-Short, s.v. "Blasphemia"; Liddell-Scott, s.v. βλασφημ-έω, -ία; and A. Blaise, *Dictionnaire latin-français des auteurs chrétiens* (Paris, 1954), s.v. "Blasphemia," 2: "parole outrageante (contre un homme ou contre la divinité) ... (au temps de St Augustin, on commence à ne plus employer ce mot qu'au sens de blasphème contre Dieu)." Tertullian and Jerome retain the older sense; Liddell-Scott rather questionably understand Luke 23:39 thus.

6. Pézard, pp. 277–82, esp. 277 ff. and 92 ff.

7. See reviews cited above, n. 2 of chap. 1.

8. The antecedent of "its" (*sua*) might conceivably be *deïtade* rather than the more obvious *natura*.

9. Berger, pp. 688–89, s.v. "Sacrilegium."

10. *Cod.* 9. 29. 1: "Qui divinae legis sanctitatem aut nesciendo confundunt aut neglegendo violant et offendunt, sacrilegium committunt" (ed. Krueger, p. 385). Quoted by Aquinas, *S.T.* II-II q.99 a.2 obj. 1, from Gratian, dictum post C.17 q.4 c.29 (ed. Friedberg, 1:822–23): "Qui autem de ecclesia vi aliquem exemerit, vel in ipsa ecclesia, vel loco, vel cultui, sacerdotibus, et ministris aliquid iniuriae inportaverit, ad instar publici criminis et lesae maiestatis accusabitur, et convictus, sive confessus, capitali sententia a rectoribus provinciae ferietur, sicut in primo libro *Codicis* legitur, titulo *de episcopis et clericis* et lege: 'Si quis in hoc genus sacrilegii proruperit,' et in *Digestis* titul. *Ad legem Iuliam pecuniarum* [*var.* peculatus] *repetundarum*, l. ultima, § 1. Conmittunt etiam sacrilegium qui contra divinae legis sanctitatem aut nesciendo conmittunt, aut negligendo violant et offendunt; aut qui de principali iudicio disputant, dubitantes, an is dignus sit, quem princeps elegerit; vel qui intra provinciam, in qua provinciales et cives habentur, offitium gerendae ac suscipiendae amministrationis desiderant, lib. 9. *Codicis* titulo *de crimine sacrilegii*."

11. *Gl. ord.*, on *Cod.* 9. 29. 1, ad v. *committunt*: "Accusabitur ergo coram praeside, qui non obedit legi evangelii: et una cum episcopo cognoscet contra laicum."

12. Ibid., ad v. *omittunt*: "Errando in articulis fidei, vel rebaptizando per errorem vel negligentiam."

13. Ibid., ad v. *committunt*: "Et quod dicit sacrilegium, dic, id est quasi [with references]"; *Gl. ord.*, on *Cod.* 9. 29. 2, ad v. *sacrilegii*: "i.e. quasi, ut supra lege proxima";

and *Gl. ord.*, on *Cod.* 9. 29. 3, ad v. *sacrilegii*, quoted below, in n. 17 of this chap.

14. *Cod.* 9. 29. 2, ed. Krueger, p. 385: "Disputari de principali iudicio non oportet: sacrilegii enim instar est dubitare, an is dignus sit, quem elegerit imperator." Cited by Gratian; see above, n. 10 of this chap.

15. *Casus*, on *Cod.* 9. 29. 2, ed. Cologne, 1612: "Elegit princeps aliquem ut esset praeses in aliqua provincia, vel magistratus in aliqua civitate in qua civis est, desiderare non debet administrationem, puta ut sit potestas in ea: alioquin crimen sacrilegii committit, nisi ex indulgentia principis hoc fuit ei concessum."

16. *Cod.* 9. 29. 3, ed., Krueger, p. 385: "Ne quis sine sacrilegii crimine desiderandum intellegat gerendae ac suscipiendae administrationis officium intra eam provinciam, in qua provincialis et civis habetur, nisi hoc cuidam ultronea liberalitate per divinos adfatus imperator indulgeat."

17. *Gl. ord.*, on *Cod.* 9. 29. 3, ad v. *sacrilegii*: "id est quasi: et est ratio quia per gratiam multa fierent, et quia nemo propheta, etc."

18. *S.T.* II-II q.99 a.1 in corp., ed. Parma, 3:360: "Et ideo omne illud quod ad irreverentiam rerum sacrarum pertinet, ad iniuriam Dei pertinet, et habet sacrilegii rationem."

19. *S.T.* II-II q.99 a.1 ad 1, ed. Parma, 3:360: "Et sic per quamdam nominis extensionem illud quod pertinet ad irreverentiam principis, scilicet disputare de eius iudicio, an oporteat ipsum sequi, secundum quamdam similitudinem sacrilegium dicitur."

20. *S.T.* II-II q.99 a.1 ad 2: "Et ideo id quod fit in iniuriam populi christiani, scilicet quod infideles ei praeficiantur, pertinet ad irreverentiam sacrae rei. Unde rationabiliter sacrilegium dicitur."

21. *S.T.* II-II q.99 a.2 in corp., ed. Parma, 3:361: "Sicut enim Damascenus dicit in lib. 4 *orthod. Fid.* [c. 3, circa med.], 'purpura regale indumentum facta honoratur et glorificatur; et si quis hanc perforaverit, morte damnatur,' quasi contra regem agens; ita etiam si quis rem sacram violat, ex hoc ipso contra Dei reverentiam agit; et sic per irreligiositatem peccat."

22. *S.T.* II-II q.99 a.2 obj. 1, ed. Parma, 3:360: "Videtur quod sacrilegium non sit peccatum speciale. Dicitur enim 17, q. 4 in append. Grat., ad cap. *Si quis suadente*: 'Committunt sacrilegium qui in divinae legis sanctitatem aut nesciendo committunt, aut negligendo violant et offendunt.' Sed hoc fit per omne peccatum: nam peccatum est 'dictum vel factum, vel concupitum contra legem Dei,' ut Augustinus dicit 22 *contra Faustum* [c.27 in princ.]. Ergo sacrilegium est generale peccatum." Blackfriars' trans., ed. T. Gilby, vol. 40 (New York and London, 1968), p. 117.

23. *S.T.* II-II q.99 a.2 ad 1, ed. Parma, 3:361: "Ad primum ergo dicendum, quod illi dicuntur [sacrilegium] in divinae legis sanctitatem committere, qui legem Dei impugnant, sicut haeretici et blasphemi, qui ex hoc quod Deo non credunt, incurrunt infidelitatis peccatum; ex hoc vero quod divinae legis verba pervertunt, sacrilegium incurrunt." Blackfriars' trans., 40:119 (later editions omit the word that I have bracketed above).

24. *Mon.* 3. 13. 5 (trans. Nicholl, p. 88): "If it [the Church] had received the power [to confer authority upon the Roman Prince] from God this would have been as a result either of divine law or of natural law, because whatever is derived from nature is derived from God; though the converse is not true." Cf. above, chap. 5, at n. 165.

[401]

25. The confusion of tongues now appears to be a law of nature, and since art must follow nature, an artificial language must follow the laws imposed by God on natural language: otherwise it is sacrilegious.

26. See above, chap. 5, after n. 28.

27. *Mon.* 3. 4. 6–11 (trans. Nicholl, pp. 68–69, first sentence altered and paragraphs supplied): "[6] Hoc viso, ad meliorem huius et aliarum inferius factarum solutionum evidentiam advertendum quod circa sensum misticum dupliciter errare contingit: aut querendo ipsum ubi non est, aut accipiendo aliter quam accipi debeat. [7] Propter primum dicit Augustinus in *Civitate Dei* [16. 2]: 'Non omnia que gesta narrantur etiam significare aliquid putanda sunt, sed propter illa que aliquid significant etiam ea que nichil significant actexuntur. Solo vomere terra proscinditur; sed ut hoc fieri possit, etiam cetera aratri membra sunt necessaria.' [8] Propter secundum idem ait in *Doctrina Cristiana* [1. 36], loquens de illo aliud in Scripturis sentire quam ille qui scripsit eas dicit, quod 'ita fallitur ac si quisquam deserens viam eo tamen per girum pergeret quo via illa perducit'; et subdit: 'Demonstrandum est ut consuetudine deviandi etiam in transversum aut perversum ire cogatur.' [9] Deinde innuit causam quare cavendum sit hoc in Scripturis, dicens: 'Titubabit fides, si *Divinarum Scripturarum* vacillat autoritas.' [10] Ego autem dico quod si talia fiunt de ignorantia, correctione diligenter adhibita ignoscendum est sicut ignoscendum esset illi qui leonem in nubibus formidaret; si vero industria, non aliter cum sic errantibus est agendum, quam cum tyrampnis, qui publica iura non ad communem utilitatem secuntur, sed ad propriam retorquere conantur. [11] O summum facinus, etiamsi contingat in sompniis, ecterni Spiritus intentione abuti! Non enim peccatur in Moysen, non in David, non in Iob, non in Matheum, non in Paulum, sed in Spiritum Sanctum qui loquitur in illis. Nam quanquam scribe divini eloquii multi sint, unicus tamen dictator est Deus, qui beneplacitum suum nobis per multorum calamos explicare dignatus est."

28. E.g., *Mon.* 3. 3. 7, 18; *Inf.* xix, 88 ff. Note that popes are especially left in the arena at the end of *Mon.* 3. 3; cf. text above, chap. 5, after n. 30.

29. *S.T.* II-II q.154 a.10, ed. Parma, 3:519 (English Dominican trans. [London, 1921], pp. 155–56): "Sed contra est quod Augustinus dicit, 15 *de Civ. Dei* [c.16, a med.], quod 'si iniquum est aviditate possidendi transgredi limitem agrorum, quanto est iniquius libidine concumbendi subvertere limitem morum?' Sed transgredi limitem agrorum in rebus sacris est peccatum sacrilegii. Ergo pari ratione subvertere limitem morum libidine concumbendi in rebus sacris facit sacrilegii vitium. Sed libido concumbendi pertinet ad luxuriam. Ergo sacrilegium est luxuriae species. — Respondeo dicendum, quod sicut supra dictum est [implic. q.99 a.1, et a.2 ad 2, et I-II q.18 a.7], actus unius virtutis, vel vitii ordinatus ad finem alterius, assumit speciem illius; sicut furtum quod propter adulterium committitur, transit in speciem adulterii. Manifestum est autem quod observatio castitatis, secundum quod ordinatur ad cultum Dei, fit actus religionis, ut patet in illis qui vovent et servant virginitatem, ut patet per Augustinum in lib. *de Virginitate* [c. 8]. Unde manifestum est quod etiam luxuria, secundum quod violat aliquid ad divinum cultum pertinens, pertinet ad speciem sacrilegii, et secundum hoc sacrilegium potest poni species luxuriae."

30. On the classification of sacrilege according "to persons dedicated to God's worship, to consecrated places, and to other sacred things," see *S.T.* II-II q.99 a.3, ed. Parma, 3:361 (Blackfriars' trans., 40:121).

31. *Bermondi Choveronii caesarei pontificiiq. viris doc. praestantissimi, in sacrosanctioris Lateranen. concilii (concordata vocant) titulum de publicis concubina. commentaria,* ed. in *Tractatus illustrium in utraque tum pontificii, tum caesarei iuris facultate iurisconsultorum* ..., vol. 11, pt. 1 (Venice, 1584), fols. 145va–195rb, at fol. 160ra, under the rubric *"De peccato sodomitico"* (158va–160rb), nos. 31–32. For this discovery I am indebted to the curious erudition of Professor John F. McGovern, who in fact had referred me to the passage for its claim that Virgil was a sodomite: "Apud Deum sodomia intantum est detestabilis ut illa nocte, qua redemptor fuit natus omnes sodomitae subito perierunt et dicunt quidam illa nocte Vergilium peremptum fuisse, qui quamplurimum tactus erat illo vitio sodomitico" (ibid., nos. 30–31).

32. See *Pauly's Realencyclopädie der classischen Altertumswissenschaft, Supplement,* vol. 7 (Stuttgart, 1950), pp. 1204–12, s.v. "Semiramis 1," by Th. Lenschau.

33. Matt. 7:5 (NEB).

34. C.32 q.7 cc.12–14, ed. Friedberg, 1:1143. All are found earlier in Ivo of Chartres' *Panormia* 9. 115, 105, 106.

35. C.32 q.7 c.12: *"Ambrosius in libro de Patriarchis* [1. 6. 52]. Offerebat sanctus Loth filiarum pudorem. Nam etsi illa quoque flagiciosa inpuritas erat, tamen minus erat secundum naturam coire, quam adversus naturam delinquere. Preferebat domus suae verecundiae hospitalem gratiam, etiam apud barbaras gentes inviolabilem."

36. C.32 q.7 c.14: *"Idem* [probably referring to a preceding canon in some earlier collection rather than to Augustinus in Gratian's c. 13] *contra Iovinianum, lib. I."* Professor David Heimann, who is editing Jerome's treatise of the same title for the *CCL,* assures me that is not the source.

37. *Confessions* 3. 8. 15, ed. P. Knöll (Teubner, 1909), as reprinted in Loeb Classical Library with W. Watts' translation (1631), rev. W. H. D. Rouse (Cambridge, Mass., and London, 1912), 1:126–28; Gratian's variants from Friedberg, 1:1143: "Itaque flagitia, quae sunt contra naturam, ubique ac semper detestanda [*var.* repudianda] atque punienda sunt, qualia Sodomitarum fuerunt. Quae si omnes gentes facerent, eodem criminis reatu divina lege tenerentur, quae non sic fecit homines, ut hoc [*var.* illo] se uterentur modo. Violatur quippe ipsa societas, quae cum deo nobis esse debet, cum eadem natura, cuius ille [*var.* ipse] auctor est, libidinis perversitate polluitur."

38. Unless otherwise stated, I quote the Watts-Rouse translation (see above, n. 37 of this chap.); sometimes I have preferred the revision of Watts made by E. B. Pusey (Everyman's Library, 1907); occasionally I have conflated the two or tacitly made my own revisions. Ever since "The Waste Land," the opening sentence of book 3 will be remembered by literate English readers in Pusey's translation, with the cadence improved by "then," apparently inserted by T. S. Eliot himself (see his note to verse 307).

39. On *securitas,* see Hugh Pope, *Saint Augustine of Hippo: Essays Dealing with His Life and Times and Some Features of His Work* (1937; reprint by Image Books, Garden City, N.Y., 1961), n. 43 of chap. 5 (p. 395; cf. p. 84).

40. *Conf.* 3. 2. 3: "Sed [illa vena amicitiae] quo vadit? quo fluit? ut quid decurrit in torrentem picis bullientis,* aestus inmanes taetrarum libidinum, in quos ipsa mutatur, et vertitur per nutum proprium de caelesti serenitate detorta atque deiecta?" *"He

[403]

alludes to the sea of Sodom [Tacitus *Hist*. 50. 5], which is said to bubble out a pitchy slime, into which other rivers running, are there lost in it. And like the lake itself, remain unmoveable: wherefore it is called the Dead Sea" (Watts' note).

41. "Such is men's blindness, that they even brag of their own owl-eyedness."

42. Opinion is divided on Augustine's age at this point. *Conf*. 3 covers "his residence at Carthage from his seventeenth to his nineteenth year" (Pusey's headnote). The conversion to philosophy is placed at age eighteen by H. I. Marrou, *A History of Education in Antiquity* (Mentor ed., 1964, p. 397). However, three precise references to the event are cited by V. J. Bourke, *Augustine's Quest of Wisdom* (Milwaukee, Wis., 1945), p. 17: "Sed liber ille ipsius exhortationem continet ad philosophiam et vocatur Hortensius … cum agerem annum aetatis undevicensimum" (*Conf*. 3. 4. 7); cf. *Soliloquia* 1. 10. 17 (ed. Migne, *PL*, 32:878), and *De beata vita* 1. 4 (ed. Migne, *PL*, 32:961). By Roman idiom (Lewis-Short, s.v. "Ago," II.D.5) he accordingly had completed his nineteenth year; yet the crucial phrase can be interpreted "I was living my nineteenth year," i.e., was completing it, and hence was eighteen in fact and "going on nineteen."

43. Col. 2:8–9: "Videte ne quis vos decipiat per philosophiam, et inanem fallaciam [seductionem] secundum traditionem hominum, secundum elementa [huius] mundi, et non secundum Christum: quia in ipso inhabitat omnis plenitudo divinitatis corporaliter." Text in [brackets] as quoted by Augustine; Douay-Rheims trans.

44. *Conf*. 3. 4. 8: "hoc tamen solo delectabar in illa exhortatione, quod non illam aut illam sectam, sed ipsam quaecumque esset sapientiam ut diligerem et quaererem et adsequerer et tenerem atque amplexarer fortiter…." On this experience, see, above all, A. D. Nock, *Conversion* (Oxford, 1933), pp. 184, 261.

45. Ibid.: "Et quidquid sine hoc nomine fuisset, quamvis litteratum et expolitum et veridicum, non me totum rapiebat."

46. *Conf*. 3. 5. 9: "Itaque institui animum intendere in scripturas sanctas, et videre, quales essent."

47. Ibid.: "Non enim sicut modo loquor, ita sensi, cum attendi ad illam scripturam, sed visa est mihi indigna, quam Tullianae dignitati compararem. Tumor enim meus refugiebat modum eius, et acies mea non penetrabat interiora eius. Verum tamen illa erat, quae cresceret cum parvulis, sed ego dedignabar esse parvulus et turgidus fastu mihi grandis videbar."

48. Ibid.: "Et ecce video rem non compertam superbis neque nudatam pueris, sed incessu humilem, successu excelsam, et velatam mysteriis, et non eram ego talis, ut intrare in eam possem, aut inclinare cervicem ad eius gressus."

49. *Conf*. 3. 6. 10: "Et dicebant: 'veritas et veritas,' et multum eam dicebant mihi, et nusquam erat in eis, sed falsa loquebantur non de te tantum, qui vere veritas es, sed etiam de istis elementis mundi, creatura tua, de quibus etiam vera dicentes philosophos transgredi debui prae amore tuo." Watts-Rouse trans., rev.

50. *Conf*. 3. 6. 11: "Vae, vae! quibus gradibus deductus in profunda inferi, quippe laborans et aestuans inopia veri, cum te, deus meus … cum te non secundum intellectum mentis, quo modo praestare voluisti belvis, sed secundum sensum carnis quaererem." Watts-Rouse trans., rev. from Pusey.

51. Ibid.: "Offendi illam mulierem audacem, in opem prudentiae, aenigma Salomonis, sedentem super sellam in foribus et dicentem: panes occultos libenter edite et aquam dulcem furtivam bibite. Quae me seduxit, quia invenit foris habitantem in

oculo carnis meae, et talia ruminantem apud me, qualia per illum vorassem." Watts-Rouse trans., rev.

52. *Conf.* 3. 4. 7; 3. 11. 5.

53. Prov. 1:5–6: "Audiens sapiens, sapientior erit: et intelligens, gubernacula possidebit. Animadvertet parabolam, et interpretationem, verba sapientum, et aenigmata eorum." —"A *riddle* [*aenigma*] is a comparison or analogy which enforces a lesson when the hearer discerns its intention and is able to complete it" (*Oxford Annotated Bible*, on Prov. 1:5–6, citing, e.g., Prov. 25:14, 26:7, 30:18–19). I have no doubt that the *Comedy* was framed as just such an *aenigma sacrum*.

54. Prov. 9:10–18: "Principium sapientiae, timor Domini [repeated from 1:7; cf. Ps. 110:10, Eccles. 1:16]: et scientia sanctorum, prudentia. 11. Per me enim multiplicabuntur dies tui, et addentur tibi anni vitae. 12. Si sapiens fueris, tibimetipsi eris: si autem illusor, solus portabis malum. 13. Mulier stulta et clamosa, plenaque illecebris, et nihil omnino sciens, 14. Sedit in foribus domus suae super sellam in excelso urbis loco, 15. Ut vocaret transeuntes per viam, et pergentes itinere suo: 16. Qui est parvulus, declinet ad me. Et vecordi locuta est: 17. Aquae furtivae dulciores sunt, et panis absconditus suavior. 18. Et ignoravit quod ibi sint gigantes, et in profundis inferni convivae eius."

55. *Conf.* 3. 7. 12: "Nesciebam enim aliud, vere quod est, et quasi acutule movebar, ut suffragarer stultis deceptoribus, cum a me quaereretur...," and "quid in scriptura diceremur, ad imaginem dei, prorsus ignorabam."

56. *Gl. ord.* on Prov. 9:15, ad vv. *ut vocaret*, ed. *Textus Biblie* (Lyons: Mareschal, 1520), 3:318r: "Vocat heresis ad perfidiam sepe catholicos: quos iter rectum agere: et viam huius seculi transire citius velle: atque ad eternam patriam festinare conspicit." The woman of Proverbs has special allurements for the Dantist, if I am correct in seeing her as the original of the *puttana sciolta* or *fuia* who, with her giant lover, appears in the Terrestrial Paradise and flirts with the pilgrim (*Purg.* xxxii, 148–60; cf. *Purg.* xxxiii, 44–45). I developed this view in a paper, "Dante's Razor and Gratian's D.XV," given at the Sixth Conference on Medieval Studies (Kalamazoo, Mich., May 1971).

57. The end of the excursus is clearly marked when he returns to the Manichaeans (*Conf.* 3. 10. 18).

58. *Conf.* 3. 7. 13: "Et non noveram iustitiam veram interiorem non ex consuetudine iudicantem, sed ex lege rectissima dei omnipotentis, qua formarentur mores regionum et dierum pro regionibus et diebus, cum ipsa ubique ac semper esset, non alibi alia nec alias aliter; secundum quam iusti essent Abraham et Isaac et Iacob et Moyses et David, et illi omnes laudati ore dei; sed eos ab imperitis iudicari iniquos iudicantibus ex humano die [1 Cor. 4:3] et universos mores humani generis ex parte moris sui metientibus; ..." Pusey's trans., with his phrase "human judgment" altered to "man's day," the Douay-Rheims version of "humano die."

59. Ibid.: "Numquid iustitia varia est et mutabilis? sed tempora, quibus praesidet, non pariter eunt; tempora enim sunt." Watts-Rouse trans., rev. from Pusey.

60. Quoted above, n. 37 of this chap.

61. *Conf.* 3. 8. 16: "Sed hoc vindicas, quod in se homines perpetrant, quia etiam cum in te peccant, inpie faciunt in animas suas, et mentitur iniquitas sibi: sive corrumpendo ac pervertendo naturam suam, quam tu fecisti et ordinasti; vel inmoderate

utendo concessis rebus vel in non concessa flagrando in eum usum, qui est contra naturam: . . ." Watts-Rouse trans., rev. from Pusey.

62. *Conf.* 3. 9. 17: "Ea iusta est societas hominum, quae servit tibi."

63. *Conf.* 3. 10. 18: "Haec ego nesciens, inridebam illos sanctos servos et prophetas tuos. Et quid agebam, cum inridebam eos, nisi ut inriderer abs te, sensim atque paulatim perductus ad eas nugas. . . ."

64. *Conf.* 8. 12. 30: "Stans in ea regula fidei, in qua me ante tot annos ei [Monicae] revelaveras."

65. *Conf.* 3. 12. 21: "Respondit enim me adhuc esse indocilem, et quod inflatus essem novitate haeresis illius, et nonnullis quaestiunculis iam multos inperitos exagitassem, sicut illa indicaverat ei. 'Sed' inquit 'sine illum ibi. Tantum roga pro eo dominum: ipse legendo reperiet, quis ille sit error et quanta inpietas.'" Watts-Rouse trans., rev. from Pusey.

66. On the vices opposed to *scientia* and *intellectus*, see Thomas, "De caecitate mentis et hebetudine sensus," *S.T.* II-II q.15.

List of Works Cited

Every work, whether primary or secondary, that I have cited in the notes has been included in this list. It does not include works that I have consulted but have not cited, so this is neither a comprehensive nor a critical bibliography of the studies of *Inferno* xv. Consequently this is not a substitute for the extensive bibliography given by Pézard, pp. 411–33 (see also note 1 of chapter 1 above). The abbreviations used in the entries below are those that are listed at the beginning of this book.

Accademia della Crusca (Florence). *Vocabulario degli Accademici della Crusca.* 5th ed. 11 vols. Florence, 1863–1923.

Acta sanctorum. Edited by J. Bolland et al. Feb., vol. 3. 3d ed. Paris and Rome, 1865.

Aharoni, Y., and Avi-Yonah, M., eds. *The Macmillan Bible Atlas.* New York, 1968.

Alain de Lille. *Opera omnia.* = Migne, *PL*, vol. 210.

Andrieu, M., ed. *Les ordines romani du haut moyen-âge.* Vol. 4. Spicilegium sacrum Lovaniense, no. 28. Louvain, 1956.

———. *Le Pontifical romain au moyen-âge.* Studi e testi, vols. 86–88. Vatican City, 1938–40.

Anselm of Havelberg. *Dialogorum libri III.* In Migne, *PL*, 188:1139–1248.

Artinian, R. "Dante's Parody of Boniface VIII." *Dante Studies* 85 (1967): 71–74.

Auerbach, E. "Figura." *Archivum Romanicum* 22 (1938): 436–89.

———. *Neue Dantestudien.* Istanbuler Schriften, no. 5. Istanbul, 1944.

———. *Scenes from the Drama of European Literature: Six Essays.* New York, 1959.

———. *Typologische Motive in der mittelalterlichen Literatur.* Schriften und Vorträge des Petrarca-Instituts Köln, no. 2. Krefeld, 1953.

Augustine. *De civitate Dei libri XI–XXII.* Edited by B. Dombart and A. Kalb. — *CCL*, vol. 48. Turnhout, 1955.

———. *Confessions.* Translated by W. Watts [1631]; revised by W. H. D. Rouse. Loeb Classical Library. 2 vols. Cambridge, Mass., 1912.

———. *The Confessions of St. Augustine.* Translated by E. B. Pusey [1838]. Everyman's Library. London, 1907.

———. *Epistulae 185–270.* Edited by A. Goldbacher. = *CSEL*, vol. 57. Vienna, 1911.

———. *Quaestionum in Heptateuchum libri VII; Locutionum in Heptateuchum libri VII.* Edited by I. Fraipont. In *CCL*, vol. 33, pp. 1–465. Turnhout, 1958.

———. *Sermo 339.* In Migne, *PL*, 38:1480–82.

Bailey, Derrick S. *Homosexuality and the Western Christian Tradition.* London, 1955.

Barbi, M. "La lettura di Benvenuto da Imola e i suoi rapporti con altri commenti." *Studi danteschi* 16 (1932): 137–56; 18 (1934): 79–98.

Barraclough, G. *The Medieval Papacy.* New York, 1968.

———. *Papal Provisions.* Oxford, 1935.

Bayley, C. C. *War and Society in Renaissance Florence: The "De militia" of Leonardo Bruni.* Toronto, 1961.

Becker, M. B. "Dante and His Literary Contemporaries as Political Men." *Speculum* 41 (1966): 665–80.

———. "A Study in Political Failure: The Florentine Magnates, 1280–1343." *Mediaeval Studies* 27 (1965): 246–308.

Bede. *Explanatio Apocalypsis.* In Migne, *PL,* 93:129–206.

———. *Libri quatuor in principium Genesis usque ad nativitatem Isaac et eiectionem Ismahelis adnotationum.* Edited by C. W. Jones. = *CCL,* vol. 118A. Turnhout, 1967.

Bennett, C. E. *New Latin Grammar.* 3d ed. Boston, 1918.

Benson, Robert L. *The Bishop-Elect: A Study in Medieval Ecclesiastical Office.* Princeton, N.J., 1968.

Benvenuto da Imola. *Benevenuti de Rambaldis de Imola comentum super Dantis Aldigherij "Comoediam."* Edited by J. P. Lacaita. Florence, 1887.

Berger, A. *Encyclopedic Dictionary of Roman Law.* = *Transactions of the American Philosophical Society,* n.s., vol. 43, pt. 2. Philadelphia, 1953.

Bernard of Clairvaux. *De consideratione ad Eugenium papam.* In *S. Bernardi Opera,* ed. J. Leclercq and H. M. Rochais, 3:379–493. Rome, 1963.

Bertoni, G. *Cinque "letture" dantesche.* Modena, 1933.

Biagi, G., ed. *"La Divina Commedia" nella figurazione artistica e nel secolare commento.* Vol. 1: *Inferno.* Turin, 1924.

———. *Le novelle antiche.* Florence, 1880.

Bible. *The Bible: An American Translation.* Edited by J. M. Powis Smith and E. J. Goodspeed. Chicago, 1935.

———. *Biblia sacra vulgatae editionis.* Edited by C. Vercellone. Rome, 1861. Reprint. Paris, 1891.

———. *The Holy Bible containing the Old and New Testaments and the Apocrypha, translated . . . by His Majesty's special command* [i.e., the Authorized Version of King James, A.D. 1611].

———. *The Holy Bible: Revised Standard Version . . . Being the Version Set Forth A.D. 1611, Revised A.D. 1881–1885 and A.D. 1901. . . .*

———. *The Holy Bible Translated from the Latin Vulgate.* Rheims, 1582, and Douay, 1609. Revised by R. Challoner [1749–50]. Reprint. New York, 1899.

———. *The New English Bible with the Apocrypha.* Oxford and Cambridge, Eng., 1970.

———. *The New Testament in the Original Greek.* Edited by B. F. Westcott and F. J. A. Hort. Cambridge, Eng., 1881. Reprint. New York, 1951.

———. *The Oxford Annotated Bible.* Edited by H. G. May and B. M. Metzger. New York, 1962.

———. *Septuaginta.* Edited by A. Rahlfs. 8vo edition. Stuttgart, 1935.

———. *Textus biblie cum Glosa ordinaria, Nicolai de Lyra Postilla. . . .* 6 vols. Lyons: Mareschal, 1520.

Bibliotheca hagiographica Latina antiquae et mediae aetatis. Vol. 1. Brussels, 1898.

Black, H. C., ed. *Black's Law Dictionary*. 4th ed. St. Paul, Minn., 1951.

Blaise, A. *Dictionnaire latin-français des auteurs chrétiens*. Paris, 1954.

Bliss, W. H. See s.vv. "Great Britain. Public Record Office."

Boccaccio, G. *Il comento alla "Divina Commedia."* Edited by D. Guerri. Vol. 3. Scrittori d'Italia, vol. 86. Bari, 1918.

["Boccaccio, Il Falso."] *Chiose sopra Dante*. Florence: [Lord Vernon], 1846.

Boethius. *Philosophiae consolatio*. Edited by L. Bieler. = CCL 94. Turnhout, 1957.

Bourke, V. J. *Augustine's Quest of Wisdom*. Milwaukee, Wis., 1945.

Bracton, Henry de. *Bracton on the Laws and Customs of England*. Edited and translated by S. E. Thorne. 2 vols. Cambridge, Mass., 1968.

Brandileone, F. "Perché Dante colloca in Paradiso il fondatore della scienza del diritto canonico." *Atti della Accademia nazionale dei Lincei, Rendiconti della classe di scienze morali, storiche e filologiche*, 6th ser. 2 (1926): 65–149. Reviewed by F. Ruffini, *Studi danteschi* 13 (1928): 119–25; and by P. Fournier, *Revue historique de droit français et étranger*, 4th ser. 6 (1927): 565–68.

Brixius, J. M. *Die Mitglieder des Kardinalkollegiums von 1130–1181*. Berlin, 1912.

Brugnoli, G. "Donato." *Enciclopedia dantesca* 2:568–69. Rome, 1970.

Brunetto Latini. *"Li livres dou tresor" de Brunetto Latini*. Edited by F. J. Carmody. University of California Publications in Modern Philology, vol. 22. Berkeley and Los Angeles, 1948.

——. *La "Rettorica" di Brunetto Latini*. Edited by F. Maggini. Florence, 1915.

Bruns, H. T., ed. *Canones apostolorum et conciliorum saeculorum IV. V. VI. VII*. Bibliotheca ecclesiastica, edited by A. Neander, no. 1. 2 vols. Berlin, 1839.

Bury, Richard de. *The "Liber epistolaris" of Richard de Bury*. Edited by N. Denholm-Young. Roxeburghe Club. Oxford, 1950.

Cassiodorus. *Expositio in psalterium*. In Migne, *PL*, 70:9–1056.

Ceva, Bianca. *Brunetto Latini: L'uomo e l'opera*. Milan and Naples, 1965.

Chaplais, P. "English Arguments Concerning the Feudal Status of Aquitaine in the Fourteenth Century." *Bulletin of the Institute of Historical Research* 21 (1946–48): 203–13.

Charity, A. C. *Events and Their Afterlife: The Dialectics of Christian Typology in the Bible and Dante*. Cambridge, Eng., 1966.

Chenu, M. D. *Toward Understanding Saint Thomas*. Translated by A.-M. Landry and D. Hughes. Chicago, 1964.

Chiaudano, M. "Dante e il diritto romano." *Giornale dantesco* 20 (1912): 37–56, 94–119.

Choveronius, Bermondus. *In sacrosanctioris Lateranen. concilii (concordata vocant) titulum de publicis concubina. commentaria*. In *Tractatus illustrium in utraque tum pontificii, tum caesarei iuris facultate iurisconsultorum* . . . , vol. 11, pt. 1, fols. 145ra–195rb. Venice, 1584.

Congar, Y. "L'ecclésiologie de S. Bernard." *Analecta sacri ordinis Cisterciensis* 9 (Rome, 1953): 136–90.

Corpus iuris canonici. Edited by Aemilius Friedberg. 2 vols. Leipzig, 1879–81.

—— [with *Glossa ordinaria*.] [Vol. 1:] *Decretum divi Gratiani* . . . ; [vol. 2:] *Decretales Gregorii Noni pontificis* . . . ; [vol. 3:] *Liber VI. Decreta[lium]*. . . . *Clementinae: Clementis Quinti Constitutiones . . . Extravagantes XX. Ioannis Vigesimisecundi . . . Extravagantes communes*. . . . Lyons: Apud Hugonem & haeredes Aemonis à Porta [vol. 3, apud Hugonem à Porta], 1548 [*Liber sextus*, 1549].

Corpus iuris civilis. Vol. 1: *Institutiones,* edited by P. Krueger. *Digesta,* edited by T. Mommsen. 3d ed. Berlin, 1882. Vol. 2: *Codex Iustinianus,* edited by P. Krueger. Berlin, 1880. Vol. 3: *Novellae,* edited by R. Schoell and G. Kroll. Berlin, 1895.

Corpus iuris civilis Iustinianei cum Accursii commentariis [i.e., the *Glossa ordinaria*]. . . 5 vols. Cologne: Stephanus Gamonetus, 1612.

Corti, M. "Le fonti del *Fiore di virtù* e la teoria della 'nobilità' nel Duecento." *Giornale storico della letterature italiana* 136 (1959): 1–82.

Cosmo, U. *Guida a Dante.* 2d ed., edited by B. Maier. Maestri e compagni, no. 4. Florence, 1962.

Cross, F. L., ed. *The Oxford Dictionary of the Christian Church.* Rev. ed. London, 1958.

Curtius, E. R. *European Literature and the Latin Middle Ages.* Translated by W. R. Trask. Bollingen Series, no. 36. London, 1953.

Cuttino, G. P. "Historical Revision: The Causes of the Hundred Years War." *Speculum* 31 (1956): 463–77.

Cynus (Cino da Pistoia). *Cyni Pistoriensis in Codicem et aliquot titulos primi Pandectorum tomi, id est, Digesti veteris, doctissima commentaria.* Frankfurt, 1578. Reprint. Turin, 1964.

Damon, P. "Adam on the Primal Language: 'Paradiso' 26.124." *Italica* 38 (1961): 60–62.

Dante Alighieri. *The Comedy of Dante Alighieri, the Florentine.* Translated by D. L. Sayers. 3 vols. New York, 1963.

———. *"La Commedia" secondo l'antica vulgata.* Edited by G. Petrocchi. 4 vols. Le opere di Dante Alighieri: Edizione nazionale a cura della Società dantesca italiana, no. 7. Milan: Mondadori, 1966–67.

———. *Il Convito: The Banquet of Dante Alighieri.* Translated by E. P. Sayer. London, 1887.

———. *Il Convivio.* Edited by G. Busnelli and G. Vandelli. 2d ed., revised by A. E. Quaglio. Opere di Dante, edited by V. Branca et al., vols. 4 and 5. Florence, 1964.

———. *Il Convivio.* Edited by M. Simonelli. Testi e saggi di letterature moderne: Testi, no. 2. Bologna, 1966.

———. *The Convivio of Dante Alighieri.* Translated by P. H. Wicksteed. Temple Classics. London, 1903.

———. *Dante's Convivio.* Translated by William W. Jackson. Oxford, 1909.

———. *Dante's Lyric Poetry.* Edited and translated by K. Foster and P. Boyde. Oxford, 1967.

———. *Dantis Alagherii Epistolae: The Letters of Dante.* Edited and translated by P. Toynbee. 2d ed. Oxford, 1966.

———. *De vulgari eloquentia.* Edited by A. Marigo. 3d ed., revised by P. G. Ricci. Opere di Dante, edited by M. Barbi, vol. 6. Florence, 1957.

———. *La Divina Commedia.* Edited by N. Sapegno. = *La letteratura italiana: Storia e testi,* vol. 4. Milan and Naples, 1957.

———. *"La Divina Commedia" . . . col commento Scartazziniano rifatto da G. Vandelli.* 19th ed. Milan, 1965.

———. *"La Divina Commedia" commentata da G. A. Scartazzini . . . riveduta e corretta da G. Vandelli.* 5th ed. Milan, 1907. 6th. ed. Milan, 1911.

———. *The Divine Comedy.* Translated, with a commentary, by Charles S. Singleton. 6 vols. Bollingen Series, no. 80. Princeton, 1970–75.

———. *The Divine Comedy of Dante Alighieri.* Translated by John D. Sinclair. 3 vols.

London: John Lane, 1939–46. Rev. ed. London: John Lane; New York: Oxford University Press, 1948. Reprint. New York: Oxford University Press, Galaxy Books, 1961.

———. *The Inferno: A Verse Rendering for the Modern Reader.* Translated by J. Ciardi. New York, 1954.

———. *The Inferno of Dante Alighieri.* Translated by J. A. Carlyle [1849, rev. 1867]. Revised by H. Oelsner. Temple Classics. London, 1900.

———. *Monarchia.* Edited by G. Vinay. Florence, 1950.

———. *Monarchia.* Edited by P. G. Ricci. Le opere di Dante Alighieri: Edizione nazionale a cura della Società dantesca italiana, no. 5. Milan, 1965.

———. *"Monarchy" and Three Political Letters.* Translated by Donald Nicholl. Library of Ideas. London: Weidenfeld and Nicolson, 1954.

———. *Le Opere di Dante: Testo critico della Società dantesca italiana.* 2d ed. Florence, 1960.

———. *The Paradiso of Dante Alighieri.* Translated by P. H. Wicksteed. Temple Classics. London, 1899.

———. *The Purgatorio of Dante Alighieri.* Translated by T. Okey. Temple Classics. London, 1901.

———. *A Translation of the Latin Works of Dante Alighieri.* Translated by A. G. Ferrers Howell and P. H. Wicksteed. Temple Classics. London, 1904.

———. *"La vita nuova" di Dante Alighieri con il commento di Tommaso Casini.* 3d ed., edited by L. Pietrobono. Florence, n.d. Reprint. Florence, 1968.

Davidsohn, R. "I campioni nudi ed unti." *Bullettino della Società dantesca italiana,* n.s. 7 (1899–1900): 39–43.

———. "I campioni 'nudi ed unti' (*Inf.* xvi, 19)." *Bullettino della Società dantesca italiana,* n.s. 9 (1901–2): 185–87.

———. *Forschungen zur älteren Geschichte von Florenz.* 4 vols. Berlin, 1896–1908. Reprint. Turin, 1964. [Titles to vols. 3 and 4 omit *"älteren."*]

———. *Geschichte von Florenz.* 4 vols. Berlin, 1896–1927.

———. *Storia di Firenze.* 8 vols. Florence, 1956–68.

Davis, Charles T. "Brunetto Latini and Dante." *Studi medievali,* 3d ser., vol. 8, no. 1 (1967), pp. 421–50.

———. *Dante and the Idea of Rome.* Oxford, 1957.

Deferrari, R. J. *A Latin-English Dictionary of St. Thomas Aquinas.* Boston, 1960.

Dekkers, E., ed. *Clavis patrum Latinorum, qua in novum "Corpus Christianorum" edendum optimas quasque scriptorum recensiones a Tertulliano ad Bedam commode recludit E. Dekkers. . . .* 2d ed. = *Sacris erudiri,* vol. 3. Steenbrugge, 1961.

Del Giudice, G. *Carlo Troya: Vita pubblica e privata, studi, opere.* Naples, 1899.

Delhaye, P. *Pierre Lombard: Sa vie, ses oeuvres, sa morale.* Publications de l'Institut d'études médiévales à Montréal: Conférence Albert-le-Grand, 1960. Paris, 1961.

D'Entrèves, A. P[asserin]. *Dante as a Political Thinker.* Oxford, 1952.

Dictionnaire de droit canonique. Edited by R. Naz. 7 vols. Paris, 1935–65.

Dictionnaire des lettres françaises. Edited by G. Grente et al. Vol. 1: *Le moyen âge,* edited by R. Bossuat et al. Paris, 1964.

Dino Compagni. *La cronaca di Dino Compagni delle cose occorrenti ne' tempi suoi.* Edited by I. Del Lungo. *RIS²,* vol. 9, pt. 2. Città di Castello, 1907–16.

Dizionario biografico degli italiani. Vol. 1. Rome, 1960. In progress.

Donatus. *Ars grammatica.* Edited by H. Keil in his *Grammatici latini,* 4:367–402. Leipzig, 1864.

———. *De partibus orationis ars minor.* Edited by H. Keil in his *Grammatici latini,* 4: 355–66. Leipzig, 1864.

Donno, D. J. "Dante's Argenti: Episode and Function." *Speculum* 40 (1965): 611–25.

———. Review of F. Fergusson, *Dante,* Masters of World Literature Series (New York, 1966). In *Speculum* 42 (1967): 136–39.

Du Cange, Charles Du Fresne, sieur. *Glossarium mediae et infimae Latinitatis.* Edited by L. Favre. 10 vols. Niort, 1883–87. Reprint. Graz, 1954.

Dümmler, E., ed. *Epistolae Karolini aevi.* Vol. 2. = *MGH, Epistolae,* vol. 4. Berlin, 1895.

[Dupuy, P., ed.] *Histoire du différend d'entre le pape Boniface VIII et Philippes le Bel roy de France.* Paris, 1655.

Emden, A. B. *A Biographical Register of the University of Oxford to A.D. 1500.* Vol. 1. Oxford, 1957.

Enciclopedia cattolica. 12 vols. Vatican City, 1948–54.

Enciclopedia dantesca. Vol. 1. Rome, 1970. In progress.

Enciclopedia italiana di scienze, lettere ed arti. 36 vols. Rome and Milan, 1929–39.

Encyclopaedia Britannica. 11th ed. 28 vols. Cambridge, Eng., 1910–11.

Esposito, E. *Gli studi danteschi dal 1950 al 1964.* Rome, 1965.

Eubel, C. *Hierarchia Catholica Medii Aevi; sive, Summorum pontificum, s. R. e. cardinalium, ecclesiarum antistitum series.* . . . Vol. 1. Münster, 1898. 2d ed. Münster, 1913.

Falletti, L. "Guillaume Durand." In *Dictionnaire de droit canonique,* 5:1014–75. Paris, 1953.

Fanfani, P., ed. *Commento alla "Divina Commedia" d'Anonimo Fiorentino del secolo XIV.* 3 vols. Collezione di opere inedite o rare dei primi tre secoli della lingua, vols. 15–17. Bologna, 1866–74.

Fasoli, G. "La pace del 1279 tra i partiti bolognesi." *Archivio storico italiano* 91 (1933): 49–75.

———, and Sella, P., eds. *Statuti di Bologna dell'anno 1288.* 2 vols. Studi e testi, vols. 73 and 85. Vatican City, 1937–39.

Feine, H. *Kirchliche Rechtsgeschichte.* Vol. 1. 3d ed. Weimar, 1955.

Filipini, F. "Il grammatico Prisciano nell'*Inferno* dantesco." *Archiginnasio: Bulletino della Biblioteca communale di Bologna* 12 (1917): 23–31. Reviewed by A. Aruch in *Bullettino della Società dantesca italiana,* n.s. 24 (1917): 184–85.

Fiorelli, P. "Accorso." *Dizionario biografico degli italiani,* 1:116–21. Rome, 1960.

———. "Accorso da Reggio." *Dizionario biografico degli italiani,* 1:121–22. Rome, 1960.

———. "Minima de Accursiis." *Annali di storia del diritto* 2 (1958): 345–59. Reviewed by F. Mazzoni, *Studi danteschi* 38 (1961): 359.

Flores historiarum. Edited by H. R. Luard. Rerum Britannicarum Medii Aevi scriptores ["Rolls series"], no. 95. 3 vols. London, 1890.

Fournier, P. See review cited above s.v. "Brandileone, F."

Friedberg, Aemilius, ed. *"Quinque compilationes antiquae" nec non "Collectio canonum Lipsiensis."* Leipzig, 1882.

———. See also *Corpus iuris canonici.*

Gams, P. B. *Series episcoporum ecclesiae catholicae.* Regensburg, 1873.

Gaudemet, J. *L'Eglise dans l'Empire romain (IVᵉ–Vᵉ siècles). = Histoire du droit et des institutions de l'Eglise en Occident*, edited by G. Le Bras, vol. 3. Paris, 1958.

Gerhoh of Reichersberg. *De investigatione Antichristi.* In *MGH, Libelli de lite imperatorum et pontificum saec. XI et XII conscripti*, 3:304–95. Hanover, 1897.

Ghellinck, J. de. "Pierre Lombard." *Dictionnaire de théologie catholique*, 12:1941–2019. Paris, 1935.

Gibbon, E. *History of the Decline and Fall of the Roman Empire.* Edited by J. B. Bury. 10th ed. Vol. 3. London, 1944.

Gillingham, J. B. "Why Did Rahewin Stop Writing the Gesta Frederici?" *English Historical Review* 83 (1968): 294–303.

Gilson, E. *Dante et la philosophie.* Etudes de philosophie médiévale, vol. 28. Paris, 1939.

———. *Dante the Philosopher.* Translated by D. Moore. New York, 1949. Facsimile reprint with the title *Dante and Philosophy.* New York, 1963.

Gough, H. *Itinerary of King Edward the First throughout His Reign, A.D. 1272–1307.* Paisley, Scotland, 1900.

Gozzadini, G. "Il palazzo detto di Accursio." *Atti e memorie della R. Deputazione di storia patria per le provincie di Romagna*, 3d ser. 1 (1883): 425–50.

Grayson, C. " 'Nobilior est vulgaris': Latin and Vernacular in Dante's Thought." In *Centenary Essays on Dante by Members of the Oxford Dante Society*, pp. 54–76. Oxford, 1965.

[Graziolo de' Bambaglioli.] *Il commento più antico e la più antica versione latina dell' Inferno di Dante, dal codice di Sandaniele del Friuli.* Edited by A. Fiammazzo. Udine, 1892.

Great Britain. Public Record Office. *Calendar of Entries in the Papal Registers Relating to Great Britain and Ireland: Papal Letters.* Vol. 1: *A.D. 1198–1304.* Edited by W. H. Bliss. London, 1893.

———. *Calendar of the Close Rolls Preserved in the Public Record Office: Edward I, A.D. 1272–1279.* London, 1900.

———. *Calendar of the Close Rolls Preserved in the Public Record Office: Edward I, A.D. 1279–1288.* London, 1902.

———. *Calendar of the Patent Rolls Preserved in the Public Record Office: Henry III, 1247–1258.* London, 1908.

———. *Calendar of the Patent Rolls Preserved in the Public Record Office: Edward I, A.D. 1272–1281.* London, 1901.

———. *Calendar of the Patent Rolls Preserved in the Public Record Office: Edward I, A.D. 1281–1291.* London, 1893.

———. *Statutes of the Realm.* Vol. 1. London, 1810.

Great Britain. Record Commission. *The Parliamentary Writs and Writs of Military Summons, Together with the Records and Muniments Relating to the Suit and Service Due and Performed to the King's High Court of Parliament and the Councils of the Realm, or Affording Evidence of Attendance at Parliaments and Councils.* Edited by Sir F. Palgrave. Vol. 1. London, 1827.

Gregory the Great. *The Book of Pastoral Rule.* Translated by J. Barmby. In *A Select Library of Nicene and Post-Nicene Fathers of the Christian Church*, 2d ser., edited by P. Schaff and H. Wace, vol. 12, pt. 2, pp. 1–72. New York, 1895.

———. *Homiliae in Ezechielem.* In Migne, *PL*, 76:785–1072.

———. *Homiliae XL in Evangelia.* In Migne, *PL*, 76:1075–1312.

————. *Pastoral Care.* Translated by Henry Davis. Ancient Christian Writers, no. 11. Westminster, Md., 1950.

————. *Regula pastoralis.* In Migne, *PL,* 77:10–128.

Hammond (C. S.) & Co., Inc. *Atlas of the Bible Lands.* Maplewood, N.J., 1959.

Haskins, G. L. "Francis Accursius: A New Document." *Speculum* 13 (1938): 76–77.

————. "Three English Documents Relating to Francis Accursius." *Law Quarterly Review* 54 (1938): 87–94.

————, and Kantorowicz, E. H. "A Diplomatic Mission of Francis Accursius and His Oration before Pope Nicholas III." *English Historical Review* 58 (1943): 424–47.

Helm, R. "Priscianus." In *Pauly's Realencyclopädie der classischen Altertumswissenschaft,* vol. 22, pt. 2, cols. 2328–46. Stuttgart, 1954.

Herde, P. *Beiträge zum päpstlichen Kanzlei- und Urkundenwesen im dreizehnten Jahrhundert.* Münchener historische Studien, Abt. geschichtl. Hilfswissenschaften, no. 1. 2d ed. Kallmünz, 1967.

Hollander, R. *Allegory in Dante's "Commedia."* Princeton, N.J., 1969.

Hostiensis (Henry of Susa). *Henrici de Segusio cardinalis Hostiensis iur. utr. monarchae celeberrimi in primum (quartum) Decretalium liber commentaria [= Lectura].* Venice, 1581. Reprint. Turin, 1965.

————. *Summa aurea.* Basel, 1573.

Huck, A., ed. *Synopse der drei ersten Evangelien.* 2d ed. Freiburg i.B., 1898.

Hugh of Saint-Cher (Hugo de Sancto Caro). *Sacrorum Bibliorum Vulgatae editionis concordantiae Hugonis cardinalis ordinis praedicatorum.* Revised by F. Lucas [1617] and H. Phalesius [1677]. Venice, 1719.

Hunt, W. "Edward I (1239–1307)." In *Dictionary of National Biography,* 17:14–30. London, 1889.

Innocent III. *De quadripartita specie nuptiarum.* In Migne, *PL,* 217:921–68.

————. *De sacro altaris mysterio.* In Migne, *PL,* 217:773–916.

————. *Die Register Innocenz' III.* Edited by O. Hageneder and A. Haidacher. Vol. 1. Graz and Cologne, 1964.

————. *Sermo II, in consecratione pontificis maximi.* In Migne, *PL,* 217:653–60.

————. *Sermo III, in consecratione pontificis: De quatuor speciebus desponsationum, et praeconiis Romanae Ecclesiae; de spirituali conjugio episcopi cum ecclesia sua, et bonis conjugii.* In Migne, *PL,* 217:659–66.

Isidore, Pseudo [Isidore Mercator]. *Decretales Pseudo-Isidorianae.* Edited by P. Hinschius. Leipzig, 1863.

Jacopo della Lana. *"Comedia" di Dante degli Allagherii col commento di Jacopo della Lana bolognese.* Edited by L. Scarabelli. 2d ed. 3 vols. Bologna, 1866–67.

Jacopo di Dante Alighieri. *Chiose alla cantica dell' Inferno di Dante Alighieri scritte da Jacopo Alighieri.* Edited by Jarro [G. Piccini]. Florence, 1915.

Jaeger, W. *Paideia: The Ideals of Greek Culture.* Translated by G. Highet. 3 vols. New York, 1944.

Jaffé, P., ed. *Regesta pontificum Romanorum ab condita Ecclesia ad annum post Christum natum MCXCVIII.* 2d ed., edited by G. Wattenbach, S. Loewenfeld, F. Kaltenbrunner, and P. Ewald. 2 vols. Leipzig, 1885–88.

Jerome. *Commentarii in prophetas minores [Osee, Ioelem, Amos, Abdiam, Ionam, Michaeam].* Edited by D. Vallarsi and revised by M. Adriaen. = *CCL,* vol. 76. Turnhout, 1969.

——. *Commentariorum in Esaiam libri I–XI* and *XII–XVIII*. Edited by M. Adriaen. = *CCL*, vols. 73 and 73A. Turnhout, 1963.

——. *Commentariorum in Ezechielem libri XIV*. In Migne, *PL*, 25:15–512.

——. *Commentariorum in Hiezechielem libri XIV*. Edited by F. Glorie. = *CCL*, vol. 75. Turnhout, 1964.

——. *Commentariorum in Matheum libri IV*. Edited by D. Hurst and M. Adriaen. = *CCL*, vol. 77. Turnhout, 1969.

——. *Commentarius in Ecclesiasten*. Edited by M. Adriaen. In *CCL*, 72:249–361. Turnhout, 1959.

——. *Epistulae*. Vol. 1. Edited by J. Hilberg. = *CSEL* 54. Vienna, 1910.

——. *Hebraicae quaestiones in libro Geneseos*. Edited by P. de Lagarde. In *CCL*, 72:1–56. Turnhout, 1959.

——. *In Hieremiam libri VI*. Edited by S. Reiter. = *CCL*, vol. 74. Turnhout, 1960.

——. *Liber interpretationis Hebraicorum nominum*. Edited by P. de Lagarde. In *CCL*, 72:59–161. Turnhout, 1959.

Kantorowicz, E. H. "Dante's 'Two Suns.'" In his *Selected Studies*, pp. 325–38. Locust Valley, N.Y., 1965.

——. *The King's Two Bodies: A Study in Mediaeval Political Theology*. Princeton, N.J., 1957.

Kantorowicz, H. U. "Accursio e la sua biblioteca." *Rivista di storia del diritto italiano* 2 (1929): 35–62, 193–212.

Kay, R. "Dante's Razor and Gratian's D.XV." Forthcoming.

——. "Dante's Unnatural Lawyer: Francesco d'Accorso in *Inferno* XV." In *Post Scripta: Essays on Medieval Law and the Emergence of the European State in Honor of Gaines Post*, edited by J. R. Strayer and D. E. Queller. = *Studia Gratiana* 15:147–200. Rome, 1972.

——. "An Episcopal Petition from the Province of Rouen, 1281." *Church History* 34 (1965): 294–305.

——. "Martin IV and the Fugitive Bishop of Bayeux." *Speculum* 40 (1965): 460–83.

——. "Priscian's Perversity: Natural Grammar and *Inferno* XV." *Studies in Medieval Culture* 4 (Kalamazoo, Mich., 1974): 338–52.

——. "Rucco di Cambio de' Mozzi in France and England." *Studi danteschi* 47 (1970): 49–57.

——. "The Sin of Brunetto Latini." *Mediaeval Studies* 31 (1969): 262–86.

Keeney, B. C. "The Medieval Idea of the State: The Great Cause." *University of Toronto Law Journal* 8 (1949): 48–71.

Keil, H., ed. *Grammatici latini*. Vols. 2–4. Leipzig: Teubner, 1855–64. Reprint. Hildesheim, 1961.

Kennan, E. "The 'De consideratione' of St. Bernard of Clairvaux and the Papacy in the Mid-Twelfth Century: A Review of Scholarship." *Traditio* 23 (1967): 73–115.

Kern, F., ed. *Acta Imperii, Angliae et Franciae ab a. 1267 ad a. 1313*. Tübingen, 1911.

Klingner, F. *De Boethii Consolatione Philosophiae*. Philologische Untersuchungen, vol. 27. Berlin, 1921.

Kuttner, S. "The Father of the Science of Canon Law." *Jurist* 1 (1941): 2–19.

——. "Zur Entstehungsgeschichte der Summa de casibus poenitentiae des hl. Raymund von Penyafort." *Zeitschrift der Savigny-Stiftung für Rechtsgeschichte, Kanonistische Abteilung* 39 (1953): 419–34.

Laistner, M. L. W. *Thought and Letters in Western Europe, A.D. 500 to 900.* 2d ed. London, 1957.

Lami, G., ed. *Sanctae ecclesiae Florentinae monumenta.* 4 vols. Florence, 1758.

Lampertico, F. "Dei fatti d'arme combattuti al palude e del vescovo Andrea de' Mozzi." In *Dante e Vicenza,* pp. 42–87. Vicenza: Accademia Olimpico di Vicenza, 1865.

Landgraf, G., ed. *Historische Grammatik der lateinischen Sprache.* 2 vols. Leipzig, 1894–1903.

Langlois, C. V. "Nova Curie." *Revue historique* 87 (1905): 55–79.

Le Bras, G. *Institutions ecclésiastiques de la chrétienté médiéval.* = *Histoire de l'Eglise,* edited by A. Fliche et al., vol. 12, pts. 1–2. Paris, 1959–64.

——— et al. *L'âge classique, 1140–1378: Sources et théorie du droit.* = *Histoire du droit et des institutions de l'Eglise en Occident,* edited by G. Le Bras, vol. 7. Paris, 1965.

Lenschau, T. "Semiramis 1." *Pauly's Realencyclopädie der classischen Altertumswissenschaft, Supplement,* 7:1204–12. Stuttgart, 1950.

Leroquais, V. *Les bréviaires manuscrits des bibliothèques publiques de France.* 5 vols. Paris, 1934.

Leumann, M., and Hofmann, J. B. *Lateinische Grammatik.* 2 vols. Handbuch der Altertumswissenschaft, edited by I. von Müller, sec. 2, pt. 2. Munich, 1926–28. Reprint (with vol. 2 revised by A. Szantyr). Munich, 1963–65.

Lewis, T., and Short, Charles, eds. *A New Latin Dictionary Founded on the Translation of Freund's Latin-German Lexicon.* Edited by E. A. Andrews. Rev. ed. by T. Lewis and Charles Short. New York, 1879.

Lexikon für Theologie und Kirche. 2d ed. 11 vols. Freiburg i.B., 1957–67.

Liddell, H. G., and Scott, R., eds. *A Greek-English Lexicon.* 9th ed., revised by Henry Stuart Jones et al. Oxford, 1940.

Lodge, E. C. *Gascony under English Rule.* London, 1926.

Lo Nigro, S., ed. *"Novellino" e conti del duecento.* Turin, 1963.

Lubac, H. de. *Exégèse médiévale: Les quatre sens de l'Ecriture.* 4 vols. Paris, 1959–64.

Lunt, W. E. *Financial Relations of the Papacy with England to 1327.* Mediaeval Academy of America. Publications no. 33. Cambridge, Mass., 1939.

———, ed. *The Valuation of Norwich.* Oxford, 1926.

Maccarrone, M. *Chiesa e stato nella dottrina di papa Innocenzo III.* Lateranum, n.s., an. 6, nos. 3 and 4. Rome, 1940.

———. "Il terzo libro della *Monarchia.*" *Studi danteschi* 33 (1955): 5–142.

———. *Vicarius Christi: Storia del titolo papale.* Lateranum, n.s., an. 18, nos. 1–4. Rome, 1952.

McGovern, John F. "The Conquest of Geryon." *Studies in Medieval Culture* 6–7 (1976): 129–34.

Malagola, C. "L'Archivio di stato di Bologna dalla sua istituzione a tutto il 1882." *Atti e memorie della R. Deputazione di storia patria per le provincie di Romagna,* 3d ser. 1 (1882–83): 145–220.

Mann, H. K. *Lives of the Popes in the Middle Ages.* Vols. 9–17. London, 1925–32. [J. Hollnsteiner coauthor, vol. 16; vols. 9–12, 2d ed.]

Marrou, H. I. *A History of Education in Antiquity.* Translated by George Lamb. New York, 1956. Reprint. New York, 1964.

———. *Saint Augustin et la fin de la culture antique.* BEFAR[1], no. 145. Paris, 1938.

Marsiglio of Padua. *Defensor pacis.* Edited by R. Scholz. = *MGH, Fontes iuris Germanici antiqui,* [no. 7]. 2 vols. Hanover, 1932–33.

Martène, E., and Durand, U., eds. *Veterum scriptorum et monumentorum historicorum, dogmaticorum, moralium, amplissima collectio.* 9 vols. Paris, 1724–33.

Marzi, D. *La cancelleria della repubblica fiorentina.* Rocca San Casciano, 1910.

Masi, E. "Fra savi e mercanti suicidi del tempo di Dante." *Giornale dantesco* 39 (1936): 199–238.

Masseron, A. "Brunetto Latini réhabilité?" [Review of Pézard.] *Les lettres romanes* 5 (1951): 99–128, 187–98.

Mazzoni, F. Review of Pézard. *Studi danteschi* 30 (1951): 278–84.

Mazzuchelli, G. *Gli scrittori d'Italia; cioé notizie storiche, e critiche intorno alle vite, e agli scritti dei letterati italiani.* Vol. 1, pt. 1. Brescia, 1753.

Meijers, E. M. *Etudes d'histoire du droit.* Edited by R. Feenstra and H. F. W. D. Fischer. 3 vols. Leiden, 1956–59.

Midrash Rabbah, Translated into English. Edited by H. Freedman and M. Simon. 13 vols. in 10. London: Soncino Press, 1939.

Moreni, D., ed. *Mores et consuetudines ecclesiae Florentinae.* Florence, 1794.

Munk, Connie M. "A Study of Pope Innocent III's Treatise *De quadripartita specie nuptiarum.*" Ph.D. dissertation in history, University of Kansas. [Lawrence], 1975.

Munz, P. *Frederick Barbarossa.* London, 1969.

———. "Why Did Rahewin Stop Writing the Gesta Frederici? A Further Consideration." *English Historical Review* 84 (1969): 771–79.

Nardi, B. *Dante e la cultura medievale.* Bari, 1942.

———. "Dante e la filosofia." *Studi danteschi* 24 (1940): 5–42.

Naz, R. See s.vv. "*Dictionnaire de droit canonique.*"

New Catholic Encyclopedia. 15 vols. New York, 1967.

Nock, A. D. *Conversion: The Old and the New in Religion from Alexander the Great to Augustine of Hippo.* Oxford, 1933.

Ober, L. "Die Translation der Bischöfe im Altertum." *Archiv für katholisches Kirchenrecht* 88 (1908): 209–29, 441–65, 625–48; 89 (1909): 3–33.

Oculus pastoralis; sive, Libellus erudiens futurum rectorem populorum. In *Antiquitates Italicae Medii Aevi,* edited by L. A. Muratori, 4:93–128. Milan, 1741.

Orchard, B., et al., eds. *A Catholic Commentary on Holy Scripture.* London, 1953.

Ottokar, N. *Il comune di Firenze alla fine del Dugento.* Florence, [1926]. 2d ed. Biblioteca di cultura storica, no. 69. Turin, 1962.

Otto of Freising and Rahewin. *Gesta Friderici I imperatoris.* = *MGH, Scriptores rerum Germanicarum,* vol. 46. 3d ed., edited by B. de Simson. Hanover and Leipzig, 1912.

Palandri, E. "L'archivio vescovile di Firenze: Appunti storici e inventario sommario del materiale più antico." *Rivista delle biblioteche e degli archivi,* n.s. 4 (1926): 167–200 and *169–*191 [page numbers repeated by error].

———. "Il vescovo Andrea de' Mozzi nella storia e nella leggenda dantesca." *Giornale dantesco* 32 (1931): 91–118.

Palgrave, F. See s.vv. "Great Britain. Record Commission."

Paoletti, L. "Benvenuto da Imola." In *Dizionario biografico degli italiani,* 8:691–94. Rome, 1966.

Papal registers. See s.vv. "Registers, papal."

Pellegrini, F., ed. "Il Serventese dei Lambertazzi e dei Geremei." *Atti e memorie della*

R. Deputazione di storia patria per le provincie di Romagna, 3d ser. 9 (1891): 22–71, 181–224; 10 (1892): 95–140.

Perrin, J. W. "Legatus in Roman Law and the Legists." Ph.D. dissertation, University of Wisconsin, Madison, 1964.

Peter Lombard. *"Libri IV sententiarum" studio et cura pp. Collegii S. Bonaventurae in lucem editi.* 2 vols. 2d ed. Quaracchi, 1916.

Peultier, E., et al., eds. *Concordantiarum universae Scripturae sacrae thesaurus.* 2d ed. Paris, 1939.

Pézard, A. *Dante sous la pluie de feu (Enfer, chant* xv*).* Etudes de philosophie médiévale, no. 40. Paris, 1950.

———. "La langue italienne dans la pensée de Dante." *Cahiers du sud*, an. 38, no. 308 (1951), pp. 25–38.

Pickering, F. P. *Literature and Art in the Middle Ages.* London, 1970.

Pietro Cantinelli. *Petri Cantinelli Chronicon (AA. 1228–1306).* Edited by F. Torraca. = *RIS²*, tome 28, pt. 2. Città di Castello, 1902.

Pocquet du Haut-Jussé, B. A. "Le second différend entre Boniface VIII et Philippe le Bel: Note sur l'une de ses causes." In *Mélanges Albert Dufourcq: Etudes d'histoire religieuse*, pp. 73–108. Paris, 1932.

Pope, Hugh. *Saint Augustine of Hippo: Essays Dealing with His Life and Times and Some Features of His Work.* London, 1937. Reprint. New York, 1961.

Portier, L. Review of Pézard. *Revue des études italiennes*, n.s. 1 (1954): 5–19.

Post, Gaines. "Masters' Salaries and Student-Fees in the Mediaeval Universities." *Speculum* 7 (1932). 181–98.

———. "Philosophantes and Philosophi in Roman and Canon Law." *Archives d'histoire doctrinale et littéraire du Moyen Age* 21 (1955; an. 29, 1954): 135–38.

———. *Studies in Medieval Legal Thought: Public Law and the State, 1100–1322.* Princeton, N.J., 1964.

———; Giocarinis, K.; and Kay, R. "The Medieval Heritage of a Humanistic Ideal." *Traditio* 11 (1955): 195–234.

Potthast, A., ed. *Regesta pontificum Romanorum inde ab a. post Christum natum MCXCVIII ad a. MCCCIV.* 2 vols. Berlin, 1874–75.

Powicke, F. M. *King Henry III and the Lord Edward.* 2 vols. Oxford, 1947.

Pozzi, J. P. *"De episcoporum transmigratione et quod non temere judicentur regule quadraginta quattuor": Libellus ex tomo XVIII Vallicelliano editur, inroductione* [sic] *historico iuridica auctus.* Rome: Pontificia Universitas Lateranensis, Institutum Utriusque Juris, 1959.

———. "Le fondement historique et juridique de la translation des évêques depuis les premiers documents du droit canonique au Décret de Gratien." Dissertation, Faculté de droit, Université de Paris, 1953.

Previté-Orton, C. W. *A History of Europe from 1198 to 1378.* 3d ed. London, 1951.

Priscian. *Institutionum grammaticarum libri XVIII.* Edited by M. Hertz. In *Grammatici latini*, edited by H. Keil, vols. 2 and 3. Leipzig, 1855–59.

Public Record Office. See s.vv. "Great Britain. Public Record Office."

Queller, D. E. *The Office of Ambassador in the Middle Ages.* Princeton, N.J., 1967.

Quillet, J. *La philosophie politique de Marsile de Padoue.* Paris, 1970.

Rabanus Maurus. *Expositio super Ieremiam prophetam.* In Migne, *PL*, 111:793–1271.

[Rahewin.] *Dialogus de pontificatu sanctae Romanae ecclesiae.* Edited by H. Boehmer.

In *MGH, Libelli de lite imperatorum et pontificum saeculis XI. et XII. conscripti*, 3:526–46. Hanover, 1897.

———. See also s.vv. "Otto of Freising and Rahewin."

Record Commission. See s.vv. "Great Britain. Record Commission."

Reeves, M. "Marsiglio of Padua and Dante Alighieri." In *Trends in Medieval Political Thought*, edited by B. Smalley, pp. 86–104. Oxford, 1965.

Regesta pontificum Romanorum. See s.vv. "Jaffé, P., ed." and "Potthast, A., ed."

Registers, papal. *Les registres d'Innocent IV* [1243–1254]. Edited by E. Berger. BEFAR², no. 1. Paris, 1884–1921.

———. *Les registres d'Alexandre IV* [1259–1261]. Edited by C. Bourel de la Roncière et al. BEFAR², no. 15. Paris, 1895–1959.

———. *Les registres d'Urbain IV (1261–1264)*. Edited by J. Guiraud. BEFAR², no. 13. Paris, 1899–1958.

———. *Les registres de Clément IV (1265–1268)*. Edited by E. Jordan. BEFAR², no. 11. Paris, 1893–1945.

———. *Les registres de Nicolas III (1277–1280)*. Edited by J. Gay and S. Vitte. BEFAR², no. 14. Paris, 1898–1938.

———. *Les registres de Martin IV (1281–1285)*. Edited by F. Olivier-Martin et al. BEFAR², no. 16. Paris, 1901–35.

———. *Les registres d'Honorius IV* [1285–1287]. Edited by M. Prou. BEFAR², no. 7. Paris, 1888.

———. *Les registres de Nicolas IV* [1288–1292]. Edited by E. Langlois. BEFAR², no. 5. Paris, 1886–1893.

———. *Les registres de Boniface VIII* [1294–1303]. Edited by G. Digard et al. BEFAR², no. 4. Paris, 1884–1935.

———. See also s.vv. "Innocent III," "Jaffé, P., ed.," and "Potthast, A., ed."

Repertorium fontium historiae medii aevi, primum ab Augusto Potthast digestum, nunc cura collegii historicorum e pluribus nationibus emendatum et auctum. 3 vols to date. Rome: Istituto storico italiano per il medio evo, 1962–.

Reynolds, Barbara, ed. *The Cambridge Italian Dictionary*. Vol. 1: *Italian-English*. Cambridge, Eng., 1962.

Richardson, Alan, ed. *A Theological Word Book of the Bible*. New York, 1951.

Riley, H. T., ed. *Chronica monasterii S. Albani*. 12 vols. in 7. Rerum Britannicarum Medii Aevi scriptores ["Rolls series"], no. 28. London, 1863–76.

Ruffini, F. See review cited above s.v. "Brandileone, F."

Runciman, S. *The Sicilian Vespers*. Cambridge, Eng., 1958. Reprint. Baltimore, Md., 1960.

Russell, Frederick H. *The Just War in the Middle Ages*. Cambridge Studies in Medieval Life and Thought, 3d ser., vol. 8. Cambridge, Eng., 1975.

Rymer, T., ed. *Foedera*. 4th ed. Vol. 1. London, 1816.

Sacchetto, A. "Le chant des trois florentins." *Annales du Centre universitaire méditerranéen* 6 (1952–53): 117–81. = *Travaux de la Société d'études dantesques du Centre universitaire méditerranéen*, 6:148–87. Also reprinted as "Il canto dei tre fiorentini (XVI dell'*Inferno*)" in his *Dieci letture dantesche*, pp. 25–56. Florence, 1960.

Salimbene. *Chronica fratris Salimbene*. Edited by O. Holder-Egger. = *MGH, Scriptores*, vol. 32. Hanover and Leipzig, 1905–13.

Sanesi, E. "Maestro Perfetto da Castelfiorentino, canonico di S. Reparata." *Miscellanea storica della Valdelsa* 39 [1931]: 144–51.

———. "Un ricorso del capitolo fiorentino alla signoria alla fine del sec. XIII." *Rivista storica degli archivi toscani* 3 (1931): 141–61.

———. "Del trasferimento di messer Andrea dei Mozzi da Firenze a Vicenza." *Studi danteschi* 22 (1938): 115–22.

Sanford, E. M. "The Lombard Cities, Empire, and Papacy in a Cleveland Manuscript." *Speculum* 12 (1937): 203–8.

Santini, P. "Sui fiorentini 'che fur sì degni.'" *Studi danteschi* 6 (1923): 25–44.

Sarti, M., and Fattorini, M. *De claris archigymnasii Bononiensis professoribus a saeculo XI usque ad saeculum XIV.* 2d ed., edited by C. Albicini and C. Malagola. 2 vols. Bologna, 1888–96. Reprint. Turin, 1962.

Savigny, F. C. von. *Geschichte des römischen Rechts im Mittelalter.* 2d ed. Vol. 5. Heidelberg, 1850. Reprint. Bad Homburg, 1961.

Sbaralea, J. H., ed. *Bullarium Franciscanum.* Vol. 3. Rome, 1765.

Scherillo, M. *Alcuni capitoli della biografia di Dante.* Turin, 1896.

Schevill, F. *History of Florence.* New York, 1936. Facsimile reprints with the title *Medieval and Renaissance Florence.* New York, 1961 and 1963.

Schizzerotto, G. "Uguccione da Pisa, Dante e la colpa di Prisciano." *Studi danteschi* 43 (1966): 79–83.

Schmitz-Kallenberg, L. *Urkundenlehre,* pt. 2: *Papsturkunden.* Grundriss der Geschichtswissenschaft, edited by A. Meister, vol. 1, pt. 2. Leipzig and Berlin, 1913.

Schulte, J. F. von. *Die Geschichte der Quellen und Literatur des canonischen Rechts von Gratian bis auf die Gegenwart.* 3 vols. Stuttgart, 1875–80. Reprint. Graz, 1956.

Selmi, F., ed. *Chiose anonime alla prima cantica della "Divina Commedia" di un contemporaneo del poeta.* Turin, 1865.

Senior, W. "Accursius and His Son Franciscus." *Law Quarterly Review* 51 (1935): 513–16.

Singleton, C. S. *An Essay on the "Vita nuova."* Cambridge, Mass., 1958.

Smalley, B. *The Study of the Bible in the Middle Ages.* 2d ed. New York, 1952.

Smith, A. L. *Church and State in the Middle Ages.* Oxford, 1913.

Sorbelli, A., ed. *Corpus chronicorum Bononiensium.* = RIS², tome 18, pt. 1, vol. 2. Città di Castello, 1910–38.

Stegmüller, F. *Repertorium Biblicum Medii Aevi.* 7 vols. Madrid, 1950–61.

Stickler, A. M. "Decretisti bolognesi dimenticati." *Studia Gratiana* 3 (1955): 377–410.

———. *Historia iuris canonici latini: Institutiones academicae.* Vol. 1: *Historia fontium.* Turin, 1950.

Stubbs, W. *The Constitutional History of England.* 3d ed. Vol. 2. Oxford, 1883.

Talmud. *The Babylonian Talmud, Seder Nezikin.* Edited by I. Epstein. Vol. 3: *Sanhedrin.* Translated by J. Shachter and H. Freedman. London: Soncino Press, 1935.

Thomas Aquinas. *Sancti Thomae Aquinatis doctoris angelici Ordinis Praedicatorum opera omnia secundum impressionem Petri Fiaccadori Parmae 1852–1873 photolithographice reimpressa.* New York: Musurgia, 1948.

———. *Summa Theologiae.* Blackfriars' translation. Edited by Thomas Gilby. Vol. 40: *(2a2ae. 92–100).* New York: McGraw-Hill Book Co., 1968.

———. *The "Summa theologica" of St. Thomas Aquinas.* Translated by fathers of the English Dominican province. 20 vols. London, 1911–25.

Tierney, B. *Foundations of the Conciliar Theory: The Contribution of the Medieval Canonists from Gratian to the Great Schism.* Cambridge Studies in Medieval Life and Thought, n.s., vol. 4. Cambridge, Eng., 1955.

———. *"Natura id est deus:* A Case of Juristic Pantheism?" *Journal of the History of Ideas* 24 (1963): 307–22.

———. " 'Tria quippe distinguit iudicia . . . ' A Note on Innocent III's Decretal *Per venerabilem.*" *Speculum* 37 (1962): 48–59.

Tommaseo, N., and Bellini, B., eds. *Dizionario della lingua italiana.* 4 vols. Turin, 1861–79.

Toy, C. H. "Ecclesiastes." *Encyclopaedia Britannica,* 11th ed., 8:849–53. Cambridge, Eng., 1910.

Toynbee, P. *A Dictionary of Proper Names and Notable Matters in the Works of Dante.* 2d ed., revised by C. S. Singleton. Oxford, 1968.

Trummer, J. "Mystisches im alten Kirchenrecht: Die geistige Ehe zwischen Bischof und Diözese." *Österreichisches Archiv für Kirchenrecht* 2 (1951): 62–75.

Ughelli, F. *Italia sacra.* 2d ed., revised by N. Coleti. 10 vols. Venice, 1717–22.

Villani, Filippo. *Liber de civitatis Florentiae famosis civibus.* Edited by G. C. Galletti. Florence, 1847.

———. *Le vite d'uomini illustri fiorentini.* Translated and edited by G. Mazzuchelli. Annotated by F. Gherardi Dragomanni. Collezione di storici e cronisti italiani editi ed inediti, vol. 7. Florence, 1847.

Villani, Giovanni. *Cronica di Giovanni Villani.* Edited by F. Gherardi Dragomanni. Collezione di storici e cronisti italiani editi ed inediti, vols. 1–4. Florence, 1844–45.

———. *Villani's Chronicle, Being Selections from the First Nine Books of the "Chroniche Fiorentine" of Giovanni Villani.* Translated by R. E. Selfe and edited by P. H. Wicksteed. 2d ed. London, 1906.

Vogel, C., and Elze, R., eds. *Le pontifical romano-germanique du dixième siècle.* 2 vols. Studi e testi, vols. 226–27. Vatican City, 1963.

Waley, D. P. *The Papal State in the Thirteenth Century.* London, 1961.

Walther, H., ed. *Proverbia sententiaeque latinitatis medii aevi: Lateinische Sprichwörter und Sentenzen des Mittelalters in alphabetischer Anordnung.* Carmina medii aevi posterioris latina, no. 2. 5 vols. Göttingen, 1963–67.

Watt, J. A. "The Theory of Papal Monarchy in the Thirteenth Century: The Contribution of the Canonists." *Traditio* 20 (1964): 179–317.

———. "The Use of the Term 'Plenitudo Potestatis' by Hostiensis." In *Proceedings of the Second International Congress of Medieval Canon Law,* edited by S. Kuttner and J. J. Ryan, pp. 161–87. Monumenta Iuris Canonici, series C, vol. 1. Vatican City, 1965.

Webster's New International Dictionary of the English Language. 2d ed. Springfield, Mass., 1934.

Wieruszowski, H. "Brunetto Latini als Lehrer Dantes und der Florentiner (Mitteilungen aus Cod. II, VIII, 36 der Florentiner Nationalbibliothek)." *Archivio italiano per la storia della pietà* 2 (1959): 171–98.

Wilkins, E. H., and Bergin, T. G., eds. *A Concordance to the "Divine Comedy" of Dante Alighieri.* Cambridge, Mass., 1965.

Wilks, M. *The Problem of Sovereignty in the Later Middle Ages: The Papal Monarchy with Augustinus Triumphus and the Publicists.* Cambridge, Eng., 1963.

Williamson, Edward. "De beatitudine huius vite." *Annual Report of the Dante Society* 76 (1958): 1–22.

Young, Robert. *Analytical Concordance to the Bible.* 4th ed. Edinburgh, 1881.

Zoppi, G. B. *Gli animali nella "Divina Commedia."* Venice, 1892. Offprint from *L'Alighieri*, vols. 2–3.

Indices of Citations

1. BIBLE

A. *Old Testament*

Indices of Citations

B. *New Testament*

[427]

Indices of Citations

2. THE TWO LAWS

A. *Roman Law*: Corpus juris civilis

B. *Canon Law*: Corpus juris canonici

3. AQUINAS

4. DANTE

A. *Divina Commedia*

Indices of Citations

B. *Minor Works*

General Index